Family Law for the Paralegal

Family Law for the Paralegal

Family Law for the Paralegal

CONCEPTS AND APPLICATIONS

Second Edition

Mary E. Wilson
Northern Essex Community College

Boston   Columbus   Indianapolis   New York   San Francisco   Upper Saddle River
Amsterdam   Cape Town   Dubai   London   Madrid   Milan   Munich   Paris   Montreal   Toronto
Delhi   Mexico City   São Paulo   Sydney   Hong Kong   Seoul   Singapore   Taipei   Tokyo

Editorial Director: Vernon R. Anthony
Executive Editor: Gary Bauer
Editorial Project Manager: Linda Cupp
Editorial Assistant: Tanika Henderson
Director of Marketing: David Gesell
Marketing Manager: Stacey Martinez
Senior Marketing Assistant: Les Roberts
Production Project Manager: Clara Bartunek
Manager Central Design: Jayne Conte
Cover Designer: Suzanne Behnke
Manager, Rights and Permissions: Karen Sanatar
Image Permission Coordinator: Mike Lackey
Cover Art: © Creatas Images/Thinkstock, © David Sacks/Thinkstock, © Jupiterimages/Getty Images,
 © Jupiterimages/Getty Images
Full-Service Project Management: Sandeep Rawat/Aptara®, Inc.
Printer/Binder: Edwards Brothers Inc.
Cover Printer: Lehigh / Phoenix, Hagerstown
Text Font: Minion Pro

Credits and acknowledgments borrowed from other sources and reproduced, with permission, in this textbook
appear on appropriate page within text or on page 581.

Library of Congress Cataloging-in-Publication Data

Wilson, Mary E.
   Family law for the paralegal / Mary E. Wilson. — 2nd ed.
      p. cm.
   Previous ed. has sub-title: Concepts and applications.
   Includes bibliographical references and index.
   ISBN-13: 978-0-13-510948-9
   ISBN-10: 0-13-510948-5
   1. Domestic relations—United States.   2. Legal assistants—United States—Handbooks,
manuals, etc.   I. Title.
   KF505.W555 2013
   346.7301'5—dc23

                                                    2011039396

10 9 8 7 6 5 4 3 2 1

ISBN-10:   0-13-510948-5
ISBN-13: 978-0-13-510948-9

Dedication

This book is dedicated to:

My partner in life and in this work, Richard A. Tauson,
who encourages me to accept uncertainty and embrace adventure

My mother, Florence Ruth Purcell Wilson,
who is an abiding source of love and inspiration

My father, the Honorable Robert Gardiner Wilson Jr.,
who set the bar high

My professors, the Honorable John E. Fenton Jr. and John G. Schuler, who made a difference,

and

My students, past, present, and future, who keep me learning and who make it all worthwhile

BRIEF CONTENTS

CONTENTS

CHAPTER 8   Child Custody   248

PREFACE

FROM THE AUTHOR

Welcome to *Family Law for the Paralegal: Concepts and Applications, 2nd edition.* As you embark on your study of family law, I want to share a few thoughts with you about the nature, purpose, and scope of this text.

One of its primary purposes is to introduce you to basic principles of family law and procedure. Although the focus is on traditional terminology and generic topics, an effort is made to alert you to the considerable variation that exists in both law and procedure from jurisdiction to jurisdiction. Each chapter provides opportunities for you to consider issues through the lens of your own state and the facts of a particular case.

A major purpose of this text is to foster development of your practical skills and self-confidence so that you are better prepared to transition to the workforce well equipped to carry out your responsibilities as a valued member of a family law team or as a resource in a general practice that addresses domestic as well as other matters. The text focuses specifically on the role of the family law paralegal afforded the opportunity to be involved in all phases of legal representation, including, for example, interviewing clients, maintaining client contact in emotionally charged contexts, preparing discovery requests, drafting pleadings, conducting research, engaging in creative problem solving, and preparing for and assisting at trial.

Every effort has been made to ensure that the material provided is current and accurate, including URL addresses. However, sources of information and the law continually evolve. The success of a client's case may ultimately turn on a recently decided case or a newly passed statute. Practical applications and exercises throughout the text are designed to emphasize the need to continually update your knowledge base, particularly with respect to the governing law and procedure where you are employed.

Family law is an exciting and rapidly evolving area of substantive law. As you will learn in this text, it is no longer solely about who is to blame for the breakup of the marriage and who gets the kids and the house. You may well be surprised and challenged by the range of topics it encompasses.

Now take a deep breath and enjoy your adventure in family law!

Mary E. Wilson

TEXTBOOK FEATURES

This text is designed to effectively meet the needs of two primary audiences: students who want an interesting, readable text that presents course content in a manner designed to build their knowledge base, strengthen their skills, and enhance their job prospects and performance; and instructors who want to employ diverse teaching strategies but who often lack the time or the resources to develop course materials that will promote conceptual, critical-thinking, problem-solving, interpersonal, and technical job skills. To this end, each chapter in this text includes the following features that illuminate, explain, and apply legal concepts:

Narrative Features

Chapter Opening Scenario.   The scenario is designed to pique the reader's interest and place the chapter content in context. Each scenario anticipates one or more of the exercises at the end of the chapter.

Learning Objectives.   The objectives essentially introduce the basic content and organization of the chapter.

Paralegal Applications.   Each chapter includes a number of real-world applications and exercises designed to reinforce substantive content, illustrate applications in the workplace, and promote critical thinking and class discussion. Many expose students to ideas, concepts, beliefs, and points of view different from their own.

Paralegal Practice and Drafting Tips.   Tips provide nuggets of information that enhance job performance by giving paralegals an "edge" in the workplace. They provide a level of practical detail not usually available in texts or reached in class lectures.

Cases.   The text contains a broad selection of excerpts from current and landmark cases, some with accompanying questions designed to promote case analysis, application of legal concepts, critical-thinking skills, and lively class discussion. Full texts of a majority of featured opinions are accessible on the Companion Website and in the New MyLegalStudiesLab.

Exhibits.   Each chapter contains a series of exhibits that summarize and visually illustrate a variety of concepts, forms, terms, principles, etc., reinforcing the chapter content in another format. Many of the exhibits highlight multistate variations in approaches to specific family law topics and issues in order to sensitize the reader to the importance of researching and applying the law and procedure applicable to a particular case.

End-of-Chapter Concept Reinforcement and Developing Your Paralegal Skills Exercises

Key Terms.   A list of chapter-specific key terms appears at the end of each chapter. Context-specific definitions are provided in chapter margins for emphasis as well as in a Glossary at the end of the text.

Review Questions.   A series of review questions are presented at the end of each chapter to focus and reinforce content review.

Focus on the Job.   An extensive hypothetical is provided at the end of each chapter that builds on the opening scenario and calls for students individually, in pairs, or in small groups to complete a work assignment, such as drafting a pleading, preparing a discovery request, or conducting an interview.

Focus on Ethics.   Attention to ethical concerns permeates the text. In particular, each chapter includes an end-of-chapter exercise that requires the student to analyze, discuss, and/or recommend a response to a situation usually related to the Focus on the Job hypothetical with reference to a specific code of paralegal conduct.

Focus on Case Law.   This Focus requires the student to address a particular case in some fashion (IRAC, brief, oral or written responses to a series of questions, etc.).

Focus on State Law and Procedure.   This end-of-chapter activity requires the student to relate chapter content to his or her home state by locating a form, statute, case, etc., and completing a related assignment.

Focus on Technology.   This focus provides a list and brief description of selected websites related to the chapter content as well one or more online assignments.

Internet Links.   The second edition of this text identifies nearly 400 URLs for forms, statutes, cases, and resources related to chapter content, many of which provide information relating to all fifty states. The links are accessible on the Companion Website and in the MyLegalStudiesLab. In addition, Appendix B identifies websites of general interest by topic and Appendix C provides URLs for each state for students and instructors wanting to access state forms and/or statutes. All of the URLs were operational as of January 2012.

HIGHLIGHTS OF THE SECOND EDITION

- Total of fourteen rather than fifteen chapters
- Chapters have been resequenced to provide a more seamless flow
- New/combined chapter on Marriage and Evolving Alternatives
- New/combined chapter on Cohabitation and Premarital Agreements
- New extended segment on adjudication of paternity, including forms
- Identification of nearly 400 Internet links to forms, statutes, cases, and resources related to chapter content
- Expansion of URLs for each state for accessing forms and/or statutes
- New charts and references to resources for learning how various issues are treated in all fifty states and the District of Columbia
- Identification of potential portfolio products at the end of each chapter
- Recent cases incorporated in chapter narratives, Paralegal Applications, Paralegal Practice Tips, and Focus on Case Law activities
- Continued focus on material designed to strengthen paralegal skills
- New opportunities to learn more about:

  Locating hidden assets

  Using the Internet (including social networking sites) as an informal discovery tool

  Exploring the impact of circumstances such as military deployment and incarceration

  Researching international adoption, the Hague Convention and international custody disputes

  Illustrating property division settlements

  And more. . .

CHAPTER ORGANIZATION AND ADDITIONAL NEW COVERAGE

Chapter 1 Introduction to a Family Law Practice

In its condensed form, this chapter still performs important functions. The focus is on the nature of a contemporary family law practice from the perspective of the paralegal. What is family law? What kinds of cases are covered? What is the paralegal's role? What basic resources does the paralegal use? What ethical principles guide the paralegal's professional conduct? The chapter introduces but does not duplicate the content of later chapters. The Focus on Case Law has been changed to a case that emphasizes the nature, importance, and value of services performed by skilled paralegals and the legitimacy of charging clients for those services. New Internet links emphasize codes of ethics and related articles, cases, and ethics commission opinions as well as basic forms for fee agreements and letters of engagement.

Chapter 2 Cohabitation and Premarital Agreements

This is a "new" chapter that combines coverage of cohabitation and premarital agreements and reduces duplication of material. The focus is on two kinds of couples: those who are choosing to live together and not marry and those about to marry, each of whom seeks to establish his or her respective rights and obligations. The chapter still includes an exhibit on forms of relief available to cohabitants when their relationships dissolve (with examples) along with a detailed sample premarital agreement, which provides drafting tips that build paralegal skills and emphasize potential jurisdictional variations. New Paralegal Practice Tips bring attention to a variety of recent cases. Internet links focus on cases, samples of documents executed by cohabitants, the Uniform Premarital Agreement Act, and statutory variations among states.

Chapter 3 Marriage and Emerging Alternatives

This is a "new" chapter that merges material on marriage with information about alternative "family" statuses. It addresses the concerns that a separate chapter on "marriage" is unnecessary and that the impact of same-sex relationships "isn't relevant in our state." Tables listing statutes governing marriage in each state, identifying common law marriage jurisdictions, and describing the positions of each state regarding same-sex marriage and alternative relationships establish that, whatever one's opinion may be, no state has remained unaffected by developments in this realm. This new organizational approach helps to clarify the rights, benefits and obligations/duties that flow from traditional marriage, same-sex marriage, and other legal statuses (particularly civil unions and domestic partnerships) under state and federal law and the District of Columbia as of January 2012. Added Internet links emphasize cases, statutory variations in types of marriage (including putative and covenant marriages) and other recognized relationships, and examples of forms used to seek judicial recognition of a common law marriage, permission to marry without delay, and establishment or dissolution of a domestic partnership. The new Focus on Case Law is on a 2006 Colorado case involving a minor and common law marriage.

Chapter 4 Annulment

This chapter has been condensed by reducing coverage of historical approaches to annulment and by selecting a limited number of representative cases. The shorter length will work better for faculty who treat this topic as the "flip side of the marriage coin" when they address marriage, and yet it is still substantial enough to support a full class session, if desired. The Focus on Case Law has been changed to a more recent case. Links focus on cases, variations in statutory provisions governing annulment (including grounds), and forms petitioning for annulment.

Chapter 5 The Divorce Process

What was good about this comprehensive chapter in the first edition is even better in the second edition without an increase in length. The major enhancement is the inclusion of more than fifty Internet links, forty of which are to a wide array of divorce-related forms used in a variety of states. The skeletal outline of the divorce process has been reformatted, the *Blanchflower* case has been converted to a shorter Paralegal Application, coverage of ADR has been condensed, less immediately relevant cases and paralegal applications have been eliminated, and the discussion of religion and divorce has been reduced to a couple of basic references. The new Focus on Case Law is a 2010 Indiana case involving a defendant in the military serving overseas.

Chapter 6 Discovery and Financial Statements

The basic content and structure of this chapter have remained the same, but new material has been added with respect to uncovering hidden assets and the use of the Internet (and especially social networking sites) as discovery tools. The Focus on Case Law has been changed to a case involving problems arising from a wife's "electronically" spying on her husband. The links focus on standardized forms used in some states for formal discovery requests (including requests for admissions and documents as well as interrogatories), ethics opinions related to electronic discovery, and variations in financial affidavit forms in several states.

Chapter 7 Parenthood

This chapter now logically precedes the other chapters specifically related to children. The content has been reorganized somewhat and priorities for coverage have been adjusted. Nonessential historical material has been eliminated, and coverage of "interested parties" and of the more complex material on ART has been eliminated or refined, including the lengthy *Johnson v. Calvert* case excerpt. The major addition to the chapter is new and extended coverage of the process for adjudicating paternity (with related forms), coverage unavailable in any other family law paralegal text on the market as this text goes to print. The other key addition is more than thirty Internet links, twenty-one of which are to forms related to establishment of parentage. A link is also provided to state-by-state coverage of disestablishment of paternity. The new Focus on Case Law allows the student to choose from among three cases to brief: the first concerning a paternity contest, the second involving former same-sex partners, and the third addressing a disestablishment case. The Focus on State Law and Procedure has been changed to a more practical exercise. The student is given a fact pattern and is asked to draft a Complaint for Paternity that would be appropriate in his or her jurisdiction.

Chapter 8 Child Custody

This chapter remains an especially strong chapter and its basic content on substantive and procedural law has remained unchanged. However, a few additions are well worth mentioning: Forty-five Internet links are included, many to examples of custody-related forms, several to cases, and some to resources that provide state-by-state summaries and links to custody laws. There is increased attention to international custody issues, and the new Focus on Case Law involves two Hague Convention cases that reached opposite results based on their respective fact patterns. A new 2010 Kentucky case is provided that addresses a child custody dispute between two former same-sex parents, and grandparent visitation is the topic of the Focus on State Law and Procedure.

Chapter 9 Child Support

Additions to this chapter include the conversion of a lengthy case to a new and more focused Paralegal Application on imputation of income and the addition of a Paralegal Application on incarceration as a basis for modification of child support orders. The major new feature is the inclusion of forty Internet links, several to cases and more than twenty to examples of child-support-related forms in multiple states. Some of the forms are UIFSA- and Title IV-D–driven forms, some are child support guidelines worksheets and calculators (including shared-custody models), and some relate to enforcement measures (notice of lien, income withholding, etc.).

Chapter 10 Spousal Support

The major new feature in this chapter is the addition of twenty-five Internet links, ten of which are to cases and five to spousal-support-related forms. Some links provide state-by-state information and links to specific state laws. In addition, a key table has been reformatted and a couple of nonessential cases have been eliminated.

Chapter 11 Property Division

There are seventeen new links in this chapter. Also added in this edition is a "Property Division Illustration," basically a proposed marital balance sheet for allocation of a specific couple's assets and liabilities upon divorce. This Paralegal Application helps prepare students for the Focus on the Job assignment at the end of the chapter.

Chapter 12 Separation Agreements

The primary strength of this chapter is the detailed sample separation agreement it provides complete with drafting tips. The chapter can be used to bring together many of the topics addressed in a family law course, or it can be read earlier in a semester to introduce the issues that will be covered as the course progresses. Ten Internet links are provided, six to cases and four to alternative models of marital/ dissolution agreements.

Chapter 13 Family Violence

Some of the material in this chapter has been condensed, particularly the statistical data and detailed coverage of successive editions of VAWA legislation. The major addition is the inclusion of forty-two links: three to statutes, four to cases, eighteen to resources (many of which provide state-by-state information on topics such as mandated reporter laws, definitions of various forms of abuse, etc.), and seventeen to forms, including, for example, petitions for protection, reporting forms, a request for a permanency-planning hearing, CHINS-related forms, forms that comply with the Indian Child Welfare Act, an order for removal, and a petition for care and custody of an unborn child.

Chapter 14 Adoption

The section of this chapter on types of adoption has been reformatted and simplified, and material has been added on international adoption. However, the major new feature is the addition of more than forty links, nine to cases, more than five to resources that provide state-by-state information on various topics related to adoption (safe haven laws, putative father registries, open records laws, etc.), and more than twenty to adoption-related forms, including, for example, forms for consent to adoption by various parties including the child, requests to access closed records, a petition for adult adoption, a petition and order to terminate parental rights, ICPA forms required in interstate adoptions, and a putative father registration form.

MYLEGALSTUDIESLAB VIRTUAL LAW OFFICE EXPERIENCE FOR FAMILY LAW

The Family Law MyLegalStudiesLab Virtual Law Office Experience is a multimedia course program including integrated e-books designed to provide students with the tools they need to confirm their mastery of legal concepts and applications and then apply their knowledge and skills in a workplace context. They watch realistic video scenarios, work with case files and documents, and use the technology tools they will find in the law office to do the work a paralegal will be asked to do in practice. Throughout the course students build a portfolio of work that demonstrates that they have the training and experience employers are seeking.

- **Students engage in a workplace experience throughout the course as a law office intern**

- **Students see behind closed doors in law offices and in the courts**

- **Students build a comprehensive portfolio of workplace products to show potential employers**

- **Students can test their mastery of concepts and concept application by taking quizzes and receiving feedback and a link to e-book content**

Within the MyLegalStudiesLab, students can access a wealth of resources to complete assignments at any time including:

- *Ask the Law Librarian Instructional Videos* to answer students' research and writing questions

- *Ask Technical Support* for technology and legal software support

- *Forms File* contains examples of commonly used legal documents for the major legal specialties.

- *Case Materials* contain all of the case information and documents needed to complete assignments

ACCIDENT SCENE

PROGRAM BENEFITS AND INSTRUCTOR RESOURCES FOR MYLEGALSTUDIESLAB VIRTUAL LAW OFFICE EXPERIENCE FOR FAMILY LAW

- Measurable outcomes for both knowledge of substantive law and procedure and development of workplace skills.
- MyLegalStudiesLab content is book-specific with an integrated e-book built into the program.
- All course outcomes are assessed and include all AAFPE-recommended learning objectives.
- Legal Concept and Legal Application quiz questions feed an instructor gradebook.
- Assessments for all Virtual Law Office Experience assignments include grading rubrics.
- Instructor supplements, including the Instructor's Manual, PowerPoint Lecture Screens, and Test Generator, have been upgraded and include the Virtual Law Office Assignment teaching notes and rubrics.
- All videos within the Lab are also available on DVD in a high-resolution format for use in the classroom.
- For selected assignments use of legal software is integrated into the Virtual Law Office Experience to be assigned at the instructor's option.

A MyLegalStudiesLab access code with or without the Pearson eText can be packaged with the print textbook at a value price or can be purchased standalone in a bookstore or online.

MyLegalStudiesLab Virtual Law Office Experience w/Pearson eText Packages

A MyLegalStudiesLab Virtual Law Office Experience access code with or without the Pearson eText can be purchased online at *www.mylegalstudieslab.com.* Either access code can also be packaged with the print textbook at a value price. Please contact your local representative for packaging options.

SUPPLEMENTS

COMPANION WEBSITE FOR STUDENTS

Students can access a wealth of textbook-related resources at www.pearsonhighered.com/wilson. This online Companion Website includes the following for each chapter: learning objectives and links to cases, statutes, forms (such as motions, pleadings, and discovery requests), and additional resources including multistate summary charts, statistics, and other supplemental material.

INSTRUCTOR SUPPLEMENTS

Instructor's Manual With Test Item File

The Instructor's Manual contains chapter objectives, chapter overviews, model syllabi, lecture outlines, supplementary class activities, and suggested answers to end-of-chapter assignments.

PEARSON MYTEST ELECTRONIC TESTING PROGRAM

Pearson MyTest is a powerful assessment generation program that helps instructors easily create and print quizzes and exams. Questions and tests can be authored online, allowing instructors ultimate flexibility and the ability to efficiently manage assessments anytime, anywhere. Educator access to MyTest is already included in Pearson's Instructor Resource Center (IRC) Educator suite. Simply go to www.pearsonmytest.com and log in with your existing IRC login name and password.

PowerPoint Lecture Presentation Package

The Instructor's Manual, Test Generator, and PowerPoints Package can be downloaded from our Instructor's Resource Center. To access supplementary materials online, instructors need to request an instructor access code. Go to www.pearsonhighered.com/irc, where you can register for this code. Within forty-eight hours of registering, you will receive a confirming e-mail including an instructor access code. Once you have received your code, locate your text in the online catalog and click on the "Instructor Resources" button on the left side of the catalog product page. Select a supplement and a log-in page will appear. Once you have logged in, you can access instructor material for all Pearson textbooks.

ACKNOWLEDGMENTS

Primary thanks go to my partner, Richard Tauson. Ric has been my number-one supporter and most constructive critic. His long hours of research, attention to detail, manuscript preparation, and review were invaluable. His patience, and that of friends and family, makes many things possible.

Much appreciation is due the Commonwealth of Massachusetts Trial Court Law Library—Lawrence Division—and the Northern Essex Community College Library (most especially Librarians Gail Stuart and Louise Bevilacqua). I also want to thank my paralegal program colleagues for providing input and encouragement, as well as my family law students at Northern Essex for their enthusiastic pilot-testing of several of the Paralegal Applications, research assignments, ethics exercises, and drafting projects.

Finally, I want to thank personnel at Prentice Hall for their guidance, assistance, and support, especially Gary Bauer, Linda Cupp, and Clara Bartunek. Thanks also are due the following reviewers for their helpful suggestions regarding the first and/or second edition:

Richard Q. Barrett, *Simpson College*
Heidi Getchell-Bastien, *Northern Essex Community College*
Erma Hart, *Wharton County Junior College*
Annette R. Heim, *University of North Carolina–Charlotte*
Jennifer Jenkins, *South College*
Tracy Kaiser, *Manor College*
Heidi K. Koeneman, *Ivy Tech Community College, Fort Wayne*
Genia Lee, *McNeese State University*
Elaine S. Lerner, *Kaplan University*
June Peterson-Gleason, *College of Lake County*
Beth R. Pless, *Northeast Wisconsin Technical College*
Annalinda Ragazzo, *Bryant and Stratton College*
Cheryl Reinhart, *Pulaski Technical College*
Joan Stevens, *Loyola University of Chicago*
Laura Tolsma, *Lansing Community College*
Buzz Wheeler, *Highline Community College*
And, most especially, Julia O. Tryk, *Cuyahoga Community College*

ABOUT THE AUTHOR

MARY E. WILSON is a graduate of Suffolk University Law School in Boston, Massachusetts. In addition to her law degree, she earned a Master's in Education from Boston University and a Bachelor's Degree from Middlebury College in English and Psychology. She presently is a member of the American Bar Association Family Law Section and is admitted to the practice of law in Massachusetts and New Hampshire. Having retired as a full professor in 1997, she now is an adjunct faculty member at Northern Essex Community College in Haverhill and Lawrence, Massachusetts, where she teaches courses in the paralegal and criminal justice programs. In her more than thirty-five years of teaching at both public and private institutions, she has designed and taught a variety of behavioral science, education, and law courses. She has also directed a statewide training program for foster parents and social workers through the Massachusetts Community College system and has authored training manuals on child discipline and working with abused and neglected children. A former department chair, she has also served as a director and dean at Northern Essex.

Exhibits (EX), Cases (CA), and Paralegal Applications (PA)

chapter 1

INTRODUCTION TO A FAMILY LAW PRACTICE

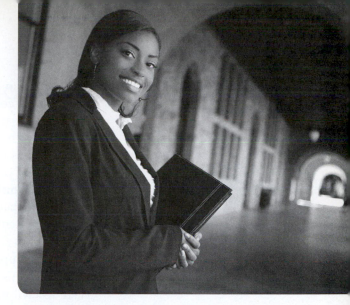

Annamaria Santiago did well in her paralegal coursework in college, and graduated with honors. This morning she starts work at a law firm that specializes in family law. While driving to the office, she recalls how each chapter of her family law textbook began with a factual scenario related to the content of the chapter and ended with challenging exercises based on that scenario. Now those challenges will involve real people and their well-being, and she will be called upon to use her skills to deal with them. As her feelings of anxiety and excitement build, she recalls her father once telling her that the Chinese expression for "crisis" is made up of two characters. One means danger and the other, opportunity. That expression captures how she feels today. She has the opportunity to become one of the "experienced and trusted" paralegals about whom she has read, provided she remains mindful of her responsibilities and ethical duties.

LEARNING OBJECTIVES

After reading this chapter and completing related assignments, you should be able to:

- describe the nature and scope of a contemporary family law practice

- identify ways in which technology has impacted the practice of family law

- describe the role of a paralegal in a family law practice

- identify the major objectives of an initial client interview

- explain why fee agreements and time sheets are important

- list primary legal research resources used by family law paralegals

- identify basic ethical principles that guide the professional conduct of family law paralegals

The Evolving Nature and Scope of a Family Law Practice

Family law is the body of law that deals with marriage, divorce, custody, adoption, support, paternity, and other domestic relations issues. It addresses the rights and obligations of individuals in the formation, continuation, and dissolution of marriages and other "family" relationships. The practice of family law has changed dramatically over the past four decades. A "traditional" pre-1970 family law practice focused primarily on proving fault in divorce and alimony cases. Judges were essentially the sole arbiters of disputes between adversarial parties represented by dueling attorneys. Today the scope of a contemporary family law practice tends to be more multidimensional. The courts commonly encourage parties to resolve their differences through mediation and negotiation rather than litigation, often resulting in mutual agreements and uncontested final hearings in which many parties proceed *pro se* with the assistance of court personnel.

Family law
the body of law that deals with marriage, divorce, custody, adoption, support, paternity, and other domestic relations issues, including matters related to nonmarital family units

Pro se
[Latin: for himself or on his or her own behalf] without legal representation

1

Given an awareness that approximately half of all first marriages end in divorce, many couples now elect to execute premarital agreements or, in the alternative, to postpone or forgo marriage entirely and negotiate cohabitation or "living-together" agreements. The legal definition of marriage itself is evolving. For centuries marriage has been defined as the legal union of one man and one woman, and the right to marry has enjoyed sustained constitutional protection. As the millennium approached, however, the national social, religious, political, and legal debate about the rights of homosexuals generally, and same-sex partners in particular, began to increasingly focus on demands for equal protection and freedom from discrimination based on sexual orientation in the family law context. At present, several states, municipalities, and private employers are granting status to same-sex relationships in a variety of forms ranging from marriage to civil unions and domestic partnerships, to family status-based benefit programs.

When couples who do marry subsequently divorce, the courts now pay minimal attention to fault unless the "misconduct" has economic consequences for the marital unit. They also no longer uniformly cast the husband in the role of breadwinner and the wife in the roles of homemaker and primary caretaker of the children. Today, both partners are viewed as making economic and noneconomic contributions to the marriage. Alimony is gender neutral by law, if not in actual practice, and marital assets usually are divided equally or are assigned on the basis of principles of fairness depending on the jurisdiction.

In a majority of states, divorcing parents now are at least initially perceived as having equal rights to custody of the children of their marriage. Historically the right of those parents to raise their children as they see fit has been staunchly protected by judges and legislators. However, that protection has begun to erode as the courts have chosen, in some circumstances, to tip the balance in favor of the best interests of children and to recognize "rights" of third parties. Adoptive parents are no longer the sole option for third-party parental status. Individuals such as grandparents, "psychological" parents, co-parents, and others are increasingly seeking and being granted an opportunity to play a significant parenting role in children's lives even if against the wishes of the "actual" parents.

Four decades ago, babies were produced as a result of a man and a woman engaging in sexual relations. In the last three decades, advances in reproductive technology initially led to artificial insemination and surrogate parenting arrangements. Now the horizon appears limitless. Among other options, we have *in vitro* fertilization, cryopreserved embryos subject to disposition upon divorce, postmortem reproduction, and cytoplasmic egg donation, in which genetic material is transferred from one woman's eggs to another's, creating two genetic mothers.

Up until the 1970s, creation and enforcement of substantive family law and policy were primarily left to the states. However, since that time, the federal government has assumed a leadership role in creating national standards, rules, and regulations impacting family law in areas such as taxes, jurisdiction, paternity, child support enforcement, bankruptcy, adoption, and family violence. In addition to being partially shaped by federal law, family law is also increasingly influenced by model acts promulgated by the National Conference of Commissioners on Uniform State Laws for consideration by the states. These Acts promote uniform legislation and policy in many areas, such as premarital agreements, parentage, assisted conception, marital property, custody, and child support.

PARALEGAL PRACTICE TIP

www.nccusl.org is the website for the National Conference of Commissioners on Uniform State Laws. All of the Uniform Acts can be accessed at this site along with Enactment Status Maps and information about pending related legislation that can be viewed by state. You can find a link to this site at www.pearsonhighered.com/wilson in the companion website material for Chapter 1 under "Resources."

THE IMPACT OF TECHNOLOGY ON A FAMILY LAW PRACTICE

It is not solely the substantive and procedural aspects of family law that have changed. Electronic technology has dramatically altered the practice of law and the ways in which law firms create, receive, obtain, store, and retrieve information. Wireless laptops, smart cell phones, personal digital assistants (PDAs), voice mail, and fax machines were just a beginning. The "paperless" office is looming on the horizon. To compete in a digital age and properly serve clients, members of the family law team must be aware of the potential of technology and its advantages and disadvantages. A full discussion of this topic is beyond the scope of this text, but it is appropriate to at least mention some of the implications of technological advances for a family law practice.

- Some jurisdictions now manage dockets electronically and permit electronic filing. This will likely be the standard in the not-too-distant future.
- Under federal and state law, subject to evolving procedural rules, data retained in electronic form by a party is discoverable, just as information contained in a client's or opponent's file cabinet is if not protected by privilege or other consideration.
- Parties have an obligation to preserve evidence and may be sanctioned by the court for willfully destroying relevant electronic files and documents, such as financial records and e-mails.
- *Ex parte* motions may be needed to preserve evidence when there is a strong likelihood that necessary electronic documents may be altered or destroyed prior to production.
- Servers and freestanding storage media (tapes, disks, and memory "sticks," etc.) are gradually replacing cumbersome file cabinets since digitally stored data is far more conveniently organized, accessible, compact, and transportable. Faxes are replacing the U.S. mail, and texting and e-mail are taking the place of the telephone and written letter.
- Computer "forensics" experts are becoming as commonplace as traditional private investigators as they "cybersleuth" to gather information to support a client's case.
- Software products designed to support law practices now allow attorneys to manage caseloads, client lists, documents, and billing far more efficiently.
- At trial, attorneys are increasingly using PowerPoint and other media presentations (often created by paralegals) to highlight elements of the client's case, for example, to illustrate proposed parenting schedules or the dissipation of marital assets over time.

Ex parte
without advance notice to or hearing argument from the opposing party based on the urgency of the matter or the harm that might otherwise result

PARALEGAL PRACTICE TIP

Paralegals need to be aware of their firm's records maintenance, retention, and destruction policies as well as applicable federal or state rules. Problems can arise when, for example, a client exercises the right to request his or her "file." Technically, the "file" is the property of the client, but in the age of digital technology, what constitutes the "file" and where is it located? If the client wants to receive a copy of his or her file in electronic form, the firm may be required to deliver it in digital format. See the New Hampshire Bar Association Ethics Committee Opinion #2005–06/3 on this topic available at *www.nhbar.org*. You can find a link to this site at *www.pearsonhighered.com/wilson* in the companion website material for Chapter 1 under "Resources."

PARALEGAL PRACTICE TIP

Parties in family law cases often have several actions pending at the same time. Those matters may involve tax, corporate, bankruptcy, criminal, evidence, tort, property, contract, intellectual property, juvenile delinquency, child care and protection, probate, and immigration law.

- The family law team can now perform most research online without necessarily either maintaining costly and extensive in-house libraries or visiting law libraries.

A family law practice presents challenges and opportunities for paralegals. Progressing through this text, the reader will see that family law not only encompasses divorce law and related issues but also touches on many other areas of substantive law. It tests interviewing, research, organizational, computer, and problem-solving skills. It poses challenging new ethical dilemmas. Last, but not least, it stretches to the maximum the emotional stamina of practitioners.

The Role of a Paralegal in a Family Law Practice

PARALEGAL PRACTICE TIP

The NALA-based definition adopted in the state of South Dakota Rules of Professional Conduct can be located at *www.legis.state.sd.us*. You can find a link to this site at *www.pearsonhighered.com/wilson* in the companion website material for Chapter 1 under "Statutes."

The National Association of Legal Assistants defines paralegals as a distinguishable group of persons who through formal education, training, and experience, have knowledge and expertise regarding the legal system and substantive and procedural law which qualify them to do work of a legal nature under the supervision of an attorney.[1]

The role of a paralegal in a family law practice is shaped by four primary forces:

- **The size of the practice:** In a small practice, the paralegal may be called upon to function as a legal assistant, a secretary, and a receptionist. In a larger practice, the paralegal is more likely to be utilized as a *true* legal support person.
- **The style and expectations of the supervising attorney:** Some attorneys have high expectations of paralegals and delegate a wide range of responsibilities. Others provide close supervision and delegate only the most fundamental tasks.
- **The scope of the practice:** Although the major focus of most family law practices continues to be on divorce, as a member of a family law team a paralegal may have an opportunity to address a broad range of matters including, for example, establishment of paternity, enforceability of cohabitation agreements, grandparent visitation, termination of parental rights, and issues raised by same-sex relationships. Some family law practitioners specialize in particular aspects of family law such as alternative dispute resolution, appellate law, child support collection and enforcement, international adoption, or matters involving the care and protection of children.
- **The skill of the paralegal:** Initially, entry-level paralegals are likely to focus on completing standardized forms, drafting routine correspondence, preparing basic discovery requests, scheduling meetings, and preparing invoices. More experienced paralegals may organize trial notebooks, search for hidden assets, prepare pretrial memoranda, and draft appellate briefs.

PARALEGAL PRACTICE TIP

Job descriptions can be deceiving and no single job description applies in all settings. When interviewing for a position, a candidate should try to get a sense of how paralegals actually are treated and utilized in the practice. Do they function as legal assistants or legal secretaries? Knowing in advance can help promote realistic expectations and enhance later job satisfaction.

The job description of a paralegal in a family law practice is, in many respects, like a generic paralegal job description. The sample description provided in Exhibit 1.1 presumes a highly skilled paralegal and a family law attorney willing to delegate responsibilities and provide appropriate supervision. Paralegal Application 1.1 provides a series of practical suggestions designed to supplement the formal job description and improve the paralegal's efficiency, productivity, and job satisfaction.

EXHIBIT 1.1 Paralegal Job Description

The following functions are performed by paralegals under the direction and supervision of a licensed attorney. The terms "draft" and "prepare" refer to a preliminary writing to be approved and signed by the attorney, if required.

- Develop office management systems: record keeping, filing, billing, calendaring of meetings and court dates, etc.
- Screen potential clients for conflicts of interest
- Conduct or participate in initial and follow-up interviews with the client and record notes in memoranda for the supervising attorney and the file
- Prepare letters of engagement (or nonengagement) and fee agreements as directed
- Maintain communication with the client throughout the period of representation
- Gather preliminary information and documents essential to the case
- Prepare release and authorization forms necessary to obtain copies of documents such as employment records, income tax returns, financial records, medical records, police reports, and social service agency records and reports
- Research legal issues and assist in drafting briefs and memoranda
- Draft initial complaints/petitions and responsive pleadings such as answers and counterclaims, along with accompanying documents such as affidavits for review, approval, signature(s), filing, and service
- Draft motions for temporary orders and other forms of relief, along with supporting affidavits and proposed orders, if required
- Assist the client in gathering data on income, expenses, assets, and liabilities and in preparing financial statements
- Draft and edit successive versions of stipulations/agreements between the parties
- File pleadings and other documents with appropriate transmittal letters and copies as directed and arrange for service, if necessary
- Check calendars and schedule hearings as required and then mark all appropriate calendars
- Schedule meetings as directed with mediators, clients, opposing counsel, witnesses, experts, etc.
- Draft discovery requests and review and analyze responses received from opposing parties
- Review, analyze, and draft responses to discovery requests received from opposing parties
- Monitor deadlines to confirm that all are met by the paralegal, the supervising attorney, and the opposition
- Review and analyze property inventories and documentation of values and proof of ownership
- Facilitate activity and payment of accountants, appraisers, **guardians *ad litem*,** experts, private investigators, and other agents as needed
- Assist with preparation of trial materials such as pretrial memoranda, exhibits, PowerPoint and other media presentations, trial notebooks, etc.
- Assist with preparation and orientation of witnesses (including clients) as directed
- Draft any necessary post-trial materials such as **Qualified Domestic Relations Orders (QDROs),** deeds, and other documents transferring assets as ordered
- Draft post-trial pleadings, motions, etc., such as notices of appeal, motions to enforce judgment, requests for modification, etc., as warranted
- Draft letters concluding representation, including the attorney's opinion as to the tax-deductible portion of fees paid (i.e., the amount attributable to the provision of tax advice and analysis)

Guardian *ad litem*
a person, usually a lawyer, appointed by the court to conduct an investigation and/or represent a party who is a minor or otherwise unable to represent himself or herself in a legal proceeding; the guardian's role may be limited to investigation of a particular matter, such as custody

Qualified Domestic Relations Order (QDRO)
a court order directing the administrator of a pension plan to pay a specified portion of a current or former employee's pension to an alternate payee to satisfy a support or other marital obligation

THE FAMILY LAW PARALEGAL'S ROLE IN THE CLIENT INTAKE PROCESS

A paralegal is often a prospective client's first contact with a family law practice. This contact typically occurs by telephone when the client calls to schedule a meeting with the attorney. The initial interview (sometimes called an initial consultation

Paralegal **Application 1.1**

Tips for Effective Job Performance and Satisfaction

There are many tasks effective family law paralegals perform that do not appear in formal job descriptions but that have the potential to significantly improve job performance and satisfaction. Several of these appear below:

- Maintain checklists regarding the tasks commonly performed and use them to guide and double-check your work. Several such lists are provided throughout this text. For example, what are the elements of a separation or marital agreement? What materials need to be filed with a complaint/petition for divorce? What steps should be followed when serving or responding to various types of discovery requests? What kinds of property are subject to division upon divorce? Which statutes and court rules apply to the matters most commonly encountered on a daily basis in a family law practice?

- Maintain lists of key governing statutes and case law on a variety of issues, particularly those that establish standards for the court as it makes decisions. For example, what is the standard in the jurisdiction for assessing a custodial parent's request to relocate to another state or country with his or her child? Under what circumstances will a court "impute" income to a party who is understating income on a financial statement? Such lists are very useful when drafting pretrial memoranda or appellate briefs or when considering the kinds of information to include in motions and supporting affidavits.

- Develop your own "tickler" (reminder) system with respect to various dates (hearings, etc.) and deadlines (discovery, etc.).

- Keep models/templates of various kinds of motions, pleadings, discovery requests, and types of correspondence (transmittal letters, confirmation of hearings and appointments, letters of engagement, etc.). Many forms are now available on disks accompanying practice manuals and online through court-sponsored sites and the like. These resources can save you significant time and prevent reinvention of the wheel, BUT remember to verify which forms and formats are mandatory and/or currently in use and to tailor each document to the specific facts of the client's case.

PARALEGAL PRACTICE TIP

There are many useful resources available containing examples of checklists and common correspondence, etc. See, for example, Mark Chinn, *Forms, Checklists and Procedures for the Family Lawyer,* published by the American Bar Association (ABA).

- Proofread and never solely rely on computer spell- and grammar-check. Accuracy is essential. Errors reflect poorly on the paralegal and the attorney and can have costly consequences.

PARALEGAL PRACTICE TIP

Use of an incorrect address can result in a failure of proper service of a complaint or published notice. A transposition of figures on a financial statement can impact client credibility and, if not detected, the nature of a property settlement. For example, a stock portfolio worth $849,456 may be incorrectly valued at $489,456, and a client settles for a "50%" share of $244,728 rather than $424,728! If the error is discovered at a later date, the "injured" client may seek relief from the divorce judgment and pursue a malpractice claim against his or her attorney.

- When given an assignment, make a note of the date you receive it and the date by which it is to be completed. Listen and be sure you understand the instructions. Repeat them if necessary. If warranted, ask for feedback as you move forward with the task. It is a strength rather than a weakness to recognize your limitations and when you need guidance and supervision.

- When overwhelmed with a multiplicity of tasks to be performed, prioritize them with your supervisor.

- Be respectful of other members of the family law team and other professional colleagues, both in and out of the office.

- Learn the names of court personnel and others you communicate with in your professional capacity and address them by name.

- Be alert to the unique practices and procedures of various courts and agencies the firm deals with on a regular basis and to any idiosyncrasies of contact personnel in those settings.

- Maintain high standards of professional ethics. If something doesn't feel right, check it out; it probably isn't!

- Keep your skills current, and participate in continuing legal education programs (preferably with the encouragement and financial support of the firm).

- Be aware of your own personal biases and remember, everyone is entitled to representation. Personal, moral, or religious beliefs should not compromise competent advocacy. If you perceive a personal conflict, bring it to the attention of your supervisor.

- Be prepared for the often physically and emotionally draining nature of the job. Family law is perhaps the most stressful area of legal practice. Much too often, hearts are broken, dreams are shattered, children are used as pawns by angry combatants, finances are exhausted, and no one is a "winner." To maintain a healthy perspective in the midst of such emotional chaos, be sure to "have a life" apart from the job!

Paralegal Application 1.2

Initial Client Intake Interview CheckList

The primary objectives of an initial client intake interview are to:

- identify the nature of the client's need for services
- establish whether or not any conflict of interest exists that would prohibit or restrict representation
- discuss the client's goals and expectations for the representation and indicate what the firm can and cannot do with respect to those goals
- determine whether or not the attorney is able *and* willing to represent the client and whether or not the client wants to retain the attorney
- discuss the scope of representation and potential fees, costs, and payment terms
- introduce the primary members of the family law team and describe their respective roles, emphasizing the paralegal's greater accessibility and the cost efficiency of having the paralegal perform certain tasks and maintain routine communication with the client
- describe the nature and scope of attorney-client confidentiality and privilege
- identify any urgent deadlines or emergency situations needing immediate attention
- confirm and/or gather all information called for in an initial Client Intake Form
- agree on a course of action and plan for follow-up, including execution of a fee agreement, completion of a comprehensive client questionnaire tailored to the subject matter of the representation, and identification of materials to be gathered

or intake interview) is occasionally conducted over the telephone, but most often involves a face-to-face meeting in which the participants essentially screen each other. It is an important meeting, because it sets the tone for a future working relationship. Paralegal Application 1.2 provides a checklist identifying the primary objectives of an initial meeting with a prospective client.

Given the purposes of an initial intake interview, it is advisable that an attorney conduct it, at least in part. The kinds of decisions needing to be made, such as whether or not to accept the case, setting the fee, and determining an appropriate course of action, are all decisions that the attorney must make. It is difficult, if not impossible, for a paralegal to accomplish the same purposes without engaging in the **unauthorized practice of law.** A common compromise approach is to divide the meeting into two parts: The attorney conducts the first part and makes the legal decisions while the paralegal takes notes, observes the client, and records any follow-up activity needed and/or requested by either the client or the attorney. The paralegal should listen to the client's words and also observe his or her body language, being alert to potential "red flags." For example, are there any signs of deception? Does it appear the client intends to lie in court regarding assets or conduct? Does the client give any indication of being a victim or perpetrator of abuse? Is the client uncertain about the course of action he or she wants to pursue (e.g., divorce or reconciliation)? If the client and attorney agree on the terms, purposes, and scope of the representation, the paralegal may then be asked to conduct the second portion of the meeting, which is essentially an information-gathering session.

Interviewing, even if only to collect data, is a skill that usually develops with practice and experience. The paralegal may want to consult some of the many resources available on basic interviewing techniques and structuring interviews in the legal context. Research can be helpful, but good interviewing flows primarily from strong interpersonal skills that allow the paralegal to exercise:

- an unconditional positive regard (a nonjudgmental respect and acceptance) for the client
- an ability to focus on, listen to, and hear the client

PARALEGAL PRACTICE TIP

Occasionally the meeting will be taped with the consent of the client, but many attorneys find that taping inhibits the openness and free flow of the interview.

Unauthorized practice of law (UPL) engaging in the practice of law without a license

PARALEGAL PRACTICE TIP

Some attorneys use a comprehensive client questionnaire to guide the initial interview, but such forms may be overwhelming for the client, detract from the spontaneity of the meeting, and force attention on "nitty-gritty" items usually best left to follow-up by the paralegal and the client. An example of a generic client intake form suitable for use in a family law case is available on the companion website in the material related to Chapter 1 under "Forms" at *www.pearsonhighered.com/wilson*.

Letter of engagement
a letter from an attorney to a client confirming that the attorney agrees to represent the client in a particular legal matter

Letter of nonengagement
a letter from an attorney to an individual confirming that the attorney will NOT be representing that individual with respect to a particular legal matter

PARALEGAL PRACTICE TIP

Sample engagement letters can be found at *www.americanbar.org* and *www.tba.org/tnbarms/tba_settingupgupractice/engagementletter.doc*. You can find links to these sites at *www.pearsonhighered.com/wilson* in the companion website material for Chapter 1 under "Resources."

a capacity to empathize with the client while maintaining an appropriate professional demeanor (See Paralegal Application 1.3.)

Following the initial interview, the paralegal will customarily perform the following tasks:

- Draft a **letter of engagement** or a **letter of nonengagement** (or declination) if the attorney does not accept the case. Attorneys elect to decline cases for one or more reasons that may include:
  - the prospective client's inability to pay
  - the likelihood that the person is raising frivolous or baseless claims
  - the person's unrealistic expectations or stated intent to "do whatever is necessary" to prevail, including concealing assets and lying under oath in court
  - the existence of a conflict of interest
  - a case complexity that calls for a level of skill and expertise far beyond that of the attorney such that accepting the case would violate the attorney's ethical duty to provide competent representation
- Prepare an interview summary for the supervising attorney, including highlights, issues, concerns, and follow-up matters
- Prepare a fee agreement based on the attorney's instructions and make arrangements to have it signed by both the client and the attorney
- Open a client file and ensure that the client's name is promptly added to the firm's master client list to facilitate future conflicts checks

Paralegal **Application 1.3**

Basic Interviewing Tips for Paralegals

- Determine how the client would like to be addressed, e.g., by his or her first name or by a professional title such as Dr.
- Communicate with the client in plain English and avoid the use of "legalese" unless the client has a legal background.
- Adopt a style you are comfortable with and then tailor it as much as possible to the client's communication style. Each client is different. Some will feel free to present a spontaneous, open-ended narrative but will eventually need a degree of structure in the form of focused questions. Others will need to be encouraged, reassured, and drawn out.
- Focus on the client and maintain eye contact as much as possible unless the client is from a cultural background that views eye contact as hostile or threatening (as in certain Native American cultures). Be sensitive to the fact that for people from some backgrounds, it is especially difficult to discuss "private failures" that bring shame to the family.
- Use a basic interview format as a guide, but be flexible, allowing the client to tell his or her story without interruption. The gaps can always be filled in later.
- Assuming the interview is not taped, strike a balance between focusing on the client and note taking.

Note taking can be distracting and convey the message that the client is being ignored. It helps to explain to the client the purpose of note taking and to develop a personal shorthand for abbreviating common terms.
- Be prepared for a variety of emotions to be expressed in the context of the interview, given the emotionally charged nature of issues commonly addressed in a family law practice.
- Be empathetic when appropriate, but try to keep focused on the progression of the interview. If it appears the client might benefit from a referral to a mental health professional or other resource, suggest that possibility to the supervising attorney.
- Avoid the temptation to interject your own life story. A certain amount of small talk is appropriate at the outset to establish an initial rapport, but remember, the client may be paying by the hour and will not appreciate the banter when the bill arrives!
- If the firm is going to represent a client you find offensive or threatening, remain objective in the context of the interview but later bring your concerns to the attention of your supervisor. If the client becomes extremely hostile or assaultive, remove yourself to a safe location if possible and call for assistance.

- Send the client any documents needing to be completed and/or signed, such as:
  - a client questionnaire
  - a financial statement
  - release forms authorizing the attorney to seek and receive information concerning the client from third parties such as hospitals, doctors, accountants, social service agencies, and the Internal Revenue Service

THE IMPORTANCE OF FEE AGREEMENTS AND BILLING

Fee Agreements

One of the major sources of malpractice actions and tension between attorneys and clients relates to fees and costs. Fee agreements are designed to help prevent such problems. A **fee agreement** is a contract between an attorney and a client, and a failure of either party to comply with its terms may give rise to an action for breach of contract or malpractice. An effective fee agreement:

- is executed at the outset of the representation
- describes the rights and responsibilities of both the attorney and the client
- is written in plain terms and in the language of the client if he or she is non-English speaking
- clearly describes the scope of the legal services to be performed (and the tasks that will not be performed, if appropriate)
- specifies the fees to be charged for professional employees working on the client's case including the lead attorney, associate attorneys, and paralegals
- identifies the kinds of costs the client will be responsible for, including, for example, filing fees, telephone calls, travel, postage, and copying charges
- spells out the circumstances under which the attorney may terminate the representation

Exhibit 1.2 identifies the most common types of fee agreements used by attorneys. A developing trend in legal representation, and particularly with respect to family law matters, is toward "**unbundling**" legal services provided to parties proceeding in part *pro se*. This option affords the client the benefit of legal services when needed at reduced overall expense. When permitted, rather than comprehensive representation, the client retains the attorney to perform certain discrete tasks for a fee. In order to prevent abuse, confusion, and misunderstanding, fee agreements in such cases (**limited-scope agreements**) must be carefully drafted to specify the precise tasks to be performed, such as researching a specific issue or drafting a particular document to be filed under the client's signature. The agreement should also indicate any major blocks of services, such as trial preparation, court appearances, or post-divorce services, that the attorney will not perform.

Fee agreement
a contract between an attorney and a client regarding payment for the attorney's professional services

PARALEGAL PRACTICE TIP

Attorneys are usually permitted to withdraw, and in some instances must withdraw, from representation of a client if continued representation would result in a violation of the law or an ethical rule or if the attorney's representation is impaired by a conflict of interest or by his or her physical or mental condition. If litigation has already begun, permission of the court may be required to withdraw.

Unbundling of legal services
an alternative to full representation in which an attorney performs discrete tasks rather than comprehensive representation in a legal matter, usually at a substantial overall savings to the client

Limited-scope agreement
an agreement between an attorney and a client that specifically limits the nature and extent of the professional representation to be provided

PARALEGAL PRACTICE TIP

In some states, if the attorney actually drafts a document and the client files it, the document must be marked "prepared by counsel" in order to avoid a lack of candor before the court.

EXHIBIT 1.2 Types of Fees

Flat fee	A fixed dollar amount is charged to handle a specific legal matter, such as the negotiating and drafting of a cohabitation agreement.
Hourly rate	The attorney charges the client for each hour worked on the case (usually billing in tenths of an hour) plus fees (filing, recording, etc.), costs (telephone, postage, copying, etc.), and other expenses (such as travel).
Retainer (1)	This term is sometimes used in general to describe the contract between the attorney and the client, particularly with respect to fees.

PARALEGAL PRACTICE TIP

An example of a fee agreement suitable for use in a family law case can be found at *www.pearsonhighered.com/wilson* in the companion website material related to Chapter 1 under "Forms."

PARALEGAL PRACTICE TIP

Throughout this text, an effort is made to provide examples of cases, laws, and procedural rules of many states. A major reason for providing these illustrations is to sensitize the reader to the critical importance of knowing and adhering to the applicable law and rules governing a specific matter in a particular jurisdiction. For example, in New York, an attorney representing a client in a domestic relations matter is required to provide the client with a statement of the client's rights and responsibilities with respect to fees.[3] To learn more about the New York rules visit *www.nysba.org*. You can find a link to this site at *www.pearsonhighered.com/wilson* in the companion website material for Chapter 1 under "Resources."

PARALEGAL PRACTICE TIP

Attorneys and paralegals often spend far more time on cases than is eventually billed to the client. The decision as to how much of the time spent is ultimately billed to the client is made by the attorney.

EXHIBIT 1.2 *(Continued)*

Retainer (2)	The client advances a lump-sum payment to an attorney for deposit in a client trust fund account. The attorney withdraws funds from the retainer as the client incurs fees and costs. If the retainer is exhausted and the representation has not yet concluded, the client is asked to provide an additional amount or to continue payments on some other basis. Any unused portion of a retainer is returned to the client at the conclusion of the representation.
Retainer (3)	Occasionally an attorney is paid a retainer for the purpose of making him- or herself readily available to the client whenever needed. A retainer of this type, in effect, pays the attorney for declining other employment.
Contingent fee	The attorney is paid a certain percentage of the amount recovered by the client in a settlement or court judgment (plus fees and costs). Common in personal injury cases, contingent fees based on results obtained usually are not permitted in divorce cases, as they have a tendency to fuel litigation and discourage settlement or reconciliation. Limited exceptions to the general rule may apply when, for example, reconciliation is no longer a possibility or an attorney is retained for the sole purpose of recovering a debt owed to a client in the form of unpaid alimony or delinquent child support payments.
Split fee	The dividing of a fee between attorneys is permissible under certain circumstances (e.g., the total fee is in reasonable proportion to the work performed, and the client consents).[2] Dividing a fee for legal services with a nonattorney is not permitted.

Billing

Billing is viewed by some practitioners as a burden but clearly a necessary one. If not properly managed, it is a potential source of malpractice actions. Keeping accurate track of time spent on a case and for what specific purpose needs to become an automatic function, an integral part of each attorney's and paralegal's *modus operandi*. The costs of paralegal services are recoverable as a component of overall attorneys' fees, if those costs are reasonable, for appropriate services, and properly documented.[4] Therefore, paralegals are required to keep track of the time they spend working on client files. This is customarily accomplished through the use of time sheets (commonly electronic) that include the client's name, file/docket number, time spent, and nature of services performed. (See Exhibit 1.3.) These records provide the documentation necessary to support client billing.

LEGAL RESEARCH IN A FAMILY LAW PRACTICE

One of the most important functions a family law paralegal performs is legal research. Research is not merely a job requirement, it is an ethical obligation. A failure to conduct adequate research may expose an attorney to liability for malpractice. For example, in a case in which it upheld a lower court's award of $100,000 to an attorney's former client, the California Supreme Court held that "Even as to doubtful matters, an attorney is expected to perform sufficient research to enable him to make an informed and intelligent judgment on behalf of his client."[5]

In doing their research, paralegals draw on a rich variety of resources. Paralegal Application 1.4 provides a description of the components of a paralegal's basic family law library.

EXHIBIT 1.3 Sample Time Sheet

Law Offices of Robert G. Wilson, III
7 Faneuil Marketplace
Boston, Massachusetts 02180

TIME SHEET

Employee:_____

Date	Client/ Case	File#	Time hours & tenths	Description of Services Performed		Cost Code
				1. Research 2. Drafting 3. Meeting/ interview 4. Telephone 5. Office/ conference	6. Correspondence 7. Travel 8. Copying 9. Court 10. Other: _____	1. Filing fees 2. Travel 3. Copies 4. Postage 5. Other _____

TOTALS:

Employee signature: _____

PARALEGAL PRACTICE TIP

In the event that the reader has not yet completed a course in legal research and writing, a list and brief description of "Major Research Resources and Related Terminology" used in this text is available at *www.pearsonhighered.com/wilson* in the companion website material for Chapter 1 under "Resources."

PARALEGAL PRACTICE TIP

Several cases and statutes are referenced throughout the text that are "good law" as of the spring of 2011. However, the law is constantly evolving, and attorneys and paralegals must always verify that they are referencing appropriate governing law, using up-to-date forms, and following currently applicable rules and procedures. This means continually checking pocket parts, advance sheets, and legal publications, and shepardizing cases and statutes before using them.

PARALEGAL PRACTICE TIP

Paralegals are often surprised to learn that consistent with an ethical duty of candor before the court, attorneys have an obligation to bring to its attention not only controlling primary authority that supports the client's position but also contradictory primary authority if opposing counsel fails to do so.[6] In the face of unfavorable controlling authority, every effort must be made to distinguish the facts of the client's particular case from the facts of "controlling" case law.

Paralegal **Application 1.4**

The Paralegal's Basic Family Law Library

The legal materials most often utilized by a family law paralegal on a day-to-day basis are the following:

- **The state's statutory code,** primarily those sections governing domestic relations matters such as marriage, divorce, custody, child support, spousal support, property division, adoption, and related jurisdictional requirements
- **Court rules** governing domestic relations practice and procedure
- **Case law** contained in state, regional, and Supreme Court reporters with "pocket parts." (Most states and regions also have digests containing brief summaries of court opinions.)
- **Practice manuals** providing a wealth of information about substantive law and procedure as well as forms and useful checklists
- **Form books** containing forms for use in a variety of actions
- **A legal dictionary,** such as the current edition of *Black's Law Dictionary*
- **A citation manual,** such as the *Bluebook*

- **Legal newspapers** often published weekly by state bar associations and available in libraries and by subscription. They provide current information on recent cases, legislative developments, legal trends and publications, state and local bar association activities, etc.

Codes, Rules of Procedure, and reporters are available in law and college libraries, many law offices, and online through law libraries and commercial databases such as Lexis-Nexis, WESTLAW, and Loislaw. In some states they may also be available through state-sponsored public sites at no cost, although the commercial databases are generally more likely to be accurate and up-to-date. Throughout this text, various websites are highlighted in Paralegal Practice Tips and in the end-of-chapter activity called Focus on Technology. Several of these sites contain links to laws on a variety of topics on a state-by-state basis. A list of websites of interest last visited in the fall of 2011 is available in Appendix B. Appendix C provides URLs where basic family law statutes and forms for many of the fifty states can be accessed.

Ethics
the standards or rules of conduct to which members of a profession are expected to conform

Jurisdiction
a geographical area in which a certain law or procedure is governing; the authority of a court to issue enforceable orders concerning a particular type of legal matter, person, or thing

Subject matter jurisdiction
the authority of a court to hear and decide a particular type of claim or controversy

Personal jurisdiction
the authority of a court to issue and enforce orders binding a particular individual; sometimes called *in personam* jurisdiction

In rem jurisdiction
[Latin: against a thing] the authority a court has over a property or thing rather than over a person

PARALEGAL PRACTICE TIP

Although there is a significant amount of useful material available free on the Internet, the reader is reminded that much of it is anonymous, unregulated, and unmonitored. Caution needs to be exercised. Remember that information located on the Internet that is referenced in documents submitted to the court needs to be cited. Rule 18 of the *Bluebook* provides rules for citing Internet sources.

PARALEGAL PRACTICE TIP

The following is a sample of the state codes available online:

> *www.law.justia.com* Michigan
> *www.legis.wisconsin.gov* Wisconsin
> *www.in.gov* Indiana (select the "Legislative" link on the home page)
> *www.leg.state.nv.us* Nevada (select the "law library" link on the home page)
> *www.michie.com/California,/Colorado,/Delaware,/Maryland,/Mississippi,/Tennessee,/Vermont,/Wyoming, and/PuertoRico*

Ethical Rules That Guide the Paralegal's Professional Conduct

Ethics are standards or rules of conduct to which members of a profession are expected to conform. *Black's Law Dictionary* (8th edition) specifically defines legal ethics as "The minimum standards of appropriate conduct within the legal profession involving the duties that its members owe one another, their clients, and the courts." Across the country, there exist a number of paralegal codes and guidelines for practice,

Paralegal Application 1.5

A Common Research Challenge—Jurisdictional Issues

There are two primary meanings of **jurisdiction** in the legal context:

1. A geographical location, such as a country, circuit, state, or county, in which a certain body of law is governing or a particular procedure is required. The potential impact of a jurisdiction on the rights and interests of individuals can be significant.

PARALEGAL PRACTICE TIP

The impact of jurisdictional variations is potentially significant for family law clients. For example, will fault grounds for divorce be available? Will marital property be divided equally or equitably? Will alimony be a potential option? Can a particular person adopt or be adopted? How will same-sex relationships be treated?

2. The authority of a court to hear a case and issue enforceable orders concerning:
   - A particular type of legal matter = **subject matter jurisdiction**
   - A particular person = **personal jurisdiction**
   - A particular property or thing = ***in rem* jurisdiction.**

Virtually every case involves a consideration of jurisdictional issues. In a majority of cases, these issues are relatively straightforward. For example, the parties to a divorce and their children all live in one state and all of their property is located in that state. However, some cases are jurisdictionally complex. They may involve multiple parties and property located in several different states. Where a document is prepared, a property is located, or an action is brought may determine the outcome of that case. Attorneys often assign paralegals to research jurisdictional issues and gather information necessary for the attorney to make informed recommendations and decisions. Paralegals do not need to understand all the subtle intricacies of jurisdictional issues, but they need to be able at least to ask the right questions, know where to look for possible answers, and recognize the kinds of facts that will be necessary to support a client's position.

sometimes called canons or rules of professional responsibility. Some related to paralegals are written by attorneys for attorneys such as the American Bar Association's Model Guidelines for the Utilization of Legal Assistants and similar rules promulgated by state bar associations. Some are written, at least in part, by paralegals under the auspices of professional paralegal associations at the local, state, or national level, such as the National Federation of Paralegal Associations (NFPA) or the National Association of Legal Assistants (NALA). (See Appendix A.)

Codes specifically applicable to paralegals do not exist in every state. However, each state does have a code governing the conduct of attorneys practicing law within its jurisdictional boundaries. These codes are backed by sanctions, such as suspension or disbarment. The sanctions may be imposed as a result of the attorney's own direct actions or due to the actions of paralegals and others employed by the attorney under the **doctrine of *respondeat superior.*** Under this doctrine, the lawyer may be held vicariously liable for acts of the paralegal performed within the scope of employment provided:

- the lawyer knows of or ratifies the conduct, or
- the lawyer has supervisory authority over the paralegal, knows of the conduct at a time when the consequences of the harm could be avoided, and fails to take remedial action, or
- the lawyer fails to exercise adequate supervision over the paralegal

Codes of conduct for paralegals commonly are not backed by sanctions, although organizations such as the NFPA urge a move in that direction. However, paralegals may be sanctioned by a state in some circumstances, particularly those involving the unauthorized practice of law. (See Case 1.1.) Even if not sanctioned by the state for ethical violations, paralegals may lose their jobs and their professional reputations or be sued for actions taken outside of the scope of employment that resulted in harm to a client. In addition, a paralegal is not insulated as an employee from potential criminal liability if he or she knowingly participates in criminal activity such as "borrowing" client funds from a trust account to pay for law school tuition.

The vast majority of law firms maintain **malpractice** insurance to cover negligence of attorneys and other employees within the scope of their employment. Malpractice complaints in the area of family law typically involve:

- failure to properly advise a client
- failure to investigate the nature and extent of marital assets
- failure to protect pension or retirement rights
- failure to draft appropriate terms for a property settlement agreement or proposed divorce decree
- failure to give proper notice
- failure to timely perfect an appeal
- failure to ensure the payment of money or the transfer of property[7]

Clearly, no matter how hard members of a family law team work, few family law cases can be described as "total victories," and sometimes mistakes are made. Dissatisfied clients sometimes seek redress but are not necessarily successful, absent particularly egregious promises or conduct on the part of the attorney. An attorney who acts in good faith and in an honest belief that his advice and acts are well founded and in the best interest of his client usually will not be held liable for a mere error of judgment or for a mistake in a point of law which has not yet been clearly settled.[8]

PARALEGAL PRACTICE TIP

The Model Code of Ethics and Professional Responsibility and Guidelines for Enforcement promulgated by the National Federation of Paralegal Associations can be found at *www.paralegals.org.* You can find a link to this site at *www.pearsonhighered.com/wilson* in the companion website material for Chapter 1 under "Resources."

PARALEGAL PRACTICE TIP

The ABA's Model Guidelines for Utilization of Legal Assistants can be found at *www.americanbar.org.* You can find a link to this site at *www.pearsonhighered.com/wilson* in the companion website material for Chapter 1 under "Resources."

Doctrine of *respondeat superior* [Latin: let the superior make answer] the doctrine under which an attorney is held vicariously liable for the acts of his or her employees performed within the scope of employment

Malpractice intentional or negligent professional misconduct of an attorney that may occur in the form of a failure to properly supervise a paralegal

PARALEGAL PRACTICE TIP

If paralegals "hold themselves out" as attorneys or as possessing a higher level of legal skills, they may be held to that higher standard in a civil action.

PARALEGAL PRACTICE TIP

Some states require attorneys to notify clients in writing if they do not maintain a certain level of malpractice insurance.

CASE **1.1** *Columbus Bar Association v. Thomas,* 109 Ohio St. 3d 89, 2006 Ohio 1930, 846 N.E.2d 31 (2006)

BACKGROUND

William Thomas was employed by attorney James Watson for several years as a paralegal/legal assistant. In 2002, Attorney Watson was recovering at home for several months after sustaining a serious injury. During that period, he relied on his legal assistant to perform duties subject to his supervision and approval. Thomas, who was not licensed to practice law in Ohio, exceeded the authority granted to him and acted independently on behalf of Richard Zahner in a divorce case. He prepared and filed an answer and counterclaim as well as a motion for a restraining order and a supporting affidavit. Zahner denied that the signature on the affidavit was his although Thomas had notarized it by using Attorney Watson's notary seal and signing Watson's name. Without Watson's knowledge, authority, or approval, Thomas also drafted a letter to Zahner describing the domestic relations process and giving legal advice on his case. He signed the attorney's name on the letter. In response to Watson's instructions, he also prepared objections to a magistrate's order in the case, but did not obtain Watson's approval of the filing or specific authorization to sign it on his behalf.

While working for Watson during 1997, Thomas also assisted a relative, Inez Faulkes, with preparation of her will and, following her death, prepared legal documents regarding the estate using Watson's signature but without his knowledge or review.

Based on these facts, the Board on the Unauthorized Practice of Law of the Ohio Supreme Court found that Thomas had engaged in the unauthorized practice of law and also found that he had not cooperated in the board proceedings. Based on lack of cooperation, the flagrancy of the violations, and harm to third parties, the board recommended a $10,000 civil penalty representing $5,000 for each count (Zahner and Faulkes cases). (No. UPL 05–01)

FROM THE OPINION

We agree that respondent engaged in the unauthorized practice of law. Section 2(B)(1)(g), Article IV, Ohio Constitution confers on this court original jurisdiction regarding admission to the practice of law, the discipline of persons so admitted, and all other matters relating to the practice of law. A person who is not admitted to the practice of law pursuant to the Supreme Court Rules for the Government of the Bar engages in the unauthorized practice of law when he or she provides legal services to another in this state. . . .

The practice of law is not limited to appearances in court. It also embraces the preparation of papers that are to be filed in court on another's behalf and that are otherwise incident to a lawsuit. . . .

We have specifically held that a lay employee engages in the unauthorized practice of law by preparing legal documents for another to be filed in domestic-relations court without a licensed attorney's oversight. *Cleveland Bar Assn. v. Para-Legals, Inc.,* 106 Ohio St. 3d 455, 2005 Ohio 5519, 835 N.E.2d 1240. Providing legal counsel by a layperson in preparing another person's will also constitutes the unauthorized practice of law. . . . Further, unauthorized practice occurs when a layperson renders legal advice in the pursuit of managing another person's legal actions and proceedings before courts of law. . . .

Rules prohibiting the unauthorized practice of law are "intended to protect Ohio citizens from the dangers of faulty legal representation rendered by persons not trained

(Continued)

in, examined on, or licensed to practice by the laws of this state." *Disciplinary Counsel v. Pavlik* (2000), 89 Ohio St.3d 458, 461, 2000 Ohio 219, 732 N.E.2d 985. Thus, although laypersons may assist lawyers in preparing legal papers to be filed in court and managing pending claims, those activities must be carefully supervised and approved by a licensed practitioner. . . . Because respondent lacked this professional oversight, his actions with respect to Zahner and Faulkes violated the prohibitions against the unauthorized practice of law.

To discourage such practices, we agree that a civil penalty is warranted, but we find the recommended $10,000 civil penalty to be excessive. Respondent did not appear before the board; however, he did cooperate during relator's investigation by being deposed twice and candidly admitting many of the facts underlying relator's complaint. From this testimony, we are convinced that respondent did not understand, despite his years of experience as a legal assistant, the extent to which he had overstepped the bounds of that role. We find what the panel and board conceded was possible: that respondent believed, although he was seriously mistaken, that he had Watson's permission to prepare and sign documents on his behalf.

Respondent is enjoined from engaging in acts constituting the unauthorized practice of law, including preparing and filing in court papers to determine the legal rights of others and offering legal advice to others about how to protect those rights. We also order respondent to pay a civil penalty of $5,000 pursuant to Gov.Bar R. VII(8)(B) and VII(19)(D)(1)(c). Costs are taxed to the respondent.

Judgment accordingly.

SIDEBAR

What do you think of the Ohio Supreme Court's decision in this case? Was the court too hard on the legal assistant? Too lenient? Should the attorney have been sanctioned for a failure to properly supervise his employee?

Because of its importance, the topic of paralegal ethics is sometimes covered in a separate semester-long course. In this text, an effort is made to weave ethical considerations into all of the chapters, each of which includes a Focus on Ethics exercise. Paralegal Application 1.6 provides an initial introduction to paralegal dos and don'ts likely to be relevant in the family law context.

Paralegal **Application 1.6**

Paralegal Ethics in a Nutshell

- The paralegal may participate in an initial interview with a prospective client under an attorney's direction **BUT** may not solicit clients, accept or reject cases on behalf of the firm, or set any fee for representation.
- The paralegal may be paid a reasonable fee for services and receive bonuses and profit-sharing plan benefits unrelated to a specific case **BUT** may not split legal fees with an attorney.

- The paralegal can provide to a client factual information that is a matter of public record (such as a court's order or the content of a statute) and may relay advice from the attorney to the client **BUT** may not give legal advice to or counsel a client, as that would constitute an unauthorized practice of law (practice of law without a license).

(Continued)

The giving of legal advice to a client involves an exercise of professional judgment based on knowledge of the law. It includes advising a client about his or her rights and responsibilities, recommending a course of action, or predicting an outcome. For example, if a client asks what a counterclaim for divorce is, the paralegal can provide a definition (based on an established source such as a legal dictionary) but cannot advise the client as to whether or not and why he or she should file a counterclaim.[9]

- The paralegal may communicate with opposing counsel as directed by the supervisor **BUT** may not communicate directly with an opposing party who is represented by counsel unless that party's counsel consents to the contact.
- The paralegal may assist in maintaining a relationship with a client, **BUT** the attorney must maintain control over the relationship.
- The paralegal may complete tasks delegated by an attorney (such as drafting pleadings and discovery requests), **BUT** the tasks must be performed under the supervision of the attorney, be subject to the attorney's review and approval, and merge with the attorney's work product.
- In a majority of states, the paralegal's name may appear in a firm's letterhead or on the paralegal's business card, **BUT** the paralegal's title and nonattorney status must be clearly indicated and the paralegal may not be a partner with a lawyer when any of the activities of the partnership include the practice of law.
- The paralegal should communicate to the supervising attorney confidential information provided by the client **BUT** must not reveal those confidences to anyone else in or outside of the firm, not even a spouse or a parent. The confidentiality rule extends to all communication relating to representation of a client.

Special care needs to be exercised when utilizing cell phones, e-mail, and fax machines or leaving files open on a desk or on a computer screen where passersby may see them.

- The paralegal may perform work on a case in which the firm represents multiple parties in a particular matter (sometimes called joint or common representation) if permitted under governing rules of professional conduct **BUT** otherwise must avoid conflicts of interest and bring them to the attention of the attorney.

Do not allow yourself to be seduced by your skills or your job, however tempting it may be, especially when pressured by a person for assistance. Preparing documents for an uncontested divorce without the supervision of an attorney constitutes the unauthorized practice of law. "Common sense dictates that the drafting of even a simple complaint or an uncomplicated petition for dissolution of marriage requires at least some degree of legal knowledge or skill." [10]

- The paralegal may prepare and sign basic correspondence as directed by a supervisor (such as transmittal cover letters or letters confirming appointments, etc.) **BUT** may not sign actual **pleadings** (informing an adverse party of the nature of a claim or defense) or **motions** (applications to the court for an order) filed with the court and requiring the attorney's signature. The attorney's signature is a certification that the attorney has read the pleading and that, to the best of his or her knowledge, it is filed in good faith, that there are grounds to support it, that it is supported by existing law (or by a good-faith argument for extension, modification, or reversal of existing law), and that it is not filed for the purpose of delaying the underlying action or harassing the opposing party.
- The paralegal may assist and "represent" clients at a variety of administrative hearings (such as before the Social Security or Veterans Administration or a workman's compensation board)[11] **BUT** generally may not represent a client in court. The family law paralegal may assist an attorney in court with the court's permission and provided the paralegal is introduced and his or her role clearly indicated. However, some states allow paralegals to appear in court with clients in uncontested matters or domestic violence cases.
- The paralegal must seek to maintain a high level of competence **BUT** should not perform tasks for which he or she is unqualified. The client is entitled to competent representation.

Pleading
a document in which a party to a legal proceeding sets forth or responds to a claim, allegation, defense, or denial

Motion
a written or oral request that a court issue a particular ruling or order

Conflicts of Interest

An attorney (and by extension members of the family law team) has a duty of undivided loyalty to the client. Any situation that interferes with that duty and the exercise of independent judgment may place a client at a disadvantage and impair the capacity of team members to competently and zealously advocate for the client. Situations that constitute **conflicts of interest** arise in a variety of contexts. When a conflict exists disqualifying one attorney or paralegal in a firm from working on a case, the disqualification may be imputed to the entire firm. However, sometimes disqualification may not be necessary if an "**ethical wall**" can be created around the employee who creates the conflict. With respect to paralegals, the NFPA Model Code defines an "ethical wall" as a "screening method implemented in order to protect a client from a conflict of interest. An ethical wall generally includes, but is not limited to, the following elements: (1) prohibit the paralegal from having any connection with the matter; (2) ban discussions with or the transfer of documents to or from the paralegal; (3) restrict access to files; and (4) educate all members of the firm, corporation, or entity as to the separation of the paralegal (both organizationally and physically) from the pending matter."[12] Paralegal Application 1.7 presents some examples of ethical dilemmas encountered by paralegals in a family law practice.

Protection of Attorney-Client Communications

The protection of communications between attorney and client arises in two areas of law, each of which is governed by its own rules:

- The **attorney-client privilege** (and work product doctrine) in the law of evidence applies in proceedings in which the lawyer is called as a witness or is required to produce evidence relating to a client. The "privilege" belongs to the client and prevents the attorney from disclosing attorney-client communications subject to limited exceptions. It is based on state and federal rules of evidence.
- The **rule of attorney-client confidentiality** is established in codes of professional ethics. It refers to the attorney's duty not to reveal *any* information relating to representation of the client, not merely "confidences" or "secrets." Some firms require employees to sign agreements in which they promise not to reveal client information. Violation of the agreement may result in loss of employment and, in some states, criminal sanctions. The duty is triggered even if the individual came in only for a consultation and later retains another attorney.

Conflict of interest
a situation or circumstance that interferes with the attorney's or a paralegal's duties of zealous advocacy and loyalty to the client

Ethical wall
a screening mechanism designed to protect a client from a conflict of interest by preventing one or more lawyers (or paralegals) within a firm from participating in any legal matter involving that client

Attorney-client privilege
the client's right to refuse to disclose and to prevent the attorney from disclosing confidential communications between the client and the attorney unless the communication concerns future commission of a serious crime; the privilege is established by statute

Rule of attorney-client confidentiality
the duty of an attorney not to reveal any information relating to representation of a client; the rule is an ethical rule established in codes of professional conduct

Paralegal **Application 1.7**

Paralegal Ethical Dilemmas Involving Conflicts of Interest

PARALEGAL PRACTICE TIP

For a good discussion of paralegal conflict-of-interest issues, visit the website of the NFPA at *www.paralegals.org.* You can find a link to this site at *www.pearsonhighered./com/wilson* in the companion website material for Chapter 1 under "Resources."

- At law firm A, Mikayla worked on Charlie Morgan's criminal case. He was charged with statutory rape and was eventually acquitted following a brief trial. During the representation, she was privy to a considerable amount of confidential information about Charlie. Two months after his acquittal, she got a job nearer to her home as a paralegal at firm B. In her

first week there, she became aware that her new employer was representing Ava Morgan, Charlie's wife, in her action for divorce. Although not the same matter, the divorce action was substantially related to the criminal case, as Ava was suing her husband for divorce on the grounds of adultery with a series of young women. The paralegal's duty to the earlier client did not end when the relationship or prior employment ended. In such circumstances, the paralegal must promptly bring the conflict to the supervisor's attention, because it would not be apparent in a conflicts check against the firm's master client list. In this set of facts and especially in a small firm, it is unlikely the conflict can be overcome (even with

(Continued)

creation of an "ethical wall" around the paralegal), and the disqualification may extend to other members of the firm as well. However, if the nature of the later action had been totally unrelated to the earlier representation (such as drafting of a bill of sale for an automobile) and the former client consented, the paralegal's new employer might be permitted to represent the former client's adversary.

- Brooke's supervisor has just agreed to represent Jackie Notar, who has a two-year-old daughter named Shayla. Shayla's dad is Jackie's ex-boyfriend, Scott, and he is seeking sole custody of their child. Jackie has told her attorney that she is living alone and never uses drugs despite Scott's claims to the contrary. Brooke's cousin, Martin, is Jackie's present boyfriend, and Brooke knows that he is living with Jackie and that drugs and drug paraphernalia are openly present in the home and frequently used by the couple in front of the child. Brooke believes strongly that Jackie is not a fit mother for Shayla and that Scott appears to be a great dad. Brooke nevertheless has a duty of loyalty to Jackie. If her bias against Jackie is so strong that it interferes with her work performance, Brooke must bring the conflict to the supervising attorney's attention. Whether or not she continues to work on the case, she should also share with her supervisor the information that has come to her attention through her cousin.

- Against his own better judgment, Hank develops an intimate relationship with a client, Liz, after working closely with her for almost a year. Liz initially was heartbroken when her husband sued her for divorce. Hank tried to comfort and reassure her that there is life after divorce. He hopes that her new life will be with him. However, that hope soon may be dashed because Liz's husband is seeking to reconcile with his wife. Hank's interests are now potentially at odds with Liz's in light of their personal relationship. If the personal relationship interferes with his capacity to work on her case, Hank must bring the situation to his supervisor's attention. Paralegals should strive to avoid even the appearance of impropriety in their professional lives. It is therefore generally ill-advised to engage in personal relationships with clients.

- Dennis invests his modest savings in a start-up computer company owned by a client of the firm where he is employed. The client, Bonnie, is in the midst of a bitter divorce and doesn't want her husband to benefit in any way from her company. Bonnie has told both Dennis and his supervisor that she intends to run the company into the ground so that her husband never sees a dime from it. A conflict arises if the business relationship compromises undivided loyalty to the client and creates competing interests, as it appears to do in this instance. Some "business relationships" with clients do not create conflicts of interest. For example, no conflict is created if Bonnie owns the only insurance company in the small town where they both live and work and Dennis insures his automobile through that company.

- Klara is very attentive to ethical conduct. She is concerned that her supervisor, Belle, is violating ethical rules by representing both parties to an uncontested no-fault divorce action. Joint representation (also sometimes called common or multiple representation) is usually considered inappropriate in family law cases. However, the ABA Model Rules of Professional Conduct do not impose a blanket prohibition on common representation. In some circumstances, if the parties are allegedly in agreement, they consent to joint representation, and the attorney explains the risks and reasonably believes neither client will be disadvantaged, in some states the attorney will be permitted to represent both parties.

For the duty and the privilege to apply, the client must have communicated the information to the attorney (or his or her paralegal) in confidence for the purpose of obtaining legal advice from a person acting as a legal professional.

Although members of the family law team are obligated to maintain client confidentiality, there are exceptions to this general rule established by court rules and codes of ethics on a state-by-state basis. The attorney usually may reveal confidential information:

- If the client consents to the release of information, preferably in a writing that sets forth what can be released, when, to whom, and under what circumstances
- If the attorney reasonably believes the client is about to engage in conduct that will result in serious bodily harm or death or the wrongful execution of

another and there is a movement toward also including serious financial harm, such as the depletion of a company's retirement fund

- If a third person is present when the client "confides" in his or her attorney or paralegal, the disclosure is not protected by the attorney/client privilege (This might occur, for example, if the client were to communicate with the attorney in a restaurant or a crowded elevator or in the presence of her best friend, whom she wanted to have present at a meeting with the attorney for moral support.)
- To the extent necessary to establish a claim or defense on behalf of the lawyer, for example, in litigation between the attorney and the client in a malpractice action or a suit for nonpayment of fees
- If necessary to rectify a client fraud in which the lawyer's services were used without his or her knowledge

Paralegal **Application 1.8**

Ethics and E-mail

E-mail has tremendous potential for facilitating communication between counsel and members of the family law team and their clients. Messages are transmitted over a variety of networks in a largely open environment and often include attachments such as financial statements or agreements. As such, they are vulnerable to misuse, alteration, and interception. They may also run afoul of the attorney's duty to protect the confidentiality of client communications. The paralegal needs to be aware of the firm's policy with respect to e-mail communications. The firm may, for example:

- prohibit e-mail communication with clients.
- utilize encryption software to help ensure the security of communications.

- include boilerplate language on every e-mail (and facsimile) stating that the message is private and confidential and intended only for the recipient and that if it is received by another in error, it should be returned to the sender and may not be copied or destroyed.
- advise clients of the risks and benefits of communication by e-mail and have them sign a waiver consenting to communication by that means if they wish to do so.

Can you think of other ways of protecting e-mail communications?

Paralegal **Application 1.9**

Ethics and Firm Websites

The majority of law firms today maintain websites (often developed by paralegals) that are designed in part to market their services to prospective clients. They customarily provide a description of the firm, including areas of specialization, background information on the attorneys employed by the firm and their respective areas of expertise, and sometimes informational material on legal topics. It is important to be sure that the content that appears on such sites complies with applicable state bar regulations and any laws governing advertising and solicitation. Although the states vary, the U.S. Supreme Court has held that the public has a right to learn about the availability and cost of legal services and that attor-

neys have a constitutional right to advertise, although that advertising may be subject to reasonable regulation by the states.[13]

For example, it is reasonable to require that the advertising not be false or misleading (e.g., it should not guarantee results). Although they may advertise to the general public, attorneys ordinarily are not permitted to solicit business directly from strangers (e.g., persons who are neither relatives nor already clients). The distinction between advertising and solicitation relates to the fact that personal contact tends to subject prospective clients to undue pressure when they are most vulnerable (hence the phrase "ambulance chasing").

CHAPTER SUMMARY

A family law practice can be exhilarating and heartbreaking. It tests the skills and ethical integrity of practitioners and provides opportunities for creative and constructive problem solving in the midst of family chaos and disruption. Family law is also one of the most rapidly evolving areas of legal practice, as it tracks many of the social, political, and economic issues of the day. It is also one of the most essential areas, given that approximately half of all first marriages end in divorce and more than half of all children under eighteen are being raised in one-parent households. At the individual level it addresses issues at the core of people's personal and intimate lives, usually in the context of a dispute. Members of a family law team are in a position to help shape the lives and futures of these adults and children. The paralegal is an invaluable member of that team.

This text is designed to introduce paralegals to the body of **substantive** and **procedural law** governing family-related matters and related disputes. This first chapter touches on fundamental topics such as research, jurisdiction, client intake, fee agreements, billing, and the paralegal's role in a family law practice. Because ethical issues and challenges permeate every area of practice, the broad topic of paralegal ethics is introduced. Each subsequent chapter addresses at least one ethical dilemma encountered by paralegals in the family law

context. Paralegals rarely receive formal on-the-job training in ethical conduct. They must, therefore, build on what they learn in their coursework. They must internalize basic ethical principles in the interest of their own professional integrity and success. They must also do so because, as members of the family law team, their misconduct or negligence may expose their supervising attorney and the firm to liability and sanctions. Basic training as a paralegal that includes a family law course is simply the beginning. The law is continually evolving, and some of the material in law-related textbooks is outdated as soon as the books go into print. Therefore, a career in law and the fulfillment of the ethical duty to maintain one's competence require ongoing education through attending seminars and workshops, reading legal publications, and utilizing other strategies for updating knowledge and skills.

Substantive law
laws that relate to rights and obligations/duties rather than to technical procedures

Procedural law
the technical rules for bringing and defending actions before a court or administrative agency

CONCEPT REVIEW AND REINFORCEMENT

KEY TERMS

Attorney-client privilege	*In rem* jurisdiction	Procedural law
Conflict of interest	Jurisdiction	*Pro se*
Doctrine of *respondeat superior*	Letter of engagement	Qualified Domestic Relations Order (QDRO)
Ethical wall	Letter of nonengagement	
Ethics	Limited-scope agreement	Rule of attorney-client confidentiality
Ex parte	Malpractice	Subject matter jurisdiction
Family law	Motion	Substantive law
Fee agreement	Personal jurisdiction	Unauthorized practice of law
Guardian *ad litem*	Pleading	Unbundling of legal services

REVIEW QUESTIONS

1. Define family law and identify the kinds of issues that are addressed in a family law practice.
2. Identify a minimum of three ways in which technology is influencing the practice of family law.
3. Describe the role of a paralegal in a family law practice.
4. Identify the primary purposes of an initial client interview, and describe the potential role played by the paralegal.

5. Describe the characteristics of an effective fee agreement, and identify the various types of fee agreements that may be used in divorce cases.
6. List the kinds of resources included in a basic family law library.
7. Identify at least five ethical "dos" that should guide the professional conduct of paralegals.
8. Distinguish between the attorney-client privilege and the ethical rule of attorney-client confidentiality.

DEVELOPING YOUR PARALEGAL SKILLS

FOCUS ON **THE JOB**

This activity provides students with an opportunity to role-play an initial client interview.

The Facts

Maria Santiago has decided to divorce her husband, Tony, after a troubled fifteen-year marriage. Attorney Schornstein has tentatively agreed to represent her in this matter and has scheduled an initial intake interview. Attorney Schornstein's paralegal will participate in the interview.

The Assignment

Your class should be divided into groups of three. One student in each group will play the role of Attorney Schornstein, another the client, Maria Santiago, and the third will function as the attorney's paralegal. Role-play an initial interview, applying the information you have learned thus far about interviewing and the purposes of an initial client intake interview. Refer to Paralegal Applications 1.2 and 1.3 for guidance.

FOCUS ON **ETHICS**

This focus on ethics asks you to consider some of the ethical issues that arise when documents are accidentally sent to opposing counsel by facsimile.

The Ethical Dilemma

Assume that you are a paralegal working for Attorney Chen on a divorce case involving William and Elizabeth Beauregard. Attorney Chen represents Elizabeth, who is convinced that William is attempting to conceal marital assets. His attorney, Hugh Hechtl, telephones you to say that his paralegal will be faxing a copy of William's financial statement for Attorney Chen's information. When you go to the fax machine, you discover that the paralegal apparently accidentally faxed not only the promised statement but also an attached note from William that reads: "H—— This is the revised statement and the version I want to give her. I took a few accounts out and upped my expenses! She'll never know the difference. WB"

What ethical concerns arise in this situation? What do you think you should do? Would your response be the same if the wife had found the note at home and brought it in to Attorney Chen? Do you find any guidance in the ethical canons for paralegals promulgated by the National Association of Legal Assistants (see Appendix A)? Does your state's bar association or code of professional responsibility for attorneys address circumstances like this? Present your responses to these questions in a 1–2 page paper.

PARALEGAL PRACTICE TIP

The American Bar Association Model Rules of Professional Conduct (2010 edition), Rule 4.4 (b), states, "A lawyer who receives a document relating to the representation of the lawyer's client and knows or reasonably should know that the document was inadvertently sent shall promptly notify the sender." An earlier version of the rule and related ethics opinions had provided that the document was to be returned or destroyed and not used by the attorney who received it (in the interest of respecting attorney-client confidentiality). Each state Bar Association has its own rules, and virtually all are based on the ABA Model Rules. The ABA Model Rules can be found at *www.americanbar.org* along with information regarding state adoptions. You can find a link to this site at *www.pearsonhighered.com/wilson* in the companion website material for Chapter 1 under "Resources."

FOCUS ON **CASE LAW**

This activity requires you to brief a case that addresses the topic of fees for services provided by paralegals.

The Assignment

Read the court's opinion in *McMackin v. McMackin*, 651 A.2d 778 (1993), and then brief the case using the format provided on the companion website for this text or one prescribed by your instructor.

PARALEGAL PRACTICE TIP

The case can be found at *www.pearsonhighered.com/wilson* in the companion website material related to Chapter 1 under "Cases" and in the Case Resources Section of the MyLegalStudiesLab. A format for briefing a case appears in Chapter 1 "Resources" on the companion website.

FOCUS ON **STATE LAW AND PROCEDURE**

This activity requires the student to locate the rules governing the ethical conduct of attorneys and paralegals in his or her state in the context of a particular fact pattern.

The Assignment

Attorney Niskala has recently moved to your state and joined the small family law firm where you are employed.

She is a very conscientious attorney and wants to be certain she abides by the rules governing attorney conduct in your state, including any rules relating to the utilization and supervision of paralegals. She also wants to learn whether there are any rules of ethics governing the conduct of paralegals. She has asked you to research these questions and report your results to her in a one-page internal memo. You can use the following format:

Memorandum

To: Attorney Niskala

From: *Your Name, Paralegal*

Re: *The topic of the assignment*

Date: *Insert date*

Description of the assignment: *What is it that you have been asked to do?*

Results of Research: *What did you find and where?*

FOCUS ON **TECHNOLOGY**

In addition to the links provided throughout the chapter, this activity provides a series of useful websites for reference along with technology-related assignments for completion.

Companion Website

www.pearsonhighered.com/wilson

The reader is urged to make frequent use of the companion website for this text. It contains links to Websites of Interest provided in each chapter; full opinions of many of the cases featured in the text; a selection of illustrative forms and statutes; and a variety of resources such as sample motions, discovery requests, and checklists. The website is organized by chapter, and a document will appear in the material for the chapter of the text in which it is mentioned unless otherwise indicated.

Websites of Interest

www.abanet.org

This is the website for the American Bar Association. The Model Code of Professional Responsibility, Model Guidelines for Utilization of Paralegal Services, and links to state ethics rules can be located at this site.

www.DivorceStatistics.org

An interesting variety of statistics about divorce can be found at this site.

www.findlaw.com

This site can be used to access a wide range of information related to divorce and other family law matters, such as child custody, child support, paternity, grandparents' rights, adoption, and domestic violence. Links to many state statutes and forms are provided.

www.legalethics.com

This site provides summaries of and links to recently published articles on a number of topics related to legal ethics. It also provides links to other ethics-related sites.

www.nala.org

This is the site of the National Association of Legal Assistants (NALA).

www.paralegals.org

This is the site of the National Federation of Paralegal Associations (NFPA).

Note: The NALA and NFPA sites contain information regarding News & Events, Positions & Issues, Continuing Legal Education, Legal Resources, Opportunities, Networking, etc., for paralegals as well as links to other law-related sites.

Assignments

1. Find out if your state's statutory code is available at no cost on the Internet. If so, what is the address (URL, or Uniform Resource Locator) where it can be accessed? Appendix C and *www.findlaw.com* may be useful resources as you complete this task.
2. Assume that you are assigned to create the home page for the website of the firm where you are employed. Locate the rules governing legal advertising in your state, if any, to guide your plan. Then create a design after having visited at least five websites of other attorneys practicing in your state.
3. Go to the website for the National Association of Legal Assistants at *www.nala.org* to locate that association's criteria for certification as a paralegal. Would you qualify?
4. Locate and review the American Bar Association's Model Guidelines for Utilization of Legal Assistant Services, available for download at *www.abanet.org/legalservices/paralegals*.

PORTFOLIO PRODUCTS

1. Brief of the *McMackin* case on fees for paralegal services
2. Report on ethics issues that arise in a hypothetical fact pattern
3. Memorandum on codes of ethics in a specific jurisdiction

chapter 2

COHABITATION AND PREMARITAL AGREEMENTS

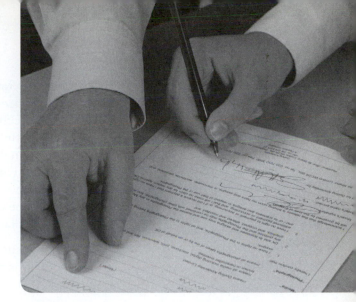

Tran and Malia are both in their sixties. They have been seeing each other for six months and enjoy their relationship tremendously. They have decided to live together and they intend to remain intimate partners for the rest of their lives. Each of them is semiretired after a successful career and each has been self-supporting for some time. Tran thinks they will marry eventually but he just wants them to live together for now. Malia has said, "Whatever you want is fine with me."

Introduction

A broad objective of this chapter and the next is to introduce the reader to the dramatic evolution that is taking place in contemporary society around legal recognition of marital and nonmarital intimate relationships. In this chapter, our primary focus is on issues related to two kinds of couples: those who choose to live together and not get married and those who plan to marry in the relatively near future. Increasingly parties in such circumstances proactively seek to establish and protect their rights and obligations with respect to each other. We will first consider the definition and prevalence of cohabitation; the documents that cohabitants may use to establish their respective rights and responsibilities including cohabitation or living-together agreements; and the remedies potentially available to former cohabitants when their relationship ends. Our focus will then shift to the purpose, nature, and enforcement of premarital agreements—agreements executed by persons about to marry in hopes of minimizing problems if their upcoming marriage later ends in a divorce or legal separation.

Cohabitation

With the changes that have taken place in the landscape of family and social life in this country, cohabitation has become a mainstream behavior for many American couples. **Cohabitation** is broadly defined as two unmarried persons living together in an intimate relationship.

LEARNING OBJECTIVES

After reading this chapter and completing related assignments, you should be able to:

- define cohabitation
- identify various kinds of documents cohabiting partners can use to create and protect their rights
- explain what a cohabitation agreement is
- identify forms of relief potentially available to cohabiting partners if their relationship terminates
- describe the nature and purpose of a premarital agreement
- identify commonly accepted legal requirements for a valid premarital agreement
- list the kinds of provisions a basic premarital agreement contains
- identify trends regarding the enforceability of premarital agreements
- describe the paralegal's potential role with respect to cases involving cohabitation and premarital agreements

Cohabitation
two unmarried people living together, commonly in an intimate relationship

PARALEGAL PRACTICE TIP

A wealth of data about types of households can be accessed at *www.census.gov/acs.* This is the site for the U.S. Census Bureau's American Community Survey. You can find a link to this site at *www. pearsonhighered.com/wilson* in the companion website material for Chapter 2 under "Resources."

Although the term traditionally has been used to refer to heterosexual couples, it technically encompasses both opposite and same-sex relationships.

In the United States, a number of agencies and organizations gather data about cohabiting couples. However, we have no uniform definition of cohabitation or any national legal registration system that encompasses two people living together in an intimate relationship as a nonmarital "family unit." Thus far, the best measure demographers have developed to gauge the living arrangements of U.S. residents is the Census Bureau's data on household types and relationships. A variety of the available data sources tell us the following:

- A Census Bureau survey has estimated married-couple households at 49.7%—a new minority.[1]
- In 2010, fewer than 22% of all households were "traditional" households (a married couple with one or more minor children under the age of 18).[2]
- In 2008, of the 6.4 million unmarried couples living together, approximately 90% were of the opposite sex and 10% were of the same sex.[3]
- Approximately 75% of cohabiters say they plan to marry their partners, and roughly half marry within five years of moving in together; approximately 40% break up within five years; and about 10% remain in an unmarried relationship for five years or longer.[4]

PARALEGAL PRACTICE TIP

Even though laws relating to cohabitation and consensual sexual behavior are rarely enforced,[5] the paralegal should find out if they are still "on the books" in his or her jurisdiction, particularly if the parties are interested in executing an enforceable cohabitation agreement. Some states still have laws prohibiting male-female cohabitation as lewd and lascivious behavior.[6] The offense is typically a misdemeanor punishable by a short prison term and/or a fine. For example, the relevant Michigan statute appears in a section of the state penal code with other "Indecency and Immorality" offenses. It provides that "Any man or woman, not being married to each other, who lewdly and lasciviously associates and cohabits together, and any man or woman, married or unmarried, who is guilty of open and gross lewdness and lascivious behavior, is guilty of a misdemeanor. . . . "[7]

There are distinct differences between marriage and cohabitation. (See Exhibit 2.1.) The legal effect of these differences is not always fully appreciated by unmarried couples who choose to live together for a host of personal reasons:

- The parties may view a period of cohabitation as a trial marriage.
- One or both of them may not want the social and personal commitment or responsibilities implicit in the marital relationship.
- Many female partners have increased their level of economic independence and become "liberated" from the constraints of rigid gender roles and societal pressure to marry.
- Parties who were previously married and experienced the emotional and financial costs of messy divorces may want to be in a relationship that is easier and less expensive to terminate should it fail.
- The parties may view cohabitation as a convenient way to reduce taxes, housing costs, and other living expenses.
- One or both of the parties may have considerable assets they want to protect in the event their relationship ends.
- The parties may be unable to marry legally (e.g., polygamists, same-sex couples in all but a small minority of states, and first cousins living in a state that does not permit them to marry).

PARALEGAL PRACTICE TIP

Visit *www.ncsl.org* to find a report (5/2010) on the status of state laws on the marriage of first cousins, which is banned in approximately half the states. You can find a link to this site at *www.pearsonhighered. com/wilson* in the companion website material for Chapter 2 under "Resources."

EXHIBIT 2.1 Marriage and Cohabitation—A Comparison

MARRIAGE	COHABITATION
To enter a marriage, the parties must satisfy certain requirements that vary state to state but customarily include a minimum age for marrying without parental consent, a license, and a ceremony.	In states where cohabitation is legal, parties may freely elect to cohabit without satisfying any formal requirements.
A marriage is terminated by formal legal process.	A period of cohabitation can be terminated without legal process.
In virtually all states, children born during a marriage are presumed to be offspring of the husband and wife, and each spouse owes them a duty of support for however long the law requires.	There is no presumption of paternity/parentage when a child is born to a female partner in a cohabiting couple and therefore there is no parallel duty of child support during or after the period of cohabitation.
After termination of a marriage, both parents of minor children generally have custody and visitation rights absent a finding of unfitness.	Absent establishment of paternity/parentage, a former partner has no custody or visitation rights following termination of a period of cohabitation with the legal parent of a child.
Division of property upon termination of marriage is governed by state law absent an enforceable premarital agreement (or postmarital agreement, where permitted)	Division of property may be based on an agreement of the parties, sometimes embodied in the provisions of a cohabitation agreement. In the event of a disagreement, absent evidence of "true" ownership of property or an enforceable express agreement, a party may seek equitable relief through the courts in most states.
In most states, spousal support may be awarded to a former spouse based on one party's need and the other party's ability to pay.	Absent a contractual agreement to the contrary, a cohabiting partner will not be ordered to pay support to the other partner following termination of their relationship.

Since the social pressure against living together has significantly lessened and cohabitation is no longer a crime in most states, why don't couples simply live together and not worry about formalizing their relationships through contractual agreements and/or establishing a legally recognized status? Consider the following hypothetical situation.

Imagine having lived with a man for ten years in a committed, monogamous relationship that you both intend to "last forever." Imagine going to pick him up at an airport and being greeted by airline personnel who advise you that he has experienced a heart attack midair and is being rushed to a hospital emergency room. You race to the hospital and the first question you are asked is "Are you a family member?" And that is only the beginning of a series of painful events with devastating consequences. You cannot be admitted to see him in intensive care. You cannot be advised of his condition due to federal privacy regulations, and you cannot consent to his medical treatment, although you know his wishes. You cannot write checks on his bank account to pay his obligations. If he dies, you have no say in the funeral and burial arrangements, and yet only you know what he would want. You cannot enter the home where you have lived together because when it was purchased by the

PARALEGAL PRACTICE TIP

Visit *www.health.state.ny.us/forms* to find forms and information about health care proxies in the state of New York. You can find a link to this site at *www.pearsonhighered/wilson* in the companion website material for Chapter 2 under "Forms."

Health care proxy
a document granting another person the authority to make health care decisions for the grantor in the event of his or her incapacity

Durable power of attorney
a document that grants someone authority to act in the grantor's stead for convenience and/or in the event of incapacity; the authority survives incapacity but terminates on the death of the grantor

Joint tenant with right of survivorship
a form of ownership of property by two or more persons in which each tenant owns an identical interest in the property, and each joint tenant has a right of survivorship in the other's share

PARALEGAL PRACTICE TIP

Some retirement accounts and related death benefit options restrict beneficiaries to a mandatory class of persons usually including spouses, ex-spouses, and minor or otherwise dependent children.

PARALEGAL PRACTICE TIP

These documents need to be carefully drafted, particularly in situations involving same-sex couples. Family members who did not know about or who refuse to accept the couple's relationship may challenge the validity of the document on grounds such as fraud or undue influence should one of the partners die and the other partner benefit over relatives.

two of you, it was put in his name only. You cannot access his safe deposit box, even though you have valuable personal property in it. You cannot inherit through him if he dies without a will, because you have no legally recognized interest in his estate. The two of you are, in effect, legal strangers.

What could you have done to protect each other in the event of such a tragedy? Lawyers have utilized a wide range of devices in an effort to establish rights and responsibilities between cohabiting partners. These devices are designed primarily to control the legal consequences for the parties in the event of disability or termination of their relationship by death or separation. Cohabitants are commonly advised to do the following:

- **Execute health care proxies** in which each of you designates the other as the person entitled to obtain information regarding your condition and consent to the specifics of your care if you are unable to make medical decisions for yourself.
- **Execute durable powers of attorney** in which each of you designates your partner as the person authorized to act on your behalf with respect to a wide range of matters including, but by no means limited to, banking and business affairs in the event of disability or incapacitation.
- **Execute wills** in which you each designate the other as your personal representative and make appropriate provisions for him or her.
- **Purchase property as joint tenants with a right of survivorship** in case one of you dies while you still own the property.
- **Purchase life insurance policies** designating each other as primary beneficiaries.
- **Execute and fund trusts** that provide for each other under a variety of circumstances, such as the death or disability of a partner.
- **Designate your partner as a primary beneficiary on 401(k)s, IRAs, and/or other retirement accounts** not otherwise restricted.
- **Execute a joint-partnership agreement** if you intend to invest in property jointly and/or operate a business together.
- **Execute a cohabitation/partnership agreement**.

COHABITATION AGREEMENTS

Historically, because of a strong public policy favoring marriage, the legal system has not provided cohabiting couples with a procedure for dissolving their relationships and resolving their disputes. Unlike marriage, absent a legally conferred status such as a domestic partnership or civil union, cohabiting partners do not automatically become entitled to particular rights and benefits when they decide to live together. If they want to establish rules and principles to govern particular aspects of their relationship and/or if they want to secure certain rights or assume specific responsibilities, then they need to do so by executing a contract, a cohabitation agreement (in addition to whatever other documents they may elect to create).

PARALEGAL PRACTICE TIP

Although our focus in this segment of the chapter is on cohabitation agreements between intimate partners, living-together agreements may also be executed by roommates residing together primarily for convenience and financial reasons and without any sexual involvement. The parties may be friends or strangers who connect with each other through, for example, postings on bulletin boards, newspaper ads, or online resources such as Craig's List. The focus of such agreements is usually on household responsibilities, financial obligations (e.g., for rent, utilities, phone, and food), and "rules" with respect to such topics as smoking, drinking, overnight guests, and pets.

A **Cohabitation Agreement** (sometimes called a Cohabitation Contract, a Living-Together Agreement, or a Nonmarital Agreement) is a private contract between two parties living together in a nonmarital relationship, which establishes mutually agreed-upon rights and responsibilities, many of which married persons obtain by statute, agreement, and custom. Cohabitation agreements are similar to, but usually do not contain all the provisions of, a premarital agreement.

A cohabitation agreement is not a replacement for a will, a health care proxy, a durable power of attorney, or a deed to property protecting a surviving partner in the event the other dies. It also does not necessarily have the same force and effect after marriage as a premarital agreement. It does, however, provide the parties with an opportunity to identify, negotiate, and reach agreement with respect to their expectations, both financial and personal. Such agreements reflect the general trend toward couples' private ordering of their legal rights and responsibilities. They are designed, in part, to avoid unanticipated and sometimes disastrous results when children are born, a party develops a long-term illness or dies, the relationship terminates, or a common law marriage is claimed by one of the parties.

A majority of states now permit, and in many instances encourage, unmarried cohabiting couples to contract legally with each other, although sometimes the parties may need to seek the assistance of the courts to enforce those agreements. An individual provision of a cohabitation agreement may be held unenforceable because it violates a law, constitutional right, or strong public policy (such as an agreement to have children, to abort a pregnancy should one occur, or to pay a partner each time the parties engage in a particular sexual act). If the provision is so offensive that it taints the entire agreement, the whole agreement may be ruled unenforceable. However, even if not enforceable, the document may be presented in a legal proceeding as evidence of the parties' intentions with respect to certain issues, such as how they agreed to treat the property accumulated during the term of their cohabitation. Paralegal Application 2.1 identifies some of the provisions most commonly included in cohabitation agreements.

> **Cohabitation Agreement**
> an agreement between two unmarried individuals who live or intend to live together, defining their intentions, rights, and obligations with respect to one another while living together and upon termination of their relationship

PARALEGAL PRACTICE TIP

Even if the parties have expectations with respect to their sexual relationship, caution should be exercised when including language on this topic. A court may not enforce an agreement if cohabitation is prohibited in the jurisdiction or if it appears that financial support is being provided solely in exchange for sexual services, thereby constituting a contract for prostitution. The courts will not enforce an agreement to commit a crime. The phrase "**meretricious sex**" is commonly used to refer to unlawful or illicit sexual relations.

> **Meretricious sex**
> unlawful or illicit sexual relations, such as prostitution or sexual relations outside of marriage

Paralegal **Application 2.1**

Cohabitation Agreements—Common Provisions

PARALEGAL PRACTICE TIP

An example of a Sample Cohabitation Agreement available online can be found at _www.family.findlaw.com_. You can find a link to this site at _www.pearsonhighered.com/wilson_ in the companion website material for Chapter 2 under "Forms."

Models of cohabitation agreements may be located online, in form and practice books, and often in office files (paper and/or electronic). However, it is important to adapt the content of a particular agreement to the unique circumstances of the parties and to governing state law. The paralegal may be asked to gather information about

(_Continued_)

the client's intentions, locate appropriate models, and draft for review a proposed agreement tailored to the client's needs. Because there is little statutory or case law governing the contents of cohabitation agreements beyond the requirements of basic contract law, they tend to be more varied than premarital agreements although they contain many of the same kinds of provisions. They commonly include the following in a signed, witnessed, and notarized document:

- A number of standard **boilerplate** provisions that identify the parties, the purpose of the agreement, and the state's law that will govern its interpretation and enforcement.

PARALEGAL PRACTICE TIP

The governing law chosen must be that of a state with which the parties have some connection (e.g., they must live, work, or plan to relocate there). Care should be taken to select a state that recognizes and enforces cohabitation agreements. To learn more about your state's position regarding enforcement of such agreements, visit *www.divorcesource.com/tables/domesticagreements.shtml*. A link to this site can be found at *www.pearsonhighered.com/wilson* in the companion website material for Chapter 2 under "Resources."

- A description of the consideration for the agreement (usually the parties' mutual promises) making clear that the agreement is not based on a promise to provide sexual services.
- A statement regarding the effective dates of the agreement including when it will become effective; whether it will be affected by temporary separations (as when one party is away on business for extensive periods); the timing of periodic reviews, if any; and the circumstances under which it will terminate and become null and void.
- A statement of the parties' agreement about how they will represent their relationship to the public and whether or not they intend it to potentially ripen into a common law marriage. If they do eventually marry, will the agreement become null and void or will it become the parties' premarital agreement?

PARALEGAL PRACTICE TIP

If the parties want their cohabitation agreement to serve as their premarital agreement should they eventually marry, the agreement must expressly state that intention, satisfy any jurisdictional requirements for a valid premarital agreement, and be executed with all the appropriate formalities.

- A description of the parties' agreement with respect to the waiver of any rights such as the right to claim a common law marriage, the right to claim any form of maintenance or support if the relationship terminates, the right to share in the pension or retirement accounts of the other party, or the right to make any claim on the other's estate in the event of death (except as otherwise provided or to enforce a debt against the estate).
- A statement of the parties' understanding with respect to the division of household and other joint expenses during the period of cohabitation. This portion of the agreement may appear in the form of an itemized budget and may also address personal expenses including health insurance.
- The parties' agreement regarding the treatment of income and property acquired during the period of cohabitation. How will jointly purchased property be titled? Will one party have any claim to appreciation in the value of the other's separate property?
- The parties' agreement with respect to treatment of debts and obligations acquired prior to and during the cohabitation period by either or both parties.
- A statement of intentions with respect to having and raising children. Although provisions concerning child-related matters such as custody and support remain under the jurisdiction of the court and are not necessarily enforceable, parties sometimes want to at least clarify their expectations in this area.
- Acknowledgments that the parties have disclosed their respective assets and liabilities and that they have been represented by separate counsel during negotiation and execution of the agreement.

PARALEGAL PRACTICE TIP

The parties to a cohabitation agreement may approach a single attorney to have their agreement drafted. Even though the parties' interests may not presently be antagonistic, they may be at a later date. Because a law firm may not ethically represent parties with adverse interests, each party should retain his or her own counsel in connection with drafting and/or reviewing their agreement. If only one party is represented, the agreement should indicate that both knew which party was represented, and that the other party was aware of his or her right to representation. Occasionally, the parties may use a collaborative law approach to developing their agreement or they have one attorney mediate creation of the document, and then each party consults separate counsel to review it.

- A statement that the document represents the parties' entire agreement.
- A description of if, when, and how the agreement can be modified or amended and how related disputes will be resolved.
- If any provision of the agreement is held to be invalid, will the remainder of the agreement be deemed valid and enforceable (a severability clause)?

- The agreement may contain additional provisions related to the parties' particular needs and circumstances. For example, do they expect to engage in business together? Will they have pets? Does either of them have a child from a prior relationship or a dependent adult for whom he or she is responsible? Who will do the shopping, cooking, and household chores? Are there any unique health needs? Are there any personal habits or idiosyncrasies the parties want to address such as smoking or personal hygiene?

FORMS OF RELIEF ABSENT A COHABITATION AGREEMENT

Prior to the 1970s, the law essentially denied any rights to unmarried cohabitants following a period of cohabitation. The contention was that granting financial and property rights to unmarried couples would demean the institution of marriage and condone "meretricious" or illicit sex. Although legislatures have been compelled to assume a more active role in regulating nonmarital relationships over the past decade, for more than thirty years the courts have carried the primary responsibility for establishing rules governing the rights of cohabitants when their relationships dissolve in the absence of an agreement. The seminal decision in this area is the high-profile case *Marvin v. Marvin,* decided by the California Supreme Court in 1976. (See Case 2.1.) Viewing the case as an alimony action between two unmarried cohabitants, the media coined the term **palimony** to describe it.

Without abandoning the strong public policy favoring marriage, the *Marvin* court strongly endorsed the now widely held principle that when the facts warrant it, the courts should fashion appropriate equitable remedies for cohabitants to avoid hardship or injustice.

Palimony

a term that originated in the media, palimony refers to a court-ordered allowance paid by one cohabitant to the other after their relationship terminates; recognized in some states by case law, but generally not by statute

CASE **2.1** *Marvin v. Marvin,* 18 Cal.3d 660, 557 P.2d 106, 134 Cal. Rptr. 815 (1976)

FROM THE OPINION

During the past 15 years, there has been a substantial increase in the number of couples living together without marrying. Such nonmarital relationships lead to legal controversy when one partner dies or the couple separates. . . .

Plaintiff avers that in October of 1964 she and defendant "entered into an oral agreement" that while "the parties lived together they would combine their efforts and earnings and would share equally any and all property accumulated as a result of their efforts whether individual or combined." Furthermore, they agreed to "hold themselves out to the general public as husband and wife" and that "plaintiff would further render her services as a companion, homemaker, housekeeper and cook"; . . . in return defendant agreed to "provide for all of plaintiff's financial needs and support for the rest of her life."

Plaintiff alleges that she lived with defendant from October of 1964 through May of 1970 and fulfilled her obligations under the agreement. During this period the

(Continued)

PARALEGAL PRACTICE TIP

You can find the opinion in the *Marvin* case at *www.pearsonhighered. com/wilson* in the companion website materials for Chapter 2 under "Cases" and in the Case Resources Section of the MyLegalStudiesLab.

parties as a result of their efforts and earnings acquired in defendant's name substantial real and personal property, including motion picture rights worth over $1 million. In May of 1970, however, defendant compelled plaintiff to leave his household. He continued to support plaintiff until November of 1971, but thereafter refused to provide further support.

On the basis of these allegations plaintiff asserts two causes of action. The first, for declaratory relief, asks the court to determine her contract and property rights; the second seeks to impose a constructive trust upon one half of the property acquired during the course of the relationship.

In the case before us plaintiff, . . . maintains that the trial court erred in denying her a trial on the merits of her contention. Although the trial court did not specify the ground for its conclusion that plaintiff's contractual allegations stated no cause of action, defendant offers some . . . theories to support the ruling. . . .

Defendant first and principally relies on the contention that the alleged contract is so closely related to the supposed "immoral" character of the relationship between plaintiff and himself that the enforcement of the contract would violate public policy. He points to cases asserting that a contract between nonmarital partners is unenforceable if it is "involved in" an illicit relationship. . . .

Numerous other cases have upheld enforcement of agreements between nonmarital partners in factual settings essentially indistinguishable from the present case. . . .

. . . The fact that a man and a woman live together without marriage, and engage in a sexual relationship, does not in itself invalidate agreements between them relating to their earnings, property or expenses. . . . Agreements between nonmarital partners fail only to the extent that they rest upon consideration of meretricious sexual services. . . .

The principle that a contract between nonmarital partners will be enforced unless expressly and inseparably based upon an illicit consideration of sexual services not only represents the distillation of the decisional law, but also offers a far more precise and workable standard than that advocated by defendant. . . .

In summary, we base our opinion on the principle that adults who voluntarily live together and engage in sexual relations are nonetheless as competent as any other persons to contract regarding their earnings and property rights. Of course, they cannot lawfully contract to pay for the performance of sexual services, for such a contract is, in essence, an agreement for prostitution and unlawful for that reason. But they may agree to pool their earnings and to hold all property acquired during the relationship in accord with the law governing community property; conversely they may agree that each partner's earnings and property acquired from those earnings remains the separate property of the earning partner. So long as the agreement does not rest upon illicit meretricious consideration, the parties may order their economic affairs as they choose, and no policy precludes the courts from enforcing such agreements.

Both plaintiff and defendant stand in broad agreement that the law should be fashioned to carry out the reasonable expectations of the parties. . . .

. . . the cases denying relief do not rest their refusal upon any theory of "punishing" a "guilty" partner. Indeed, to the extent that denial of relief "punishes" one partner, it

(Continued)

necessarily rewards the other by permitting him to retain a disproportionate amount of the property. Concepts of "guilt" thus cannot justify an unequal division of property between two equally "guilty" persons.

Other reasons advanced in the decisions fare no better. The principal argument seems to be that "[equitable] considerations arising from the reasonable expectation of . . . benefits attending the status of marriage . . . are not present [in a nonmarital relationship]" (*Vallera v. Vallera* . . .). But, although parties to a nonmarital relationship obviously cannot have based any expectations upon the belief that they were married, other expectations and equitable considerations remain. The parties may well expect that property will be divided in accord with the parties' own tacit understanding and that in the absence of such understanding the courts will freely apportion property accumulated through mutual effort. We need not treat nonmarital partners as putatively married persons in order to apply principles of implied contract, or extend equitable remedies; we need to treat them only as we do any other unmarried persons.

The argument that granting remedies to the nonmarital partners would discourage marriage must fail; . . . Although we recognize the well-established public policy to foster and promote the institution of marriage, . . . perpetuation of judicial rules which result in an inequitable distribution of property accumulated during a nonmarital relationship is neither a just nor an effective way of carrying out that policy.

The mores of society have indeed changed so radically in regard to cohabitation that we cannot impose a standard based on alleged moral considerations that have apparently been so widely abandoned by so many. Lest we be misunderstood, however, we take this occasion to point out that the structure of society itself largely depends on the institution of marriage and nothing we have said in this opinion should be taken to derogate from that institution. The joining of the man and woman in marriage is at once the most socially productive and individually fulfilling relationship that one can enjoy in the course of a lifetime.

We conclude that the judicial barriers that may stand in the way of a policy based upon the fulfillment of the reasonable expectations of the parties to a nonmarital relationship should be removed. As we have explained, the courts now hold that express agreements will be enforced unless they rest on an unlawful meretricious consideration. We add that in the absence of an express agreement, the courts may look to a variety of other remedies in order to protect the parties' lawful expectations.

The courts may inquire into the conduct of the parties to determine whether that conduct demonstrates an implied contract or implied agreement of partnership or joint venture . . . or some other tacit understanding between the parties. The courts may, when appropriate, employ principles of constructive trust . . . or resulting trust. . . . Finally, a nonmarital partner may recover in quantum meruit for the reasonable value of household services rendered less the reasonable value of support received if he can show that he rendered services with the expectation of monetary reward.

Since we have determined that plaintiff's complaint states a cause of action for breach of an express contract, and, as we have explained, can be amended to state a cause of action independent of allegations of express contract, we must conclude that the trial court erred in granting defendant a judgment on the pleadings.

The judgment is reversed and the cause remanded for further proceedings consistent with the views expressed herein.

(Continued)

PARALEGAL PRACTICE TIP

Courts in some states have refused to provide relief to cohabitants when their relationship terminates or do so only under certain circumstances. For example, in Minnesota, if sexual relations between the parties are contemplated, a cohabitation agreement between them will be enforceable only if it is written and signed by the parties and enforcement is sought after termination of the relationship. Sexual relations may be contemplated but must not be the basis for the agreement. The pertinent Minnesota Statutes, 513.075 and 513.076, are accessible at *www.pearsonhighered.com/wilson* in the companion website materials for Chapter 2 under "Statutes."

PARALEGAL PRACTICE TIP

This judgment established that the plaintiff was entitled to have her cause of action heard. On remand, however, the Superior Court did not find that the parties had an enforceable express contract but did award her a sum of $104,000 so that she could prepare to reenter the job market and become self-supporting.

Putative spouse
a person who believes in good faith that his or her invalid marriage is legally valid

Quasi-marital property
property treated as if it was acquired by the parties during the marriage even though the marriage was never valid; property acquired during a marriage in a non-community-property state that would be marital property if acquired in a community property state

SIDEBAR

In its opinion, the California Supreme Court also discussed California decisions addressing the impact of the state's Family Law Act establishing no-fault divorce in California. It noted that in the *Cary* case (34 Cal. App.3d 345, 109 Cal. Rptr. 862 (1973)), the Court of Appeals reasoned that the Act was designed to eliminate fault as a basis for dividing marital property. It further opined that once fault is excluded, nothing distinguishes the property rights of a nonmarital "spouse" living in a family relationship from those of a "**putative spouse**" who is entitled to half the parties' "**quasi-marital property**." The California Supreme Court determined that this reasoning may be applied by analogy to cohabiting couples who believe they are in a spouselike relationship. Do you agree?

When a marriage dissolves, the spouses have property rights that are identified by statute and applied by the courts. Cohabitants lack such established rights (unless contained in an enforceable agreement or afforded under a civil union or comparable statute). Absent a guiding legal framework, when cohabitants seek relief, the courts must consider each petition on a fact-intensive case-by-case basis. Paralegal Application 2.2 describes the kinds of information a paralegal may be required to gather in a cohabitation case. A summary of the primary legal theories various courts have relied on to provide relief to cohabitants is provided in Exhibit 2.2.

Paralegal **Application 2.2**

Gathering Information in a Cohabitation Case

In a "palimony" case, the paralegal may be asked to gather information in an effort to shape and develop support for the client's case and anticipate opposing arguments and defenses that may be raised. Answers to questions such as the following may be obtained directly from the client and/or other individuals through interviews and also from documents.

- When, where, and why did the parties decide to live together?
- Did either party relocate, change employment, or make any other major changes in order to cohabit?
- What were the dates during which the parties lived together?
- What was the understanding with respect to the sexual relationship between the parties, if any? What specifically was said? To what extent, if at all, was sexual activity a consideration for the agreement? What was the nature of the parties' sexual relationship before and during the period of cohabitation? Was it exclusive?

- Did the parties discuss their intentions with respect to marriage, and, if so, to what did they agree?
- What, if any, commitments were made regarding:
  - housing: rental or purchase and payment of related costs?
  - payment of household expenses: food, utilities, etc.?
  - homemaking responsibilities: cooking, cleaning, etc.?
  - medical insurance and expenses?
- How did the parties describe their relationship to their families, employers, friends, and the general public? Did they call each other spouses, companions, partners, roommates, significant others, etc.?
- How did the parties manage their finances? Did they have joint and/or separate bank accounts?
- What was said and agreed to with respect to the parties' separate property and property accumulated during the period of cohabitation?

(Continued)

- Were there any discussions and/or agreements concerning: children, the making of wills or other legal documents (such as powers of attorney and health care proxies), or the giving of gifts to each other during the cohabitation period?
- Were any other commitments made and, if so, what were they?
- How, and to what extent, were the parties involved in each other's business activities, and what was the agreement, if any, with respect to that involvement?
- Did either party ever compensate the other for services rendered during the cohabitation period and, if so, for what and in what manner and amount?
- Were any of the parties' agreements written down or recorded? Were any notes taken?
- Were there witnesses to any of the agreements made?

- What are the names and addresses of witnesses who may be able to testify regarding the parties' relationship and express or implied agreements?
- What documents exist to support any of the above, (e.g., lease agreements, deeds to property, checking and savings account statements, tax returns, loan applications, etc.)?
- Are there any **defenses** available to either party, such as fraud, undue influence, **unclean hands**, lack of capacity, etc.?

Defense
a defendant's stated reason why a plaintiff has no valid claim or why the court should not grant the relief requested

Unclean hands
the principle that a party should not be granted relief if he or she has acted unfairly, wrongfully, or illegally

EXHIBIT 2.2 Legal Bases for Granting Relief to Cohabitants Upon Dissolution of Their Relationship

Legal Basis for Relief	Definition	Example	
Express contract	This is a contract that is created by an actual articulated agreement of the parties as to certain terms of their relationship. The parties negotiate and "express" the terms to each other. As with other contracts, an express contract requires an offer, acceptance, and consideration (other than sexual services). Absent a cohabitation agreement evidencing the parties' intentions, express contracts can be difficult to prove and usually turn on the relative credibility of the parties.	Marlene and Walter decide to live together. They agree that during the period of their cohabitation (however long it may last), they will equally contribute to expenses, jointly perform household chores, and share equally in whatever assets they accumulate. Although they do not actually commit them to writing, they openly discuss these terms and agree that they are fair. Following the "Marvin Doctrine," many courts are likely to enforce this agreement.	**Express contract** a contract that is created by an actual articulated agreement of the parties as to certain terms of their relationship expressed orally or in writing
Implied-in-fact contract	This is a judicially created contract. The intentions of the parties are inferred from their conduct given the facts and surrounding circumstances. Even though its terms may not have been actually discussed or "expressed," a court may reasonably conclude there was an agreement based on the parties' actions.	Marlene and Walter agree to cohabit and they live together for seven years. They open joint checking and savings accounts into which they both make contributions. The couple shares most expenses equally, and household furnishings, etc., are purchased with commingled funds. Many of their friends assume that they are married. Based on these facts, a court could reasonably find an implied agreement to share assets accumulated during the relationship.	**Implied-in-fact contract** a judicially created contract, the existence of which is inferred from the conduct of the parties

(Continued)

EXHIBIT 2.2 (*Continued*)

Quasi-contract/implied-in-law contract a contract imposed by a court to prevent unjust enrichment of one party at the expense of the other	**Quasi-contract/ Implied-in-law contract**	While express or implied-in-fact contracts are based on the actual language or conduct of the parties, in a quasi-contract, the court imposes contractual obligations on the parties to avoid unjust enrichment of one party at the expense of the other. It is a "legal fiction" created by the court in the absence of an express agreement.	Marlene gives up her job as an accountant in order to perform the couples' household chores and to take care of Walter's three-year-old son. She provides seven years of household and childcare services at a considerable benefit to Walter. A court may now treat her services as part of a bargained-for exchange rather than as a gift and require him to make some payment to her. Based on a **quantum meruit** (as much as is deserved) approach, the court may award Marlene the reasonable value of services she rendered less any payments actually received. An economist may testify as to the estimated economic value of the services in the open marketplace.
Quantum meruit [Latin: as much as he deserved] a basis for establishing damages or providing relief based on the reasonable value of services one person has provided to another			
Resulting trust a trust created by the court when one party contributes funds or services toward the acquisition of property and the title to that property is held in the name of the other party	**Resulting trust/ Purchase money resulting trust/ Implied trust**	A **resulting trust** is created by the court when one party contributes funds or services toward the acquisition of property and the title to that property is in the name of the other party. It is imposed by the court on an asset for the benefit of a contributing party when it is demonstrated that he or she did not intend for the other party to have all or any ownership rights. The trustee (the one who "owns"/has title to the property) is deemed by the court to hold the property for the benefit of the beneficiary (the one who provided the funds).	Marlene and Walter purchase a small condo titled and mortgaged in Walter's name because of his better credit history, but Marlene pays the entire deposit of $25,000 and also pays the monthly mortgage payments out of her inheritance from her brother's estate. A court may reasonably find that Marlene did not intend for Walter to have ownership of the property, but rather that he holds title to the condo for her benefit.
Constructive trust a trust imposed by the court on an asset of a party who improperly or wrongfully acquired the property	**Constructive trust**	A **constructive trust** is imposed by the court on an asset of a party who improperly or wrongfully acquired the property. It is not based on the parties' intentions, but rather is designed to prevent unjust enrichment. The trustee (the holder of the property) is in effect ordered by the court to convey the property to the beneficiary (the wronged party).	Shortly before Marlene and Walter stopped living together, without Walter's knowledge or consent, Marlene took all of the funds out of the joint checking and savings accounts to which they each had contributed. The total amount taken was $24,000. A court may find that she holds at least 50% of that amount in a constructive trust for Walter's benefit and order her to pay him that amount.

EXHIBIT 2.2 *(Continued)*

Implied partnership/ Joint venture	Similar to an implied-in-fact contract, when the cohabiting partners work together in a business venture that is owned by one of the parties, the court creates an **implied partnership** or joint venture (more limited than a partnership) based on the conduct of the parties and then distributes the assets and liabilities of the business based on principles of fairness.	When Marlene and Walter began living together, Walter had a small sailboat chartering business. While she was at home, Marlene learned all she could about operating and marketing such a business. She spent about six hours a day for several years working to build the business. When the couple ceased living together, the business had grown to nearly forty times its value when they moved in together due primarily to her labors. Although she and Walter had no formal employment or partnership agreement, a court may hold that the chartering business represents a joint venture of the parties and that Marlene is entitled to a portion of its value.
Putative spouse doctrine	A putative spouse is a person who reasonably believes he or she entered a valid marriage, until some impediment to the marriage is discovered that renders the marriage invalid. Some courts will provide relief to an innocent "spouse" in such situations. This doctrine is sometimes extended to provide for other "innocent" unmarried partners.	Walter and Marlene initially met when he was forty years old and she was fifteen and they began living together when Marlene was seventeen. To celebrate, they went on a vacation to an Indian Reservation in South Dakota. While there, they participated in a traditional celebration that Walter convinced Marlene was a wedding ceremony. Marlene, albeit naively, continued to believe they were married until they eventually ceased living together several years later. A court may apply the putative spouse doctrine to afford Marlene some degree of relief.

Implied partnership
a judicially created partnership, the existence of which is inferred from the conduct of the parties

Postmarital agreement
an agreement made by two people already married to each other who want both to continue their marriage and also to define their respective rights upon separation, divorce, or death of one of the spouses. These agreements have been called "reconciliation agreements" in some states. They allow spouses to resolve financial issues and focus energy on other aspects of their marriage.[9] Postnuptial agreements have been expressly approved by statute and/or case law in approximately half the states, but at least two states (Ohio and Oklahoma) bar them.

Separation agreement
an agreement made between spouses, in anticipation of a divorce or a legal separation, concerning the terms of the divorce or separation and any continuing obligations of the parties to each other

Premarital agreement
an agreement made by two persons about to be married defining for themselves their respective rights, duties, and responsibilities in the event their marriage terminates by death, annulment, separation, or divorce

What Is a Premarital Agreement and What Is Its Purpose?

A premarital agreement is one of several kinds of agreements made by adults entering into, presently in, or exiting from a relationship with another adult. In addition to **cohabitation agreements**, others include **postmarital agreements**[8] and **separation agreements.**

A **premarital agreement** (sometimes called a premarital contract, prenuptial agreement, or antenuptial agreement) is an agreement made by two persons about to be married. The agreement is an effort by the parties to define for themselves rights, duties, and responsibilities that flow from the marital relationship and that otherwise would be regulated and determined by state law upon death, annulment, separation, or divorce. What usually happens in a premarital agreement is that one

PARALEGAL PRACTICE TIP

To learn about premarital (antenuptial) agreements in the state of Connecticut, visit *www.jud.ct.gov*. You can find a link to this site at *www. pearsonhighered.com/wilson* in the companion website material for Chapter 2 under "Resources."

Public policy

an idea or principle that is considered right and fair and in the best interest of the general public

Per se invalid

invalid in and of itself, standing alone, without reference to any additional facts or circumstances

Void

invalid and of no legal effect

PARALEGAL PRACTICE TIP

The opinion in the *Posner* case is available at *www.pearsonhighered. com/wilson* in the companion website material for Chapter 2 under "Cases" and in the Case Resources Section of the MyLegalStudiesLab.

or both of the parties agree to give up spousal support, an equal or equitable division of property, or other rights they might be entitled to under state law. Despite past fears that premarital agreements encourage divorce, they may actually promote marriage. People may choose to marry who might not do so without the personalized "safety net" the premarital agreement provides in the event the marriage does not last.

Premarital Agreements in Perspective

One of the primary **public policies** that legislatures and courts in the United States historically have supported is one favoring the marital relationship as the fundamental structural unit of society. In support of that policy they have legislated and decreed regulations designed to protect the institution of marriage and family members in the event of death or divorce. These regulations have been influenced by prevailing societal views about sexual morality, the vulnerability of children, and gender-related issues including the respective roles and relative power of men and women in society.

Although courts had, for many years, enforced premarital agreements that addressed property distribution upon death,[10] agreements made in contemplation of marriage that anticipated the possibility of divorce were viewed as **per se invalid** until the 1970s. The basic concern was that the party who would benefit most from the agreement (usually the male partner) would be motivated to terminate the marriage and the female partner would be left destitute. This perception has gradually changed over the past four decades along with views about men and women, fault-based divorce, and the institution of marriage generally. We now live in a society in which the rate of divorce has risen and few presume that marriage is a permanent union. As a result, we have an increasing number of individuals, both male and female, taking steps to develop their own approaches to distribution of property upon divorce or death. A premarital agreement is one vehicle for accomplishing this end.

The opinion in the landmark *Posner* case (see Case 2.2) describes the shift in public policy from one that presumed and promoted the permanence of marriage to one that acknowledges and enforces, under certain conditions, agreements regulating rights upon the dissolution of marriage. In *Posner*, the wife appealed the portion of the divorce decree that awarded the divorce to her husband and alimony to her in the amount of $600 a month pursuant to the terms of a premarital agreement between the parties. The wife's position was that, consistent with prior case law, the agreement should not be enforced. The court held that such agreements should no longer be considered **void** as contrary to public policy when the divorce is pursued in good faith on proper grounds.

CASE **2.2** *Posner v. Posner*, 233 So. 2d 381 (Fla. 1970)

FROM THE OPINION

At the outset, we must recognize that there is a vast difference between a contract made in the market place and one relating to the institution of marriage.

It has long been the rule in a majority of the courts of this country and in this state that contracts intended to facilitate or promote the procurement of a divorce will be declared illegal as contrary to public policy. . . .

(Continued)

The state's interest in the preservation of the marriage is the basis of the rule that . . . an antenuptial agreement by which a prospective wife waives or limits her right to alimony or to the property of her husband in the event of a divorce or separation, regardless of who is at fault, has been in some states held to be invalid. . . .

There can be no doubt that the institution of marriage is the foundation of the familial and social structure of our nation and, as such, continues to be of vital interest to the State; but we cannot blind ourselves to the fact that the concept of the "sanctity" of a marriage—as being practically indissoluble, once entered into—held by our ancestors only a few generations ago, has been greatly eroded in the last several decades. . . .

With divorce such a commonplace fact of life, it is fair to assume that many prospective marriage partners whose property and familial situation is such as to generate a valid antenuptial agreement settling their property rights upon the death of either, might want to consider and discuss . . .—and agree upon, if possible—the disposition of their property and the alimony rights of the wife in the event their marriage, despite their best efforts, should fail. . . .

We know of no community or society in which the public policy that condemned a husband and wife to a lifetime of misery as an alternative to the opprobrium of divorce still exists. And a tendency to recognize this change in public policy and to give effect to the antenuptial agreements of the parties relating to divorce is clearly discernible. . . .

SIDEBAR

What are the major reasons for not recognizing premarital agreements? What are the major reasons for enforcing them? If you were presently contemplating getting married, would you want to have such an agreement? Why?

What Kinds of Individuals and Couples Might Want to Execute a Premarital Agreement?

Once thought of as appropriate only for the rich and famous, premarital agreements are becoming increasingly more common. This is not all that surprising when one considers that about half of first marriages end in divorce. Although statistics are scarce, according to one source, some twenty percent of remarried couples use premarital agreements, and they have quintupled in overall frequency over the past twenty years.[11]

Premarital agreements are particularly appropriate for parties in circumstances such as the following:

- There is a significant age difference between the parties.
- One or both of the parties have substantial property of their own including real estate, investments, businesses, and retirement accounts.
- A party has an interest in a family business that he or she wants to "keep in the family."
- A party is responsible for taking care of third parties such as elderly parents or siblings with disabilities.

PARALEGAL PRACTICE TIP

The more common premarital contracts become, the less sensitive a topic they are for couples approaching marriage. However, sometimes meetings with individuals negotiating premarital agreements can be tense. Although generally optimistic about the future, most individuals recognize that marriage can be a challenge and that many initially happy unions fail. A premarital agreement is about as close as the parties can come to obtaining an insurance policy in case things do not work out as they hope.

- One of the parties is pursuing a degree or license in a potentially lucrative field such as medicine, and the other party will be supporting the couple through an extended education program.
- Both of the parties have been out of high school for several years, remained single, and had an opportunity to accumulate significant property.
- One of the parties is giving up a successful career in order to be a "stay-at-home" parent.
- One or both of the parties have children or grandchildren from a previous marriage.
- One of the parties is involved in a speculative business venture that may result in a significant increase or loss in wealth.
- One or both of the parties want to ensure a new spouse's inheritance, especially if, upon marriage, the new spouse will lose his or her right to a Social Security benefit or alimony from a prior spouse.
- One or both of the parties suffered through a prior divorce that was emotionally and financially devastating, and they do not want to repeat the experience.

PARALEGAL PRACTICE TIP

An alternative approach to developing agreements tailored to the unique circumstances of the two people about to be married involves use of the relatively nonadversarial **collaborative law** process. When the collaborative law process is used, "the written agreement is prepared last and only after the partners have discussed the issues and concerns important to them and their shared life, and have reached shared agreements about those concerns. The collaborative agreement becomes a mutually developed blueprint for the marriage."[12] Although the parties still have to address challenging questions and require the assistance of specially trained counsel during the process, the "difference is that the collaborative process provides a safe and supportive setting . . . and . . . enhances the couple's togetherness rather than emphasizing their separateness."[13]

Collaborative law
an approach to reaching agreements and resolving differences that stresses cooperation, joint problem solving, and the avoidance of litigation

How Are Premarital Agreements Developed?

The usual approach to creating a premarital agreement is that the parties first discuss the possibility of executing an agreement and their reasons for doing so. Then one of the parties (customarily the one with the greater incentive and the most to protect) selects an attorney to draft an agreement. The other party ideally retains a second attorney to review the agreement, recommend revisions, and advise him or her before signing. Occasionally the parties will utilize traditional **mediation** to resolve their differences concerning the proposed terms of their agreement.

Mediation
an approach to resolving differences in which a neutral third person helps the parties identify their differences, consider their options, and structure a mutually acceptable agreement

Fiduciary
a person who owes another a duty of good faith, trust, loyalty, and candor

PARALEGAL PRACTICE TIP

Cohabitation agreements are customarily viewed as basic contracts by the courts. They are subject to a lower standard than premarital agreements because they do not involve an interspousal relationship

What Are the Legal Requirements for a Valid Premarital Agreement?

Unlike contracts negotiated in the business world involving strangers who deal at arm's length, a premarital agreement is a contract between two individuals presumably engaged in a relationship of mutual trust and confidence. Given the couple's special relationship, courts often impose additional requirements and a higher standard of care on the parties, whom the courts view as having a **fiduciary** duty to one another, a special duty of fairness in dealing.

Although states vary with respect to specific requirements for validity, generally a premarital agreement must satisfy the following three requirements:

1. the basic requirements applicable to all contracts
2. the requirement of **procedural fairness,** meaning fairness in the negotiation and execution of the agreement
3. the requirement of **substantive fairness,** which means fairness in the actual terms of the agreement

Procedural fairness
fairness in the negotiation and execution of an agreement

Substantive fairness
fairness in the specific terms of an agreement

PARALEGAL PRACTICE TIP

The Focus on Technology activity at the end of this chapter identifies a selection of state statutes governing premarital agreements. Try locating some additional statutes by navigating four of the state codes available online at no cost. Links to the following sites can be found at *www.pearsonhighered.com/wilson* in the companion website material for Chapter 2 under "Statutes:" MAINE: *www.legislature.maine.gov/legis/statutes*; INDIANA: *www.in.gov/legislative*; KANSAS: *www.kslegislature.org*; and NORTH DAKOTA: *www.legis.nd.gov.*

THE BASIC REQUIREMENTS APPLICABLE TO ALL CONTRACTS

1. There must be an offer and acceptance (generally evidenced by the parties' signatures on a written agreement).
2. The parties must have the legal capacity to contract in terms of age and mental competence.
3. The subject matter of the contract must not be illegal (i.e., the parties cannot agree to commit an illegal act).
4. The contract must be supported by **consideration,** a bargained-for exchange of something of value (usually the mutual promise to marry in the case of premarital agreements, although courts may look for additional consideration when one party appears to gain everything and give up nothing).
5. There must be a "**meeting of the minds.**"

Consideration
a bargained-for exchange or mutual promises underlying the formation of a contract

Meeting of the minds
a shared understanding with respect to the terms and conditions of a contract

PARALEGAL PRACTICE TIP

Most contracts, including premarital agreements, must satisfy a state's **Statute of Frauds,** which specifies the kinds of contracts that must be in writing and signed in order to be enforced. A contract in consideration of marriage is one of the traditional Statute of Frauds exceptions to oral contract validity. Since the states differ on the requirements for a valid premarital agreement, it is important to determine whether the validity or enforcement of a premarital agreement at issue may be subject to an exception in the particular Statute of Frauds governing the case.[14]

Statute of Frauds
the requirement that certain types of contracts be in writing, such as a contract that by its terms cannot be completed within a year, a contract in consideration of marriage, or a contract for the sale of land

THE REQUIREMENT OF PROCEDURAL FAIRNESS[15]

The focus of procedural fairness is on fairness during the negotiation and execution of the agreement. In assessing procedural fairness, the courts usually will look at the surrounding circumstances to answer such questions as the following:

- Was each party represented by independent counsel?
- Was there adequate disclosure by each of the parties of the nature and value of their assets and liabilities?
- Was there sufficient time to discuss, negotiate, and reflect on the agreement prior to execution?

PARALEGAL PRACTICE TIP

Consider the following example: A husband residing in a community property state such as California, Arizona, Texas, or Idaho has a right to 50% of his spouse's earnings from the date of marriage. If a man is going to enter a premarital agreement in one of those states, he needs to understand how his rights and responsibilities under state law may be altered by the agreement. He should have a reasonable opportunity to consult with independent counsel of his own choosing.

- Was there any fraud, duress, or undue influence in the negotiation or execution of the agreement?

Was each party represented by independent counsel? Even though the parties are generally not antagonistic as they look forward to their forthcoming marriage, they do have "adverse" interests. When they execute their agreement, each of them is being asked to waive or vary certain rights to which they would otherwise be entitled upon divorce, separation, or death. This is an especially important consideration when the parties are of unequal bargaining power, such as when one party is much more highly educated and financially sophisticated than the other. (See Paralegal Application 2.3.)

Was there adequate disclosure by each of the parties of the nature and value of their assets and liabilities? Virtually all states require some degree of financial disclosure but vary with respect to how much is necessary. Some states require full disclosure, while others provide that a general picture of one's financial worth is enough. Many states allow a party to waive his or her right to seek or receive disclosure. Ideally financial disclosure should accurately and adequately reveal a party's assets, liabilities, and net worth to protect against later claims of fraud or misrepresentation. The preferred form of disclosure is a separate schedule of income, assets, and liabilities for each of the parties that is referenced in the body of the agreement and appended as an exhibit. Completed financial affidavits, tax returns, and other documents such as deeds and appraisals may also be attached. The paralegal is often involved in the collection, review, and/or preparation of these materials.

In assessing adequacy of disclosure, a court is likely to ask: Given the surrounding circumstances, did both parties have, or should they have had, sufficient knowledge of the other's worth such that each of them could make an informed decision with respect to the terms of the agreement? Generally, there is no "meeting of the minds" with respect to the contract if one party was provided inadequate information regarding the other's assets and the value of the rights waived.

Paralegal Application 2.3

Representation by Independent Counsel

It is difficult, if not impossible, for one attorney to represent the interests of both parties to a premarital agreement. The conflict of interest inherent in such a multiple representation leaves the attorney open to allegations of ethical misconduct. In an effort to protect against such a result, the following steps may be taken:

1. If one party declines to seek counsel, it is wise for the attorney representing the other party to confirm in writing to both parties which of them he or she represents and to strongly advise and explain why it is important that the other party seek independent counsel. This should be done in the best interests of the client *and* the attorney. The paralegal may be asked to draft such a letter.

2. Many agreements now contain statements to be signed by counsel and/or by the parties under oath confirming that each has been instructed to seek legal counsel to advise them of their respective potential statutory rights in the property of the other and the effect that execution of the agreement will have on those rights. The paralegal should keep this option in mind when assisting in the drafting of an agreement, particularly one involving an unrepresented party.

3. In some states, prohibitions against multiple representation require that the nonrepresented individual provide a written statement acknowledging the fact that the sole attorney is not protecting his or her interests. This requirement affords additional protection against a later malpractice claim for the attorney representing the other party.

Was there sufficient time to discuss, negotiate, and reflect on the agreement prior to execution? Although the time period between execution of the agreement and the marriage ceremony is not necessarily determinative, it is a factor the courts will consider in evaluating the validity of an agreement. The best advice is to allow reasonable time for negotiation and review. Some states automatically invalidate any premarital agreement that is signed on the day of the wedding. In general, the longer the time period (within limits) between when a party was presented with the agreement and when it was executed, the greater the likelihood the execution will be deemed voluntary, but the states go both ways. Generally, timing will be considered in the context of the nature, scope, and complexity of the agreement. A simple agreement the parties discussed for months addressing one bank account of modest value may well be considered valid even if presented for review and signature on the wedding eve. On the other hand, a complex agreement covering millions of dollars of diverse assets between a party with significant bargaining power and an individual with little power, few assets, and much to lose warrants ample time for review and deliberation with the assistance of competent, independent counsel. Although many courts will consider whether each of the parties had the background, experience, and time necessary to evaluate options and the consequences of choices to be made, there is not always a requirement that a party actually understand the legal effect of the terms of the agreement.[18] *Ignorantia legis non excusat!* (See Case 2.3, the *Simeone* case, later in this chapter.)

Was there any fraud, duress, or undue influence in the negotiation or execution of the agreement? Ideally, the parties should be equals in the process. However, because they are involved in a special relationship, they tend to be more vulnerable making agreements than strangers would be negotiating in the business world. They may be eager to please each other. One partner may dominate or even abuse the other emotionally or physically. One of the parties may have limited English skills and/or may rely on the other, blindly trusting that individual's superior knowledge and skill. One of the ways in which some attorneys try to protect against a later claim that an agreement was executed under undue influence or duress is to have the parties and their respective attorneys all present at the execution and to videotape the event. A paralegal may be asked to schedule this taping and should be certain the necessary equipment is available and in good working order.

PARALEGAL PRACTICE TIP

When the execution of the agreement is videotaped, a series of questions such as the following may be asked of each party:

1. Have you had an opportunity to review the agreement and the attached documents?
2. Please identify the attached documents.
3. Have you had an opportunity to consult with counsel of your own choosing and to ask questions regarding the agreement and the attached documents?
4. Do you understand the terms of the agreement?
5. Are you satisfied with those terms?
6. Have you disclosed all of your assets and liabilities and is a summary of them attached to the agreement?
7. Has anyone made any promises to you other than what is contained in the agreement?
8. Are you presently under the influence of any drug or condition that might impair your ability to understand what you are signing?
9. Do you have any questions?
10. Are you prepared to sign the agreement at this time?

Paralegal Application 2.4

Elderly Clients

Premarital agreements provide an especially useful vehicle for addressing the challenges and fears the elderly face with respect to marriage and remarriage late in life. Among other goals, seniors want to protect and preserve wealth, benefits from previous marriages, and relationships and interests of their children. They also want to avoid the partner's financial obligations related to health care and other debts.[19]

Agreements involving elderly clients or other clients whose competency may be questioned require special consideration. Many attorneys require elderly clients to obtain an **Affidavit of Competency** from a physician prior to execution of legal documents such as wills, powers of attorney, or premarital agreements to help protect against later claims that the documents were executed under undue influence. Paralegals may be asked to work with clients to facilitate this task.

Affidavit of Competency
an affidavit from a physician that an individual is competent to perform a particular act

---

PARALEGAL PRACTICE TIP

A New York court has defined an "unconscionable bargain" as one which "no person in his or her senses and not under delusion would make on the one hand, and no honest and fair person would accept on the other, the inequality being so strong and manifest as to shock the conscience and confound the judgment of any person of common sense." *Morad v. Morad*, 27 A.D.3d 626, 812 N.Y.S.2d 126 (2006).

Unconscionable
so substantially unfair in terms or result as to shock the conscience

Waiver
the giving up of a right or privilege

PARALEGAL PRACTICE TIP

Agreements increasingly tie waivers and alimony provisions to the length of the marriage. The longer the marriage, the greater the likelihood and amount of alimony.

THE REQUIREMENT OF SUBSTANTIVE FAIRNESS

Substantive fairness refers to fairness in the actual terms of the agreement. A few states require the agreement to be fair to both parties. Some take the position that people are free to make "bad bargains,"[20] but most courts will not enforce an agreement if its terms are so unfair to one of the parties that they "shock the conscience of the court." Generally, the scope of the inquiry with respect to substantive fairness is whether the terms of the agreement are fair and not **unconscionable.** Under normal contract review (U.C.C. §2–302), unconscionability is determined at the time of execution. States vary with respect to whether the determination of fairness is made only as of the date of execution or also at the time of performance.

Substantive Fairness at the Time of Execution

Fairness at the time of execution involves a review of the agreement as written, and the court will consider such matters as the following:

Is the division of property *per se* unfair or unconscionable at the time of execution? Given that the purpose of a premarital agreement is to allow the parties to alter the usual division of property at divorce and/or death, it is likely that the agreement will result in an unequal division of property. The court will consider fairness under the parties' circumstances. An agreement that calls for one party to receive everything while the other receives nothing and will end up on public assistance is likely to be scrutinized closely and not be enforced.

Is an agreement to waive alimony or spousal support fair at the time of execution? In most states, an agreement that limits or waives spousal support is likely to be deemed valid if it is entered into freely, with knowledge of the rights waived, after adequate disclosure by both parties, and without undue influence. This is especially likely to be the case if the **waiver** is made by a party with ample assets at the time the agreement is signed. A waiver providing for the allowance of alimony under certain extreme and unforeseen circumstances (serious illness, etc.) or a waiver that is effective only if the marriage lasts less than a certain number of years is also likely to be enforceable.

Substantive Fairness at the Time of Performance

A consideration of fairness at the time of performance (upon divorce or death) allows a court to take a "second look" and consider whether terms that were fair at the time of execution are still fair at the time of enforcement. Generally the focus is on whether, due to unforeseen circumstances, an agreement that was once fair and reasonable has become so unfair that its enforcement would be unconscionable. There is no precise definition of "unconscionable" that binds all courts. Rather the assessment is made on a case-by-case basis.

Preparation for Drafting a Premarital Agreement

Paralegal Application 2.5 identifies several of the tasks that should be performed prior to the actual drafting of a premarital agreement.

Paralegal **Application 2.5**

In Anticipation of an Agreement—Tasks for the Attorney and the Paralegal

- The attorney should advise the client of the basic law governing rights and responsibilities upon separation, divorce, annulment, or death.
- The attorney should advise the client of the law regarding premarital agreements and their enforceability.
- The attorney should discuss the importance of independent representation for the prospective spouses.
- The attorney should learn what the client's motivations and goals are so that a decision can be made as to whether or not a premarital agreement is the most appropriate means for accomplishing the client's objectives. This may involve an assessment of any federal income tax, gift tax, and estate tax consequences of various options.
- Necessary background information and copies of documents need to be gathered including the following, a task often accomplished by or at least with the assistance of the paralegal:
  - the names, addresses, ages, and social security numbers of the parties
  - the date of the intended marriage and the flexibility with respect to that date
  - information regarding prior marriages and children/grandchildren of both parties and any related obligations (child support, spousal support, etc.)

- information regarding all forms of income and assets of the parties (including expected assets). A threshold value may be set for assets that should be identified (e.g., any property valued at over $5,000 or $25,000 based on the size of the parties' estates). A paralegal or the attorney will often work with the client to be certain that all kinds of assets of value are included (collections, stock portfolios, antiques, etc.).
- copies of potentially relevant documents, including, for example, trusts, deeds, retirement plans, court orders (e.g., for property division, support, or other judgments), insurance policies, and appraisals of real estate, artwork, jewelry, and the like
- information regarding debts/liabilities of each of the parties
- information about any unique and/or foreseeable circumstances (such as one party already having been diagnosed with a debilitating or terminal disease or special needs of any children of a party, such as severe physical or mental impairments)
- The paralegal should confirm current requirements for premarital agreements in the state of execution, such as whether any particular kinds of provisions are prohibited and whether the agreement must be witnessed, notarized, and/or recorded.

What Kinds of Provisions Does a Premarital Agreement Contain?

Each premarital agreement is unique because it reflects the intentions of two specific people, each with his or her own goals and needs. However, agreements commonly include:

1. A preamble (introductory segment) that identifies the parties and describes their intentions
2. Schedules of each party's assets and liabilities, which may include anticipated gifts and inheritances that are reasonably certain and of known value
3. A definition of "separate property" and a description of how each party's "separate property" and its appreciation and proceeds, if sold, will be treated in the event of death or divorce
4. A definition of marital or "joint property" and a description of how marital property of various kinds (real estate, jewelry, other personal property) will be treated and what role, if any, contribution will play
5. A statement of the rights each party will have to alimony or spousal support if the marriage ends in a legal separation or divorce, or a waiver of those rights
6. A provision relating to death benefits or waivers thereof

The Uniform Premarital Agreement Act (UPAA) provides that the parties also are free to contract with respect to personal rights and obligations during their marriage, provided the terms do not violate public policy or existing statutes. They may want to include provisions relating to several aspects of their life together. One or more of these terms may taint the entire agreement and render it void and unenforceable. An attorney may want to confirm with the client in writing that there is no guarantee that a particular provision will be enforced by the courts. Paralegal Application 2.6 identifies some potentially problematic terms.

Paralegal Application 2.6

Potential Red Flags

- The parties cannot agree to engage in criminal activity.
- The parties may include provisions relating to child custody and support but they cannot bargain away the rights of third persons (their children). Such provisions will be subject to approval by the court that retains jurisdiction over child-related issues. For example, an agreement that children from a party's prior marriage may not live with the parties may be held unenforceable as a violation of public policy and not in the best interests of the children.

(Continued)

In some countries where the civil law is based on the teachings of Islam, agreements contain both religious and secular provisions. If a party seeks enforcement of such an agreement at the time of a divorce action in the United States, the court may make an effort to separate provisions that are secular and enforceable from those that are religious in nature and not enforceable.

- Terms that tread on constitutional rights may not be enforceable, such as:
  - An agreement to raise children in a particular religion may be viewed as violating a party's (or a child's) right to freedom of religion,[21] although a court may enforce a provision that a party be required to participate cooperatively in obtaining a religious separation or annulment.[22]
  - An agreement to work or render certain services may be deemed a form of involuntary servitude if enforced by the court.
- Terms that invade a party's "right to privacy" are unlikely to be enforced, such as:

A New York case (*Avitzur*) was the first case decided by any state's highest court pertaining to the execution of a *get*, a Jewish divorce. If interested in this topic, read the article available at *www.jlaw.com*, *A Suggested Antenuptial Agreement: A Proposal in the Wake of Avitzur* by Rabbi J. David Bleich. A link to this site can be found at *www.pearsonhighered.com/wilson* in the companion website material for Chapter 2 under "Resources."

- A promise to perform certain sexual acts or to engage in sexual relations according to a particular schedule.[23]
- A promise to use contraception or not to have an abortion.
- A promise not to have children.[24]
- Courts may not enforce a promise to prosecute or not prosecute a divorce action.
- Certain "spousal" waivers of retirement benefits may not be valid and enforceable if made prior to marriage under the requirements of the Employee Retirement Income Security Act (ERISA) and the Retirement Equity Act (REA). (See 29 U.S.C. Section 1055.)[25]

EXHIBIT 2.3 Sample Premarital Agreement

PREMARITAL AGREEMENT
PREAMBLE

THIS AGREEMENT is made this _____ day of _____, 2012, by and between *Name of prospective spouse A* of _____ *address*, _____, _____ ("*first name*") and _____ *Name of prospective spouse B* of _____ *address*, _____ ("*first name*"), _____ collectively referred to as "the parties."

DRAFTING TIP

The preamble establishes the identity of the parties.

RECITALS

WHEREAS,

A. The parties plan to be married in _____ *city, state* _____ on or about _____ *date* _____, 2012. Neither of the parties has been married previously.

DRAFTING TIP

Reference should be made in this part of the agreement to any prior marriages and existing children or grandchildren of either or both of the parties, if applicable.

B. Each recognizes that the other is gainfully employed and possesses property and assets independently acquired prior to their intended marriage such that each is able to provide for his or her own individual needs. Each desires to enter this agreement realizing that either or both of the parties' financial, health, or other circumstances may change substantially in the future.

Some attorneys include social security numbers, a practice that can be helpful if a party later needs to be located. Others do not include them in an effort to prevent identity theft, as premarital agreements eventually may become public documents if recorded in Registries of Deeds or if filed as part of the pleadings in a divorce action or estate administration.

EXHIBIT 2.3 (*Continued*)

DRAFTING TIP

Paragraph B lays the basis for a determination that the agreement is fair at the time of execution. It also makes clear that the parties intend their agreement to take effect with full knowledge of the uncertainties of life such as early retirement, fluctuations in income, health problems, or pursuit of a new career. This helps defend against a later claim that a certain change was unforeseeable, such as poor health or a financial failure.

C. The parties intend by this Agreement to define and fix their respective rights and obligations to each other with regard to spousal support and to any property now owned or hereafter acquired before or after the date of their marriage, in the event of the termination of their marriage by death or legal process.

DRAFTING TIP

Paragraph C addresses the basic purpose of the agreement.

D. A owns certain property, both real and personal, as listed on Exhibit 1 attached hereto and incorporated herein, the nature and approximate value of which has been fully disclosed to B prior to execution of this Agreement. Also listed on Exhibit 1 and previously disclosed to B is A's indebtedness exclusive of his personal expenses.

E. B owns certain property, both real and personal, as listed on Exhibit 2 attached hereto and incorporated herein, the nature and approximate value of which has been fully disclosed to A prior to execution of this Agreement. Also listed on Exhibit 2 and previously disclosed to A is B's indebtedness exclusive of her personal expenses.

DRAFTING TIP

Paragraphs D and E and the Schedules that will be attached to the agreement as Exhibits 1 and 2 address the requirement of disclosure of assets and liabilities. Some agreements provide that these schedules will be updated on a periodic basis without affecting the nature, validity, or effect of the underlying agreement.

DRAFTING TIP

Sometimes the agreement will include a paragraph that provides that disclosures of property will be kept confidential absent consent or legal necessity. This is particularly appropriate when a party's business interests are listed and he or she would be disadvantaged if the document is made part of a public record and a competitor becomes aware of sensitive information.

DRAFTING TIP

Other related exhibits may also be attached such as copies of trusts, tax returns, and appraisals.

F. The parties acknowledge that each has had an adequate opportunity to negotiate, review, and consider the terms of this Agreement prior to execution; that each has been advised

EXHIBIT 2.3 *(Continued)*

by independent counsel of his or her individual choice as to his or her rights as a spouse under the law and the legal effect of the Agreement on those rights; that each believes the provisions of the Agreement are fair, just, and reasonable; that each understands, assents to, and intends to be bound by its provisions; and that each enters the Agreement freely, voluntarily, and without any duress, undue influence, or illegal consideration.

DRAFTING TIP

Paragraph F addresses procedural fairness in the negotiation and execution of the agreement, including the requirement that it be freely and voluntarily executed. The reference to counsel of individual choice makes clear that each party chose and retained his or her own independent attorney and not one chosen by the other party. The content presumes that counsel has described the applicable state's approach to allocation of property upon divorce and death so both parties appreciate what they are gaining and/or giving up in the agreement.

G. This Agreement shall become effective only upon the marriage of the parties within a period of one (1) year from the date hereof, and, if such marriage is not solemnized within said period, then this Agreement shall be null and void.

DRAFTING TIP

The one-year time frame is intended to protect against such a long period passing that the nature of the assets and liabilities of the parties may have changed in some significant manner.

NOW THEREFORE, in consideration of the mutual promises and covenants set forth herein, the parties mutually agree as follows:

DRAFTING TIP

This paragraph identifies the consideration that supports the agreement.

AGREEMENTS

1. **Definition of Separate Property**
   For purposes of this Agreement, "separate property" shall be defined as:
   a. all assets in which each presently has an interest exclusive of the other as shown on the Schedules contained in Exhibits 1 and 2;
   b. any inheritances, gifts, bequests, or devises received by either of them after the date of the parties' marriage;
   c. all appreciation, reinvestments, and proceeds of sale or redemption of any of the above property after the date of the parties' marriage;
   d. any property designated as separate property by both parties in writing after the date of their marriage; and
   e. any income earned by either party during the marriage including salaries and bonuses.

DRAFTING TIP

"Separate property" must be carefully defined because each party is giving up an interest he or she might otherwise have in the other party's separate property. The definition of separate property provided here is broad. For example, some agreements do not designate income earned by a party during the marriage as separate property.

(Continued)

PARALEGAL PRACTICE TIP

Some agreements include a "sunset provision" that terminates the agreement after a certain number of years. Such clauses are used primarily by wealthier parties concerned about the impact of a potential short-term marriage.

EXHIBIT 2.3 *(Continued)*

DRAFTING TIP

This definition does not include as separate property retirement benefits (pension, profit sharing, deferred compensation, etc.) because potential rights in certain retirement plans cannot be waived by a nonspouse under ERISA. However, the agreement could include a provision that the other party will agree to execute a waiver after an appropriate period post marriage.

DRAFTING TIP

Sometimes the agreement will specify whether ownership of property will be exclusively determined by title or whether one party's contributions (financial or nonfinancial) to appreciation in the value of the other party's property will be considered in some manner. For example, what happens if the parties purchase a boat together and each contributes to its purchase and maintenance but not equally? The agreement may also address the effect of commingling of assets and income or future increases in the value of separate property.

2. **Separate Property During Marriage**
   Each party agrees to keep and retain the sole ownership and control of any property held as his or her separate property as herein defined without interference from the other and in the same manner as if the marriage had not occurred.

3. **Separate Obligations of the Parties**
   Obligations of a party incurred prior to the marriage shall remain the separate obligations of that party. The other party shall not be liable for those obligations, and shall be indemnified and held harmless from them by the responsible party. Such existing obligations shall be paid from the separate property of the responsible party.

DRAFTING TIP

It is important to address liabilities as well as assets in premarital agreements. This provision could be expanded to address liabilities incurred during marriage by either or both of the parties.

4. **Definition of Marital Property**
   For purposes of this Agreement, with the exception of either party's separate property as herein defined, marital property ("Marital Property") shall be defined as all property accumulated by the parties during the marriage until the date of the death of either party or the date on which any legal action for separation, annulment, or divorce is commenced. Marital property shall also include any property designated as marital property by both parties in writing after the date of the marriage.

DRAFTING TIP

This paragraph sets the date of the filing of an action as a key date. Other options might be the date of separation, the date of divorce, etc.

DRAFTING TIP

In the event of an annulment, if the marriage was *void ab initio* (invalid from the outset), no valid marriage will ever have occurred and the agreement will never have taken effect, absent a provision that addresses this circumstance.

PARALEGAL PRACTICE TIP

Given the broad definition of separate property in this agreement, each party may be in a position to transfer significant assets by will, trust, gift, or otherwise to children from a prior marriage, other parties, charities, or the spouse, if he or she chooses to do so.

EXHIBIT 2.3 (*Continued*)

DRAFTING TIP

Most often agreements address income and asset issues. At this point in the agreement, however, the parties may choose to include provisions regarding various aspects of their life together. Some agreements will address how various responsibilities will be managed during the marriage. How will bank accounts be set up? How will payment of bills be handled? Who will perform various household responsibilities? What are the parties' intentions with respect to childrearing roles and responsibilities? Provisions that pertain to medical, disability, life insurance, and long-term care expenses and insurance are especially appropriate in agreements involving elderly and/or disabled parties. Occasionally an agreement will address behavioral issues such as excess spending, gambling, drinking, drug abuse, or infidelity during the marriage. Although such provisions may clarify expectations of the parties, some of them may be unenforceable.

5. **Marital Property Upon Termination of the Marriage**
   a. In the event of termination of the marriage by legal proceedings, all assets then jointly owned by the parties as joint tenants, tenants by the entirety, or otherwise and not herein defined as separate property shall be divided equally between the parties.

DRAFTING TIP

This particular agreement provides for an equal rather than an equitable division of marital property regardless of the jurisdiction in which legal process is commenced and whether it is a community property or equitable distribution state. Parties to other agreements may elect different options.

DRAFTING TIP

This agreement adopts what some call a "three-pot" approach to property: "his," "hers," and "theirs." Some parties will set forth further provisions requiring the transfer of an asset of one party to the other party or creation of an asset for the other party's benefit (for example, a lump sum payment; a health, disability, or life insurance policy for the other's benefit; or transfer of an asset to the other party such as a vacation home). This is particularly likely if the agreement contains a waiver of spousal support or estate claim and/or a party is giving up employment or an alimony payment from a prior spouse as a result of the upcoming marriage. Such provisions are sometimes tied to the length of the marriage.

   b. In the event of the termination of the marriage by the death of a party, all assets defined as marital property shall become the sole property of the surviving party and thus be excluded from the decedent's estate. The surviving party shall own said property subject to any liens, mortgages, or encumbrances secured by the property.

DRAFTING TIP

It is important to specify if the marital property will be transferred subject to encumbrances pursuant to the agreement (by contract rather than by inheritance). Otherwise, the decedent's estate would not receive the asset but would be liable for the decedent's share of the encumbrances.

(Continued)

EXHIBIT 2.3 *(Continued)*

PARALEGAL PRACTICE TIP

It is important to check the law governing agreements, both statutory and case law, that may impact the content of the agreement. Waivers of spousal support are especially subject to variations. In Louisiana, for example, by statute (LSA-C.C. art. 2329) spouses before or during marriage have the right to enter agreements "as to all matters that are not prohibited by public policy." By case law, parties may waive permanent spousal support but not temporary support in their prenuptial agreements based on public policy. See, e.g., *Barber v. Barber,* 38 So. 3d 1046 (2010).

6. **Mutual Waivers**
   a. Waiver of Rights to Property: In the event of termination of the marriage by divorce or annulment, each party agrees not to assert any claim of any kind to the separate property of the other as herein defined. This waiver shall not apply to marital property.
   b. Waiver of Rights to Maintenance and Support: In the event of a legal separation, divorce, or annulment, the parties agree to waive any rights to spousal support or maintenance of any kind to which either might otherwise be entitled. The parties agree that this provision may be entered as a complete defense by either party in response to an action for alimony. The parties further agree that nothing herein shall be deemed a waiver of either party's right to claim child support for support of any minor children born to or legally adopted during their marriage.

DRAFTING TIP

The parties cannot waive rights or obligations pertaining to child custody and support which remain subject to the jurisdiction of the court.

DRAFTING TIP

This model sets forth a waiver of spousal support. If, in the alternative, it provided for support, the agreement could spell out a method for determining the appropriate amount to be paid. It could also identify the circumstances in which payment of alimony would commence, be modified, or terminate. For example, the amount could be tied to a certain event (e.g., disability, reduction in income) or the length of the marriage (i.e., the longer the marriage, the greater the amount of support). Some agreements provide for reductions or elimination of support if there is proof of adultery by the recipient spouse during the marriage.

DRAFTING TIP

The enforceability of spousal support waivers in premarital agreements varies from state to state and they may not be effective if enforcement would bring about an "unconscionable" result.

   c. Waiver of Estate Claims: In the event of the death of one of the parties, each party hereby relinquishes and waives all rights, claims, and interests that he or she may have or acquire as surviving spouse, heir at law, or otherwise in the estate of the other party.

DRAFTING TIP

Paragraphs a and b are waivers of statutory rights upon divorce, and c is a waiver of rights upon death. It is common to specifically list the scope of the rights being waived upon death of a party (the right to inherit as a spouse under the state's laws of descent and distribution, the right to claim a distributive or forced share as a surviving spouse, the right to petition to serve as administrator of the deceased spouse's estate, etc.).

7. **Wills/Trusts**
   Nothing contained herein shall preclude or prevent either party from freely executing a will or settling a trust that confers benefits on the other party, or from nominating the other party as executor or trustee, or from exercising any power of appointment in favor of the other party.

EXHIBIT 2.3 (*Continued*)

Under contract law, judges look to "the four corners" of the agreement (the "face" of the written instrument) to determine what the parties intended at the time the agreement was executed. Sometimes, however, if an agreement is ambiguous, the court will go outside the contract and hear testimony ("parol evidence") from witnesses, not to create terms but rather to clarify the parties' intentions with respect to specific existing terms.

DRAFTING TIP

A premarital agreement is a contract and generally not a replacement for a will though its terms are customarily enforceable as claims against the estate of a party who dies. However, if the agreement is executed with all the formalities of a will, a party may assert that it serves as a will "substitute." Clients should consider their agreement and wills in tandem. Even though the parties may waive statutory rights in the agreement, they are still free to voluntarily make provisions for each other.

8. **General Provisions**
   a. Entire Agreement
      The parties agree that this Agreement contains their entire understanding and that there have been no additional promises, representations, or agreements made to either party by the other, oral or written, except as set forth herein.

DRAFTING TIP

A paralegal should maintain a complete file including successive drafts, revisions suggested by either party, and written confirmations of telephone exchanges, etc. Even though an agreement may never be challenged, if it is, the contents of a complete file can be very valuable as forensic evidence for use in court.

   b. Modification
      This Agreement may be modified, amended, or rescinded at any time after the solemnization of the marriage, only by a subsequent written agreement between and signed by the parties.

DRAFTING TIP

This paragraph leaves the door open for the parties to alter or rescind their agreement at a later date if their circumstances alter. However, modification provisions should not be included in a jurisdiction where postmarital agreements are prohibited. In such jurisdictions, inclusion of a modification provision may cause rescission of the entire agreement.

   c. Waiver of Breach or Default
      No waiver of breach or default with respect to a provision of this Agreement shall be deemed a waiver of any subsequent breach or default.

DRAFTING TIP

This provision means that if a party allows the other party to default on a particular obligation under the agreement, he or she is not waiving the right to object to a subsequent default on that or any other provision.

   d. Binding Effect
      This Agreement shall be binding on the parties hereto and their respective legal representatives, heirs, successors, and assigns.

(*Continued*)

EXHIBIT 2.3 (*Continued*)

DRAFTING TIP

The agreement binds the parties with respect to each other but is not necessarily binding on third parties such as creditors or bona fide purchasers of property without notice. To ensure that the agreement will be enforceable against a purchaser of a piece of real estate, for example, a copy of the agreement should be recorded in the appropriate Registry of Deeds. Some states have statutes that specifically address this issue.[26]

   e. Severability
      In the event any provision of this Agreement shall be held illegal, invalid, or otherwise unenforceable, such holding shall not invalidate or render unenforceable any other provisions hereof, and the offending provision shall be severed from this Agreement and be null and void and of no force and effect.

DRAFTING TIP

Severability clauses are common in most contracts. They are especially important in premarital agreements when a client insists on including a provision that is likely to be unenforceable (such as a term that the parties will have no children or must practice a particular religion).

   f. Governing Law
      This Agreement shall be governed, controlled, and interpreted under the laws of the state of _____.

DRAFTING TIP

The law of the state where the parties will reside is usually designated. If another state is chosen, the parties must have a significant connection with that state, presently or after marriage. Given that laws vary from state to state, this provision anticipates a possible "conflict of law" question. For example, the parties may agree that the law of Maryland will govern but they eventually divorce in California. According to basic choice of law principles, the California court will apply Maryland law in construing the agreement unless the result of doing so would violate strong public policy in California. This is a potentially important choice given the degree to which states vary in their approaches to dividing property upon divorce and to determining the validity of premarital agreements.[27]

DRAFTING TIP

Some agreements include a provision that sets out the steps to be taken in the event of a dispute regarding any terms of the agreement in addition to judicial relief (a party seeking to enforce an agreement can sue for breach of contract and seek specific performance). It may include options such as mediation and arbitration.

DRAFTING TIP

The provisions in this last section of the sample premarital agreement are "boilerplate" to a considerable extent. Boilerplate is standard language commonly used in a particular kind of document that usually does not require negotiation. However, as with all documents, care must be taken to tailor even boilerplate to jurisdictional requirements and the facts of a case at hand.

PARALEGAL PRACTICE TIP

The state designated to govern the agreement will affect the terminology used. For example, in a community property state "marital property" may be termed "community property."

EXHIBIT 2.3 *(Continued)*

IN WITNESS WHEREOF, the parties have signed, sealed, and acknowledged this Agreement on the day and year indicated below.

Witness_____

Prospective spouse A_____

Date:_____

Witness_____

Prospective spouse B_____

Date:_____

DRAFTING TIP

Certifications by notaries, etc., should be provided in a form appropriate to the jurisdiction. It is important to verify and comply with applicable procedural rules, such as witness requirements and the like. Even if not required, each page of the agreement and any attached exhibits should be signed or initialed to protect against later claims that a particular provision was not included in the original agreement.

EXHIBIT 1

SCHEDULE OF ASSETS FOR Prospective Spouse A.

(abbreviated in length)

Assets	Fair Market Value	Adjustments	Net Value
Real Estate:			
Personal Property:			
Bank accounts			
Stocks and securities			
Retirement funds			
Life insurance			
Antiques			
Jewelry			
Collections			
Vehicles including boats, etc.			
Other			
Total			
Liabilities			
(List)			
Total			
Net Worth:			

Date: _____

                                                  Signature of prospective spouse A

I hereby acknowledge that I have received and reviewed this schedule of assets and liabilities.

Date: _____

                                                  Signature of prospective spouse B

(Continued)

PARALEGAL PRACTICE TIP

EXHIBIT 2 will be the Schedule of Assets and Liabilities for Prospective Spouse B.

What Are the Trends Regarding Enforceability of Premarital Agreements?

PARALEGAL PRACTICE TIP

Despite statutory requirements for validity of premarital agreements, the courts sometimes are moved to find ways of enforcing agreements where one or both of the parties have not strictly complied with the requirements. It is important to research both statutes and case law to discover potential "loopholes"! See, e.g., *Dove v. Dove,* 285 Ga. 647, 680 S.E.2d 839 (2009).

Each state sets forth by statute and/or case law its own requirements for what constitutes a valid and enforceable agreement. Some states invest premarital agreements with a presumption of validity as long as certain requirements are satisfied.[28] If there is never a controversy surrounding the agreement and the parties simply abide by its provisions, enforceability does not become an issue. However, if challenged, the burden of proof of invalidity is on the party challenging enforcement of the agreement. There are basically three approaches to determining enforceability: the Uniform Premarital Agreement Approach, the traditional Fairness Approach, and the contemporary Freedom to Contract Approach.

THE UNIFORM PREMARITAL AGREEMENT ACT'S POSITION ON ENFORCEABILITY

Approximately half of the states have adopted the Uniform Premarital Agreement Act, approved by the National Conference of Commissioners on Uniform State Laws in 1983. The goal of the UPAA is to create uniformity and increased enforceability of premarital agreements through ordinary contract principles.

PARALEGAL PRACTICE TIP

Visit *www.nccusl.org* to see which states have enacted the Uniform Premarital Agreement and where legislation may be pending. You can find a link to this site at *www.pearsonhighered.com/wilson* in the companion website material for Chapter 2 under "Resources." As of 2011, the following states and the District of Columbia had adopted the UPAA in whole or in part: Arizona, Arkansas, California, Connecticut, Delaware, Hawaii, Idaho, Illinois, Indiana, Iowa, Kansas, Maine, Montana, Nebraska, Nevada, New Jersey, New Mexico, North Carolina, North Dakota, Oregon, Rhode Island, South Dakota, Texas, Utah, Virginia, West Virginia, and Wisconsin. Even in states that have not enacted the UPAA, its provisions frequently reflect trends in the law and are often considered by the courts.

Under §6 of the UPAA, premarital agreements will not be enforced if:
. . . the party against whom enforcement is sought proves that:

a. [he or she] did not execute the agreement voluntarily; or
b. the agreement was unconscionable when it was executed and, before execution of the agreement, that party

   i. was not provided a fair and reasonable disclosure of the property or financial obligations of the other party,
   ii. did not voluntarily and expressly waive, in writing, any right to disclosure of the property or financial obligations of the other party beyond the disclosure provided, and
   iii. did not have, or reasonably could not have had, an adequate knowledge of the property and financial obligations of the other party.

In general, subject to §6, the UPAA favors enforcement of the terms of premarital agreements as long as they do not lead to an unconscionable result. That determination is one to be made by the court as a matter of law. However, the act states a specific position with respect to provisions designed to modify or eliminate spousal support. If enforcement would result in a party becoming eligible for public assistance upon divorce or separation, the act provides that a court may order the other party to provide support to the extent necessary to prevent that result.

ENFORCEABILITY OF PREMARITAL AGREEMENTS IN STATES THAT HAVE NOT ADOPTED THE UPAA

The Traditional View—The Fairness Approach

After years of not enforcing premarital agreements that addressed rights upon divorce, following *Posner*, states have increasingly considered premarital agreements on a case-by-case basis, focusing attention on whether an agreement at issue constitutes a valid contract and is substantively and procedurally fair. The "traditional view" treats premarital agreements as contractual agreements between people who bear a special "fiduciary" relationship to one another and therefore holds them to a higher standard than contracts between strangers. It is essentially a fairness approach. Some states that apply this approach look only to fairness at the time of execution of the agreement. Other states have adopted a "**second look**" or "second glance" doctrine examining agreements to determine if they remain fair at the time of performance (i.e., divorce). (See Paralegal Application 2.7.)

Second look doctrine
an approach to determining enforceability of premarital agreements adopted by some courts that involves examining the terms of a premarital agreement for fairness at the time of performance as well as at the time of execution

PARALEGAL PRACTICE TIP

When working on a case that involves a premarital agreement, it is important to know what the current criteria for enforceability are in the applicable jurisdiction based on both statutes and case law. For example, in a "contract" approach jurisdiction, the party challenging validity of the agreement will have to show that the agreement did not satisfy the basic requirements of a contract, that the contract was the result of fraud or duress, or that a term was unconscionable in some fashion at the time of execution. In a "second look" fairness approach jurisdiction, courts will focus primarily on procedural fairness at the time of execution, and substantive fairness both at the time of execution and at performance. Knowing what has to be proved or defended against should guide the paralegal's information-gathering efforts. Paralegal Application 2.7 describes information-gathering needs in a "second look" jurisdiction.

Paralegal **Application 2.7**

Information-Gathering Needs If a Premarital Agreement Is Challenged in a "Second Look" Jurisdiction—Tasks for a Paralegal

- Obtain a copy of the agreement and the file if available.
- Locate the state statute governing premarital agreements, if any, so it can be determined if its requirements were met.
- Research state case law on point.
- Research circumstances surrounding the drafting and execution of the agreement such as:

  Who suggested the agreement?

  Who drafted it?

  Was each party represented? How was counsel obtained and who paid for the representation?

  What was the timing of the drafting and execution?

  What financial disclosures were made and how complete and accurate were they?

  What were the parties' respective financial circumstances, education levels, and business backgrounds?

  Was there any history of threats or emotional or physical abuse prior to execution of the agreement?

  Was the execution taped?

- Identify potential witnesses with whom either party may have discussed the agreement, including attorneys, financial advisors, friends, and family members.
- Find out how circumstances have changed since the execution of the agreement. What are the current financial circumstances of each of the parties? Have children been born to the marriage? Has one of the parties developed a serious health problem?
- Recommend a discovery strategy, if warranted. Discovery methods for premarital agreement controversies are the same as for divorce: Interrogatories, Depositions, Requests for Admissions, Production of Documents, or Mental Examinations, and informal methods such as interviews, examination of public records, etc.

The "Contemporary Approach"—A Freedom to Contract Approach

In more recent years, there has been a trend away from subjecting premarital agreements to a higher standard and toward treating them as basic contracts. Contract law protects both freedom to contract and expectations that the terms of an agreement will be met by each of the contracting parties. Under contract law, absent proof of fraud, misrepresentation, or duress, agreements will be enforced unless enforcement will bring about an "unconscionable" result. Absent such a result, parties are free to make hasty, unfair bargains against their own self-interest. A party cannot avoid performance of a contract simply because it seems unfair, unreasonable, or to his or her disadvantage. However, a court may elect to reform a portion of the agreement to limit the effects of an unforeseen hardship for the benefit of a seriously disadvantaged or abused party.

The opinion in the Pennsylvania case of *Simeone v. Simeone* describes how and why this trend has evolved in response to broad societal changes. (See Case 2.3.) In *Simeone*, the wife appealed a lower court's decision upholding the validity of the premarital agreement that she and her husband had executed on the eve of their wedding in 1975. At the time, the wife was an unemployed twenty-three-year-old nurse. Her spouse was a thirty-nine-year-old neurosurgeon earning $90,000 a year with an additional $300,000 in assets. She signed the agreement without the advice of an attorney or knowing which legal rights she was giving up. The terms of the agreement limited her to support payments of $200 per week in the event of separation or divorce, up to a maximum of $25,000. When the premarital agreement was upheld and her petition for further alimony was denied by the Superior Court, she appealed to the Pennsylvania Supreme Court.

CASE **2.3** *Simeone v. Simeone,* 525 Pa. 392, 581 A.2d 162 (1990)

PARALEGAL PRACTICE TIP

The opinion in the *Simeone* case is available at *www.pearsonhighered. com/wilson* in the companion website material for Chapter 2 under "Cases" and in the Case Resources Section of the MyLegalStudiesLab.

FROM THE OPINION

There is no longer validity in the implicit presumption that supplied the basis for . . . earlier decisions. Such decisions rested upon a belief that spouses are of unequal status and that women are not knowledgeable enough to understand the nature of contracts that they enter. Society has advanced, however, to the point where women are no longer regarded as the "weaker" party in marriage, or in society generally. Indeed, the stereotype that women serve as homemakers while men work as breadwinners is no longer viable. Quite often today both spouses are income earners. Nor is there validity in the presumption that women are uninformed, uneducated, and readily subjected to unfair advantage in marital agreements. Indeed, women nowadays often have substantial education, financial awareness, income, and assets.

Accordingly, the law has advanced to recognize the equal status of men and women in our society. . . . Paternalistic presumptions and protections that arose to shelter women from the inferiorities and incapacities that they were perceived as having in earlier times have, appropriately, been discarded. . . .

. . . Traditional principles of contract law provide perfectly adequate remedies where contracts are procured through fraud, misrepresentation, or duress. . . . Prenuptial agreements are contracts, and, as such, should be evaluated under the same criteria as are applicable to other types of contracts. . . . Absent fraud, misrepresentation, or duress, spouses should be bound by the terms of their agreements.

(Continued)

Contracting parties are normally bound by their agreements, without regard to whether the terms thereof were read and fully understood and irrespective of whether the agreements embodied reasonable or good bargains. . . . *Ignorant[i]a legis non excusat.*

Accordingly we find no merit in a contention raised by the appellant that the agreement should be declared void on the ground that she did not consult with independent legal counsel. To impose a *per se* requirement that parties entering a premarital agreement must obtain independent legal counsel would be contrary to traditional principles of contract law, and would constitute a paternalistic and unwarranted interference with the parties' freedom to enter contracts.

Further, the reasonableness of a prenuptial bargain is not a proper subject for judicial review. . . .

. . . If parties viewed an agreement as reasonable at the time of its inception, as evidenced by their having signed the agreement, they should be foreclosed from later trying to evade its terms by asserting that it was not in fact reasonable. . . .

Further, everyone who enters a long-term agreement knows that circumstances can change during its term, so that what initially appeared desirable might prove to be an unfavorable bargain. Such are the risks that contracting parties routinely assume. . . .

We are reluctant to interfere with the power of persons contemplating marriage to agree upon, and to act in reliance upon, what *they* regard as an acceptable distribution scheme for their property. A court should not ignore the parties' expressed intent by proceeding to determine whether a prenuptial agreement was, in the court's view, reasonable at the time of inception or at the time of divorce. . . .

. . . we do not depart from the longstanding principle that a full and fair disclosure of the financial positions of the parties is required. . . .

SIDEBAR

Read the full opinion in the *Simeone* case available on the companion website. After reading the opinion, do you agree with the outcome? Why? What do you think the requirements should be in order for a premarital agreement to be valid and enforceable?

Paralegal **Application 2.8**

An Enforceable Agreement? What Do You Think?

The facts

Joseph and Susan were married in March of 1990, when he was forty-seven and she was forty-one. They had known each other in high school, dated occasionally in the 1970s, and renewed their acquaintance in 1987. Joseph proposed marriage in 1989 on condition that Susan sign a premarital agreement, which she agreed to do. At the time of the marriage, she was living with her daughter from her first marriage in a two-bedroom house. She was working as a secretary earning $25,000 a year. She owned no real property and had few assets. On request of Susan's attorney, two weeks before the agreement was signed, Joseph disclosed assets indicating his net worth was between $108 and $133 million. Although she requested a significant share of those assets during negotiations, she eventually settled for an agreement providing that, in the event of divorce, she would receive the marital home free of encumbrances, yearly support of $35,000 until her death or remarriage with an annual cost-of-living increase, an automobile, and medical insurance until her death or remarriage. Both attorneys were present when Susan and Joseph executed the agreement and the signing was recorded.

(Continued)

The videotape shows Joseph's attorney reciting the terms and the parties communicating their understanding and consent. They also acknowledged that they each had counsel of their own choice, exchanged financial disclosure, and understood what their rights would be in the absence of an agreement. Although the wife testified at the time of the divorce that she did not want to sign and felt ill on that day, the tape revealed no sign of distress, resistance, or unwillingness to sign.

In March 1998, the husband filed for divorce. The trial court held that the agreement was invalid because it was not fair and reasonable at the time of execution or enforcement. The husband appealed.

Sidebar

How would this appeal most likely be decided under the traditional fairness approach? Why? How would it be decided under the freedom to contract approach applying an unconscionability standard? Why? How do you think it should be decided? What additional information would you like to have?

PARALEGAL PRACTICE TIP

To learn how the Massachusetts Supreme Judicial Court decided the case, go to *www.pearsonhighered. com/wilson* and read the opinion in *DeMatteo v. DeMatteo*, 436 Mass. 18, 762 N.E.2d 797 (2002), available in the companion website material for Chapter 2 under "Cases" and in the Case Resources Section of the MyLegalStudiesLab.

The Role of the Paralegal in Cohabitation and Premarital Agreement Cases

The paralegal applications provided in this chapter address several aspects of the paralegal's role in matters involving cohabitation and premarital agreements. The nature of that role in a specific instance depends primarily on whether the case involves the negotiation and execution of an agreement, the enforceability of an already existing agreement, or the absence of an agreement.

When there is no agreement, the paralegal's role is driven by the facts and circumstances of the individual case. When an agreement is involved, the tasks to be performed will depend on whether the case is at the negotiation and execution stage or at the enforcement stage. In these contexts, an experienced paralegal may perform the following tasks:

Tasks Common to Both Stages

- participate in meetings with the client as requested by the supervisor
- research the jurisdictional requirements for valid and enforceable agreements
- help the client and the attorney gather necessary information and documents
- maintain communication with the client
- schedule meetings with the client, the other party and his or her attorney, and any other essential individuals (e.g., mediators, etc.)
- prepare related forms and correspondence (including fee agreements and confirmation of meetings)
- track/monitor progress on the case and ensure that required timelines are met

Negotiation and Execution of the Agreement

- prepare exhibits for use in negotiations
- draft successive versions of an agreement and related schedules and attachments based on instructions from the supervising attorney
- review proposed agreements from the other party for consistency with the client's position and agreed-upon terms based on information provided by the supervisor
- make arrangements for obtaining an affidavit of competency, if appropriate
- arrange for execution of the agreement, including taping if desired

Enforcement of an Existing Agreement

- draft appropriate pleadings for review and in the event of a divorce be certain that the client's Complaint for Divorce (or Answer) puts the court on notice as to the existence of the agreement and the client's position with respect to potential enforceability
- prepare related memoranda based on research as requested
- draft discovery materials such as interrogatories, requests for admissions, requests for production of documents, requests for physical or mental examinations, and proposed questions for depositions
- draft responses to discovery requests, working with the client and the supervising attorney
- assist with preparation for hearings or a trial on the merits, including drafting pretrial memoranda for review, preparing exhibits, and arranging for service of subpoenas on potential witnesses, if needed
- help identify and prepare prospective witnesses

CHAPTER **SUMMARY**

When most people think of a family law practice, the image that often comes to mind is of a couple engaged in a bitter battle fueled by attorneys and an adversarial and impersonal legal system. The parties are struggling to divide the pieces of a failed relationship at a time when they can't even communicate with each other and their future may end up being decided by a stranger in a black robe according to laws they don't agree with or even understand. Fortunately, this scenario occurs less and less frequently as most courts today encourage parties to resolve their differences without costly litigation and attorneys make greater use of collaboration and alternative dispute resolution methods. Perhaps equally influential is the fact that couples choosing to marry or simply live together as unmarried partners increasingly recognize at the outset that relationships can fail and that more than half of all marriages end in divorce. At a time when they are looking forward to their life together, many of these couples elect to develop their own personalized blueprints for the future. They anticipate the problems that may arise and they create agreements designed to minimize those problems and resolve them in advance at a point in time when they view each other as partners rather than adversaries. These cohabitation/living-together and premarital agreements are the primary focus of this chapter.

The early part of the chapter addresses cohabitation. The kinds of documents cohabitants can execute to create and protect their rights with respect to each other are identified, including, for example, cohabitation agreements, wills, trusts, health care proxies, beneficiary designations, and powers of attorney. Attention is also given to the theories used by courts to provide relief to cohabitants when their relationship terminates and they have no written agreement. The nature, purpose, and development of premarital agreements are then discussed, and a detailed model of a basic comprehensive agreement is provided, accompanied by extensive drafting tips. Many of the provisions in the agreement (particularly boilerplate language regarding disclosure, governing law, severability, and the like) may also appear in cohabitation agreements. Different approaches to determining whether or not a premarital agreement should be enforced are discussed, including a traditional fairness assessment (at both the time of execution and the time of performance), a freedom to contract approach, and the position of the Uniform Premarital

Agreement Act adopted in slightly more than half the states and the District of Columbia.

    Because cohabitation and premarital agreements are relatively recent developments, their origins and evolution are highlighted in pertinent case excerpts. Throughout the chapter a number of tasks also are identified that a supervisor might assign to a paralegal, with particular emphasis on gathering information, drafting agreements and other documents tailored to the client's specific needs, and researching enforceability issues. Several paralegal applications and tips are provided which are designed to alert the paralegal to special problems related to the drafting, execution, and enforcement of cohabitation and premarital agreements. An effort is made to highlight jurisdictional variations and ethical issues.

PARALEGAL PRACTICE TIP

Although premarital agreements providing for rights upon divorce were unenforceable for generations, that has clearly changed and we now have new issues to consider. The highly controversial topic of same-sex marriage will no doubt be debated over the next decade on public policy grounds favoring a traditional definition of marriage as the legal union of one man and one woman. In a state that allows same-sex marriage, a premarital agreement between the parties may well be enforceable, at least with respect to matters governed by that state's law. Whether or not it will be enforceable in any other state remains to be seen.

CONCEPT REVIEW AND REINFORCEMENT

KEY **TERMS**

Affidavit of Competency	Implied partnership/Joint venture	Quasi-contract/implied-in-law contract
Boilerplate	Joint tenant with right of survivorship	Quasi-marital property
Cohabitation	Meretricious sex	Resulting trust/Purchase money
Cohabitation agreement	Palimony	resulting trust/Implied trust
Constructive trust	*Per se* invalid	Second look doctrine
Consideration	Postmarital agreement (postmarital	Separation agreement
Defense	contract, postnuptial agreement)	Substantive fairness
Durable power of attorney	Premarital agreement (premarital	Unclean hands
Express contract	contract, antenuptial agreement)	Unconscionable
Fiduciary	Procedural fairness	Uniform Premarital Agreement Act
Health care proxy	Public policy	(UPAA)
Ignorantia legis non excusat	Putative spouse	Void
Implied-in-fact contract	*Quantum meruit*	Waiver

REVIEW **QUESTIONS**

1. Describe how the *Marvin* decision reflects a change in society's view of cohabitation over the past few decades.
2. Identify five documents cohabitants can execute in order to define their respective rights and responsibilities and protect and provide for each other.
3. Identify and give examples of three theories a court might rely on to justify relief to cohabitants when their relationship terminates and they have no enforceable agreement.
4. Describe the nature and purpose of a premarital agreement and explain why such agreements are becoming increasingly more common.
5. Distinguish between substantive and procedural fairness and give an example of each.

6. List at least five of the provisions most commonly included in premarital agreements.
7. Identify three terms individuals may want to include in an agreement that may not be enforceable and explain why. In this context, explain the importance of a severability clause in an agreement.
8. Describe the historical trend from nonenforceability to enforceability of premarital agreements reflected in the *Posner* case.
9. Explain the difference between a freedom to contract and a fairness approach to enforcement. What is the significance of the *Simeone* case, the second look doctrine, and the UPAA in this context?
10. Describe the role of the paralegal in cases involving cohabitation and premarital agreements.

DEVELOPING YOUR PARALEGAL SKILLS

FOCUS ON **THE JOB**

In this activity, the student has an opportunity to collaborate with other students in drafting a cohabitation agreement tailored to a detailed fact pattern.

The Facts

Tran Ng and Malia Barach have been going out for six months. Although they are very happy and plan to spend the rest of their lives together, for a number of reasons they have decided to live together and postpone marriage for a while.

Both parties are semiretired after long and successful careers, he as an engineer, she as a college dean. He is sixty-five years old, was married once before for twenty-two years, and has three adult children and four grandchildren. She is sixty-three years old and a widow (receiving Social Security benefits through her deceased husband), and has no children or grandchildren.

His Primary Assets	Her Primary Assets
Vacation home on the New Jersey shore (assessed at $350,000)	Vacation cottage in Beverly Farms, Massachusetts (assessed at $200,000)
Artworks valued at about $40,000	State pension
Bell Laboratories pension	36-foot sailboat valued at $50,000
30-foot trawler valued at $125,000	Condominium in North Conway, New Hampshire (assessed at $250,000)
401(k) valued at $350,000	Jewelry valued at $27,000
Investment portfolio (current value $325,000)	Investment portfolio (current value $225,000)

Tran and Malia plan to purchase a new home in your state. Tran will pay a $200,000 down payment, and Malia will get a mortgage for $200,000 and make the associated payments. The deed and mortgage will be in Malia's name only, but they intend that the property will belong to them equally. They will share all home maintenance, utility, and daily living expenses equally and will pay those expenses from a joint account to which they will both contribute. Malia intends to do a significant amount of landscaping to improve and maintain their new home. Tran plans to add a music/art room to the house for his enjoyment and at his expense. Tran is concerned about Malia's housekeeping and has decided he wants to pay for daily maid services. The couple will share grocery shopping and cooking chores. Each party will maintain an individual bank account in addition to their joint account. Each party intends to work part time. Tran will work in a marine supply store two days a week and both parties will teach one or two courses at a local college. Each will be entitled to his or her own earnings. Malia anticipates no inheritance through her family. Tran anticipates a substantial inheritance when his mother dies.

It does not bother them if other people think of or treat them as if they are married, but they have no intention of entering a marriage, common law or otherwise, for at least a year. They do share an intimate and sexual relationship and anticipate that will continue, but that is not the reason why they are moving in together. The couple expects to continue their current lifestyle and do considerable traveling together, particularly by boat. Malia has a beagle, "Spike," and, because Tran is allergic to dogs, she has agreed to not have Spike inside the house or on the boat and to be totally responsible for all expenses related to the dog.

The parties intend their agreement to take effect upon signing and to be unaffected by any periodic, temporary separations. It will terminate only when the parties sign a written declaration of termination or have lived separate and apart for a continuous six-month period. Neither party expects to benefit under the will of the other at this point, but each is free to make whatever provisions he or she wishes. Neither party intends to make a claim for any kind of support if their relationship should terminate even if permitted under current or future legislation. However, each does agree to do the following within thirty days of executing their agreement:

- Establish a $500,000 life insurance policy for the benefit of the other.
- Designate the other as his or her health care proxy.
- Execute a durable power of attorney naming the other as his or her attorney-in-fact in the event of incapacitating disability, etc.

The agreement will be executed in your state and the parties also intend that it be governed by the law of your state, if permitted. (If such agreements are contrary to law or public policy in your state, assume you live in a nearby state where they are permitted.) If either party breaches the agreement, attorney's costs will be paid by the nonprevailing party. Tran's attorney will draft the agreement for review and input from Malia. Malia will have her attorney, Nancy Riggs, review the document once it is drafted. She says she trusts Tran and whatever he wants is fine with her. Besides, she doesn't want to spend any more money on a lawyer than she has to.

The Assignment

Either individually or working in teams of three—one person playing the role of Tran, one the role of Malia, and the third the role of Tran's attorney, Juliana Dahl—draft a cohabitation agreement that is tailored to the above fact pattern. Assign local addresses within your state to each of the parties and counsel. Your draft should reflect what you have learned from reading this chapter, class discussion, and any additional research you may have done or are required by your instructor to do. You should begin by determining if there are any requirements for a valid cohabitation agreement in your jurisdiction and locating a variety of appropriate models in form books and/or online.

FOCUS ON **ETHICS**

In this activity, the students will draft a letter addressing the ethical issue of dual representation.

The Assignment

Assume that in the above fact pattern, Malia does not believe she needs to have another attorney advise her with respect to the negotiation and execution of the proposed agreement. She has told both Tran and his attorney, Juliana Dahl, how she feels and that she trusts both of them to be fair with her. Assume that you are the paralegal for Attorney Dahl. Draft a letter to Malia for your supervisor's review and signature in which you explain why it is strongly advised that she be represented by independent counsel and what the potential risks are of failing to do so. Indicate, if she insists on not obtaining counsel, what steps, if any, need to be taken in an effort to protect your client against a later allegation that the agreement was unfair in its terms or execution or that it was the product of fraud or duress, etc. The tone of the letter needs to be firm but also reflect sensitivity to the situation.

FOCUS ON **CASE LAW**

In this activity, the student is required to locate and brief a case involving the enforceability of a premarital agreement in his or her jurisdiction.

The Assignment

Locate the most recently decided case in the state where you live addressing the enforceability of a premarital agreement and the standard to be applied in making that determination. Read the case and then brief it. If there is no case law on point in your state, select a case from a neighboring state.

PARALEGAL PRACTICE TIP

If needed, a format for briefing cases is available at *www.pearson-highered.com/wilson* in the companion website material for Chapter 1 under "Cases" and in the Case Resources Section of the MyLegalStudiesLab.

FOCUS ON **STATE LAW AND PROCEDURE**

In this activity, the student is asked to research whether a premarital agreement is likely to be enforced in his or her state, given a hypothetical fact pattern. If there is no state law on point, the student should assume that the UPAA has been adopted.

Fact Pattern

Richard Marshall is a very wealthy seventy-two-year-old retired engineer who recently married a thirty-five-year-old model. He has been married three times and is paying alimony to two of his three prior spouses. He also has five much loved adult children and twelve grandchildren whose futures he wants to secure when he dies. He told Elaine before they wed that he definitely wanted no more children and she agreed. Richard's assets total over $4 million, and Elaine's add up to approximately $300,000, plus she is still working and earns about $250,000 a year. They generally disclosed their respective assets and liabilities prior to the marriage and executed a premarital agreement drafted by Richard's attorney, James Schornstein. Richard disclosed information about all of his real estate, retirement accounts, antique car collection, yacht, and investments. He "overlooked" disclosing several valuable paintings he inherited from his grandmother that are on display in a New York museum. He has never had them appraised but believes they are worth over a million dollars.

Richard's attorney delivered the agreement to Elaine the day before their lavish wedding. Elaine elected not to have an independent lawyer review the document, in part because there was no time to do so because she was busy with the wedding plans. She told Richard and his attorney that she trusted them and whatever "Rich" wanted was fine with her. Elaine failed to reveal that the week before the wedding she learned she was two months pregnant. She did not tell Richard about their "love child" until two months after their marriage. Richard was so upset by this turn of events that he promptly filed for divorce. He wants the court to enforce the parties' premarital agreement, which provides that, if the parties are married for less than two years, Elaine receives only what she brought into the marriage and no form of continuing support. Elaine does not want the agreement enforced and wants a substantial spousal support award for a six-year period, until the baby enters elementary school and she returns to work. She says that Richard should not be allowed to benefit from the agreement because he never told her about the paintings, and she only recently found out about them from her friend, Johnnie Rasmussen, at a museum fundraiser. She retains Attorney Olga Carroll to represent her in this matter. Assume that you are Attorney Carroll's paralegal and that she has asked you to research the enforceability of the agreement at issue in your state. Prepare a memorandum describing the results of your research and

your conclusion with respect to Elaine's chances of prevailing. Your report should be in a basic internal memo format such as the following:

Memorandum

To: Olga Carroll, Esq.

From: *Your Name, Paralegal*

File Reference: *Name of client (followed by case caption with a docket number if provided by your instructor)*

Re: *Enforceability of Premarital Agreement*

Date:

Description of Issue/Assignment: *What is it that you have been asked to do?*

Results of Research: *What did you learn about the enforceability of premarital agreements in your state?*

Application to the Case: *Apply the law (case and statutory) to the facts of the case at issue.*

Conclusion: *What is the likelihood that Elaine will prevail with respect to the enforceability of the premarital agreement?*

FOCUS ON **TECHNOLOGY**

In addition to the links throughout the chapter, this activity provides a series of useful websites for reference, along with technology-related assignments for completion. Links to the websites are located at *www.pearsonhighered.com/wilson* in the companion website material for Chapter 2 under "Resources."

Websites of Interest

www.deltabravo.net

This is the website for the Separated Parenting Access and Resource Center (SPARC). A Sample Pre-Nuptial Agreement can be located at this site. Be sure to remember that forms located online must be carefully reviewed to be sure that they comply with governing law and that they can be tailored to the specific needs of the parties.

www.divorcenet.com

This site contains information on a number of family law topics. Search by topic and/or by state.

www.divorcesource.com

Click on divorce laws and then search by topic and/or state. Links are provided to both articles and sites for cases. Cases reflecting the positions of several states regarding enforceability of cohabitation agreements can be found at *www.divorcesource.com/tables/domesticagreements.shtml*. Some material on this site cannot be viewed without a subscription (available at a modest fee).

www.findlaw.com

This site contains a wide range of information about family law, marriage, living together, premarital agreements,

and other topics related to the content of this chapter. A copy of a sample cohabitation agreement can be found at this site.

www.jlaw.com

The focus of this site is on Jewish law in a variety of topical areas. An example of a premarital agreement is provided (without any guarantee as to enforceability).

www.legalforms.com

This is an example of a site where individuals can purchase premarital agreement packages. There is no guarantee that the material provided satisfies particular states' current requirements, although the packages are promoted as state-by-state products.

www.palimony.com

The stated goal of this website is to provide a one-stop source of resources and information for unmarried couples (heterosexual or same-sex) who are living together as domestic partners or are considering doing so. The Resources section includes an extensive set of links to information and resources. The site also includes articles about cohabitation agreements. It focuses primarily on the state of California.

http://www.unmarried.org

This is the website for the Alternatives to Marriage Project. The site provides information and statistics on cohabitation, living single, domestic partner benefits, common law marriage, etc.

Assignments

1. Locate three models of formats for cohabitation agreements online. In your opinion, which of the three would be most useful as a model for developing a cohabitation agreement for the parties in the Focus on the Job assignment in this chapter?

2. Visit *www.divorcesource.com/tables/domesticagreements.shtml* and see if you can determine your state's position with respect to the enforceability of premarital agreements.

3. See what you can learn online about the "palimony" case of the late Johnnie Cochran, renowned attorney (89 Cal. App.4th 283, 106 Cal. Rptr.2d 899 Cal. App. 2001). Did he prevail?

4. Using online resources, determine whether or not your state has adopted the Uniform Premarital Agreement Act. Be sure to verify whatever you learn.

5. Assume that the firm where you are employed wants to develop a "common questions and answers" information/fact sheet regarding premarital agreements. Search the Web for ideas on what should be included in such a sheet. Start with *www.findlaw.com*.

6. To learn more about the law governing premarital agreements in various states, locate the following statutes through online resources:

Minn. Stat. § 519.11 (2010)	Minnesota
ORC Ann. 3103.06 (2011)	Ohio
N.C. Gen. Stat. § 52-10 (2010)	North Carolina

PORTFOLIO PRODUCTS

1. Cohabitation agreement
2. Letter to a client's prospective spouse re the need for independent representation
3. Brief of a state case on premarital agreements
4. Internal memorandum re enforceability of a premarital agreement

chapter 3

MARRIAGE AND EMERGING ALTERNATIVES

> Mary, a fifteen-year-old girl who lives in Texas, has fallen madly in love with her first cousin, Marty, a twenty-three-year-old professional bull rider on the rodeo circuit who lives in Massachusetts. She has hatched a plan for them to wed and live happily ever after in Colorado. Marty is not so sure they can "get away with it."

Introduction

Once upon a time, there was a nation whose prime-time television shows included *I Remember Mama* and *Father Knows Best*. These programs featured storybook-perfect intact traditional families; characters playing highly gendered roles; and classic moral themes. Cohabitation was viewed as "living in sin" and constituted a crime in virtually all states. "Gay" meant cheerful and lighthearted, and "domestic agreements" referred to contracts with hired help to perform household chores.

The above description is clearly a white, middle-class, "idealized" portrait of the nuclear family projected by the media of the day. Although a reality for some, it failed to capture the fact that throughout this country's history, the nature of the nuclear family has adapted to societal conditions such as war, racism, and economic depression, and it continues to do so today. Although the majority of adults in the United States still marry at least once in their lifetimes, significant changes in our society have resulted in expanded, publicly acknowledged, and legally recognized concepts of marriage and the family unit that encompass a wide range of lifestyles and diverse living arrangements. A number of forces have promoted this broader and more flexible view of both the family and intimate relationships: the women's rights, fathers' rights, and gay rights movements; a decreased emphasis on marriage as a defining event in life (particularly for women); an increased social acceptance of alternative lifestyles; and a greater protection of the right to privacy in sexual conduct between consenting adults.

In chapter 2 we discussed cohabitation, the generic term for same-sex or different-sex persons living together without being married or having any other legally recognized status. In this chapter we will first

LEARNING OBJECTIVES

After reading this chapter and completing related assignments, you should be able to:

- explain how and why the concept of "family" has evolved over the past fifty years

- distinguish among different types of marriage

- identify ways in which the states regulate and restrict the fundamental right to marry

- identify common requirements for valid ceremonial and common law marriages

- identify and describe legal statuses accorded same-sex couples in various states including domestic partnerships and civil unions

- distinguish among the rights, benefits, and obligations that flow from traditional marriage, same-sex marriage, civil unions, and domestic partnerships

- describe the potential role of a paralegal in cases involving marriage and alternative family relationships focus on issues related to various types of marriage, including the controversial category of same-sex marriage. We will then turn our attention to the most common alternative legal statuses created by states, municipalities, and employers to give unmarried partners a variety of benefits that are customarily available only to spouses, including but not limited to civil unions and domestic partnerships.

PARALEGAL PRACTICE TIP

The Louisiana legislature enacted the first covenant marriage legislation in the country in 1997, creating a two-tiered system of marriage in that state and defining covenant marriage as:

> . . . a marriage entered into by one male and one female who understand and agree that the marriage between them is a lifelong relationship. Parties to a covenant marriage have received counseling emphasizing the nature and purpose of marriage and the responsibilities thereto. Only when there has been a total and complete breach of the marital covenant commitment may the non-breaching party seek a declaration that the marriage is no longer legally recognized.

Divorce is granted on the following grounds only: adultery, sentence of death or imprisonment at hard labor for a felony, physical or sexual abuse, abandonment of the marital home for a year, or living separate and apart continuously without reconciliation for two years.

La. Rev. Stat. Ann. § 9:272274

To learn about covenant marriage in Arizona visit *www.azcourts.gov.* You can find a link to this site at *www.pearsonhighered.com/wilson* in the companion website material for Chapter 3 under " Resources."

PARALEGAL PRACTICE TIP

The content of Exhibit 3.1 focuses on types of marriage common in the United States. However, throughout history, four fundamental forms of marriage have existed across the world: (1) monogamy; (2) polygyny (one man with several wives); (3) polyandry (one woman with several husbands); and (4) group marriage. The term *polygamy* encompasses both polygyny and polyandry. The various forms are rooted deeply in the cultures, religious beliefs, and social mores of the societies in which they appear.

PARALEGAL PRACTICE TIP

To learn more about the Uniform Marriage and Divorce Act visit *www. nccusl.org.* A primary objective of Uniform Acts in general is to promote legislative uniformity among the states. This particular Act is treated more as a "Model" than a "Uniform" Act. It suggests approaches to certain areas of family law and is cited frequently but does not call out for uniform acceptance by the states. Also visit *www.law.cornell.edu* to find links to the text of the Act in the eight states where it has been adopted in whole or in part. You can find links to both of these sites at *www.pearsonhighered.com/wilson* in the companion website material for Chapter 3 under "Resources."

EXHIBIT 3.1 Types of Monogamous Marriage

Ceremonial Marriage	Available in all 50 states, a ceremonial marriage customarily requires a license and solemnization in a ceremony performed by a person authorized by statute to perform weddings. The ceremony may be civil (performed by a government official/Justice of the Peace), religious (performed by a religious cleric), or, in the case of Native Americans, conducted according to tribal customs.
Covenant Marriage	A covenant marriage is a form of ceremonial marriage available in a small number of states including Arkansas, Arizona, and Louisiana, and under consideration in others. It developed in response to concerns about high divorce rates and the ease with which no-fault divorces are granted. It emphasizes the seriousness of the decision to marry and the goal of permanence in marital relationships. As a result, covenant marriages are more difficult to enter and exit than traditional ceremonial or common law marriages.
Common Law Marriage	A common law marriage is created by the conduct of the parties rather than in a formal ceremony. As of June 2011, common law marriages can be entered in a limited number of states, e.g., Alabama, Colorado, Iowa, Kansas, Montana, Rhode Island, South Carolina, Texas, Utah, and the District of Columbia. In New Hampshire, common law marriage is recognized for purposes of inheritance and death benefits only. The requirements for a common law marriage usually include capacity and intent to marry, cohabitation, and a holding out to the public as husband and wife.[1]
Same-Sex Marriage	As of January 2012, same-sex marriages can be entered into in Connecticut, Iowa, Massachusetts, New Hampshire, New York,

EXHIBIT 3.1 *(Continued)*

	Vermont, and the District of Columbia. Same-sex marriage is, in some respects, comparable to traditional marriage, with the important exceptions that the parties are of the same sex, the marriage is not recognized under federal law as of January 2012 and the extent to which it will be recognized in other jurisdictions is still unclear.
Putative Marriage	The putative marriage doctrine is recognized in a limited number of states. Section 209 of the Uniform Marriage and Divorce Act defines a putative spouse as follows: "Any person who has cohabited with another to whom he is not legally married in the good faith belief that he was married to that person is a putative spouse until knowledge of the fact that he is not legally married terminates his status and prevents acquisition of further rights. A **putative spouse** acquires the rights conferred upon a legal spouse, including the right to maintenance following termination of his status, whether or not the marriage is prohibited (Section 207) or declared invalid (Section 208)." The presumed marriage may be either common law or ceremonial in nature. The doctrine does not make the marriage valid, but it does allow the courts to treat it as a valid marriage for purposes of property division and spousal support.

PARALEGAL PRACTICE TIP

The Illinois statute concerning putative spouses can be seen at *www.pearsonhighered.com/wilson* in the companion website material for Chapter 3 under "Statutes."

Putative spouse
a person who believes in good faith that his or her invalid marriage is legally valid

Marriage—Definitions and Historical Perspective

DEFINITIONS

In 1810, the Massachusetts Supreme Judicial Court described marriage as follows:

> Marriage is . . . a civil contract, founded in the social nature of man, and intended to regulate, chasten, and refine, the intercourse between the sexes; and to multiply, preserve, and improve the species. It is an engagement, by which a single man and a single woman, of sufficient discretion, take each other as husband and wife. From the nature of the contract, it exists during the lives of the two parties, unless dissolved for causes which defeat the object of marriage . . . .[2]

In 2003 (193 years later), the same court, in a sharply divided decision, defined marriage as "the voluntary union of two persons as spouses, to the exclusion of all others."[3] The court held that "Limiting the protections, benefits and obligations of civil marriage to opposite sex couples violates the basic premises of individual liberty and equality under law protected by the Massachusetts Constitution."[4]

The above definitions reflect the fact that the way we define **marriage** depends to a considerable extent on prevailing social, cultural, and political environments. The first definition mirrors our early marriage laws, which, in a majority of the states, were based on English common law. It is moral in tone and emphasizes the union of a man and a woman and the procreative function of marriage. The second definition falls at the other end of the spectrum, where marriage involves two "persons" who voluntarily enter a "union" with each other.

Marriage
a legal status that two people attain by entering a government-approved and regulated contract with each other; a civil contract between a man and a woman or between two same-sex partners in a state that permits marriage of partners of the same sex

PARALEGAL PRACTICE TIP

The New York statute concerning the property of married women effective on February 17, 1909, can be seen at *www.pearsonhighered.com/wilson* in the companion website material for Chapter 3 under "Statutes."

HISTORICAL PERSPECTIVE

The history of marriage in the United States has its roots in ecclesiastical and English common law. Under common law, upon marriage a husband and wife became one, and that one was embodied in the husband. The wife became entitled to support by her husband, but essentially lost her independent legal status. Although she retained title to any real property she owned in her own name when she wed, her husband acquired an exclusive right to manage, control, and collect all income from that property. She lost her right to own personal property, and any she did own became her husband's. She could not execute a contract or a will, and any executed prior to marriage were automatically revoked. She could not sue or be sued in her own name. She could be employed but any income she received belonged to her husband.

PARALEGAL PRACTICE TIP

In the eight **civil law** or **community property states** influenced primarily by Spanish civil law (Arizona, California, Idaho, Nevada, New Mexico, Texas, and Washington) or French civil law (Louisiana), the wife's independent legal identity technically did not merge with her husband's, and property acquired during marriage generally constituted "community property" belonging to both spouses. However, the spouses were not "equals." As under the common law tradition, the husband held complete control over his wife's property and earnings during the marriage.

Civil law

one of the two primary legal systems in the Western world, originating in the Roman Empire and influential in several parts of the world and a small number of states

Community property states

states in which a husband and wife hold property acquired during the marriage (exclusive of gifts and inheritances) in common, with each spouse entitled to a one-half interest in the property upon divorce

Married Women's Property Acts

state statutes that extended to women various property rights denied them under common law, including ownership and control of property

By the mid to late nineteenth century, the situation of women began to improve somewhat as the states passed **Married Women's Property Acts**. The acts were passed partly in response to pressure from reformers seeking equality for women in political, social, and domestic arenas. Generally, they eliminated several of the disabilities of married women. Despite this initial progress, it was not until the 1960s that a variety of forces converged and brought about fundamental change in both society and the law relating to marriage and the family: men and women both wanting to escape stereotypic roles; fathers wanting to parent their children and take care of their homes; women seeking economic independence; men wanting to be free of financial burdens upon divorce; gay and lesbian individuals wanting to have their identities and lifestyles acknowledged and respected; and both married and unmarried heterosexual couples wanting to shape the contours of their own relationships.

Paralegal **Application 3.1**

The Promise to Marry—What If You Say You Will and Then You Won't?

At one time, a mutual promise to marry was recognized as a legally enforceable contract, although the courts fell short of ordering **specific performance** of its terms. The remedy was in the form of an action for **breach of promise**. The essence of a breach of promise action was the failure to honor the promise to marry. If a prospective spouse acted in a fraudulent manner toward his or her prospective spouse, the courts sought to place the injured party (usually the woman) in the position he or she would have been in had the marriage taken place. The injured party could seek damages for pain and suffering, **expectation damages** for loss of an anticipated lifestyle, and **reliance damages** to recover for actions taken and expenses incurred as a result of the mutual promise to marry.

Few defenses to a breach of promise action were available, with the exception of proof that the plaintiff was "unchaste" during the period of the engagement. By the early 1900s, however, it had become apparent that breach of contract actions were often abused, that damages were too difficult to measure, and that the courts were not an appropriate forum for dealing with the emotional trauma of "broken hearts." The romance of engagement also began to give way to the more practical view that it made little sense to penalize people for refusing to enter marriages that were doomed to fail. As a result, by the middle of the century, more than half of the states had passed **Anti-Heartbalm Statutes** abolishing breach of contract actions. In the current no-fault era, what remains of the earlier breach of

(Continued)

contract action in most states is at best an action seeking **compensatory damages** for out-of-pocket costs incurred as a natural result of the engagement. These expenses might include, for example, the cost of a nonreturnable wedding dress and nonrefundable deposits and other **liquidated damages** paid in connection with cancellation of a reception hall reservation or the booking of a band.

PARALEGAL PRACTICE TIP

The Illinois Anti-Heartbalm Statute enacted in 1947 can be seen at *www.pearsonhighered.com/wilson* in the companion website material for Chapter 3 under "Statutes."

The courts are divided with respect to treatment of the "engagement" ring and commonly take one of three positions:

- Because the ring is the traditional symbol of the commitment to marry, some courts view it as a gift that is contingent on the marriage taking place. To avoid unjust enrichment, if the engagement is broken, the ring should be returned regardless of which party breaks the engagement. The same rule may be applied to wedding gifts or other large gifts made to a party in contemplation of a forthcoming marriage.

PARALEGAL PRACTICE TIP

For the giving of the ring to be a completed gift, the following elements must be satisfied:

- The ring must actually be "delivered" to the **donee** by the **donor**
- The transfer of the ring must have been voluntary
- At the time of the transfer, the donor must have intended to relinquish title, dominion, and control over the ring
- There must be no consideration for, or condition on, the giving of the ring and
- The donee must accept the ring

- Some view the giving of the ring as a completed and irrevocable gift and thus nonreturnable.
- Still other courts look to the facts of each case, giving particular attention to which party broke the engagement and why and whether or not it appears from the circumstances that the gift was conditional on the agreement to marry (the engagement itself) or on the occurrence of the actual marriage.

Breach of promise

under common law, the breaking of an engagement without justification, entitling the innocent party to damages

Expectation damages

compensation awarded for the loss of what a person reasonably anticipated from a contract or transaction that was not completed

Reliance damages

damages awarded to a plaintiff for losses incurred from having acted in reliance on a contract that was breached by the other party

Anti-Heartbalm Statutes

state laws that abolish the cause of action for breach of promise

Compensatory damages

damages sufficient to compensate an injured person for a loss suffered

Liquidated damages

an amount agreed to in a contract as the measure of damages to be paid by the breaching party to the nonbreaching party

Donee

the one to whom a gift is made

Donor

the one who gives a gift

Paralegal Application 3.2

The Marriage Broker Business

Although "arranged" marriages are accepted in many cultures, under common law, marriage broker contracts, in which a person was paid to secure a spouse for another person, were considered void and unenforceable. Consider the extensive network of dating services doing business today in this country, many of which promise to locate lifetime partners for their customers and then feature the couples they introduced who subsequently married. Think also about the reality TV shows that involve contests in which the ultimate prize is a rose, a ring, and a spouse. Do you think such commercial ventures should

be permitted? Should they be licensed or otherwise monitored and regulated? Read the opinion in *Ureneck v. Cui*, 59 Mass. App. Ct. 809, 798 N.E.2d 305 (2003). Do you agree with the decision in that case? Why?

PARALEGAL PRACTICE TIP

The opinion in *Ureneck v. Cui* can be accessed at *www.pearsonhighered.com/wilson* in the companion website material related to Chapter 3 under "Cases" and in the Case Resources Section of the MyLegalStudiesLab.

Marriage—A Fundamental Right

In the 1967 landmark decision *Loving v. Virginia*, the U.S. Supreme Court definitively established that marriage is a fundamental right under the due process clause of the Constitution:

> The freedom to marry has long been recognized as one of the vital personal rights essential to the orderly pursuit of happiness by free men. . . . Marriage is one of the "basic civil rights of man," fundamental to our very existence and survival.[5]

However, the right to marry is not absolute, and the states are permitted to regulate or restrict it to a reasonable extent. Examples of cases in which the courts have held that state law impermissibly restricted the right to marry include the *Loving* case referenced above. In that case, the U.S. Supreme Court struck down Virginia's antimiscegenation law prohibiting marriage between white and "colored" persons. (See Case 3.1.) Examples of other statutes found to have impermissibly restricted the right to marry include the following:

- In *Zablocki v. Redhail*,[6] the U.S. Supreme Court struck down a Wisconsin statute requiring proof that child support payments due from a prior marriage were being met and prohibiting noncustodial parents behind in those payments from marrying. The Court indicated that other collection methods were available to accomplish the intended purpose without encroaching on the fundamental right to marry.
- In *Salisbury v. List*,[7] a federal court struck down a blanket prohibition against allowing prisoners with life sentences to marry except when certain conditions were met. Subsequently, in 1987, the U.S. Supreme Court held that a Missouri law denying confined persons the right to marry was unconstitutional. The Court observed that many important elements of marriage, such as expressions of emotional support, eligibility for receipt of government benefits, property rights, and the legitimation of children, remain after taking into account the limitations of prison life. The Court held that a prisoner should not be deprived of the right to marry unless exercise of the right would be inconsistent with the status of the prisoner or with legitimate penological objectives of the corrections system. The state's general interest in rehabilitation and security were deemed insufficient justifications for denial of the fundamental right to marry.[8]

CASE **3.1** *Loving v. Virginia*, 388 U.S. 1, 87 S. Ct. 1817, 18 L. Ed. 1010 (1967)

BACKGROUND

In this case, a couple, Mildred Jeter (an African-American) and Richard Loving (a white man), challenged Virginia's antimiscegenation law. Similar statutes were still in effect at the time in sixteen other states as well. In June of 1958, the parties, residents of Virginia, traveled to the District of Columbia, where they married under the law of that jurisdiction. They subsequently returned to Virginia, where they were indicted and found guilty of violating the state's ban on interracial marriage. They were sentenced to one year in jail, a sentence that was suspended provided they left Virginia and did not return for twenty-five years. In his opinion, the trial judge stated:

(Continued)

Almighty God created the races white, black, yellow, malay and red, and he placed them on separate continents. And but for the interference with his arrangement there would be no cause for such marriages. The fact that he separated the races shows that he did not intend for the races to mix.

The convictions were upheld on appeal. The couple relocated to the District of Columbia and filed a motion in the Virginia trial court to vacate their convictions on the ground that the statutes they violated were unconstitutional. The motion was denied and, on appeal, the Virginia Supreme Court of Appeals upheld the constitutionality of the statutes and the convictions. The appeal to the U.S. Supreme Court followed, and the statute was held to violate the Equal Protection Clause of the Fourteenth Amendment by restricting a person's choice of a spouse based on racial classifications. The Court also held that the right to marry is a fundamental right under the Due Process Clause.

FROM THE OPINION

This case presents a constitutional question never addressed by this Court: whether a statutory scheme adopted by the State of Virginia to prevent marriages between persons solely on the basis of racial classifications violates the Equal Protection and Due Process Clauses of the Fourteenth Amendment. . . .

The two statutes under which appellants were convicted and sentenced are . . . . § 2058 [and § 2059] of the Virginia Code:

"Leaving the state to evade law.—If any white person and colored person shall go out of this State, for the purpose of being married, and with the intention of returning, and be married out of it, and afterwards return to and reside in it, cohabiting as man and wife, they shall be punished as provided in sect. 2059. . . ."
"Punishment for marriage.—If any white person intermarry with a colored person, or any colored person intermarry with a white person, he shall be guilty of a felony and shall be punished by confinement in the penitentiary for not less than one nor more than five years."

. . . Penalties for miscegenation arose as an incident to slavery and have been common in Virginia since the colonial period. The present statutory scheme dates from the adoption of the Racial Integrity Act of 1924, passed during the period of extreme nativism which followed the end of the First World War. . . .

I. In upholding the constitutionality of these provisions . . . , the Supreme Court of Appeals of Virginia referred to its 1955 decision in *Naim v. Naim,* 197 Va. 80, 87 S. E. 2d 749. . . . In *Naim,* the state court concluded that the State's legitimate purposes were "to preserve the racial integrity of its citizens," and to prevent "the corruption of blood," "a mongrel breed of citizens," and "the obliteration of racial pride," obviously an endorsement of the doctrine of white supremacy. *Id.,* at 90, 87 S. E. 2d, at 756. The court also reasoned that marriage has traditionally been subject to state regulation without federal intervention, and, consequently, the regulation of marriage should be left to exclusive state control by the Tenth Amendment.

While the state court is no doubt correct in asserting that marriage is a social relation subject to the State's police power, . . . the State does not contend in its argument before this Court that its powers to regulate marriage are unlimited notwithstanding the commands of the Fourteenth Amendment. . . . [T]he State contends that, because its miscegenation statutes punish equally both the white and the Negro participants in an interracial marriage, these statutes, despite their reliance on racial classifications, do not constitute an invidious discrimination based on race. . . .

. . . the Equal Protection Clause requires the consideration of whether the classifications drawn by any statute constitute an arbitrary and invidious discrimination.

(Continued)

The clear and central purpose of the Fourteenth Amendment was to eliminate all official state sources of invidious racial discrimination in the States. . . .

There can be no question but that Virginia's miscegenation statutes rest solely upon distinctions drawn according to race. . . . Over the years, this Court has consistently repudiated "distinctions between citizens solely because of their ancestry" as being "odious to a free people whose institutions are founded upon the doctrine of equality." *Hirabayashi v. United States*, 320 U.S. 81, 100 (1943). . . . [I]f they are ever to be upheld, they must be shown to be necessary to the accomplishment of some permissible state objective, independent of the racial discrimination which it was the object of the Fourteenth Amendment to eliminate. . . .

There is patently no legitimate overriding purpose independent of invidious racial discrimination which justifies this classification. The fact that Virginia prohibits only interracial marriages involving white persons demonstrates that the racial classifications must stand on their own justification, as measures designed to maintain White Supremacy. We have consistently denied the constitutionality of measures which restrict the rights of citizens on account of race. There can be no doubt that restricting the freedom to marry solely because of racial classifications violates the central meaning of the Equal Protection Clause.

II. These statutes also deprive the Lovings of liberty without due process of law in violation of the Due Process Clause of the Fourteenth Amendment. The freedom to marry has long been recognized as one of the vital personal rights essential to orderly pursuit of happiness by free men.

Marriage is one of the "basic civil rights of man," fundamental to our very existence and survival. *Skinner v. Oklahoma*, 316 U.S. 535, 541 (1942). . . . To deny this fundamental freedom on so unsupportable a basis as the racial classifications embodied in these statutes, classifications so directly subversive of the principle of equality at the heart of the Fourteenth Amendment, is surely to deprive all the State's citizens of liberty without due process of law. The Fourteenth Amendment requires that the freedom of choice to marry not be restricted by invidious racial discriminations. Under our Constitution, the freedom to marry, or not marry, a person of another race resides with the individual and cannot be infringed by the State.

These convictions must be reversed.

SIDEBAR

Despite this ruling, the remnants of antimiscegenation statutes were still evident nearly twenty years later when the U.S. Supreme Court held in *Palmore v. Sidoti*[9] that a state cannot impose an indirect penalty on a person who marries another of a different race by depriving him or her of child custody based on race. The full opinion in the *Loving* case can be found at *http://www.law.cornell.edu*. You can find a link to this site at *www.pearsonhighered.com/wilson* in the companion website material for Chapter 3 under "Cases" and in the Case Resources Section of the MyLegalStudiesLab.

Paralegal **Application 3.3**

Is a Contract Enforceable If It Restricts an Individual's Right to Marry?

The facts

Rabbi Zaltman does not want his beloved daughter, Alexandra, to marry outside of the Jewish faith in which she has been raised. On the occasion of her graduation from college, he gives her a check for $500,000 on condition that, if she ever marries, she will marry only a Jewish man. She agrees, endorses the check, deposits the funds in her account, and spends the full amount over the next five years. At that time, she marries a Catholic man,

(Continued)

Patrick Michael Madden. Outraged, her father seeks to recover the $500,000.

Sidebar

Should the court enforce the agreement and require the return of the $500,000 or should it find the contract unenforceable because enforcement of its terms by the court would restrict the daughter's fundamental right to marry? Would it make any difference if the father had sought a promise that the daughter never marry? Not marry for a period of five years? Not marry until she completed medical school? Should the courts as agents of the state become "entangled" in such disputes?

A total prohibition against marriage is unlikely to be enforced by a court even if both parties initially agreed to the terms of the contract. However, a partial or limited restriction that serves a useful purpose may be enforceable. Is an interest in maintaining a particular cultural or religious tradition a sufficiently useful purpose? Explain your response.

PARALEGAL PRACTICE TIP

In weighing the government's interest against a constitutional right or principle such as the right to marry, the courts apply what is called a "strict scrutiny" test. The test essentially involves a two-part inquiry:

- First, does the state have a compelling interest that justifies the regulation restricting the fundamental right as it applies to a particular class of persons?
- Second, is the statute sufficiently narrowly drawn so as to avoid unnecessary abridgments of the right?

Marriage Requirements

Although marriage is a contract between the parties, it is a contract regulated by the government. Having established that marriage is a fundamental right that cannot be restricted unreasonably by the states, what kinds of restrictions can and do the states legitimately impose? We cannot simply marry anyone wherever and whenever we please. Each of the states has established its own requirements that couples must satisfy in order to marry. Although there are variations, the requirements are fairly standard state to state. There are basically two types: requirements relating to legal capacity to marry and technical requirements governing particular kinds of marriages. (See Exhibit 3.2 State Statutes—Marriage Requirements.)

PARALEGAL PRACTICE TIP

At *www.law.cornell.edu* you can locate a comprehensive table of state marriage requirements and related links to state codes. To find a link to this site, go to *www.pearsonhighered.com/wilson* and look in the companion website material for Chapter 3 under "Resources." See also Exhibit 3.2 in this chapter of the text.

REQUIREMENTS RELATING TO LEGAL CAPACITY TO MARRY

Restrictions on legal capacity to marry fall into six main categories:

- Sex of the parties
- Age of the parties
- Marital status of the parties
- Degree of relationship between the parties by blood (consanguinity) and marriage (affinity)
- Mental capacity of each party
- Physical capacity of each party

A failure to comply with these restrictions may affect the validity of a marriage and is usually raised in the context of an annulment action.

Sex of the Parties

As of January 2012, all but six states and the District of Columbia require that the parties to a marriage be of different sexes, male and female. (See Exhibit 3.5.) This may seem like a reasonably straightforward requirement, but in this era of advanced medical technology, several courts have had to address (in annulment, custody, adoption, wrongful death, and probate cases) the issue of the sex of a transsexual individual who has successfully undergone sex reassignment surgery. In New Jersey, the state's highest court has held that the "new" sex is the operative sex for determining marital status and legal rights.[10] Courts in other states (such as Florida and Texas) have held that a person's sex at birth is controlling.[11]

Age of the Parties

At common law, the minimum age of consent for marriage was twelve for a female and fourteen for a male. Every state now establishes by statute the minimum age at which parties may marry without parental consent, usually eighteen. The basic rationale for this restriction is the assumption that individuals need to have attained at least some degree of maturity before they can appreciate the nature of marriage, understand the rights and responsibilities that flow from it, and be capable of bearing and raising children in a healthy and responsible family environment. There are, however, several common exceptions to the general rule:

- Youths within an age range such as between sixteen and eighteen may be permitted to marry if they have the consent of a parent or guardian and/or the court.
- Courts may waive the age requirement if the female is pregnant.
- If one or both of the parties is emancipated, the court may grant a request for waiver of the age requirement. **Emancipation** may be established in a number of ways and generally includes no longer living with one's parents and being self-supporting.

Even if a party marries while underage, he or she may ratify the marriage by remaining with the spouse in a marital relationship after attaining the statutory age of consent.

PARALEGAL PRACTICE TIP

The Mormon Church repudiated the practice of polygamy in 1890, but periodic, and high-profile, news stories, such as the removal of more than 450 children from the Yearning for Zion compound in Texas in the spring of 2008, indicate it is still practiced by a number of Mormon fundamentalists. For more information on this topic, visit *www.religioustolerance.org*. You can find a link to this site at *www.pearsonhighered.com/wilson* in the companion website material for Chapter 3 under " Resources."

Marital Status of the Parties

Each of the parties must be "free" to marry in the sense that neither is married to another individual still living at the time of the marriage. **Bigamy**, a crime in all states (usually a misdemeanor), is defined as entering a second marriage while a prior marriage is still valid. **Polygamy**, also a crime, refers to a situation in which one individual (usually a male) has multiple spouses at the same time.[12]

Most states provide that bigamous and polygamous marriages are **void**, but if at least one party enters the marriage in good faith, the impediment is eventually removed (by death or divorce), and the parties continue to live together in a marital relationship, the marriage may be considered valid from the date the impediment was removed.

Degree of Relationship Between the Parties by Blood (Consanguinity) and Marriage (Affinity)

States establish, by statute, restrictions on the degrees of relationship that can exist by consanguinity and affinity in order for two persons to marry. Such regulations are based primarily on the state's interests in promoting family harmony, protecting

---

PARALEGAL PRACTICE TIP

To see a form used by a minor to request the court's permission to marry (with parental consent), visit *www.vermontjudiciary.org/eforms*. You can find a link to this site at *www.pearsonhighered.com/wilson* in the companion website material for Chapter 3 under "Forms."

Emancipation
the point at which a child is considered an adult and granted adult rights; usually occurs at the age of majority or upon the occurrence of certain acts or events such as marriage or entering the armed services

PARALEGAL PRACTICE TIP

Some anti-incest taboos are based on broad cultural, political, and social rather than genetic concerns. For example, among the Navajo, incest has been based on membership in one of several major "clans," each potentially consisting of hundreds of people, resulting in a rule that a person must not be intimate with anyone in either the father's ("born for") clan or the mother's ("born to") clan.

Bigamy
the act of entering a subsequent marriage while a prior marriage of one or both of the parties is still in effect; in most states constitutes a criminal offense if committed knowingly; a ground for annulment and/or divorce in all states

Polygamy
the state of having more than one spouse at the same time

Void
invalid and of no legal effect

children from sexual exploitation, and limiting the genetic transmission of negative recessive traits (such as hemophilia and congenital deafness). These regulations are designed to be consistent with provisions of state criminal codes regarding crimes such as **incest**.

Consanguinity provisions specify impermissible blood relationships in marriage such as parent and child, sister and brother (of the whole or half blood), and uncle and niece. Several states still prohibit the marriage of first cousins based on an assumption that such marriages result in genetic defects in children due to inbreeding. Rather than totally restricting the right of first cousins to marry, it has been suggested that this concern can be effectively addressed by providing genetic counseling for parties to such unions[13] or, as provided in some states, by permitting marriage only after the parties have passed their procreative years (e.g., both are over age sixty-five). The Uniform Marriage and Divorce Act permits first cousins, as well as individuals related to one another through adoption, to marry.

Affinity provisions establish impermissible unions based on relationships created by marriage rather than by blood, such as a wife and her father-in-law or a husband and his sister-in-law. Several states have eliminated restrictions based on affinity. Some states that have not eliminated them provide that the prohibitions are lifted when the person who created the prohibited relationship dies. There are also variations among the states with respect to the impact of relationships created by adoption or through step-parents.

Mental Capacity

Initially, the requirement that the parties have sufficient mental capacity to marry was based to some extent on a fear that mentally deficient individuals would marry, bear similarly limited children, and create financial and social burdens for society at large. Today, mental capacity most often becomes an issue in cases where a party is seriously ill, of advanced age, under guardianship, or under the influence of drugs or alcohol at the time of the marriage ceremony. It should be noted that even if a person lacks mental capacity a majority of the time, courts have held that he or she can contract a valid marriage in a "lucid interval."

Lack of sufficient mental capacity is described in the following excerpt from an opinion of a North Dakota court:

> While there has been a hesitancy on the part of the courts to judicially define the phrase "unsound mind," it is established that such [a] term has reference to the mental capacity of the parties at the very moment of inception of the marriage contract. Ordinarily, lack of mental capacity, which renders a party incapable of entering into a valid marriage contract, must be such that it deprives him of the ability to understand the objects of marriage, its ensuing duties and undertakings, its responsibilities and relationship. There is a general agreement of the authorities that the terms "unsound mind" and "lack of mental capacity" carry greater import than eccentricity or mere weakness of mind or dullness of intellect.[14]

Physical Capacity

Historically, the presence of "incurable diseases" acted as a bar to marriage in some states. In a small number of states (such as Nebraska[15]) applicants for a marriage license still must be free of syphilis, creating a particular dilemma for a clerk issuing licenses in a state (such as Ohio) where blood tests have been eliminated but the restriction remains in force.

Incest
sexual intercourse between two people who are too closely related for some purpose as defined by civil and criminal statutes; a term used in some states to describe prohibited degrees of consanguinity and affinity in the marriage context

Consanguinity
a blood relationship between individuals

Affinity
relationship by marriage (i.e., the relationship a spouse has to the blood relatives of the other spouse)

PARALEGAL PRACTICE TIP

Visit *www.ncsl.org* to find a report (5/2010) on the status of state laws on the marriage of first cousins, which is banned in approximately half the states. To find a link to this site, go to *www.pearsonhighered.com/wilson* in the companion website material for Chapter 3 under "Resources."

TECHNICAL REQUIREMENTS FOR A CEREMONIAL MARRIAGE

In addition to satisfying the legal requirements for capacity to marry, the states also establish fairly consistent technical requirements for ceremonial marriages. These requirements commonly include the following components:

- an application for a license
- a medical certificate or provision of information concerning certain diseases
- a license
- a waiting period
- a ceremony
- recording of the license/marriage certificate

When one or more of these "requirements" are not met, the marriage usually still will be upheld, given the strong public policy favoring the validity of marriages. Some states expressly provide by statute that if the marriage is lawful in all other respects and is consummated in the belief of either party that it is lawful, the marriage will be deemed valid notwithstanding any failure to satisfy a technical requirement. The penalty for noncompliance is usually in the form of a modest fine. However, falsifying public documents may carry a heavier penalty, including a period of incarceration.

Application for a License

The parties pay a fee and file a written application for a license to marry (sometimes called a notice of intention) usually in the county where they intend to marry. Both parties complete the application and sign it under pain and penalty of perjury. If one of the parties is seriously ill or in the armed services, a parent, guardian, or the other party may be permitted to provide the absent party's information. Customarily, the application requires the following:

- the parties' names and the names they intend to use once married
- their places of residence
- their birthplaces and ages (Documentation may be required, especially when there is reasonable doubt as to a party's stated age.)
- their parents' names
- the number of any prior marriages of each party and the means by which they were terminated or dissolved (Some states require documentation such as a death certificate or a divorce decree.)
- Some forms also require the parties to affirm a general statement that there are no legal impediments to the marriage such as a prohibited degree of blood relationship between the applicants.

PARALEGAL PRACTICE TIP

Under common law, a wife automatically assumed her husband's surname upon marriage, a practice consistent with the doctrine of marital unity. This tradition has faded somewhat. States may address the topic by statute, case law, or procedural rules or practices. For example, in New York, the parties are given notice that their names will not automatically change upon marriage, and they are asked to indicate the names they intend to use after marriage on the application for a marriage license. Search for information about getting married in New York at *www.health.state.ny.us*. You can find a link to this site at *www.pearsonhighered.com/wilson* in the companion website material for Chapter 3 under "Resources."

The parties will also be asked to provide any information required by the state's child support enforcement agency, including their respective Social Security

PARALEGAL PRACTICE TIP

To see the Massachusetts' provisions governing marriage requirements visit *www.lawlib.state.ma.us*. "Chapter 207 Section 42" specifically addresses the effect of an irregularity in solemnization on the validity of a marriage. You can find a link to this site at *www.pearsonhighered.com/wilson* in the companion website material for Chapter 3 under "Statutes."

PARALEGAL PRACTICE TIP

A copy of the Application for a Marriage License for the State of Hawaii can be found at *www.pearsonhighered.com/wilson* in the companion website material for Chapter 3 under "Forms."

numbers. Ideally, given the present-day emphasis on privacy rights and the potential for identity theft, the number should be provided on a separate form for submission to the agency and should not become a part of the public record.

Medical Certificate

Historically, the requirement of physical examinations and/or blood tests was designed to determine whether either party had incurable tuberculosis or a sexually transmitted disease such as syphilis, or if the female had been vaccinated for rubella unless she was past her childbearing years. Today, many of the states have eliminated this requirement, largely because of advances in medical technology and an increased emphasis on privacy. However, some still require the filing of a medical certificate indicating that the parties have undergone certain laboratory tests within a specified period prior to filing their application. Others require that information regarding AIDS and other sexually transmitted diseases be provided to marriage applicants.

License

The license is issued by the statutorily designated authority, usually within a specified period after the application is made.

Waiting Period

Some states establish a waiting period (commonly not more than three days) between application for and issuance of a license, although the period may be waived by statute under certain conditions or by the court on a Motion for a Marriage Without Delay. The general purpose of the waiting period is to promote deliberate consideration of the decision to marry.

Ceremony

A ceremony is performed, usually by a religious cleric, a Justice of the Peace, or another governmental official authorized by statute to perform such functions. During the ceremony, the parties express their intentions to marry in the presence of witnesses. Some states (such as Colorado and Texas) allow **proxy marriages**, in which the marriage ceremony takes place with one of the parties absent. A third-party agent is given authority to act on behalf of the missing person. Situations in which proxy marriages occur include those involving a party serving in the armed services and stationed overseas, a person who is incarcerated, or an American citizen who enters a proxy marriage with someone in another country, thereby qualifying that person for citizenship. Given the potential for abuse, proxy marriages generally are not favored.

PARALEGAL PRACTICE TIP

Some states permit individuals who have been "ordained" online to perform ceremonies. Massachusetts has a procedure by which an individual may apply for a special one-day designation to perform/solemnize marriages. M.G.L. 207 § 39 provides that the governor may "designate any other person to solemnize a particular marriage on a particular date and in a particular city or town. . . ." To see the form used for requesting a one-day authorization to perform a marriage visit *www.lawlib.state.ma.us.* You can find a link to this site at *www.pearsonhighered.com/wilson* in the companion website material for Chapter 3 under "Forms."

Recording of the License/Marriage Certificate

The individual who performs the ceremony records the license or certificate of marriage in the public office designated by statute within a certain time frame (usually from three to ten days).

PARALEGAL PRACTICE TIP
To read the West Virginia statute on premarital testing, visit *www.pearsonhighered.com/wilson* and look in the companion website material for Chapter 3 under "Statutes."

PARALEGAL PRACTICE TIP
To see a Motion for Marriage Without Delay, visit *www.lawlib.state.ma.us.* A link to the site can be found at *www.pearsonhighered.com/wilson* in the companion website material for Chapter 3 under "Forms."

Proxy marriage
a marriage ceremony in which a designated agent stands in for and acts on behalf of one of the absent parties (prohibited in most states)

PARALEGAL PRACTICE TIP
In some states, one document serves as the Notice of Intention to Marry and the Certificate of Marriage. See, e.g., Vermont's Certificate of Marriage, which can be found at *www.vermontjudiciary.org/eforms.* A link to this site is available at *www.pearsonhighered.com/wilson* in the companion website material for Chapter 3 under "Forms."

EXHIBIT 3.2 State Statutes—Marriage Requirements

Alabama Ala. Code Tit. 30 Ch. 1	**Kentucky** Ky. Rev. Stat. Tit. XXXV, Art. 402	**North Dakota** N.D. Cent. Code Tit. 14, Ch. 14-03
Alaska Alaska Stat. Tit. 25, Ch. 5	**Louisiana** La. Civil Code Bk. 1, Tit. 4, Ch. 1	**Ohio** Ohio Rev. Code Ann. Tit. 31, Ch. 3101
Arizona Ariz. Rev. Stat. Tit. 25 Ch. 1	**Maine** Me. Rev. Stat. Ann. Tit. 19A, Pt. 2, Ch. 23	**Oklahoma** Okla. Stat. Tit. 43
Arkansas Ark. Code: Tit. 9, Sub. 2, Ch. 11	**Maryland** Md. Fam. Law Code Tit. 2	**Oregon** Or. Stat. Tit. 11, Ch. 106
California Cal. Fam. Code, Div. 3	**Massachusetts** Mass. Gen. Laws Ch. 207	**Pennsylvania** Pa. Cons. Stat. Tit. 23, Pt. II
Colorado Colo. Rev. Stat. Tit. 14 Art. 2. Pt. 1	**Michigan** Mich. Comp. Laws Ch. 551	**Rhode Island** R.I. Gen. Laws Tit. 15, Ch. 1-3
Connecticut Conn. Stat. Tit. 46b, Ch. 815e	**Minnesota** Minn. Stat. Dom. Rel. Code, Ch. 517	**South Carolina** S.C. Code Tit. 20, Ch. 1
Delaware Del. Code Tit. 13, Ch. 1	**Mississippi** Miss. Code Tit. 93, Ch. 1	**South Dakota** S.D. Codified Laws Tit. 2 Ch. 25-1
District of Columbia D.C. Code Div. VIII, Tit. 46, Sub. 1, Ch. 4	**Missouri** Mo. Stat. Tit. 30, Ch. 451	**Tennessee** Tenn. Code Tit. 36, Ch. 3
Florida Fla. Stat. Ch. 741.01-741.212	**Montana** Mont. Cod: Tit. 40, Ch. 1	**Texas** Tex. Family Code Ann. Tit. 1 Ch. 1, 2
Georgia Ga. Code Art. 9-3-1–19-3-68	**Nebraska** Neb. Rev. Stat. Ch. 42, Art. 1	**Utah** Utah Code Tit. 30, Ch. 1
Hawaii Haw. Rev. Stat. Div. 3, Tit. 31, Ch. 572	**Nevada** Nev. Rev. Stat. Tit. 11, Ch. 122	**Vermont** Vt. Stat. Tit. 15 Ch. 1; Tit. 18, Part 6, Ch. 105
Idaho Idaho Code Gen. Laws, Tit. 32, Ch. 2, 3 and 4	**New Hampshire** N.H. R.S.A. Tit. XLIII, Ch. 457	**Virginia** Va. Code Tit. 20 Ch. 2, 3
Illinois Ill. Comp. Stat. Ch. 750 ILCS, 5, Parts II and III	**New Jersey** N.J. Rev. Stat. Tit. 37, Ch. 1	**Washington** Wash. Rev. Code Tit. 26, Ch. 26.04
Indiana Ind. Code Tit. 31, Art. 11, Ch. 1-6	**New Mexico** N.M. Stat. Ch. 40, Art. 1	**West Virginia** W. Va. Code Ch. 48 Art. 2
Iowa Iowa Code Tit. XV, Sub. 1, Ch. 595	**New York** N.Y. Cons. Laws Dom. Rel. Law Art. 2, and 3	**Wisconsin** Wis. Stat. The Family Ch. 765
Kansas Kan. Stat. Ch. 23, Art. 1	**North Carolina** N.C. Gen. Stat. Ch. 51	**Wyoming** Wyo. Stat. Tit. 20, Ch. 1, Art. 1

PARALEGAL PRACTICE TIP

There are those who argue that the common law marriage doctrine should be revived because it protects the interests of women, especially poor women and women of color. A greater percentage of these segments of the population do not marry but live with partners for extended periods and/or have children. When their relationships break up or their partners and breadwinners die, they are left without benefits and protections available to common law spouses. Courts increasingly try to find ways of providing relief in such cases.[16]

Requirements for a Common Law Marriage

At the end of the nineteenth century, the U.S. Supreme Court ruled that common law marriages are valid unless prohibited by a state.[17] At that time, they were recognized in most states. However, because of the potential for abuse (especially when the existence of a common law marriage is claimed after the death of a party), and the argument that they promote immoral behavior, such marriages are not usually favored even in jurisdictions where they are authorized. However, abuse should not be presumed, given that people opt for common law marriage for a variety of legitimate reasons including, but not limited to, convenience, lack of expense, and a desire to minimize involvement with either the government or religious bodies.

The requirements for a valid common law marriage vary slightly in states that allow this form of union. They customarily include the following:

- The parties must have the legal capacity to marry.
- They must intend and simultaneously agree to be married. (Some states require that the agreement be expressed; others will infer an agreement from the conduct of the parties.)
- They must cohabit (although consummation may not be required).
- They must hold themselves out to the public as husband and wife.

The popular belief that the parties to a common law marriage must cohabit for a specific length of time is largely a misconception. However, the New Hampshire statute does include a time requirement. (See Exhibit 3.3.) In all states where common law marriage is permitted, with the exception of New Hampshire, once a common law marriage is established, it carries with it the same rights, benefits, and duties as a traditional ceremonial marriage, and children born to the parties are legitimate. It also must be formally dissolved by divorce if the relationship terminates and either or both of the parties wish to marry another.

EXHIBIT 3.3 New Hampshire Statute Concerning Cohabitation: New Hampshire Revised Statutes Annotated 457:39

FROM THE STATUTE

457:39 Cohabitation, etc.—Persons cohabiting and acknowledging each other as husband and wife, and generally reputed to be such, for the period of three years, and until the decease of one of them, shall thereafter be deemed to have been legally married.

EXHIBIT 3.4 Common Law Marriage States

Alabama	Montana
Alaska until 1/1/64	Nebraska until 1923
California until 1895	Nevada until 3/29/43
Colorado (age restriction: must be over 18)	New Hampshire (for probate purposes only)
District of Columbia	New Jersey until 1/12/39
Florida until 1/1/68	New York until 4/29/33

(Continued)

PARALEGAL PRACTICE TIP

In states where they are permitted, the requirements for a valid common law marriage may be set forth in statutes and/or case law. The applicable Iowa statute can be found at *www.legis.iowa.gov.* You can find a link to this site at *www.pearsonhighered.com/wilson* in the companion website material for Chapter 3 under "Statutes."

PARALEGAL PRACTICE TIP

To see a form used in Utah to seek judicial recognition of a common law marriage, visit *www.utcourts.gov/howto/family/.* You can find a link to this site at *www.pearsonhighered.com/wilson* in the companion website material for Chapter 3 under "Forms."

PARALEGAL PRACTICE TIP

The New Hampshire Cohabitation Statute is unusual in two respects:

1. It includes a requirement that the parties cohabit for at least three years.
2. It is applicable only in the context of inheritance or death benefit claims.

PARALEGAL PRACTICE TIP

Most states will recognize a common law marriage that is valid in the state where it was entered. When the existence of a common law marriage is asserted, it is important to check states that presently permit such marriages and under what circumstances. It is also important to check whether the alleged marriage was entered in a state that no longer recognizes common law marriage but formerly did and did so at a time when the parties resided in that state. Visit *www.ncsl.org,* the site of the national conference of state legislatures, as a starting point for researching the status of common law marriage in the United States. You can find a link to this site at *www.pearsonhighered.com/wilson* in the companion website material for Chapter 3 under "Resources."

EXHIBIT 3.4 (*Continued*)

Georgia until 1/1/97	Ohio until 10/10/91
Idaho until 1/1/96	Oklahoma until 1998
Illinois until 6/30/1905	Pennsylvania until 2005
Indiana until 1/1/58	Rhode Island
Iowa	South Carolina
Kansas (age restriction: must be over 18)	South Dakota until 7/1/59
Michigan until 1/1/57	Texas (called: informal marriages)
Minnesota until 4/26/41	Utah (enacted 1987; Condition: if validated by a court or administrative order)
Mississippi until 4/5/56	Wisconsin until 1913
Missouri until 3/3/21	

Paralegal Application 3.4

Information Gathering in a Common Law Marriage Case

In a case in which a client is alleging the existence of a common law marriage, a paralegal may be asked to gather information from the client and other sources regarding the following:

- the date and circumstances under which the parties met
- any children born to or adopted by the parties
- the parties' decision to live together—when and how it was made
- details regarding when, where, and for how long the parties have lived together
- details regarding travel by the parties, if any, to other states that recognize common law marriage

PARALEGAL PRACTICE TIP

Is it possible to enter a common law marriage by accident? Occasionally a party will claim he or she entered a common law marriage because the couple annually vacationed in a state that permits common law marriage and in that state held themselves out as married. See, e.g., *Collier v. Milford,* 537 A.2d 474 (Conn. 1988).

- the nature of the parties' relationship, including whether or not they engaged in sexual relations

- details regarding the parties' financial arrangements, including payment of expenses, maintenance of bank and credit card accounts, etc.
- the parties' history with respect to payment of taxes—were joint returns filed?
- the existence and location of documents pertaining to any property, real or personal, owned by the parties, individually or jointly
- the existence and location of documents executed by the parties, such as wills, health care proxies, powers of attorney, trusts, insurance policies, etc.
- details regarding any oral or written agreement between the parties regarding marriage, including why they did not enter a traditional ceremonial marriage
- details regarding the parties' social life and how they have represented themselves to others
- names and contact information for individuals familiar with the parties as friends, relatives, and business associates who regard and treat them as husband and wife
- the existence and location of other evidence of the parties' intent, such as inscriptions on photographs, engraving on jewelry, inclusion of the parties' names and marital relationship in family trees and bibles, etc.

Marriage as a Source of Rights, Benefits, and Obligations

According to an audit report of the U.S. General Accounting Office, under federal and state law, there are more than one thousand rights and duties that flow from a valid heterosexual marriage, either ceremonial or common law. Some of the most important of these include the following:

PARALEGAL PRACTICE TIP

Given that same-sex marriages are not recognized under federal law as of January 2012, the rights and obligations conferred on parties to same-sex marriages are limited to those extended under state law. State-created legal statuses, such as domestic partnerships and civil unions, extend varying degrees rights, benefits, and obligations of married persons to nonmarital partners. For an authoritative but complex summary of 1,138 of the federal statutory provisions in the United States Code in which marital status is a factor in determining or receiving benefits, rights, and privileges, see a report entitled *Categories of Laws Involving Marital Status* (commonly referred to as "Rights and Responsibilities of Marriages in the United States"), an enclosure to a letter found at *www.gao.gov/archive/1997/og97016.pdf* or *www. gao.gov/new.items/d04353r.pdf*. You can find links to these sites at *www.pearsonhighered.com/wilson* in the companion website material for Chapter 3 under "Resources."

- Each spouse is entitled to receive support from and has a duty to provide support to the other spouse.
- Absent a valid and enforceable premarital agreement to the contrary and subject to the statutory provisions of state law, parties to a valid marriage acquire an interest in all "marital property" acquired by the spouses during their marriage (generally exclusive of property received by a spouse through an inheritance or gift from a third party). A spouse may seek division of the marital property upon divorce.
- When the marital property is divided, one spouse may receive payment of a portion of the other spouse's pension. Given an exception to the general federal policy prohibiting assignment of retirement interests, a Qualified Domestic Relations Order (QDRO) issued by the court may make a spouse an alternate payee under an employee spouse's pension plan.
- In some states, spouses may hold title to real property as tenants by the entirety, a form of ownership available only to spouses, which grants each spouse a right in the whole property. Generally, if title to the marital residence is held in this form, the property will not be able to be seized by the creditors of a debtor spouse.
- Absent an enforceable premarital agreement, each spouse is entitled to inherit property from his or her spouse. If the spouse dies **intestate**, the surviving spouse will inherit property to the extent provided in the **laws of descent and distribution** in force in the state where the deceased spouse was domiciled at death. Essentially, these laws specify that the estate of the deceased will be distributed among his or her closest relatives (spouse, children, parents, siblings, etc.).
- Provided any necessary conditions are satisfied (such as age or a minimum length of marriage), spouses are entitled to receive certain governmental benefits, such as Social Security administration and veterans' benefits after the death of a wage earner or veteran.
- A divorced, separated, or surviving spouse may be entitled to continued employer-provided health insurance coverage for a specific period, generally up to thirty-six months under the Consolidated Omnibus Budget Reconciliation Act of 1985 (COBRA).
- In *tort* law, the existence of a valid marriage still is a threshold requirement in most states to recover for "loss of consortium" resulting from the negligent conduct of another. **Consortium** commonly includes a loss of services, companionship, support, guidance, comfort, affection, and, in the case of spouses, a loss of sexual relations. For example, if an individual is paralyzed as a result of the negligence of a drunk driver, then his or her spouse may seek to recover for loss of consortium.

PARALEGAL PRACTICE TIP

Attorneys often advise clients to protect their estates while a divorce is pending by executing wills that dispose of their property as they wish. If they fail to do so and die without a will before the divorce is final, their property will be distributed according to the applicable state's law of descent and distribution.

Intestate
dying without leaving a valid will

Laws of descent and distribution
the laws governing inheritance of property by heirs when a decedent dies without leaving a valid will. Usually, a surviving spouse will inherit the entire estate or will receive half of it, with the other half being distributed to any surviving children in equal shares. If the spouse dies testate (with a will) and the will largely disinherits or fails to make adequate provisions for the surviving spouse, some states allow him or her to "waive the will" and claim a "forced share" of the estate as set by statute.

Tort
a civil wrong (other than breach of contract) for which a court provides a remedy, usually in the form of money damages; the wrong must involve harm resulting from breach of a duty owed to another

Consortium
companionship, affection, and, in the case of spouses, sexual relations, that one is entitled to receive from another based on existence of a legal relationship (e.g., husband-wife, parent-child)

- Surviving spouses are also eligible to file claims for the wrongful death of their marital partners. For example, if Carlos dies as a result of an explosion caused by the installation of a faulty furnace, his wife may file a wrongful death action against the installer and the manufacturer of the furnace. As callous as it may sound, damages are measured by the monetary value of the decedent to the surviving spouse in terms of loss of reasonably expected income as well as loss of consortium.
- Marriage customarily confers the ability to make medical decisions on behalf of a spouse in times of crisis or incapacity.
- A nonresident alien who marries a U.S. citizen obtains permanent resident status (if no deportation proceeding is pending), although the marriage will be treated as conditional until two years after the marriage takes place.[18]
- A spouse generally cannot be criminally charged as an accessory-after-the-fact for harboring or concealing his or her spouse after the latter has committed a felony.
- The law values the important functions served by confidential communications in a variety of contexts (attorney-client, priest-penitent, doctor-patient), and the relationship between husband and wife is one of those contexts. The husband-wife or **marital communications privilege** prohibits compelled disclosure of statements made by spouses to each other within the privacy of the marital relationship. It does not apply to actions the spouse may have seen or to written communications. It also does not apply in civil actions for divorce, separation, custody, spousal or child support, or in criminal actions for nonsupport, incest, or abuse.

Marital communications privilege
the privilege that allows a spouse to refuse to testify, and to prevent others from testifying, about confidential communications between spouses during their marriage; does not apply in certain contexts, such as cases involving child custody and/or abuse

PARALEGAL PRACTICE TIP

The husband-wife privilege protects the privacy of spouses against third persons and against the state in some circumstances. It also protects spouses from each other to a degree by placing limitations on the extent to which a spouse may use private surveillance to "spy on" the other spouse while a divorce is pending and the parties are living separate and apart. For example, a client may need to be cautioned by counsel regarding any federal or state prohibition against electronically recording phone conversations with his or her spouse while a divorce action is pending.[19]

Same-Sex Marriage

A client asks her partner, "Can I, Kelly Sue, take thee, Dorothy Ann, to be my wedded spouse from this day forward?" As is the case with most legal questions, the answer is "It depends." The first same-sex marriages were performed in April of 2001 in the Netherlands. A small number of other countries have elected to permit them since that time, including Belgium and Canada. And on May 17, 2004, after decades of battling for the right to do so, over one thousand same-sex couples successfully obtained marriage licenses in cities and towns across the Commonwealth of Massachusetts. Some regard that monumental event as just the beginning. Some view it as the beginning of the end of the institution of marriage. Few are without an opinion on the subject.

Once the Supreme Court established marriage as a fundamental right in the *Loving* case in 1967, same-sex couples across the United States began challenging state laws restricting that right to heterosexual couples primarily as discriminatory denials of equal protection and due process. Initially, plaintiffs in states such as Kentucky and Minnesota hit a brick wall. The courts reasoned that the Due Process Clause did not encompass same-sex couples because of the traditional and essential nature of marriage as a union between a man and a woman. Statutes restricting marriage to heterosexual couples were held to serve the states' legitimate interests in protecting the traditional family as the fundamental building block of society, promoting procreation within the family environment, and discouraging illegal sexual activity between unmarried and, specifically, same-sex partners.

Cracks in the brick wall began appearing in the 1990s as the question of whether same-sex partners have a right to marry started to become as controversial and hotly debated an issue in the field of family law as is abortion. In its 1993 decision in *Baehr v. Lewin*,[20] the Hawaii Supreme Court declined to find that same-sex couples have a right to marry, but it did hold that denial of the right *might* constitute a denial of equal protection under the Hawaii state constitution. On remand, the trial court ordered the state to stop denying marriage licenses to same-sex couples, holding that the marriage ban was not necessary for the protection of children as had been alleged by the state. The door that appeared to open while that decision was on appeal slammed shut on same-sex marriage in that state when the voters supported a constitutional amendment that gave the legislature the authority to limit marriage to opposite-sex couples. The legislature promptly passed a statute expressly stating that a valid marriage "shall be only between a man and a woman."[21]

Finally in 2003, plaintiffs in the *Goodridge* case in Massachusetts prevailed where others had not when the Massachusetts Supreme Judicial Court held that denying same-sex couples the right to marry constituted a denial of equal protection under the state's constitution.[22] Whatever position one holds with respect to same-sex marriage, it is well worth reading the lengthy *Goodridge* opinion. It touches on the vast majority of the questions raised in the cases and public debate surrounding this topic:

- What is the definition of marriage?
- What is the function of marriage?
- Is procreation the primary purpose of marriage?
- Does it make a difference if children are created through "noncoital" rather than "coital" means of reproduction?
- What is the "optimal setting" in which to raise children?
- Are heterosexual parents "better" parents than same-sex parents?

PARALEGAL PRACTICE TIP

In its 2008 decision, *In re Marriage Cases,* the California Supreme Court opined that "In contrast to earlier times, our state now recognizes that an individual's capacity to establish a loving and long-term committed relationship with another person and responsibly to care for and raise children does not depend upon the individual's sexual orientation." 43 Cal. 4th 757 at 782, 183 P.3d 384 at 400, 76 Cal. Rptr. 683 at 701 (2008).

- Is the *sine qua non* of marriage an exclusive commitment between two individuals regardless of gender?
- Does particular statutory language limit marriage to heterosexual couples?
- Does the fundamental right to marry extend to same-sex couples?
- Does equal protection require that the right to marry be granted to same-sex couples?
- Do due process considerations require the right to marry be afforded to same-sex couples?
- Does the state have a legitimate and/or compelling interest in confining marriage to heterosexual couples, and, if so, what is it?
- What standard/test applies to restrictions on the right to marry: Rational basis? Strict scrutiny?
- Is restricting marriage to heterosexual couples cost-effective?
- What are the respective roles of the legislature and the judiciary in addressing the issue of same-sex marriage?
- What role should the electorate play in the decision-making process?

- What influence do antigay prejudices have in influencing (clouding) decisions regarding same-sex marriage?
- How do religious, moral, and ethical convictions influence decisions in this area?
- Will permitting same-sex marriage destabilize the social order?
- What are the rights, benefits, and duties that come with legal marital status?
- How does denying same-sex couples the right to marry impact those couples and their children?
- Does denial of the right to marry create a population of second-class citizens?
- Does extending the right to marry to same-sex couples "trivialize" or devalue the institution of marriage?

PARALEGAL PRACTICE TIP

An excerpt from the lengthy opinion in this case is available at *www.pearsonhighered.com/wilson* in the companion website material related to Chapter 3 under "Cases" and in the Case Resources Section of the MyLegalStudiesLab.

CASE **3.2** *Goodridge v. Department of Public Health,* 440 Mass. 309, 98 N.E.2d 941 (2003)

BACKGROUND

The plaintiffs in this case were fourteen individuals, seven couples, from five Massachusetts counties. They had been in committed same-sex relationships for periods ranging from four to thirty years. In March and April of 2001, each of the couples had applied for and been denied marriage licenses on the ground that Massachusetts did not recognize same-sex marriage. The couples then filed suit in Superior Court against the Department of Public Health (and the Commissioner), seeking a judgment that the exclusion of the couples, and other qualified same-sex couples, "from access to marriage licenses, and the legal and social status of civil marriage, as well as the protections, benefits, and obligations of marriage" violated state law, including the Massachusetts Constitution. The Superior Court judge dismissed the plaintiffs' claim. He concluded that the plain wording of the relevant Massachusetts marriage statutes precluded marriage between members of the same sex. With respect to the constitutional claims, the judge held that the marriage exclusion did not offend "the liberty, freedom, equality or due process provisions of the Massachusetts Constitution," and that the Massachusetts Declaration of Rights did not guarantee a fundamental right to same-sex marriage. He concluded that the prohibition rationally furthered the state's legitimate interest in safeguarding the primary purpose of marriage—procreation—because opposite-sex couples are more likely to have children and to do so without relying on "inherently more cumbersome" noncoital means of reproduction. The ruling was successfully appealed to the Massachusetts Supreme Judicial Court, which found that the marriage ban violated both equal protection and due process clauses of the state constitution. The court effectively modified the common law definition of marriage and then stayed implementation of the ruling for 180 days so that the legislature could conform the state's marital laws to the decision.

FROM THE OPINION

. . . Marriage is a vital social institution. The exclusive commitment of two individuals to each other nurtures love and mutual support; it brings stability to our society. For those who choose to marry, and for their children, marriage provides an abundance of legal, financial, and social benefits. The question before us is whether, consistent with the Massachusetts Constitution, the Commonwealth may

(Continued)

deny the protections, benefits, and obligations conferred by civil marriage to two individuals of the same sex who wish to marry. We conclude that it may not. The Massachusetts Constitution affirms the dignity and equality of all individuals. It forbids the creation of second-class citizens. . . .

We are mindful that our decision marks a change in the history of our marriage law. Many people hold deep-seated religious, moral and ethical convictions that marriage should be limited to the union of one man and one woman, and that homosexual conduct is immoral. Many hold equally strong religious, moral, and ethical convictions that same-sex couples are entitled to be married. . . . Neither view answers the question before us. Our concern is with the Massachusetts Constitution. . . .

Barred access to the protections, benefits, and obligations of civil marriage, a person who enters into an intimate, exclusive union with another of the same sex is arbitrarily deprived of membership in one of our community's most rewarding and cherished institutions. That exclusion is incompatible with the constitutional principles of respect for individual autonomy and equality under law.

PARALEGAL PRACTICE TIP

Technically, there is no "same-sex marriage statute" in Massachusetts. The same laws and procedures that govern traditional marriage apply as well to same-sex marriage. On the Notice of Intention to Marry (the application for a license), the parties are now designated Party A and Party B. This is the basic approach taken in other states that permit same-sex marriage, although the District of Columbia does have a brief statutory provision specifically addressing this topic (D.C. Code section 64-401). It can be found at *www.dccouncil.washington.dc.us.* You can find a link to this site at *www.pearsonhighered.com/wilson* in the companion website material for Chapter 3 under "Statutes."

Paralegal Application 3.5

Same-Sex Marriage: Which Camp Are You In?

"A battle for the hearts and minds of the American people is being waged, and the battleground is the institution of public marriage."[23]

The warriors fall into four main camps:

- Those who seek to preserve marriage in its traditional form, viewing it as a crucially important social, cultural, religious, and legal institution. Justice Antonin Scalia articulated the fear driving this camp in his dissent in *Lawrence v. Texas*, the case in which the U.S. Supreme Court held it unconstitutional for a state to prosecute consenting same-sex adults for engaging in private sexual conduct that does not involve prostitution. He expressed his view that the majority in that case "largely signed onto the so-called homosexual agenda" and effectively decreed "the end of all morals legislation" causing "massive disruption of the current social order."[24] This camp does not want to extend any legally recognized status to same-sex couples.

- Those who support same-sex marriage and believe that its adoption on a nationwide basis is inevitable. This position has been described as follows:

   Attempts to amend constitutions so as to make legal marriage impossible for same-sex couples are futile. . . . Where such amendments have been adopted, they will eventually be repealed or invalidated, because the "incoming tide," i.e., the long-term international trend, will eventually bring full legal equality to our fellow human beings who happen to be lesbian and gay individuals, or members of same-sex couples, with or without children.[25]

- Those who would abolish civil marriage. "The law should not define, regulate, or recognize marriage. Marriage—the structured, publicly-proclaimed, communally-supported relationship of mutual commitment—should become solely a religious and cultural institution with no legal definition or status.

(Continued)

. . . Culturally, marriage no longer plays the role in our society it once did."[26] In this option, with a variety of religious models to choose from, the door might open to polygamous marriages.

- Those who believe marriage should continue to be restricted to heterosexual couples but that under the Equal Protection Clause of the Constitution, an alternative legal status according equivalent rights (such as civil unions) should be established for same-sex couples.

Sidebar

As responsible citizens and voters, we will each be called upon to consider this issue over the next decade. Which position do you presently espouse? Why? Are you persuaded in any respect by the *Goodridge* decision?

PARALEGAL PRACTICE TIP

For many years, some states have had **Marriage Evasion Statutes** under which a marriage may not be recognized if the parties leave their state of residence and go to another state with more lenient marriage rules for the sole purpose of marrying there and with the intention of returning to their home state following the marriage. In many instances, these statutes serve the same purpose as a mini-DOMA.

Marriage Evasion Statutes

laws designed to prevent a resident of State A from going to State B to get married if the marriage would have been illegal in State A. State A may elect to not recognize the marriage. These laws were primarily designed to prevent underage couples from crossing state borders to enter into marriages that they couldn't legally enter into in their home states. They now may be applied to same-sex couples who go to another state to enter a marriage not permitted in their state of residence.

Defense of Marriage Act (DOMA)

a federal law restricting the definition of marriage to the union of one man and one woman for purposes of federal law and allowing the states to deny full faith and credit to same-sex marriages valid in a sister state

Federal and Interstate Recognition of Marriage

The choice-of-law rule traditionally applied with respect to interstate recognition of marriage provides that the validity of a marriage will be determined according to the law of the state in which it was entered. This common law rule is reinforced by Article IV, Section 1 of the U.S. Constitution, which provides that "Full Faith and Credit shall be given in each State to the public Acts, Records, and judicial Proceedings of every other state." Guided by these principles, the states have historically validated out-of-state marriages, even if a marriage would have been prohibited under local law (for example, a marriage between first cousins valid in Massachusetts is recognized and given effect in a state that does not permit such marriages under its own law). This approach appeared to work satisfactorily, until same-sex marriage and other nonmarital family forms came onto the scene.

Following the *Baehr* case in Hawaii, opponents of same-sex marriage became alarmed that another state might do exactly what Hawaii had almost done and what Massachusetts eventually did in 2003 (and a handful of other states and the District of Columbia have done since)—legalize same-sex marriage. In response, at the federal level, Congress passed the **Defense of Marriage Act (DOMA)** in 1996. The Act does not go so far as to declare same-sex marriages illegal, but it does provide that, for purposes of federal law, "the word 'marriage' means only a legal union between one man and one woman as husband and wife, and the word 'spouse' refers only to a person of the opposite sex who is a husband or wife."[27]

The practical effect of this legislation is to deny to same-sex married couples all of the rights and privileges granted under federal law to heterosexual married couples. The Act further provides that no state can be forced to recognize a same-sex marriage, stating:

No State, territory, or possession of the United States, or Indian tribe, shall be required to give effect to any public act, record, or judicial proceeding of any other State, territory, possession, or tribe respecting a relationship between persons of the same sex that is treated as a marriage under the laws of such other State, territory, possession, or tribe or a right or claim arising from such relationship.[28]

Following the federal lead, many states have enacted legislation in the form of statutes (commonly called mini-DOMAs) banning same-sex marriage and, in some states, civil unions and domestic partnerships as well. (See Exhibit 3.5.)

The future of initiatives opposing recognition of same-sex relationships is unclear. There continues to be some measure of public support and legislative commitment to passage of a Federal Marriage Amendment to the U.S. Constitution. The amendment would define marriage as the union of a man and a woman and could be used to overrule state or local protections for same-sex couples and their children. To become part of the Constitution, the amendment would need to be approved by two-thirds of both houses of Congress and then be ratified by the legislatures of three-fourths of the states. How strong and successful the lobby for such an amendment may be is falling into question with support dwindling at the highest levels of government. For example, the U.S. Supreme Court decided not to stop enforcement of the same-sex marriage law that went into effect in the District of Columbia in May 2010. In addition, President Obama initially directed the Department of Justice (DOJ) to stop defending DOMA in federal challenges, leaving any legal defense of the 1996 statute up to Congress. However, in July of 2011, executive opposition to DOMA became more active and direct when the DOJ filed papers in a lawsuit filed by an attorney with the 9th US Circuit Court of Appeals, whose partner was denied benefits based on DOMA. The DOJ argues in their brief that the Defense of Marriage Act violates the U.S. Constitution's guarantees of equal protection.

EXHIBIT 3.5 State Positions on Same-Sex Marriage and Evolving Alternative Relationships as of October 2011

Note: Broad constitutional ban means a ban on extension of spousal rights to partners in any form of same-sex relationship including, for example, domestic partnerships and civil unions.

State	Position
ALABAMA	-Broad constitutional ban 2006
ALASKA	-Constitutional amendment restricting marriage to man and woman 1998
ARIZONA	-Constitutional amendment restricting marriage to man and woman 2008
ARKANSAS	-Broad constitutional ban 2004
CALIFORNIA	-Domestic partnerships 1999, expanded 2005 (equivalent spousal rights)
	-Same-sex marriages between 6/16/2008 and 11/4/2008
	-Recognizes validly entered same-sex marriages from other states
	-Constitutional amendment restricting marriage to man and woman 2008 (challenged under federal law)
COLORADO	-Designated beneficiaries, limited spousal rights 2009
	-Constitutional amendment restricting marriage to man and woman
CONNECTICUT	-Same-sex marriage 2008
DELAWARE	-Civil unions effective 1/12/2012
	-Statute restricting marriage to man and woman
DISTRICT OF COLUMBIA	-Same-sex marriage 2010
	-Domestic partnerships (health care benefits)
	-Recognizes validly entered same-sex marriages, civil unions, and domestic partnerships
FLORIDA	-Broad constitutional ban 2008
GEORGIA	-Broad constitutional ban 2004
HAWAII	-Civil unions effective 1/1/2012
	-Reciprocal beneficiaries
	-Statute restricting marriage to man and woman
	-Recognizes validly entered same-sex marriages, domestic partnerships, and civil unions as civil unions
IDAHO	-Broad constitutional ban 2006

(Continued)

(Continued)

PARALEGAL PRACTICE TIPS

A comprehensive, current, and authoritative view of the status of same-sex marriage, civil unions, domestic partnerships, rights, and debates around the world does not exist. The website of the International Lesbian and Gay Association, *www.ilga-europe.org* publishes a country-by-country status report on the European countries. A useful reference for information on the various states is *www.ncsl.org*, the National Conference of State Legislatures website. The online encyclopedia *www.wikipedia.org* provides both historical and current information along with valuable links to many additional sources, including federal and state statutes. It includes detailed references to many of the states that have confronted this issue judicially and legislatively. Keep in mind that online resources are useful starting points, but information should be verified before use. Links to these sites can be found at *www. pearsonhighered.com/wilson* in the companion website material for Chapter 3 under "Resources."

PARALEGAL PRACTICE TIP

Domestic partnerships and civil unions are important vehicles for recognition of nonmarital relationships on the international scene as well as in the United States, with the trend being most apparent in Europe. Beginning with Denmark in 1989, civil unions, under one name or another, have been established in many other countries, including, but not limited to, Israel, Norway, Sweden, France, Germany, Portugal, Finland, New Zealand, Switzerland, and the United Kingdom. As of January 2007, Belgium, Canada, the Netherlands, Spain, and South Africa have also permitted same-sex marriage. The extent to which relationships formed in these nations will be recognized by courts in this country remains to be seen.

PARALEGAL PRACTICE TIP

Some statutes/marriage amendments "appear to ban same-sex couples only from the institution of marriage; . . . Other amendments, however, employ a variety of textual prohibitions designed to prevent both courts and legislators from creating any legal status similar to marriage. For example, Nebraska's constitution states, 'the uniting of two persons of the same sex in a civil union, domestic partnership, or other similar same-sex relationship shall not be valid or recognized in Nebraska.' Other state amendments prohibit ". . . receipt of the 'incidents,' 'benefits,' or 'rights' of marriage by same sex couples. . . ."[29] Some states have found ways of having it both ways. For example, Wisconsin has a broad ban but has also established a legal status of domestic partnerships which the legislature describes as "not substantially similar to that of marriage." Wis. Stat. § 770.001.

PARALEGAL PRACTICE TIP

When working on a case involving a couple in a same-sex relationship, paralegals need to research the law governing such relationships in the appropriate jurisdiction. For example, Illinois permits civil unions and also recognizes (as civil unions in Illinois) same-sex marriages, civil unions, or "substantially similar legal relationships" (other than common law marriage) that are legally formed outside of Illinois.

EXHIBIT 3.5 (*Continued*)

ILLINOIS	-Civil unions effective 6/1/2011 -Statute restricting marriage to man and woman
INDIANA	-Statute restricting marriage to man and woman
IOWA	-Same-sex marriage 2009 -Recognizes validly entered same-sex marriages but not civil unions and domestic partnerships
KANSAS	-Statute defining marriage as between a man and woman -Constitutional ban on extension of spousal rights to same-sex relationships repealed
KENTUCKY	-Broad constitutional ban 2004
LOUISIANA	-Broad constitutional ban 2004
MAINE	-Domestic partnerships 2004 -Statute restricting marriage to man and woman -Marriage equality legislation signed in May 2009 repealed by ballot November 2009
MARYLAND	-Domestic partnerships (limited and no registry) -Recognizes validly entered same-sex marriages 2010 (Attorney General Opinion) but not civil unions and domestic partnerships -Statute restricting marriage to man and woman
MASSACHUSETTS	-Same-sex marriage effective 2004
MICHIGAN	-Broad constitutional ban 2004
MINNESOTA	-Statute restricting marriage to man and woman
MISSISSIPPI	-Constitutional amendment restricting marriage to man and woman 2004
MISSOURI	-Constitutional amendment restricting marriage to man and woman 2004
MONTANA	-Constitutional amendment restricting marriage to man and woman 2004
NEBRASKA	-Broad constitutional ban 2000
NEVADA	-Domestic partnerships 2009 Equivalent spousal rights -Constitutional amendment restricting marriage to man and woman 2002
NEW HAMPSHIRE	-Same-sex marriage 2010
NEW JERSEY	-Civil unions 2007 -Domestic partnerships (heterosexual partners over age 62) -Recognizes valid same-sex marriages, civil unions, and domestic partnerships
NEW MEXICO	-Recognizes validly entered same-sex marriages 2011 (Attorney General Opinion)
NEW YORK	-Same-sex marriage (2011) -Recognizes validly entered same-sex marriages, civil unions, and domestic partnerships in limited circumstances
NORTH CAROLINA	-Statute restricting marriage to man and woman
NORTH DAKOTA	-Broad constitutional ban 2004
OHIO	-Broad constitutional ban 2004
OKLAHOMA	-Broad constitutional ban 2004
OREGON	-Domestic partnerships 2008 Equivalent spousal rights -Constitutional amendment restricting marriage to man and woman 2004 -No prohibition against recognition of validly entered out-of-state relationships as domestic partnerships
PENNSYLVANIA	-Statute restricting marriage to man and woman

EXHIBIT 3.5 (*Continued*)

PUERTO RICO	-Statute restricting marriage to man and woman
RHODE ISLAND	-Civil unions (2011)
	-Conflict between Attorney General and state Supreme Court recognition of validly entered same-sex marriages
SOUTH CAROLINA	-Broad constitutional ban 2006
SOUTH DAKOTA	-Broad constitutional ban 2006
TENNESSEE	-Constitutional amendment restricting marriage to man and woman 2006
TEXAS	-Broad constitutional ban 2005
UTAH	-Broad constitutional ban 2004
VERMONT	-Same-sex marriage 2009
	-Recognizes validly entered same-sex marriages, civil unions, and domestic partnerships
VIRGINIA	-Broad constitutional ban 2006
WASHINGTON	-Domestic partnerships 2007/ 2009 Equivalent spousal rights
	-Recognizes validly entered civil unions and domestic partnerships
	-Statute restricting marriage to man and woman
WEST VIRGINIA	-Statute restricting marriage to man and woman
WISCONSIN	-Domestic partnerships 2007/2009
	-Constitutional amendment restricting marriage to man and woman 2006
WYOMING	-Statute restricting marriage to man and woman

PARALEGAL PRACTICE TIP

In addition to having been the first state to enact same-sex marriage, Massachusetts was the first state to challenge the federal DOMA on federal constitutional grounds. In July 2010, a federal judge ruled in two separate lawsuits that the federal DOMA is unconstitutional. In one, *Commonwealth of Massachusetts v. Health and Human Services,* 698 F. Supp. 2d 234 (D. Mass 2010), the court ruled DOMA violates the Tenth Amendment of the Constitution by taking from the states powers that the Constitution gives to them. In the other case, *Gill v. Office of Personnel Management,* 699 F. Supp. 2d 374 (D. Mass. 2010), the court ruled that DOMA violates the equal protection principles embodied in the Due Process Clause of the Fifth Amendment, in an effort to "disadvantage a group of which it disapproves." To learn about the topic of same-sex marriage, including state and federal cases initiated in Massachusetts, visit *www.lawlib.state.ma.us.* You can find a link to this site at *www.pearsonhighered.com/wilson* in the companion website material related to Chapter 3 under "Resources."

PARALEGAL PRACTICE TIP

The paralegal should keep in mind that the same term may mean different things in different jurisdictions, at different times, or in different contexts. For example, traditionally the adjective "meretricious" has had a negative connotation and has been associated primarily with illicit sexual conduct. The state of Washington previously has looked beyond the traditional meaning of the word "meretricious" and used the phrase "meretricious relationship" in case law to refer to a "stable, marital-like relationship, where both parties cohabit with knowledge that a lawful marriage between them does not exist." Factors the court considered in determining whether or not a meretricious relationship exists "included, but were not limited to: continuous cohabitation, duration of the relationship, purpose of the relationship, pooling of resources and services for joint projects, and the intent of the parties." Once a meretricious relationship was established, a trial court could evaluate the interest each party had in the property acquired during the relationship and make an equitable distribution of that property. Although a meretricious relationship was not considered the same as a marriage, the court focused on property that would have been community property had the parties been married. See, e.g., *In re Marriage of Lindsay,* 101 Wash.2d 299 at 304–5; 678 P.2d 328 (1984). See also *Connell v. Francisco,* 127 Wash.2d 339, 898 P.2d 831 (Wash. 1995).

Alternative Nonmarital Relationships

Recognition of heterosexual and same-sex nonmarital relationships in the United States, thus far, has run along a continuum from cohabitation to marriage. Labels abound, definitions overlap, and each model has its own advantages and limitations. In Chapter 2 we addressed cohabitation, sometimes referred to as the umbrella under which all nonmarital relationships fall. But cohabitation standing alone is not a legally recognized status and affords little protection unless formalized in an enforceable cohabitation agreement. In the first part of this chapter, we looked at issues related to traditional and same-sex marriage. In the last part, we will consider legally recognized alternative nonmarital statuses including adult adoption, functional family status, domestic partnerships (sometimes called meretricious or reciprocal beneficiary relationships), and civil unions. Because there are no fixed definitions of these relationships that are consistent from state to state or country to country, the definitions provided in this chapter are generic. It is also impossible to provide a set list of benefits and obligations that flow from any status as they also vary from state to state and from time to time. Whatever variations may exist, however, the rationale for extending benefits to same-sex partners in particular remains the same. Legislators in Oregon have expressed it this way:

> Many gay and lesbian Oregonians have formed lasting, committed, caring and faithful relationships with individuals of the same sex, despite long-standing social and economic discrimination. These couples live together, participate in their communities together and often raise children and care for family members together, just as do couples who are married under Oregon law. Without the ability to obtain some form of legal status for their relationships, same-sex couples face numerous obstacles and hardships in attempting to secure rights, benefits and responsibilities for themselves and their children. Many of the rights, benefits and responsibilities that the families of married couples take for granted cannot be obtained in any way other than through state recognition of committed same-sex relationships. This state has a strong interest in promoting stable and lasting families, including the families of same-sex couples and their children. All Oregon families should be provided with the opportunity to obtain necessary legal protections and status and the ability to achieve their fullest potential.[30]

PARALEGAL PRACTICE TIP

To view a Petition for Adult Adoption go to *www.vermontjudiciary.org/ eforms.* A link to this website can be found at *www.pearsonhighered. com/wilson* in the companion website material for Chapter 3 under "Forms."

ADULT ADOPTION

Adult adoption can sometimes provide a means of achieving a recognizable family status for same-sex couples. However, it is rarely used and is permitted in only a small number of states. From the parties' perspective, it is a desirable option in that it creates a relationship that brings with it a full array of family benefits. However, it is limited in that it generally cannot be dissolved if the parties' relationship later terminates. From the perspective of the courts, it is often viewed as distorting the intended purpose of adoption, the creation of a parent-child relationship.[31]

FUNCTIONAL FAMILY STATUS

Some courts extend at least limited rights to nonmarital partners in certain circumstances by applying a functional family approach that focuses on the "reality of family life"[32] and the nature of the partners' relationship rather than on definitions of family limited to persons related by blood, marriage, or adoption. Concentrating on the intimacy and strength of the bond between the parties, courts consider factors such as the following:

- how long the couple has lived together
- whether or not the relationship is exclusive
- the degree of the couple's emotional commitment
- the extent to which their finances are commingled
- how committed each of the partners is to supporting the other economically
- the manner in which the parties have conducted themselves in their daily lives (roles, sharing of household responsibilities, etc.)
- how they have represented themselves to the outside world

(See Paralegal Application 3.6.)

Paralegal **Application 3.6**

Would You Evict?

Fact Pattern

Miguel and Leslie were same-sex partners who lived together in a rent-controlled apartment for more than a decade until Leslie died. Leslie was the tenant of record, and after his death, the landlord tried to evict Miguel, claiming that he had no right to occupy the apartment, given the applicable rent-control statute. The statute provided that a landlord could not evict a "surviving spouse of the deceased tenant or some other member of the deceased tenant's family who has been living with the tenant of record." The landlord claimed Miguel was neither Leslie's spouse nor a member of his family. Miguel claimed that the interpretation and application of the statute should not be restricted by rigid legal distinctions based solely on a definition of family as individuals related by blood, marriage, or adoption. Rather, the definition should be extended to include two lifetime partners whose relationship is long term and characterized by an emotional and financial commitment and interdependence. Miguel and Leslie had lived together for more than ten years and were regarded by each other and their friends as spouses. They had attended family and other functions as a couple. Miguel considered the apartment his home, used the address on his driver's license and passport, and received his mail there. They had shared all household obligations and maintained joint bank and credit card accounts. Leslie had also granted Miguel power of attorney so that he could make necessary medical, financial, and personal decisions for him during his illness.

PARALEGAL PRACTICE TIP

The opinion in *Braschi v. Stahl Associates Co.* is available at *www.pearsonhighered.com/wilson* in the companion website material related to Chapter 3 under "Cases" and in the Case Resources Section of the MyLegalStudiesLab.

Sidebar

How do you think this case should be decided and why? What is the purpose of such laws? Spouses would automatically have qualified to remain in the apartment. Is it fair to require nonmarital partners to prove the nature and quality of their relationship in order to be protected by the rent-control law? To see how New York's highest court decided this case, read the opinion in *Braschi v. Stahl Associates Co.*, 74 N.Y.2d 201, 543 N.E.2d 49, 544 N.Y.S.2d 784 (1989).

DOMESTIC PARTNERSHIPS

The American Law Institute (ALI) has defined domestic partners as "two persons of the same or opposite sex, not married to one another, who for a significant period of time share a primary residence and a life together. . . ."[33] According to the ALI, factors indicating the existence of a domestic partnership include, among others, oral statements, commingled finances, economic dependency, specialized roles, naming beneficiaries, emotional and sexual intimacy, community reputation, commitment or attempted marriage ceremony, common household, and joint procreation, childrearing, or adoption.

PARALEGAL PRACTICE TIP

The content of domestic partnership statutes is not uniform. For example, California recognizes domestic partnerships for same-sex partners and also for opposite-sex couples when at least one of the partners is age 62 or older. The state of Maine extends domestic partnership eligibility to both heterosexual and homosexual partners and defines domestic partners as "2 unmarried adults who are domiciled together under long-term arrangements that evidence a commitment to remain responsible indefinitely for each other's welfare."[34]

Domestic partnership
a status granted to an unmarried couple who live together and receive a variety of economic and noneconomic benefits customarily granted to spouses

PARALEGAL PRACTICE TIP

To see the Nevada statute listing the rights and duties of domestic partners in that state visit *www.leg. state.nv.us/law1.cfm*. You can find a link to this site at *www. pearsonhighered.com/wilson* in the companion website material for Chapter 3 under "Statutes."

PARALEGAL PRACTICE TIP

For information and forms related to declaring and terminating a domestic partnership in Wisconsin, visit *www.wilawlibrary.gov/topics/ familylaw/domesticpartner.php*. The site also provides information about the benefits that flow from a domestic partnership in Wisconsin and a "Domestic Partnership Protections Reference Guide." You can find a link to this site at *www.pearsonhighered. com/wilson* in the companion website material related to Chapter 3 under "Resources."

Under the law, a **domestic partnership** is a status granted to an unmarried couple who live together and receive a variety of economic and noneconomic benefits customarily granted to spouses. Some states refer to domestic partnerships as reciprocal or designated beneficiary relationships. The status may be available to heterosexual couples but in most instances is limited to same-sex couples. In a few jurisdictions, domestic partnership status is granted and regulated by the state. Hawaii (a civil union jurisdiction effective 1/1/2012) was the first state to offer a form of domestic partnership status to its employees in 1997. As of June 2011, the following states extend domestic partner status to same-sex, and in some cases heterosexual, partners: California, Colorado, Maine, Maryland, Nevada, Oregon, Washington, and Wisconsin. Several smaller governmental units, such as counties, cities, and municipalities, confer limited domestic partnership benefits on employees but not a comprehensive legal status.[35] Many private companies and educational institutions also afford some employee benefits to domestic partners under certain conditions. (See Exhibit 3.6.)

To become domestic partners, the couple usually must qualify for and register their relationship with the appropriate state agency. Typical requirements for qualification include the following:

- The parties are at least age eighteen.
- Each partner is unmarried and is not a party to another domestic partnership.
- Their relationship is exclusive.
- They share a residence.
- They agree to be jointly responsible for each other's basic living expenses.
- They are not related in a way that would prevent them from legally marrying under applicable state law.
- They agree that if their relationship ends, they will file a certificate of dissolution.

Domestic partnership status granted under state law generally is less extensive than civil union status in terms of the nature and extent of benefits provided. However, the benefits obtained through a domestic partnership vary by state and may be extensive. The rights and benefits granted under the California statute are particularly expansive. The applicable California statute states in part: "(a) Registered domestic partners shall have the same rights, protections, and benefits, and shall be subject to the same responsibilities, obligations and duties under law, . . . as are granted to and imposed upon spouses."

Each state that authorizes the creation of domestic partnerships establishes the means by which they can be terminated. Typically, termination is accomplished either by filing a form with the appropriate governmental office or by filing a termination action in the appropriate court. In California, for example, domestic partners who satisfy certain requirements can file with the Secretary of State's Office a Notice of Termination of Domestic Partnership, which will be effective six months after filing without a trial or a hearing if not revoked in the interim. As of November 2011, the requirements for proceeding in this manner include:

- Both parties want to terminate the partnership.
- The partnership has been in existence for less than five years.
- No children were born to or adopted by the parties, and neither party is pregnant at the time of filing the Notice.
- Neither owns land or buildings.
- The value of the parties' community property, if any, is less than $33,000.
- The parties have less than $5,000 in community obligations.
- The parties have prepared and executed a property settlement agreement (or have no community property).
- Neither party is requesting money or support from the other.
- Neither party has separate property valued in excess of $33,000.

If these conditions are not satisfied, an action for termination can be filed in Superior Court and the parties are entitled to a hearing and trial before a judge.

EXHIBIT 3.6 Employers That Lead the Way—Is the Client Missing Anything?

BUSINESSES

In response to changes in company policy and/or pressure from unions and other advocates, over the past two decades a significant number of employers have broadened their eligibility requirements for receiving benefits, most to both opposite- and same-sex partners and some only to the latter. The Village Voice union was the first in the nation to fight successfully for benefits for domestic partners and has had them since 1982. Companies providing benefits only to same-sex couples usually premise the decision on cost considerations, and the fact that same-sex partners generally do not have the choice to legalize their relationships through marriage. The primary benefits most commonly extended include medical insurance, life insurance, relocation, and bereavement leave. Some of the major employers extending benefits include Levi Strauss & Company, Ben and Jerry's Ice Cream, Disney Corporation, Lotus, and Apple Computer. Several businesses also offer benefits to their customers. For example, many insurance companies (such as USAA and AAA) extend family coverage for health and auto policies to unmarried couples who demonstrate a long-term, financially interdependent relationship even though they are not technically "domestic partners."

COLLEGES AND UNIVERSITIES

A number of academic institutions have extended benefits to domestic partners (primarily same sex) as well. Among the earliest to do so were Harvard University, Princeton University, Stanford University, the University of Chicago, and the University of Iowa. The benefits extended usually include health and dental insurance and bereavement and parental leave. Some institutions also extend housing benefits, recreational facilities privileges, and eligibility for tuition remission and scholarship opportunities.

PARALEGAL PRACTICE TIP

Extensive information about domestic partnerships in California, including forms for declaring and terminating a partnership, can be found at *www.sos.ca.gov*. You can find a link to this site at *www.pearsonhighered.com/wilson* in the companion website material for Chapter 3 under "Resources."

PARALEGAL PRACTICE TIP

The future of public sector employer benefits is at risk in states with broad constitutional bans against extension of benefits to partners in any form of same-sex relationship. In May of 2008, for example, the Michigan Supreme Court ruled that the state's 2004 ban on gay marriage also blocks domestic partner benefits for gay employees extended by the University of Michigan and other public sector employers.

PARALEGAL PRACTICE TIP

For information about entering a marriage or a civil union in New Jersey, visit *www.state.nj.us/health/ vitalcivilunion_apply.shtml*. You can find a link to this site at *www.pearsonhighered.com/wilson* in the companion website material for Chapter 3 under "Resources."

Civil union
a formal legal status that provides a same-sex couple with the rights, benefits, protections, and responsibilities that a married heterosexual couple has under state but not federal law

PARALEGAL PRACTICE TIP

Similar to earlier "reciprocal beneficiaries" legislation in Hawaii, Vermont's civil union law also contained a "reciprocal beneficiaries" provision, which provided benefits to nongay or nonlesbian couples, who also were not eligible to marry. By December of 2006, Vermont had issued over 8,000 licenses for civil unions, and more than 80% of them involved couples from out of state.

PARALEGAL PRACTICE TIP

To see New Jersey's detailed "declarations concerning civil unions," go to *www.njleg.state.nj.us*. You can find a link to this site at *www.pearsonhighered.com/wilson* in the companion website material for Chapter 3 under "Statutes."

CIVIL UNIONS

In contrast with most domestic partnership laws, **civil unions** are essentially designed to afford same-sex partners the same benefits, protections, and responsibilities that married spouses have under state law. The dissolution of a civil union also parallels dissolution of a marriage and the same forms generally are utilized. Although some believe civil unions represent a significant advance for same-sex couples, the "separate but equal" model falls short of full equality, as the parties are still denied the vast array of rights available to opposite-sex married partners under federal law and their relationship is not legally designated as a "marriage," a right of vital importance to many same-sex partners.

Although now a same-sex marriage jurisdiction, Vermont was the first state to enact civil unions in 2000. In 1999, the Vermont Supreme Court ruled in *Baker v. State*[36] that same-sex couples were entitled under Chapter 1, Article 7 of the Vermont State Constitution to the same benefits and protections afforded under Vermont law to heterosexual married couples. The ruling did not require the issuance of marriage licenses but rather ordered the legislature to create an "equivalent statutory alternative" that would afford essentially the same benefits to same-sex couples as are extended to married couples under Vermont law. After extensive and heated debate (including opposition from the Vermont Bar Association, which had endorsed same-sex marriage), the legislature finally passed H.B. 847, which went into effect on July 1, 2000.

In order to be united in a civil union, the partners typically must meet the following requirements:

- Neither may be a party to another civil union, marriage, or domestic partnership/reciprocal beneficiary relationship.
- Both parties must be of the same sex.
- The parties may not be close family members.
- Both must be at least eighteen years of age.
- Both must be mentally competent.
- Neither party may be under a guardianship, unless the guardian consents in writing.

PARALEGAL PRACTICE TIP

Keep in mind that several states have granted different statuses to same-sex partners at different points in time and governing law may need to be researched in greater depth in some situations. For example, New Jersey permitted domestic partnerships before enacting civil unions, Connecticut and New Hampshire permitted civil unions before adopting same-sex marriage, and California allowed same-sex marriage for a brief period, although as of this writing, it does not. Usually, partners who have entered one type of relationship in a state need to terminate that status before entering another legally recognized relationship in the same or a different state. For example, in New Hampshire, if a same-sex couple previously entered a civil union in that state they must file a Petition for Civil Union Dissolution before entering a same-sex marriage. You can locate the form used for this purpose at *www.courts.state.nh.us*. You can find a link to this site at *www.pearsonhighered.com/wilson* in the companion website material for Chapter 3 under "Forms."

As of October 2011, civil union states included Hawaii (effective 1/1/2012), Illinois (effective 6/1/2011), New Jersey, and Rhode Island. Generally speaking, civil unions afford more extensive and significant rights than do domestic partnerships. For example, prior to that state becoming a same-sex marriage jurisdiction, the Connecticut civil union legislation provided that "parties to a civil union shall have the same benefits, protection and responsibilities under law as granted to spouses in a marriage, which is defined as the union of one man and one woman."[37] The legislation further provided that the terms "spouse," "family," "immediate family," "dependent," and "next of kin" as well as any other term denoting spousal relationship was construed to include a party to a civil union.

Implications for the Future

The mix of approaches to family status and nonmarital relationships described in this chapter and summarized in Exhibit 3.5 has sent shock waves into the social fabric of this country that reverberate into its legal system as well. No state has been entirely unaffected, and even the federal government has elected to become involved in an area traditionally left to the states. Virtually every area of substantive law has been impacted: probate, tax, contract, immigration, health care, corporate, tort, criminal, conflict/choice of law, and most visibly constitutional law as same-sex partners persist in challenges to state and federal laws on equal protection and due process grounds. The impact is felt most heavily in family law. Even if states do not recognize couples by affording them a specific legal status or rights, it is impossible to ignore the increasing numbers of individuals living in nontraditional family structures (including both same-sex and heterosexual couples). These relationships challenge long established family law principles and procedures. They generate complex disputes, often involving multiple states and even nations. As this trend persists, lawmakers and the courts will be pressured to develop basic family law policies and procedures designed to address the needs of couples who cannot or do not wish to marry and those who are eligible to enter a variety of legally sanctioned relationships.

PARALEGAL PRACTICE TIP

States that have recognized same-sex marriage, domestic partnerships, and civil unions may afford state tax benefits to parties to such relationships. However, as of November 2011, federal tax law does not afford the same benefits to nonmarital families as it does to married persons. Parties to such relationships must be aware of how they will be treated under federal tax law. For example, under federal tax law, the amount an employer contributes for a domestic partner's health insurance coverage is includable in the employee's taxable income unless the partner qualifies as a dependent of the employee under the federal tax code.

PARALEGAL PRACTICE TIP

In some situations, the recognition of rights for same-sex partners has led to challenges by heterosexual partners whose rights are less protected. For example, in *Irizarry v. Chicago Board of Education,* 251 F.3d 604 (U.S. App. 2001), a heterosexual woman who had been living with her opposite-sex partner for over twenty years raised an unsuccessful equal protection challenge to the Chicago Board of Education's policy of extending "spousal health benefits" to domestic partners, but only if the domestic partner was of the same sex as the employee.

The Paralegal's Role

In 1965, this chapter would have been one-fifth as long and the content would have been cut-and-dried. It was a different era then. There really weren't what one would call "marriage" cases, and when there were, a paralegal's role would have been minimal. It might entail such tasks as obtaining certified copies of marriage certificates, preparing for an annulment action, or documenting the incidents of a traditional or common law marriage in a small number of cases. But we are in a new era. The past five decades have been a time of steady evolution in the structure of family life and intimate relationships in the United States, a trend that promises to continue for the foreseeable future. Going forward, the paralegal's role in this area will be determined by two major factors:

- The prevailing law in the jurisdiction where the paralegal is employed. For example, is it a domestic partnership, civil union, or same-sex marriage state? A state that vigorously opposes all quasi-marital statuses? A state in transition?
- The degree to which the firm in which the paralegal is employed extends its expertise into areas of substantive law impacted by developments described in this chapter. For example, will the firm handle probate, contract, immigration, and tax law as well as family law? Will it take on constitutional challenges?

Issues related to intimate relationships between different- and same-sex partners are now at the heart of heated political, religious, social, and cultural controversies, and pose cutting-edge legal questions that are likely to intensify in the next decade. Some paralegals will inevitably have an opportunity to work with attorneys, legislators, courts, and other interested parties engaged in answering those questions.

CHAPTER **SUMMARY**

In this chapter, we have reviewed:

- the evolution of marriage and other forms of family unions;
- the significance of the right to marry as a "fundamental" right and the ways in which it can be regulated by the states;
- the various types of marriage and emerging alternatives and the requirements for establishing each of them;
- the rights, benefits, and obligations that flow from marriage, domestic partnerships, and civil unions; and
- the trends and controversy surrounding same-sex relationships.

We learn in this course that today fewer people are choosing to marry and increasing numbers of those who do marry eventually divorce. Marriage has become the focal point for a variety of causes including the gay, gender, religious, and states' rights agendas. It has become a political football at the national and local levels. It is now treated as an economic partnership between alleged equals who are increasingly privately structuring their "marital" rights. It is also decreasingly the environment in which children are born and raised, as new forms of legal relationships are established.

Whatever view an individual espouses, we can be certain that the federal government and the states will continue to take a strong interest in marriage and the family as the fundamental social unit through which culture, values, and wealth are transmitted from one generation to the next. The Massachusetts Supreme Court's 4–3 decision in the *Goodridge* case has fueled the fire. Its impact is being felt across the nation. The constitutionality of the Defense of Marriage Act itself is being called into question as there are those who strongly contend that Congress does not have the power to limit the effect of the Full Faith and Credit Clause of the Constitution. The decade ahead promises to be a dynamic one for family law practitioners and their paralegals!

CONCEPT REVIEW AND REINFORCEMENT

KEY **TERMS**

Adult adoption	Consortium	Marital communications privilege
Affinity	Covenant marriage	Marriage
Anti-Heartbalm Statute	Defense of Marriage Act (DOMA)	Marriage Evasion Statute
Bigamy	Domestic partnership	Married Women's Property Acts
Breach of promise	Emancipation	Polygamy
Civil union	Functional family status	Proxy marriage
Common law marriage	Incest	Putative spouse
Compensatory damages	Laws of descent and distribution	
Consanguinity	Liquidated damages	

REVIEW **QUESTIONS**

1. Describe how the definitions of "marriage" and "family" have evolved over the past 200 years.
2. Describe the significance of the Supreme Court's decision in *Loving v. Virginia*.
3. Identify the common requirements for a ceremonial marriage and indicate what the consequence usually is for failure to comply with a technical requirement.
4. Identify the usual requirements for a valid common law marriage.
5. Identify a minimum of six rights and benefits that flow from a valid ceremonial or common law marriage.
6. Describe the significance of the *Goodridge* case decided by the Massachusetts Supreme Judicial Court in 2003. Identify three arguments in favor of same-sex marriage and three against it.
7. Describe the position of the federal government with respect to same-sex marriage and identify the form in which it is expressed.

8. Respond to the following questions regarding domestic partnerships and civil unions:
   a. Identify the common requirements for establishing a domestic partnership and a civil union.
   b. Identify the most common benefits of a domestic partnership and a civil union.
   c. Identify three states that allow domestic partnerships and three that permit civil unions.
9. Identify the biggest drawback of domestic partnerships, civil unions, and same-sex marriage in comparison with traditional marriage.
10. Describe the functional family approach as it might apply to resolution of a dispute between two former cohabitants.

DEVELOPING YOUR PARALEGAL SKILLS

FOCUS ON **THE JOB**

This assignment requires the student to research requirements for a valid marriage in three different states and apply them to a hypothetical fact pattern.

The Facts

Mary W. is a fifteen-year-old girl who resides in Texas. She believes she has fallen madly in love with a man, Marty C., who rides bulls on the rodeo circuit. He is a resident of Massachusetts and is twenty-three years old. Mary says they were bound to find each other because, looking at their family histories, they have discovered they are actually first cousins. Mary says she has done her legal homework and that she and Marty have come up with a plan. Because her mother opposes the marriage, Mary is going to get her stepfather to consent to the marriage in writing. Then she will go to Massachusetts and she and Marty will get married there and then move to Colorado, where she is firmly convinced they will live happily ever after. Mary spoke with your supervisor, Attorney McGuigan, about this at a recent family party. He is not interested in becoming involved in the case, as he knows Mary's mother personally. However, he says that it

would be a good exercise for you, his paralegal, to research the legal issues relating to Mary's circumstances.

The Assignment

Research the law in ~~Texas, Massachusetts, and Colorado~~ N.C. to determine whether or not Mary and Marty can enter a valid marriage in any of those states under the circumstances described. You will need, at the least, to look at:

- the minimum age for marrying with and without parental consent in each state
- the circumstances under which a minimum age requirement may be waived in each state
- whether or not first cousins are permitted to marry in any of the states
- whether any of the states has a marriage evasion law that might affect the validity of any purported marriage
- whether any of the states permits common law marriages and, if so, under what circumstances

Summarize your research and conclusions in a memorandum to Attorney McGuigan. For help getting started, the following sites may be useful: *www.ncsl.org* and *www.findlaw.com*.

FOCUS ON **ETHICS**

In this activity, the student will prepare a short paper about ethical concerns related to the substance of an interview with a client.

The Assignment

Assume that you are Attorney McGuigan's paralegal and that he has been retained to advise Mary in the above fact pattern. He has asked you to interview her and prepare a brief report about what you learn and your general impressions of Mary. Assume that the fact pattern reflects the basic content of the interview with one exception: Mary tells you that she plans to forge her mother's signature consenting to the marriage. She is confident she can do it because she has "been doing it for years on report cards and absence slips at school." She directs you not to tell Attorney McGuigan about this little scheme, because he knows her mom and would "tell on her." Write a one- to two-page paper in which you describe what you plan to do about what happened in the interview. Indicate how the ethical canons for paralegals promulgated by the National Association of Legal Assistants (contained in Appendix A) apply to this situation.

FOCUS ON **CASE LAW**

In this Focus, the student has an opportunity to see an example of how a judicial decision regarding common law marriage led to a change in the law relating to minors in Colorado.

The Assignment

Read the case *In re the Marriage of J.M.H. and Willis Rouse and Concerning Weld County Department of Social Services,* 143 P.3d 1116 (Colo. App. 2006). Also look at 14-2-109.5 and 14-2-104(3) of the Colorado Revised Statutes, which are available online at *www.michie.com/colorado*. In a one- to two-page paper, describe the case and indicate how it would have been decided differently if the subsequent change in the law had been in effect at the time the case was heard.

PARALEGAL PRACTICE TIP

The *In re the Marriage of J.M.H. and Willis Rouse and Concerning Weld County Department of Social Services* opinion is available at *www.pearsonhighered.com/wilson* in the companion website material related to Chapter 3 under "Cases" and in the Case Resources Section of the MyLegalStudiesLab.

FOCUS ON **STATE LAW AND PROCEDURE**

In this exercise, students are required to research governing law in their respective jurisdictions with respect to marriage and alternative legally recognized statuses.

The Assignment

Research the law of your state (constitutional, statutory, and case law) to determine answers to the following questions, and present your findings in a written report:

1. What are the requirements for a valid marriage? Exhibit 3.2 might help you get started.
2. What is the minimum age for a person to marry and are there any exceptions to the rule?
3. Does your state allow common law marriages and, if so, what requirements must be satisfied?
4. Does any law in the state where you live make provisions for domestic partnerships, civil unions, or same-sex marriage? If so, identify the applicable statute(s) and the related requirements and benefits.
5. Has your state enacted any constitutional or statutory provision banning or otherwise restricting legal recognition of same-sex relationships in your state or elsewhere? Exhibit 3.5 may be of some assistance, but given the rapidity with which the laws change in this area, current provisions should be researched. The National Conference of State Legislatures website (*www.ncsl.org*), *www.law.cornell.edu*, and the online encyclopedia *www.wikipedia.org* may also be useful resources as starting points. All information gleaned from these sites should be verified prior to use. Links to all three of these sites can be found at *www.pearsonhighered.com/wilson* on the companion website material related to Chapter 3 under "Resources."

FOCUS ON **TECHNOLOGY**

In addition to the links provided throughout the chapter, this Focus provides a series of useful websites for reference, along with technology-related assignments for completion.

Websites of Interest

Links to the following websites are provided at *www.pearsonhighered.com/wilson* in the companion website material for Chapter 3 under "Resources."

www.aclu.org

Information is available on this site regarding domestic partnerships, civil unions, and same-sex marriage. Search by key word.

www.findlaw.com

This site contains useful information on family law, marriage, domestic partnerships, civil unions, and other topics related to the content of this chapter. Search by key word. Accuracy and currency of information should be verified prior to use.

www.hrc.org

This is the website of the Human Rights Campaign. Search the site for information about domestic partnerships and civil unions.

www.infoplease.com

This site is an online encyclopedia that provides a wide range of information on a variety of topics. Of particular relevance to this chapter is "A Primer on Same-Sex Marriage, Civil Unions, Domestic Partnerships, and Defense of Marriage Acts" and a link to a comprehensive report on the status of related legislation in each state and countries around the world. References should be verified to be sure they are current.

www.lambdalegal.org

This site provides extensive information regarding states, municipalities, and other entities offering domestic partnership and civil union benefits. As with other sites, the information provided should be verified before use.

www.law.cornell.edu

This is an academically based site that is very informative. Among other resources, it provides a comprehensive table of state marriage requirements and provides related links to state codes.

www.legalout.com

This is a website established by a Georgia lawyer and gay rights activist. It is essentially an online document preparation service for the lesbian, gay, bisexual, and transgender community. In addition to document preparation, LegalOut offers document storage and sharing, news blogs, links to activist sites, and a referral network of lawyers sympathetic to LGBT causes.

www.michie.com

As of June 2011, statutory codes for the following could be accessed at this site: California, Colorado, Delaware,

Maryland, Mississippi, Tennessee, Vermont, Wyoming, and Puerto Rico. Use the URL followed by /name of the state.

www.ncsl.org

This is the website for the National Conference of State Legislatures. It provides reports and summaries of state laws in several areas, such as common law marriage, covenant marriage, marriage between first cousins, same-sex marriage, domestic partnerships, and civil unions.

www.sos.ca.gov/

This site is maintained by the office of the California Secretary of State. Considerable information about domestic partnerships in California can be accessed with a "domestic partnership" search. Links are provided to information about registration, forms and fees, related legislation, and a "Frequently Asked Questions" resource with further links.

www.unmarried.org

This is the website for the Alternatives to Marriage Project. It contains information and statistics on cohabitation, living single, domestic partner benefits, common law marriage, etc.

www.usmarriagelaws.com

This site provides a summary of marriage laws of the states and selected countries. Information should be verified prior to use.

Assignments

1. Use the Internet to determine whether your state provides for domestic partnerships, civil unions, or same-sex marriage. If so, what are the requirements and benefits of the law(s)?
2. Identify two online resources that support same-sex marriage and two that oppose it. In a two-page paper, briefly outline the arguments pro and con.

PORTFOLIO PRODUCTS

1. Memorandum regarding the validity of a potential marriage based on a fact pattern involving three states
2. Paper on ethical issues that arise in a client interview
3. One- to two-page paper on the interrelationship between a Colorado case and a statute involving common law marriage in that state
4. Written report on governing law in the student's jurisdiction with respect to marriage and alternative legally recognized statuses

chapter 4
ANNULMENT

Audrey's husband, John, recently told her that he'd initially married her only because she was pregnant and that he'd never had any intention of staying married. She is heartbroken and wants to have their marriage annulled. John says he no longer feels the way he did when they got married. He loves his wife and son and there is no way he wants their marriage to terminate by annulment or divorce.

LEARNING OBJECTIVES

After reading this chapter and completing related assignments, you should be able to:

- describe the nature, purpose, and effect of an annulment

- identify the differences between annulment and divorce

- explain the difference between a void and a voidable marriage

- describe the procedure for obtaining an annulment

- list a minimum of five grounds for annulment

- identify potential defenses to an annulment action

- describe the potential role of a paralegal in an annulment case

. . . if every misrepresentation made by the wooer or the wooed were to pave the way to a courthouse for a disappointed spouse suddenly made aware of unsuspected and deliberately concealed frailties of the other, society would indeed have reached a pretty pass. Shall the wife be entitled to nullify her solemnly accepted status if, forsooth, in the face of previous protestations to the contrary, her husband reveals himself as the possessor of a bewitching glass eye or a set of pearly false teeth. . . ? Of course not, for such fraud has not the slightest bearing on the objectives of matrimony. . . . *Caveat emptor [Let the buyer beware]* is the harsh but necessary maxim of the law.[1]

Definition of Annulment

Marriage
a civil contract between a man and a woman or between two same-sex partners in a state that permits marriage of partners of the same sex; a legal status that two people attain by entering a government-approved and regulated contract with each other

In chapter three, we discussed **marriage**, a civil contract between a man and a woman or between two same-sex partners in a state that permits same-sex marriage. In order for a marriage to be valid, the parties must satisfy the basic legal requirements for entering a marriage contract. There must be an offer, acceptance, and consideration; the parties must have capacity to contract under applicable state law; the subject matter of the contract must not be illegal; there must be a meeting of the minds; and the contract must be freely entered and not the product of fraud or duress. In this chapter, we consider the other side of the marriage coin. When one or more of the requirements for a valid marriage are not met, the marriage may potentially be annulled. The marriage contract may be either **void *ab initio*** (it never existed because of a legal impediment) or **voidable** (able to be rescinded or revoked in an action by a party to the contract who has been wronged or, in some circumstances, by a third party whose rights are impacted by the contract).

An **annulment** is the legal procedure for declaring that a marriage is null and void. Strictly speaking, the term "annulment" refers to nullification of a voidable marriage, a marriage capable of being nullified because of a circumstance existing at the time it was established (such as undue influence or fraud). If no action is taken to annul a voidable marriage, the marriage will continue to be deemed valid. On the other hand, if a marriage is void *ab initio* because it is prohibited by law (such as when a prior marriage of one of the parties has never been terminated by death, divorce, or annulment), the marriage is automatically null and void, invalid from the outset, although a legal declaration of nullity is customarily necessary to establish that a legal marriage never existed. Many states do not distinguish between void and voidable marriages in their statutes, but courts sometimes refer to the common law distinction that grew out of early **ecclesiastical (church) law.**

PARALEGAL PRACTICE TIP

Several religions provide for annulment in one form or another. For example, although there are divergent views of Muslim family law, each provides for annulment—in effect, "cancellation" of a marriage—if a serious deficiency arises in either party, such as "chronic madness," serious disease, or an inability to fulfill "conjugal obligations" for an extended period. The civil laws that provide for such an annulment without the necessity of a divorce are solidly grounded in Islamic beliefs, principles set forth in the Koran, and the rulings of Imams (religious leaders). An annulment under the principles of Muslim family law thus represents both a secular (civil) and a religious event.

To learn about annulment in the Catholic faith, visit *www.catholicnewsagency.com*. A link to this site can be found at *www.pearsonhighered.com/wilson* in the companion website material for Chapter 4 under "Resources." A Declaration of Nullity issued by an Ecclesiastical Tribunal of the Roman Catholic Church is recognized by the Church but not by the state. Before marrying again, a marriage must also be dissolved under the civil law by divorce or annulment.

Divorce and Annulment: A Comparison

Depending on the circumstances of the case, a party may ask a court to dissolve a marriage, annul it, or issue a declaratory judgment regarding the validity of the marriage. Annulment is a viable option for terminating a marriage when appropriate grounds exist and when it better meets a party's personal and strategic needs than a fault or no-fault divorce. For example, clients may prefer an annulment because divorce is contrary to their religion or because they want to avoid having to pay alimony. Exhibit 4.1 summarizes the major differences between an annulment and a divorce.

Occasionally the law of a state and the facts of a particular case are such that a party may seek either a divorce or an annulment based on the same ground. For example, in Tennessee, an annulment may be sought on the ground that a previous marriage was still in existence at the time of a subsequent marriage (unless the former spouse has been absent for five years or more and is not known to be living). Tennessee law also provides as a ground for divorce that "either party has knowingly entered into a second marriage, in violation of a previous marriage, still subsisting."[2] In the case of marriages that are void due to the continuing existence of a prior marriage, decrees of divorce or annulment have the same practical effect

Void *ab initio*
of no legal effect from the outset; a contract is void *ab initio* if it seriously offends law or public policy

Voidable marriage
a marriage capable of being nullified because of a circumstance existing at the time it was established; the marriage remains valid unless and until it is declared invalid by a court of competent jurisdiction

PARALEGAL PRACTICE TIP

The Texas statutes governing annulment distinguish between void and voidable marriages. They can be seen at *www.statutes.legis.state.tx.us*. You can find a link to this site at *www.pearsonhighered.com/wilson* in the material related to Chapter 4 under "Statutes."

Annulment
the legal procedure for declaring that a marriage is null and void because of an impediment existing at its inception

Ecclesiastical law
the law governing the doctrine and discipline of a particular church. For centuries, the Catholic Church, and subsequently the ecclesiastical courts of England, regarded a marriage, once entered, as indissoluble. Although there technically was no divorce under ecclesiastical law, certain "canonical disabilities" existing at the time of the marriage ceremony were viewed as entitling parties to an annulment, essentially a religious ruling that no marriage ever existed between the parties. These disabilities included, for example, *consanguinity, affinity,* and *impotence.*

of providing a public record declaring that the purported marriage is invalid, void from its inception, and a legal nullity.

PARALEGAL PRACTICE TIP

Because generally only marital property is subject to division upon divorce and spousal support obligations are based on the existence of a valid marriage, when a marriage is terminated by annulment or by divorce on the ground of bigamy, no property division or alimony will be awarded by the court as "incidents of divorce." If there was no marriage, there is no "marital property" to divide and there is no "former spouse" to pay or receive alimony.[3]

PARALEGAL PRACTICE TIP

Even if not technically required to establish rights between the parties with respect to each other in a marriage that is void from the outset, it is often desirable to obtain an annulment formally declaring the marriage null and void when third parties are impacted, such as lenders who may act with respect to the parties under a belief that they are married. A Declaration of Annulment or a Declaration of Validity of Marriage may also be essential when the rights of individuals are being determined in the probate context. For example, what are the rights of someone who claims to be a "surviving spouse" when the validity of a marriage is in question? Such issues may be especially problematic in states that recognize common law marriage.

Quasi-marital property

property treated as if it was acquired by the parties during the marriage even though the marriage was never valid

EXHIBIT 4.1 Differences Between Divorce and Annulment

Annulment	Divorce
In an annulment action, one or both of the parties claim that a purported marriage is not valid and does not exist.	A divorce severs a marriage the parties acknowledge exists.
The ground for annulment exists at the time the marriage relationship is formed.	In the vast majority of cases, the cause for divorce arises after the marriage was established.
An annulment declares an alleged marriage to be null and void *ab initio*.	A divorce terminates a legal marriage as of the date of divorce.
If a marriage is annulled, the parties generally regain the legal status they had before the marriage occurred.	Traditionally, after a divorce, the parties have a continuing legal status as former spouses with respect to division of property, custody of children, and child and spousal support.
Certain rights or entitlements, such as worker's compensation benefits or occasionally alimony from a previous marriage that terminated upon a recipient's remarriage, may be revived upon annulment of the later marriage.	Worker's compensation or alimony benefits flowing from a prior marriage will generally not be revived upon dissolution of the recipient's later marriage.
In some states, annulment will result in the extinguishing of interests in property acquired during the purported marriage. In other states, the interests may be preserved in whole or part through application of equitable remedies, such as the putative spouse doctrine (in effect, treating the property as **quasi-marital property**).	Upon divorce, property acquired during the marriage is divided between the parties based on equitable division or community property principles absent an enforceable agreement to the contrary.
An annulment establishes that no valid marriage ever existed. Because the right to potentially receive spousal support flows from a valid marriage, there customarily is no right to spousal support following an annulment.	Subject to limitations in some states, spousal support may be awarded based on one party's need and the other party's ability to pay.
If the parties obtain an annulment establishing that no valid marriage ever existed between them, they must each file amended returns (as unmarried persons) for all tax years within a three-year period of limitations.[4]	Divorced spouses may file a joint tax return for the year in which their divorce is granted provided they are married for some portion of that tax year.

Procedure for Obtaining an Annulment

Under common law, in the absence of a controlling statute to the contrary, a void marriage was absolutely void from its inception (void *ab initio*) and continued to be so. Technically, no judicial pronouncement was necessary to annul the marriage and restore the parties to their original rights. The states now vary with respect to whether or not a decree is necessary to invalidate a void marriage. In Connecticut, for example, in the *Davis* case, the court determined that a marriage deemed void *ab initio* should be declared so by the court rather than by the parties simply asserting its invalidity. The case involved two nineteen-year-old residents of Connecticut who went on an automobile ride with some friends. In the context of the fun-filled occasion, the "wife" dared the "husband" to marry her. He accepted the dare, a license for the marriage was obtained in New York State, and the ceremony was performed there by a Justice of the Peace. Neither party intended at the time to assume a marital status and the parties never cohabited after the ceremony.[5]

When annulments are sought, procedures vary from state to state. The pleading that initiates a suit to annul a marriage may be called a Complaint or Petition for Annulment, a Libel for Annulment (or for a Judgment of Nullity), or a Petition for Declaration of Invalidity of Marriage, among other options. Sometimes a party who is not able to file for an annulment will seek clarification as to his or her marital status by filing a **declaratory judgment** action or an action to affirm the validity of a marriage. When a Complaint for Annulment is filed, the process is essentially the same as with other actions. The defendant is served and files an Answer, and, if the case is contested, related motions may be filed, discovery sought, and negotiations conducted. Once the court conducts an evidentiary hearing and establishes the legal status of the marriage, it may address any potentially related issues, such as property division, spousal support, child custody, and child support. As with other kinds of proceedings, the court will eventually issue a decree.

BURDEN OF PROOF

In order to obtain an annulment, proper grounds must exist and the party seeking the annulment must act within any applicable time limitations. Because there is a presumption that a marriage is valid, the burden of proving it is not rests with the party challenging its validity. The general standard of proof in a civil action is **preponderance of the evidence**. However, the standard of proof in an annulment action is commonly the higher burden of **clear and convincing evidence**. Nevada, for example, established this standard in the *Irving* case in 2006. In annulment cases involving allegations of fraud, "Nevada courts will now require a party seeking to annul a marriage on the grounds of fraud to prove the fraud with clear and convincing evidence. Nevada law favors this higher **burden of proof** because of a strong public policy in favor of marriage and against annulment."[6]

STANDING TO PETITION FOR ANNULMENT

Generally either party to a purported marriage has **standing** to seek an annulment absent authority to the contrary. However, in some states, only an "innocent" party may be able to seek relief in the form of annulment. In most states, a parent or guardian of a child may file a petition when parental consent was required for marriage and was not provided or the age of the child was misrepresented.

A conservator or guardian of an adult may file a complaint for annulment on behalf of a ward. In a 2005 case, for example, a conservator filed a complaint alleging that his ward lacked the mental capacity to enter into a contract of marriage and that the defendant exerted undue influence on her. The ward's treating neurologist testified that the ward was unable "to understand and appreciate the benefits, obligations and responsibilities of marriage" well before the time of the marriage ceremony, that her condition was steadily deteriorating, and that she had no lucid intervals. Since she also had already been declared incompetent by a court, her ability to enter into contracts or other legally significant acts had been terminated. An appellate court affirmed a trial court's annulment of the marriage.[7]

Courts in several states have addressed the question of whether or not an administrator or executor of a decedent's estate may seek an annulment on behalf of a deceased "spouse" after he or she has died.[8] The prevailing rule is that a void marriage may be annulled after the death of one of the parties, absent a statute or case law to the contrary. The validity of void "marriages" may be challenged by someone who claims to be a surviving spouse as well as by third parties, such as children of the decedent. With a voidable marriage, such as one in which a man marries a woman solely to obtain **green card** status, third parties (including beneficiaries under the will of a decedent) are generally not permitted to seek an annulment of the decedent's marriage post death.[9] Although some courts have held that annulment actions may be commenced after the death of a person entitled to an annulment by a person or persons whose legal rights depend on whether the marriage was valid or void, some place restrictions on such actions if, for example, the marriage was followed by cohabitation and the birth of children.[10]

Grounds for Annulment

Particularly with the advent of no-fault divorce, courts are more likely than ever to hold to strict standards for granting annulments and to apply the doctrine of *caveat emptor* (Latin: let the buyer beware) when it comes to marriages that fail to meet the parties' expectations. Generally, a party may not challenge the validity of a marriage based on the express or implied representations of the other party "with respect to such matters as character, habits, chastity, business or social standing, financial worth or prospects, or matters of similar nature. It is conclusively presumed that each of the parties made his or her own independent investigation and was satisfied with the result. . . ."[11] However, annulment still is an option for parties to an alleged "marriage" in some situations.

Specific grounds for annulment vary considerably from state to state. Commonly, grounds are of two types:

1. Grounds relating to legal capacity to marry, customarily rendering the marriage void *ab initio*:
   - **nonage**/underage
   - **consanguinity**
   - **affinity**
   - **bigamy**/polygamy
   - physical incapacity or disease (in a limited number of jurisdictions)

Green card
a document (registration card) evidencing a resident alien's status as a permanent resident of the United States; a "green card marriage" is a sham marriage in which a U.S. citizen marries a foreign citizen for the sole purpose of allowing the foreign citizen to become a permanent U.S. resident

PARALEGAL PRACTICE TIP

The term "incest" is used in some state statutes to describe prohibited degrees of consanguinity and affinity.

Nonage
below the minimum age established by law to perform a particular act

Consanguinity
a blood relationship between individuals

Affinity
the relationship a spouse has to the blood relatives of the other spouse; relationship by marriage

Bigamy
the act of entering a subsequent marriage while a prior marriage of one or both of the parties is still in effect

2. Grounds relating to intent to marry, customarily rendering the marriage voidable:

   - fraud
   - lack of consent
   - duress
   - undue influence
   - **impotence**
   - underage

Based on prevailing public policies, all states establish the "marriages" that are prohibited and therefore void from the outset. For example, a majority of states expressly prohibit marriage when a prior marriage of either or both parties is still in existence (bigamy/polygamy), when the parties are too closely related by blood (consanguinity), when the parties are of the same sex, or when one or both of the parties are "too young" to marry even with parental consent according to state law (nonage). A decreasing number prohibit marriage when the parties are too closely related by marriage (affinity) or when one or both have an incurable, sexually transmitted disease.

Most states also identify by statute the grounds for annulment of a voidable marriage based on some circumstance existing at the time a marriage was established, such as a lack of free consent or consent based upon a fraudulent representation by one of the parties to the other. Some states, such as Delaware and North Dakota, grant annulments only on grounds enumerated by statute. Other states (such as Kansas) have statutes setting forth some grounds but do not consider them to be the exclusive potential grounds for annulment. A small number of states (such as Florida) have no specific statutory provisions laying out grounds for annulment of voidable marriages.

Impotence

lack of capacity to procreate due to inability to have sexual intercourse or to incompetent sperm or ova

Paralegal **Application 4.1**

Know the Law in Your Jurisdiction

Because there is considerable variation state to state, it is important to know the law governing grounds for annulment and prohibited marriages as well as the procedural rules applicable to a particular annulment action. Examples of some of the unique provisions in effect in certain jurisdictions include the following:

- In Hawaii, a statute expressly provides as a ground for annulment that one of the parties was afflicted by a "loathsome disease" at the time of the marriage that was unknown to the party seeking an annulment. (HRS §580–21 (6))
- A small number of states list "joke," "jest," or "dare" as a ground for annulment. Among these states are Colorado (CRS §14–10–111 (1)(f)) and Delaware (13 Del. C. §1506 (a)(6)).
- Rhode Island provides special exceptions to the prohibited marriages statute with respect to consanguinity

(Continued)

and affinity for marriages allowed by Jewish religious law (R.I. General Laws §15–1–4).

- Virginia will grant an annulment when, prior to the marriage, either party was, without the knowledge of the other, a prostitute (Va. Code Ann. §20–89.1(b)).
- In Mississippi, a cause for annulment is the "Pregnancy of the wife by another person, if the husband did not know of the pregnancy" (Miss. Code Ann. §93–7–3 (e)).
- Being under the influence of alcohol or drugs at the time of the marriage is a ground for annulment in several states, such as Texas (§6.105) and Illinois (750 ILCS 5/301 (1)).
- Wisconsin prohibits marriages between persons closer in kin than second cousins unless the parties are first cousins and the woman is 55 or one party is sterile (Wis. Stat. §765.03 (1)). Utah has a similar provision (Utah Code Ann. §30–1–1 (2)(b)).
- Several states provide by statute or case law that a marriage voidable due to fraud or lack of mental capacity may not be annulled if the parties freely cohabit after knowledge of the fraud or restoration of mental capacity.
- Several states require that annulment actions be brought within limited time frames after the impediment is known, such as sixty or ninety days or one or two years. In Wisconsin, with the exception of cases involving bigamy, annulments of marriages prohibited by law must be sought within ten years (Wis. Stat. §767.313 (1)(d)).

NONAGE/UNDERAGE

A marriage entered by an underage party in violation of state law may be deemed void or voidable if not ratified. Marriage laws in every state establish the minimum age under which a party may not marry (usually termed nonage). With the exception of California, they also provide a minimum age under which a party may not marry without the consent of a parent or guardian or the permission of the court. The minimum age may also vary if the female is pregnant or has given birth to a child out of wedlock. If an underage party goes to another state where he or she is of legal age, marries, and soon after returns to the state where he or she resides, some states will consider the marriage invalid (under so-called marriage evasion laws), while others will take the position that the marriage cannot be annulled, as it is valid where it was performed.

BIGAMY

It is a requirement in every state that in order for a marriage to be valid, all prior marriages, if any, must have been terminated by death, annulment, or dissolution prior to entering the subsequent marriage. If terminated by divorce, the divorce must be final under the law of the jurisdiction where it was granted and any waiting period must have expired before a subsequent marriage takes place. Applications for marriage licenses customarily require that information regarding the termination of any prior marriages be provided (for example, the date of death of the last prior spouse or the date and jurisdiction in which the last decree of dissolution was entered).[12]

When a party is seeking to annul a marriage based on the contention that the other party was still married to another individual in another state or another country, proof will need to be presented to the court documenting the prior marriage and the fact that the earlier spouse is still alive.[13] If the other party claims the earlier marriage has been dissolved, proof of dissolution needs to be presented to the court as a defense.

IMPOTENCE

In general, parties to a marriage reasonably anticipate having a sexual relationship with their spouse after marriage. **Impotence,** or lack of a party's capacity to have sexual intercourse, may be a ground for annulment when the other party did not know of the condition at the time of the marriage. It may make the marriage voidable at the election of the unknowing party. However, that party may **ratify** the marriage by continuing to live with the other party and claiming a marital status under the law and before the general public. Unlike grounds such as bigamy and consanguinity, impotence is usually viewed as a ground available only to a party to the marriage and not to third persons, given the nature of proof required.

Failure to **consummate** a marriage (or a concealed intent not to do so) is not necessarily a ground for annulment, but a willful refusal to consummate a marriage and/or cohabit without good cause may be. Even if the ground for annulment is not specifically impotence or lack of consummation, as a practical matter it is often easier to obtain an annulment when the marriage has not been consummated. Concealment of prior homosexuality may not be a sufficient ground for annulment, but concealment of one's sexual preferences and/or limitations at the time of marriage may be sufficient. A unique challenge arises when courts are called on to consider the validity of a marriage in which one of the partners is a transsexual. (See Paralegal Application 4.2.)

Ratification
acceptance or confirmation of a previous act thereby making it valid from the moment it was done

Consummation
making a marriage complete by engaging in sexual intercourse

Paralegal Application 4.2

To Be a He or Not to Be a He—Should It Matter?

Courts in Florida, Kansas, New Jersey, New York, Ohio, and Texas have addressed issues related to marriages involving postoperative transsexual persons. In *M.T. v. J.T.,* a New Jersey court not only upheld the validity of a marriage involving a transsexual but also denied an annulment to a husband sought on the ground that his wife was a male-to-female transsexual. In explaining its rationale, the court stated:

> In sum, it has been established that an individual suffering from the condition of transexualism is one with a disparity between his or her genitalia or anatomical sex and his or her gender, that is, the individual's strong and consistent emotional and psychological sense of sexual being. A transsexual in a proper case can be treated medically by certain supportive measures and through surgery to remove and replace existing genitalia with sex organs which will coincide with the person's gender. If such sex reassignment surgery is successful and the postoperative transsexual is, by virtue of medical treatment, thereby possessed of the full capacity to function sexually as a male or female, as the case may be, we perceive no legal barrier, cognizable social taboo, or reason grounded in public policy to prevent that person's identification at least for purposes of marriage to the sex finally indicated.[14]

States other than New Jersey have tended to apply the narrow traditional meaning of male and female, basing sexual identity on the individual's chromosomal makeup as the test rather than on concepts of "gender identity" or "self-identity." In a case decided in 2004, for example, a Florida Court of Appeals reversed and remanded a trial court ruling granting a divorce and custody of his adopted child to a female-to-male transsexual husband. The court held that Florida law "does not provide for or allow such marriages" and essentially agreed with the wife's position that the parties' marriage was void *ab initio.*[15]

PARALEGAL PRACTICE TIP

The New Jersey and Florida opinions referenced in Paralegal Application 4.2 are both provided in their entirety at *www.pearsonhighered.com/wilson* in the companion website material for Chapter 4 under "Cases" and in the Case Resources Section of the MyLegalStudiesLab. (See *M.T. v. J.T.,* 140 N.J. Super. 77, 355 A.2d 204 (1976) and *Kantaras v. Kantaras,* 884 So. 2d 155 (Fla. App. 2004)).

Sidebar

Which position do you think the courts should take on this issue? Should it make a difference if the parties are both aware of the sex change at the time the marriage is entered?

FRAUD

In order for a state to permit a marriage to be annulled on the basis of fraud, the fraud generally must be more than the type of fraud that would be sufficient to rescind an ordinary business contract. The fraud must directly affect the marital relationship in some manner. It must go to "the essentials of marriage." The elements of fraud are described in Paralegal Application 4.3.

Courts are reluctant to annul a marriage for fraud unless the defrauded party would not have entered the marriage except for the fraud. Decisions are made on a case-by-case basis, because what is considered essential to a marriage by one party may be of considerably less significance to another. Fraud related to personal characteristics or habits is generally not considered sufficient to justify annulment of a marriage. Annulments are also rarely, if ever, granted solely based on fraud or misrepresentation of a purely financial nature (business interests, financial worth or prospects, etc.) even when a perpetrator of the fraud admits to misrepresenting financial circumstances or deceiving the other party with respect to allegedly joint-business ventures.[16]

Examples of fraud that some courts have deemed go to the essentials of marriage have included fraud related to undisclosed intentions to not consummate a marriage, sexual orientation, the ability to have children, a woman's concealment of her pregnancy by another man, prior marital status, chastity, promises about religion, and matters of health or drug abuse.[17] The Superior Court of New Jersey granted an annulment to a wife because the husband told her after they had married that he wanted to have children despite the fact that he had signed a premarital agreement in which he stated that he did not wish to have children. The court held that this situation constituted fraud relating to an essential element of the marriage contract.[18] The Minnesota Supreme Court declined to grant an annulment to a husband who discovered after marriage that his wife had been committed to a mental institution prior to their marriage. After the marriage, she had a relapse and was again committed. In denying the annulment, the court reasoned that the wife had not actively concealed her prior commitment and that her husband had never inquired about it.[19]

However, there are some physical conditions that do present a sufficient ground to warrant an annulment under certain circumstances, such as when a party to a marriage conceals from his or her spouse the existence of an incurable sexually

PARALEGAL PRACTICE TIP

Civil annulments are sometimes sought based on the failure of one of the parties to live up to a premarital promise to practice a particular religious faith. Whether or not a court will grant an annulment in such circumstances tends to turn on the extent to which religion is central to the marriage and permeates multiple facets of marital life and culture (diet, dress, language, social life, etc.). See, e.g., *In re the Marriage of Linda A. and Robert S. Owen*, 2002 Cal. App. Unpub. LEXIS 1500.

Paralegal **Application 4.3**

The Elements of Fraud

If a husband seeks an annulment on fraud grounds based on the fact that his wife lied to him about being pregnant so that he would marry her, he needs to plead and prove all of the elements of fraud:

   a. a false representation by the wife—she told him she was pregnant when she was not

   b. the wife's knowledge of the falsity—she knew she was not pregnant

   c. the misrepresentation concerns an essential of the marital relationship—childbearing and rearing are essentials of the marital relationship

   d. the wife's intention that the husband act on the representation—she told him she was pregnant so that he would marry her

   e. his reliance on the truth of the representation—he believed her and married her as a result of the misrepresentation

   f. he sustained injury as a result of the misrepresentation—he entered a marriage he would otherwise not have entered transmitted disease (e.g., syphilis or HIV/AIDS). For example, in an unpublished California appellate decision in 2004, a court found that substantial evidence supported a trial court's finding that a wife's concealment of her incurable and highly transmittable syphilitic condition was a fraud going to the essence of the marriage, which warranted granting a judgment of annulment to the husband (who following the marriage had applied to the Immigration and Naturalization Service for a green card for his wife). The court concluded that "a spouse's concealment of a medical condition or sexually transmittable disease that does not absolutely foreclose intercourse or child-bearing, but nevertheless endangers the life and health of the other spouse or their offspring, is so destructive of marital intimacy and the potential for procreation that it goes to 'the very essence of the marital relation.' . . ."[20]

LACK OF CONSENT, DURESS, AND UNDUE INFLUENCE

Marriage is a contract and, like other contracts, may be voided by a lack of mental capacity of one or both of the parties. For a marriage to be valid there needs to be a shared intent to assume the rights and duties of marriage. Each party to a marriage must be capable of consenting at the time of the marriage and must be able to understand and appreciate the benefits, obligations, and responsibilities of marriage. A person who is mentally limited or incompetent for some purposes may still legally consent to marriage in a lucid moment. The standard is generally lower than it would be for a contract under the Uniform Commercial Code for a business transaction. Absent evidence to the contrary, it is generally assumed that an individual who is getting married basically understands what marriage is and wants to be married to his or her partner.

Several states set out by statute grounds for annulment that are related to lack of consent at the time the marriage was solemnized. For example, a party may be incapable of consenting due to a mental condition, duress, undue influence, or the effects of intoxicants of some kind. The lack of consent may also be expressed in statutes as a "lack of mutual assent" to the marriage relationship. If the marriage has been followed by cohabitation or otherwise ratified, consent grounds are usually unavailable.

Undue influence is generally said to occur where there has been a fraudulent influence over the mind and will of another to the extent that an action of that person is not freely done, but rather is the act of the one who procures the result. **Duress** is an extreme form of undue influence involving threats or force. Annulment actions on these grounds may be able to be brought by third parties as well as by a "spouse" and may, in some circumstances, be brought after the death of a party. (See Case 4.1.)

Undue influence
the improper use of power or trust in a way that deprives a person of his or her free will and substitutes another's purposes in its place

Duress
a threat of harm made to compel a person to do something contrary to his or her free will or judgment

CASE **4.1** *Estate of Goodwin v. Foust-Graham,* 171 N.C. App. 707, 615 S.E.2d 398 (2005)

BACKGROUND

Under North Carolina law, the marriage of a person who is incapable of contracting from want of will is voidable. It will remain valid until it is declared void in a legal action. Prior to this case, North Carolina courts had annulled marriages on the basis of duress, but neither the North Carolina Supreme Court nor an appellate court in the state had addressed "undue influence" as a ground for annulment.

(Continued)

PARALEGAL PRACTICE TIP

The full opinion in the *Estate of Goodwin v. Foust-Graham* case is available at *www.pearsonhighered.com/wilson* in the companion website material for Chapter 4 under "Cases" and in the Case Resources Section of the MyLegalStudiesLab.

FROM THE OPINION

In the instant case, there was evidence pertaining to each of the factors that our Supreme Court has identified as relevant in analyzing undue influence. . . . Specifically, Goodwin was elderly at the time of the marriage, and there was testimony tending to establish that he was suffering from dementia and/or Alzheimer's disease. It is not disputed that he was subject to constant association with, and supervision by, Foust-Graham and that he had little association with his family or friends in the months immediately preceding the marriage. The marriage left Goodwin's previously existing estate plan in doubt and placed Foust-Graham in a position to take action that would substantially reduce the amount that Goodwin's daughter would inherit. Further, there was evidence that Foust-Graham procured the marriage, including Goodwin's apparent confusion as to why he was at the magistrate's office, the fact that Foust-Graham had driven Goodwin to the magistrate's office, and the fact that the marriage was undertaken suddenly. Accordingly, the jury could find that Goodwin was subject to undue influence, that Foust-Graham had the opportunity and disposition to exert undue influence, and that the marriage occurred as a result of undue influence. . . . a finding of undue influence is tantamount to a finding that Goodwin was incapable of contracting from want of will, . . .

SIDEBAR

To what extent do you agree with the outcome in this case?

Defenses to an Annulment Action

The most commonly raised defenses to an annulment action are:

- Compliance with state statutes governing marriage
- Ratification of the marriage by subsequent conduct
- Consummation of the marriage
- Laches
- Equitable estoppel
- Judicial estoppel
- Unclean hands

COMPLIANCE WITH STATE STATUTES GOVERNING MARRIAGE

As described in Chapter 3, each state lays out by statute a series of technical "requirements" for a valid marriage. Those requirements generally include an application for and issuance of a license to marry signed under pain and penalty of perjury by persons eligible to marry (with parental consent or court approval if necessary), a marriage certificate, a ceremony performed by someone licensed in the state to perform marriages, and the return of an executed marriage certificate to the appropriate keeper of public records. Although a party may claim that failure to comply with such requirements should render a marriage void, states generally do not treat as void or voidable marriages contracted in violation of technical or procedural statutory requirements.[21]

Although misstatements on applications for marriage licenses usually do not provide a sufficient basis for an annulment, in some cases they will. For example, a

North Carolina Court of Appeals applying Georgia law held that an annulment was appropriate when a wife indicated under oath on a Georgia application for a marriage license that she had been married twice before, when in fact she had been married seven times.[22]

RATIFICATION OF THE MARRIAGE BY SUBSEQUENT CONDUCT

When a marriage is voidable, such as the marriage of a minor without parental consent, it can be ratified by the minor once he or she reaches the age of majority. Ratification is normally accomplished by the parties voluntarily continuing to live together as husband and wife after the minor attains the age of majority. Because of the strong public policy favoring marriage, most states establish, by statute or case law, a time frame within which the injured party (the minor) must disaffirm the marriage.

CONSUMMATION OF THE MARRIAGE

In considering a complaint for annulment, courts may consider whether or not there has been cohabitation following a marriage. Cohabitation is evidence that the parties have been validly married, but it is not dispositive, nor is it essential to establish a marriage, particularly when there has been sexual intercourse prior to marriage.

Generally, if a voidable marriage is consummated with knowledge of an impediment, it will be considered to have been ratified. A Florida court, for example, has held that a marriage that has been consummated cannot be annulled on the basis of fraud alone.[23] There are also circumstances in which the parties may marry with full understanding that the marriage will never be consummated, as when one of the parties is incarcerated for life without possibility of parole or conjugal visitation.

LACHES

The defense of **laches** is an equitable doctrine that precludes a litigant from asserting a claim if his or her unreasonable delay in raising the claim has prejudiced the opposing party. It is based on the notion that courts should not come to the aid of a party who has knowingly "slept on his rights" to the detriment of the other party.[24]

Laches
unreasonable delay in pursuing a right or claim that prejudices the other party's rights

EQUITABLE ESTOPPEL

A party may raise **equitable estoppel** as a defense when a person, by conduct, induces a second person to rely, to his or her detriment, on the statements or conduct of the first person. The person who asserts a claim of estoppel must have reasonably relied on the acts or representations of the other and have had no knowledge or means of knowing the facts. Assume, for example, that Bonnie (who is from California) tells her "boyfriend," John, that she is suffering from a terminal disease and hopes with all her heart that he will marry her before she dies even though they will never be able to consummate their marriage because of her "condition." John is deeply touched by her request. He relocates his home and business to California and marries Bonnie. One year later, after she has cleaned out his bank account, Bonnie tells John that she is not in fact ill and that they are not

Equitable estoppel
preventing a party from asserting a claim or a defense because it would be unfair to an opposing party to do otherwise

really married because their so-called marriage was never consummated. In response to her claim for annulment, he raises the defense of equitable estoppel. She lied to him and he relied on her representations, and as a result he says that based on principles of fairness, the court should "estop" her from denying the validity of the marriage.

In exceptional circumstances, some jurisdictions permit a marriage to be created by equitable estoppel to mitigate the effects of fraud and protect the rights of innocent persons who otherwise would be adversely affected. In marriage by estoppel, a marriage is presumed to be valid even though technically it is not. This defense is generally available only with respect to voidable but not void marriages. For example, courts are highly unlikely to apply the doctrine when parties enter a bigamous marriage, even if neither party was aware of the impediment.[25]

JUDICIAL ESTOPPEL

A variation on equitable estoppel is **judicial estoppel**, a doctrine designed to protect the courts (as well as good-faith litigants). Judicial estoppel is an equitable doctrine designed to prevent a party from gaining an unfair advantage over another party by making inconsistent statements on the same issue in different lawsuits. As a North Carolina court phrased it, ". . . our courts do not permit the submission of new theories, not previously argued, because the law does not permit parties to swap horses between courts in order to get a better mount. . . ."[26] In the *Pickard* case decided by a North Carolina Court of Appeals in 2006, the court applied this doctrine and upheld a district court's denial of an annulment to a petitioner. (See Case 4.2.)

CASE **4.2** *Pickard v. Pickard*, 625 S.E.2d 869 (N.C. App. 2006)

Carl Pickard and his wife, Jane, had been married by a Cherokee Indian in the Native American tradition in June of 1991. The parties had received a North Carolina license and certificate of marriage and filed it with the appropriate Register of Deeds. Both of the parties believed the ceremony was legally sufficient to bind them in marriage and they lived together and conducted themselves as husband and wife for the next eleven years. In 1998, the husband petitioned the court to adopt his wife's adult biological daughter. He provided the court with a sworn statement that he was "the stepfather of the adoptee, having married her natural mother." He also listed his marital status as "married." The clerk of the county superior court subsequently filed a decree of adoption based on his assertions. When the husband subsequently sought an annulment in 2002, he alleged that the marriage ceremony was not properly solemnized because the Cherokee Indian who performed it was not qualified to conduct a marriage ceremony. Because the husband had earlier represented himself to the court in the adoption proceeding as married, the court in effect held that the issue of his marital status was **res judicata**, and he was judicially estopped from later claiming his marriage was not valid. The appellate court noted that it also would impose an unfair detriment on the wife if it were to undo an eleven-year marriage by allowing the husband to proceed with his inconsistent position.

SIDEBAR

Do you agree with the court's decision?

Judicial estoppel
an equitable doctrine designed to prevent a party from gaining an unfair advantage over another party by making inconsistent statements on the same issue in different lawsuits

PARALEGAL PRACTICE TIP

The full opinion in the *Pickard* case can be accessed at *www.pearsonhighered.com/wilson* in the companion website material related to Chapter 4 under "Cases" and in the Case Resources Section of the MyLegalStudiesLab.

Res judicata
an issue that has been definitively settled by judicial decision; the three essential elements are: (1) an earlier decision on the issue, (2) a final judgment on the merits, and (3) the involvement of the original parties

PARALEGAL PRACTICE TIP

Attorneys will advise clients in annulment cases that they need to revise their respective wills if they have executed them, particularly if they still want to provide for their "spouse." An annulment will revoke the designation of the "spouse" as executor and will also automatically revoke gifts and bequests in a will made to a "surviving spouse" unless the will expressly states otherwise. If no will exists, one should be prepared and executed.

UNCLEAN HANDS

The doctrine of **unclean hands** provides that "he who comes into Equity must come with clean hands."[27] If a plaintiff in an equity action has, through his or her own misconduct, injured or damaged the defendant, the court should not allow that plaintiff to benefit as a result of his or her own misdeeds. The application of the doctrine is limited to misconduct connected with the matter in litigation.

Unclean hands
the principle that a party should not be granted relief if he or she has acted unfairly, wrongfully, or illegally

Consequences of an Annulment

FOR THE PARTIES

The general rule is that if a marriage ends in an annulment, property division and spousal support provisions technically do not apply as they would in divorce. However, some states with annulment statutes specifically provide that the court may grant alimony and custody and support orders for any minor child, as in the case of divorce.[28] Other states provide for the parties by applying equitable principles on a case-by-case basis. For example, courts in some states (particularly community property states such as California, Texas, and Washington) may declare a marriage void and yet grant a putative spouse, who innocently believed the marriage was valid, a share of the couple's quasi-marital property. Such states use a good-faith analysis to determine whether either of the parties had reason to believe the marriage was invalid. In a 2004 case, the Nevada Supreme Court applied the **putative spouse** doctrine as a basis for dividing the parties' property. (See Case 4.3.) Even though the putative spouse may be deemed entitled to a share of the quasi-marital property, the marriage itself is considered void.

Putative spouse
a person who believes in good faith that his or her invalid marriage is legally valid

PARALEGAL PRACTICE TIP

The full opinion in the *Williams* case is available at *www.pearsonhighered.com/wilson* in the companion website material for Chapter 4 under "Cases" and in the Case Resources Section of the MyLegalStudiesLab.

CASE **4.3** *Williams v. Williams,* 97 P.3d 1124 (Nev. 2004)

FROM THE OPINION

This is a case of first impression involving the application of the putative spouse doctrine in an annulment proceeding. Under the doctrine, an individual whose marriage is void due to a prior legal impediment is treated as a spouse so long as the party seeking equitable relief participated in the marriage ceremony with the good-faith belief that the ceremony was legally valid. A majority of the states recognize the doctrine when dividing property acquired during the marriage, applying equitable principles, based on community property law, to the division. However, absent fraud, the doctrine does not apply to awards of spousal support. While some states have extended the doctrine to permit spousal support awards, they have done so under the authority of state statutes.

We agree with the majority view. Consequently, we adopt the putative spouse doctrine in annulment proceedings for the purposes of property division and affirm the district court's division of property. However, we reject the doctrine as a basis for awarding equitable spousal support. Because Nevada's annulment statutes do not provide for an award of support upon annulment, we reverse the district court's award of spousal support.

On August 26, 1973, appellant Richard E. Williams underwent a marriage ceremony with respondent Marcie C. Williams. At that time, Marcie believed she was divorced from John Allmaras. However, neither Marcie nor Allmaras had

(Continued)

obtained a divorce. Richard and Marcie believed they were legally married and lived together, as husband and wife, for 27 years. In March 2000, Richard discovered that Marcie was not divorced from Allmaras at the time of their marriage ceremony.

In August 2000, Richard and Marcie permanently separated. In February 2001, Richard filed a complaint for an annulment. Marcie answered and counterclaimed for one-half of the property and spousal support as a putative spouse. In April 2002, the parties engaged in a one-day bench trial to resolve the matter.

At trial, Richard testified that had he known Marcie was still married, he would not have married her. He claimed that Marcie knew she was not divorced when she married him or had knowledge that would put a reasonable person on notice to check if the prior marriage had been dissolved. . . .

The district court found that Marcie had limited ability to support herself. The district court also concluded that both parties believed they were legally married, acted as husband and wife, and conceived and raised two children. Marcie stayed at home to care for and raise their children. Based on these facts, the district court granted the annulment and awarded Marcie one-half of all the jointly-held property and spousal support. The district court did not indicate whether its award was based on the putative spouse doctrine or an implied contract and quantum meruit theory. . . .

A marriage is void if either of the parties to the marriage has a former husband or wife then living. Richard and Marcie's marriage was void because Marcie was still married to another man when she married Richard. Although their marriage was void, an annulment proceeding was necessary to legally sever their relationship. An annulment proceeding is the proper manner to dissolve a void marriage and resolve other issues arising from the dissolution of the relationship.

Under the putative spouse doctrine, when a marriage is legally void, the civil effects of a legal marriage flow to the parties who contracted to marry in good faith. That is, a putative spouse is entitled to many of the rights of an actual spouse. A majority of the states have recognized some form of the doctrine. . . .

The doctrine has two elements: (1) a proper marriage ceremony was performed, and (2) one or both of the parties had a good-faith belief that there was no impediment to the marriage and the marriage was valid and proper. "Good faith" has been defined as an "honest and reasonable belief that the marriage was valid at the time of the ceremony." Good faith is presumed. The party asserting lack of good faith has the burden of proving bad faith. Whether the party acted in good faith is a question of fact. Unconfirmed rumors or mere suspicions of a legal impediment do not vitiate good faith "so long as no certain or authoritative knowledge of some legal impediment comes to him or her." However, when a person receives reliable information that an impediment exists, the individual cannot ignore the information, but instead has a duty to investigate further. Persons cannot act "blindly or without reasonable precaution." Finally, once a spouse learns of the impediment, the putative marriage ends.

We have not previously considered the putative spouse doctrine, but we are persuaded by the rationale of our sister states that public policy supports adopting the doctrine in Nevada. Fairness and equity favor recognizing putative spouses when

(Continued)

parties enter into a marriage ceremony in good faith and without knowledge there is a factual or legal impediment to their marriage. Nor does the doctrine conflict with Nevada's policy in refusing to recognize common-law marriages or palimony suits. . . . As a majority of our sister states have recognized, the sanctity of marriage is not undermined, but rather enhanced, by the recognition of the putative spouse doctrine. We therefore adopt the doctrine in Nevada.

We now apply the doctrine to the instant case. The district court found that the parties obtained a license and participated in a marriage ceremony on August 26, 1973, in Verdi, Nevada. The district court also found that Marcie erroneously believed that her prior husband, Allmaras, had terminated their marriage by divorce and that she was legally able to marry Richard. In so finding, the district court also necessarily rejected Richard's argument that Marcie acted unreasonably in relying on Allmaras' statements because she had never been served with divorce papers and that she had a duty to inquire about the validity of her former marriage before marrying Richard.

. . . The district court was free to disregard Richard's testimony, and substantial evidence supports the district court's finding that Marcie did not act unreasonably in relying on Allmaras' representations. The record reflects no reason for Marcie to have disbelieved him and, thus, no reason to have investigated the truth of his representations. . . .

Community property states that recognize the putative spouse doctrine apply community property principles to the division of property, including determinations of what constitutes community and separate property. Since putative spouses believe themselves to be married, they are already under the assumption that community property statutes would apply to a termination of their relationship. There is no point, therefore in devising a completely separate set of rules for dividing property in a putative spouse scenario. . . .

States are divided on whether spousal support is a benefit or civil effect that may be awarded under the putative spouse doctrine. Although some states permit the award of alimony, they do so because their annulment statutes permit an award of rehabilitative or permanent alimony. At least one state, however, has found alimony to be a civil effect under the putative spouse doctrine even in the absence of a specific statute permitting an award of alimony.

Nevada statutes do not provide for an award of alimony after annulment. . . .

. . . We adopt the putative spouse doctrine and conclude that common-law community property principles apply by analogy to the division of property acquired during a putative marriage. However, the putative spouse doctrine does not permit an award of spousal support in the absence of bad faith, fraud or statutory authority. Therefore, we affirm that portion of the district court's order equally dividing the parties' property and reverse that portion of the order awarding spousal support.

SIDEBAR

Do you agree with the outcome? How reasonable is it for a spouse to rely on the oral and undocumented representations of a former spouse that their marriage is dissolved? What would you do in the same circumstances? What do you think the result should be if one of the parties entered the marriage with knowledge of the impediment and does not qualify as a putative spouse?

Alimony commonly terminates upon the recipient's remarriage. If that "re-marriage" is subsequently annulled, the recipient may claim that the payor should have to resume paying alimony, as there was no valid subsequent marriage. Courts use a variety of approaches to address this question including the following:

- Alimony obligations revive after void but not voidable remarriages of alimony recipients.
- Alimony automatically terminates on the remarriage of the recipient regardless of subsequent events furthering interests of finality and certainty for the obligor when the obligee elects to look to another for support.
- The revival decision is made on a case-by-case basis.
- The decision is driven by the language of the parties' separation agreement if the issue is specifically addressed in an agreement incorporated in the court's decree.

(See the Focus on Case Law at the end of this chapter and read the *Fredo* case that addresses this issue).

An annulment decree may revive a party's previous legal status in other respects in some circumstances. For example, annulment of a surviving spouse's second marriage may entitle that spouse to reinstatement of Social Security and worker's compensation death benefits flowing from a prior marriage. The rationale behind reinstatement is that the burden of death and injury should be carried by industry.

FOR THE CHILDREN

PARALEGAL PRACTICE TIP

In some cases, the court in a state where a child of annulment is considered illegitimate may accomplish a positive result by applying the law of another state if the child in question was born in and would be considered legitimate under that state's law.

In most states, children born to marriages that are subsequently annulled are deemed "legitimate" for legal purposes under state law. Some states, such as Nebraska and Iowa, specifically provide by statute that children born to annulled marriages are legitimate unless a court decrees otherwise. However, there are isolated exceptions. For example, in Mississippi, children born to incestuous marriages are not considered legitimate.

Rather than being termed "illegitimate," children of annulled marriages typically are described as being "born out of wedlock." The courts generally will treat them as legitimate whenever possible within the law to achieve a desirable result. When an annulment is granted, they usually will make orders for the care, custody, and maintenance of the parties' children, and, with the exception of inheritance rights, most other disabilities of "illegitimacy" have been eliminated as well by statute or constitutional interpretation. However, children of annulment may need to establish legal parentage to inherit from or through a parent or to claim some benefits such as the rights to file a wrongful death or workman's compensation claim for injury to a parent. They are also required to go through extra bureaucratic steps to establish their rights to a variety of federal dependent-based benefits or to establish citizenship.

Although alimony obligations of a prior spouse are usually not revived by annulment of a recipient's subsequent marriage, annulment of a child's marriage during his or her minority usually will revive the child's unemancipated status and also revive a parent's child support obligation. "Public policy directs that parents financially support their minor children, even if those children make unwise decisions. Moreover, assuming the parent with the support obligation might rely on the validity of the child's marriage in making financial plans, that period of reliance would not last indefinitely but only until the child would otherwise become emancipated."[29]

PARALEGAL PRACTICE TIP

When multiple states are involved in an annulment case, a conflict-of-law issue may arise. The general rule is that if a marriage would be valid in the state where it was entered (for example, a common law marriage), it will be valid in the state where a party is domiciled at the time of the annulment action unless it violates a strong public policy of that state. However, some states have marriage evasion statutes providing that if domiciliaries of that state go to another state solely to evade a marriage restriction, marry in the second state, and then return to their home state, the home state may refuse to recognize the "marriage."

The Paralegal's Role in an Annulment Case

The tasks most commonly performed by a paralegal in an annulment case are:

- Researching the law governing annulment in the applicable jurisdiction and in other jurisdictions as well, if appropriate
- Preparing related memoranda based on research as requested
- Gathering information and documentation essential to preparation of necessary documents, discovery requests, pleadings, and correspondence
- Scheduling and participating in interviews as assigned
- Drafting complaints/petitions, motions, supporting affidavits, and proposed orders or responses to complaints/petitions
- Drafting discovery requests, if necessary, such as proposed interrogatories, deposition questions, requests for admissions, requests for production of documents and things, and requests for physical or mental examinations
- Assisting in preparation for hearings or trial, including drafting pretrial memoranda for review, organizing documents and exhibits, etc.
- Preparing subpoenas for witnesses, if necessary
- Helping to prepare the client as well as witnesses appearing for the client
- Tracking progress on the case and being certain that any timelines are met
- Making sure the client is kept informed of progress and upcoming deadlines, hearings, discovery matters, etc.
- Acting as a conduit for providing information such as brochures, prepared charts, instructions, and frequently-asked-questions (FAQs) sheets

CHAPTER SUMMARY

Prior to the emergence of no-fault divorce in the 1970s, divorce actions all were based on grounds such as cruel and abusive treatment, adultery, abandonment, imprisonment, and chronic alcohol abuse. The process was especially painful and antagonistic and often presented difficult problems of proof. Annulment actions sometimes provided an alternative but not necessarily an emotionally and financially less costly one. Although not everyone would agree, divorce today has become somewhat more streamlined and humane. No longer does one spouse have to demonize the other spouse if irreconcilable differences have developed that have caused the breakdown of the marriage. As a result, although annulment is still an appropriate option in some cases, no-fault divorce now may present some couples with a more desirable route to terminating their marriage.

This chapter first addresses the meaning of annulment and the distinction between an alleged marriage that is void *ab initio* (a marriage that never came into being because of a legal impediment that existed at the time of the marriage) and a voidable marriage (one that remains valid until declared invalid by a court of competent jurisdiction). After clarifying the differences between annulment and divorce, the basic procedural requirements for obtaining an annulment are briefly described. Various grounds for annulment are reviewed and illustrated, such as bigamy, impotence, fraud, nonage, duress, and undue influence. Also referenced are some of the more common defenses to an annulment action such as compliance with state law, laches, ratification, consummation, estoppel (equitable and judicial), and unclean hands. The paralegal's role in an annulment action is referenced throughout the chapter, with emphasis on the particular importance of being aware of local law and procedure and jurisdictional variations.

CONCEPT REVIEW AND REINFORCEMENT

KEY **TERMS**

Affinity	Equitable estoppel	Putative spouse
Annulment	Fraud	Quasi-marital property
Bigamy	Green card	Ratification
Clear and convincing evidence	Impotence	*Res judicata*
Consanguinity	Incest	Standing
Consummation	Judicial estoppel	Unclean hands
Declaratory judgment	Laches	Undue influence
Duress	Marriage	Void *ab initio*
Ecclesiastical law	Nonage	Voidable marriage

REVIEW **QUESTIONS**

1. Define and distinguish between a marriage that is void *ab initio* and one that is voidable and give an example of each.
2. Distinguish between annulment and divorce.
3. Describe the procedure for obtaining an annulment and identify the kinds of individuals who have standing to bring annulment actions.
4. Identify five grounds for annulment and give an example of each.
5. Identify five potential defenses to an annulment action.
6. Identify consequences of an annulment for the parties and for their children.
7. Describe the role of a paralegal in an annulment action.

DEVELOPING YOUR PARALEGAL SKILLS

FOCUS ON **THE JOB**

In this activity, the student will draft a complaint for annulment based on a specific fact pattern.

The Facts

John and Audrey Morrison had a nonmarital relationship that began in 2007. John is an attorney and a partner in a law firm. Audrey is a certified public accountant. In the spring of 2011, Audrey became pregnant. John claimed that the pregnancy was Audrey's fault and her responsibility and told her she should get an abortion as soon as possible. He said the pregnancy should be terminated because he was not prepared to be a father at that point in his life. A devout Catholic for her entire life, Audrey was determined not to have an abortion. She and John had a series of arguments on the subject, and Audrey became so upset by the situation that she went to a therapist and was put on strong medication that calmed her down but clouded her thinking. John believed she was suicidal and in an effort to prevent that outcome, agreed to marry her prior to the birth of their child. He felt very pressured and, although he didn't tell her at the time of the marriage, he did not plan to live together as husband and wife after the child was born, nor did he intend to remain married. He just wanted to stop her tirades and nagging and thought that if she felt their child was "legitimate," she would accept whatever happened between the two of them. He was quite wrong on several fronts. After the baby was born, a healthy boy named John Morrison, Jr., John decided he wanted to remain married and raise the boy as a couple. He told Audrey that he was very happy as a family man and that he couldn't believe what he had initially intended to do. When she questioned him further and he told her about his earlier plan, she immediately went wild, took the baby, ran out of the house calling him all sorts of names, and went to live with her sister. The following week she went to meet with an attorney, your supervisor, in order to file for an annulment of their marriage based on her husband's conduct and intentions at the time the parties were married.

The Assignment

Locate the proper form for bringing an annulment action in the state where you live. Then complete the form for review assuming that you are a paralegal in the firm representing Audrey in the above fact pattern. The firm is Wilson and Tauson, LLP, located at 390 Main Street, your city or town, state, and zip code, and the attorney handling the case is Juliana Wilson, Esq. Audrey is living with her sister at 2 Woodbine Road in your city or town, and John continues to reside at 3 River Road in your city or town (where the parties last resided together). They were married on October 28, 2011, in a Catholic church in your state (choose a location, if necessary) and were both residents of the state when they wed.

FOCUS ON **ETHICS**

In this activity the student is asked to identify and address ethical issues that arise in the context of a client interview.

The Assignment

Assume the facts in the Focus on the Job hypothetical. Assume further that you have been asked to interview the client, Audrey Morrison, in order to gather background information about the facts of the case so that Attorney Wilson can determine whether or not an annulment is a viable option. During the interview with the client, she tells you, among other things, that she is heartbroken. She had believed that she and her husband were a happy couple, totally compatible, and committed to each other. She further reveals that they had been having sexual relations during the entire period of their relationship and relatively brief marriage. You recall something from your paralegal training about how an annulment cannot be obtained if the parties cohabit and engage in sexual relations after their marriage.

You tell Audrey what you recall but reassure her that she doesn't have to worry, as she can still get out of her relationship with John by filing for a divorce instead of an annulment. Audrey tells you that you don't understand. She is a devout Catholic and divorce is simply not an option for her. She leaves the office sobbing hysterically. You try to go after her but the phone rings and you have to answer it, as you are the only one in the office at the time. When Attorney Wilson returns, she asks how the interview went and when you tell her what happened, she is not pleased to say the least. She asks you if you have any idea what you have done and tells you to leave the office and not return until you figure it out and spell out in writing the ethical errors you made. She also directs you to suggest an appropriate course of action. Do as she has requested, applying the ethical canons for paralegals promulgated by the National Association of Legal Assistants contained in Appendix A of this text. Your response should be in the form of a memorandum to Attorney Wilson.

FOCUS ON **CASE LAW**

This activity provides the student with an opportunity to analyze an annulment case using an IRAC format.

The Assignment

Read the opinion *Fredo v. Fredo,* 49 Conn. Supp. 489, 894 A.2d 399 (Conn Super. 2005), and then analyze the case using an IRAC format:

Identify the ISSUE.

Identify the RULE of law.

ANALYZE the case in terms of how the rule of law applies to the facts of the case.

Draw a CONCLUSION.

PARALEGAL PRACTICE TIP

The opinion in the *Fredo* case is available at www.pearsonhighered.com/wilson in the companion website material related to Chapter 4 under "Cases" and in the Case Resources Section of the MyLegalStudiesLab.

FOCUS ON **STATE LAW AND PROCEDURE**

In this activity, the student is asked to research the grounds for annulment in his or her jurisdiction.

The Assignment

Locate the grounds for annulment in the state where you are studying family law. You may need to check both statutes and case law. Remember to consider statutes restricting capacity to marry (age, sex, etc.) as well as statutes or cases setting forth grounds related to intent (fraud, duress, etc.).

FOCUS ON **TECHNOLOGY**

In addition to the links contained in the chapter, this activity provides a series of technology-related assignments for completion.

Assignments

1. Learn more about annulment in the Catholic Church at *www.catholicnewsagency.com*

2. Locate online the forms for bringing an action for annulment in three states other than your own. Links provided in the chapter and *www.forms.justia.com* may be of some assistance in completing this task.

3. Visit *www.findlaw.com* and see what you can locate in the way of information about annulment.

PORTFOLIO PRODUCTS

1. Complaint for Annulment
2. Memorandum on ethical issues in a hypothetical case
3. Analysis of an annulment case in an IRAC format

4. List of grounds for annulment in the student's jurisdiction

chapter 5
THE DIVORCE PROCESS

Divorce Decree

All is not well with David and Marie's fifteen-year marriage. He is convinced she has twice disrupted his educational goals by getting pregnant. Now, he says, she has begun drinking and not taking proper care of the children and the marital home. She claims he has abused her emotionally and physically, is obsessed with neatness, and is involved with another woman at work. He has decided to move out of the house and file for divorce.

Historical Perspective

Historically, the states have exercised considerable control over the marital relationship: its creation, its maintenance, and its termination. Until the early 1970s, a family law practice that focused on divorce law was largely a litigation practice, because in order to get a divorce under state law, one of the parties had to prove that there was serious wrongdoing by the other party. Even when both parties wanted to end the marriage, as was often the case, the focus still was on fault and blame. Frequently, the system either trapped people in painfully unhappy and shallow marriages or forced them to deceive the court about their true circumstances in order to fit into the fault mold and obtain a divorce.

The "culture of divorce" has changed dramatically since the 1970s. The emergence of **no-fault divorce** in all fifty states was the most dramatic catalyst in this evolution, and it has been buttressed by:

- an emphasis on divorce as an economic event in which spouses are viewed as equal partners in the marriage
- the institution of child support guidelines
- the codification of criteria to guide decisions pertaining to custody, alimony, and property division
- the introduction of parenting plans and programs
- the creation of support systems and user-friendly court procedures for parties proceeding *pro se*

LEARNING OBJECTIVES

After reading this chapter and completing related assignments, you should be able to:

- describe how the "culture of divorce" has evolved over the past four decades
- list the four primary methods of altering the marital status
- identify the basic stages of the divorce process
- distinguish among the six major alternative dispute resolution methods used in the family law context
- provide examples of jurisdictional issues that may arise in divorce cases
- identify the most common fault and no-fault grounds for divorce
- list defenses available to defendants in divorce actions
- describe the role of the paralegal at each major stage of the divorce process

No-fault divorce
divorce based on an irremediable breakdown of the marital relationship rather than on the fault of one or both of the parties

Pro se
[Latin: for himself or on his or her own behalf] without legal representation

- a reduction in litigation due to an increased use of alternative approaches to dispute resolution and the collaborative efforts of attorneys to make the divorce process more civil
- a judicial and societal movement toward respect for autonomy and privacy in family relationships.

Methods of Altering a Marital Relationship

There are four primary court proceedings used by parties seeking to separate and/ or dissolve their marriage:

- Divorce
- Legal separation
- Separate maintenance
- Annulment

Each of these requires that there be grounds for altering the marital status. The grounds for the first three may be traditional **fault grounds** (such as adultery and cruel and abusive treatment) or **no-fault grounds** (irreconcilable differences, living separate and apart, etc.). The grounds for annulment differ in that it is the validity of the marriage itself, rather than the relationship between the parties, that is faulty.

DIVORCE

Depending on the state, a divorce may be called an absolute divorce, a dissolution of marriage, or a **divorce a vinculo matrimonii**. A **divorce** is a judicial determination that a marriage is legally terminated. Both ceremonial and common law marriages require judicial intervention to effect a termination and permit the parties to remarry. A divorce may be obtained on the basis of no-fault grounds in all fifty states and also on fault grounds in a majority of states. Termination of the marital status does not necessarily terminate duties arising upon marriage, such as spousal maintenance, nor does it eliminate responsibility for the custody and support of children of the marriage. It also does not automatically provide for the division of marital property. In a bifurcated or divisible divorce, the dissolution of marriage is resolved in one proceeding, and all other issues such as property division and child custody are resolved in one or more later separate proceedings in the same or another state.

PARALEGAL PRACTICE TIP

When parties who are legally separated decide they want a divorce, the conversion is not automatic. They must petition the court to accomplish their purpose. To find an example of a "Stipulation and Order Converting Legal Separation to Divorce," visit *www.wicourts.gov*. A link to this site can be found at *www. pearsonhighered.com/wilson* in the companion website material related to Chapter 5 under "Forms." Check "Form 4110" to see that, in Wisconsin, as in many states, the form for seeking a legal separation is the same as the form for seeking a divorce.

LEGAL SEPARATION

Legal separations are most often sought by parties who are not yet ready to divorce for a variety of personal reasons or who are opposed to divorce on religious grounds. A decree of **legal separation** establishes the rights and obligations of two spouses

---

Fault grounds
grounds for divorce based on the fault of one of the parties

No-fault grounds
grounds for divorce based on an irremediable breakdown of the marital relationship rather than on the fault of one or both of the parties

Divorce *a vinculo matrimonii*
[Latin: from the chains or bonds of marriage] an absolute divorce that frees the parties to marry

Divorce
a judicial determination that a marriage is legally terminated

PARALEGAL PRACTICE TIP

A list of terms used to describe or refer to divorce and a summary of selected statistics on divorce are provided at *www.pearsonhighered. com/wilson* in the companion website material related to Chapter 5 under "Resources."

Legal separation
a judicial determination that allows the parties to live separate and apart without dissolving their legal relationship as husband and wife; sometimes called a limited divorce

who wish to live separate and apart but remain married. The obligations can then be enforced by the court. Depending on the state it may be called a judicial separation, a limited divorce, or a **divorce *a mensa et thoro***. Grounds must exist to support an action for a legal separation and are essentially the same as would be used in the divorce context. The end result is not the same, however, because the marriage is not actually terminated and the parties are not free to remarry. The court can make alimony and child custody and support awards, grant a party freedom from interference by the other party, and incorporate a separation agreement executed by the parties that addresses these issues as well as division of property in some states. The agreement should state clearly whether or not various terms of the agreement will continue to be binding on the parties if they eventually divorce or reconcile. If the parties do subsequently reconcile, the court's order of legal separation is still in force until it is vacated, one of the parties dies, or the marriage is formally terminated by annulment or a full divorce. Several states permit the conversion of a legal separation into a divorce after a period of time set by statute.

SEPARATE MAINTENANCE

An action for **separate maintenance** or separate support is usually an option in jurisdictions that do not grant legal separations. It, too, may require the existence of grounds that are essentially the same as the grounds for divorce. It serves the same purpose of allowing the parties to live apart under a court order that defines the terms of the separation, including provisions for spousal and child support, insurance coverage, occupancy and maintenance of the former marital home, etc. In some states, child custody is determined in a separate action. A decree granting separate maintenance does not terminate the marriage, permanently divide the parties' property, or permit either of the parties to remarry. Separate maintenance decrees can be enforced in the same manner as support awards in the context of a divorce or a legal separation. They also remain in effect, even if the parties reconcile, until such time as vacated by the court, one of the parties dies, or the marriage is terminated by divorce.

ANNULMENT

As indicated in Chapter 4, an **annulment** is a judicial determination that a marriage never existed. The marriage may be either **void *ab initio*** or **voidable** because of the existence of a defect at the inception of the marriage, such as a prior existing marriage of one of the parties or inability of a party to enter a valid marriage due to nonage, lack of mental capacity, duress, etc.

The Divorce Process—A Skeletal Road Map

For the client, the decision to seek a divorce is often a monumental, life-altering event that takes place after months, even years, of deliberation. When the client comes to the attorney's office, he or she often feels the hard part is over and a divorce is just around the corner. However, it can be a rude awakening to discover that getting a divorce, even on an uncontested basis, usually takes months, and hotly contested divorces may drag on for years. Although the vast majority of divorce actions are settled and do not proceed to trial, approximately 10% still do. This chapter first provides a description of the various stages of the full process in a contested case and then describes variations in the process in uncontested cases.

Divorce *a mensa et thoro*
[Latin: divorce from bed and board] a legal separation

PARALEGAL PRACTICE TIP

An action for separate support may also be brought by a guardian of a minor child. If the family is receiving public assistance and the state's Title IV-D agency believes that one of the spouses/parents has the ability to pay support and is not doing so, then that agency may also bring an action for separate support.

Separate maintenance
court-ordered spousal support while the parties are living separate and apart but not divorced

PARALEGAL PRACTICE TIP

To see a Complaint for Separate Support, visit *www.lawlib.state.ma.us*. A link to this site can be found at *www.pearsonhighered.com/wilson* in the companion website material for Chapter 5 under "Forms."

Annulment
the legal procedure for declaring that a marriage is null and void because of an impediment existing at its inception

Void *ab initio*
of no legal effect from the outset; a marriage contract may be void *ab initio* if it seriously offends governing law or public policy

Voidable
capable of being nullified by a court of competent jurisdiction

PARALEGAL PRACTICE TIP

Sometimes courts provide helpful guidance to parties seeking a divorce. To see some of the ways in which courts in Alaska have done this, visit *www.courts.alaska.gov.* You can find a link to this site at *www. pearsonhighered.com/wilson* in the companion website material for Chapter 5 under "Resources."

Every state establishes its own procedural rules for divorce/dissolution actions. In some states, they are the same as for civil actions in general. In others they are specific to domestic relations cases, and still others use a combination of the two. The basic steps in the process in a contested case are outlined in skeletal form in Exhibit 5.1. The role played by a paralegal in the process depends both on the specific paralegal's level of experience and also on the policies and procedures of individual law firms and supervisors. Whenever actions are taken by a paralegal, such as filing a document or communicating with a client, it is presumed that the actions are taken only with a supervisor's approval.

PARALEGAL PRACTICE TIP

The assumption in this outline is that the client is the plaintiff. The defendant who knows that the spouse intends to file for divorce may meet with an attorney at the outset, or he or she may not do so until after being formally served.

Appearance
a document filed with the court by an attorney, indicating that he or she will be representing one of the parties in a matter before the court

EXHIBIT 5.1 A Skeletal Outline of the Basic Process in a Contested Divorce Case

1. The Plaintiff's attorney conducts an initial interview with the client.
2. The attorney identifies the primary issues in the case (grounds for divorce, custody, child and spousal support, property division, need for emergency orders, etc.).
3. The attorney explores the potential for mediation, counseling, etc. (This may occur at any point during the process and may occur more than once.)
4. The attorney identifies and resolves any jurisdictional questions and determines the proper forum and court in which to file the action for divorce.
5. The Plaintiff's attorney drafts and files a Complaint for Divorce on the client's behalf and also files an **Appearance**.
6. The Summons and Complaint are served on the Defendant and the Return of Service is filed with the court.
7. The Defendant files an Answer (which may include a Counterclaim for Divorce) *or* files a Motion to Dismiss and Defendant's attorney files an Appearance (General or Limited).
8. The Plaintiff and Defendant file and serve Motions for Temporary Orders and for other purposes, if appropriate (protect assets, vacate marital home, appoint appraiser or GAL, etc.).
9. The Parties conduct discovery if warranted and feasible given their assets and liabilities.
10. One or both parties draft Separation/Marital Agreement(s) for discussion.
11. The Parties/counsel engage in negotiations. (Negotiations may occur throughout the process.)
12. The Parties' counsel prepare a Separation Agreement addressing uncontested issues.
13. The Parties prepare for and attend a Pretrial Conference.
14. The Parties prepare for Trial.
15. If the case does not settle, the Trial takes place.
16. The Court issues a Decree/Judgment.
17. Follow-up matters are addressed (transfers of property, execution of QDROs, etc.).
18. The Parties file posttrial Motions and/or an Appeal, if warranted.
19. The Parties seek to enforce the Judgment, if necessary (contempt actions, etc.)
20. The Parties seek modifications of the Judgment, if appropriate, based on substantial changes in circumstances

PARALEGAL PRACTICE TIP

Although the attorneys are responsible for making the legal decisions during a divorce action, other members of the family law team are actively involved in the process and all major decisions are made with the client's consent.

The Initial Interview in a Divorce Case

An initial interview sets the tone for the working relationship between the client and the family law team. Some law firms and legal resources provide client questionnaires and interview checklists for suggested use in initial interviews. However, many practitioners find it more practical, productive, and economical to have the client complete a detailed questionnaire at home. The interview can then be used to establish a relationship with the client, obtain answers to important threshold questions, and address fundamental preliminary matters. (See Paralegal Application 5.1.) Subsequent interviews can focus in more detail on particular issues, such as the potential grounds for divorce, the nature and extent of the marital estate, completion of the financial statement, and child-related issues.

PARALEGAL PRACTICE TIP

Occasionally, clients interview a series of attorneys before retaining specific counsel. In such situations, some attorneys will conduct brief, exploratory interviews at no charge. Others will charge a flat fee or full hourly rate. Once such an interview takes place, a conflict of interest may exist should the attorney subsequently be contacted by the opposing party in the matter, a situation not uncommon in smaller communities.

Paralegal **Application 5.1**

The Client's Initial Interview with the Family Law Team

PARALEGAL PRACTICE TIP

An example of a basic client questionnaire for use in a divorce case is available at *www.pearsonhighered.com/wilson* in the companion website material related to Chapter 5 under "Resources."

An initial interview is customarily conducted by the attorney with or without the presence and assistance of the paralegal. If the paralegal does participate, he or she is usually asked to take notes and prepare an intake memorandum confirming information gathered, agreements reached, and follow-up needed. If the paralegal is asked to interview the client, the following list can be used to guide the process, but it must be customized to avoid any unauthorized practice of law. Whatever role the paralegal plays, communications within the interview are confidential.

1. Get acquainted with the client. Establish a comfortable rapport, being sensitive to the emotionally charged nature of the topics discussed, the cultural background of the client, and any unique communication issues and/or barriers. Invite the client to ask questions at any point during the interview.
2. Obtain sufficient background information about each party and any children of the marriage (including ages and current addresses) so that basic jurisdictional questions can be assessed and a thorough conflicts check can be completed.
3. Learn more about why the client has contacted the firm and what his or her short- and long-term goals are. If the client appears to have unrealistic expectations, it is useful to establish at the outset that there are no winners in divorce and no guar-

antees about the outcome, no matter how hard the team works or how much the client pays. Discuss alternatives to divorce, including legal separation and annulment (if appropriate). Ask if the parties have engaged in counseling or mediation and/or are willing to do so. The attorney may suggest such options, especially if the client appears to be uncertain about whether or not the marriage really is irretrievably broken or if mediation eventually may be required by the court.
4. If the client is intent on seeking a divorce, identify the primary reasons for doing so (e.g., Have the parties simply "grown apart"? Is one or both of them involved in a new relationship? Are there financial problems?).
5. Inquire about the spouse's knowledge of the pending action and likely response. Will the action be joint or contested? Have any prior actions been filed? Is the spouse presently represented by counsel? If so, obtain contact information. If not, is he or she likely to be?
6. Obtain a preliminary client history, basic financial information (major assets, employment of both spouses, dependence on public assistance, etc.), and additional information about any children of the marriage, such as the existence of special needs, problems, or talents. Is either party responsible for additional children from other relationships? With whom are the children residing and what arrangements exist for visitation, if any? If participation in a parent education program is recommended or required by the court, provide information about approved programs in the area.
7. Did the parties execute a pre- or postmarital agreement?

(Continued)

8. Identify any potential emergency issues. Are there any immediate financial or housing needs? If there is a history of abuse of either or both of the spouses and/or the children, have the police or social services been contacted? With what result(s)? Suggest that the client prepare a personal safety plan if abuse of either the client or the children is known or suspected.

PARALEGAL PRACTICE TIP

If there is a history of abuse, copies of relevant documents should be obtained from appropriate law enforcement and social service sources.

9. Determine whether or not there will be any immigration issues as a result of the divorce.
10. Determine if there are any religious considerations involved.
11. Describe the firm's approach to cases, the roles played by various members of the family law team, fees, and billing policies and procedures. Some attorneys address these topics at the outset before the nature and potential scope of the case are determined. However, that approach has a tendency to distract a client, who then may spend the balance of the interview quietly obsessing about cost rather than paying attention to the substance of the interview.
12. Does the client have any questions or concerns?

PARALEGAL PRACTICE TIP

Firms frequently have informational materials available for perusal in office reception areas, including, for example, "Ten Most Commonly Asked Questions About Divorce" sheets; flowcharts outlining the steps involved in the divorce process comparing contested and uncontested options; blank copies of personal safety plans for victims of abuse; lists of community resources for spouses and children; descriptions of alternative dispute resolution options; information regarding times and locations of state-approved parenting programs; blank financial statements; lists and descriptions of services available through the state's Title

IV-D agency; and blank child support guideline worksheets. The paralegal may be responsible for ensuring that such material is up-to-date and in good supply. To see an example of a "Ten Most Commonly Asked Questions About Divorce" sheet developed by an attorney, visit *www.anthonypiazza.com*. You can find a link to this site at *www.pearsonhighered.com/wilson* in the companion website material for Chapter 5 under "Resources."

If the decision is made to accept the case and the client agrees to the terms of engagement, the attorney should outline the process of getting a divorce and identify the next steps to be taken by the client and members of the family law team. A contact person at the firm should be designated (customarily the paralegal rather than the attorney, partially in an effort to control costs).

Some firms give the client "homework" assignments to complete at this point, including, but not necessarily limited to, the following:

- Complete a client questionnaire.
- Complete a preliminary financial statement for review.
- Photograph the contents of the marital home.
- Keep a daily journal highlighting matters related to the case, such as abuse, parenting and financial issues (e.g., the dissipation of marital funds).
- Gather and/or make copies of important documents such as deeds, tax returns, passports, social security cards, and bank account statements.
- Remove valuable separate property (e.g., jewelry, family heirlooms) from the marital home for safekeeping lest it mysteriously disappear!

Some firms provide (or recommend that the client create) a notebook to organize documents related to the divorce, such as pleadings, financial affidavits, court orders, and discovery requests. If desired, the paralegal may be assigned to help the client organize his or her "notebook." If nothing else, assignments and a notebook may help to create in the client a sense of some control over the process.

After the initial interview, members of the family law team will perform a number of important follow-up tasks:

Fee agreement
a contract between an attorney and a client regarding payment for the attorney's professional services

Letter of engagement
a letter from an attorney to a client confirming that the attorney agrees to represent the client in a particular legal matter

PARALEGAL PRACTICE TIP

A sample fee agreement is provided at *www.pearsonhighered.com/wilson* in the companion website material related to Chapter 1 under "Forms.".

- **Complete and execute a Fee Agreement and a letter of engagement.** The attorney must establish the fees to be charged for services performed by various members of the family law team. The paralegal may draft the agreement or "fill in the blanks" on a boilerplate fee agreement used by the firm and ensure that two originals are signed by both the client and the attorney before placing one in the office file. The second original goes to the client.

PARALEGAL PRACTICE TIP

If the prospective client decides not to retain the attorney or the attorney elects not to accept the case, a **letter of nonengagement/declination** should be drafted to confirm that decision in order to avoid any misunderstanding or a later malpractice action for failure to perform legal services. No reason needs to be given for declining the case. The person should be advised of any upcoming deadlines or matters requiring immediate attention with or without the assistance of another attorney. The paralegal may be assigned the task of drafting this letter.

Letter of nonengagement
a letter from an attorney to an individual confirming that the attorney will *not* be representing that individual with respect to a particular legal matter

- **Establish a file and a tracking system.** The paralegal usually sets up "the file" (both paper and electronic) and performs several related activities throughout the case:
  - marks all appropriate calendars with deadlines, appointment and hearing dates, etc.
  - develops a personal "tickler" (reminder) system
  - monitors follow-up activities and deadlines
  - tracks the case maintaining a chronology of activity
- **Gather preliminary information and documents necessary to shape the nature and theory of the case.** The paralegal usually assists in gathering information, working with both the client and the supervising attorney, and then collects, organizes, and maintains a comprehensive filing system with appropriate subheadings (pleadings, witnesses, discovery, financial statements, research, etc.). The attorney uses this material to develop a theory of the case: What relief will the client seek? Why is the client entitled to that relief? What law and evidence support the client's position? What is the nature of the opposing party's case and how can it be countered?
- **Determine if there is a need to seek emergency relief.** It may be determined during conversations with the client that circumstances warrant the filing of *ex parte* motions (motions without advance notice to the defendant). Some, such as a restraining order to protect the client and/or the children, to protect marital assets, or to prevent removal of the children from the jurisdiction, may need to be filed immediately. Others, such as motions for temporary custody and child support, may be filed with the complaint for divorce or shortly thereafter. The paralegal may:
  - suggest warranted forms of relief to the attorney
  - draft *ex parte* motions for review and signature (along with affidavits and proposed orders, if required)
  - help the client prepare an application for a restraining/protective order

PARALEGAL PRACTICE TIP

Visit *www.courts.wa.gov/forms.* to see a Motion for an Ex Parte Restraining Order. (Washington) You can find a link to this site at *www.pearsonhighered.com/wilson* in the companion website material for Chapter 5 under "Forms"

PARALEGAL PRACTICE TIP

To see a Petition for a Restraining Order visit *www.wicourts.gov.* (Wisconsin) A link to this site can be found at *www.pearsonhighered.com/wilson* in the companion website material for Chapter 5 under "Forms."

Dispute Resolution Options in Family Law Cases

When a divorce case proceeds to trial, the parties essentially lose control over the making of decisions affecting not only their lives but also the lives of their children, if any. Given the cost of litigation in time, money, and emotional stress, nonjudicial means of resolving differences offer the parties potentially more

PARALEGAL PRACTICE TIP

In some states, attorneys are required to certify to the court that they have advised their clients about the availability of divorce resolution alternatives to conventional litigation. To see the certification form used in New Jersey that must be signed by both attorney and client, visit *www.judiciary.state. nj.us.* A link to this site can be found at *www.pearsonhighered.com/wilson* in the companion website material for Chapter 5 under "Forms."

Alternative dispute resolution (ADR)
a procedure for settling a dispute by means other than litigation, such as mediation or arbitration

PARALEGAL PRACTICE TIP

When the parties are having trouble resolving disputes relating to custody or property division, etc., a party may ask the court to order mediation. To see a form used for this purpose in Wisconsin, visit *www.wicourts.gov.* A link to this site can be found at *www. pearsonhighered.com/wilson* in the companion website material for Chapter 5 under "Forms."

Parenting coordinators
individuals, usually appointed by the court, who assist with design and implementation of parenting agreements and enforcement of decrees in high-conflict cases involving minor children

PARALEGAL PRACTICE TIP

In direct negotiation, attorneys are usually not involved until contacted by the parties when they have already reached their own agreement, or as many of its elements as they can.

Mediation
an approach to resolving differences in which a neutral third person helps the parties identify their differences, consider their options, and structure a mutually acceptable agreement

productive alternatives that allow them to exercise more control over both the process and the end result. Although the alternatives to litigation also carry a price tag, they are usually considerably less costly financially. They are also more likely to lead to a mutually agreed-upon resolution of the parties' differences in a fraction of the time a fully litigated case would take. In addition, the rules governing most alternative dispute resolution (ADR) proceedings require, with limited exceptions, that information shared in that context remains confidential. On the other hand, court proceedings are open to the public, and most documents filed become part of a public record.

The courts strongly encourage the use of **alternative dispute resolution (ADR)** options, sometimes explicitly in court rules or standing orders (as in Texas). In some circumstances they require participation in court-affiliated mediation services, particularly with respect to child-related issues. In Massachusetts, attorneys are required to sign a statement that they have advised their clients of the availability of court-facilitated mediation.

ADR options can be used at any stage of the process. More than one option may be used and on more than one occasion, if desired. However, the earlier they are used, the more effective they are likely to be. Research also shows higher levels of satisfaction and compliance with mediated agreements than with litigated decrees. In the short run, the parties each play a greater role in shaping the outcome of their case and, in the long run, in shaping their futures. There are several dispute resolution alternatives to litigation in the family law context. The most common methods are identified and described in Exhibit 5.2.

PARALEGAL PRACTICE TIP

An emerging option for alternative dispute resolution in family law cases is parenting coordination. **Parenting coordinators** have a limited scope of responsibility. They are most commonly appointed by a court to deal with design and implementation of parenting agreements in high-conflict cases and cases in which children may be at risk. Parenting coordinators mediate disputes and, in some instances, are granted limited decision-making authority in an effort to reduce the number of return trips to court. To see a sample Motion to Appoint a Parenting Coordinator visit *http://www.utcourts.gov/howto/family/.* You can find a link to this site at *www.pearsonhighered.com/wilson* in the companion website material for Chapter 5 under "Forms."

EXHIBIT 5.2 Common Methods of Alternative Dispute Resolution in Family Law Cases

- **Direct negotiation between the parties.** The parties negotiate directly with each other in person, by telephone, and by mail (including e-mail). They initially operate without the assistance of any professional, legal or otherwise, in an effort to reach as many terms of their agreement as possible. Because of the power imbalance in the relationship, direct negotiation usually is not appropriate in high-conflict cases or cases in which there is a history of abuse between the parties.
- **Mediation.** The parties may participate in **mediation** voluntarily or be ordered to do so by the court. In this process, a neutral third person, called a mediator, facilitates discussion of issues and negotiation between the parties and occasionally their attorneys. Typically, the mediation takes place in one or a series of face-to-face meetings, as needed. Occasionally the mediator will "caucus" with each client individually within a session. The primary role of the mediator is to overcome barriers that prevent the parties from reaching agreement. Mediators focus on resolving issues rather than on winning and losing. The role of the parties' attorneys in mediation varies. Whether they actually attend and participate in the sessions or not, attorneys commonly brief their clients about the process, help define issues and goals

EXHIBIT 5.2 (*Continued*)

for the mediation, and act as consultants before and after the sessions. They also review any draft agreements from the mediation before they are executed. Most attorneys and mediators do not consider mediation an appropriate option when there is a continuing history of concealing or destroying assets and/or abuse between the parties.

PARALEGAL PRACTICE TIP

The attorney's role is different from the mediator's in the sense that an attorney has an ethical duty to advocate zealously for the client and obtain the most favorable settlement possible. The mediator, on the other hand, is impartial, does not advocate the position of either side, and is committed to reaching a "fair deal," one that will serve both parties and the family as a whole in the long run. Given these differences, the roles of the mediator and attorney may work at cross-purposes in the mediation context.

- **Collaborative law.** Collaborative law "combines the positive problem-solving focus of mediation with the built-in lawyer advocacy and counsel of traditional settlement-oriented representation. . . . In collaborative practice, specially trained lawyers agree to represent clients in negotiating a divorce with both parties and their lawyers committing to settle the case without litigation. While the clients cannot be prohibited from later switching to litigation, the lawyers are disqualified from representation should that happen."[1]

- **Negotiation through counsel.** This is the traditional and most common model of negotiating divorce settlements. Proposals (written and/or oral) are usually exchanged between the attorneys until an agreement is reached or the parties come to an impasse with respect to unresolved issues. The parties participate in the process mostly through counsel and occasionally in four-way conferences (sometimes mandated by the court). Initial proposals rarely reflect the parties' bottom lines, and the negotiation process frequently involves considerable give-and-take and a series of compromises before a settlement is reached. Each topic may be addressed separately, but usually no agreement is finalized on a single major issue until a comprehensive agreement is reached.

PARALEGAL PRACTICE TIP

Four-way meetings can be productive, but clients should be prepared for them in advance. Which issues will be discussed at the meeting? What are the client's goals with respect to those issues? Where is there room for compromise? What is the other side likely to propose? What kind of response will be called for? How should the client conduct himself or herself?

- **Neutral case evaluation.** This option is customarily used later in the process, after completion of discovery and the parties' positions have been on the table for some time. Although those positions may have crystallized, there is a strong incentive for the parties to settle, given the stress and expense associated with an imminent trial. In a **neutral case evaluation,** an experienced trial attorney or judge provides the parties with a reality check. The evaluator listens to a summary of the conflict by each side and offers an opinion about settlement potential and a prediction about the likely outcome if the matter proceeds to trial. The evaluator then makes an attempt to resolve the case.

PARALEGAL PRACTICE TIP

Depending on how far the case has proceeded, the attorneys will provide various documents to the evaluator in advance of the actual case evaluation session(s), including the complaint and the answer, the parties' financial statements, pretrial memoranda, and the like. The attorneys may or may not attend the actual meeting(s). Whether they attend or not, they customarily brief their clients regarding the nature of the process, its goals, and the potential alternative outcomes.

(*Continued*)

Collaborative law
an approach to reaching agreements and resolving differences that stresses cooperation, joint problem solving, and the avoidance of litigation

Neutral case evaluation
a process in which a neutral third party, usually an experienced trial attorney or judge, listens to the parties' positions and offers an opinion about settlement potential and the likely outcome if the matter proceeds to trial

EXHIBIT 5.2 (*Continued*)

Arbitration

a process in which one or more neutral third persons who are trained arbitrators hear arguments, review evidence, and render a decision with respect to the issues selected for arbitration by the parties involved in a dispute

Binding arbitration

arbitration in which the parties agree to abide by the arbitrator's decision as final and unappealable

Nonbinding arbitration

arbitration in which the parties are free to accept or reject the arbitrator's decision

- **Arbitration.** In **arbitration,** one or more neutral third parties who are trained arbitrators hear arguments, review evidence, and render a decision with respect to the issues identified by the parties for arbitration. The arbitrator is often an attorney and is usually affiliated with a professional organization such as the American Arbitration Association. Arbitration is used less frequently than mediation prior to divorce. It is used more commonly post divorce pursuant to a dispute resolution provision in the parties' separation agreement in which they agree to submit certain kinds of disputes to arbitration if they cannot be resolved by the parties or with assistance of counsel. In **binding arbitration,** the parties agree to abide by the arbitrator's decision. In **nonbinding arbitration,** the parties can accept or reject the decision. In the context of the actual arbitration, the attorney presents the client's position and the evidence. The parties may testify and respond to questions from both counsel and the arbitrator. Any decision reached by the arbitrator remains subject to review by the court, which usually is unwilling to relinquish its decision-making authority, particularly with respect to child-related issues.[2] However, with respect to other kinds of issues, courts usually will not disturb an award that results from binding arbitration unless the arbitration process itself was flawed in some manner, such as by fraud or corruption.

PARALEGAL PRACTICE TIP

The parties' attorneys describe the process to their clients and assist them in shaping the arbitration in advance to some extent by recommending the arbitrator, identifying the questions to be addressed, and limiting the range of remedies the arbitrator can consider. The parties can also decide whether the arbitration will be binding or nonbinding.

The paralegal's role in the alternative dispute resolution context generally includes the following:

- being familiar with the various forms of dispute resolution utilized in the jurisdiction
- maintaining lists of local ADR specialists, with pertinent information on each
- preparing any required forms
- scheduling ADR sessions/meetings
- helping the attorney prepare for conferences/meetings
- attending settlement meetings to listen and take notes on the parties' respective positions and any agreements reached
- communicating with ADR resources and arranging for payment
- drafting agreements based on understandings reached by the parties in various forms of ADR
- drafting provisions relating to dispute resolution for inclusion in separation agreements

Jurisdictional Issues in Divorce Actions—What Is the Proper Forum?

Jurisdictional questions must be addressed at the outset of every case. In many instances, the answers are straightforward: The parties and their children live in the same county within a single state, own no real estate, and possess minimal personal property. In others, the answers are far more complex and eventually may have to be resolved by the court. For example, the whereabouts of a party may be unknown or the parties may live in different states and have three children, two of whom are residing with the father and one with the mother; and each may own personal property, real estate, and business interests in multiple states. The paralegal's role with respect to jurisdictional issues usually involves researching the applicable statutory and governing case law and gathering the facts needed by the attorney to determine where a given action should be filed. In complex situations, the law of multiple states will need to be researched along with potential **conflict-of-law** issues.

Jurisdiction in a family law case is primarily a matter of state law and procedure subject to overriding federal constitutional limitations as interpreted by the U.S. Supreme Court. From a jurisdictional perspective, there are basically two facets of divorce actions: (1) dissolution of the marital status and (2) corollary matters, such as division of the marital estate (property division), custody, and support issues. Most divorce actions involve both facets. In these cases, the court hearing the matter needs to have subject matter jurisdiction over family law matters, personal jurisdiction over both of the parties, and *in rem* jurisdiction over the property in dispute. (See Exhibit 5.3.)

Conflict of law
a conflict arising out of a difference between the laws of two jurisdictions, such as two states or two nations

EXHIBIT 5.3 Jurisdiction in Divorce Actions

Type of Jurisdiction	How It Is Acquired	What the Court Can Do
Subject matter jurisdiction is the authority of a court to hear and decide a particular type of claim or controversy.	Subject matter jurisdiction is conferred by a state statute authorizing the court to hear and decide divorce actions. It cannot be created by agreement of the parties.	A court can hear divorce actions if authorized to do so by state statute provided (a) the plaintiff satisfies the state's applicable residency requirements, if any, and (b) the defendant is given proper notice of the action and an opportunity to be heard.
Personal jurisdiction is the authority of the court to issue and enforce orders binding a particular individual.	In order for the court to exercise personal jurisdiction over a defendant, he or she must have notice of the action and an opportunity to be heard. Personal jurisdiction is acquired over a defendant by personal service of process, consent, or substituted service (e.g., by mail or publication in a newspaper) or under a state's long-arm statute if the defendant is a nonresident who has sufficient minimum contacts with the state.	The court can issue enforceable orders binding a defendant in a divorce action regarding alimony, child support, and property division.
***In rem* jurisdiction** is the authority a court has over a thing (including the marital status of the plaintiff in some states) rather than over a person.	A state court can exercise its powers over property located inside of that state's boundaries. In order to acquire *in rem* jurisdiction over a marital status, the plaintiff must be domiciled in the state and reasonable notice of the action must be given to the defendant by a means authorized by state statute.	The court can issue orders affecting the parties' property located within the state's boundaries. However, even if the court has personal jurisdiction over a defendant, the court's power to distribute marital property located outside of the state may be limited.

Subject matter jurisdiction
the authority of a court to hear and decide a particular kind of claim or controversy

Personal jurisdiction
the authority of a court to issue and enforce orders binding a particular individual; sometimes called *in personam* jurisdiction

***In rem* jurisdiction**
the authority a court has over a property or thing rather than over persons located within its jurisdictional borders

When the plaintiff satisfies applicable residency requirements, the appropriate court will be able to exercise subject matter jurisdiction over dissolution of the marriage, even if the defendant is beyond the reach of the court, provided he or she is given proper notice. The subject matter is the marital status of the plaintiff. It is the basic "thing" being addressed in the action. It is possessed by each of the spouses and exists, for jurisdictional purposes, in any state where either of the spouses resides. Other related matters, such as property division and child-related issues, may also be addressed only if additional jurisdictional requirements are met.

Although it is not favored, occasionally a court may be willing to divide or bifurcate a divorce proceeding under unusual circumstances (such as advanced age or illness). In a **bifurcated divorce,** the court dissolves the marriage but does not adjudicate other issues, such as support, custody, and property division. It may reserve jurisdiction over those issues until a later date or leave them to be determined by the courts of another state that has jurisdiction over the defendant, the marital property, and/or the parties' children.

In this chapter we are concerned with jurisdiction as it relates to actions for divorce in particular and specifically with the answers to the following five questions as they apply in an individual case:

1. Does the plaintiff satisfy the state's residency requirements?
2. Which court has subject matter jurisdiction over divorce and related matters?
3. Does the court have personal (*in personam*) jurisdiction over the defendant?
4. Does the court have *in rem* jurisdiction over the property involved in the action?
5. In which specific court should the complaint for divorce be filed—i.e., where is venue proper?

DOES THE PLAINTIFF SATISFY THE STATE'S RESIDENCY REQUIREMENTS?

Each state as a sovereign has a rightful and legitimate concern in the marital status of persons domiciled within its borders. . . . it is plain that each state can alter within its own borders the marriage status of the spouse domiciled there, even though the other spouse is absent.[3]

In order to file for divorce in a particular state, the general rule is that one of the parties must satisfy its domicile or residency requirement for bringing such actions. There is considerable variation in residency requirements, ranging from six weeks in states such as Idaho and Nevada to six months in Pennsylvania, and one year in approximately one-fifth of the states, including, for example, Rhode Island and Iowa. Even when there is a basic residency requirement, however, there are frequently exceptions that may or may not work to the client's advantage. For example, in Maryland, there is no residency requirement unless the cause of the marital breakdown occurred outside of the state (one year) or if the ground for the action is insanity (two years). Tennessee and Massachusetts have residency requirements of six months and one year, respectively, unless the party bringing the action is domiciled in the state and the cause of the marital breakdown arose within the state, in which case there is no requirement. Some states, such as Texas and California, also have county residency requirements.

The U.S. Supreme Court speaks of **domicile** when addressing the issue of a state's power to dissolve a marriage. The states speak in terms of residency (or, in some instances, both domicile and residency). The distinctions can be confusing and have occasionally led to challenges with respect to the validity of a divorce.

Bifurcated divorce
a divorce in which the dissolution of marriage is resolved in one proceeding, and all other issues, such as property division and child custody, are resolved in one or more later, separate proceedings in the same or another state

Domicile
a person's legal residence; the place one considers his or her permanent home and to which he or she intends to return when away

Your domicile is the place you consider your permanent home and to which you intend to return when away. Your residence may, in fact, be your domicile. However, you may have several residences where you reside on occasion, but only one domicile. Where one is domiciled is a question of law and fact. The court will look at several factors when determining an individual's domicile, such as:

- how long the person has resided in a particular state
- whether the person has a long-term lease on the property where he or she is living
- whether the party owns property in the state
- where the party votes
- which state issued the party's driver's license
- where his or her car is registered and serviced
- where he or she pays income taxes
- what his or her mailing address is for billing purposes
- where the person is employed
- whether the person is an employee-at-will or has a long-term employment contract
- where the person's extended family lives

WHICH COURT HAS SUBJECT MATTER JURISDICTION OVER DIVORCE AND RELATED MATTERS?

"Subject matter jurisdiction" refers to a court's authority to hear and render a decision with respect to a particular type of case. All divorce matters are brought in state rather than federal courts. Subject matter jurisdiction is conferred by state statutes and the parties cannot confer it on a court by agreement. Each state determines the court authorized to grant divorces within its jurisdiction. In many states, there are specialized family courts, and in others, divorce actions are heard in courts of general jurisdiction, such as superior courts, chancery courts, circuit courts, or courts of common pleas that hear other kinds of matters as well. A court can have subject matter jurisdiction sufficient to dissolve a marriage, even if it lacks personal jurisdiction over a defendant, as long as the plaintiff is domiciled in the state. It is the plaintiff's relationship with the state where the action is filed that matters. However, if a plaintiff travels to another state solely for the purpose of obtaining a divorce, the defendant-spouse, particularly one who did not receive actual notice of the action, may be able to attack the validity of the divorce decree for lack of proper subject matter jurisdiction.

DOES THE COURT HAVE PERSONAL (*IN PERSONAM*) JURISDICTION OVER THE DEFENDANT?

It has long been the rule that a valid judgment imposing a personal obligation or duty in favor of the plaintiff may be entered only by a court having jurisdiction over the person of the defendant. The existence of personal jurisdiction, in turn, depends upon the presence of reasonable notice to the defendant that an action has been brought and a sufficient connection between the defendant and the forum State as to make it fair to require defense of the action in the forum. (Citations omitted.)[4]

In order for a court to issue an order that will be enforceable against a particular defendant (such as an order for property division or spousal support), it must have personal jurisdiction over that defendant. Given the Fourteenth Amendment's

PARALEGAL PRACTICE TIP

The jurisdictional rules governing child custody and support actions are addressed in Chapters 8, 9, and 10.

Long-arm statute

a statute setting forth the circumstances in which a state may exercise personal jurisdiction over a nonresident defendant; identifies the minimum contacts a defendant must have with the state where the statute is in effect

PARALEGAL PRACTICE TIP

To see a survey of long-arm statutes in all fifty states, Google "Long-Arm Statutes: A Fifty-State Survey."

PARALEGAL PRACTICE TIP

Phrasing can be critically important not only in court orders but also in requests for relief. The client wants to ask the court to order actions which are within its power to order.

PARALEGAL PRACTICE TIP

The opinion in the *Russo* case can be accessed at *www.pearsonhighered.com/wilson* in the companion website material related to Chapter 5 under "Cases" and in the Case Resources Section of the MyLegalStudiesLab.

The *Russo* case provides an example of how important phrasing can be when requesting relief involving the disposition of out-of-state property in a divorce.

requirements of due process and procedural fairness, a defendant is entitled to reasonable notice and an opportunity to be heard in the matter at issue and is also protected from being hailed into court in a state with which he or she has no connection. There are four primary means of acquiring personal jurisdiction over a defendant in a domestic relations proceeding that are consistent with due process requirements:

- **Presence.** Personal service of process on a nonresident defendant while physically present in the state as a temporary resident, visitor, or otherwise. The U.S. Supreme Court has held that a nonresident of a state is subject to the jurisdiction of that state if he is properly served while physically present in the state.[5]
- **Domicile.** Actual service of process or substituted (or constructive) service over a defendant who is domiciled in the state by publication in the paper and mailing the summons and complaint to the defendant's last known address.
- **Consent.** The defendant, even a nonresident defendant, may voluntarily consent to the court's jurisdiction by accepting service or by appearing and defending the action.
- **Minimum contacts.** Each state has a **long-arm statute** that identifies the kinds of minimum contacts a nonresident defendant may have with the state that are sufficient to give rise to personal jurisdiction over a nonresident defendant with notice of the action. The focus is usually on more recent contacts. The basic premise is that it is fair and reasonable to exercise personal jurisdiction in certain circumstances. State statutes vary but generally include provisions such as the following (some of which are tailored to domestic relations cases):
  - The defendant conducts business in the state.
  - The defendant contracts to provide services in the state.
  - The defendant has caused tortious injury by an act or omission in the state.
  - The defendant has an interest in real property located within the state.
  - The defendant has maintained a residence in the state (most often a marital residence).
  - The defendant is subject to an order of alimony, property division, parentage of a child, child custody, or child support issued by a court in the state.
  - The litigation relates to some action of the nonresident defendant within the state.
  - The defendant had sexual relations in the state that may have resulted in the birth of a child to the parties.

DOES THE COURT HAVE *IN REM* JURISDICTION OVER THE PROPERTY INVOLVED IN THE ACTION?

A state court with subject matter jurisdiction has authority over real property located within the state's boundaries and can issue orders with respect to that property. A court can distribute property within its jurisdiction pursuant to a divorce decree, but if the property in dispute is immovable (such as a piece of real estate or mining rights) and is located in another state, the court's powers may be limited.

The *Russo* case[6] provides an illustration of what can be subtle differences in interpreting and applying personal and *in rem* jurisdiction. In *Russo*, a Pennsylvania trial court ordered the parties to sell real property located in the state of Ohio and divide the proceeds. The defendant husband appealed that portion of the divorce judgment, alleging that the court lacked jurisdiction to distribute property located outside of Pennsylvania. The husband argued that jurisdiction extended only to property located in Pennsylvania and that a Pennsylvania court could not exercise *in rem* jurisdiction over real or personal property located outside the state. The appellate court held that when the trial court ordered the parties to sell the Ohio property, it was not exercising *in rem* jurisdiction over the property. Rather, it was ordering the parties, over whom it had personal jurisdiction, to sell the property and distribute the proceeds.

Paralegal Application 5.2

Jurisdictional Issues—What Do You Think?

Case 1 Fact Pattern

The parties in this case were married in Connecticut in 1979. In 1999, the wife filed for divorce in Connecticut, where she was domiciled. Her husband had left Connecticut in 1985. The parties had married, had a child, and received public assistance for several years in Connecticut. They had also filed joint tax returns in that state. The wife saw the husband when he visited family members in Connecticut in 1986 and 1989 but had not seen him since. The wife filed for divorce in Connecticut. The divorce was awarded, along with alimony and counsel fees. The husband appealed, claiming the court lacked personal jurisdiction over him.

Sidebar

Do you think it was fair and reasonable for the Connecticut court to exercise personal jurisdiction over the defendant? Why? Read the opinion in *Panganiban v. Panganiban*, 736 A.2d 190 (Conn. Ct. App. 1999) and see if you agree with the court's decision.

PARALEGAL PRACTICE TIP

The *Panganiban* opinion can be accessed at *www.pearsonhighered.com/wilson* in the companion website material related to Chapter 5 under "Cases" and in the Case Resources Section of the MyLegalStudiesLab.

Case 2 Fact Pattern

In 1987, a wife who was domiciled in Virginia went to Hawaii to marry a man who was a U.S. Marine stationed there. The parties subsequently lived at duty stations in Virginia Beach, Virginia, from 1996 to 1999 and in Guantanamo Bay for a year, at which time the husband was reassigned to Camp Pendleton in California. The wife, initially without the husband's knowledge, decided to return to live in Virginia because of the husband's admitted infidelity and a generally deteriorating marital relationship. She filed for divorce in Virginia and the husband was served with the summons and complaint while he was in Virginia visiting with the parties' children. The husband claimed that the Virginia court lacked both subject matter and personal jurisdiction. He alleged that neither party qualified as a bona fide resident or domiciliary of Virginia and that the court lacked personal jurisdiction over him because he was fraudulently induced to come to Virginia by the actions of the wife and would not have been there otherwise. The wife asserted that for purposes of subject matter jurisdiction, both parties were bona fide residents of Virginia based on the following evidence:

- One of the family's vehicles was still registered, licensed, and titled in Virginia.
- Each of them possessed a Virginia driver's license while they lived in Cuba.
- They held accounts in Virginia banks.
- The wife had a brother, sister, and brother-in-law living in Virginia.
- Prior to her marriage, the wife filed taxes in Virginia.
- The parties lived in Virginia for three years prior to moving to Cuba, and the wife returned to Virginia to reestablish her residency.
- When she left Virginia to go to Cuba, the wife left solely because of her husband's military orders.

Under Virginia law, the issue of subject matter jurisdiction requires a determination of the plaintiff's domicile and bona fide residency in the state of Virginia for at least six months prior to the filing of the action for divorce.

Sidebar

In your opinion, did the Virginia court have subject matter jurisdiction sufficient to dissolve the marriage? Why? Do you think the court properly exercised personal jurisdiction over the defendant? Explain your response. Read the opinion in *Blackson v. Blackson*, 579 S.E.2d 704 (Va. Ct. App. 2003) to see if you agree with the court's decision.

PARALEGAL PRACTICE TIP

The *Blackson* opinion can be accessed at *www.pearsonhighered.com/wilson* in the companion website material related to Chapter 5 under "Cases" and in the Case Resources Section of the MyLegalStudiesLab.

IN WHICH SPECIFIC COURT SHOULD THE COMPLAINT FOR DIVORCE BE FILED?

Venue
refers to the geographical location within which a particular action should be filed

This question asks where venue will be proper. **Venue** refers to the particular geographical location within the state where the action should be filed—in which city, town, or county. As with subject matter and personal jurisdiction, the states establish rules governing venue. Typically, in a divorce action, venue will be proper in the county where the defendant resides, where the plaintiff resides, or where the parties last resided together as husband and wife.

Grounds for Divorce

Ground for divorce
the reason for filing the action, the basis on which relief is sought in a divorce action; may be either a fault or no-fault ground

Divorce is a creature of statute, and each state establishes its own **grounds for divorce,** the reasons it considers sufficient to warrant the termination of a marriage. The statutory scheme in Tennessee (see Exhibit 5.4) is one of the most comprehensive. Similar to divorce statutes in just over 60% of the states, it includes

PARALEGAL PRACTICE TIP

In several of the states, some of the statutory grounds for divorce are also potential grounds for annulment, such as impotency (e.g., in Massachusetts), bigamy (e.g., in Ohio), and fraud (e.g., in Connecticut).

EXHIBIT 5.4 Tenn. Code Ann. § 36–4–101. Grounds for Divorce from Bonds of Matrimony

FROM THE STATUTE

The following are causes of divorce from the bonds of matrimony:

1. Either party, at the time of the contract, was and still is naturally impotent and incapable of procreation;
2. Either party has knowingly entered into a second marriage, in violation of a previous marriage, still subsisting;
3. Either party has committed adultery;
4. Willful or malicious desertion or absence of either party, without a reasonable cause, for one (1) whole year;
5. Being convicted of any crime that, by the laws of the state, renders the party infamous;
6. Being convicted of a crime that, by the laws of the state, is declared to be a felony, and sentenced to confinement in the penitentiary;
7. Either party has attempted the life of the other by poison or any other means showing malice;
8. Refusal, on the part of a spouse, to remove with that person's spouse to this state, without a reasonable cause, and being willfully absent from the spouse residing in Tennessee for two (2) years;
9. The woman was pregnant at the time of the marriage, by another person, without the knowledge of the husband;
10. Habitual drunkenness or abuse of narcotic drugs of either party, when the spouse has contracted either such habit after marriage;
11. The husband or wife is guilty of such cruel and inhuman treatment or conduct towards the spouse as renders cohabitation unsafe and improper, which may also be referred to in pleadings as inappropriate marital conduct;
12. The husband or wife has offered such indignities to the spouse's person as to render the spouse's position intolerable, and thereby forced the spouse to withdraw;
13. The husband or wife has abandoned the spouse or turned the spouse out of doors for no just cause, and has refused or neglected to provide for the spouse while having the ability to so provide;
14. Irreconcilable differences between the parties; and
15. For a continuous period of two (2) or more years that commenced prior to or after April 18, 1985, both parties have lived in separate residences, have not cohabited as man and wife during such period, and there are no minor children of the parties.

both no-fault grounds (e.g., irreconcilable differences or living separate and apart) and fault grounds (e.g., adultery or cruel and abusive treatment). Most divorces are granted on a no-fault basis. Although no-fault divorce is generally less costly, both emotionally and financially, some clients insist on pursuing fault grounds for personal reasons such as anger, revenge, and a desire to publicly establish themselves as "blameless" for the failure of the marriage.

NO-FAULT GROUNDS

No-fault grounds for divorce are grounds that do not require a party to prove that the other party is to "blame" for the breakdown of the marriage. Marital misconduct is largely irrelevant. Each state establishes its own no-fault grounds or standards, and approximately 40% of the states have eliminated fault grounds entirely and have only a single no-fault standard. The two most common no-fault grounds are:

- irreconcilable differences
- living separate and apart

PARALEGAL PRACTICE TIP

To see a statute in a state that has no fault grounds and grants divorces solely when there is "an irretrievable breakdown of the marriage relationship" see the Minnesota statute at *www.mncourts.gov*. You can find a link to this site at *www.pearsonhighered.com/wilson* in the companion website material for Chapter 5 under "Statutes."

PARALEGAL PRACTICE TIP

When parties have entered a **covenant marriage**, a no-fault divorce is generally not an option. Arizona provides an interesting example of a state that is a "no-fault" state but because it recognizes "covenant marriages" that usually can be dissolved only on fault grounds, it has a statute specifically addressing grounds for dissolution of a covenant marriage. To see that statute, visit *www.azleg.gov*. You can find a link to this site at *www.pearsonhighered.com/wilson* in the companion website material for Chapter 5 under "Statutes."

Irreconcilable Differences (Also Called Irretrievable or Irremediable Breakdown of the Marriage or Incompatibility)

Whatever it may be called, the core of **irreconcilable differences** as a ground for divorce is that the marriage has broken down and is beyond repair, and one or both of the parties want to terminate it. Some jurisdictions require that the parties actually live separate and apart for a period of time prior to filing. Others recognize the economic challenges faced by many divorcing spouses and allow the parties to continue living under the same roof, provided they do not engage in "marital relations" during the period of "separation." When this ground is alleged on an uncontested or joint basis, the court's inquiry is generally limited. The parties may be asked to briefly describe the nature of the differences that have caused the breakdown, approximately how long they have persisted, whether the parties have sought counseling or participated in some form of alternative dispute resolution in an effort to resolve their differences and save the marriage, and whether they believe the marriage has irretrievably broken down.

If a divorce action on this ground is contested, proof must be presented regarding the nature and extent of the parties' differences that have resulted in the alleged breakdown of the marriage. The breakdown may be due to an inability to communicate, or to serious disagreements between the parties about finances, childrearing issues, value systems, or marital priorities, or the parties may simply have grown apart and developed such divergent interests and incompatible lifestyles that they can no longer live together in a "normal" marital relationship. Whatever the explanation, the court's task is to determine that the marriage is beyond repair without examining the individual conduct of the parties in fault terms.

Covenant marriage
a type of marriage that emphasizes the permanence of marriage; a kind of marriage in which the parties participate in counseling prior to the marriage, accept marriage as a lifelong commitment, and agree not to seek a divorce absent a total and complete breach of the marriage covenant

Irreconcilable differences
a no-fault ground for divorce, the essence of which is that the marriage has irreparably broken down due to serious differences between the parties

PARALEGAL PRACTICE TIP

From a practical perspective, if one of the parties is intent on obtaining a divorce and the other is adamantly opposed, the breakdown is self-evident. However, that alone may not be seen by the court as enough.

Living Separate and Apart for a Specified Period of Time

The essence of this no-fault ground is that the marriage has broken down and, as a result, the parties are **living separate and apart**. Marital fault is essentially irrelevant as long as the parties have lived apart for the requisite period of time. There is considerable variation in state statutes with respect to the length of time the parties must have lived separate and apart (commonly from one to three years), whether the period of separation must be uninterrupted by attempts at reconciliation, whether the parties are living apart pursuant to a court order, whether the decision to separate is mutual, whether the separation is voluntary (e.g., not due to incarceration, hospitalization, or military service), and whether or not the parties must actually have lived under separate roofs.

When this ground is alleged and contested, evidence should be produced to establish the nature and length of the separation. This is accomplished through the testimony of witnesses familiar with the parties' living arrangements and documents such as leases, rent receipts, and telephone bills.

Living separate and apart
a no-fault ground for divorce based on the fact that, due to a breakdown of the marriage, the parties have lived apart from each other for a requisite period of time

PARALEGAL PRACTICE TIP

A single divorce action may involve assertion of multiple alternative grounds by one or both parties. In a Virginia case, for example, the husband alleged four fault grounds (desertion, adultery, sodomy, and cruelty) and the wife cross-complained, alleging no-fault grounds. See *Jones v. Jones,* 2004 Va. App. LEXIS 455. The trial court's decree awarded the divorce to the wife, finding that the parties had lived separate and apart for more than the required one-year period.

PARALEGAL PRACTICE TIP

Paralegals need to familiarize themselves with the applicable rules and statutes in their respective jurisdictions so they are aware of specific requirements. The applicable Utah statute, for example, provides for a divorce on this ground "when the husband and wife have lived separately under a decree of separate maintenance of any state for three consecutive years without cohabitation."[7]

FAULT GROUNDS

The most common fault grounds include:

- adultery
- desertion/abandonment
- cruelty
- habitual drunkenness or drug abuse
- criminal conviction and incarceration

Adultery

Adultery as a ground for divorce commonly means voluntary sexual intercourse between a married person and a person other than his or her spouse, usually called the co-respondent. However, the language in state statutes varies. If the statute specifies intercourse with a "person other than the spouse," then it may encompass adultery committed with a person of either sex. If the statute is silent on this point, the courts usually look to relevant case law and/or criminal statutes. (See Paralegal Application 5.3.) A majority of the states that have addressed this issue have concluded that adultery is not limited to heterosexual intercourse.

Adultery
voluntary sexual intercourse between a married person and a person other than his or her spouse; a fault ground for divorce recognized in some states

Criminal conversation
a tort action for adultery brought against a third party who has sexual intercourse with another's spouse; abolished as a cause of action in most jurisdictions

PARALEGAL PRACTICE TIP

On rare occasions, a wronged spouse may bring a tort action for **criminal conversation** against a third party who has committed adultery with the plaintiff's spouse.

PARALEGAL PRACTICE TIP

In some jurisdictions, if adultery is alleged, the name of the alleged co-respondent must be provided in the complaint for divorce, and the individual must be served. In others, the adultery may be alleged, but in order to name the third party, the petitioner must file a motion with the court for permission to disclose the name. The latter approach helps to reduce the number of baseless and malicious allegations. To see the New Hampshire statute regarding service on the co-respondent go to *www.gencourt.state. nh.us*. You can find a link to this site at *www.pearsonhighered.com/wilson* in the companion website material for Chapter 5 under "Statutes."

Some states require that in order to claim adultery, both the petitioner and the respondent must be residents of the state where the divorce action is brought. Most states require that adultery involve actual sexual intercourse, although, because of its nature, the act usually may be proved by circumstantial evidence. Mere suspicions or the opportunity to commit adultery is not enough. Evidence of an "adulterous disposition" is usually established by evidence such as public displays of intimacy observed by others, e-mails and other forms of correspondence referencing sexual activity, unexplained absences and travel, and contracting of a venereal disease. In some states, the circumstantial evidence must be substantial, such as when a wife gives birth to a child genetically unrelated to her husband.

Paralegal Application 5.3

Adultery—Does the Sex of the Partner Matter?

When adultery is alleged, does it make any difference whether the extramarital relationship is with a partner of the same sex? A majority of the courts that have addressed the issue have held that it does not. Those courts have found that from the perspective of the injured spouse, an extramarital relationship is just as devastating whatever the specific sexual acts performed by the promiscuous spouse and regardless of the sex of the co-respondent. Some have opined that a homosexual affair may be even more devastating.

The minority view on this issue is reflected in a New Hampshire case, *In the Matter of Blanchflower and Blanchflower*, 150 N.H. 226, 834 A.2d 1010 (2003), decided before that state implemented its civil union legislation in 2008 and same-sex marriage in 2010. In the *Blanchflower* case, a husband sued for divorce on the ground of adultery, alleging that his wife had engaged in a "continuing adulterous affair" with the co-respondent, a woman, resulting in the irremediable breakdown of the parties' marriage. The co-respondent sought to dismiss the petition, contending that a homosexual relationship between two people, one of whom is married, did not constitute adultery under the state statute. The trial court disagreed but the New Hampshire Supreme Court agreed. Before addressing the merits, the court insisted

that the case was not about the status of homosexual relationships in our society or the formal recognition of homosexual unions but rather addressed only the narrow question of whether a homosexual relationship between a married person and another constituted adultery within the meaning of RSA 458:7, II.

Because the statute did not define adultery, the court chose to rely on dictionary definitions and an analogy to the state's criminal statute in reaching its decision. The court opined that according to Webster's Dictionary, the plain and ordinary meaning of adultery is "voluntary sexual intercourse between a married man and someone other than his wife or between a married woman and someone other than her husband." *Webster's Third New International Dictionary 30* (unabridged ed., 1961). Although the definition did not specifically state that the "someone" with whom one commits adultery must be of the opposite gender, it did require sexual intercourse (coitus), and coitus was defined as requiring "insertion of the penis into the vagina." The state's criminal adultery statute also required sexual intercourse: "A person is guilty of a class B misdemeanor if, being a married person, he engages in sexual intercourse with another not his spouse or, being unmarried, engages in sexual intercourse with another known by him to be

(Continued)

married." RSA 645:3. The court declined to read into the statute that the adultery fault ground is based upon the fundamental concept of marital loyalty and public policy's disfavor of one spouse's violation of the marriage contract by engaging in acts of a sexual nature with another, be they heterosexual or homosexual. It held that to do otherwise would preempt the legislature's role in matters of public policy and change beyond recognition a well-established ground for divorce resulting in countless new marital cases alleging adultery for strategic purposes. The dissent opined that consistent with the overall purpose of New Hampshire's fault-based divorce law, the word "adultery" in RSA 458:7 II should be interpreted to mean a spouse's extramarital intimate sexual activity with another, regardless of the specific intimate sexual act performed, the marital status, or the gender of the third party.

Sidebar

Read the opinion in this case. Do you agree with the position of the majority or the dissent? Explain your response. Was the dissent suggesting the creation of a new ground for divorce? Did the majority insist that the definition of adultery as a ground for divorce is forever fixed? How would a change come about? Do you think that the outcome in this case would be any different today, given the fact New Hampshire now permits same-sex marriage?

PARALEGAL PRACTICE TIP

The *Blanchflower* opinion can be accessed at *www.pearsonhighered.com/wilson* in the companion website material related to Chapter 5 under "Cases" and in the Case Resources section of the MyLegalStudiesLab.

Paralegal Application 5.4

Adultery Postseparation—A Ground for Divorce?

Clients who have already separated from their spouses often ask if it is okay for them to "date" while the divorce action is pending. The paralegal should refer the question to the attorney and avoid providing a response that might constitute the giving of legal advice to the client. For a case in which a New York court granted a divorce to a wife based on her husband's postseparation adultery,

see *Golub v. Ganz*, 22 A.D.4d 919, 802 N.Y.S.2d 526 (2005). Although many courts would not view a "new" relationship in terms of a potential fault ground for divorce, they may look for dissipation of the marital estate that occurs in conjunction with the new relationship. Do you think postseparation relationships should be considered in the divorce context? Why?

Desertion/abandonment
a fault ground for divorce in some states; the plaintiff must show that the defendant deliberately and without consent left the marital relationship with no intention to return, and that the absence has continued for a specified continuous period of time (customarily a year or more)

Constructive desertion
a situation in which a spouse's objectionable conduct is so abusive or otherwise intolerable that it renders continuation of the marital relationship impossible and forces the "innocent spouse" either to move out or move into a separate area within the marital residence in order to maintain his or her health, safety, or self-respect

Desertion/Abandonment

To obtain a divorce on the ground of **desertion/abandonment**, the petitioner usually must show that the defendant deliberately and without consent left the marital relationship with no intention to return, and that the absence has continued for a specified continuous period of time (customarily a year or more). The desertion must be unnecessary and without sufficient cause. Since it also must be voluntary, an absence due to military service, incarceration, or institutionalization in a mental or other facility such as a rehabilitation center will not constitute desertion.

When abandonment is alleged, it involves abandonment of the relation between the husband and wife and not necessarily the house in which they live. The desertion may be **constructive desertion** if a spouse's objectionable conduct is so abusive or otherwise intolerable that it renders continuation of the marital relationship impossible and forces the "innocent spouse" either to move out or to move into a separate area within the marital residence in order to maintain his or her health, safety, or self-respect. The spouse who leaves has a defense to a claim by the other party of desertion and also has his or her own ground for divorce.

A refusal of sexual relations and/or moving to a separate bedroom may form the basis of a ground for divorce (such as desertion or cruelty), depending on the facts of the case.[8] An unjustifiable refusal for an extended period (a year or more) may be sufficient unless the refusal is based on sexually abusive conduct of the defendant or a reasonable suspicion of his or her infidelity. For example, in a Virginia case, an appellate court held that a wife's refusal of sexual relations did not constitute desertion when the husband engaged in recurring extramarital sexual relations without using protection. His conduct was deemed to constitute cruelty.[9]

Cruelty

Cruelty is frequently termed **cruel and abusive treatment,** cruel and inhumane treatment, indignities, physical and mental cruelty, or treatment that endangers health and reason. Although a single act may be sufficient if it is atrocious or severe, cruelty usually involves a course of conduct. In some states (such as Illinois), the cruelty must constitute "extreme and repeated physical or mental cruelty."[10] Particularly in states with a limited number of specific fault grounds, cruelty is often used as a catchall ground. For example, excessive drinking, drug addiction, or failure to provide for the needs of the family when there is an ability to do so may cause such severe emotional stress that a court may deem the conduct cruel and abusive.

Cruelty generally encompasses both acts of physical violence and the reasonable apprehension thereof and also "acts and conduct the effect of which is calculated to permanently destroy the peace of mind and happiness of one of the parties to the marriage and thereby render the marital relationship intolerable."[11] Nagging, temper tantrums, name-calling, rudeness, cursing, and criticism usually are not sufficient to constitute cruelty, although they may be, depending on the known vulnerabilities of a specific plaintiff and an intention to cause pain and anguish.[12] Some states require that the plaintiff demonstrate proof of the harm suffered as a result of the defendant's conduct, such as medical records, medications prescribed for stress, counseling sought, significant weight loss or gain, and sleep disturbances. (See Case 5.1.)

Cruel and abusive treatment
a fault ground for divorce available in some states; conduct that is so physically or mentally damaging that it endangers the spouse's health, safety, or reason

CASE 5.1 *Pfoltzer v. Pfoltzer,* 9 A.D.3d 615, 779 N.Y.S.2d 668 (N.Y. App. Div. 2004)

FROM THE OPINION

Appeal from an amended judgment of the Supreme Court . . . entered March 7, 2002 . . . granting plaintiff a divorce, upon a decision of the court.

Supreme Court granted plaintiff a divorce following the parties' 15-year marriage on the ground of cruel and inhuman treatment. Defendant appeals, arguing that there was insufficient evidence upon which to grant plaintiff a divorce on this ground. Noting that Supreme Court's determination as the factfinder on this issue will not be lightly disturbed by this Court . . . , we disagree with the defendant's contention and accordingly affirm.

Domestic Relations Law § 170 (1) provides that a divorce will be granted on a theory of cruel and inhuman treatment after a showing "that the conduct of the defendant so endangers the physical or mental well being of the plaintiff as renders it unsafe or improper for the plaintiff to cohabit with the defendant." "[I]n order to make out a prima facie case of cruel and inhuman treatment, a party must show

(Continued)

something more than 'mere incompatibility' and 'serious misconduct [must] be distinguished from trivial'" (citations omitted). While a high degree of proof of serious or substantial misconduct was required in this case owing to the long duration of the parties' marriage . . . , we are satisfied that plaintiff made such a showing. . . .

The evidence revealed that defendant has engaged in a constant barrage of harassing and controlling behavior toward plaintiff, often underscored by harsh religious accusations. According to plaintiff, defendant has alienated him from certain members of his family and he was forced to obtain a temporary order of protection to remove his personal items from the marital residence following his departure therefrom. He also obtained an order of protection preventing defendant from continuing to make harassing telephone calls. The record further reveals that defendant has engaged in a course of verbal and mental abuse by harassing and embarrassing plaintiff with public accusations that he has loathsome personal hygiene, has engaged in sexual-related criminal conduct and that he suffers from a particular venereal disease, as well as Acquired Immune Deficiency Syndrome.

The evidence also sufficiently established that the anguish and embarrassment suffered by plaintiff has had an effect on his physical and mental health thus providing a basis for finding that cohabitation with defendant would be either unsafe or improper. . . . Plaintiff was receiving medical treatment for a stress-related ulcer at the time of the trial and had been receiving mental health counseling for some time to address his depression and to help him understand and overcome the abusive relationship between himself and defendant. Indeed for a one-year period in the latter part of the parties' marriage, plaintiff had been prescribed medication to treat his depression caused by the turmoil in the marriage.

Mercure, J.P., Crew III, Lahtinen and Kane, JJ., concur.

Ordered that the amended judgment is affirmed, without costs.

SIDEBAR

Read the opinion in this case. Do you agree that the defendant's conduct was sufficient to warrant a divorce? Explain your response.

Habitual Drunkenness or Drug Abuse

This ground is most commonly called habitual drunkenness, but the precise terminology may vary. In Massachusetts, it is called "gross and confirmed habits of intoxication."[13] The Georgia statute includes both "habitual intoxication" and "habitual drug addiction" as independent grounds for divorce.[14] Some states require that the abuse have continued for a certain period. The Illinois statute, for example, reads, "the respondent has been guilty of habitual drunkenness for the space of 2 years" and "the respondent has been guilty of gross and confirmed habits caused by the excessive use of addictive drugs for the space of 2 years."[15]

Criminal Conviction and Incarceration

The state statutes that include criminal conviction and incarceration as a ground for divorce vary with respect to the type of crime committed, the jurisdiction in which the crime was committed, the length of the sentence, and whether or not the respondent is/was actually confined. The pertinent Maryland statute lists as a ground "conviction of a felony or misdemeanor in any state or in any court of the United States if before the filing of the application for divorce the defendant has: (i) been sentenced to serve at least 3 years or an indeterminate sentence in a penal institution; and (ii) served 12 months of the sentence."[16] The Georgia statute specifies that the offense be one that involves "moral turpitude."[17] In Ohio, the respondent must be incarcerated at the time the complaint is filed.[18] The Virginia statute addresses the potential impact of a subsequent pardon.[19]

Examples of some of the less common statutory fault grounds for divorce include the following:

- The respondent has inflicted the spouse with a sexually transmitted disease.[20]
- Either party has joined any religious sect or society that professes to believe the relation of husband and wife is unlawful and has refused to cohabit for a six-month period.[21]
- Insanity under certain conditions. For example, a ground in Connecticut is the legal confinement of a spouse "in a hospital or hospitals or other similar institution because of mental illness, for at least an accumulated period totaling five years within the period of six years next preceding the date of the complaint."[22]
- "Excessively vicious conduct toward the complaining party or a minor child of the complaining party, if there is no reasonable expectation of reconciliation."[23]
- "Willful neglect of the respondent to provide for the petitioner the common necessaries of life."[24]
- "Any gross neglect of duty."[25]

PARALEGAL PRACTICE TIP

The **marital communications privilege,** which prevents a spouse from testifying in court about confidential communications with the other spouse during their marriage, usually does not apply in divorce actions or cases in which the defendant is alleged to have committed a crime against the spouse and/or their children. However, if adultery is alleged and is still a crime in the jurisdiction, the defendant may claim a Fifth Amendment right against self-incrimination if questioned about the existence of an adulterous relationship that falls within the applicable statute of limitations period.

Marital communications privilege
the privilege that allows a spouse to refuse to testify, and to prevent others from testifying, about confidential communications between the spouses during their marriage

Defenses to a Divorce Action

Defenses to a divorce action commonly include:

- Lack of subject matter jurisdiction.
- Lack of personal jurisdiction.
- Lack of proper venue.
- Forum *nonconveniens.*
- Lack of proper service of process.
- Failure of the complaint to state a claim upon which relief can be based. The plaintiff has alleged a ground for divorce that is not available in the jurisdiction.
- The matter is *res judicata.* The marital status previously has been dissolved as in an action for divorce or annulment in another state or country.
- Invalidity of the marriage.

Defense
a defendant's stated reason why a plaintiff has no valid claim or why the court should not grant the relief requested

When the divorce action is based on one or more fault grounds, additional defenses may be available. These "traditional" defenses have their origins in common law and include the following:

- **Condonation**. This defense is used when the defendant asserts that the petitioner has, in effect, condoned the alleged blameworthy conduct, such as an adulterous affair, by forgiving it to the extent that he or she has resumed "normal" marital relations with the defendant spouse, who, with forgiveness, regains innocence. As an Illinois court described it in a 2005 decision,

Condonation
the forgiveness of a matrimonial offense

Provocation
a traditional defense claiming that the plaintiff provoked the conduct alleged in the complaint and therefore should be denied relief

Recrimination
a defense raised when the defendant alleges the plaintiff has also committed a marital wrong and therefore should not be granted a divorce

Doctrine of comparative rectitude
in the divorce context, the granting of a divorce to the party who is least at fault when both parties have committed marital wrongdoing

Dual divorce
a divorce granted to both parties

Connivance
a traditional defense in which the defendant alleges the plaintiff consented to, or participated in, the act complained of in the complaint

Collusion
a determination by the court that the parties should not be granted a divorce because they jointly deceived the court as to the true nature and purpose of the action

"Condonation in the law of divorce is the forgiveness of an antecedent matrimonial offense on condition that it shall not be repeated and that the offender shall thereafter treat the forgiving party with conjugal kindness."[26]

- **Provocation.** When this defense is raised, the defendant is claiming that the plaintiff provoked the conduct alleged in the complaint. For example, if the alleged ground for divorce is desertion/abandonment, the defendant may defend by saying that the plaintiff's excessive drinking and drug use forced a departure from the marital home for the defendant's safety and protection.

- **Recrimination.** Eliminated in several states, this defense is raised when the defendant claims that the plaintiff has also committed a marital wrong such as adultery and thus should not be granted a divorce. Some states have adopted the **doctrine of comparative rectitude** to deal with situations in which both parties are at fault. Under the doctrine, a court grants the divorce to the party whose wrongdoing is least serious. Other courts occasionally award **dual divorces**, in which each party is granted the divorce.

- **Connivance.** Connivance is an appropriate defense when the plaintiff allegedly consented to or created the opportunity for the defendant to commit the act complained of in the complaint. For instance, if the petitioner alleges habitual drunkenness as a ground for divorce, the defendant may defend stating that the plaintiff both participated in and promoted the defendant's drinking and actively sabotaged his or her efforts to seek treatment.

- **Collusion.** Collusion is less a defense than a legal bar to a divorce. Collusion is a determination by the court that the parties should not be granted a divorce because they had an agreement to, in effect, deceive the court as to the nature and true purpose of the action. Essentially they conspired to fabricate a reason for the divorce when no legally recognized ground existed. Although far more common in the fault era, collusion is not unheard-of today. For example, in an Oklahoma case in 2005, a court vacated a divorce decree based on the fact that the husband and wife sought a divorce with no intention of separating and solely for the purpose of increasing the wife's public benefits in support of her chronic illness.[27]

PARALEGAL PRACTICE TIP

Before raising a common law defense, the paralegal needs to research whether or not "traditional" defenses are still available to defendants in the jurisdiction. For example, Minnesota provides by statute that the defenses of condonation, connivance, collusion, recrimination, insanity, and lapse of time are abolished. (Minn. Stat. §518.06) Florida law provides in Title VI Chapter 61 (61.044) that the defenses of condonation, collusion, recrimination, and laches are abolished.

Drafting and Filing of the Complaint

A divorce action technically begins when a Complaint/Petition is filed with the court and the defendant is served. The **Complaint** (or Petition for Dissolution) is the main pleading in a divorce case. It sets forth the nature of the action, the requested relief, and the basis of the court's jurisdiction over the action. It usually calls for the following information:

Complaint
the main pleading in a case that sets forth the nature of the action and the request for relief

- names and addresses of the parties
- date and place of the parties' marriage

- date when the parties separated/last resided together as husband and wife
- names and dates of birth of any minor children
- alleged ground(s) for the divorce
- declaration regarding property in a community property state
- the request (or "prayer") for relief (e.g., division of property, custody, child and/or spousal support, maintenance of insurance, sale of the marital home, resumption of maiden name), usually including a final open-ended request for any further relief the court deems fair and equitable

The complaint should be prepared in a manner that complies with applicable state statutes and procedural rules re grounds, format, jurisdiction, venue, etc. In a complaint, the parties are commonly referred to as the plaintiff and the defendant. In a petition they are usually called the petitioner and the respondent. If the petition for divorce is a joint petition, the parties are usually labeled petitioner and co-petitioner. A copy of a Complaint for Absolute Divorce used in the state of Maryland is provided in Exhibit 5.5.

PARALEGAL PRACTICE TIP

In some states, the plaintiff will be limited in the judgment to the relief requested in the complaint and cannot request additional forms of relief (such as alimony) at a later date. In some instances, the court may not be authorized to grant more relief than is requested.

PARALEGAL PRACTICE TIP

If there is a premarital agreement between the parties, it is important that the complaint put the court on notice of its existence—for example, by attaching a copy and asking that the court enforce (or not enforce) the premarital agreement executed by the parties on a certain date.

PARALEGAL PRACTICE TIP

A majority of the states now make Complaints/Petitions for Divorce available online. Examples include the following:

NEW HAMPSHIRE: *www.courts.state.nh.us*
INDIANA: *www.in.gov/judiciary/forms*
MONTANA: *courts.mt.gov*
WYOMING: *www.courts.state.wy.us*

Links to these sites can be found at *www.pearsonhighered.com/wilson* in the companion website material related to Chapter 5 under "Forms."

The paralegal is often asked to draft the complaint/petition. Before doing so, the proper jurisdiction and venue should be confirmed with the attorney based on the facts of the case (where each of the parties resides, where the parties last lived together as husband and wife, where the children are located, etc.). The next step is to determine whether the court mandates the use of specific forms or formats. The paralegal then drafts the document using the appropriate form—complaint, joint petition, etc. Many states now provide divorce forms online, and many practice manuals include disks with model forms. Careful attention must be given to using jurisdictionally appropriate terminology. For example, some states use the terms "divorce" and "dissolution" interchangeably. Others, such as Ohio, use "dissolution" strictly to refer to uncontested actions.

PARALEGAL PRACTICE TIP

Even in an uncontested joint petition, a ground must be indicated (e.g., the parties are seeking a divorce due to irreconcilable differences that have caused the irremediable breakdown of the marriage). Typically one party's attorney will complete the necessary documents for review by the other party's attorney and the clients prior to signing and filing.

PARALEGAL PRACTICE TIP

Many states mandate the use of uniform preprinted forms or formats for various purposes. Some states also have special rules governing the use of computer-generated forms. For example, there may be a requirement that the form be printed on a particular color or weight of paper or that the origin of the form be noted (e.g., cgf—computer-generated form—marked on a bottom corner of the form).

PARALEGAL PRACTICE TIP

To see a Joint Petition for Simplified Dissolution of Marriage in an Illinois county visit *www.cookcountyclerkofcourt.org*. A link to this site can be found at *www.pearsonhighered.com/wilson* in the companion website material for Chapter 5 under "Forms."

EXHIBIT 5.5 Complaint for Absolute Divorce

Courtesy of the State of Maryland

Circuit Court for _____ **Case No.** _____
                        City or County

Name   Name

Street Address   Apt. #   Street Address   Apt. #

City   State Zip Code Area Telephone   City   State Zip Code Area Telephone
                         Code   Code

Plaintiff   **Defendant**

COMPLAINT FOR ABSOLUTE DIVORCE
(DOM REL 20)

I, _____ , representing myself, state that:
          Your Name

1. The Defendant and I were married on_____
                                       Month   Day   Year
   in_____ in a ☐ civil ☐ religious ceremony.
      City/County/State where Married   (Check One)

2. *Check all that apply:*
   ☐ I have lived in Maryland since:_____
                                      Month/Year
   ☐ My spouse has lived in Maryland since: _____
                                              Month/Year
   ☐ The grounds for divorce occurred in the State of Maryland.

3. *Check one:*
   ☐ We have no children together (skip paragraphs 5 and 6) or
   ☐ My spouse and I are the parents of the following child(ren:)

   _____   _____   _____   _____
        Name   Date of Birth   Name   Date of Birth
   _____   _____   _____   _____
        Name   Date of Birth   Name   Date of Birth
   _____   _____   _____   _____
        Name   Date of Birth   Name   Date of Birth

4. I know of the following related cases concerning the child(ren) or parties (such as domestic violence, paternity, divorce, custody, visitation, termination of parental rights, adoption or other cases):

   Court   **Case No.**   **Kind of Case**   **Year Filed**   **Results or Status (if known)**

   _____   _____   _____   _____   _____
   _____   _____   _____   _____   _____
   _____   _____   _____   _____   _____

5. I have been a party, witness, or otherwise involved in the following cases about custody or visitation of the child(ren) :

   State   **Court**   **Case No.**   **Date of Child Custody Determination**

   _____   _____   _____   _____
   _____   _____   _____   _____

   Attach the most recent court order for the above-referenced court cases.

(Continued)

EXHIBIT 5.5 (*Continued*)

6. I know of the following people, not parties to this case, who have physical custody of, or claim rights of legal custody or physical custody of, or visitation with the child(ren) :

_____	_____
Name	Current Address
_____	_____
Name	Current Address
_____	_____
Name	Current Address

7. The child(ren) are currently living with:_____
   Name

8. The child(ren) have lived in the following places, with the persons indicated during the last five years:

Time Period	**Place**	**Name(s)/Current Address of Person(s) with whom Child Lived**
_____	_____	_____
_____	_____	_____

9. It is in the best interests of the child(ren) that I have (*check all that apply*):

   ☐ joint ☐ sole physical custody of _____
   (Check One)   Name of Children

   ☐ joint ☐ sole legal custody of _____
   (Check One)   Name of Children

   ☐ visitation with_____
                                        Name of Children

10. I ☐ am ☐ am not seeking alimony because_____
    (Check One)

11. (You do not have to complete paragraph 11 if you are not asking the court to make decisions about your property.) My spouse and/or I have the following property (*check all that apply*)

    ☐ House(s)   ☐ Furniture

    ☐ Pensions   ☐ Bank account(s) and investment(s)

    ☐ Motor Vehicle(s)   ☐ Other _____

    ☐ Debts (attach list)

12. My grounds for absolute divorce are: (*check all that apply*)

    ☐ **Two-Year Separation** - From on or about_____, my spouse and I have lived
                                              Month/Day/Year
    separate and apart from each other in separate residences, without interruptions, without sexual intercourse, for more than two years and there is no reasonable expectation that we will reconcile.

    ☐ **Voluntary Separation** - From on or about_____, my spouse and I by mutual and
                                              Month/Day/Year
    voluntary agreement have lived separate and apart from one another in separate residences, without interruption, without sexual intercourse, for more than 12 months with the express purpose and intent of ending our marriage, and there is no reasonable expectation that we will reconcile.

    ☐ **Adultery** - My spouse committed adultery.

    ☐ **Actual Desertion** - On or about_____, my spouse, without just cause or reason,
                                        Month/Day/Year
    abandoned and deserted me, with the intention of ending our marriage. This abandonment has continued without interruption for more than 12 months and there is no reasonable expectation that we will reconcile.

EXHIBIT 5.5 (*Continued*)

☐ **Constructive Desertion** - I left my spouse because his/her cruel and vicious conduct made the continuation of our marriage impossible, if I were to preserve my health, safety, and self-respect. This conduct was the final and deliberate act of my spouse and our separation has continued without interruption for more than 12 months and there is no reasonable expectation that we will reconcile.

☐ **Criminal Conviction of a Felony or Misdemeanor** - On or about_____, my
  Month/Day/Year
spouse was sentenced to serve at least three years or an indeterminate sentence in a penal institution and has served 12 or more months of the sentence.

☐ **Cruelty/Excessively Vicious Conduct Against Me or my minor child** - My spouse has persistently treated me or my minor child cruelly and has engaged in excessively vicious conduct rendering continuation of the marital relationship impossible if I am to preserve my health, safety, and self-respect, and there is no reasonable expectation that we will reconcile.

☐ **Insanity** - On or about_____, my spouse was confined to a mental institution,
  Month/Day/Year
hospital, or other similar institution and has been confined for 3 more years. Two doctors competent in psychiatry will testify that the insanity is incurable and there is no hope of recovery. My spouse or I have been a resident of Maryland for at least two years before the filing of this complaint.

FOR THESE REASONS, I request (*check all that apply*):

☒ An Absolute Divorce

☐ A change back to my former name;_____
                                            Full Former Name

☐   ☐ Sole ☐ Joint physical custody of the minor child(ren).
            (Check One)

☐   ☐ Sole ☐ Joint legal custody of the minor child(ren).
            (Check One)

☐ Visitation with the minor child(ren).

☐ Use and possession of the family home for up to three years from the date of the divorce.

☐ Use and possession of the family use personal property for up to three years from the date of the divorce.

☐ Child support (Attach Form DOM REL 30 or DOM REL 31).

☐ Health insurance for the child(ren).

☐ Health insurance for me.

☐ My share of the property or its value.

☐ Transfer of family use personal property.

☐ A monetary award (money) based on marital property.

☐ Alimony (Attach Form DOM. REL 31).

☒ Any other appropriate relief.

I, _____ , solemnly affirm under the penalties of
              Your Name
perjury, that the contents of this document are true to the best of my knowledge, information and belief.

_____   _____
           Date   Signature

Once completed, reviewed, and signed, the Complaint is filed, accompanied by the filing fee and any other required documents. Although the states vary with respect to the additional documents that must be filed, most require the following:

- A certified copy of the Marriage Certificate (with a certified translation if in a foreign language)
- A Disclosure Affidavit concerning any orders in force or pending regarding care, custody, and support of the parties' minor children, if any

- A Financial Statement (must be updated at trial and every time a motion with financial implications is heard)
- A Military Affidavit if the defendant/respondent is unlikely to appear or is in the service and will not be able to appear
- A Bureau of Vital Statistics Form used to collect data on divorcing couples

The attorney customarily also files an Appearance at this point, indicating that he or she will be representing the plaintiff in the divorce action. The paralegal may drafts the Appearance (or completes the court's appearance form) and files it after it is reviewed and signed.

The paralegal often gathers the necessary documents and files the complaint along with the accompanying documents and a transmittal letter to the court when directed to do so by the supervisor. The paralegal needs to be familiar with filing requirements and practices in the jurisdiction (in person, by mail, electronically, etc.). Copies of all documents filed should also be placed in the client's file and sent to the client.

When the complaint is filed, the court clerk assigns a docket number and issues a summons. The docket number should appear on all subsequent documents and correspondence related to the action. Sometimes the summons is completed by court staff, but in some counties necessary information is filled in by a member of the family law team, usually the paralegal.

Occasionally, third parties may be joined in a divorce action. For example, if one of the spouses creates a sham trust, allegedly for someone else's benefit; makes

Memorandum of *lis pendens*
a notice that ownership and disposition of certain real property is subject to a pending legal action, and that any interest acquired during the pendency of that action is subject to its outcome; usually filed in a Registry of Deeds where the property is located

Declaratory judgment
a binding adjudication that establishes the rights, status, or other legal relations between the parties

a substantial "loan" to a sibling; holds property in the names of other persons; or otherwise transfers property in a scheme designed to deprive the other spouse of a fair share of the marital assets, the third party may be drawn into the divorce, usually by use of an "equity" complaint for a **declaratory judgment** and/or injunctive relief. Some states add financial institutions, putting them on notice that the assets they hold are subject to a court order, thereby facilitating discovery with respect to those assets.

PARALEGAL PRACTICE TIP

To see an example of a Summons for Divorce, visit *www.judicial.state.sc.us/forms*. (South Carolina) You can find a link to this site at *www.pearsonhighered.com/wilson* in the companion website material for Chapter 5 under "Forms."

Service of the Complaint and Return of Service

Service of the Summons and Complaint must comply with all applicable local rules and customarily must be made within a specified period after the filing date (usually sixty to ninety days). The **summons** informs the defendant that he or she has been sued and needs to answer within a certain period (usually twenty to thirty days) or risk possibility of a default judgment. **Service of process** is usually accomplished by:

Summons
a formal notice from a court informing a defendant of an action filed against him or her and ordering the defendant to respond and answer the allegations of the plaintiff within a certain period or risk entry of a default judgment

Service of process
delivery of a summons and complaint to a defendant in a manner consistent with state and federal law; usually accomplished by personal "in-hand" service by an authorized individual such as a sheriff or by publication in a newspaper and mailing to the defendant's last known address

- **Acceptance of service**—If a defendant is aware (by whatever means) of the summons, he or she may, for example, go voluntarily to a courthouse, receive the summons, and sign a form acknowledging service.
- **Personal service**—An approved process server delivers the summons into the hand of the defendant. The server then completes the "return of service" information indicating the summons has been served (or that service was attempted on multiple occasions but not accomplished). The proof of service information on the summons must be completed by the process server, who certifies when, where, and how service was made. The completed summons is returned by the server to either the court or the attorney's office, depending on local rules. The original is kept in the court's file, and a copy should be placed in the client's file.

PARALEGAL PRACTICE TIP

When the defendant is personally served or accepts service, it is called "actual service" and gives the court personal jurisdiction over the defendant.

PARALEGAL PRACTICE TIP

To see an example of an Affidavit of Service, visit *www.wicourts.gov*. You can find a link to this site at *www.pearsonhighered.com/wilson* in the companion website material for Chapter 5 under "Forms."

- **Publication in a local newspaper and mailing to the defendant's last known address**—Service may be made by this means if the defendant is evading service or his or her whereabouts are unknown (requires permission of the court).

The paralegal must be familiar with the rules and procedures governing service of process and will usually perform the following related tasks:

- Complete the summons, if required.
- Maintain a list of approved process servers and fees. Process servers usually include sheriffs, constables, marshals, etc. Some jurisdictions permit service by a disinterested adult.

- Make arrangements for proper service and alert the client as to where and when it is likely to be made in case there are safety issues to address.

PARALEGAL PRACTICE TIP

To see an example of a form requesting the court's permission to serve a defendant by publication, visit *http://www.courts.state.co.us*. A link to this site can be found at *www.pearsonhighered.com/wilson* in the companion website material for Chapter 5 under "Forms."

- If service is by publication, draft a Motion for Permission to Serve by Publication, if required. If approved, mail a copy of the order of notice of the action, the complaint, and the summons by certified mail to the defendant's last known address, and arrange for publication in the appropriate newspaper(s).

PARALEGAL PRACTICE TIP

To see some interesting tips on locating people to effect service, visit *www.courts.alaska.gov*. You can find a link to this site at *www.pearsonhighered.com/wilson* in the companion website material for Chapter 5 under "Resources."

- If the defendant is located in another state or nation, research and arrange to have him or her properly served in that location.
- Track and ensure that service is properly completed and documented and advise the supervisor and client to that effect.
- Return proof of service to the court, if necessary, keeping copies for the client and the file.
- Arrange for payment of the process server's fee.

PARALEGAL PRACTICE TIP

Occasionally, a party may want or need to amend a Complaint, for example, to correct an error in an address in the original filing, provide the name of a co-respondent, or add a fault or no-fault ground for divorce. Local rules dictate whether the Complaint can be amended with or without the permission of the court, and it may depend on whether or not the Complaint already has been served. The paralegal may be asked to draft a Motion to Amend the Complaint, along with a supporting Affidavit and Proposed Order, if required.

Defendant's Response to the Complaint

The defendant's initial pleading is customarily an **Answer** to the complaint/petition for divorce, which must be filed within the period set by statute or procedural rule. In the answer, the defendant admits, denies, or indicates lack of information sufficient to respond to each of the paragraphs/allegations in the complaint. The defendant may also:

- Raise any defenses he or she has to the allegations in the Complaint (such as condonation, existence of a binding premarital agreement, etc.).

PARALEGAL PRACTICE TIP

If a defendant receives notice and fails to respond to a Complaint, he or she may not be permitted to seek relief at a later date. However, courts are reluctant to issue default judgments in divorce cases and customarily will not do so without a hearing.

- Include a **counterclaim** for divorce and his or her own request for relief. If the defendant also wants a divorce, it is good practice to file a counterclaim (even if the grounds are the same as in the Complaint, e.g., irreconcilable differences). In the event the other party subsequently withdraws his or her Complaint, the date the counterclaim is filed will be preserved and there is no need to start the process all over again. In the alternative, if the parties are able to reach an agreement, the contested claims may be converted to a joint uncontested action, and the parties can proceed on that basis.

Answer
a pleading filed by a defendant in response to a plaintiff's complaint, setting forth the defendant's defenses and counterclaims

PARALEGAL PRACTICE TIP

To see an example of a standard Answer form in West Virginia, visit *www.state.wv.us*. You can find a link to this site at *www.pearsonhighered. com/wilson* in the companion website material for Chapter 5 under "Forms."

Counterclaim
a defendant's claim against the plaintiff

Motion to Dismiss
a request that the court dismiss the case because of some procedural or other defect, such as lack of jurisdiction or failure to state a claim on which relief can be based

When responding to a complaint for divorce on behalf of a nonresident defendant, careful consideration must be given to the nature of the response. In appropriate circumstances, in lieu of an answer, the defendant may file a **Motion to Dismiss** (for lack of subject matter or personal jurisdiction, improper venue, or deficiencies in service, etc.) and *not* an Answer. If a nonresident defendant files an Answer, he or she will trigger personal jurisdiction. If the defendant is represented, his or her attorney should file a limited appearance for the sole purpose of contesting jurisdiction. Any personal appearance by a nonresident defendant will confer full personal jurisdiction on the court even if the defendant appears solely to seek dismissal of the action. The paralegal may be asked to draft whichever response will be filed.

Once the plaintiff's attorney is notified that the opposing party has retained counsel, all communication from the firm should be with that attorney and not directly with the party he or she represents. Direct communication between the parties themselves is virtually impossible to avoid, even when restraining orders have been issued. Such communication is a double-edged sword. Voluntary resolution of differences and maintenance of a civil, even positive, relationship between the parties is encouraged, particularly when children are involved and /or resources are limited. However, in high-conflict cases or when there is a considerable power differential between the parties, communication is best left to counsel. In either situation, a client should always consult counsel before signing or otherwise finalizing any agreements with the other party.

Motions for Temporary Orders and Other Purposes

Temporary orders
orders designed to protect the parties and maintain the status quo while a matter is pending before the court

Motion
an oral or written request that the court issue a particular ruling or order

Affidavit
a first-person statement signed under oath laying out facts in support of the motion

Pendente lite
Latin: while the action is pending

At this point in a divorce case, one or both of the parties may file a request for **temporary orders,** most often addressing custody and support issues. Usually the request is made in the form of a **motion** (a request to the court for an order) accompanied by an **affidavit.** In some states, requests for temporary relief may or must be made in one motion or in separate motions or may be contained in the initial complaint or the answer. Requests for temporary orders are driven by the needs and problems of each individual case. They are designed to maintain the status quo and protect the client, if necessary, *pendente lite* (Latin: while the action is pending). Because of their potential to subtly impact "permanent" orders, absent an emergency, some attorneys prefer to postpone the decision to file for temporary orders until after sufficient discovery is conducted.

The parties may file additional motions as the action progresses, addressing other issues such as the following:

- removal of children from the state on a temporary basis while the litigation is pending

- protection of marital assets held by third parties, such as banks or investment firms (requires financial statement)
- preservation of marital assets, requesting that the other party be enjoined from disposing of or encumbering a specific asset

- attorney's fees and costs *pendente lite* to allow the party to maintain the action (usually requires an affidavit of the attorney, a schedule of anticipated expenses, a financial statement, etc.)
- use and occupancy of the marital home and responsibility for related expenses (requires a financial statement), including a request that one of the parties vacate the marital home, if necessary (see Exhibit 5.6 for a sample of a Motion to Vacate the Marital Home)
- appointment of an investigator, custody evaluator, and/or guardian *ad litem* (GAL)
- restraining order for protection from abuse (may be based on a complaint rather than a motion, depending on the jurisdiction and circumstances)
- appraisals of major assets such as the marital home
- consolidation with the divorce action of one or more actions, such as a prior order from another court that is still in force relating to protection from abuse, to child custody, and/or to occupancy of the marital home

Because of their nature, some of these motions may be filed ***ex parte*** (without advance notice to the opposing party). For example, the purpose of a motion for an order restraining transfer or dissipation of marital assets, or to prevent removal of the minor children from the jurisdiction, may be totally defeated if advance notice is provided. *Ex parte* motions usually must be accompanied by an affidavit setting forth the nature of the emergency and how the giving of notice would pose a substantial risk of harm.

Most states issue "automatic restraining orders" that are effective with regard to the plaintiff upon filing of the Complaint and to the defendant when served with the Summons and Complaint. The orders generally remain in effect while the matter is pending unless modified by agreement of the parties or by order of the court. These orders usually restrain transfer or disposal of any of the parties' property (except to cover reasonable living or ordinary business expenses), incurring of debt, and changing of any insurance or pension beneficiaries. The client may need to be alerted to or reminded about the existence of these orders.

The court may choose to appoint a **guardian *ad litem*** in cases where custody is contested, even if not requested by the parties. The guardian is likely to request

Ex parte motion

a motion made without advance notice to the opposing party; a motion considered and initially ruled on by the court without hearing from both parties, based on the urgency of the matter or the harm that might otherwise result

Guardian *ad litem*

a person, often a lawyer, appointed by the court to conduct an investigation and/or represent a party who is a minor or otherwise unable to represent himself or herself in a legal proceeding; the guardian's role may be limited to a particular matter, such as custody

EXHIBIT 5.6 Sample of a Motion to Vacate the Marital Home

STATE OF NEW HAMPSHIRE

HILLSBORO COUNTY

SUPERIOR COURT　　　　　　　　　　　　　　　DOCKET NO. XXXXXXX

JANE TURNER,	)	
Plaintiff	)	
	)	PLAINTIFF'S
v.	)	MOTION TO VACATE THE
	)	MARITAL HOME
JAMES TURNER,	)	
Defendant	)	
	)	

NOW COMES JANE TURNER, plaintiff in the above-captioned matter, and respectfully requests this Honorable Court order the defendant, JAMES TURNER, to vacate the marital home forthwith.
In support of her motion, the plaintiff states as follows:

1. The parties were married at Fort Myers, Florida, on November 16, 1998, and are presently residing in the marital residence at 306 North Dunstable Road, Nashua, New Hampshire, together with the parties' two minor children, Calvin Turner, age 10 years (DOB April 16, 2001), and Elizabeth Turner, age 7 years (DOB June 11, 2003).
2. The plaintiff has filed a Complaint for Divorce (Docket No. XXXXXXX) on the grounds of irreconcilable differences that have caused the irretrievable breakdown of the marriage.
3. The defendant's abusive behavior in the home has caused the plaintiff severe emotional stress and physical side effects. Moreover, tension caused by the defendant's actions and disagreements pertaining to the pending action for divorce are causing the parties' minor children emotional trauma and distress.
4. The relationship between the parties has significantly deteriorated in the five months since the Divorce Complaint was filed and conflict between the parties has escalated to a level that requires that the parties live apart.
5. It is in the best interests of the children that they remain in the marital home with the plaintiff, who has been their primary caretaker since birth.

In further support of this Motion, the plaintiff submits the accompanying Affidavit, which is herein incorporated by reference.

WHEREFORE, for the reasons set forth above and in the plaintiff's Affidavit, the plaintiff requests that this honorable Court order the defendant to vacate the marital home forthwith.

　　　　　　　　　　　　　　　　　　　　　　　Respectfully submitted,
　　　　　　　　　　　　　　　　　　　　　　　Jane Turner
　　　　　　　　　　　　　　　　　　　　　　　By her attorney,

Date:_____　　　　　　　　　　　_____

　　　　　　　　　　　　　　　　　　　　　　　Attorney's name
　　　　　　　　　　　　　　　　　　　　　　　Attorney's address
　　　　　　　　　　　　　　　　　　　　　　　Attorney's telephone number
　　　　　　　　　　　　　　　　　　　　　　　Attorney's Bar number

CERTIFICATE OF SERVICE

I, (*Plaintiff's Attorney*), hereby certify that I have today served the above Motion and accompanying Affidavit, and Proposed Order on the Defendant, James Turner, by first-class mail to the office of his attorney, (*name and address of defendant's attorney*), together with notice that the Motion has been marked for hearing before the presiding Justice sitting in the _____ Court at 8:30 a.m. on Monday, May 16, 2011.

Date: _____　　　　　　　　　　_____

　　　　　　　　　　　　　　　　　　　　　　　Name of Plaintiff's Attorney

from each party a variety of documents, such as pleadings, reports in the parents' possession, and medical records. Releases will need to be provided where necessary. The guardian usually interviews the parents, the children, school personnel, day care providers, pediatricians, and others to gather information about the children's history and current home and school environment. The guardian may then make a custody recommendation to the court, which it may accept or reject. Counsel is customarily permitted to question the GAL at trial regarding the report and the basis for any findings and recommendations. The report is usually impounded and not part of the public record, to protect the privacy of the children and the parties.

HEARINGS ON MOTIONS

Motions are usually heard in what commonly are called motion sessions, in which the court hears several motions in a sequence essentially controlled by the clerk. Sometimes the sequence will be determined in advance and specific time blocks will be allocated for each case. Usually, the docket is posted in the courthouse on the date of the hearing. Many courts require that all parties and attorneys expecting to be heard report at the same time (e.g., 8:00 a.m.). The clerk will "call the list" to confirm that all necessary individuals are present and determine whether there are any special needs, such as for an interpreter or a referral for mediation or a meeting with a family service worker.

In many states, if the parties have not already reached agreement with respect to the subject matter of the motion prior to coming to court, they will be required to meet with a family service worker or court-based mediator to see if the matter can be resolved prior to the hearing. If an agreement is reached by the parties, it is reduced to a written **stipulation** and submitted to the court for consideration. If the matter is not resolved, the family service worker may submit a recommendation, and the motion will be argued before the court.

Motion hearings are usually quite brief, and rules of evidence are rarely strictly followed, unlike in a trial. In some states, the parties are required to be present for hearings unless their absence is excused by the court. When a party fails to appear without explanation or excuse, the moving party must file a **military affidavit** in accordance with the Soldiers and Sailors Relief Act,[28] stating under pain and penalties of perjury that the absent party is currently not serving in the armed services.

PARALEGAL PRACTICE TIP

To see an example of a Military Affidavit, visit *www.vermontjudiciary.org/eforms*. You can find a link to this site at *www.pearsonhighered.com/wilson* in the companion website material related to Chapter 5 under "Forms."

The paralegal may perform the following tasks related to temporary orders and other motions:

- Gather information necessary to draft, support, and file the motion (or oppose it).
- Draft motions, supporting affidavits, and proposed orders, if required, for review.
- File and send copies of the documents to the client and opposing counsel with transmittal cover letters when approved and signed.

PARALEGAL PRACTICE TIP

To see an example of a Motion for Appointment of a Guardian *ad Litem*, visit *www.flcourts.org*. You can find a link to this site at *www.pearsonhighered.com/wilson* in the companion website material for Chapter 5 under "Forms."

PARALEGAL PRACTICE TIP

Throughout the process, consideration should be given to the availability of alternative dispute resolution options. In some states litigants are required to mediate. When a court orders that a case be diverted for conciliation or mediation services at any point, it places a subtle but especially strong pressure on the parties and counsel to settle the matter at issue.

Stipulation

an agreement between the parties concerning some matter; may be filed with the court to be entered as an order

Military affidavit

an affidavit submitted by a party stating under pain and penalties of perjury that an absent party is currently not serving in the armed services

PARALEGAL PRACTICE TIP

To see an example of a Stipulation for Temporary Orders, visit *www.wicourts.gov*. You can find a link to this site at *www.pearsonhighered.com/wilson* in the companion website material related to Chapter 5 under "Forms."

- Assist with preparation of accompanying financial statement and child support guidelines worksheet if necessary.
- If the court permits scheduling in advance by counsel, check all appropriate calendars (including those of opposing counsel) and arrange to mark motions for hearing or diversion to court conciliation or mediation services, if appropriate (often the procedure with child-related motions). If the hearing date is known at the time of service, include it in the certification along with the time and place for the hearing.
- Be certain that hearing dates are marked on all appropriate calendars and on the firm's "docket control system" if applicable. The client should also be notified of the date. The attorney will usually describe the nature of the proceeding to the client and will review the roles of each party, counsel, and the court.
- Assist with preparation for motion hearings.

In order to carry out these responsibilities, the paralegal must keep current with respect to the rules governing various aspects of motion practice, including special rules of civil procedure for domestic relations courts, local court rules, and practices of various courts and judges. For example:

- Are uniform forms for motions, affidavits, and proposed orders required?
- How far in advance of a hearing must a motion be served? In an emergency, may a party request and be granted a "short order of notice" reducing the required notice period?
- Can motions be filed and/or served electronically?
- What are the procedures for scheduling motion hearings in the court where the motion is filed? Some courts permit counsel to schedule dates in advance and serve notice of the hearing date along with the motion if there has been prior consultation with opposing counsel. Other courts strictly control scheduling and mark motions only after they are filed with the court and without any opportunity for input from counsel.
- When a party opposes a motion for temporary orders, does the court require submission of a memorandum or affidavit in opposition to the motion, or does it simply rely on testimony presented at the hearing on the motion?
- Is the motion being filed governed by rules over and above those regulating domestic relations matters? For example, motions to protect marital assets may need to comply with nondivorce procedural rules (such as motions for **trustee process** that in effect freeze assets of the other party, directing a third-party holder of the assets, such as a bank, to hold them in trust, pending resolution of the action).

Trustee process
a legal process by which a third party holds the property of a party in trust at the direction of a court

PARALEGAL PRACTICE TIP

The paralegal should maintain a file of clerks/contacts in each court and agency with which the office has frequent contact. It is always helpful to establish a network and be able to refer to personnel by name. It also is a good idea to maintain a record of any of the "idiosyncrasies" of particular courts and special instructions and "pet peeves" of particular judges!

Discovery
the process of gathering information relevant to a matter at issue; includes both formal and informal methods

Discovery

Discovery is a pretrial process for obtaining information relevant to the divorce proceeding. Although it is sometimes used as a "fishing expedition," its proper focus is on relevant, unprivileged information pertaining to all issues involved in a case, such as custody, support, and property division. Its primary purposes are:

- to learn about the claims and defenses of the other side
- to understand the strengths and weaknesses of the case from the perspective of each of the parties
- to avoid surprises at hearings and at trial
- to promote settlement

Discovery is governed by procedural rules, limitations, and timelines that must be carefully followed. The paralegal must master these rules and any related amendments or variations county to county. The state may require specific basic kinds of mandatory discovery/production within a certain time period following service of the complaint (e.g., forty-five days). In addition, informal discovery may be completed by the entire family law team with the assistance of the client. Formal discovery methods available in every state include:

- Interrogatories
- Depositions
- Requests for Production of Documents or Things or Entry Upon Land
- Requests for Admissions
- Requests for Medical or Physical Examinations

There are several discovery-related motions that may be filed. The most common include the following:

- Motion for a Protective Order to limit discovery
- Motion to Compel Discovery (and impose sanctions, if appropriate)
- Request for Status Conference regarding discovery to clarify issues, resolve disputes, and outline a plan, methods, and timeline (such conferences may be required by the court)
- Motion for Fees to cover the costs of various discovery initiatives, such as accountants, appraisers, and the like

The paralegal's role in all kinds of discovery (formal, informal, electronic, etc.) is discussed at considerable length in Chapter 6, "Discovery and Financial Statements."

Negotiation and Drafting of the Separation Agreement

If the parties reach agreement on all unresolved issues following discovery, a **separation agreement** can be drafted, reviewed, and executed, and the case can move forward on an uncontested basis. If the parties have resolved some, but not all, issues, a partial separation agreement can be drafted that addresses all issues not in dispute. Whether the agreement is full or partial, the parties customarily request that the court incorporate it into the divorce judgment. Depending on its terms, the agreement either will "merge" into the judgment and lose its separate identity, or it will "survive" (with the exception of child-related provisions) as an independent contract with legal significance apart from the judgment. The concepts of "merger" and "survival" are discussed more fully in Chapter 12, which focuses entirely on the topic of separation agreements. It

Separation agreement
an agreement made between spouses in anticipation of divorce or legal separation concerning the terms of the divorce or separation and any continuing obligations of the parties to one another

provides drafting advice, a comprehensive model of a complete agreement, and a description of the primary tasks the paralegal may perform with respect to separation agreements.

Pretrial Activities

States vary with respect to the specific nature and sequencing of activities that take place between the time the parties reach an impasse regarding one or more issues and decide to proceed to trial and the date of the actual trial. Typically the following activities occur, although they may be labeled differently in various jurisdictions.

- The moving party files a *Request for Pretrial Conference/Hearing*, if required (may be in the form of a request for a trial that automatically triggers a court-ordered pretrial conference/hearing). The paralegal for the moving party may draft the request (or prepare the required form for signature and filing).
- The court issues a *Pretrial Conference Notice and Order* indicating what is required at the pretrial conference/hearing. When the notice is received, the paralegal will mark the assigned pretrial conference date, place, and presiding judge on all appropriate calendars and advise the client of the date and location in writing.
- Many states require that a *four-way conference* be held at this point prior to the formal pretrial conference.
- Each side prepares a *Pretrial Memorandum*, which customarily must address the following:
  - procedural history of the case
  - uncontested issues
  - contested issues, including contested issues of fact (finances, parenting skills, etc.) and contested issues of law (custody, alimony, attorney's fees, etc.), including the status of agreement with respect to each issue
  - status of discovery and time frame for completion (usually must be completed prior to filing a request for trial)
  - list of exhibits (including written objections, if any)
  - list of proposed witnesses (including experts)
  - property values (agreed on and disputed)
  - estimated length of trial

An experienced paralegal may be asked to prepare the first draft of the Pretrial Memorandum.

- The *Pretrial Conference* is held and the court reviews the topics covered in the parties' memoranda. The judge/marital master who conducts the hearing usually strongly urges the parties to settle their differences and avoid the necessity of a trial. Some judges even will suggest how they are likely to rule on particular issues.
- Following the pretrial conference, if there is a need to complete further discovery and/or there is any potential for settlement, the court may, at the request of counsel or on its own initiative, schedule one or more status conferences.
- If and when the parties arrive at a clear impasse, one or both of them will file a *Request for Trial*. The paralegal may draft the Request or prepare the required form for signature and filing.

- The court then issues a *Pretrial Order* and assigns a trial date. The paralegal should mark the trial date on all appropriate calendars and notify the client in writing.

The Trial

PREPARATION FOR TRIAL

The opposing sides prepare for trial, although negotiations often continue in hopes the case can be settled "on the courthouse steps," thereby avoiding further litigation expense and emotional trauma. The nature, extent, and cost of trial preparation depend on the type, number, and complexity of disputed issues to be addressed at trial. For example, some couples may be able to resolve all issues with the exception of the disposition of the marital home, an issue they can argue in a half-day trial with only the parties as witnesses and an agreed-upon appraisal of the property. Others may be unable to agree on any issues and maintain fixed positions with respect to the grounds for divorce, alimony, property division, and child custody and support. In such cases, the trial may take a matter of weeks and involve extensive testimony of witnesses (including experts, private investigators, employers, and GALs, among others), complex exhibits, sophisticated audiovisuals and computer graphics, business and property valuations, etc.

Whatever the scope of the trial, an experienced paralegal may play a major supportive role in all aspects of trial preparation. Some tasks are common to virtually all trials, no matter what their scope. The members of the family law team need to:

- **Verify that all required documents have been filed or are ready for filing,** including a current Financial Statement, Child Support Guidelines Worksheet, and Parenting Plan, if necessary.
- **Request and confirm a stenographer** if necessary, to preserve the record for possible appeal. Some court stenographic services now offer an option of plugging into the stenographer's computer and obtaining a simultaneous transcription during the trial.
- **Prepare witnesses** for questions likely to be asked in both direct and cross-examination. Witnesses cannot be told what to say, but they can be given advice with respect to how to most effectively answer questions and handle themselves in the face of various styles of questioning by opposing counsel. Preparation may include a trip to the courthouse to orient potential witnesses to the environment and nature of the proceedings. The client also needs to be familiar with and understand the exhibits to be presented and their significance to the case.
- **Prepare/assemble a Trial Notebook.** (See Paralegal Application 5.5.)
- **Draft Trial Memorandum of Law, and Proposed Findings of Fact, Conclusions of Law, and Judgment, if required.** Counsel for each party is customarily required to prepare these documents in anticipation of trial, with a focus on contested issues and the factors the court will consider when making decisions regarding those issues:
  - **Trial Memorandum of Law.** The Trial Memorandum essentially lays out the basic facts of the case along with the client's arguments regarding contested issues supported by appropriate authority (statutory law, case law, secondary

Trial notebook
a term used loosely to describe the organizational system used by an attorney to assemble all of the material needed for a trial

Proposed Findings of Fact
facts that a party asks a court to accept as true

Conclusions of Law
statements as to how governing law applies to a case

PARALEGAL PRACTICE TIP

To see an example of a form for a court's Findings of Fact, Conclusions of Law, and Judgment, visit *www.wi-courts.gov*. You can find a link to this site at *www.pearsonhighered.com/wilson* in the companion website material for Chapter 5 under "Forms."

PARALEGAL PRACTICE TIP

Increasingly, courts are requesting that certain documents, such as Trial Memoranda, Proposed Findings of Fact, Conclusions of Law, and Proposed Orders, be submitted in both hard copy and electronic formats, partially in anticipation that the court may adopt all or a significant portion of a party's submission. The chances of this happening are significantly increased when the proposals are realistic and consistent with governing authority.

sources, etc.). This document provides the court with references to potential authoritative support for its findings.

- **Proposed Findings of Fact:** In Proposed Findings of Fact, the attorney (on behalf of the client) asks that the court accept certain facts as true, such as the date and length of the marriage, the parties' ages and health status, their education and employability, and their respective contributions to the marriage. In most cases, the parties will stipulate, or agree to, a number of basic facts in advance of trial so that proof will not need to be presented with respect to those matters.

- **Conclusions of Law:** Conclusions of Law are statements for the court's potential adoption as to how governing law should apply to the case from the client's perspective. For example, the attorney may propose conclusions such as the following based on the facts of the case at hand:

  - That the court has jurisdiction over the case and the parties (based on the particular statutes authorizing jurisdiction)

  - That a judgment of divorce should be entered when the court is satisfied that the parties' marriage is so irretrievably broken that it cannot be remedied and the parties can no longer live together (referencing the state's no-fault statute and possibly case law or other authority)

  - That, in dividing the parties' property, the court may consider the source of assets, particularly if acquired through inheritance or a party's family of origin (based on the applicable state statute and case law or other authority)

  - That custody decisions are to be guided by the best-interests-of-the-child standard and there is a presumption against awarding custody to a parent who has a documented history of abuse (based on statute and case law)

- **Proposed Judgment.** A Proposed Judgment is a judgment written from the client's perspective that the court is urged to adopt as its own. An example of a Proposed Judgment appears in Exhibit 5.7.

Paralegal **Application 5.5**

The Trial Notebook

In all cases to be tried, no matter how uncomplicated, *organization* is critical. Thorough preparation is extremely important to the success of a case and leaves a favorable impression on the court (and the client!). The term "trial notebook" is used loosely to describe the organizational system used by an individual attorney to assemble all of the materials needed for trial. The physical form of the trial notebook may vary—it may truly take the form of an indexed loose-leaf binder or it may be in the shape of a series of well-labeled files organized in boxes if necessary. It often comprises multiple "notebooks":

- **The Trial Notebook.** This notebook essentially contains a script for the attorney that organizes ma-

terials according to each stage of the trial: an overall trial outline, an opening statement, outlines of witness examinations (and potential questions for cross-examination), identification and description of all exhibits, excerpts of deposition transcripts and interrogatories to be used, and a closing argument.

- **Supplemental notebooks.** These notebooks organize all of the material related to the case that may or may not be needed at trial, including, but not necessarily limited to:

  - a notebook containing all pleadings and rulings with those that are central to the case, clearly tabbed, and accessible if needed

(Continued)

- a notebook containing tabbed discovery materials with accompanying summaries
- a notebook containing clearly indexed financial information, including financial statements of each party, tax returns, bank records, credit card statements, mortgage applications, pay stubs, pension data, etc.
- a witness notebook containing subfiles for each witness in alphabetical order, including curriculum vitae, deposition summaries/transcripts, correspondence, etc. This notebook may include appraisals of various assets (real estate, collections, businesses, etc.), medical reports, and reports of investigators, including court-ordered evaluations.
- a notebook containing indexed research files by issue (for example, when a party can be granted a greater than 50% share of the marital assets, child support awards outside of the guidelines, or designation of certain assets as marital property). If any seminal cases may be referenced at trial, four copies of relevant opinions should be available "just in case" (one for the court, one for the stenographer, and the other two for counsel).
  - an indexed notebook containing correspondence with the court, opposing counsel, the client, and others, organized separately and usually by date with the most recent appearing first

- Some courts, particularly in complex cases, require counsel to prepare indexed **Exhibit Notebooks** for the convenience of the court and to save considerable trial time sorting through and marking exhibits during the trial. Four copies usually are prepared: one for each attorney, one for the court, and one for use with witnesses who are testifying. The Exhibit Notebook generally contains:
  - The plaintiff's exhibits (disputed and undisputed)
  - The defendant's exhibits (disputed and undisputed)
  - Copies of current financial statements for each party
  - The GAL's report if the guardian will be called as a witness by either party
  - Stipulations of the parties with respect to such issues as tax matters, property values, and business valuations. (Depending on the court, these may be read into the record.)

Exhibit notebook
a notebook, prepared for the convenience of the court and counsel, containing all exhibits to be introduced at trial by either or both parties

In more complex trials, there are additional tasks that the family law team may need to complete prior to trial, including the following:

- Prepare **subpoenas** for people (including the GAL, if warranted) and subpoenas *duces tecum*. A subpoena is a document ordering a witness to appear and provide testimony in a court hearing or trial. A **subpoena *duces tecum*** requires the witness to bring with him or her certain documents such as bank, pension, or employment records.
- Obtain certified copies of public documents as appropriate, for example, certified copies of related legal proceedings conducted in other jurisdictions.
- Gather documentation regarding any expert witnesses so that the court will be positioned to qualify them as "experts" able to render expert opinions.
- Prepare **Motions *in Limine*** and memoranda in support of or in opposition to admissibility of particular evidence.
- Prepare a Motion to Assess Counsel Fees, if warranted.
- Prepare a Complaint for any arrearages in payments due under temporary orders.
- Create PowerPoint presentations, illustrative graphics, etc., that will clearly illustrate major points and complex topics in a "simplified" form for the court.

Subpoena
a document ordering a witness to appear and provide testimony in a legal proceeding, such as a deposition, court hearing, or trial

Subpoena *duces tecum*
a subpoena ordering a witness to appear in a legal proceeding such as a deposition, court hearing, or trial and to bring with him or her specified documents, records, or things

Motion *in limine*
a motion asking the court to exclude or limit the use of certain evidence at trial

THE TRIAL

The trial in a contested case is a full trial involving opening and closing statements, presentation of each party's case through direct and cross-examination of witnesses, and introduction of evidentiary exhibits. The usual standard of proof in divorce cases is **preponderance of the evidence** (i.e., it is more likely than not that the facts alleged are true). The trial is intended to resolve all disputed issues. Divorce trials are open to the public although rarely attended except in higher-profile cases. Some states, such as New York and Texas, permit jury trials in divorce cases.

Although the attorney presents the client's case, the paralegal may perform several functions during the trial:

- With the court's permission, the paralegal may attend the trial and be seated at the counsel table with the client and the attorney. Counsel will introduce the paralegal by name and will indicate his or her paralegal status. The paralegal may then assist counsel by quickly locating needed documents, pointing out relevant materials, and providing support and encouragement to the client.
- Both the paralegal and the client may make notes during the trial regarding important issues, documents needed, ideas for additional questions, portions of exhibits to counter the defendant's testimony, etc.
- The paralegal is available to make needed copies and phone calls and confirm the arrival of a scheduled witness (or track down an absent witness!).

Preponderance of the evidence
a standard of proof requiring that the evidence show that it is more likely than not that an alleged fact is true or false as claimed

THE JUDGMENT

After the case is presented, the judge reviews the evidence, testimony, etc., and makes a decision on the merits of the case. Some judges render decisions promptly, and others take a matter of weeks, even months, depending in part on the complexity of the case. Customarily, the judge first enters an **Interlocutory Decree (or a Decree *Nisi*)** along with accompanying findings of fact and conclusions of law. An interlocutory decree is not final, and the parties are technically still married until a final decree issues. If they reconcile in the interim period, a **Motion to Vacate the Judgment** may be filed. The **Final Judgment** (sometimes called the Judgment Absolute) usually enters automatically in most jurisdictions after a specified period of time (commonly thirty to ninety days). The paralegal should obtain certified copies of the decree and send them to the client, who will need them for a variety of postdivorce matters, such as changing accounts and insurance policies.

Interlocutory Decree/Decree *Nisi*
an interim decree; a decree that is not final

Motion to Vacate the Judgment
a motion requesting the court to nullify or cancel a judgment before it becomes final

Final Judgment/Judgment Absolute
the court's final decision determining the rights of the parties and issues in dispute

PARALEGAL PRACTICE TIP

To see an example of a Stipulation and Order Vacating a Judgment of Divorce or Legal Separation, visit *www. wicourts.gov*. (Wisconsin) You can find a link to this site at *www.pearsonhighered.com/wilson* in the companion website material for Chapter 5 under "Forms."

Postdivorce Proceedings

Depending on the circumstances of each case, a variety of postdivorce proceedings may be necessary.

EXHIBIT 5.7 Example of a Proposed Judgment

STATE OF_____

_____COUNTY
FAMILY COURT
DOCKET NO:_____

TIFFANY HEALEY,)
Plaintiff)
) PLAINTIFF'S
v.) PROPOSED JUDGMENT
)
NOEL HEALEY,)
Defendant)

All interested persons having been notified in accordance with law and after hearing, it is adjudged *nisi* that a divorce be granted to the Plaintiff for the cause of irretrievable breakdown of the marriage (*cite statute*) and that upon the expiration of ninety (90) days from entry of this judgment it shall become absolute unless, upon application of any person within such period, the court shall otherwise order. It is further ordered that:

1. The Agreement of the parties dated April 1, 2011, is incorporated and merged in this judgment and hereafter shall have no independent legal significance.
2. The property located at 1125 Marlboro St., _____, shall be conveyed to the wife by the husband within one hundred and twenty (120) days of this date.
3. The parties shall have joint legal custody of the minor child, Bethany Healey, and physical custody shall be with the mother with reasonable rights of visitation to the father consistent with the parenting plan filed with this court and dated April 1, 2011.
4. The husband shall pay child support in the amount of $465.00 per month payable on the first day of each month commencing on June 1, 2011, said amount being consistent with this state's guidelines for child support.
5. Each party shall be responsible for his or her own health insurance and uninsured medical, dental, and/or psychiatric expenses, and the father shall maintain health insurance for the benefit of the minor child.
6. Each party shall pay his or her own legal fees and costs.

_____
Presiding Justice

Dated:_____

POST-TRIAL MOTIONS

Post-trial motions may include the following:

- **Motion to Alter and Amend the Judgment** to correct factual and substantive errors
- **Motion for a New Trial,** alleging that prejudicial errors made during the trial affected the outcome. This motion usually must be brought promptly (e.g., within ten days).
- **Motion for Relief From Judgment,** based on fraud, mistake, or newly discovered evidence, etc. This kind of motion usually must be brought within a reasonable period (e.g., within a year after entry of judgment). When the motion is allowed, the court may modify its initial judgment or vacate it and order a new trial.

PARALEGAL PRACTICE TIP

To see an example of a motion for a new trial, Google "Sample Form 40 Motion for New Trial."

PARALEGAL PRACTICE TIP

To review a variety of appellate forms used in the state of Washington, visit *www.courts.wa.gov/forms.* The state of Alaska has an extensive self-help appeals process that guides the litigant through the process and provides necessary forms. You can find this material by visiting *http://www.courts.alaska.gov.* Links to both of these sites can be found at *www.pearsonhighered.com/wilson* in the companion website material for Chapter 5 under "Forms."

Appellant

the party bringing an appeal of a lower court's judgment

Appellee

the party against whom an appeal is brought

The paralegal may be asked to draft these motions with careful attention to governing rules and strict timelines. Prior to doing so, he or she will need to obtain a copy of the transcript of the trial or portions of it, as necessary.

APPEAL OF A FINAL JUDGMENT

Occasionally, a client will elect to appeal a final judgment or the portion of it that is adverse. The party filing the appeal is called the **appellant** and the opposing party is the **appellee.** The appeals process is governed by procedural rules and strict time standards that must be satisfied throughout the process, and an appeal can be dismissed for failure to meet a deadline. The appeal is usually heard by an intermediate appellate court unless the state does not have one, in which case it goes directly to the state's highest court. A decision of an intermediate appellate court usually can be appealed to the state's highest court.

PARALEGAL PRACTICE TIP

Appeals, etc., are usually subject to statutes of limitations that must be honored. For example, in a 2006 Texas case, following the death of her former husband, a woman unsuccessfully sought relief when she learned that, shortly before he'd died, he had changed his will in favor of his current wife. The change violated a provision of the parties' divorce decree that required all finances and insurance policies through the time of divorce be granted to the ex-wife. A Texas appellate court held that her claim was subject to a two-year statute of limitations governing family law actions rather than by the longer six-year statute of limitations governing contracts.[29]

An appellate court does not retry the case. The appeal is based on the record of what took place at the trial court level. New evidence is not introduced. The focus is on whether the trial court made any errors in applying the law to the facts of the case or abused its discretion and made findings of fact unsupported by the evidence. Great deference is shown to the trial court's findings, because that court was in the best position to hear and assess the credibility of the witnesses.

The basic steps in the appeals process are the following:

- The appellant files a notice of appeal in the appropriate court within the required period after the final judgment (usually the date of the decree *nisi*).
- The appellant designates the portion of the trial court materials he or she wants in the record on appeal (including any relevant portions of the transcript), and the appellee may cross-designate materials.
- The clerk assembles the record and then dockets the case with the appeals court.
- The parties submit briefs (first the appellant, then the appellee), and, after the submissions, the appellant has an opportunity to respond to the appellee's brief.
- The court may decide the appeal based on the briefs and the record or may hear oral argument.
- The appellate court affirms, reverses (in whole or in part), and/or remands for a new trial consistent with its opinion.

The paralegal may:

- Draft the notice of appeal for review, signature, and filing.
- Monitor the appeals process (deadlines, notice of appeal, submission of materials, etc.).

- Contact a stenographer and make arrangements to have the relevant portions of the transcript prepared and filed.
- Research and draft the appellate brief, although such assignments are generally given only to highly skilled and experienced paralegals.

COMPLAINT FOR MODIFICATION

Either party may, at some point after judgment, find it necessary to file a Complaint (or Motion, depending on the jurisdiction) for Modification of child custody, child support, or spousal support (where permitted) based on a substantial change in circumstances (such as a change in employment status, income, marital status, residence, and/or health). The court may issue temporary orders while the modification action is pending and discovery is conducted, if necessary. The paralegal may be asked to research and draft the Complaint for Modification (or the Answer to a Complaint if representing the defendant) for review, signature, and filing. Absent an agreement between the parties, the court will issue its order after a hearing on the merits.

COMPLAINT FOR CONTEMPT

An existing order of the court remains valid until the court declares otherwise. However, it is not uncommon for clients simply to decide they should not have to comply with an order because of changed circumstances, such as the loss of a job or development of a serious medical problem, or because the other party is not abiding by the terms of the decree in some manner. For example, if the noncustodial parent fails to pay child support, the custodial parent may unilaterally decide to deny visitation without the court's authorization.

When a party fails to comply with the terms of the judgment, the other party may file a Complaint for Contempt (sometimes called a Petition for Contempt or a Motion to Enforce Litigant's Rights). The paralegal may be asked to research and draft the Complaint for Contempt (or the Answer to a Complaint if representing the defendant) for review, signature, and filing. In addition to holding a defendant in contempt, several other remedies may be requested to enforce the decree, such as garnishment of wages or a declaration of a **constructive trust** over property, depending on the nature of the defendant's noncompliance with the court's order. There may be a statutory presumption that attorney's fees will be awarded to the prevailing party in a contempt action but, if not, they should be requested. After a hearing, the court will issue its order. The paralegal should ensure that a copy is sent promptly to the client.

PARALEGAL PRACTICE TIP

If the parties executed a separation agreement that survived the divorce judgment as an independent contract, the agreement may serve as a bar to modification of non-child-related provisions or may set forth the conditions under which modifications can occur.

Constructive trust
a trust imposed by the court on an asset of a party who improperly or wrongfully acquired the property

PARALEGAL PRACTICE TIP

To see an example of a Petition for Contempt, visit *http://www.courts.state.nh.us.* You can find a link to this site at *www.pearsonhighered.com/wilson* in the companion website material for Chapter 5 under "Forms."

PARALEGAL PRACTICE TIP

If the parties' separation agreement survives as an independent contract, relief may also be sought in a **court of equity** (for **specific performance** of the contract).

Court of equity
a court that has authority to decide controversies in accordance with rules and principles of equity (principles of fairness)

Specific performance
a remedy for breach of contract in which the court orders the breaching party to complete the contract as promised

Follow-up Matters

After the divorce is final, a number of follow-up tasks may need to be completed by one, the other, or both of the parties with or without the assistance of the attorney who handled the divorce. These actions may include, for example:

- Preparation of deeds transferring real property interests
- Preparation and processing of a **QDRO**
- Transfer of stock ownership, etc.
- Closing of joint accounts
- Payment of joint debts
- Drafting of a petition for name change if desired and not addressed as part of the divorce action
- Preparation of a new estate plan (may include a will, trust, health care proxy, etc.)

If any of these tasks fall within the attorney's scope of employment, the paralegal may monitor their completion to ensure they are carried out in a timely manner.

The initial fee agreement/letter of engagement should specify the point at which the attorney's responsibility to the client with respect to the case will end and, specifically, whether or not it includes postdivorce activity. Even with a clear agreement, it is wise to send the client a letter of termination of services when the representation concludes, noting any need for follow-up in various areas. Some attorneys conduct closing interviews with the client in which they review the representation from start to finish, discuss the results obtained, identify matters requiring the client's attention, and answer any questions the client may have.[30]

The Uncontested Scenario

This chapter has focused in large part on the divorce process in a contested case. However, it is estimated that more than 90% of divorce cases proceed on an uncontested basis. Although generally considerably less costly in terms of time and dollars, an uncontested divorce can still be very costly emotionally. The two primary ways in which a divorce is uncontested are (1) when the divorce is sought jointly by the parties and (2) when the defendant does not oppose the divorce and either participates without opposition or fails to respond at all. The following material briefly outlines the process when the divorce is jointly sought by the parties, who may proceed *pro se* or with the assistance of counsel at each stage.

- The parties make the decision to dissolve their marriage on an uncontested (and usually no-fault) basis with or without having participated in counseling and/or contacting attorneys.
- The parties (with or without the assistance of dispute resolution options) negotiate the terms of an agreement resolving all of their marital rights and obligations and dividing their personal property and realty.
- The parties identify the proper forum in which to file their action for divorce.
- The parties draft and file their Joint Petition for Divorce, usually accompanied by the following:
  - Filing fee (or request for waiver, if eligible)
  - Certified copy of the parties' marriage certificate
  - Joint affidavit of irretrievable breakdown of the marriage

Qualified Domestic Relations Order (QDRO)
a court order directing the administrator of a pension plan to pay a specified portion of a current or former employee's pension to an alternate payee to satisfy a support or other marital obligation

- The Financial statements
- Fully executed separation agreement
- The Affidavit disclosing any care and custody proceedings, if the parties have minor children
- The Certificates of Completion of Parent Education Program, if required
- Parenting Plan, if required
- Child Support Guidelines Worksheet, if there are minor children
- Income Assignment Worksheet, if applicable

- The parties request a final hearing (sometimes called a Request for Trial).
- The final hearing takes place, and the court renders a Judgment.

Some courts require that both parties (and/or their respective attorneys) be present at the final hearing unless an absence is excused by the court. However, the trend is toward minimizing court appearances, and some jurisdictions no longer require either party to be present in a joint action. Hearings on joint petitions are customarily quite brief (five to fifteen minutes). However, a limited number of questions are usually asked so that it is apparent the court has made some inquiry and not simply rubber-stamped the parties' agreement. If the parties are represented, the court may have counsel question their clients. If a party is unrepresented, the court will conduct the questioning. The questions are very basic and usually address the following:

- parties' names and addresses
- facts about the marriage: when and where the parties married and when and where they last lived together as husband and wife
- names and ages of minor children, if any
- parties' shared belief that the marriage is irretrievably broken
- the separation agreement: Have the parties read it, discussed it with counsel, understood its terms, and signed it voluntarily?

The court may then ask specific questions on key issues, such as insurance coverage, custodial arrangements, wage assignment, and waivers of spousal support. It is important that the parties understand the terms of the agreement so they can respond intelligently if asked about them.

Even in an uncontested divorce, postdecree activity is sometimes warranted, including:

- Posttrial motions
- Actions to enforce the judgment (contempt actions, etc.)
- Modifications of the judgment (based on substantial change in circumstances)

PARALEGAL PRACTICE TIP

Even if the case is uncontested, if the court reviews the agreement and considers it grossly one-sided, the judge may continue the matter until the seemingly disadvantaged party consults with an attorney and provides documentation to the court that he or she has done so.

CHAPTER **SUMMARY**

The "culture of divorce" has changed dramatically over the past four decades from a fault-based system that made litigation inevitable to one that emphasizes the parties' capacity to resolve their differences without blame and courtroom battles. The focus has shifted from a preoccupation with fault and morality to one emphasizing economics and the nature of marriage, and particularly of parenthood, as a partnership that does not necessarily end upon divorce. The no-fault model recognizes the complexity of human relationships and the likelihood that in any given marriage, no one party bears full responsibility for its success or failure.

Couples who want to separate or dissolve their relationship have four potential legal options, depending on the facts of their case: divorce, legal separation, separate support, and annulment. For some individuals, it is also important to seek a religious termination of the marital relationship that will allow them to remarry within their faith.

Although the bulk of the content of this chapter describes the sequence of events in a contested case, approximately 90% of divorces are obtained without the necessity of a trial. To some extent, this is the result of an increasing emphasis by the legal profession, including the courts, on the use of alternative methods of resolving disputes, such as direct negotiation between the parties, mediation, collaborative law, negotiation through counsel, neutral case evaluation, and arbitration.

The content of this chapter highlights the basic stages of the divorce process. Depending on his or her skills and experience, the paralegal may play a key role at virtually every stage of the divorce process in both uncontested and contested cases. Various aspects of that role are described in this chapter.

CONCEPT REVIEW AND REINFORCEMENT

KEY TERMS

Adultery
Alternative dispute resolution
Annulment
Answer
Appearance
Appellant
Appellee
Arbitration
Bifurcated divorce
Collusion
Complaint
Conclusions of Law
Condonation
Connivance
Constructive desertion
Counterclaim
Cruel and abusive treatment
Defense
Desertion/abandonment
Discovery
Divorce
Divorce *a mensa et thoro*
Divorce *a vinculo matrimonii*
Domicile

Dual divorce
Exhibit notebook
Ex parte motion
Fault grounds
Fee agreement
Final Judgment/Judgment Absolute
Ground for divorce
Guardian *ad litem* (GAL)
In rem jurisdiction
Interlocutory Decree/Decree *Nisi*
Irreconcilable differences
Legal separation
Letter of engagement
Letter of nonengagement/declination
Living separate and apart
Long-arm statute
Marital communications privilege
Mediation
Memorandum of *lis pendens*
Military affidavit
Motion
Motions *in limine*
Motion to Dismiss
Motion to Vacate the Judgment

Neutral case evaluation
No-fault divorce
No-fault grounds
Nonbinding arbitration
Parenting coordinator
Pendente lite
Personal jurisdiction
Preponderance of the evidence
Proposed Findings of Fact
Pro se
Provocation
Recrimination
Separate maintenance
Separation agreement
Service of process
Stipulation
Subject matter jurisdiction
Subpoena
Subpoena *duces tecum*
Summons
Temporary orders
Trial notebook
Venue

REVIEW QUESTIONS

1. Describe how the "culture of divorce" has changed over the past forty years.
2. Identify the four legal proceedings parties use to separate from each other or dissolve their marriage, and give examples of when each of them might be appropriate.
3. Define "bifurcated divorce" and identify a circumstance in which one might occur.
4. Identify the six most common dispute resolution options used in divorce cases. What are the primary differences among them ?

5. Define subject matter, personal (*in personam*), and *in rem* jurisdiction in the divorce context and indicate how each is acquired by a court.
6. Identify the primary difference between a fault and a no-fault ground for divorce and give a common example of each.
7. Identify a minimum of five potential defenses to a divorce action.
8. Describe the nature and purpose of a complaint.
9. Identify the primary ways of serving process and describe the nature and purpose of a long-arm statute.

10. Identify the two most common responses of a defendant to an action for divorce and indicate the differences between them.
11. Describe the nature and purpose of temporary orders.
12. Identify a minimum of five kinds of motions sometimes filed in divorce actions while the litigation is pending.
13. Explain why a party might choose to file a motion on an *ex parte* basis. Give an example.

14. Identify the primary purposes of discovery.
15. Describe the nature and purpose of a separation agreement.
16. Identify and describe a minimum of four major "documents" prepared in anticipation of trial.
17. Identify the most common kinds of divorce-related legal proceedings brought postdivorce.
18. Describe the role of the paralegal in the various stages of the divorce process

DEVELOPING YOUR PARALEGAL SKILLS

FOCUS ON **THE JOB**

In this Focus on the Job, the student has an opportunity to participate in an interview and draft a variety of documents tailored to the needs of the parties in a hypothetical divorce action.

The Facts

David and Marie Rogers were married on July 17, 1997, in your city and state at St. Patrick's Church. Marie was born on September 7, 1977, and David was born on October 3, 1976. Both parties were born in your city and state and were raised as devout Catholics. David no longer practices his religion, but Marie has remained very active in her local church. The children often attend Mass with her, and this is a source of considerable tension between the parties.

David and Marie were high school sweethearts. After graduation from high school, Marie remained at home with her parents. She worked as a cashier in a local Starbucks and attended "beauty school" in the evenings at the regional vocational school. She was unable to complete her course of study because her mother became very ill and Marie had to stay home and take care of her. David went off to your state's university to study mathematics.

David and Marie initially planned to get married following David's graduation from college, and in the interim, they continued to see each other during his school vacations. During his senior year, David wrote to Marie and said he wanted to date other women. Marie was devastated. During spring break, they went to Florida and, while there, had sexual relations for the first and only time prior to marriage. Marie became pregnant and, as a result of the pregnancy, the couple decided to get married. Because of David's concerns that they were rushing into marriage prematurely, they executed a premarital agreement essentially providing that any assets or liabilities a party had entering the marriage would remain that party's, and any assets and liabilities accruing during the marriage would be divided equally. Despite his reservations about the timing, David thought getting married was what he wanted and should do.

Now, in retrospect, he feels he had no choice. The wedding was held shortly after his graduation, and their son, Jon, was born on December 12, 1997. A second son, Charles, was born on May 12, 2000, and a daughter, Megan, was born on June 16, 2007.

Since their marriage, David has been employed as a math teacher at the local community college. Initially he had hoped to begin working on his master's degree in math following graduation while Marie continued her cashier's job, but the parties jointly decided it was important for Marie to stay home with Jon. Accordingly, to his great disappointment, David was unable to pursue his educational plans.

David earns $68,000 a year at his teaching job, and his family is covered on his insurance plan. He has paid into the state employees' pension fund since starting at the college in 1997 and became vested after ten years of service. He also does odd jobs for people during the summer months and on weekends and earns an additional $8,000 a year from that work. He is paid "under the table" for these odd jobs, and the couple has never paid taxes on this income. They have filed a joint return every year since they married. David has been a good provider and a devoted father to his two sons, but has had trouble relating to his daughter.

Since the birth of Jon, Marie has not been employed outside of the home. She maintains the home and is the primary caretaker of the children. At the time Marie became pregnant with Megan, David had been accepted into a master's degree program and Marie was going to return to work to help support the family. The plan was that when David completed his degree, he would then support Marie through beauty school and possibly a four-year-degree program if she wanted to go to college.

David believes that Marie got pregnant deliberately by failing to use birth control. He thinks that she was trying to sabotage his plans to return to school as she had done years before. He asked her to have an abortion, but she refused, given her strong religious beliefs. This was a major crisis in their relationship, and, during the pregnancy, the marriage began to fall apart. David's frustration kept building and he became increasingly resentful that, once again, he would have to defer his educational plans because of Marie's pregnancy.

David remained bitter and, according to Marie, has never bonded with Megan. His interaction with her has been minimal, although he continues to engage in weekend activities with the boys. He acknowledges that he has difficulties with his daughter but says he was initially the same way with his boys until they got a little older and could talk and "do things."

Since Megan's birth, Marie has experienced several bouts of severe depression. She has been briefly hospitalized twice and is seeing a therapist regularly. She gained fifty pounds during her pregnancy with Megan and has put on an additional thirty pounds since giving birth. According to David, she also has begun to drink heavily and has neglected the household and the children. On several occasions, a neighbor has found her wandering around the neighborhood so inebriated that she was unable to find her way home.

Marie claims that David has become verbally abusive and has hit her on a few occasions. He denies hitting her, but acknowledges that he sometimes may have sounded "gruff" when he was particularly upset by her conduct. He says that she has closed herself off to any emotional support from him and has refused to engage in sexual relations since she became pregnant with Megan. He admits feeling trapped and overwhelmed by Marie's problems. This is particularly painful for him because he saw his own parents weighed down by the responsibilities of several children and vowed the same thing would never happen to him.

As for the children, Megan appears to be developmentally delayed. No one is quite sure why, but her pediatrician speculates that it may be due to the problems at home. A specialized play group has been recommended, but David and Marie have not followed through on the recommendation. The pediatrician has struggled with whether or not to file an abuse and neglect complaint, but so far has opted against doing this.

A few months ago, Jon was caught shoplifting CDs from a local store, but the store let him "work off" the offense without calling the police. David and Marie also learned recently that he and several other boys have been gathering at a friend's house after school to watch pornographic videos that an older neighbor rents for them. There is some concern that they may also have involved some younger neighborhood children in this activity at the man's request. Each parent blames the other for Jon's behavior. Marie is at a loss as to how to deal with him, and David tends to be quite strict and restricts the teenager's activities when Jon is with him.

Charles is doing extremely well in school academically but has limited social skills and no friends. He largely keeps to himself and Marie says he is a real computer "geek," spending hours at a time in front of the computer screen like his father. He says he likes being with his dad because they are interested in a lot of the same things.

Things finally reached the breaking point on February 1, 2011, and David moved out of the house at 412 Hale Street, your city and town (your area code-555–2712). He has refused to go to any kind of counseling despite Marie's request, unless the whole family is involved. He has moved to a small apartment at 412 High Street, your city and town (your area code-555–3010). David sees the boys on a regular basis each weekend and has spent a little time with Megan, although Marie seems very nervous about him doing so. David claims that since he has moved out, the house has become a "pigsty," and on several occasions when he went to pick up the boys, the children were filthy, there were no clean clothes to pack for the weekend, and there was virtually no food in the refrigerator. On one Sunday, it was ten in the morning and the children asked him if they could go get some breakfast before going to his apartment. Marie was at home, asleep on the couch in the living room, and David claims he smelled alcohol all around her. Marie claims he woke her up, shook her, and threatened to choke her if she did not get her act together. David doesn't deny shaking her but does deny threatening her. He said he shook her in a desperate effort to try and get through to her. Marie acknowledges that she has a problem dealing with caring for the home and the children on her own, but says that she is not neglectful and that David is just a compulsive "neatnik," a regular "Mr. Monk" who can't stand it when everything isn't just so.

Since he left the marital home, David has been dating a co-worker, Trisha Cronin. Marie suspects that he began dating her after she got pregnant with Megan, but David denies this. Trish is also a teacher and is working on a Ph.D. in comparative literature. She loves children and is unable to have any of her own because of a chronic medical condition. She and David are planning on moving in together at the end of the spring semester.

With respect to assets, the parties own the small condominium in which Marie presently resides with the children. They paid $180,000 for it shortly after their marriage with a $20,000 down payment. It is now assessed at about $280,000, but David claims the real estate market is greatly overinflated. They still owe about $77,000 on the mortgage. The money for the down payment came half from wedding presents and half from the proceeds of an insurance settlement from an automobile accident that Marie had been in. They have about $1,800 in a savings account and owe about $3,500 in credit card debt. David has about $19,000 in his retirement account and a government bond (with a present value of $15,000) that his father gave him before the parties married and that he has kept for a rainy day or an emergency. He also has a collection of seascape paintings by local artists that he began collecting as a small boy. Marie has a collection of figurines valued at about $3,500 and also a collection of Hummel figures she inherited from her grandmother as a young child. They own basic household furnishings valued at not more than $10,000, along with two cars, a Honda and a Toyota of relatively equivalent value, both of which are paid for.

David filed for divorce on March 15, 2011. The docket number assigned to the case is 11D-1351-DI1 (or another docket number provided by your professor). David's attorney is Juliana Wilson, Esq.

390 Main Street

Your city, town, and zip code

Your area code-555–2354

Bar Number: 0283412

David's social security number is 022–34–1919.

Marie will eventually retain Attorney James Sims. His address is 30 Washington Street in your city and town. His phone number is your area code-555-2424. His Bar Number is 346271. Marie's social security number is 044–43–6704.

The Assignment

If possible, the class should be divided into an even number of groups with up to six students in each group. Half of the groups will work as a family law team representing David and the other half representing Marie. The students on each team should develop a method for assigning the following tasks (e.g., by choice or drawing assignments), unless otherwise assigned by the course instructor.

David's Team

1. Two students role-play David's initial interview, one as David and one as the paralegal.

2. Draft a Complaint for Divorce

3. Draft a Motion for Temporary Orders with a Supporting Affidavit and Proposed Order

4. Draft a Motion for Appointment of a Guardian *ad litem,* with a supporting Affidavit and Proposed Order

5. Draft a Motion for Appointment of an Appraiser with a supporting Affidavit and a Proposed Order (to appraise the value of the marital home)

Marie's Team

1. Two students role-play Marie's initial interview, one as Marie and one as the paralegal

2. Draft an Answer (and a possible counterclaim for divorce) in response to David's Complaint

3. Draft a Motion for Temporary Orders with a supporting Affidavit and Proposed Order

4. Draft a Motion for Attorney's Fees with appropriate affidavits and a Proposed Order

5. Draft a Motion for Appointment of an Appraiser with a supporting Affidavit and a Proposed Order (to appraise the value of David's art collection)

FOCUS ON ETHICS

In this activity, the student is required to draft a memo to his or her supervisor summarizing the results of an interview in which a client expressed an intention to falsely accuse her husband of sexual abuse in an effort to gain custody of their children. The student is asked to make a recommendation regarding a future course of action in light of ethical canons governing the conduct of paralegals and attorneys.

The Assignment

Assume that you are the paralegal working for the attorney representing Marie in the above comprehensive fact pattern. You were present at the initial interview conducted with her by your supervisor, Attorney Sims. It was clear during that interview that Marie's top priority is to gain custody of all three children at all costs and that she is afraid David is going to try to take them away from her because of her psychological problems, alleged drinking, and poor housekeeping. Since the initial interview you have been asked to conduct a follow-up meeting with her to discuss a potential counterclaim for divorce and a motion for temporary orders including custody. In that interview, Marie tells you that she is prepared to

falsely claim that the reason David is having trouble developing a relationship with Megan is that he has been sexually abusing her. She says in this day and age, no judge is going to take a chance awarding custody to a father who may be sexually abusing his daughter. Marie says she has heard from her divorced friends that if she can get temporary custody, she is a "shoo-in" for permanent custody. Attorney Sims does little family law work in his practice but is a respected attorney known for his diligent and zealous advocacy on behalf of his clients. He has asked you to report to him regarding the interview and to make recommendations regarding the appropriate actions to be taken with respect to the counterclaim, the motion for temporary orders, and Marie personally.

Review the ethical canons for paralegals promulgated by the National Association of Legal Assistants contained in Appendix A of this text. Also obtain a copy of the ethical standards governing attorneys in your state. You should prepare a memorandum to your supervisor reporting the result of the interview and your recommendations with this material as a backdrop or frame of reference. Use the following basic format:

Interoffice Memorandum

> **TO:** *Your supervisor*
>
> **FROM:** *Your name*
>
> **RE:** *Follow-up Interview with Marie Rogers*
>
> **DATE:**
>
> **CASE:** David Rogers v. Marie Rogers
>
> **OFFICE FILE NUMBER/ DOCKET NUMBER:**
>
> Brief description of assignment: *What is it that you have been asked to do?*

Summary of interview: *Summarize the highlights of the interview.*

Ethical issues implicated: *Identify the ethical duties the paralegal and attorney have that are related to this situation and a future course of action.*

Analysis of the issues: *Discuss the applicability of the identified ethical duties to the facts of the case.*

Recommendations: *What actions do you recommend be taken? Suggestion: You may want to consider more than one scenario.*

FOCUS ON **CASE LAW**

In this Focus, the student will brief an appeal of a case involving bifurcation of a divorce action and jurisdiction over a defendant serving overseas in the military.

The Assignment

Read the opinion in *In re Marriage of Anthony J. Harris and Teasha J. Harris,* 922 N.E.2d 626 (Indiana 2010), and then brief the case using the format on the companion website or one provided by your instructor.

PARALEGAL PRACTICE TIP

The opinion in the *Harris* case is available at *www.pearsonhighered. com/wilson* in the companion website material related to Chapter under "Cases" and in the Case Resources Section of the MyLegal-StudiesLab.

The format for briefing a case is provided in the material related to Chapter 1 under "Resources."

FOCUS ON **STATE LAW AND PROCEDURE**

In this activity, students are asked to locate and prepare a list of basic laws and procedures related to divorce proceedings in their respective jurisdictions.

The Assignment

Prepare a list of the responses to the following questions:

1. Which chapters/sections of your state code govern divorce and related matters (custody, child and spousal support, and property division)?
2. Which section(s) of your state's statutes or rules of procedure govern service of process in domestic relations matters? Be sure to indicate where your state's applicable long-arm statute is located.
3. What are the grounds for divorce in your state and where are they set forth?
4. What residency requirement, if any, must a plaintiff satisfy in your state in order to be able to file a complaint for divorce?
5. What defenses to divorce are available in your jurisdiction?
6. Do the rules and procedures governing divorce actions vary within your state, e.g., by county/circuit, or are they uniform across the state?

FOCUS ON **TECHNOLOGY**

In addition to the links provided throughout the chapter, this focus provides a series of useful websites for reference along with technology-related assignments for completion.

Websites of Interest

Links to all of the listed websites are provided at *www. pearsonhighered.com/wilson* in the companion website material for Chapter 5 under "Resources."

http://www.americanbar.org

This is the website of the American Bar Association. Go to the website and search for divorce charts containing state-by-state information, particularly Chart 4 Grounds for Divorce and Residency Requirements. Search for "Family Law in the Fifty States."

www.divorcelawinfo.com

This is the website for the Divorce Law Information Center. It offers "do-it-yourself divorce kits" and state-by-state divorce and family law information, including child support calculators. Caution should always be exercised prior to actually using unofficial forms from commercial sites.

www.divorcelinks.com

This site offers links to state and federal divorce laws by topic.

www.divorcenet.com

This site offers links to state divorce laws, indicating statutory references and brief narratives on topics such as residence, grounds for divorce, "military divorce," approaches to division of property, alimony, and child custody, visitation, and support.

www.divorcesource.com

The site provides information on divorce laws by state. It also offers an online, for-fee QDRO preparation service. Caution should be exercised as QDRO formats vary employer to employer and must satisfy the requirements of plan administrators (as well as the courts).

www.findlaw.com

This is a particularly well-organized site with access to resources for both public and professional inquirers. It provides general and state-specific information, including access to the laws of all fifty states on divorce and related topics.

Assignments

1. Determine which, if any, divorce-related forms are available online in the state in which you are studying

family law. Several states (e.g., California, Colorado, Hawaii, Maryland, Massachusetts, New Hampshire, and Wisconsin) have state-sponsored sites (through courts or law libraries) that provide basic family law forms that can be printed or completed online. (See Appendix C and sites referenced in this chapter.)

2. Locate and visit a website that contains information about divorce laws in all fifty states, and describe the range of information provided with respect to your state.

3. Many people believe that the institution and traditional significance of marriage are seriously threatened by the no-fault divorce and same-sex marriage movements in particular. A number of national organizations and initiatives such as the Alliance for Marriage, the National Marriage Project, and the covenant marriage initiative have emerged, seeking to "save" marriage. Locate online four websites, two supporting no-fault divorce and two opposing it. What are the arguments on each side? Do you think covenant marriage is a good vehicle for resolving the differences? Why?

PORTFOLIO PRODUCTS

1. Complaint for Divorce or Answer/Motion to Dismiss
2. Motion for Temporary Orders with Supporting Affidavit
3. Motion for Appointment of Guardian *ad Litem* (with Supporting Affidavit and Proposed Order) or Motion for Attorneys Fees (with Affidavit(s) and Proposed Order)
4. Motion for Appointment of Appraiser (with Supporting Affidavit and Proposed Order)
5. Memorandum re ethical issues in a hypothetical situation
6. Brief of Case: *In Re Marriage of Anthony J. Harris and Teasha J. Harris,* 922 N.E.2d 626 (Indiana 2010)
7. List of basic laws and procedures related to divorce proceedings in the student's jurisdiction

chapter 6

DISCOVERY AND FINANCIAL STATEMENTS

LEARNING OBJECTIVES

After reading this chapter and completing related assignments, you should be able to:

- describe discovery—its nature, purpose, and scope in the domestic relations context

- list examples of informal discovery in family law cases

- identify the five formal discovery methods

- describe strengths and weaknesses of the various formal discovery methods

- explain what e-discovery is and how the Internet can serve as an information-gathering tool

- identify the kinds of objections that can be made to discovery requests

- discuss the sanctions that can be imposed for failing to comply with discovery requests, rules, and orders

- explain how to locate and complete financial affidavits

- identify ways of identifying and uncovering hidden assets

- describe the roles of the client, the paralegal, and the court in the discovery process

> Walter and Renee have been married for more than three decades. Throughout the marriage he has totally controlled their finances and, it would appear, not always to his wife's benefit. Now that she has filed for divorce, he has no desire to share information with her or her attorney about whatever modest assets he may have accumulated.

Discovery is one of the working tools of the legal profession. It seems clear and has long been recognized that discovery should provide a party access to anything that is evidence in his case.[1]

Definition of Discovery

Technically, **discovery** is the formal process by which parties engaged in litigation seek factual information and materials known by and available to other parties and potential witnesses in the action. More broadly viewed, it refers both to formal techniques of discovery governed by procedural rules and to less formal investigative initiatives, such as interviews with potential witnesses and the searching of public records.

PARALEGAL PRACTICE TIP

Although students commonly learn about discovery in civil litigation courses, it is important to understand that, in many jurisdictions, governing rules may vary in the domestic relations context. It is also useful to learn how various formal and informal information-gathering methods are utilized in family law cases to facilitate settlement and provide a framework for trial preparation, if necessary.

Purpose of Discovery

In the family law context, the primary purpose of discovery is to gather as much information about a case as possible so that attorneys can make appropriate recommendations and clients can make informed decisions

Discovery
the process of gathering information relevant to a matter at issue; includes both formal and informal methods

regarding their options, including whether they should settle a case or proceed to trial. In uncontested cases or cases involving few assets and no dispute with respect to custody, little or no discovery may be sought. In more complex or hotly contested cases in which it is appropriate, extensive discovery may be pursued.

Discovery can be very expensive, but a failure to conduct adequate discovery when it is warranted can be disastrous. In some instances, the family law team may fail to achieve the best possible result for the client. In the most egregious cases, a failure to conduct or produce discovery may result in a malpractice action against an attorney. (See Paralegal Application 6.1.) In many cases, one of the parties has significantly more resources than the other and is better positioned to conduct discovery. In such situations, the court may entertain a motion for attorneys' fees to allow the disadvantaged party to pursue or defend the action in order to avoid being forced to accept a settlement based on insufficient information.

Paralegal **Application 6.1**

What If the Client Will Not Authorize Discovery?

In some circumstances, after conducting interviews and examining various documents, the attorney may tell the client that it appears the other party has removed funds from certain accounts and is "hiding" them. Further discovery could be used to trace and locate those funds, but not without expense. Even though discovery might well result in a significantly more favorable property division settlement in the long run, the client may say that he or she simply cannot afford additional legal costs and insist that no further discovery be conducted, despite the attorney's advice.

In such situations, it is wise for the attorney to have the paralegal draft a letter to the client reiterating the advice given and its potential benefits and costs. The letter also should confirm that, notwithstanding that advice, the attorney has been explicitly directed by the client not to conduct further discovery. To avoid any misunderstanding, the client may be advised that the letter is forthcoming and, in some circumstances, be asked to provide a written acknowledgment of receipt. Such a letter, promptly sent by certified mail, documenting that the advice was given and specifically declined, helps defeat a potential later claim by the client that he or she received inadequate representation to his or her financial detriment.

Scope of Discovery

Technically, the scope of discovery is limited to information and material relevant to the subject matter of the case. For example, information regarding income and expenses is directly related to issues of spousal and child support as well as property division. In addition, the information or material requested must not be protected by a **privilege** such as the attorney-client or doctor-patient privilege. Although the information sought need not necessarily be admissible as evidence in its present form, it should be designed to lead to evidence that may be admissible at the time of trial.

PARALEGAL PRACTICE TIP

Depositions in particular are sometimes used as open-ended "fishing expeditions" to obtain information, both admissible and inadmissible. Attorneys need to maintain a delicate balance between unethical questioning engaged in for an improper purpose (such as harassing or intimidating the **deponent**) and strategic questioning conducted in the good-faith belief it will lead to admissible evidence.

Privilege
a legal right or exemption granted to a person or a class of persons not to testify in a legal proceeding; generally based on the existence of a special relationship

Deposition
a method of pretrial discovery in which one party questions the other party or a third person under oath; responses to oral or written questions are reduced to writing for possible later use in a court proceeding

Deponent
the individual who is asked to respond under oath to questions asked in a deposition

In conducting comprehensive discovery, family law teams seek information pertaining to the parties and their claims, defenses, and requests for relief. As difficult as it is to explain to clients, consideration needs to be given to identifying the strengths and weaknesses of each of the parties and their respective positions.

Discovery is most commonly sought regarding:

- financial assets and liabilities
- current income and expenses
- financial and nonfinancial contributions to the marriage
- dissipation of marital assets
- employment history, including efforts to find employment
- parenting history, skills, and weaknesses
- marital misconduct, such as substance abuse, infidelity, or treatment that has endangered a party's health and safety if fault grounds for divorce continue to exist in the jurisdiction and/or conduct during the marriage is a factor the court considers when making property division decisions

Early in a case, a discovery strategy will be established. It will identify the kinds of information needed, the techniques to be utilized (both formal and informal), the sequencing of efforts, the assignment of tasks, and the projected cost. The plan may need to be modified after discussion with the client—particularly if there are financial constraints or if new informational needs are identified. Thorough research and preparation are essential, and the paralegal is often charged with considerable responsibility in the information-gathering effort. The nature and extent of an individual paralegal's role in this process is largely a function of his or her level of expertise. For example, an experienced paralegal may be asked to recommend a discovery plan and draft complex, sophisticated discovery requests. An entry-level paralegal is more likely to be asked to check "Blue Book" values, draft motions to compel, and prepare relatively standard discovery requests, such as requests for production of employment contracts, insurance policies, or bank account statements. One of the most important tasks performed by paralegals is the marking of deadlines on all appropriate calendars. This task includes both critical deadlines prescribed by rules governing discovery and related to scheduled court appearances, meetings and depositions, etc., and also self-imposed deadlines for completion of discovery-related tasks, allowing sufficient time for review and revision. Many paralegals find it useful to maintain a "tickler" file reminding themselves of upcoming review and submission dates.

Informal discovery
information gathering not governed by specific procedural rules, such as researching public records and locating "Blue Book" values

PARALEGAL PRACTICE TIP

Informal discovery may also refer to an "informal" voluntary exchange of information between the parties and/or their attorneys without the necessity of resorting to costly formal discovery. This approach obviously works best in a collaborative environment in which the parties basically trust each other and there is a shared commitment to reaching a mutually agreed-upon settlement without litigation.

PARALEGAL PRACTICE TIP

An example of a Comprehensive Client Questionnaire is available at www.pearsonhighered.com/wilson in the companion website material related to Chapter 5 under "Resources."

Informal Discovery

Informal discovery may involve a variety of measures not usually governed by procedural rules. For example, a private investigator may be hired to document that a party who claims to be disabled and unable to work is actually attending a gym "working out" and playing touch football with his old high school buddies. A search of public records may be conducted to establish that a party has purchased property in another state with his or her paramour. Marital property may be photographed to show that it has been allowed to fall into disrepair by the other party. Potential witnesses, such as coaches, counselors, school nurses, and teachers, may be interviewed to explore and document the impact of a parent's behavior on a child. The most useful resource is often the client. (See Paralegal Application 6.2.)

Paralegal **Application 6.2**

The Client as a Resource

When a client first seeks representation in a divorce action, he or she customarily is asked to respond to a Comprehensive Client Questionnaire. In addition, even before an action is filed, many attorneys ask clients to perform some initial informal discovery. The client may be asked to:

- Photograph the contents of the marital residence (house or apartment) with particular attention to any potentially valuable items such as jewelry, antiques, art work, and gun collections.
- Keep a journal concerning such topics as parenting situations reflecting the particular strengths or weaknesses of each parent, unexplained phone calls and absences from the home, incidents of abuse of any kind, work being performed "under the table," etc.
- Locate and make copies of important documents such as deeds, titles, registrations, bank account statements, credit card statements, travel materials (such as airline tickets and hotel invoices), employ-

ment records, brokerage account statements, state and federal tax returns, and mortgage applications.
- Make copies of relevant electronic documents such as e-mails and financial records if legally accessible.
- Make a list of the names, addresses, and telephone numbers of potential **lay witnesses** for the client and for the other party, and identify the matters about which they might testify.
- Make a list of the names, addresses, and contact numbers of any professionals, such as physicians, therapists, accountants, financial advisors, and appraisers, consulted by either or both of the parties for their benefit or the benefit of their children.

Lay witness
a witness who is not an expert on a matter at issue in a legal proceeding who testifies as to opinions based on firsthand knowledge

Formal Discovery Methods

Although **formal discovery** cannot be initiated until after a Complaint is filed, a considerable amount of informal discovery may be conducted while working with the client prior to filing. Such initial investigative efforts may shape the theory of a case and the action to be filed—for instance, whether a fault or no-fault Complaint for Divorce should be filed in states where both options are available. Once a Complaint is filed and served, some states initially require the parties to make **mandatory self-disclosure** of certain information before going to the effort and expense of the five traditional methods of formal discovery. (See Paralegal Application 6.3.)

Formal discovery
discovery methods that are subject to procedural and court rules

Mandatory self-disclosure
material specified by statute or court rule that each party in a particular legal action must provide to the other party within a certain period after filing and service of a summons and complaint

Paralegal **Application 6.3**

Mandatory Self-Disclosure

In addition to financial statements, some states require by rule that each party automatically provide certain other documents to the opposing party within a certain period of time after the Complaint is filed and served. The Massachusetts rule governing Mandatory Self-Disclosure of Financial Documents[2] provides that neither party can make discovery requests until mandatory disclosure is made. Absent agreement of the parties or order of the court, each party is required to deliver to the other, within forty-five days of service of the summons of an action for divorce or separate support, documents including the following:

PARALEGAL PRACTICE TIP

In most instances, mandatory self-disclosure requirements help reduce discovery costs. If a party fails to make the required disclosure within the mandatory period, the other party's attorney will usually contact the party (or the attorney, if she or he is represented) and reach an agreement with respect to what is needed and by when. If informal efforts are unsuccessful, a motion to compel compliance may be filed, and related costs may be charged to the noncompliant party by the court.

(Continued)

- federal and state tax returns and supporting documentation for the past three years (individual, limited-partnership, and privately held corporate returns)
- bank statements for the prior three years for any bank accounts held in the name of the party or jointly with another party for the benefit of either party or the parties' minor children
- the four most recent pay stubs from each employer for whom the party works
- documentation of the cost and nature of available health insurance coverage

- statements for the past three years for any securities, stocks, bonds, notes or obligations, certificates of deposit (for the benefit of either party or the minor children), 401(k), IRA, and pension plans (for all accounts listed on the party's financial statement)
- copies of any loan or mortgage applications filed within the past three years
- copies of any financial statements or statements of assets and liabilities prepared within the last three years

The five basic formal discovery methods are:

1. Interrogatories
2. Depositions
3. Requests for Admissions
4. Requests for Production of Documents or Things or Entry Upon Land
5. Requests for Physical or Mental Examinations

These methods are described in the following paragraphs and exhibits. The role of the paralegal is emphasized, given its potential importance in the discovery process.

Although the basic principles remain the same, the exact names for each of the discovery methods and the applicable procedural requirements may vary from state to state. For example, a Request for Production of Documents may be called a Demand for Documents or a Request for Production of Documents and Entry on Land, or it may be folded into a set of Interrogatories. In some states formal discovery may only be conducted by stipulation or court order. In others, it may not be necessary to file any discovery documents with the court or to file only a certain type such as a **Request for Admissions** (in New Hampshire, for example) or a **Request for a Physical or Mental Examination.** In some states, such as Tennessee, the rules may vary from county to county. Because of these variations, it is critically important for the paralegal to be familiar with applicable terminology and rules governing discovery in general and domestic relations matters in particular.

Request for Admissions
a discovery method in which a party makes written requests to an opposing party calling for an admission or denial of specific facts at issue or verification or denial of the genuineness of documents relevant to the case

Request for Physical or Mental Examination
a method of discovery in which one party requests that the court order the other party (or, in some instances, a third party) to submit to a physical or mental examination

PARALEGAL PRACTICE TIP

Some jurisdictions have special discovery rules and procedures tailored to family law/domestic relations matters. Others apply the same rules as are used in civil matters generally. Still others require reference to multiple sets of rules.

In any given case, all, none, or some of the methods will be utilized, depending on the nature and complexity of the case, how hotly it is contested, and the financial resources of the parties. The sequence in which they are used may vary, but interrogatories are most commonly propounded first. Information obtained through most formal discovery methods is provided by the respondent under oath and is potentially very helpful to the requesting party. Customarily, states impose a duty to supplement responses if circumstances change, new information comes to light, or errors are discovered.

INTERROGATORIES

Interrogatories are written requests for information sent by a party to an opposing party in a lawsuit. Interrogatories must be responded to in writing under oath within a prescribed period, usually thirty days. The period for responding may be extended under the applicable rules of procedure if the interrogatories are served by mail. Jurisdictional rules of procedure typically provide when they may be served and limit the total number of interrogatories allowed (commonly fifty or fewer, not including subparts) absent permission of the court or agreement of the parties. They can usually be served all at once or in several sets, provided the total allowable limit is not exceeded. Many attorneys prefer to serve an initial set of fewer than the maximum number and hold the balance in reserve in case information is obtained warranting additional questions that initially could not have been anticipated. The primary strengths and weaknesses of interrogatories are described in Exhibit 6.3.

In order to be effective, interrogatories should be clear and concise, such that they produce specific and usable information. For example, the answer to a question such as "Do you have any retirement income" asked of a thirty-year-old working party tells us little. The question should request specific information with respect to any and all forms of retirement programs in which the respondent is participating. If the respondent is unaware of specifics, he or she is obligated to ascertain them prior to responding and to supplement responses later, if warranted.

Interrogatories (and depositions) commonly request specific information about the opposing party with respect to the following:

- basic background information, such as address(es), age, prior marriages, and children
- educational background, training, and job skills
- past and present employment as well as future plans
- real property owned individually or jointly with others before and during the marriage
- the nature and value of personal property, such as automobiles, jewelry, and collections (guns, artwork, collectibles, etc.), owned before and during the marriage
- how a party spends his or her leisure time (personal and social life and membership in any clubs, civic organizations, etc.)
- the other party's spending habits (what he or she spends money on; where he or she shops/dines; whether he or she pays by cash or credit, etc.)
- income from all sources
- the responding party's investments, business interests, retirement accounts, interests in any trusts, anticipated inheritances, etc.
- the location(s) where the respondent stores business and financial records, including hard drives and/or other electronic storage devices

Interrogatories
a method of discovery in which one party submits a series of written questions to an opposing party to be responded to in writing within a certain period of time under pain and penalty of perjury

PARALEGAL PRACTICE TIP

A sample of the kinds of interrogatories that might be served in a fault case involving an allegation of adultery is provided at *www.pearsonhighered.com/wilson* in the companion website material for Chapter 6 under "Resources."

PARALEGAL PRACTICE TIP

In this age of technology, interrogatories may include questions seeking information about such topics as the following:

- any and all electronic mail accounts through which the party has sent or received mail during a certain period
- any and all Instant Messaging services subscribed to during a certain period
- any and all online dating or pornography distribution services subscribed to
- whether the party has formatted or destroyed any physical media storage device on any computer he or she has used during a specific period

PARALEGAL PRACTICE TIP

An example of a standardized first set of interrogatories in a marital dissolution action can be found at *www.forms.justia.com.* You can find a link to this site at *www.pearsonhighered.com/wilson* in the companion website material for Chapter 6 under "Forms." Discretion should always be exercised when using standardized forms. If their use is not mandatory, they may provide a reference, a starting point from which questions can be developed that are tailored to the client's case.

- bank accounts, safe deposit boxes, etc.
- financial liabilities
- the parties' respective strengths and weaknesses as parents, if applicable
- the opposing party's physical and mental health, treatment programs, physicians, medications, etc.
- the history of the marriage, such as prior separations, counseling sought and obtained, conduct of the parties during the marriage, and nature of changes in the parties' relationship during the marriage

Caution needs to be exercised when relying on generic sets of interrogatories from books or online or versions designed to meet the objectives in other cases handled by the office. Like all discovery requests, interrogatories should be tailored to the facts of each case. Failure to do so may give rise to accusations of harassment of the other party or to generation of unnecessary costs. In many states, courts provide standard forms online particularly for use by parties proceeding *pro se*.

Paralegal **Application 6.4**

Interrogatories—The Potential Role of the Paralegal

The paralegal must be familiar with the procedural rules in the jurisdiction governing each form of discovery in the family law context and with the established role of the paralegal in the firm where he or she is employed. *All discovery-related tasks are carried out under the direction and supervision of an attorney.* The following reflects a common, but not necessarily universal, approach with respect to interrogatories.

If Serving Interrogatories

- Review the file to identify information needed (from the opposing party in particular).
- Discuss the information needs and discovery options with the supervising attorney, who will determine a discovery strategy (which methods will be used to obtain each kind of information, when they will be used, and in what sequence).
- Draft proposed interrogatories for review by the client and the supervising attorney.
- Finalize interrogatories for review and signature(s) as required and then serve on the opposing party in the manner provided in local rules, with a copy to the client.

PARALEGAL PRACTICE TIP

The paralegal should not serve the interrogatories until the supervising attorney has indicated his or her final approval. In addition to sending them to the other party, a limited number of jurisdictions still require that interrogatories be filed with the court. Some require the parties to file a notice of filing interrogatories and a notice of responding to and/or objecting to interrogatories.

- When answers are received, review them for completeness and, if incomplete, draft a letter for the supervising attorney's signature requesting that the responses be supplemented.
- If the responding party fails to respond or to supplement his or her answers on request, draft a motion to compel responses for review and possible filing.
- Summarize the responses and recommend follow-up measures, if warranted, such as questions for a second set of interrogatories or deposition questions.

If Responding to Interrogatories

- Mark receipt and return dates on all appropriate calendars and also schedule draft and review dates for responses.
- Give a copy to the supervising attorney, who will make the legal determination as to whether any of the interrogatories call for privileged information and, thus, an objection rather than an answer, and, if appropriate, draft a motion for a **protective order**.

Protective order
a court order restricting or prohibiting a party from unduly burdening an opposing party or third-party witness during the discovery process

- Draft a letter to the client for the supervisor's signature explaining the process and enclose a copy of the interrogatories for review and preparation of initial responses within an appropriate time frame. The letter should also remind the client that all answers

(Continued)

- must be true and accurate to the best of his or her knowledge, as they are provided under oath.
- Schedule a meeting for the client with the paralegal and/or the attorney, as appropriate, to review draft responses the client provides.
- Delete nonresponsive answers, correct errors, complete incomplete responses, and note objections identified by the supervising attorney.
- If needed, draft a letter to opposing counsel requesting additional time to respond. If the request is denied, draft a motion asking the court to grant the requested extension in response time.

- Prepare final responses expressed in the light most favorable to the client, as long as the factual content is accurate and based on information provided by the client.
- Schedule a meeting in which the supervisor and the client review final responses and affix signatures in the required form.
- Serve the responses on the opposing party (and with the court, if required in the jurisdiction) along with a notice of responding to and/or objecting to interrogatories, if necessary.

DEPOSITIONS

In a deposition, one party asks the other party, or a third person who has or may have information and/or documents pertaining to the case, a series of questions to be answered under oath. The person being questioned is called the deponent. The responses given are recorded verbatim by a court reporter or other individual licensed to record testimony. In some jurisdictions, depositions may be audio- or videotaped according to procedural rules.

If the deponent is a party, a **Notice of Deposition** is sent to the deponent or his or her attorney, if represented, specifying the date, time, and location of the deposition. A party deponent is not required to bring any documents to a deposition unless specifically requested to do so. Such a request is accomplished by combining a Notice of Deposition with a Request for Production of Documents. Even if deponents fail to bring requested documents to a deposition, their memories can be "refreshed" by showing them a particular document and asking if the document refreshes their memory about the topic of a question.

Notice of Deposition
the notification sent to an opponent (or his or her attorney, if represented) of an intention to depose him or her at a certain date, place, and time

PARALEGAL PRACTICE TIP
As a courtesy and convenience, counsel will usually agree on a date, time, and place for the deposition in advance of notice to ensure the availability of counsel and the parties.

If the deponent is a third-party witness, such as an employer, the third party must be served with notice of the deposition by **subpoena**. A subpoena is a document signed by an officer of the court that requires the person who receives it to appear at the date, time, and place indicated, under penalty of law. If it is requested that the deponent bring certain documents to the deposition, the subpoena is called a **subpoena *duces tecum***. Sometimes the subpoena will specify that it can be satisfied by delivery of the requested document(s) to the requesting attorney's office within a certain period of time, and then the actual deposition need not take place. In most, if not all, jurisdictions, third-party witnesses must be reimbursed for their related travel expenses.

Subpoena
a document ordering a witness to appear and provide testimony in a legal proceeding such as a deposition, court hearing, or trial

Subpoena *duces tecum*
a subpoena ordering a witness to appear in a legal proceeding such as a deposition, court hearing, or trial and to bring with him or her specified documents, records, or things

PARALEGAL PRACTICE TIP
Blank subpoenas can generally be obtained from the court and can be filled in with appropriate information. They are then returned to the court to be issued.

Depositions usually take place in an attorney's office but may be scheduled at other mutually convenient sites, particularly if the deponent is located in another

PARALEGAL PRACTICE TIP

In cases involving complex, large, and diverse marital assets or thorny custody and visitation issues, it may be necessary to schedule one or more "deposition days," during which a series of potential witnesses are deposed. This approach to scheduling is more efficient, convenient, and cost-effective for both parties and counsel than consuming several days over a more extended period.

state. At the beginning of the deposition, the deponent is sworn in and promises to answer truthfully and to the best of his or her ability. Questions are usually asked orally (a deposition upon oral examination) but may be presented in written form. Counsel for the deponent has a limited role in the deposition and, depending on the jurisdiction, is usually restricted to clarifying information, registering objections, and indicating omissions to the deponent. The deponent customarily cannot consult with counsel prior to answering questions.

Because of the costs associated with a deposition, once noticed, counsel for the parties may discuss the nature of the information sought, and the deponent may agree to voluntarily provide it without the need for the actual deposition. Although this happens occasionally, depositions are often designed to serve multiple purposes, such as observing the demeanor of the deponent when questioned under oath, assessing his or her credibility, creating a record that can be used at trial to impeach the deponent's testimony, and "fishing" for additional useful information. In such cases, depositions are unlikely to be canceled.

EXHIBIT 6.1 Sample Deposition Questions

The following questions are presented as a sampling of the kinds of questions commonly asked at depositions. One of the strengths of depositions as a discovery technique is that questions may be modified or expanded as responses lead to new areas worthy of pursuit.

1. Where are you presently employed?
2. What is your current salary?
3. Do you receive any additional compensation such as bonuses, tips, stock incentives, etc.?
4. Does your employer reimburse any of your expenses, such as meals or travel?
5. With respect to the marital residence, what do you estimate to be its present value?
6. Are there any mortgages or other liens on the property?
7. What was the purchase price for this property?
8. What was the amount of the down payment?
9. What was the source of funds for the down payment?
10. From what source of funds has the mortgage been paid during the marriage?
11. Do you presently have any credit card debt?
12. Is there a name on any of your credit card accounts other than your own?
13. I want to show you Exhibit 2. Do you recognize this credit card statement? Would you please identify the Exhibit for the record?
14. Let's look at some of the individual items on this statement, starting with the $3,567 charge at the Casino Royale. . . .
15. Page 2 of the statement indicates a charge of $715 for a "bracelet" purchased at Shreve, Crump, and High. For whom was this bracelet purchased?
16. Let's shift gears for a moment and look at your individual tax return for the 2010 tax year. Would you please identify this return for the record?
17. Calling your attention to Schedule B, do you see any interest income listed there?
18. How about dividends?
19. I have here a Financial Statement dated April 1, 2011, signed by you and filed with the court. Would you please identify this Statement for the record and verify that it was signed by you?
20. Looking at the statement, can you tell us where your interest- and dividend-producing assets appear?

Paralegal **Application 6.5**

Depositions—The Potential Role of the Paralegal

If Taking the Deposition

- Make recommendations to the supervisor regarding witnesses who should be deposed.
- Prepare a notice of intent to take deposition if the person to be deposed is a party or a subpoena or subpoena *duces tecum* if the deponent is a nonparty.

PARALEGAL PRACTICE TIP

The paralegal should be alert to the rules governing a situation in which a subpoena is to be served in another state. A letter of request (sometimes called **letters rogatory**) is a document a court in one state issues to a court in another state requesting that the "foreign" court serve process on an individual or corporation within the foreign jurisdiction and return the proof of service for use in the pending case.

- Arrange for service of the subpoena, if applicable, and later confirm that service has, in fact, been made. If the deponent is a party, serve notice on opposing counsel or the party directly if he or she is not represented.
- Draft recommended deposition questions.
- Organize information and documents, such as responses to interrogatories, witness statements, bank records, and credit card statements, that will be useful and/or referenced at the deposition. The materials should be organized in the order in which they will be addressed in the deposition.
- If the deponent previously was required to produce documents, review them for compliance with the request.
- If items are to be presented as exhibits at the deposition, they should ideally be marked by the reporter in advance of the start of the deposition. The supervising attorney will most likely want to have at least four parallel sets of documents available: one clean copy to show to the deponent, one for the opponent's attorney, one marked up for personal use, and a fourth to give to the reporter and have admitted as an Exhibit.
- Attend, if requested by your supervisor, listen carefully, take notes, and be prepared to assist the attorney with locating any documents as appropriate or suggesting additional follow-up questions.

- Following the deposition, review the transcript (audiotape or videotape), prepare a summary (sometimes called a deposition digest), and make recommendations for follow-up.
- Arrange for any required payment to the reporter and to third-party deponents for travel expenses.

If Defending the Deposition

- If the client is responding to a subpoena *duces tecum* and there is an objection to the requested production, draft a motion for a protective order and, if there is no objection, organize the document(s) he or she is asked to produce for review by the attorney.
- If the client being deposed is a party, describe the process and assist the attorney in anticipating likely questions and preparing the client for questioning.

PARALEGAL PRACTICE TIP

Some attorneys choose to conduct mock depositions with their clients to familiarize them with the process and the types of questions likely to be asked. The sessions can also be used to identify and address potential weaknesses in the deponent's performance. It may become apparent that some clients will need help developing strategies for dealing with various styles of questioning.

- Attend the deposition, listen carefully, take notes, and be prepared to assist the attorney with locating any documents as appropriate or suggesting clarifications, gaps, or errors in responses.
- Following the deposition, request a copy of the transcript, review it for accuracy, and correct mistakes as directed by the attorney in a manner consistent with applicable rules.
- Prepare a summary and recommendations for any necessary follow-up including the supplementing of responses if appropriate.

Letters rogatory
documents issued by a court in one state to a court in another state requesting that the "foreign" court serve process on an individual within the foreign jurisdiction

REQUESTS FOR ADMISSIONS

Requests for Admission are written requests to an opposing party calling for an admission or denial of specific facts at issue or verification or denial of the genuineness of documents relevant to the case. Unlike interrogatories, which are presented in the form of questions, requests for admission (or requests to admit, as they are termed in some jurisdictions) are presented as statements of fact. They are used to confirm rather than collect information. (See Exhibit 6.2.)

Responses to requests are customarily short and include the following potential options:

- Admit the matter.
- Deny the matter.
- Indicate lack of sufficient knowledge to admit or deny the matter.
- State a specific objection to the request.
- Respond with a combination of the above (e.g., admit in part and deny in part).

A party who alleges lack of sufficient knowledge has a duty to look into the matter (examine his or her records, files, etc.) before responding. If a respondent denies a fact that is subsequently proven at trial, he or she may be assessed fees and costs incurred by the other party in proving the truth of the matter. If a party does not object to the request and fails to respond to a request for admissions within the period prescribed by the applicable rules of procedure (usually thirty days), the content of the admissions is deemed admitted without further action, and the facts or authenticity of documents need not be proved at a subsequent hearing or trial.

Requests for admission are not often utilized. This is surprising, given their potential to help parties avoid significant time and expense and narrow the issues needing to be proved at trial. They may cover facts or documents about which no dispute is anticipated, clarify disputed issues, and confirm suspicions. Requests can cover a wide range of topics, but each individual request should address only one fact, document, or signature to avoid confusion and minimize denials.

When a request calls for authentication of a document or signature (as on a Voluntary Acknowledgment of Paternity), a copy of the document at issue is attached to the request. If the responder admits that a document—a mortgage application, for example—is genuine, the application may be introduced at trial without having to be introduced through foundation testimony of the mortgage broker. The party can then be questioned about the contents of the application, which may or may not contain accurate information. When applying for a mortgage,

EXHIBIT 6.2 Sample Request for Admissions

STATE OF NEW HAMPSHIRE

HILLSBOROUGH, SS	SUPERIOR COURT
SOUTHERN DISTRICT	DOCKET NO. 12-M-0000
IN THE MATTER OF JOHN B. SMITH AND JANE SMITH	

REQUEST FOR ADMISSIONS

John B. Smith, by his attorney, submits the following requests for admission to Jane Smith:

1. I admit that my husband and I separated on four occasions during the five years of our marriage immediately preceding the filing of my pending action for divorce.
2. I admit that the attached deed to a property in Boring, Oregon, held in trust and bearing my name and signature, is authentic, genuine, and accurate.
3. I admit that the Bank North loan my husband and I obtained in 1999 was used to cover my tax liability (including interest and penalties) for previously undeclared income I earned as a waitress.
4. I admit that I have a joint bank account at First Third Bank with my friend, Alberto Bonilla.
5. I admit that I am now in good health and have been so throughout the past five (5) years.
6. I admit that my husband provided the initial down payment of $40,000 on the marital residence out of his own personal funds in 1995.
7. I admit that my husband performed all of the carpentry, plumbing, and electrical work completed over ten (10) full months when the marital home was fully renovated in 2002.
8. I admit that during our marriage, my husband was the primary caretaker of the children and the marital home.
9. I admit that the present value of the marital home is $250,000 based on an appraisal performed by a mutually agreed-upon appraiser in December of 2011.
10. I admit that I have contributed less than 30% of my income to the payment of joint expenses during the course of our marriage.
11. I admit that two weeks before filing for divorce, I withdrew $14,000 from the savings account at Bank of America held jointly with and funded by my husband.
12. I admit that I have filed a wrongful termination suit against my former employer.
13. I admit that I have been arrested for operating under the influence of drugs or alcohol on three occasions in the two years immediately preceding my filing for divorce.
14. I admit that my current employer provides insurance coverage for my spouse and my children at no additional cost to me.
15. I admit that the signature on the attached application for a $150,000 mortgage from Citizen's Bank dated December 15, 2011, is my signature.

If any of the foregoing requests for admission is denied because of lack of information or knowledge, identify the request and give a detailed account of every effort made by you or your attorney to inquire into the subject matter of the request, including the date of each effort, the person making such effort, the substance of such effort, and the information obtained by such effort.

ANY PARTY, WHO WITHOUT GOOD REASON OR IN BAD FAITH, DENIES UNDER RULE 54 ANY SIGNATURE OR FACT WHICH HAS BEEN REQUESTED AND WHICH IS THEREAFTER PROVED, MAY, ON MOTION OF THE OTHER PARTY, BE ORDERED TO PAY THE REASONABLE EXPENSE, INCLUDING COUNSEL FEES, INCURRED BY SUCH OTHER PARTY.

Respectfully submitted,
John B. Smith
By his attorney,

_____
Juliana Wilson, Esq.
Address
Telephone No.: xxx-xxx-xxxx

Dated:_____

Paralegal **Application 6.6**

Requests for Admissions—The Potential Role of the Paralegal

If Requesting Admissions

- Draft a proposed Request for Admissions based on facts, events, and documents involved in the case that may be suited to this technique.
- Review the draft with the client and the supervising attorney.
- Prepare a final draft that incorporates any corrections, additions, deletions, or edits.
- Serve the reviewed and signed request on opposing counsel and, if required, file it with the court in compliance with applicable procedural rules in the jurisdiction.
- Mark on all appropriate calendars the date when responses are due to be returned.
- If the response is incomplete or objections are raised, draft documents to implement the course of action determined by the supervising attorney. These may include a letter to and negotiation with opposing counsel and/or a motion to compel compliance with an accompanying proposed order.
- If neither responses are received nor objections filed within the prescribed response period (usually thirty days), notify the supervising attorney, and the facts contained in the request will be deemed admitted in accordance with local governing rules.

PARALEGAL PRACTICE TIP

If some or all of the requests are objected to, counsel may agree on a mutually acceptable revised request that can then be filed with the court if required. If a compromise cannot be reached, the court may consider the objections in a hearing at which both parties and their counsel are present.

If Responding to a Request

- When a request is received, bring it to the attention of the supervising attorney and (if so directed) send a copy to the client, with a cover letter describing the nature, purpose, and effect of this form of discovery and asking that the client promptly review the requests and determine whether the statements are true and accurate.
- At the attorney's direction, schedule a meeting with the client in which the attorney will review the requests and potential responses and determine whether there are grounds for objecting to any of the requests.
- Draft a proposed final response for review by the client and the attorney.
- Serve the reviewed and signed response on the opposing party and file it with the court if required.

the applicant generally presents the most positive picture possible. That party will need to be able to explain discrepancies, if any, in the financial picture he or she presents at the time of the divorce action.

REQUESTS FOR PRODUCTION OF DOCUMENTS OR THINGS

Request for Production of Documents or Things
a method of pretrial discovery in which a party makes a written request that the other party, or a third person, produce specified documents or other tangible things for inspection and/or copying

PARALEGAL PRACTICE TIP

An example of a standardized request for production from a third party can be found at *www.flcourts. org.* A link to this site can be found at *www.pearsonhighered.com/ wilson* in the companion website material for Chapter 6 under "Forms."

A **Request for Production of Documents or Things** is a written request for documents or things in the possession, custody, or control of the opposing party or a nonparty third person (such as an employer) for inspection and copying, if necessary. Requests for production of documents most commonly seek financial records and information such as bank statements, tax returns, and employment records. They also can encompass other things as well, such as diaries, collections, photographs, stock certificates, corporate by-laws, partnership agreements, trusts, deeds, wills, computers, hard drives and other files, e-mails, credit card records, airline tickets, deeds, and titles to motor vehicles, boats, recreational vehicles, etc. Occasionally requests for production will ask that large items (vehicles, artworks, antique furniture, etc.) be made available for inspection, appraisal, and/or photographing.

Electronic communications are prime targets for production requests. For example, the client might request:

- any and all printouts or computer files evidencing electronic mail between the opposing party and a named third party, whether sent or received during a certain time period.
- any and all documentation during a specific time period with regard to any cell phone, Blackberry, or other mobile communications device, including an itemization of incoming and outgoing calls, text messages, e-mails or picture files, as well as an indication of the sender and/or recipient.

As with all discovery requests, requests for production of documents and things should be tailored to the facts of each case. The request should state the time, place, and manner of production and be sufficiently specific that the responding party will be able to comply. For example, if requesting bank records, a request might read as follows: "Copies of all records of any accounts of any kind including, but not limited to, checking accounts, savings accounts, NOW accounts, Certificates of Deposit, and equity lines of credit with any bank, credit union, or other financial institution for the five years preceding the date of the request."

Discovery requests must be carefully drafted and targeted to secure specific information directly relevant to the case. Courts are unlikely to compel production if requests are overbroad. For example, in 2010, a New York court held that where a request was made supposedly for the purpose of discovering information pertinent to the value of the husband's law practice, a wife's general and unlimited-in-time request seeking access to the entirety of her husband's business and personal data stored on his office computer was overbroad. See *Schreiber v. Schreiber,* 904 N.Y.S.2d 886 (2010).

The responding party must produce all documents or things requested unless there is a valid objection. For example, the items requested may be subject to a privilege or may not be in the possession or control of the responding party. Unreasonable and irrelevant requests may constitute harassment of the opposing party or a third party. On occasion, the materials requested may contain trade secrets or material about to be but not yet copyrighted or patented. In such situations, the responding party may file a motion for a protective order, or the parties may execute a confidentiality agreement (with or without the assistance of the court) warranting that confidentiality of certain information will be protected under penalty of law for failure to do so.

Paralegal **Application 6.7**

Requests for Production of Documents and Things— The Potential Role of the Paralegal

If Serving a Request

- Review the file to identify and compile a list of documents or things needed that are in the possession or control of the opposing party or of third parties such as the IRS, a banking institution, or an employer.
- Discuss the information with the supervising attorney, who will determine a discovery strategy, including which documents and things to request and from whom.

- Draft a proposed Request for Production for review by the supervising attorney and the client.
- Finalize the request for review and signature(s) as required and then, at the supervising attorney's direction, serve it on the opposing party or third party in the manner provided in local rules.
- When production is received, compile a log and review production to confirm that it fully complies

(Continued)

with the request and, if it does not, draft a letter for the supervising attorney's review requesting that the production be supplemented.

- If the responding party continues to fail to comply, draft a motion and proposed order to compel production for review and possible filing.
- Organize the materials produced, make copies/take photographs as directed, summarize the response, and recommend follow-up measures, if warranted, such as questions for a first or follow-up set of interrogatories or deposition questions raised as a result of a review of the documents produced.

If Responding to a Request

- Mark receipt and return dates on all appropriate calendars and also schedule response draft and review dates.
- Give a copy to the supervising attorney, who will make a legal determination as to whether any of the requests call for confidential or privileged information and thus a confidentiality agreement or an objection rather than production.

- Draft a letter to the client, enclosing a copy of the request for review, and ask that he or she assemble as many of the requested materials as possible within an appropriate time frame.
- Schedule a meeting for the client with the paralegal and/or attorney as appropriate to review materials, filter out any not specifically requested, and remove any privileged documents or things based on the supervising attorney's instructions.
- If an extension is needed, notify the supervising attorney and draft a motion for extension of time for production (unless the supervising attorney negotiates a revised timeline with opposing counsel).
- Mark all appropriate calendars with revised draft, review, and return dates.
- Compile the production for delivery to the opposing party, being certain to limit it to material specifically requested and not privileged.
- Serve the materials on the opposing party in an appropriate manner after receiving authorization from the supervising attorney.

REQUESTS FOR PHYSICAL OR MENTAL EXAMINATION

Unlike other discovery techniques, because of its intrusiveness a request to have a physical or mental examination conducted usually must be sought by motion. Generally, courts will grant such requests and compel attendance of a party or third person at an examination only after a hearing in which good cause is shown. There are sometimes circumstances in which a request may be appropriate, such as when

- A party raises his or her own or the other party's mental or physical health as an issue.
- The paternity of one or more of the parties' children is challenged.
- The mental instability or physical disability of a party is raised as a reason why he or she should be denied custody.
- One of the parties seeks alimony or a disproportionate division of marital assets based on the alleged existence of a disability that makes it impossible for that party to be self-supporting.
- One of the parties seeks a divorce from the other on a fault ground that alleges the other party is a chronic alcoholic or abuser of other drugs.
- A party claims on his or her financial affidavit to have significant and continuing monthly costs for uninsured medical expenses or treatments of some kind.

PARALEGAL PRACTICE TIP

A sample Request for Physical or Mental Examination is available at *www.pearsonhighered.com/wilson* in the companion website material related to Chapter 6 under "Forms."

PARALEGAL PRACTICE TIP

The common distinction between a motion and a request in this context is that a request is usually automatically granted within a certain period after filing absent an objection. A motion customarily requires a hearing in which the court hears arguments from both sides and then issues an order.

In rare instances, requests may also be made for examination of a third person in the custody of a party. For example, if a deviation from the child support guidelines is requested because of expenses associated with a child's medical condition, an examination and assessment of the child's treatment needs may be appropriate. An examination may also be appropriate in cases in which custody is at issue and a credible allegation of physical or sexual abuse of a child is raised.

Paralegal Application 6.8

Requests for Physical or Mental Examination— The Potential Role of the Paralegal

If Requesting an Examination

- Review the case file and consider whether a physical or mental examination may be appropriate given the facts of the case and, if so, make a recommendation to the supervising attorney to that effect.
- Develop a list of proposed examiners (such lists often already exist in the resource files of a family law practice and may be maintained by a paralegal).
- If directed to do so, draft a Motion/Request for a Mental or Physical Examination and a proposed order as appropriate with an accompanying affidavit to be signed by the client in support of the motion.
- When approved and signed by the attorney, file the original request, affidavit, and proposed order with the court, serve copies on the opposing party, and mark on the calendar the date of service, the time and date of the court hearing on the request (if necessary), and the date by which any objection to the request must be filed.
- If the opposing party does not file an objection within the period prescribed by the applicable rules of procedure and/or the court allows the request, notify the supervising attorney for authorization to contact the office of the opposing counsel and make arrangements for scheduling the requested examination.
- If the opposing party does not submit to an examination within a reasonable period of time, notify the supervising attorney for authorization to prepare, file, and serve a motion to compel examination and a proposed order, with a copy to the client.

PARALEGAL PRACTICE TIP

Before or after filing of a motion to compel, counsel for the parties may be able to negotiate an agreement covering the purpose and scope of the examination; the selection process for choosing the examiner; the date, time, and place of the examination; and the use to which the information obtained will be put. If the parties are unable to reach an agreement, the open hearing will proceed. The attorney and the paralegal will very likely prepare the client for the hearing and the kinds of questions that may be asked.

- When a hearing date is set, notify the attorney, mark the date on the calendar, and notify the client (by

phone and in writing) that he or she should plan to be present for the hearing.
- If the examination subsequently occurs, be sure that the office receives a copy of the examiner's report and copies of the results of any tests for review and analysis, and suggest needed follow-up such as questions for the examiner if the report is introduced at trial.

If Responding to a Request for an Examination

- When a request is received, the paralegal will customarily arrange a meeting for the attorney to discuss the request with the client and determine how to proceed.
- If there is no objection, the attorney will usually negotiate terms, which are confirmed in writing, limiting the nature, scope, and use of the examination.
- If there is an objection, draft the objection and supporting affidavit or memorandum for review.
- After review, finalize the objection, obtain the supervising attorney's signature, and file the objection with the court within the period provided by local rules (usually thirty days).
- When a hearing date is set on the objection, notify the attorney, mark it on the calendar, and notify the client (by phone and in writing) that he or she should plan to be present.
- If the examination is to take place, the paralegal may be asked to schedule it and ensure that the client (or other person to be examined) keeps the appointment. On occasion, a paralegal may accompany the client to a medical examination. If questions arise (usually concerning the scope of the examination), the paralegal can contact the attorney for clarification and/or instructions.
- After the examination, a copy of the examiner's report and the results of any tests may be sought for review and analysis, but the client then is usually required to produce any similar medical reports in his or her custody or control. Under both state and federal law, the person examined may be required to execute releases waiving privacy rights with respect to medical records.

EXHIBIT 6.3 Summary Table Re Formal Discovery Methods

Method	Strengths	Weaknesses
INTERROGATORIES	• Interrogatories are cost-effective. • They can be designed to obtain information that can then be used as a basis for formulating other discovery requests. • They may be used to identify potential witnesses, including **experts**, physicians, and co-respondents when adultery is alleged. • Responses to interrogatories may be more complete than answers at depositions because the respondent has a duty to locate necessary information and provide complete responses.	• Interrogatories can usually be served only on parties and not on third persons. • A responding party's responses are reviewed with counsel and carefully drafted to reveal as little potentially damaging information as possible. • Responses to interrogatories are written. As a result, the requesting party does not have an opportunity to assess the respondent's credibility and potential weaknesses as a witness.
DEPOSITIONS	• Depositions can be used with both parties and nonparty witnesses, including expert witnesses. • Necessary information usually can be obtained more quickly than with other methods. • The credibility and performance of the deponent under oath can be assessed. • Follow-up and clarifying questions can be asked if further information is needed or if an answer is incomplete, evasive, or opens up a new area for inquiry.	• Depositions are expensive. The costs are in the preparation, follow-up, and analysis time as well as in the conducting of the actual deposition, court reporter time, transcript preparation, and copying, each of which varies based on the length and complexity of the deposition. • Deposition questions may reveal the deposing party's theory of the case and give the deponent a better chance to prepare for negotiation and/or trial.
REQUESTS FOR ADMISSIONS	• Requests for Admissions are cost-effective. • They can be used to narrow the issues needing to be addressed at trial. • They can be used to clarify disputed issues and to confirm suspicions. • They can reduce the facts (or validity of signatures or documents) needing to be proved at trial.	• Requests may reveal the theory of the client's case and/or available defenses.

(Continued)

EXHIBIT 6.3 (*Continued*)

REQUESTS FOR PRODUCTION OF DOCUMENTS OR THINGS OR ENTRY UPON LAND	• These requests can be used with both parties and nonparty witnesses. • They allow a party to obtain critical information from entities such as employers and the IRS. • They often yield a wealth of information that leads to further productive discovery.	• They can be expensive, depending on the nature and extent of production.
REQUESTS FOR PHYSICAL OR MENTAL EXAMINATION	• Requests may lead to discovery of otherwise privileged information.	• These requests can usually only be served on parties although the court may allow examinations of children in appropriate circumstances, such as when there are allegations of abuse. • Requests are highly intrusive and may exacerbate an already acrimonious dispute. • Usually a request must be sought by motion, and such motions are granted only upon a showing of good cause.

Electronic Discovery

In recent years technological innovation has given rise to dramatic changes in the ways we learn, do business, communicate with each other, and find our ways from place to place. We have rapidly come to rely on computers, the Internet, PDAs, smart phones, GPS, etc. Each of these innovations has brought new sources to be mined for information that can be used to support (or to refute) a client's case. These sources, in turn, require the family law team to be proficient both in exploring them and in advising clients about avoiding careless or inadvertent exposure of sensitive information. They also bring new legal and ethical boundaries as to what may be discovered, how it may be discovered, and how it may be used. These boundaries not only limit the scope of discovery, but they also impose new requirements on what the family law team must do in order to fulfill its obligation in advocating for clients.

The focus of **electronic discovery** (e-discovery) is basically on finding information stored in computers. For example, in a case involving substantial assets including business interests, it may be necessary to access computer records of employees in one or more companies or partnerships in order to establish the value of a party's interests. Even in less complex cases, e-discovery may be useful. A case in point is a marriage in which one spouse has totally controlled the marital assets and has maintained detailed electronic records of everything, from improvements on and maintenance of the marital home to income, investment, and tax records. Electronic evidence may be sought from many sources including not only spouses and employers but also friends, relatives, investment firms, and others. The approach taken depends in part on the nature of the documents sought, the reason for seeking them, the use to be made of them, and the relative likelihood of the other party altering or destroying them.

PARALEGAL PRACTICE TIP

Since technology is evolving rapidly, so are the modes and limits of e-discovery. The paralegal who keeps current with those evolutions—technological and legal—will significantly advance his or her value to a family law practice.

Electronic discovery

discovery of documents in electronic form; refers to any information created, stored, or utilized with computerized technology of any sort

Paralegal **Application 6.9**

Computer Information Storage—Some Basics

If you are a relative novice, it will be useful for you to be aware of some basics of computer information storage. Each "parcel" of information (letter, spreadsheet, picture, message, etc.) is packaged with **metadata**—data that describes the file in terms of its size, the format (coding) in which the data is stored, when it was created, when it was last modified, etc. Additional information can be stored outside the file that may be pertinent. This additional information may include previous versions of the file (together with their metadata) as well as potentially recoverable deleted versions or fragments. There may also be versions and/or related files stored on removable media such as CDs, DVDs, memory "sticks," zip drives, and freestanding backup drives. There also are ways of encoding data and hiding it in otherwise innocuous files. In addition, there are discoverable sources of information beyond computers and their periphery. These include PDAs and Smart phones (directly discoverable) and e-mail records, online backup files, and "**cloud**" computing files (all discoverable through their service providers).

Metadata
information that is stored and/or transmitted electronically together with a file or message that describes the file or message

Cloud computing
Internet-based computing in which both the software and data storage reside on an Internet site or network of sites

There are several paths that may be taken to securing e-discovery. If all that is needed is a copy of a document from a trusted source, then a simple (and inexpensive) request for the document may suffice. At the other end of the spectrum, if what is needed are complex records concerning the values of multiple business interests of an uncooperative and deceptive opposing party, an e-discovery request may require the seizure of one or more computers and ancillary equipment for detailed inspection by forensic computing experts using sophisticated tools. No matter what the complexity, every e-discovery process will include at least the following three steps in some form:

- Promptly putting opposing counsel (or the opposing party directly if he or she is unrepresented) on notice to preserve and retain data while the divorce or other matter is pending. This notice should be as specific as possible as to the information and sources that are to be preserved. If necessary, an agreement may be negotiated with respect to information that may be privileged or otherwise protected.

PARALEGAL PRACTICE TIP
A request for production/seizure of the other party's computer equipment, storage devices, etc., may be made by means of an *ex parte* motion to the court when there is a strong fear that the other party will destroy or alter the data stored on the computer equipment.

- Drafting appropriate discovery documents:
  - Requests for Production of Documents or Things to secure computers, peripheral hardware, PDAs, phones, etc., and to obtain a variety of documents: e-mails, browser histories, calendars, cell phone records, financial records, etc., not otherwise available to the client.
  - Depositions, Interrogatories, and/or Requests for Admissions to gather information about e-mail accounts, backup storage services, and cloud computing services, etc. that may then lead to requests for production.
- Securing the services of individuals able to glean the required information (within cost constraints). Sometimes these individuals may be "in-house."

PARALEGAL PRACTICE TIP
Care must be taken to make requests for data in a form the client and/or attorney can read, understand, analyze, and afford.

Paralegal **Application 6.10**

The Internet as an Informal Discovery Tool

The Internet is rife with opportunities to express thoughts and feelings; to connect with others who share social, business, political, or recreational interests, or simply to "chat" with like-minded others. It also offers a rich variety of means to search for information about people and their activities.[3]

Social Networks

A **social network** is a collection of people who are connected by something they have in common. A **social networking site** is an Internet-based service that promotes the formation of social networks by providing a means for people to describe (profile) themselves and to search for others whose public profiles match theirs in some fashion. Networks form by having people "friend" each other, thereby gaining access to more extensive private profiles. Facebook and Myspace are major U.S. social networking sites; LinkedIn is a social networking site that focuses on business and professional connections and employment opportunities; and Twitter is a site that offers both social networking and microblogging services. There are, of course, many others. Because access to an entire profile is intended only for friends, people feel cloaked from prying eyes and tend to reveal themselves in ways they might not in person—not always honestly or as they would want to appear in court. For example:

- A profile may represent a party seeking a divorce and custody as being single, childless, and interested in dating.
- A post promoting a party's professional services might reveal an "under-the-table" source of income not listed in a financial statement.
- Photographs and their captions posted on a network page or "wall" can reveal compromising relationships, possessions, activities, etc.

PARALEGAL PRACTICE TIP

By way of example, in a 2011 New York case, a former husband paying $850 a month alimony to his wife came across a video of her belly dancing vigorously on the Internet. She had previously claimed that she was unable to work because she was disabled as the result of an automobile accident. The court reduced her alimony to $400 a month when the husband sought a modification based on a "substantial change in circumstances!"

- A list of interests, group affiliations, and activities might yield names of potential witnesses and dates and places of meetings at which parties or other key people can be found.

- Social plans or experiences shared with friends might lead directly to compromising revelations. One anecdote reported in a bar association newspaper relates that an attorney who was a Facebook "friend" of a judge requested a continuance because her father had died. The judge, on a visit to the attorney's Facebook page, found posts about the attorney's week of "drinking, going out, and partying." Her Honor was not amused.[4] Even the nature of a person's collection of "friends" and how he or she relates to them is an indicator of his or her character and values.

Blogs and Forums

A **blog** (web log) is a website feature in which an individual maintains a chronicle—frequently on a single topic. Some blogs invite responsive postings by readers. A **forum** is a website feature on which a "thread" (specific topic within a subject area) or multiple simultaneous threads can be discussed. The discussion takes the form of "posts" (messages) sent by members of the forum to the other members, who then have the opportunity to send posts in response. For example, a divorce forum might have simultaneous threads on alimony, child support guidelines, assets, and who gets the dog. Yahoo.groups and Google.groups are online services that host a variety of forums. Blogs and forums are also found on websites of support groups of various kinds. Wherever found, they are sources of potentially revealing information.

Registries, Records, and Directories

When accessible to the public, sex offender registries and judicial records of convictions should be explored as a matter of course to avoid (or deliver) surprises. Online directories and locating services (some free, some at nominal cost) can be of great assistance in locating parties and witnesses. Some of these sites offer such services as providing genealogy trees and conducting background checks.

Search Engines

These are the wild cards of informal electronic discovery. Google, Yahoo, Bing, and a host of other search engines are available to explore the Internet. The student is encouraged to enter his or her own name into at least two of these search engines and see what turns up!

(Continued)

Properly seeking information from online sites can be a valuable tool. However, keep in mind that everything you find on these sites is subject to confirmation:

- It is possible that the person represented on the site is not the one controlling it.
- There is no way to know what is truthful and/or competent and what is not.
- Even pictures can be "doctored" to be misleading. A post is not proof, but it can make for a very bad day!

Social networking site
an Internet-based service that promotes the formation of social networks by providing a means for people to describe (profile) themselves and to search for others whose public profiles match theirs in some respect

Blog
a website feature in which an individual maintains a chronicle—frequently on a single topic

Social network
a collection of people connected electronically by something they have in common

Forum
a website feature on which a "thread" (specific topic within a subject area) or multiple simultaneous threads can be discussed

As new and evolving as technology is, the legal and ethical boundaries and requirements it imposes are even newer and less settled. For example:

- Is there a duty to Google? The attorney certainly has a duty to obtain information in support of the client's case, but what are the limits of that duty given an Internet that defies complete exploration?
- What are the limits of the attorney's responsibility to advise and instruct the client in self-protection?
  - Surely privacy settings and avoiding incriminating posts on a social website or blog are basic.
  - The client should be advised to protect his computers from spyware and at the same time be aware that it is a privacy violation and potentially a criminal offense to install spyware on another's computer. If the client has already done so it should be uninstalled.
  - The client should be instructed to make passwords "strong," to change them frequently, and to avoid using shared computers for sending and receiving confidential e-mail.
  - If the client plans to continue to use social networking sites, discretion needs to be exercised to avoid visiting incriminating sites, revealing intimate private details, or making derogatory remarks about others. Any transmission, whether taken out of context or not, can potentially be used against the client.
  - Although it may be tempting, the client should not wipe clean his or her hard drive(s). The courts do not look favorably on what appear to be efforts to destroy evidence. If the client "shares" a computer containing relevant information with a spouse and/or children, it may be appropriate to have it sequestered or "imaged."
  - The client should avoid leaving incriminating phone messages and should not send electronic communications relating to the divorce or other pending matters.
  - The client needs to be reminded that use of and access to electronic communications are governed to some degree by state and federal laws, and caution should be exercised if thinking of doing things like threatening an opposing party in e-mails or, in effect, "stalking" them through GPS monitoring.
- Although some electronic materials are subject to discovery or subpoena under applicable rules, a New Hampshire Bar Association Ethics Committee opinion places an ethical duty on both senders and receivers of electronic communications to prevent disclosure of confidential information.

PARALEGAL PRACTICE TIP

The New Hampshire Bar's ethics committee opinion can be accessed at *www.nhbar.org*. You can find a link to this site at *www.pearsonhighered. com/wilson* in the companion website material for Chapter 6 under "Resources." Essentially the opinion says that the sender must use reasonable care to avoid improper disclosure of confidential materials, and the receiver has a duty not to search for, review, or use confidential material contained in metadata received from opposing counsel.

- The Philadelphia Bar Association has issued an opinion to the effect that "virtual pretexting" (i.e., "friending" someone for the purpose of gaining access to a social network) and then using information derived from that network in litigation is in violation of Pennsylvania's Rules of Professional Conduct.

(See Paralegal Application 6.10.)

Objections to Discovery Requests

A party who receives a request for discovery has a duty to respond to the request. In general, a party must respond to all questions and/or requests for which there is no legally accepted objection. Objections are commonly governed by procedural rules and common practice. If there is an appropriate objection, it is usually specifically stated in lieu of an answer. It is possible for a discovery request to call for information that is both relevant and unprivileged, and yet still be objectionable because it is unduly burdensome or cumulative, or because the information sought is not within the party's possession or control. Local rules may structure the nature and registering of objections. In some jurisdictions, in a deposition, for example, the question should be answered and the objection raised for consideration at trial.

The most common objections to discovery requests are the following:

1. **The request is unduly burdensome.** For example, in a no-fault case involving few assets, the opposing party requests ten years of bank statements for an account that rarely held more than $2,000, and the parties have already essentially agreed on the division of their minimal property. Compliance with the request would be costly to the respondent and yield nothing productive for the party making the request.

2. **The request seeks discovery of material that is not relevant to the issues in the case.** In a no-fault divorce action in a jurisdiction that does not consider marital fault as a factor in property division or spousal support decisions, requests for information pertaining to marital infidelity that does not impact the parties' children are very likely irrelevant. This would particularly be the case for questions related to an affair that took place ten years earlier, after which the parties reconciled and had three children together, or to an affair that occurred during a prior marriage.

3. **The document or information requested is not within the party's possession or control.** In some marriages, one party has maintained control over the parties' finances, paying the bills, completing the tax returns, and maintaining records—often on a personal computer to which the other party has no access. In such circumstances, the other party may simply be incapable of complying with a discovery request calling for financial records.

4. **The document, thing, or information requested is protected by a privilege that is legally recognized within the jurisdiction.** The most obvious privilege is the attorney-client privilege, which protects communications between the attorney and the client as well as the attorney's "work product." **Work product** customarily includes material prepared in anticipation of the litigation, such as comprehensive financial reports prepared by accountants. Most jurisdictions recognize additional privileges, such as priest-penitent and doctor-patient privileges. A minority of jurisdictions recognize a social worker-client privilege and/or a parent-child privilege. A party may waive a

Work product
written or oral material prepared for or by an attorney in preparation for litigation either planned or in progress

PARALEGAL PRACTICE TIP

In a 2009 case, a California appellate court held that a father's medical records were discoverable, at least with respect to a neurological condition the wife claimed exposed the parties' minor son to risk. The court found the father had waived the doctor-patient privilege and that his constitutional right to privacy was outweighed by the state's compelling interest in protecting the child's best interest. See *Manela v. Superior Court of Los Angeles County, David Y. Manela, Real Party in Interest*, 177 Cal. App. 4th 1139, 99 Cal. Rptr. 3d 736 (2009)

privilege under certain circumstances. For example, if a spouse is seeking spousal support and/or a more favorable property settlement based upon an alleged health problem, information pertaining to that condition would likely be discoverable by the other party and would not be protected by a doctor-patient privilege.

5. **The information being sought is cumulative.** This objection is based on the argument that the party seeking the information previously has requested it in another request or format or already has the information in his or her possession or control.

6. **The form of the question is improper.** For example, the question is redundant or overbroad.

7. **The request is being made solely for the purpose of harassment.** For example, the request seeks information unrelated to the period of the marriage, such as details about all income earned since the date the other party was first employed as a teenager. Such a request would be irrelevant in the context of most marriages contracted by adults. However, there may be rare instances in which such information would be relevant (e.g., if a child actor married at age seventeen).

8. **A respondent may raise a Fifth Amendment right against self-incrimination if appropriate.** For example, in a state where adultery still constitutes a criminal offense, a person may refuse to answer questions relating to an adulterous affair during the time falling within the applicable statute-of-limitations period.

Financial Statements

Every state requires each party to an action for divorce, separate support (or legal separation), or child support to exchange and file with the court a document containing basic financial information about his or her respective needs, resources, and liabilities. (See Exhibit 6.4.) The document is commonly called a Financial Statement, a Financial Affidavit, or an Inventory of Assets and Liabilities, and it must be filed with the Complaint or within a certain period after the action is commenced. It is designed to provide the parties with data needed to inform their decisions, especially with respect to matters of support and property division. It also provides the court with a frame of reference for assessing the fairness of a proposed settlement or for making decisions in a contested case. The client is required to sign it under pain and penalty of perjury. Several states require that counsel also sign the document affirming that it does not contain information known by the attorney to be false. Clearly, a financial affidavit can be the single most important document presented to the court, as it not only provides essential information, but also reflects both the client's credibility and the attorney's level of preparedness.

PARALEGAL PRACTICE TIP

For students wanting to work their way though some financial statements online, check out the following (links to each of which can be accessed at *www.pearsonhighered. com/wilson* in the companion website material for Chapter 6 under "Forms."):

ARIZONA   *www.azcourts*
FLORIDA   *www.fl.courts.org*
GEORGIA   *www.georgiacourts. org*
MASSACHUSETTS   *www.lawlib. state.ma.us*

Forms for many other states are also available online at state judiciary sites, several of which are listed in Appendix C.

PARALEGAL PRACTICE TIP

Many states now make divorce forms, including financial statements, available online. In addition, there are several software packages available that allow family law practitioners to create and print financial affidavits in approved formats, although it may be necessary to indicate that the form is computer-generated and/or to print it on a particular color paper. Such programs are helpful because they automatically calculate the figures and store them for future use. However, considerable care must still be taken to ensure that the data input is accurate in initial and updated editions.

The specific format of financial statements varies from state to state, but the basic information called for is essentially the same. All forms cover income, assets, expenses, and liabilities. Assets include both real property (real estate) and personal property (such as bank accounts, stocks and bonds, cash, collections, household furnishings/antiques, and notes payable to the party). Liabilities include such items as mortgages, equity loans, car loans, credit card debt, court judgments, and debts owed. Some states, such as Massachusetts, have more than one form—one for parties of more modest means and a second, more detailed form for parties with more substantial income and assets.

PARALEGAL PRACTICE TIP

An example of a California Simplified Financial Statement is available at *www.pearsonhighered.com/wilson* in the companion website material related to Chapter 6 under "Forms."

EXHIBIT 6.4 Example of a Financial Affidavit—State of Connecticut

Courtesy of the State of Connecticut

FINANCIAL AFFIDAVIT
JD-FM-6 Rev. 1-08
P.B. 25-30

STATE OF CONNECTICUT
SUPERIOR COURT
www.jud.ct.gov

COURT USE ONLY
FINAFF
DOCKET NO.

FOR THE JUDICIAL DISTRICT OF   AT *(Address of court)*   NAME OF AFFIANT *(Person submitting this form)*

NAME OF CASE   ☐ PLAINTIFF   ☐ DEFENDANT

OCCUPATION   NAME OF EMPLOYER

ADDRESS OF EMPLOYER

A. WEEKLY INCOME FROM PRINCIPAL EMPLOYMENT *(Use weekly average not fewer than 13 weeks)*

B. ALL OTHER INCOME *(Include in-kind compensation, gratuities, rents, interest, dividends, pension, etc.)*

(continued)

PRINT   RESET

			ADDRESS			VALUE *(Est.)*	MORTGAGE	EQUITY	
4. ASSETS	**A. Real Estate**	Home	ADDRESS			VALUE *(Est.)* $	MORTGAGE $	EQUITY $	
		Other:	ADDRESS			VALUE *(Est.)* $	MORTGAGE $	EQUITY $	
		Other:	ADDRESS			VALUE *(Est.)* $	MORTGAGE $	EQUITY $	
	B. Motor Vehicles	Car 1:	YEAR	MAKE	MODEL	VALUE $	LOAN BALANCE $	EQUITY $	
		Car 2:	YEAR	MAKE	MODEL	VALUE $	LOAN BALANCE $	EQUITY $	

4. ASSETS	C. Other Personal Property	DESCRIBE AND STATE VALUE OF EACH ITEM	TOTAL VALUE $
	D. Bank Accounts	BANK NAME, TYPE OF ACCOUNT, AND AMOUNT	TOTAL BANK ACCOUNTS $
	E. Stocks, Bonds Mutual Funds	NAME OF COMPANY, NUMBER OF SHARES, AND VALUE	TOTAL VALUE $

	F. Insurance *(exclude children)*	NAME OF INSURED	COMPANY	FACE AMOUNT $	CASH VALUE $	AMT. OF LOAN $	TOTAL VALUE
				$	$	$	
				$	$	$	$

4. ASSETS	G. Deferred Compensation Plans	NAME OF PLAN *(Individual I.R.A., 401K, Keogh, etc.)* AND APPROX. VALUE	TOTAL VALUE *(less loans)* $
	H. All Other Assets		TOTAL VALUE $
	I. Total	E. TOTAL CASH VALUE OF ALL ASSETS →	$

5. HEALTH INSURANCE	NAME AND ADDRESS OF HEALTH OR DENTAL INSURANCE CARRIER *(Do not include policy number)*
	NAME(S) OF PERSON(S) COVERED BY THE POLICY

SUMMARY
(Use the amounts shown in boxes A thru E of sections 1-4.)

TOTAL NET WEEKLY INCOME (A)	$	TOTAL CASH VALUE OF ASSETS (E)	$
TOTAL WEEKLY EXPENSES AND LIABILITIES (B + D)	$	TOTAL LIABILITIES (TOTAL BALANCE DUE ON DEBTS) (C)	$

CERTIFICATION
I certify that the foregoing statement is true and accurate to the best of my knowledge and belief.

SIGNED *(Affiant)*	Subscribed and sworn to before me on	DATE	SIGNED *(Notary, Comm. of Superior Court, Assistant Clerk)*

JD-FM-6 Rev. 1-08 (Back)

PRINT   RESET

PARALEGAL PRACTICE TIP

A "Guide to Documenting Asset Values" is available at *www. pearsonhighered.com/wilson* on the companion website in the material related to Chapter 6 under "Resources."

The paralegal often is asked to coordinate preparation of financial statements. At first blush, completing an affidavit may appear to be a simple fill-in-the-blanks and tally-the-figures task. In cases involving few if any assets, completion of the form may be reasonably straightforward. Nonetheless, each affidavit requires careful attention, given its potential importance. Initially the client gathers the financial information for inclusion on the form provided by counsel or the court and completes a preliminary draft for review. Depending on the financial, organizational, literacy, and record-keeping skills of the client, as well as the size and complexity of the marital estate, the paralegal may be assigned to work with the client on this task. The paralegal should verify that the figures provided are current, accurate, able to be documented to the greatest extent possible, and understood by the client. If necessary, the client needs to be able to respond to questions about the contents of the statement posed by the court or by the other party. For example, in the context of a deposition, it is not uncommon for a party to be questioned about:

- each and every expense item
- how each figure was calculated
- what documentary evidence exists to corroborate the figures
- how any discrepancies between income and expenses can be explained

Paralegal **Application 6.11**

Pointers on Completion of Financial Affidavits

1. Instructions for completing financial affidavits should be followed carefully.
2. The Affidavit should be complete, with every space filled in with a figure, a 0, "none," or "NA" ("not applicable") as appropriate.
3. If allowed, footnotes or attachments should be used
   a. When necessary to supplement or more fully explain figures that might otherwise be confusing or misleading out of context
   b. if the form doesn't permit the party to adequately represent his or her specific circumstances
4. Although some attorneys might disagree, most believe it is better to provide a complete picture of the client's financial situation in an organized, coherent, and consistent manner. A failure to do so opens the door for attack by opposing counsel or questioning by a judge as to why certain information was not included.
5. The Affidavit should reflect a party's current financial circumstances. However, if a party's income varies seasonally, with market fluctuations, or for some other reason, averages may usually be used.
6. If weekly or monthly income and expenses do not balance, the party must be able to explain

how a shortfall is covered or where the excess income is placed. For example, if the party claims to be spending more than is earned, is he or she borrowing money, withdrawing from savings, selling assets, and/or receiving funds, gifts, or other subsidies from third parties?

7. Contested cases frequently drag on for months and involve multiple court appearances for temporary orders, motion hearings, discovery conferences, and the like. Whenever a hearing is for the purpose of addressing an issue with financial implications, such as child or spousal support or occupancy of the marital residence, a current financial affidavit is customarily required. A party must be able to explain any discrepancies between prior and current affidavits.
8. In cases involving complex assets and liabilities, it may be necessary to consult with accountants, financial advisors, appraisers, and other experts to establish values and appropriate figures to be included on financial affidavits.
9. Care should be taken that figures appearing on affidavits can be documented wherever possible and that they are consistent with other documents that may be provided to the court or available to the other party.[5]

One of the greatest challenges, particularly in cases involving substantial assets, is to determine whether or not an opposing party (or a client for that matter!) is disclosing all of his or her assets and income. In some cases, **forensic accountants** may be retained at considerable expense. However, counsel and skilled paralegals are often able to uncover hidden assets by carefully reviewing and comparing financial affidavits, tax returns, and other documents produced through formal and informal discovery measures. Ultimate accountability rests with the supervising attorney, but a paralegal with appropriate knowledge, training, and expertise is an invaluable resource.

Five of the best resources for detecting hidden assets are tax returns, bank statements, credit card statements, financial statements, and public records, all of which can be accessed legally and frequently informally. Discrepancies among these

Forensic accountant
an accountant who applies accounting principles and analysis to gather and present evidence in a lawsuit

PARALEGAL PRACTICE TIP

Clients are often the best resources for detecting errors, omissions, and outright deceit in their spouse's financial statements and tax returns.

various documents can be especially enlightening. Attorneys, paralegals, and clients can all be active sleuths in the process of searching for hidden assets. (See Paralegal Application 6.12.) The following list just touches the surface of the clues to potentially hidden assets that can be gleaned from the opposing party's tax return.

- **Dividend income:** On Schedule B, the taxpayer lists payors and amounts of dividend income received, but what about the underlying asset? Is it disclosed on the financial statement? The value of that asset can be determined with online resources to establish the dividend per share rate.
- **Royalty income:** Royalty income may be listed on schedule E for a patent or a published book or film. Has the taxpayer disclosed the value of the underlying asset?
- **Interest income:** If the taxpayer reports $1,500 of interest income and the prevailing interest rate is 3%, that means there is an underlying asset worth $50,000. Has it been disclosed?
- **Rental income:** If rental income is declared on Schedule E, have all the real estate holdings been disclosed and appraised for current market value?
- **Retirement fund contributions:** Has there been a change in the amount the taxpayer is contributing toward IRAs and other retirement funds?
- **Mortgage interest:** Did the amount of mortgage interest being claimed go up in the most recent tax year? Was the underlying property refinanced and, if so, where are the funds from the refinancing?
- **Trusts:** The tax return will reveal the existence of a trust, but what is its underlying value to the taxpayer in terms of principal and annual distributions?
- **Excise tax:** If excise tax is being paid, what are the values of the cars, trucks, and/or boats being taxed, and are those vehicles disclosed as assets?
- **Medical expenses:** When medical expenses are claimed, were they reimbursed?
- **Quarterly tax payments:** If quarterly tax payments have been made, is there a surplus that will be credited toward future tax liabilities? Has a tax refund been applied toward the next year's taxes?

Paralegal Application 6.12

The Search for Hidden Assets

In searching for hidden assets, a paralegal might explore the following:

1. Does a party report a modest income and yet live a lavish lifestyle with frequent vacations, an expensive residence with no mortgage, high-end motor vehicles, expensive clothing, and jewelry?
2. Has the other party deferred receipt of any income, raises, bonuses, or other forms of compensation to a date subsequent to the divorce? A review of past income history is often helpful in this area.
3. If the other party is self-employed and claiming a reduction in business and income since initiation of divorce proceedings, is the decline in marked contrast to past history or market trends?

4. Does the other party receive unacknowledged "perks" over and above direct salary at his or her job, such as a company car for business and personal use; subsidized housing or relocation costs; an allowance for uniforms or parking; an expense account for travel, dining, and entertainment; or club memberships?
5. Has the other party made sham or allegedly "bad" loans to a family member or friend?
6. Does the other party hold any as yet potentially valuable unexercised stock options in a company where he or she is or was employed?
7. Has the other party accumulated substantial sick, personal, or vacation time at work for which he or she may be compensated?

(Continued)

8. Has the other party accumulated a substantial number of frequent flier miles?

9. Has the other party made substantial withdrawals from various accounts for unknown or unexplained purposes, funds that do not appear in another form on an affidavit? Look especially for round-numbered amounts in multiples of $10,000.

10. What is the spouse's travel history? Does he or she receive calls or mail from another country? Does a credit card statement reflect an overnight trip to the Cayman Islands the day of or after substantial bank withdrawals? Does he or she have business interests in another country or associations with people who do?

11. Is cash being kept in a safe deposit box or in some other location?

12. What kind of business(es) is the other party engaged in? How is the income received? For example, does the party own or work at a gas station where receipts are tied to gas pump readings, or in a convenience store or restaurant where large sums of cash and tips are received and may or may not be declared or deposited in the business's accounts? Does the other party have a history of working "under the table"? Has the person postponed executing lucrative business contracts until after the divorce?

13. If the other party owns a business, are salary payments being made to nonexistent employees or close relatives or friends for work that was never performed?

14. Is cash being kept in the form of traveler's checks?

15. Has the other party set up a custodial account in the name of a child, using the child's social security number?

16. Have investments been made in certificate "bearer" municipal bonds or Series EE Savings Bonds, which are not registered with the IRS and do not appear on account statements.

17. Has the other party recently paid off mortgages or credit card balances in his or her name?

18. During the marriage, and especially recently, has the opposing party transferred assets to a relative, friend, or paramour?

Court Involvement in the Discovery Process

Courts generally affirm a party's right to conduct comprehensive and liberal discovery and prefer not to become involved in the process unless mandated by procedural rules (as in the case of Requests for Mental or Physical Examinations) or by the unique circumstances of individual cases or the conduct of counsel or the parties. The most common ways in which the courts become involved are:

1. **Discovery Conferences.**   A court may, on its own initiative, pursuant to court rule, or at the request of a party, order that a discovery conference be convened, at which time a discovery plan is developed and agreed upon. The plan typically sets out the appropriate topics for discovery, the discovery methods to be used by each of the parties, and the timeline within which discovery must be completed. Most states have in place procedures for managing discovery under the court's supervision (through a "discovery master") to ensure that the parties make reasonable and timely requests and responses.

2. **Protective Orders.**   A court will entertain a motion for a protective order brought by a party who contends, for example, that a discovery request seeks privileged information, is excessive and would lead to undue burden or expense, or is made in bad faith solely for the purpose of harassment. If the motion is granted, the court will establish limitations on discovery.

3. **Orders to Compel and Impose Sanctions for Noncompliance.**   When a party fails to comply with a discovery request, the party making the request may file a motion to compel. If granted, the discovery request then becomes, in effect, an order of the court, and a failure to comply may result in sanctions. For example, the noncomplying party may be held in contempt of court and be ordered to pay the fees the other party incurred in pursuing the matter.

PARALEGAL PRACTICE TIP

An example of a case management agreement can be accessed at *www.jud.ct.gov.* (Connecticut) You can find a link to this site at *www. pearsonhighered.com/wilson* in the companion website material for Chapter 6 under "Forms."

In especially egregious cases, if he or she is the moving party, the matter may be stayed or dismissed or the party may be prevented from introducing related evidence at trial. In some jurisdictions, prior to filing a motion to compel, the parties are required to exhaust efforts to settle the discovery dispute without the assistance of the court.

CHAPTER **SUMMARY**

This chapter provides a comprehensive survey of the discovery process—its nature, scope, purposes, and methods both formal and informal. Attention is given to the ways in which the client can contribute to information-gathering efforts. The five major formal discovery methods are described and examples are provided from family law cases: interrogatories, depositions, requests for admissions, requests for production of documents and things, and requests for physical and mental examinations. The nature, role, and importance of financial affidavits are also addressed.

Throughout the chapter, the paralegal's role in the discovery process is heavily emphasized. Several reminders are pro-

vided regarding related ethical duties and the importance of being aware of the substantive laws and procedural rules governing discovery. Additional topics relevant to discovery are also considered, including objections to discovery requests, the challenges of uncovering hidden assets, and the court's involvement in the process. Given the extent to which technology has greatly altered the manner in which businesses and individuals create, store, and retrieve information, particular attention is given to electronic discovery and the Internet as a valuable discovery tool.

CONCEPT REVIEW AND REINFORCEMENT

KEY **TERMS**

Deponent
Deposition
Discovery
Electronic discovery
Expert
Forensic accountant
Formal discovery
Informal discovery

Interrogatories
Lay witness
Letters rogatory
Mandatory self-disclosure
Notice of deposition
Privilege
Protective order
Request for Admissions

Request for Physical or Mental
   Examination
Request for Production of Documents
   or Things
Subpoena
Subpoena *duces tecum*
Work product

REVIEW **QUESTIONS**

1. Distinguish between "formal" and "informal discovery" and give an example of each.
2. Describe how the client can assist in the information-gathering process.
3. Identify each of the five formal discovery methods, and give an example of when and how each might be used in a family law case.
4. Identify the strengths and weaknesses of each of the five formal discovery methods.
5. Describe e-discovery and give three examples of when and how it might be used.

6. Identify the kinds of objections to discovery requests that can be raised.
7. Describe the nature and purpose of financial statements/affidavits.
8. Identify a minimum of five ways of concealing assets and how they might be detected.
9. Describe the role of the paralegal in the discovery process.
10. Describe the role the court plays in the discovery process.

DEVELOPING YOUR PARALEGAL SKILLS

FOCUS ON **THE JOB**

In this activity the student will develop a set of twenty interrogatories tailored to the facts of a specific case.

The Facts

Walter and Renee Albertson have been married thirty-seven years and have three adult children: Eleanor, Edward, and Walter Jr. The marriage has been rocky and each party believes that the other has been "unfaithful" on several occasions. The only confirmed affair occurred in 1996, when Renee became involved with a next-door neighbor and at one point moved in with him after Walter "threw her out" of the marital home because of the ongoing and open affair. After a month he begged her to come home. She did, and they went to counseling, reconciled, and resumed their marital relationship. However, Walter never really trusted Renee after that. As a result, he kept all of his assets as separate as possible from hers, with the exception of a joint bank account, out of which he paid all of the expenses related to the marital home as well as the food bills and car-related costs. Renee has been depositing her entire paycheck into this account, but Walter only matches what she puts in. He earns funds from four sources: social security, a modest salary as a school bus driver, an investment portfolio he established in 1980 and has maintained ever since, and money he earns doing electrical work "under the table," for which he is paid cash or "in-kind" (e.g., he does some wiring for his mechanic, and the mechanic repairs Walter's vehicle without charging him). He deposits his social security into the joint account along with about 20% of his check from the bus company. Throughout the marriage, he has maintained the couple's finances and largely kept Renee "in the dark," although he does give her a modest weekly "allowance." He has always kept extensive financial and business records on his computer. He pays his bills online and uses Turbo Tax to prepare the parties' joint tax returns.

The marital home (jointly held) is assessed at $350,000 for property tax purposes, but Walter claims it is worth closer to $500,000, based on work he has done building an addition that includes a den, bedroom, and bath with a hot tub in it. He spent the better part of a year doing the work in his free time. There is a $112,000 mortgage and a $20,000 equity loan secured by the property. The parties had to obtain the loan to cover income taxes (plus interest and penalties) due on previously undeclared income Walter had collected doing electrical work for friends and acquaintances. He asserts that he is not still doing this work, but Renee intends to hire a private detective to follow him in his free time, as she is certain he continues to work and not pay taxes on the funds collected or on in-kind services received. He claims to never have any money but went to Aruba for a week in January of 2010, allegedly alone, and has a new Toyota convertible, for which Renee believes he paid cash. She also saw a credit card statement that listed expenditures at two local jewelry stores and several local restaurants that she has not been to with him.

In December of 2009, Renee became suspicious that Walter was having an affair with his old high school sweetheart, Valentina Ferrara, with whom he "reconnected" at his fiftieth high school reunion. Valentina had recently been widowed. Walter admits that he is "in touch" with her (particularly by telephone and e-mail) but that she would never consider having an intimate relationship with him as long as he is still married. Besides, he claims that at the age of seventy, he is no longer able to function sexually. Renee believes he is seeing a doctor and has a prescription for "that little blue pill." Renee's heart is broken, and she has filed for divorce on the ground of adultery in a jurisdiction that retains fault grounds.

The Assignment

Assume that in the jurisdiction where you reside and/or are employed, when making property division decisions, the court considers both conduct during the marriage and financial and nonfinancial contribution to the marital enterprise. Using an appropriate format, draft a set of twenty interrogatories to be served on Walter. Assume that the firm where you work (Wilson and Tauson, LLP) represents Renee. The attorney handling the case is Juliana Wilson and the office is located at 390 Main Street in your hometown. What other forms of discovery do you think would be appropriate in this case and why?

FOCUS ON **ETHICS**

In this assignment, the student has an opportunity to consider the ethical issues raised when a client appears to be providing inaccurate and deceptive information on a financial affidavit.

The Assignment

Assume that Walter is your supervising attorney's client. He has given you a completed draft of his financial affidavit/

statement and claims that it accurately reflects all of his assets and liabilities. You are aware of all of the information presented in the above Focus on the Job fact pattern and are concerned that Walter's affidavit is very likely not accurate, and yet he must sign it under oath. You are also in a jurisdiction where his attorney must also sign the affidavit, indicating that to the best of his or her knowledge, the document contains no false information. Some of the things you are concerned about are that Walter has listed no credit card debt but does reflect a loan from his brother for $8,000, which he tells you should help him in the property settlement even though he doesn't really have to pay his brother back. He indicates his social security and bus driving income but reflects no income from investments or his work as an electrician, income you are reasonably certain he receives. He lists the joint account but no other accounts or cash assets. He has listed the value of the marital home as $500,000 less the mortgage and claims he doesn't have to list the equity loan because it was incurred to buy a car for Renee and he should not have to be liable for any of it. He also indicates that he pays 100 percent of the household expenses because, after all, he writes all the checks. None of this surprises you as you have disliked this client from the outset and find his conduct during the marriage reprehensible. As a paralegal, what course of action should you take, and how would you recommend the situation be addressed? Which of the ethical canons for paralegals promulgated by the National Association of Legal Assistants, contained in Appendix A, are applicable in this context? Present your recommendations in a 1–2 page paper.

FOCUS ON **CASE LAW**

In this activity, the student is asked to brief a case in which a party in a divorce proceeding installed spyware on her husband's computer in an attempt to monitor and record his communications with another woman.

The Assignment

Brief the case, *O'Brien v. O'Brien,* 899 So. 2d 1133 (Fla. Dist.App. 2005), using the format available on the companion website in the material related to Chapter 1 under "Resources," unless an alternative format is provided by your instructor. You can find the opinion at *www.pearsonhighered.com/wilson* in the companion website material related to Chapter 6 under "Cases" and in the Case Resources Section of the MyLegalStudiesLab.

FOCUS ON **STATE LAW AND PROCEDURE**

In this focus, the student is asked to research discovery-related rules, procedures, and forms in his or her jurisdiction.

The Assignment

1. Locate the rules governing the five formal discovery methods in family law cases in your jurisdiction. Does the state mandate any particular discovery forms/ formats?
2. Does your jurisdiction have any rules governing electronic discovery in family law cases?

3. What forms of mandatory self-disclosure, if any, does the state in which you reside (or are employed) require of parties to a divorce action?
4. Obtain and review a copy of your state's financial affidavit form. Assume that Walter is the client in the case you are working on and the facts are the same as in the Focus on the Job hypothetical in this chapter. Make a list of the kinds of documents and information you need to gather in order to help him complete his financial affidavit/statement.

FOCUS ON **TECHNOLOGY**

In addition to the links contained in the chapter, this activity provides a series of useful websites for reference, along with technology-related assignments for completion.

Websites of Interest

Links to all of the listed websites are provided at *www. pearsonhighered.com/wilson* in the companion website material for Chapter 6 under "Resources."

www.findlaw.com

Findlaw's Legal Technology Center has instituted an Electronic Discovery Rule Wizard, an online interactive tool to help legal professionals understand the amended Federal Rules of Civil Procedure and improve their use of e-discovery methods and procedures.

www.lectlaw.com/forma.htm

At this site, you can locate a set of interrogatories approved by the Florida State Supreme Court for use in family law cases. Go to "General Law Practice Forms" in the "Free Forms Room."

www.courtinfo.ca.gov/forms

At this California courts site you can locate a number of forms, including family law interrogatories, financial affidavits, a subpoena, and a subpoena *duces tecum*.

Assignments

1. Locate online the financial statements for five states including your own. A good place to start your search is with the websites for courts in various states.

The list of websites provided in Appendix B may be helpful.

2. Assume that you are currently married and a party to a divorce action. Complete (online, if possible) the appropriate financial affidavit/statement you would need to submit in the jurisdiction where you reside. This assignment is designed to be a private individual exercise. There is no requirement that it be shared with fellow students or the instructor, absent consent.

3. Assuming the facts in the above Focus on the Job hypothetical, draft an *ex parte* motion on Renee's behalf seeking to stop Walter from using his laptop and storage devices (such as floppy disks, CD-ROMs, flash memory devices, or any other similar type of storage device). You might want to request that he immediately produce and deposit the laptop and storage devices with the court in which the divorce action has been filed (your local family court) for examination by a recognized computer expert who may later present subsequent testimony under oath regarding relevant contents. You should consider building in provisions addressing how and by whom the contents will be examined, how privileged contents will be protected, what arrangements will be made for temporarily replacing the laptop, and who will bear related costs.

4. Using *www.findlaw.com,*
   a. Locate the federal rules of civil procedure regarding electronic discovery.
   b. Identify three current issues relating to interpretation and application of these rules.

PORTFOLIO PRODUCTS

1. Set of twenty interrogatories
2. Recommendations regarding ethical issues pertaining to completion of a financial statement
3. Brief of a case involving an electronic discovery issue
4. List of rules governing discovery matters in the student's jurisdiction
5. List of documents/information needed to complete a client's financial statement

chapter 7
PARENTHOOD

Stephen and Mary are in their early thirties. They have been seeing each other for four years and want to share a life together. The only thing needed to complete the picture is a child, but Stephen carries a rare genetic disease, and Mary had a hysterectomy due to uterine cancer when she was twenty-five years old. They have decided to search for egg and sperm donors who carry traits they consider desirable and then have Mary's best friend, Carol, serve as a surrogate mother. Carol and her husband, Chip, are all for the idea.

LEARNING OBJECTIVES

After reading this chapter and completing related assignments, you should be able to:

- identify the three parties most interested in parentage determinations

- identify the most common ways in which legal parentage is established

- describe the basic process for adjudicating paternity

- explain what paternity fraud is and how paternity may be disestablished

- identify various applications of assisted reproductive technology

- discuss some of the ways in which courts and legislatures are addressing surrogacy arrangements, cryopreserved embryos, posthumous conception, and the use of assisted reproductive technology by same-sex couples

- describe the role of the paralegal in cases involving determination of parentage

Introduction

In this chapter, we consider issues of importance to children, parents, and the government in the context of parentage determinations. We look at the most common ways of determining legal parenthood with particular attention to how paternity is established and may be "disestablished." The last section of the chapter addresses key topics and issues in the evolving area of assisted reproductive technology as a means of creating parent-child relationships.

This chapter further extends a basic theme of this text: Society and the law are confronting changes in the way people define parenthood, create families, and assign responsibility for children. Innovative means of conceiving and giving birth are expanding the diversity of nontraditional families in society by making parenthood possible for thousands of people who would otherwise be childless. Although preference for the "traditional family" is still strong, doors have opened to new bases for establishing, and in some cases disestablishing, legal parenthood.

In an era in which several individuals may have legitimate claims to parenthood in a given case, courts are called upon to address challenging questions:

- Should parenthood flow on a strict liability basis, solely from the performance of a sexual act regardless of the circumstances or intent of the parties to create a child? If so, how do we deal with cases involving nonconsensual sexual relations, statutory rape,[1] or partners who lie about the use of birth control measures?

- Should parenthood "by accident" be treated differently from parenthood by deliberate choice?
- Should parents have to act as parents in order to be considered parents?
- Should the mother's marital status determine parentage?
- Should individuals be able to assign parental status by contract?
- Should parenthood be a fixed status—once a parent, always a parent?
- Should children be permitted to have more than two "legal" parents?
- Should children have a voice in parentage determinations?
- Should same-sex partners be permitted by law to be parents (by contract, adoption, etc.)?

Later chapters will address issues related to child custody, child support, and adoption. The threshold question in this chapter is who are the child's parents? "Who's your mother?" was once a reasonably simple question to answer. Even "Who's your father?" was not that complicated, depending on the mother's marital status. However, with the emergence of reproductive technologies, even the answer to "Who's your mother?" is not so simple anymore. (See Exhibit 7.1.)

PARALEGAL PRACTICE TIP

One of the arguments often raised in opposition to legal recognition of gay co-parents is that a child needs both a mother and a father, as opposed to simply two parents, be it two mothers or two fathers. The claim is that "A child needs both a mother-figure and a father-figure in order to develop to his (or her) maximum potential. Implicit in this argument . . . is the assertion that fathers have certain traits that mothers cannot utilize or model as well as fathers can, and that mothers have certain traits that fathers cannot utilize or model as well as mothers can."[2] Do you agree?

EXHIBIT 7.1 When Is a Parent a Parent?

- **Acknowledged parent:** a parent who has executed an affidavit acknowledging parentage
- **Adoptive parent:** a person who, by means of legal process, becomes a parent of a child to whom he or she is biologically unrelated
- **Biological parent:** a blood-related parent who contributes half of the child's genetic material by means of a reproductive cell (egg or sperm); sometimes called a genetic or "natural" parent
- **Co-parent:** a person who shares childrearing responsibilities with a partner with or without benefit of a legally recognized parent-child relationship
- *De facto* **parent:** a person who has been a primary caregiver and financial supporter of a child, usually with consent of the legal parent and for a requisite period of time
- **Egg or sperm donor:** a person who donates genetic material (sometimes for a fee) to help others have a child; donors often remain anonymous and usually give up any parental rights they would otherwise have to a child they may help to create
- **Foster parent:** a person who takes care of a child for a temporary period of time, usually for a modest payment through a child welfare agency
- **Gestational mother:** a woman who carries and delivers a child to whom she may or may not be genetically related
- **Intended parent(s):** a person or couple who intend to take custody of and assume all parental rights and responsibilities for a child as a result of an adoption, a surrogacy arrangement, or some other technique of assisted reproduction; an intended parent may or may not be genetically related to the child
- **Legal parent:** a person who is recognized as a child's parent under state or federal law
- **Natural parent:** a mother or father who is a biological (genetic) parent of a child
- **Parent by estoppel:** an individual who, although not a legal parent, lives with and accepts parental responsibilities for a child and on whose emotional and financial support the child and the other parent have relied
- **Presumed father:** a man who is presumed to be the father of a child who is conceived/born during the course of his marriage to the mother (or within a certain period thereafter)
- **Psychological parent:** the individual who has the strongest "parental" bond with the child, who has provided the most significant care for the child in quality and quantity, and whom the child often regards as a "parent"

(Continued)

EXHIBIT 7.1 (*Continued*)

- **Putative father:** a man who may be the father of a child but who was not married to the child's mother at the time of birth and whose paternity has not yet been established through legal process
- **Step-parent:** a person who marries the legal mother or father of a child to whom he or she is biologically unrelated
- **Surrogate mother:** a woman who agrees to carry and deliver a baby with an understanding that she will surrender the child to the intended parents at birth or shortly thereafter; a surrogate mother may or may not be genetically related to the child

Who Are the Interested Parties?

The three parties most interested in parentage determinations are children, parents, and the government.

THE CHILD

According to U.S. Census Bureau data, "more than 13 million children in the U.S. live alone with their single mothers."[3] The precise number of these and other children who may not even know the identities of their biological fathers is virtually impossible to establish, but the numbers are significant. The impact of not knowing the identity of a parent can be monumental for a child as he or she grows into adulthood. The answer to the question "Who am I?" inevitably rests, at least in part, on the answer to the question "Where did I come from?" Even if the answer is not entirely satisfactory, it has many potential emotional, social, economic, medical, and legal advantages for a child. It helps build the child's identity and grants him or her membership in an extended family. It provides the basis for support and inheritance rights. It establishes eligibility for a host of dependent-based governmental benefits. It gives the child standing to sue for death or other harm to the parent. It opens access to potentially critical medical histories. However, despite its importance, children often confront legal obstacles when they attempt to discover their true parentage. (See Paralegal Application 7.1.)

Paralegal **Application 7.1**

Obstacles to Discovering Parentage

- **The Marital Presumption:** Under the marital presumption, a man married to a child's mother at the time of birth (or within 300 days of termination of the marriage) is presumed to be the child's father, a presumption that still carries considerable weight in many jurisdictions.
- **The Doctrine of Estoppel:** The doctrine of estoppel holds a mother and/or a man accountable for their conduct regarding paternity in some circumstances. If they act as if the man is the child's father, he may be

deemed by the courts to be the father, and neither the mother nor the "father" may be permitted to request genetic testing to deny paternity at a later date.
- **Issue Preclusion/*res judicata*:** Issue preclusion and *res judicata* principles prevent parties from relitigating in a subsequent suit an issue that was fully litigated and decided in an earlier action. For example, if the issue of paternity of a particular child is raised and decided in the context of a divorce proceeding, in most states neither party is permitted to

(Continued)

file a later paternity action seeking to have someone else designated the father of the child.

- **Reproductive Technology Statutes:** Depending on the method of assisted reproductive technology used to produce a child, states may dictate by statute who will or will not be deemed a legal parent. For example, the Uniform Parentage Act of 2000 (as amended in 2002), adopted in some states, provides that the donor of semen for use in artificial insemination (of a woman other than the donor's wife) will be treated as if he were not the father of a child thereby conceived.

PARALEGAL PRACTICE TIP

The full text of the Uniform Parentage Act can be found at *www.nccusl.org.* You can find a link to this site at *www.pearsonhighered.com/wilson* in the companion website material for Chapter 7 under "Resources."

- **Sealed Records/Confidentiality Statutes:** After an adoption is finalized, many states require that all records of the adoption be sealed, including the child's original birth certificate and any other documents that identify the child's birth parents. In most states, absent an agreement to the contrary, no one can have access to identifying information about the biological parents without a showing of good cause, such as a medical emergency.

Sidebar

Do you believe all children are entitled to know who their "real" parents are, no matter how complex or disturbing their origins may be?

Res judicata
[Latin: a thing adjudicated] an issue that has been definitively settled by judicial decision; requires three essential elements: (1) an earlier decision on the issue, (2) a final judgment on the merits, and (3) the involvement of the original parties

THE PARENTS

Once established, a parent's status as a mother or a father automatically brings with it a variety of rights and obligations that, for the most part, attach whether or not one exercises them. Much of the legislation and litigation on parenthood focuses primarily on the economic obligations of being a parent. However, in addition to rights such as the rights to potentially inherit from their children or to sue for the wrongful death of a child, parenthood also brings the commonly acknowledged satisfactions of raising children. Parental rights for married parents include, for example, the shared rights to discipline and educate their children and to make decisions regarding medical treatment, religion, place of residence, and social contacts. For unmarried or divorced parents, these rights may be more limited, because they often are shaped by law and established by the courts.

Paralegal **Application 7.2**

Will the Real Mom and Dad Please Stand?

PARALEGAL PRACTICE TIP

The opinion in the *Michael H. v. Gerald D.* case is available at *www.pearsonhighered.com/wilson* in the companion website material related to Chapter 7 under "Cases" and in the Case Resources Section of the MyLegalStudiesLab.

Generally under law, both genetic consanguinity and giving birth are recognized as legitimate means of estab-

lishing a mother-and-child relationship. But, what should happen if the two means do not coincide in one woman? (See Case 7.3 later in this chapter.) And what if, in a state that recognizes the marital presumption, the mother's husband and the child's biological father are different men?

Michael H. v. Gerald D., 491 U.S. 110, 109 S. Ct. 2333, 105 L. Ed. 2d 91 (1989): When Biology-Plus and Marital Presumption Collide[4]

The Facts

In this case, the Supreme Court dealt with two fathers, each with a bona fide claim to paternity. In 1981, a woman named Carol gave birth to a daughter named Victoria. Carol's husband, Gerald, was identified on the birth certificate as the child's father, and he lived with the mother and child on and off during the years following the birth. However, the child actually was the product of Carol's extramarital affair with a man named Michael, who was genetically determined (within a 98.7 degree of probability) to be the child's father. He, too, lived with Carol and Victoria on and off following the child's birth, during which time he established a relationship with his daughter. However, Gerald and Victoria subsequently reconciled. When Michael filed a paternity action seeking to be declared the child's legal father and to establish a right to visitation, Gerald opposed, claiming that, under California law, he was the child's father based on the marital presumption. The child asserted that she should be entitled to maintain her relationship with both *de facto* fathers.

Sidebar

Faced with the forced choice between two fathers in this case, what do you think the Court should do? Explain your response. Should it matter that the child is the product of an affair? Should the biological father be permitted to rebut the marital presumption? Must one father be rejected in favor of the other father, or do you think the courts should recognize both fathers as the child requested? Should the child's wishes be considered? To learn what the Supreme Court decided in this case, check the full opinion available on the companion website. Do you agree with the outcome? Compare the major arguments of the plurality and the dissent.

THE GOVERNMENT

The government's interest in establishing parentage is essentially economic.[5] It is motivated less by a desire to provide for the needs of an individual child than by an interest in controlling the costs of public assistance. This interest is well founded, given that under the federal definition of poverty, approximately one in five to six children in the United States lives in poverty. This statistic is at least in part due to a lack of economic support from unknown and absent fathers.[6]

The child's entitlement to support exists without regard to the parents' marital status or the nature and extent of the child's relationship with the parents. When parents are unavailable or otherwise unable to adequately provide for their children, help is often sought in a variety of forms funded by the federal government and distributed through the states. However, in order to continue to receive federal funds for this purpose, the states must take mandatory steps to contain the costs of financial support, food stamps, health insurance benefits, etc. For example, since 1975, the states have required mothers receiving public assistance or applying for IV-D services to cooperate with the state in an effort to identify and locate the child's father, who may then become a defendant in an action to recoup child support.

PARALEGAL PRACTICE TIP

To see an example of a form seeking IV-D assistance in locating a missing parent, go to *www.courts.state.va.us.* (Virginia) You can find a link to this site at *www.pearsonhighered.com/ wilson* in the companion website material for Chapter 7 under "Forms."

The Child's Legal Status

Under early common law, the child's legal status essentially depended on the marital status of his or her parents. Children were regarded as legitimate if born to married parents and illegitimate if born to unmarried parents. The child of unwed parents was deemed a *filius nullius*, a "child of no one," a bastard with a legal bond to neither parent—essentially a public ward. If the mother were married and the child was the product of an illicit affair, then legal parentage was established based on a **marital presumption** of legitimacy rather than on biological parenthood.

By the nineteenth century, the states began to move away from penalizing children for their parents' sexual misconduct and toward treating them as inno-

Filius nullius

[Latin: the son (child) of no one]

Marital presumption

the presumption that when a woman gives birth to a child while married or within 300 days of termination of the marriage, her husband is presumed to be the child's legal father cents warranting protection, support, and nurturance rather than punishment and the stigma of illegitimacy. Given the relative ease of establishing maternity based on the biological realities of pregnancy and birth, the legal bond between an unwed mother and her child was the first to be recognized, rendering children "legitimate" at least with respect to their mothers.

Establishment of the father-child relationship outside of the marital unit has been slower to evolve. However, recognizing the negative impact of illegitimacy on unwed fathers and their children, states began enacting legislation in the early 1800s providing for acknowledgment of paternity and legitimization of children whose parents subsequently married. Further progress was slow but was energized in the 1960s by that era's focus on equal rights and elimination of discrimination in many areas. In a piecemeal fashion and with mixed results, scrutiny has gradually extended to laws that treat unwed fathers differently from unwed mothers and unwed parents and their children differently from married parents and their children based solely on marital status. Consider the following developments:

PARALEGAL PRACTICE TIP

It is still the case that when a child is born to unmarried parents, no legal bond exists between the biological father and his child until "legal fatherhood" is established.

- In the 1968 *Levy* case, the U.S. Supreme Court held that Louisiana's wrongful death statute violated the Equal Protection Clause of the Constitution by denying children the right to recover for the death of their mother because they were "illegitimate."[7]
- Beginning with *Lehr v. Robertson*[8] in 1983, the U.S. Supreme Court at least began extending rights to unwed fathers in the adoption context, where they previously had none. The Court held that unlike an unwed mother, whose legal parentage is established at birth, an unwed father's rights are determined using a **"biology-plus" rule**. Under this approach, a biological connection alone is not enough. In order to be recognized as a parent under the law, the man must also act as a father and accept some measure of responsibility for his child.
- Differential treatment of unwed mothers and fathers also has implications for children in the immigration context. In *Nguyen v. Immigration and Naturalization Services*,[9] for example, the U.S. Supreme Court upheld a provision of the Immigration and Naturalization Act[10] applicable to children born outside of the country when only one parent was a citizen. The statute imposed different requirements for a nonmarital child's acquisition of citizenship based on whether the citizen parent was the unwed mother or the unwed father. According to the Act, the child of an unwed mother acquires citizenship if the mother, prior to the birth, was a citizen and met a one year residency requirement.[11] If the father was the citizen parent, he must have been a citizen when the child was born, have established a blood relationship to the child by clear and convincing evidence, have agreed to support the child until age eighteen, and have acknowledged paternity or been adjudicated the father before the child turned eighteen.[12]

Biology-plus rule
the rule that an unwed father's parental rights are worthy of constitutional protection if the father grasps the opportunity to develop a relationship with and accept responsibility for his child

PARALEGAL PRACTICE TIP

Laws that discriminate against children based on their parents' marital status continue to exist in some areas. However, to pass constitutional muster, they must serve legitimate governmental purposes such as preventing fraudulent claims for state and federal benefits. For example, it is considered reasonable to condition receipt of dependent-based benefits on an adjudication or acknowledgment of paternity.

How Is Parentage Established?

As suggested earlier, the concept of parentage was once reasonably straightforward. A child had two parents, and they were presumed to be a biological mother and her husband. Traditionally, motherhood and a mother's constitutionally protected

PARALEGAL PRACTICE TIP

Establishment of or challenges to paternity arise in a number of contexts, including custody, child support, adoption, immigration, inheritance, and health care.

rights to parent her child flow from the critical role she plays in nourishing the child in her womb and enduring the pain and risks of childbirth. The Supreme Court has described the relationship as "verifiable from the birth itself."[13] Because fatherhood has posed more of a challenge, the following material focuses primarily on establishment of paternity. We will first look at some of the basic provisions of the Uniform Parentage Act concerning establishment of legal parenthood and then consider the three primary methods of establishing paternity:

- The marital presumption
- Acknowledgment of parentage
- Adjudication of parentage

UNIFORM PARENTAGE ACT

PARALEGAL PRACTICE TIP

The full texts of the Uniform Acts referenced in this paragraph can be found at *www.nccusl.org.* You can find a link to this site at *www. pearsonhighered.com/wilson* in the companion website material for Chapter 7 under "Resources."

The Uniform Parentage Act (UPA) was first adopted by the National Conference of Commissioners on Uniform State Laws in 1973. It was subsequently revised in 2000 and amended in 2002. As of May 2011, the revised UPA has been enacted in whole or in part in a minority of the states, including Alabama, Delaware, New Mexico, North Dakota, Oklahoma, Texas, Utah, Washington, and Wyoming, and is under consideration in others, some of which presently recognize the 1973 edition of the Act. The current version creates a single, coherent act regarding parentage by integrating the 1973 UPA with the Uniform Putative and Unknown Fathers Act and the Uniform Status of Children of Assisted Conception Act. Its provisions are also consistent with the principles and requirements of two other key uniform acts, the Uniform Child Custody Jurisdiction and Enforcement Act (UCCJEA) and the Uniform Interstate Family Support Act (UIFSA). It is also consistent with paternity requirements of federal child support enforcement law in general.

The Act addresses both paternity and maternity determinations and treats marital and nonmarital children equally with respect to their legal status and rights. Although the Act acknowledges the availability of genetic testing to determine parentage, it makes clear that a biological father is not the only man who can be legally recognized as a father. Under the Act, a father-child relationship may be established in the following ways:[14]

- An unrebutted presumption of paternity
- An effective acknowledgment of paternity by the man unless the acknowledgment has been rescinded or successfully challenged
- An adjudication of paternity
- Adoption of the child by the man
- The man's having consented to an assisted reproduction procedure which resulted in the birth of a child
- An adjudication confirming the man as a parent of a child born to a gestational mother if their surrogacy agreement is valid and enforceable

THE MARITAL PRESUMPTION

PARALEGAL PRACTICE TIP

Arizona's Marital Presumption Statute can be seen at *www. azcourts.gov.* The statute identifies multiple "presumptions" and describes the circumstances under which the marital presumption specifically can be overcome. A link to the site can be found at *www. pearsonhighered.com/wilson* in the companion website material for Chapter 7 under "Statutes."

As mentioned earlier, under common law, parentage was based on the marital presumption (sometimes called the legitimacy presumption) that when a married woman gave birth to a child while the parties were married or within 300 days of termination of the marriage, the woman's husband was presumed to be the child's legal father. In the interest of preserving marriages, the general rule was that all of the potentially interested parties (the husband, the mother, the child, and the biological father) were precluded from bringing a paternity action. "Lord Mansfield's Rule" of evidence prohibited either spouse from giving testimony that the husband was not the father, even in the face of strong biological evidence to the contrary. When challenges were allowed, the presumption could be rebutted only with evidence of the husband's sterility, impotency, or nonaccess to the wife at the time of conception. The interests served by the presumption were described as follows by a Michigan Supreme Court Justice in a 2006 case:

> The presumption that children born or conceived during a marriage are the issue of that marriage is deeply rooted in our statutes and has been consistently recognized throughout our jurisprudence. . . . This presumption vindicates a number of interests, not the least of which include the interest of the child in not having his or her legitimacy called into question, the interest of the state in ensuring that children are properly supported, and the interest of both in assuring the effective operation of intestate succession. The presumption also reflects the recognition that "[t]here is no area of law more requiring finality and stability than family law."[15]

The states now generally set forth by statute or case law the rules for if, when, and by whom the marital presumption can be rebutted. Courts in several states still uphold it, even when conclusive scientific proof of biological paternity is available, at least as long as the marital unit is intact. However, in most states, a putative biological father or a husband who has reason to believe he is not the child's biological father may attempt to rebut the presumption, but usually must do so within a limited period of time. (See Case 7.2 later in this chapter.)

PARALEGAL PRACTICE TIP

The ways of rebutting the presumption are essentially the same as they were under common law. Proof may be provided that the husband was sterile or that he had no access to the mother during the probable period of conception. For example, it may be shown that the mother was residing in Illinois and her husband was stationed in Afghanistan during the relevant period.

ACKNOWLEDGMENT OF PARENTAGE

Since 1993 under federal law, all states must have in place simple procedures enabling parents to voluntarily acknowledge parentage by completing an appropriate notarized acknowledgment, stipulation, or affidavit. The document is most often called a voluntary acknowledgment or affidavit of parentage. Under federal law, the document must contain the names, addresses, birth dates, social security numbers, and signatures of both parents in addition to the name, birth date, and birthplace of the child. Depending on the state, it may also include the phone numbers of both parents, the mother's maiden name, the father's place of employment, the child's gender and custody status, and the ethnicity of the parents.

The acknowledgment may be executed (completed, signed, and witnessed) at a hospital at the time of birth usually for free or at any time thereafter prior to entry of a judicial order of parentage provided the parties' signatures are notarized. Witnesses and notaries will usually ask for a photo ID and social security number for identification purposes. In addition to hospitals, acknowledgment forms are also commonly available online, at **IV-D agencies**, social service agencies, and other locations where children and their parents receive services. The form contains, or is accompanied by, a description of the legal consequences of executing the document with respect to

PARALEGAL PRACTICE TIP

The form for voluntarily acknowledging paternity in Illinois can be seen at *www.pearsonhighered.com/wilson* in the companion website material for Chapter 7 under "Forms."

IV-D agency
the state agency charged with responsibility for enforcing child support obligations

child support, custody, visitation rights, and obligations along with notice that the acknowledgment may be rescinded within a limited sixty-day period after signing by complying with specific procedures. After it is signed, the document usually must be filed with the court or sent to the vital statistics/public records office that maintains birth records in the jurisdiction. Once executed, the document becomes the equivalent of a judicial finding of paternity subject to the sixty-day rescission period.[16] The acknowledgment then is entitled to full faith and credit in all states.

Some states have a relatively simple rescission procedure but others require a formal judicial action. The client may have to file a Complaint to Rescind Voluntary Acknowledgment or a Petition to Determine Parentage. Genetic tests will be ordered by the court, and if they exclude the petitioner as the child's father, the applicable vital statistics agency will be authorized to delete his name from the birth certificate. Because of the strong public policy favoring the finality of parentage determinations, after the sixty-day rescission period has elapsed, the acknowledgment usually can be challenged only on the grounds of fraud, duress, or mistake of fact (the alleged father honestly believed he was the child's father but has since learned that he is and always has been incapable of producing sperm). Such challenges usually can be brought within only a limited period, such as a year from the date of signing or filing.

Unmarried fathers often voluntarily acknowledge paternity without legal counsel and without benefit of the scientific certainty afforded by genetic (DNA) testing. When counsel is consulted, the client commonly is advised to confirm paternity through testing. The attorney representing a client in this situation is often present with both parties when the document is going to be signed. The attorney must be absolutely clear which of the parties he or she represents and should recommend that the other party seek legal advice before signing.

PARALEGAL PRACTICE TIP

To see an example of a form rescinding a voluntary acknowledgment of paternity form, visit *www.childsup.ca.gov*. (California) You can find a link to this site at *www.pearsonhighered.com/wilson* in the companion website material for Chapter 7 under "Forms."

PARALEGAL PRACTICE TIP

Parties under eighteen have a right to request tests without the permission of a parent or legal guardian.

PARALEGAL PRACTICE TIP

An Acknowledgment is not the same as the child's birth certificate. If the father's name does appear on the birth certificate, it is not conclusive proof of paternity. On the other hand, the Affidavit constitutes an admission of paternity and has the force of a judgment sixty days after the date on which the last party signs it. Congress has provided that the unmarried father's name may appear on a birth certificate only if the mother and father have executed an acknowledgment of parentage or there has been an adjudication of paternity.[17]

PARALEGAL PRACTICE TIP

An example of an Affidavit in Support of Establishing Paternity (initiating a IV-D case) is accessible at *www.pearsonhighered.com/wilson* in the companion website material related to Chapter 7 under "Forms."

Putative father
a man who is reputed or believed to be the father of a child but who was not married to the mother when the child was born and whose paternity has not yet been established by legal process

ADJUDICATION OF PARENTAGE

Historically, paternity actions were primarily criminal in nature and were designed to punish sexual misconduct. Today, they are largely civil proceedings that commence with the filing of a Complaint to Establish Paternity (see Exhibit 7.3) or a Petition for Declaration of Parentage. They are most often brought by mothers seeking child support, IV-D agencies on behalf of recipients of public assistance, or men seeking to establish or disestablish paternity. Under federal law, when paternity is contested, states must require genetic testing of the parties and the child, if requested. If the tests indicate paternity to a high degree of probability, a rebuttable presumption of paternity is established, and the burden shifts to the **putative father** to prove nonpaternity if he chooses and is able to do so.

The procedure for establishing paternity is governed by both state and federal law and the process varies considerably from state-to-state. A basic outline of the process is provided in Exhibit 7.2. Prior to filing a paternity case, there are several threshold questions that should be considered.

- **Standing:** Mothers, fathers (established, alleged, and others with legitimate claims), and IV-D child support enforcement agencies are the common claimants with standing. Article 6 of the Uniform Parentage Act and some states extend standing to children and additional parties, including adoption agencies, intended parents under a surrogacy agreement, and representatives of deceased, incapacitated, or minor persons.

- **Personal jurisdiction:** Because establishment of paternity will result in associated obligations including child support, the court must have personal jurisdiction over the defendant. In interstate cases, personal jurisdiction over a nonresident defendant often can be established under the long-arm statutes of the state or the Uniform Interstate Family Support Act. When personal jurisdiction cannot be obtained, IV-D agencies can initiate a case in the petitioner's state and send it to "the responding state" where the defendant resides. The responding state then will be responsible for obtaining jurisdiction and establishing paternity.

- **Subject matter jurisdiction:** Subject matter jurisdiction may reside in more than one court. Most paternity actions are brought in family courts. However, if a father's claim to paternity is based on his having raised, supported, and held the child out as his own without being the biological father, the action may have to be brought in a court with general equity jurisdiction. As a threshold requirement, the man usually will have to show that he has already established a substantial relationship with the child.

- **Venue:** Venue is usually proper in the judicial district where the child resides.

- **Statutes of limitation:** Statutes vary by jurisdiction and need to be determined based on the facts of each case. Under the Uniform Parentage Act, there is no statute of limitations on paternity actions if there is no legally established father. If there is an established father, challenges must be brought within two years of the child's birth. Federal law establishes an eighteen-year statute of limitations for bringing paternity actions for the purpose of establishing child support obligations.

- **Binding effect of judgments:** A judgment of paternity is binding with respect to the parties as in an action for divorce but is not necessarily binding on a child who is not a party to that action.

- **Potential defendant(s):** If the mother was married to a man other than the named defendant at the time she became pregnant, gave birth, or within 300 days thereafter, the husband may need to be added as a second defendant unless he has previously been determined not to be the father in another judicial proceeding. As an alternative in some states, the husband may sign a notarized affidavit denying paternity.

- **Burden of proof:** The burden of proving paternity is on the petitioner, who must prove his or her case by a preponderance of the evidence in most jurisdictions. In a small minority, clear and convincing evidence is required.

- **Legal advice:** Although not required, it is wise for anyone seeking to establish paternity to obtain legal advice to ensure that he or she fully understands the implications of a judgment of parentage. For example, if an unmarried mother wants to establish paternity solely as a stepping-stone to receiving child support, she needs to realize that if she is successful, the "father" will then have a legally enforceable right to seek custody and/or visitation. She must also accept the fact that she may be required to provide and respond to testimony and evidence regarding sexual intercourse she engaged in during the probable period of conception. An unmarried father hoping to establish a relationship with his child needs to understand that if he prevails, he will also become obligated to support the child.

PARALEGAL PRACTICE TIP

A child may discover that despite a determination of paternity in a legal proceeding involving his mother and alleged father (such as a divorce), his true biological father is another man. If the child was not a party to the prior action and his "true" father acknowledges him prior to death, the child may be able to bring an action to establish paternity and claim inheritance and other rights.

PARALEGAL PRACTICE TIP

To see examples of Complaint forms that may be filed by a mother and a IV-D Agency in Vermont, visit *www.vermontjudiciary.org/eforms.* You can find a link to this site at *www.pearsonhighered.com/wilson* in the companion website material for Chapter 7 under "Forms."

PARALEGAL PRACTICE TIP

To see the equivalent of an affidavit denying paternity used in Oklahoma, visit *www.okdhs.org/library/forms.* You can find a link to this site at *www.pearsonhighered.com/wilson* in the companion website material for Chapter 7 under "Forms."

PARALEGAL PRACTICE TIP

Although not addressed in this Exhibit, it should be noted that many Native American Tribal Codes include provisions regarding establishment of paternity that should be considered when applicable. Visit *www.wa.gov/forms* to see several Indian Child Welfare Act (ICWA) notice forms for various kinds of actions. You can find a link to this site at *www.pearsonhighered.com/wilson* in the companion website material for Chapter 7 under "Forms."

EXHIBIT 7.2 Adjudication of Paternity—The Basic Process

This outline assumes that the client rather than the state's child support enforcement (IV-D) agency is pursuing the paternity claim. Terminology and procedures will vary based on the jurisdiction, but the following provides a basic description of the process.

1. The Complaint/Petition is drafted by the party seeking to establish parentage (the Plaintiff or Petitioner). State-specific forms are widely available online, in courts, in form books, and in law office files (paper and electronic). (See example of a Complaint in Exhibit 7.3.) A separate Complaint must be drafted for each minor child whose parentage is at issue. In some states, the mother, but not the father, may file an action during the pregnancy, although paternity will not be established until after the child's birth.

PARALEGAL PRACTICE TIP

To see examples of a Petition for Adjudication of Paternity and an Answer, visit *www.courts.delaware.gov*. You can find a link to this site at *www.pearsonhighered.com/wilson* in the companion website material related to Chapter 7 under "Forms."

2. The Plaintiff completes some type of Care and Custody Disclosure Form regarding the child's custody and whereabouts. If not addressed in this form, an Affidavit Disclosing Care and Custody Proceedings will need to be filed indicating any orders pertaining to the child that are pending or that have already been entered. This includes restraining orders.

PARALEGAL PRACTICE TIP

To see an example of an Affidavit Disclosing Care and Custody Proceedings, visit *www.lawlib.state.ma.us*. (Massachusetts) You can find a link to this site at *www.pearsonhighered.com/wilson* in the companion website material related to Chapter 7 under "Forms."

3. If receiving public assistance or otherwise unable to pay, the Plaintiff completes an Affidavit of Indigency requesting that the state cover the costs of serving the Defendant.
4. The Plaintiff files the Complaint, the Affidavit Disclosing Care and Custody Proceedings (and the Indigency Affidavit, if appropriate), in the proper court. The Clerk will assign a docket number to be used on all future documents pertaining to the case.
5. The Plaintiff obtains a Summons and completes it if it has not been completed by the clerk's office.
6. The Plaintiff arranges service of the Summons, Complaint, and Affidavit on the Defendant(s) in a manner authorized in the jurisdiction.

PARALEGAL PRACTICE TIP

If the petitioner is receiving public assistance, the state's IV-D agency is joined as a party and must receive notice of all filings, notices, hearings, etc.

7. The Plaintiff files the original Summons with the court when service has been made and the server has completed the relevant section of the Summons.
8. The Defendant answers the Complaint within the required period (usually twenty to thirty days). In the Answer, the Defendant may admit or deny paternity. If paternity is admitted, the case may settle. Under federal law, if the Defendant has been properly served and fails to respond or appear, the state is required to provide for entry of a default order that serves as a legally binding determination of paternity and the basis for a child support order.

(Continued)

EXHIBIT 7.2 (*Continued*)

PARALEGAL PRACTICE TIP

Examples of Answers admitting and denying paternity can be seen at *www.pearsonhighered.com/ wilson* in the companion website material for Chapter 7 under "Forms."

PARALEGAL PRACTICE TIP

To see an example of a Motion for a Default Order used in the state of Washington, visit *www.courts. wa.gov/forms.* A link to this site can be found at *www.pearsonhighered.com/wilson* in the companion website material related to Chapter 7 under "Forms."

---

  9. The parties may be required to file Financial Statements at this point.

10. Motions for Temporary Orders related to the child may be filed by one or both parties, and hearing dates will be assigned. Many states require that proposed orders be filed with the motions. The court can issue temporary child support, custody, and health insurance orders if the Defendant has previously acknowledged paternity or if genetic marker testing has been done and the state's threshold of probability of paternity is met (usually over 95%). If emergency circumstances exist, a motion (accompanied by a supporting affidavit) may be filed on an *ex parte* basis.

PARALEGAL PRACTICE TIP

Once paternity is established and the court can issue enforceable child support orders, it sometimes chooses to order support back to the date of the child's birth.

---

11. When paternity is disputed and a party is unwilling to voluntarily submit to testing, a Motion for Genetic Marker Testing (with a supporting Affidavit) may be filed. (See Exhibits 7.4 and 7.5.) The courts will usually grant these motions when there is probable cause to believe that the parties engaged in sexual intercourse during the "probable period of conception."

PARALEGAL PRACTICE TIP

Although they are more intrusive than genetic tests, blood-typing tests are also still sometimes used. However, their use is essentially limited to excluding a man as the father of a specific child or including him as a "possible" father of a specific child.

PARALEGAL PRACTICE TIP

When the alleged father has died or is otherwise unavailable, the court can order testing of his close relatives.

---

12. Hearings on Motions take place. The parties may be required to meet with family service officers prior to hearings in an effort to reach agreement on the matter in dispute.

13. Discovery is conducted.

14. Pretrial steps are followed that track the steps outlined in Chapter 5 with respect to the divorce process. Absent a history of abuse, the court may require that the parties have a face-to-face four-way (clients and counsel) meeting in an effort to settle the case without further litigation.

PARALEGAL PRACTICE TIP

If the parties marry while the paternity action is pending, the court can still issue an order of paternity.

(*Continued*)

EXHIBIT 7.2 (*Continued*)

15. The trial takes place. The nature of evidence offered and testimony of witnesses will vary depending on the nature of the case. For example, an unmarried plaintiff mother may present the following:
    - A certified copy of the child's birth certificate signed by the "father"
    - A certified copy of a Genetic marker testing report

PARALEGAL PRACTICE TIP

Although DNA test results provide compelling evidence of biological paternity, they are not necessarily determinative of "legal" paternity. They can be admitted without foundation unless there is an objection (they were not performed at an accredited laboratory, they were tainted or tampered with, etc.).

- Evidence and testimony regarding sexual intercourse with the defendant during the probable period of conception, such as motel registration records or joint leases on an apartment where the parties lived together
- Certified copies of medical records or testimony of physicians/experts, especially if the child was born prematurely
- Documents evidencing the defendant's apparent acknowledgment of paternity, such as a letter urging the plaintiff to get an abortion and offering to pay for it, an earlier voluntary acknowledgment of paternity signed by the defendant but never filed by the mother, and bank records indicating checks received from the defendant on a regular basis allegedly for support of the child
- Testimony from witnesses who have firsthand knowledge that the Defendant has raised and supported the child and held him or her out as his own natural child

The defendant father may allege and present evidence that another man, possibly one of his relatives, had sexual access to the mother during the probable period of conception. He may challenge the validity of the genetic marker tests, claiming they were tainted or fraudulent. He may need to counter several legal "presumptions" if, for example, his name is on the child's birth certificate, he signed a voluntary acknowledgment, he was married to the mother at any relevant time, or he has held himself out as the child's father.

PARALEGAL PRACTICE TIP

Visit *www.vermontjudiciary.org/eforms* to see a parentage affidavit for a mother and for a father. Reading through these forms will give you an idea of some of the kinds of evidence that may be presented in a paternity case. You can find a link to this site at *www.pearsonhighered.com/wilson* in the companion website material for Chapter 7 under "Forms."

16. The case is dismissed or a Judgment is entered declaring that the Defendant is the child's father and ordering that his name be added to the child's birth certificate.

PARALEGAL PRACTICE TIP

To see an example of a Judgment in a paternity action, visit *www.courts.wa.gov/forms*. (Washington) You can find a link to this site at *www.pearsonhighered.com/wilson* in the companion website material for Chapter 7 under "Forms."

PARALEGAL PRACTICE TIP

If the Defendant is excluded as the father, he should request that the court officially rule that he is not the child's father.

EXHIBIT 7.3 Complaint to Establish Paternity
Courtesy of Commonwealth of Massachusetts

Commonwealth of Massachusetts
The Trial Court
Probate and Family Court Department

Division _____

Docket No. _____

COMPLAINT TO ESTABLISH PATERNITY

_____, Plaintiff   V.   _____, Defendant

1. Plaintiff, who resides at

_____   _____   _____
(Street Address)   (City/Town)   (County)

_____   _____ , is
(State)   (Zip)

☐ the ○ mother ○ father of a child born out of wedlock.

☐ a child born out of wedlock.

☐ the ○ guardian ○ custodian of a child born out of wedlock.

☐ the ○ parent ○ personal representative of the ○ mother ○ father of a child born out of wedlock.

☐ the ○ Department of Social Services ○ agency licensed under G.L. c. 28A.

☐ the Department of Revenue.

2. The child who is the subject of this complaint is:

Name _____   Date of Birth _____

_____   _____   _____ _____
(Street address)   (City/Town)   (State)   (Zip)

3. Defendant, who resides at

_____   _____   _____
(Street Address)   (City/Town)   (County)

_____ _____ , is the ○ mother ○ father of the above-named child who was born out of wedlock.
(State)   (Zip)

4. The plaintiff and defendant are not married.

5. The mother of the child was not married at the time of the child's birth and was not married within three hundred days before the birth of the child.

6. Wherefore, the plaintiff requests that the Court:

☐ adjudicate the ○ plaintiff ○ defendant to be the father of the child.

☐ order a suitable amount of support for the child.

☐ order the ○ plaintiff ○ defendant to ○ maintain ○ provide health insurance for the benefit of the child.

☐ prohibit the defendant from imposing any restraint on the personal liberty of the ○ plaintiff and/or ○ the child.

☐ grant the ○ plaintiff ○ defendant custody of the child.

☐ grant the ○ plaintiff ○ defendant visitation rights with the child.

Date _____

_____
(Signature of attorney or plaintiff, if pro se)

_____
(Print name)

_____
(Street address)

_____ _____ _____
(City/Town)   (State)   (Zip)

Tel. No. _____

B.B.O. # _____

CJ-D 106 (4/07)   C.G.F

PARALEGAL PRACTICE TIP

In Massachusetts, the appropriate form is called a Complaint for Paternity and it is available online. It may be called other things in other states such as a Petition to Establish Parental Relationship (California) or a Filiation Petition (Oregon).

PARALEGAL PRACTICE TIP

The docket number is assigned by the clerk's office when the Complaint is filed.

PARALEGAL PRACTICE TIP

If disclosing the plaintiff/petitioner's address on the Complaint will place him or her at risk, a request can be made to have it impounded. You can see an example of a "Motion for Confidential Address" at *www. courts.delaware.gov*. You can find a link to this site at *www.pearsonhigh-ered.com/wilson* in the companion website material for Chapter 7 under "Forms."

EXHIBIT 7.4 Motion for Genetic Marker Testing

PARALEGAL PRACTICE TIP

If the state's child support enforcement agency is involved in the case, it may arrange for the testing. The agency can also order testing administratively if no other man is presumed to be the child's father and the mother or the alleged father submits an affidavit that the parties had sexual relations during the probable period of conception. Although the agency can order the testing without court involvement, the court must issue the actual judgment of paternity if the tests are conclusive and uncontested.

PARALEGAL PRACTICE TIP

The parties also may voluntarily submit to testing. The test itself is painless and noninvasive and involves a simple "buccal swab" to obtain a saliva sample from inside the mouth.

PARALEGAL PRACTICE TIP

If a defendant father fails to comply with an order for testing, the court can draw an adverse inference, hold him in contempt, and issue a paternity order.

PARALEGAL PRACTICE TIP

If a party objects to the results of the genetic marker test, the objection usually must be made in writing within a specified period, commonly thirty days.

Equitable parent doctrine
a doctrine used to extend parenthood to an individual who is willing and able to assume parental rights and responsibilities and/or who has done so in the past

---

Commonwealth of Massachusetts
The Trial Court
Probate and Family Court Department

Essex County   Docket No. XXXXXXX
Susan Westcott,
Plaintiff   Motion for
v   Genetic Marker Testing
Peter Cann,
Defendant

NOW comes Susan Westcott, the plaintiff in this action who moves this honorable court as follows:

1. To order the plaintiff, defendant, and minor child to submit to genetic marker testing, with results expressed as a probability of paternity.
2. To order that the testing of the parties and the minor child be performed within thirty (30) days at a designated laboratory certified to perform such testing.

Respectfully submitted,
Susan Westcott
By her attorney

_____

Juliana Wilson, Esq
390 Main Street
Newburyport, MA 01950
978-465-1500
BBO# 55342

This Motion will be heard in the Essex County Probate and Family Court by the presiding justice sitting in Newburyport, Massachusetts on September 15, 2011, at 8:00 am.

CERTIFICATE OF SERVICE
I certify that I have served a copy of this Motion, the accompanying Affidavit in Support of the Motion, and the Notice of Hearing upon Peter Cann, 22 Surfer Lane, Newburyport, MA 01950, by first-class mail postage prepaid on September 2, 2011.

_____

Juliana Wilson, Esq.

When making parentage determinations the courts sometimes base their decisions on nonbiological grounds rather than on the results of genetic tests. In addition to the marital presumption, they may apply a variety of legal theories to justify decisions finding that a person is, for example, a *de facto* parent, a psychological parent, a co-parent, or a parent based on equitable estoppel. Such theories are used when the courts recognize the rights of individuals who have functioned as parents to maintain their relationships with the children they have helped to raise. For example, in Case 7.1, the Wisconsin Supreme Court applied the **equitable parent doctrine** against a biological father in favor of a nonbiological father in a custody case.

EXHIBIT 7.5 Affidavit in Support of Motion for Genetic Marker Testing

---

Commonwealth of Massachusetts
The Trial Court
Probate and Family Court Department

Essex County   Docket No. XXXXXXX

Susan Westcott,
Plaintiff   Affidavit in Support of Motion for
v   Genetic Marker Testing
Peter Cann,
Defendant

I, Susan Westcott, the Plaintiff in the above captioned matter do hereby swear that:

1. I am the biological mother of the minor child, Christopher Westcott, born on May 28, 2010, in Newburyport, Massachusetts.
2. I know the defendant, Peter Cann, and I had sexual intercourse with him during the probable period of conception of Christopher Westcott.
3. I had sexual intercourse with the defendant, Peter Cann, every weekend between June 21, 2009, and September 30, 2009, while we were registered at the Merromar Inn in Newburyport, MA.
4. After I became pregnant, Peter Cann wrote me a letter saying he wanted me to have an abortion and that he would pay for it.
5. Peter Cann has acknowledged to members of his family that he is Christopher's father.

Signed under pain and penalties of perjury.

_____
                                                        Susan Westcott

Date: September 1, 2011

PARALEGAL PRACTICE TIP

To see an example of a court order for paternity testing, visit *www.judicial.state.sc.us/forms*. (South Carolina) You can find a link to this site at *www.pearsonhighered.com/wilson* in the companion website material for Chapter 7 under "Forms."

Parenthood by estoppel essentially provides that a man may be designated the legal father of a child if he has held himself out as the child's father and has supported the child emotionally and financially. It is assumed that both the child and the mother have come to rely on that support and that it would be inequitable to deprive them of its continuation. A paralegal may be called on to gather information to support a claim that a father has held a child out as his own. Some of the kinds of conduct to be considered include the following:

> A man is deemed to have held out a child as his biological offspring when he engages in parental conduct such as: changing the child's diapers; feeding him; taking him to the doctor; bathing him; taking the child on visits away from the mother's home; allowing the child to call him daddy; giving the child gifts or cards; attending parent-teacher conferences or school events; giving the child his surname; voluntarily providing financial support for the child; and providing or building a loving relationship with the child. He can also put the child on his insurance, claim governmental benefits for the child under his name, or claim to be the child's father to the public at large, such as the child's school, daycare or even to friends, relatives and neighbors.[18]

CASE 7.1 *A.J. v. I.J.*, 2002 WI App 307, 259 Wis. 2d 120, 655 N.W.2d 195 (2002)

PARALEGAL PRACTICE TIP

The opinion in *A.J. v. I.J.* is available at *www.pearsonhighered.com/wilson* in the companion website material for Chapter 7 under "Cases" and in the Case Resources Section of the MyLegalStudiesLab.

BACKGROUND

In this case, a mother, Norma, gave birth to a child in January 1998 while she was married to her husband, Randy. Randy did not learn until he filed for divorce in October 1999 that the child's biological father was actually the mother's boyfriend, Brendan. The child knew only Randy as her father, although the mother did take her to Brendan's for weekly visits prior to her being sentenced to eight years in prison in May 1999. After the mother's incarceration, the child lived with Randy. In December 1999, Norma filed a counterclaim in the divorce action and alleged Brendan was the child's father. Brendan filed a motion to intervene and sought to be adjudicated the child's natural father and requested legal custody and primary physical placement of the child. The trial court denied the motion to intervene and declared Randy the child's equitable parent and awarded him custody. Norma and Brendan appealed.

FROM THE OPINION

This divorce case presents an unusual factual scenario. Randy A.J. is willing to continue supporting and providing care for a child that is not biologically his own. He seeks to maintain the parent-child relationship he established with a child born during his marriage to the natural mother, Norma I.J., despite the fact that genetic tests have established to a 99.99% degree of certainty that Brendan B. is the child's father. Norma and Brendan argue that because the genetic tests showed that Brendan is the biological father of the child, the trial court had no authority to determine that establishing Randy as the legal father and awarding him custody were in the best interests of the child. We conclude that Randy is the equitable parent of the minor child and affirm the trial court's decision that otherwise awarded Randy custody of the child.

. . .

On appeal, Brendan and Norma assert that once the parties submitted to genetic testing and the tests showed Brendan to be the biological father, the trial court erred in concluding that Wis. Stat. §§ 767.463 and 767.458 (1m) granted it the authority to conduct a best interests of the child hearing and dismiss the paternity action. Brendan and Norma further contend that once the genetic tests demonstrated that Brendan was the biological father . . . , he overcame the marital presumption.

. . .

The statute explicitly permits the court to dismiss an action to establish the paternity of a child based upon the best interests of the child only if genetic tests have not yet been taken.

. . .

The trial court next concluded that despite the fact that the genetic tests had established Brendan's parentage to a 99.99% degree of certainty, Brendan had not rebutted the marital presumption. . . . The presumption is rebutted by the results of a genetic test establishing by a statistical probability of 99.0% or higher the parentage of a man other than the man presumed to be the father under subsec. (1). Sec. 891.41(2).

. . .

(Continued)

While the trial court may have used the incorrect vehicle in the law, the court clearly felt compelled by the evidence to declare that Randy, not Brendan, should be the child's father. The trial court made unmistakable, but implicit, findings that Brendan should not be entitled to whatever foothold he had gained by reason of the genetic tests. . . . the trial court was wrong on the law, but its factual findings supported the correct result, had the proper standard been applied.

. . .

We first reiterate what we have already written—that the marital father is presumed to be the natural father unless rebutted. A genetic test showing another man to be the natural father rebuts that presumption. But that does not end the matter. Under Wis. Stat. § 767.48(1m), the natural father then only gains a *rebuttable presumption* that he is the child's parent. Thus, it is evident from the law that even if a test shows a man to be the natural father, his legal fatherhood is only presumed. Next, we must consider "how" such a presumption may be overcome. In our view, the presumption may be overcome by evidence that the marital father has so bonded with the child as to be considered the "equitable parent." . . .

Wisconsin has recognized the equitable parent doctrine. See *J.J. v. R.J.,* 162 Wis. 2d 420, 429–30, 469 N.W.2d 877 (Ct. App. 1991). The equitable parent doctrine extends the rights and responsibilities of a natural parent to a nonbiological parent seeking custody or visitation. . . . Once a court determines that a party is an equitable parent, there is no distinction between the equitable parent and any other parent; each is endowed with the same rights and responsibilities of parenthood. . . . We have permitted a mother in a divorce action to estop a nonbiological father from denying paternity in order to avoid child support obligations. . . . We have also held that for the purposes of establishing a right to a relationship with the child born to his wife but fathered by another man, the husband may utilize the status of "equitable parent" to assert an equitable estoppel defense against the child's mother instituting paternity proceedings against him. . . . Here we face the unusual situation where the mother is in prison, the child does not recognize the biological father as being her parent, and the nonbiological father not only wants to continue the parent-child relationship, but also wishes to support the child emotionally and financially by maintaining custody of the child.

The Michigan Court of Appeals faced a somewhat similar situation in *Atkinson.* . . .

. . . [T]he court concluded that the husband was entitled to be treated as a natural father under the equitable parent doctrine. . . . Thus, the custody dispute between the husband and the wife would be settled as if it were between two natural parents, based upon the child's best interests. . . .

While we acknowledge that the equitable parent doctrine has not been invoked in Wisconsin against a natural parent for the purpose of awarding custody to a nonparent, we have invoked the doctrine set forth in *Atkinson* against a natural parent for the purpose of awarding visitation to a nonparent in a situation that bears some factual similarity to this case. . . .

. . . In this case, the trial court held several days of hearings concerning the best interests of the child in which all parties participated. . . . we acknowledge that in exercising its equitable powers, the trial court did not expressly use the equitable parent doctrine to declare Randy the legal father and otherwise award him custody. However, . . . the trial court made substantial and careful findings of fact regarding

(Continued)

the relationship each party had established with the child and the conduct of the parties concerning the child's paternity and we use these findings in our analysis of the equitable parent doctrine as applied to this case. Whether the facts as found permit the application of equitable estoppel is a question of law that we review independently of the trial court's determination. . . .

During the pregnancy and up until Norma's incarceration, Randy, Norma and the child lived together. After Norma's incarceration, Randy became the sole custodian of the minor child and has continued to assume responsibility for her. The child considers Randy to be her only father and, up until the divorce proceedings, Randy believed her to be his biological daughter. The trial court found that "there clearly is a-what would otherwise be viewed as a normal parent-child relationship and bond between [Randy] and [the child], and, in fact, he has been her only parent from the standpoint of regular and daily contact and custodial care since May of 1999." . . .

Prior to the divorce proceeding, and with Norma's cooperation, Randy believed he held the status of a natural parent and assumed the rights and responsibilities of fatherhood. Norma and Brendan never took any steps to change Randy's belief despite the fact that they had suspected Brendan was the father of the child. The trial court found that it was in both Norma's and Brendan's best interests not to take any action concerning the child's paternity. Norma was involved in significant criminal legal difficulties at the time and needed Randy's financial backing. During legal proceedings, Randy supported Norma and funded the costs of her legal representation, using all of the family's cash and equity in their home. It was not until Norma was incarcerated and Randy filed for divorce that Norma raised the paternity issue.

The trial court also found that Brendan had the opportunity and ability to assume parental responsibility for the child and chose not to do so. The court determined that while Brendan saw the child on a weekly basis prior to Norma's incarceration, the relationship established between the two was not that of father and daughter. The relationship arose simply upon the event of Norma's relationship with Brendan. The trial court further determined that Brendan, having to purchase such things as diapers, formula, and some clothing for the child during her extended weekend stays prior to Norma's incarceration, in no way constituted support of the child either emotionally or financially. Finally the court noted that Brendan did not raise the issue of his paternity in this state until the child was well over three years old. . . .

The trial court also relied upon the testimony and recommendations of the psychologist. . . . She recommended that Randy remain the father of the child. . . . Finally, the court also gave due consideration to the substance abuse problems of the parties.

We have . . . determined that Brendan may not assert his parentage based on the facts as found by the trial court and the applicable law. . . . We affirm the trial court's determination that it was in the child's best interests that the court estop Norma from asserting the child's parentage. We hold that Randy is the legal father and affirm the trial court in that regard. We also hold that Randy is entitled to custody and affirm the trial court's determination on that issue.

SIDEBAR

How would you define the equitable parent doctrine? Do you agree with the court that it properly applied to the facts of this case? Explain your response.

Paralegal Application 7.3

Know Your Paternity Basics

Given the considerable variation among the states with respect to paternity actions and the rules that govern them, paralegals need to know the answers to the following questions when working on paternity cases:

- What are the various ways in which parentage can be established in your state? Acknowledgments? Paternity actions? Legitimation actions?
- Which court(s) have subject matter jurisdiction over paternity proceedings?
- How can a court establish personal jurisdiction over resident and nonresident defendants?
- Which statutes of limitations govern the bringing of various kinds of paternity actions (domestic relations, probate, tort, etc.)?

- Are there mandatory forms to be used when filing paternity actions?
- Who has standing to bring a paternity action: mother, husband, putative father, child, IV-D agency, third parties (such as co-parents, grandparents, and personal representatives)?
- What is the standard of proof in paternity actions? Preponderance of the evidence? Clear and convincing evidence?
- When and how can genetic testing be used?
- Is the marital presumption recognized and, if so, when and how can it be rebutted?
- Does the state recognize the equitable parent doctrine? (See Case 7.1.)

How Is Paternity Disestablished?

A natural consequence of the availability of DNA testing is that some putative fathers learn with scientific certainty that they are not the biological fathers of children they have been raising and supporting in good faith as their own. In many instances, they have mistakenly formally acknowledged paternity or been adjudicated fathers by the court. Although paternity judgments are binding and not easily challenged, an increasing number of states have determined by statute or case law that, in the interest of fairness, a father faced with such circumstances should be permitted to seek an order vacating an earlier paternity judgment, in effect disestablishing an existing father-child relationship.

Disestablishment of paternity a court order vacating an earlier paternity judgment or acknowledgment based on evidence the man is not the child's father, in effect disestablishing a previously existing father-child relationship

PARALEGAL PRACTICE TIP

The state has a statutory right to, in effect, **"disestablish"** parentage in some contexts. For example, the state may terminate a parent's rights if it proves parental unfitness by clear and convincing evidence. However, parental rights may not be terminated merely to advance the parents' convenience and interests, either emotional or financial.

Several states, such as Alaska,[19] Georgia,[20] Maryland,[21] and Ohio,[22] have established statutory procedures by which an otherwise legally recognized father can disestablish paternity. Based on the potentially devastating effect of disestablishment on the child, legislatures and courts in some other states have taken a more cautious approach and have expressly not permitted petitions to disestablish paternity. The child, rather than the nonbiological father, is viewed as the victim. Courts in still other states weigh the relative benefits of knowledge of the truth against disruption in the child's life. Factors these courts consider include:

- the nature and stability of the present home environment
- whether or not there is an existing relationship with a nonbiological father figure

PARALEGAL PRACTICE TIP

A copy of the Alaska Paternity Set-Aside statute can be found at *www. pearsonhighered.com/wilson* in the companion website material for Chapter 7 under "Statutes."

- the desire and willingness of the biological father to assume parenting responsibilities
- whether the child already has established a bond with the biological parent
- the motive of the party bringing the paternity or disestablishment action
- the age of the child
- whether or not the child is uncertain of his or her parentage
- the child's physical and emotional needs
- whether or not there exists a compelling medical need to establish the father's identity

PARALEGAL PRACTICE TIP

Visit *www.Clasp.org* (the Center for Law and Social Policy) to find state-by-state references to disestablishment cases. You can find a link to this site at *www.pearsonhighered. com/wilson* in the companion website material for Chapter 7 under "Resources."

The law with respect to disestablishment actions continues to evolve. When they are permitted, there is considerable variation state to state in terms of when they may be brought and by whom, whether genetic testing must be conducted prior to or as part of the petition to set aside paternity, and whether or not restitution of past child support payments will be granted.[23]

Paralegal Application 7.4

To Disestablish or Not to Disestablish—That Is the Question

In your opinion, which of the following three approaches to disestablishment should legislatures and courts adopt and why? Should they:

1. act in the interests of the nonbiological father seeking to be relieved of parental responsibility for a child he did not procreate by allowing disestablishment without consideration of the best interests of the child?

   Under Maryland law, for example, in proceedings to modify or set aside paternity declarations, a "determination of the best interests of the child in ordering . . . testing, or in the consideration of paternity, whether original or revised, is inappropriate."[24] "Simply stated, the fact of who the father of a child is cannot be changed by what might be the best interests of the child."[25] Finality of paternity determinations is outweighed by fairness to a man who is not a child's biological father. The "law will not compel one who has stood in the place of a parent to support the child after the relationship has ceased."[26]

2. act in the best interests of the child by maintaining an existing parent-child relationship and not allowing disestablishment?

   The Vermont Supreme Court has described this position as follows:

   . . . [T]he financial and emotional welfare of the child, and the preservation of an established parent-child relationship, must remain paramount. Where the presumptive father has held himself out as the child's parent, and engaged in an ongoing parent-child relationship for a period of years, he may not disavow that relationship and destroy a child's long-held assumptions, solely for his own self-interest. . . . Whatever the interests of the presumed father in ascertaining the genetic "truth" of a child's origins, they remain subsidiary to the interests of the state, the family, and the child in maintaining the continuity, financial support, and psychological security of an established parent-child relationship.[27]

3. act in the best interests of the child by allowing disestablishment on the ground that the child should have the opportunity to know his or her biological father?

   . . . [C]hildren have a profound right to know their father. They have an interest in their father's care and companionship. . . . In certain cases, it will be in the child's best interest to know the father's identity. Moreover, it is in the child's best interest to have the opportunity to establish a relationship with him.[28]

PATERNITY FRAUD

In some cases, a misunderstanding with respect to biological parenthood may be innocent. A mother truly may not know the identity of the father, or a man may choose to perpetuate a falsehood about the identity of a child's biological father out of love for his spouse and/or a child. However, in other cases, for a variety of reasons, the mother may have deliberately withheld information and/or fraudulently misled both the child and a man believing himself to be the child's father.

- She may not want contact with the biological father because of the circumstances of conception (e.g., rape).
- There may be a history of abuse by the father and she fears for her safety and/or the safety of the child.
- If she is married, she may not want to jeopardize marital harmony or financial security by revealing that the child is the product of an adulterous affair.
- She may want to place the child for adoption and fears that if the father has notice, he will delay or block the adoption.
- In an effort to receive needed public assistance, she may have responded to pressure to designate someone by naming a man she knows is not the child's father.

Although **paternity fraud** is old news, paternity fraud actions are a relatively new phenomenon made possible by advances in genetic testing. "In 1999 alone, almost one-third of 280,000 paternity cases evaluated by the American Association of Blood Banks excluded the individual tested as the biological father of the child. In a period of only one year, that is almost 100,000 men who were falsely accused of being the father of a child which, they simply did not father."[29] Paternity fraud actions may involve husbands, ex-husbands, or unmarried fathers, but they all essentially have one thing in common: a man has discovered that he has no genetic relationship to a child he formerly believed was his offspring and he no longer wants to be legally obligated for support. Much like wrongly convicted felons, some fathers greet DNA testing as a route to freedom. The U.S. Citizens Against Paternity Fraud website goes so far as to display the motto, "If the genes don't fit, you must acquit."[30] But is the cure worse than the disease? "Unlike Pinocchio, a fairy tale ending is neither guaranteed nor likely. . . . Marriages, relationships, and families end. Children are abandoned by the only fathers they ever knew. Fathers are bitter and fight to disown the nonbiological child. Children lose their sense of identity. And the damage cannot be undone."[31] (See Case 7.2.)

Paternity fraud
fraud in which a mother has intentionally misled a man into believing he is the father of a child to whom he is genetically unrelated

CASE 7.2 *Doran v. Doran,* 2003 PA Super 129, 820 A.2d 1279 (2003)

BACKGROUND INFORMATION

In this case, the Appellant, Pamela Doran (a.k.a. Smigiel), appealed an order of a Court of Common Pleas granting her former husband's petition for dismissal of a child support order dated August 24, 1994, but denying his request for restitution of previously paid support. At the time of the Petition to Dismiss, the child was almost eleven and a half years old. He was born during the parties' marriage and was about five years old at the time of the parties' divorce in 1995. The husband, William, had raised and supported the child as his own, and the wife, when asked, had assured him that the child, Billy, was his. Without his knowledge, however, Pamela had been

(Continued)

PARALEGAL PRACTICE TIP

The opinion in the *Doran* case is available at *www.pearsonhighered.com/wilson* in the companion website material related to Chapter 7 under "Cases" and in the Case Resources Section of the MyLegalStudiesLab.

sexually involved with another man at the time of conception and for a decade thereafter. In early 2001, Billy's appearance and mannerisms caused William to question that he was the child's biological father. He asked his wife to agree to DNA testing, the results of which indicated a 0% probability of paternity. Despite his request that they talk with the boy together, the mother chose to tell him the truth herself. William then "gently" removed himself from the child's life, hoping to cause him as little hurt as possible under the circumstances. He also then sought relief from the court based on his former wife's infidelity and deception, which had caused him to believe he was Billy's biological father. His Petition was granted in June 2002. In July, Pamela raised the following issues on appeal:

1. Was it reversible error for the lower court to grant the petition to dismiss child support, given that the parties were married and living together at the time of the child's birth and continued to do so for almost four years thereafter?

2. Was it reversible error to grant the petition to dismiss, given that William had maintained suspicions as to the child's paternity and yet continued to hold the child out to the public as his son even after he knew for certain that he was not the child's father?

3. Was it reversible error to grant the petition to dismiss where the decision to do so was contrary to established precedent with respect to the doctrines of "presumption of paternity" and "estoppel" for purposes of paternity and support matters?

FROM THE OPINION

Discussion

Smigiel essentially argues that the trial court should not have granted Doran's petition to dismiss child support since the presumption of paternity applies to the instant case. However, she further argues, if the presumption does not apply to the instant case, estoppel does.

"In matters involving support, a reviewing court will not disturb an order of the trial court unless there has been an abuse of discretion." *Diehl v. Beaver,* 444 Super. 91, 663 A.2d 232, 233 (Pa. Super. 1995) (citations omitted). . . .

In *Brinkley v. King,* 549 Pa. 241, 701 A.2d 176, 180 (Pa. 1997), the Pennsylvania Supreme Court set forth the analysis required to determine the paternity of a child conceived or born during a marriage:

> The essential legal analysis in these cases is twofold: first one considers whether the presumption of paternity applies to a particular case. If it does, one then considers whether the presumption has been rebutted. Second, if the presumption has been rebutted or is inapplicable, one then questions whether estoppel applies. Estoppel may bar either a plaintiff from making the claim or a defendant from denying paternity. If the presumption has been rebutted or does not apply, and if the facts of the case include estoppel evidence, such evidence must be considered.

We must first determine if the presumption of paternity applies to the instant case. "The policy underlying the presumption of paternity is the preservation of marriages." *Fish v. Behers,* 559 Pa. 523, 741 A.2d 721, 723 (Pa. 1999). "The presumption only applies in cases where that policy would be advanced by the application; otherwise, it does not apply." *Id.* (citation omitted). In this case, there is no longer an intact family or a marriage to preserve. Smigiel and Doran separated and a divorce action was pending prior to the hearing in the support matter instituted by Smigiel against Doran. Accordingly, the presumption of paternity is not applicable.

(Continued)

Having concluded that the presumption is inapplicable, we must determine whether Doran is estopped from denying paternity. "A (former) husband may be estopped from denying paternity of a child born during a marriage if either he or his wife holds the child out to be the child of the marriage." *Weidman v. Weidman*, 2002 PA Super 308, 808 A.2d 576, 577–78 (Pa. Super. 2002) (citation omitted).

Estoppel in paternity actions is merely the legal determination that because of a person's conduct (e.g., holding out the child as his own, or supporting the child) that person, regardless of his true biological status, will not be permitted to deny parentage, nor will the child's mother who has participated in this conduct be permitted to sue a third party for support, claiming that the third party is the true father. As the Superior Court has observed, the doctrine of estoppel in paternity actions is aimed at "achieving fairness as between the parents by holding them, both mother and father, to their prior conduct regarding the paternity of the child."

Fish, 741 A.2d at 723 (citation omitted).

In the instant case, Doran admitted that he held the child out as his own from the child's birth in 1990 until DNA testing excluded him as the father . . . he exercised visitation with the child and continued to support the child. Doran also stated that he continued to see the child after the DNA testing excluded him as the father. Therefore, it appears that Doran is estopped from denying his paternity.

Nevertheless, Doran argues that Smigiel's fraudulent conduct was the basis for his treating the child as his own; therefore, estoppel is precluded. Specifically, Doran argues that Smigiel assured him that he was the natural father and deceived him by failing to inform him of the truth of her unfaithfulness when he first had doubts about his paternity.

"When allegations of fraud arise in a paternity action, an estoppel analysis must proceed in a different manner than it would without such averments." *McConnell v. Berkheimer*, 2001 PA Super 224, 781 A.2d 206, 211 (Pa. Super. 2001) (citation omitted). Evidence of fraud "must be considered by the trial court in whether to apply paternity by estoppel." *Sekol v. Delsantro*, 763 A.2d 405, 410, 2000 PA Super 351 (Pa. Super. 2000) (citation omitted).

The presumption that a child born during a marriage is a child of the marriage and the doctrine of paternity by estoppel grew out of concern for the protection of the family unit; where that unit no longer exists, it defies both logic and fairness to apply equitable principles to perpetuate a pretense. In this case, application of estoppel would punish the party that sought to do what was righteous and reward the party that has perpetrated a fraud.

Id. . . . "The test for fraud is: (1) a misrepresentation, (2) a fraudulent utterance, (3) an intention by the maker that the recipient will thereby [be] induced to act, (4) justifiable reliance by the recipient upon the misrepresentation, and (5) damage to the recipient as a proximate result." *Sekol*, 763 A.2d 405 at 411 n. 7 (citation omitted).

In its decision, the trial court found that:

. . . Mr. Doran had been operating for more than a decade under the misrepresentation that he was, indeed, the child's father. This subterfuge was a direct result of the mother's intentional misstatements and deceptions to him. She deluded herself by refusing to even consider that her child might be fathered by the man with whom she had an illicit affair. She never once mentioned her meretricious relationship with this third party to her husband. Instead, she fallaciously led him to believe, at the same time as she was seeking child support

(Continued)

from him, that he was, in fact, the child's father. Had she been forthright to her spouse and explained what she had done at the time of the child's conception, her husband may certainly have acted differently. Unfortunately, her deceit, falsehoods and misrepresentations gave Mr. Doran no reason but to treat the child as his own—with love, care and respect, as only a decent human being would do under the circumstances.

Decision, 6/13/02, at 5–6.

. . .

Based on our limited standard and scope of review, we affirm. We hold that the trial court's factual findings are supported by competent evidence which is sufficient to sustain the trial court's order. Smigiel testified that she had sexual relations with Doran and another man at the time the child was conceived. When Doran became suspicious in 1996 that the child was not his, she assured him that it was even though she did not know for sure. It was not until 2001, when Doran questioned her again, that she finally admitted that she was not sure and agreed to the DNA testing. We, therefore, find that the trial court did not abuse its discretion in granting Doran's petition to dismiss the support order.

SIDEBAR

Do you agree with the holding in the case? Explain your response.

The focus of this chapter now shifts dramatically from the often painful collapse of family bonds through disestablishment to the joyful promise of assisted reproductive technology as a means of creating families once not possible. Each opens doors and presents challenges for an expanding legal horizon.

Assisted Reproductive Technology

In a family law text, a discussion of the contemporary concept of parenthood is incomplete without some consideration of the fascinating, and, for some, alarming, topic of **assisted reproductive technology (ART)**. One commentator has described the evolution of the use of this technology as follows:

> The technology of assisted reproduction, developed primarily to aid married couples with infertility, has been made available to people who are physically unable to engage in coitus, or who have an aversion to coitus. . . . It has been made available to people for whom gestation and childbirth pose unacceptable risks, and extended further toward the more controversial use of gestational mothers so that the genetic and/or intended mothers can avoid the inconvenience of going through a pregnancy. It has been made available to people who wish to avoid the risks of having children with genetically determined diseases, and extended further to sex selection and perceived enhancement of the genome of the intended child, in a word to eugenic practices. . . . ART has been utilized to enable procreation by dead people, by the use of gametes obtained with their knowledge and consent, and sometimes without, and sometimes obtained only after their death. It can potentially be used to enable procreation by fetuses who will never be born.[32]

Assisted reproductive technology (ART)
treatment or procedures designed to make parenthood possible for persons with fertility problems or individuals who are otherwise unable or personally unwilling to reproduce

Since the 1970s, hundreds of thousands of children have been conceived through ART rather than "naturally" through coitus. Most state legislatures have been reluctant to tackle this development. However, some have begun to do so, and family law practitioners addressing ART issues need to monitor developments and be aware of applicable governing laws and regulations. What does exist is limited, fragmented, and far from uniform. For example, Illinois has a comprehensive set of statutes regulating surrogacy;[33] New Hampshire has passed legislation regarding evaluation of gamete donors and use of gametes;[34] Massachusetts criminalizes experimentation on embryos before or after implantation;[35] Pennsylvania requires "all persons conducting or experimenting with *in vitro* fertilization" to file quarterly reports with the state;[36] Arkansas requires that facilities that provide *in vitro* fertilization services be certified and achieve a "reasonable success rate with both fertilization and births";[37] and several states, including Maryland,[38] have passed legislation addressing insurance coverage for persons undergoing assisted reproductive technology procedures.

Exhibit 7.6 provides definitions of some basic ART terms reflecting the breadth and complexity of this topic. We will briefly look at some of the legal issues related to a few of the ART methods listed in the Exhibit, including surrogacy, cryopreservation (freezing) of embryos and gametes, and posthumous reproduction. A concerted effort is made to reference cases and statutes from many states to illustrate the tremendous variation that exists in this rapidly evolving area. The remainder of the chapter will focus on the use of ART by same-sex couples, ethical and liability issues related to ART, and the role of the paralegal in cases involving parentage determinations.

EXHIBIT 7.6 Assisted Reproductive Technology—Basic Terminology

Artificial insemination/ intrauterine donor insemination	This procedure involves insertion of the sperm of a donor into a female's reproductive organs (fallopian tube) by a means other than sexual intercourse, with the intent to bring about a pregnancy.
Cloning	Cloning is the genetic replication of a living organism.
Cryopreservation	This process involves the freezing of gametes (eggs and sperm) or embryos to preserve them for use at a later date.
Cytoplasmic egg donation	In this procedure, genetic material is extracted from the eggs of a donor and injected into the eggs of another woman. In effect, the process technically results in the potential for a child to have two genetic mothers.
Donor	A donor is an individual who produces eggs or sperm for use in assisted conception. The donor may or may not receive compensation.
Embryo adoption	Embryo adoption is not technically an adoption. It occurs when one or more embryo donors give an embryo to a recipient with the intention that the recipient become pregnant. The recipient (and her spouse, if any) may subsequently adopt the resulting child post birth.
***In vitro* fertilization (IVF)**	An egg is fertilized by sperm outside the womb with the intention that the resulting zygote be transplanted into the reproductive system (uterus) of the genetic mother or a surrogate or that it be available for cryopreservation, donation, or research.

(Continued)

Cryopreservation
freezing and storage of genetic material for later use in procreation or research

PARALEGAL PRACTICE TIP
when donors participate in ART initiatives, it is important that they confirm in writing their intent with respect to the legal parentage of any children resulting from their donations.

Posthumous reproduction
reproduction that occurs after the
death of one or both of the gamete
donors

EXHIBIT 7.6 *(Continued)*

Posthumous reproduction	Posthumous reproduction occurs after the death of one or both of the gamete contributors.
Preimplantation genetic diagnosis (PGD)	This technique involves the biopsy of a single cell or embryo prior to implantation, usually to determine sex, detect genetic disorders, or custom-create or select embryos with desirable traits.
Surrogacy Agreement/ Contract	In a surrogacy agreement, a woman agrees to conceive a child through natural or artificial insemination or to implantation of an embryo and to relinquish her parental rights to the resulting child.
Surrogate	A surrogate is a woman who agrees to serve as the birth mother of a child for another individual or couple. She may or may not receive compensation.
Traditional surrogate	A traditional surrogate is artificially inseminated with the sperm of a man other than her husband. She is genetically related to the resulting child, whom she agrees to surrender post birth to the intended parents. Customarily she agrees to relinquish all of her parental rights.
Gestational surrogate	A gestational surrogate agrees to serve as the birth mother of a child to whom she is genetically unrelated. The genetic parents may be the intended parents, gamete donors, or a combination of the two.

Surrogacy

PARALEGAL PRACTICE TIP

A copy of Florida's statute governing
gestational surrogacy contracts can
be accessed at *www.pearsonhigh-
ered.com/wilson* in the companion
website material for Chapter 7
under "Statutes."

Surrogacy law in the United States is at best unsettled. Many states have no controlling statutory or case law. On one end of the spectrum of those that do is the state
of Michigan, which presently bans surrogacy contracts,[39] compensated or not, and
sentences anyone convicted of inducing, arranging, procuring, or otherwise assisting in the formation of a surrogacy contract with up to five years in prison and a
fine of up to $50,000.[40] At the other end of the spectrum are states such as Florida,
which permits unpaid surrogacy agreements in which at least one intended parent
is genetically related to the child and the parties follow several statutory requirements. Other states have enacted legislation specifically pertaining to surrogacy
that varies greatly in content. For example:

- Illinois provides considerable protection for parties to surrogacy agreements
  and permits prebirth establishment of the legal parentage of children of assisted conception, effective immediately upon birth.[41]
- In New Hampshire, parties to a surrogacy agreement must have their agreement judicially approved prior to impregnation.[42]
- Under Utah law, the intended mother cannot be receiving Medicaid or other
  state assistance, and she must be married to the intended father.[43]
- Although generally a surrogacy-friendly state, Virginia prohibits surrogacy
  "brokers."[44]
- The state of Washington does not permit compensated surrogacy contracts
  and will not give full faith and credit to a compensated surrogacy agreement
  executed in another state.[45]

- Nevada and several other states permit compensation of a surrogate, provided the payment is limited to necessary medical and living expenses. (See Exhibit 7.7.)[46]
- Kentucky prohibits compensation to attorneys for negotiating and drafting agreements regarding payment of surrogates.[47]

Although **forum shopping** is generally discouraged and, in some instances, not permitted by the courts, parties from one state may be permitted to execute an agreement in a more surrogacy-friendly state, provided that state has at least some connection with the matter and the result is not contrary to a strong public policy. For example, in one case, the Massachusetts Supreme Judicial Court allowed a prebirth judgment of parentage when the intended parents resided in Connecticut, the surrogate and her husband lived in New York, and the baby was scheduled to be born in Massachusetts.[48] The governing law of the jurisdiction in which a surrogacy agreement is executed must be carefully reviewed to better ensure the likelihood that the terms of the agreement will be enforceable.

Forum shopping

seeking a court in a jurisdiction that will provide the most favorable ruling in a case

In states such as California that permit parties to obtain prebirth parentage orders, an effort should be made to do so.[49] Even though the parties may execute a surrogacy agreement that provides the surrogate will relinquish the child and her "parental rights" at birth and/or an agreement is not required by statute, it is generally advisable for the intended parents to formally adopt the child postbirth in a manner consistent with state law. The consequences of a failure to do so are evident in a Connecticut case[50] in which an intended mother who never formally adopted a child born to a surrogate was treated as a third party, rather than a parent, in a custody dispute in the context of a divorce action.

When disputes about parentage stemming from surrogacy agreements reach the courts, the parties may include the surrogate mother and her husband, gamete donors, and the intended parents, who may or may not be married and who may be of the same or different sexes. The courts customarily apply one of the following four tests to determine parentage, each of which may produce a significantly different result.

EXHIBIT 7.7 Nevada Statute NRS 126.045 Governing Surrogacy Contracts

1. Two persons whose marriage is valid under chapter 122 of NRS may enter into a contract with a surrogate for assisted conception. Any such contract must contain provisions which specify the respective rights of each party, including:
   a. Parentage of the child;
   b. Custody of the child in the event of a change in circumstances; and
   c. The respective responsibilities and liabilities of the contracting parties.
2. A person identified as an intended parent in a contract described in subsection 1 must be treated in law as a natural parent under all circumstances.
3. It is unlawful to pay money or anything of value to the surrogate except for the medical and necessary living expenses related to the birth of the child as specified in the contract.
4. As used in this section, unless the context otherwise requires:
   a. "Assisted conception" means a pregnancy resulting when an egg and sperm from the intended parents are placed in a surrogate through the intervention of medical technology.
   b. "Intended parents" means a man and woman, married to each other, who enter into an agreement providing that they will be the parents of a child born to a surrogate through assisted conception.
   c. "Surrogate" means an adult woman who enters into an agreement to bear a child conceived through assisted conception for the intended parents.

Intent test

the position taken in parentage determinations that the individual(s) who set the procreative process in motion with the intent of raising any resulting children should be deemed the legal parent(s) of those children

Genetic test

the position taken in parentage determinations that the individuals who contribute a child's genetic material should be considered his or her legal parents

Gestational test

the position taken in maternity determinations that the woman who carries and gives birth to a child should be deemed the child's legal mother

Best interests of the child test

the position that determinations of legal parentage should be based upon who is best able to fulfill the social and legal responsibilities of parenthood

- **An intent test** Under this test, the individual or individuals who want to become parents and put the birth process in motion will be considered the legal parents of the resulting child. "[B]ut for the acted-on intentions of the parties, the child would not exist."[51] The California Supreme Court was the first to adopt the intent test in *Johnson v. Calvert*, a case that involved a "contest" between an intended and a gestational mother in which the court held that "she who intended to bring about the birth of a child that she intended to raise as her own is the natural mother."[52] (See Case 7.3.)

- **A genetic test** Courts that apply a genetic test in parentage determinations give priority to genetic heritage, based on the premise that genes contribute to the greatest extent in shaping the child's nature and future life. A genetic parent will be deemed a legal parent under this test. In cases in which the surrogate mother is also the genetic mother, courts are especially reluctant to terminate her parental rights. In some states, absent an enforceable agreement to the contrary, the individuals who contribute the genetic material are considered the child's legal parents. This has opened the door to decisions in which the legal parents are held to be a traditional surrogate mother and a man married to a woman other than the surrogate.

- **A gestational test** This test places the greatest emphasis on the significance of the fact that the birth mother is responsible for the health and safety of the fetus for the nine months of pregnancy. Her lifestyle, habits, and physical and psychological condition potentially have a permanent effect on the child. This test is consistent with the traditional common law approach to the establishment of maternity.

- **A best interest of the child test** This is the standard traditionally applied in the family law context with respect to matters pertaining to the custody of children. It serves to ensure that in resolving disputes affecting minor children, protection of the child will be the primary consideration. The court looks to who is best able to fulfill the social and legal responsibilities of parenthood, including not only financial support but also physical and psychological nurturing of the child, intellectual and moral guidance, and stability and continuity of care.

CASE 7.3 *Johnson v. Calvert*, 5 Cal. 4th 84, 851 P.2d 776, 19 Cal. Rptr. 2d 494 (1993), Cert. Denied 510 U.S. 874, 114 S. Ct. 206, 126 L. Ed. 2d 163 (1993)

PARALEGAL PRACTICE TIP

The opinion in *Johnson v. Calvert* can be found at *www.pearsonhighered.com/wilson* in the companion website material for Chapter 7 under "Cases" and in the Case Resources Section of the MyLegalStudiesLab.

Mark and Crispina Calvert were a married couple who wanted to have a child. Although Crispina had been forced to undergo a hysterectomy, her ovaries remained capable of producing eggs, and the couple eventually considered surrogacy.

On January 15, 1990, they signed a contract with Anna Johnson providing that an embryo created by the sperm of Mark and the egg of Crispina would be implanted in Anna, and post birth, Mark and Crispina would have and raise the resulting child "as their child." Anna agreed to relinquish "all parental rights" to the child. In return, Mark and Crispina agreed to pay Anna $10,000 in a series of installments. They also agreed to pay for a $200,000 life insurance policy on Anna's life. The zygote was implanted on January 19, 1990. Less than a month later, an ultrasound test confirmed Anna was pregnant. Unfortunately, during the pregnancy relations deteriorated between the two sides. The Calverts learned that Anna had not disclosed that she had previously suffered several stillbirths

(Continued)

and miscarriages. Anna felt the Calverts did not do enough to obtain the required insurance policy on her behalf. She also felt abandoned during an onset of premature labor in June. In July 1990, she sent Mark and Crispina a letter demanding the balance of the payments due her or else she would refuse to give up the child. The following month, Mark and Crispina filed a lawsuit, seeking a declaration they were the legal parents of the unborn child. Anna filed her own action to be declared the mother of the child, and the two cases were consolidated. The child was born on September 19, 1990, and the parties agreed to a court order providing that the child would remain with the Calverts on a temporary basis and Anna would have visitation rights. After hearing, the trial court ruled that Mark and Crispina were the child's "genetic, biological and natural" father and mother, that Anna had no "parental" rights to the child, and that the surrogacy contract was legal and enforceable against Anna's claims. The court also terminated the order allowing visitation. Anna appealed from the trial court's judgment. The Court of Appeals affirmed and the California Supreme Court granted review.

In reaching its decision, the California high Court was guided by the Uniform Parentage Act adopted in that state in 1975. The Court held that although the Act recognizes both genetic consanguinity and giving birth as means of establishing a mother-and-child relationship, California law recognizes only one natural mother. When the two means do not coincide in one woman, the mother who intends to bring about a child she intends to raise as her own will be considered the natural mother. The Court described the importance of intent in this context as follows:

> Because two women have each presented acceptable proof of maternity, we do not believe this case can be decided without enquiring into the parties' intentions as manifested in the surrogacy agreement. Mark and Crispina are a couple who desired to have a child of their own genes but are physically unable to do so without the help of reproductive technology. They affirmatively intended the birth of the child and took the steps necessary to effect in vitro fertilization. But for their acted-on intention, the child would not exist. Anna agreed to facilitate the procreation of Mark's and Crispina's child. The parties' aim was to bring Mark's and Crispina's child into the world, not for Mark and Crispina to donate a zygote to Anna. Crispina from the outset intended to be the child's mother. Although the gestative function Anna performed was necessary to bring about the child's birth, it is safe to say that Anna would not have been given the opportunity to gestate or deliver the child had she, prior to implantation of the zygote, manifested her own intent to be the child's mother. No reason appears why Anna's later change of heart should vitiate the determination that Crispina is the child's natural mother.[53]

The Court rejected Anna's arguments that surrogacy contracts violated the law and public policy prohibiting the payment for consent to adoption of a child and prebirth waivers of parental rights. Countering Anna's argument that surrogacy contracts tend to exploit poor women, the Court observed that there was as yet no proof that surrogacy contracts exploit poor women to any greater degree than economic necessity exploits them by inducing them to accept lower-paid or otherwise undesirable employment. In response to her claim that the surrogacy contract violated her constitutionally protected right to the care and custody of her child, the Court noted that she was not determined to be the mother and hence the primary maternal right did not belong to her.

SIDEBAR

This opinion remains one of the best expressions of the "intent standard" applied in a case in which the gestational mother has no biological relationship to the child

(Continued)

born as a result of a surrogacy arrangement. But what if she is not only the gestational mother but also the genetic mother as well? (See, e.g., *In the Matter of Baby M.*, 109 N.J. 396, 537 A.2d 1227 (1988)). Should the result be different? Explain your response. What role, if any, should "the best interests of the child" play? For example, what should the court do if the intended parents are unstable or substance abusers or their circumstances change dramatically during the course of the pregnancy? The dissent in *Johnson v. Calvert* opined that the best-interests-of-the-child test, rather than an intent test, should be applied by the courts in surrogacy cases in the absence of legislation.

Application of various tests to individual fact patterns can lead to widely diverse and unusual results. For example, in the high-profile case *In the Matter of Baby M.*,[54] the New Jersey Supreme Court held that a surrogacy "contract" between a biological father and a genetically related surrogate mother was against public policy and unenforceable as a matter of law. The court created a new "family" configuration for the child by awarding physical custody to the intended/biological father and visitation to the surrogate mother, who was also the child's genetic mother. In describing its reasoning for not enforcing such agreements, the court commented:

> The long-term effects of surrogacy contracts are not known, but feared—the impact on the child who learns her life was bought, that she is the offspring of someone who gave birth to her only to obtain money; the impact on the natural mother as the full weight of her isolation is felt along with the full reality of the sale of her body and her child; the impact on the natural father and the adoptive mother once they realize the consequences of their conduct. . . . The surrogacy contract is based on principles that are directly contrary to the objectives of our laws. It guarantees the separation of a child from its mother; it looks to adoption regardless of suitability; it totally ignores the child; it takes the child from the mother regardless of her wishes and her maternal fitness; and it does all of this, it accomplishes all of its goals, through the use of money.[55]

PARALEGAL PRACTICE TIP

The opinion in the *Baby M* case is available at *www.pearsonhighered.com/wilson* in the companion website material related to Chapter 7 under "Cases" and in the Case Resources Section of the MyLegalStudiesLab.

Cryopreserved Embryos

As more and more couples utilize ART to create and freeze embryos for use at a later date, it is inevitable that the courts will increasingly be called upon to resolve controversies involving the parties' rights and responsibilities with respect to those embryos. It is estimated that there are already hundreds of thousands of unused embryos in cryopreservation.[56]

Two of the contexts in which the courts have begun to address this development are when frozen embryos need to be disposed of upon divorce, and when they are used posthumously (after the death of one or both of the parties).

DISPOSITION OF FROZEN EMBRYOS UPON DIVORCE

After three decades of experience applying this technology, it has become apparent that, in addition to planning for use of *in vitro* fertilization and freezing of surplus embryos, couples also must anticipate and provide for the disposition of those embryos in the event of separation, death, divorce, or changes in plans or circumstances. Options for disposition include storing them for use at a later date, donating them for "embryo adoption"[57] or research, preserving them for an indefinite period, or thawing and discarding them.

A limited number of states have enacted legislation addressing issues specifically relating to use, storage, and disposition of preserved embryos. New Hampshire and Louisiana, for example, have provisions addressing some aspects of maintenance and duration periods for storing prezygotes outside of the body.[58] Under Louisiana law, the embryos are considered legal persons,[59] and embryo donations are essentially regulated by adoption statutes. Florida requires by statute that couples and their treating physicians execute written agreements addressing disposition of preembryos in the event of death, divorce, or other unforeseen circumstances.[60] Oklahoma law refers to embryo donation as "human embryo transfer and donation." Only biological parents may donate embryos; both the donor and the donee couples must be married; and the donee couple, the physician, and a judge in a court with jurisdiction over adoption must execute a written consent form.[61]

In the absence of legislation, courts in some states have been forced to judicially address disposition upon divorce with and without written agreements between the parties. The courts generally select from among five approaches to such cases:

1. In the absence of an agreement, favor the party seeking to avoid forced parenthood.
2. Enforce agreements of the parties.
3. Enforce agreements, but allow the parties to change their minds and modify their agreements up until implantation or destruction of the embryos.
4. Enforce agreements, but not for nonreproductive use unless permitted by state law.
5. Refuse to enforce agreements based on state law, public policy, or other considerations.

Related case law reflects a fact-based approach and a general trend toward enforcing modifiable agreements, but not compelling unwanted parenthood. In the landmark *Davis* case,[62] the Tennessee Supreme Court considered disposition of seven frozen embryos belonging to an already divorced couple, each of whom had remarried. The wife sought to donate the embryos to another childless couple, but the husband wanted them destroyed. The Tennessee Supreme Court determined that the lower court had erroneously applied a best-interests-of-the-child test (appropriate for a custody determination) and ruled that "pre-embryos are not, strictly speaking, either 'persons' or 'property,' but occupy an interim category that entitles them to special respect because of their potential for human life."[63] In reaching its decision, the Court recognized that "the right to procreational

PARALEGAL PRACTICE TIP

Clients contemplating cryopreservation should be encouraged to anticipate the possibility of posthumously conceived children and prepare wills that spell out their intentions with respect to children born as a result of assisted reproductive technology.

autonomy is composed of two rights of equal significance—the right to procreate and the right to avoid procreation."[64] The wife's interest in donating the embryos was viewed as less significant than the husband's interest in avoiding parenthood. Although the parties in this case had not executed a written agreement, the court indicated in dictum that such agreements should be upheld in the event of separation or divorce, stating, "the state's interest in the potential life of these preembryos is not sufficient to justify any infringement upon the freedom of these individuals to make their own decisions as to whether to allow a process to continue that may result in such a dramatic change in their lives as becoming parents."[65]

In the *Kass* case,[66] New York's highest court emphasized the importance of agreements stating:

> . . . [P]arties should be encouraged in advance, before embarking on IVF and cryopreservation, to think through possible contingencies and carefully specify their wishes in writing. Explicit agreements avoid costly litigation. . . . Advance directives, subject to mutual change of mind that must be jointly expressed, both minimize misunderstandings and maximize procreative liberty by reserving to the progenitors the authority to make what is in the first instance a quintessentially personal, private decision. Written agreements also provide the certainty needed for effective operation of IVF programs.[67]

Paralegal Application 7.5

Assisted Reproduction Documents

As a general rule, when parties enter into assisted reproduction arrangements, they should execute written agreements and consent forms documenting their intentions and expectations. Contracts may be between several different sets of parties, such as the following:

- between donors and intended parents
- between intended parents and surrogate parents
- between the intended parents
- between various parties and the clinics or physicians who facilitate the pregnancy and delivery
- between parents and clinics harvesting and/or storing gametes and embryos

Agreements will vary depending primarily on the type of arrangement and the residence of the parties. Because the law of assisted reproductive technology is largely unsettled, these agreements should anticipate various potential scenarios.

In preparing documents,[68] attention must be given to complying with any controlling statutory requirements and prohibitions and to carefully choosing the law to govern the agreement. Some potentially important

provisions to consider including in a surrogacy agreement in particular are the following:

- a description of the arrangements, including a timeline within which the agreement must be performed before it expires
- a provision that the parties participate in psychological and medical screening (required in some states)
- a surrogate celibacy provision to remain in effect until the fertilization process is concluded
- an indemnification clause identifying the risks involved in the process and protecting the attorney and client from liability
- a clear statement with respect to insurance coverage for the surrogate and child
- a clause addressing any compensation to be paid to the surrogate, including the amount and purpose(s) for which it is being paid (time, pain, inconvenience, medical expenses, etc., and NOT for releasing parental rights)
- a provision indicating the circumstances under which the agreement may be terminated or modified,

(Continued)

including the surrogate mother's right to abort the pregnancy (and the inability of the intended parents to compel an abortion)

- language consistent with state law addressing the surrogate's (and her spouse's, if applicable) relinquishing of parental rights and release of the child to the intended parents post birth
- a provision requiring the intended parents to accept the child even if their circumstances change or the child is born with serious health issues, etc.
- if donors are involved, a clause indicating that donors have waived any and all parental rights
- a clause covering any agreement regarding confidentiality/disclosure of information

- a clause addressing the parties' agreement with respect to post-birth contact, if any
- a provision regarding disposition of any surplus gametes and/or embryos
- an affirmation that each party has been represented by independent counsel
- a provision regarding the respective parties' rights in the event of a breach, particularly since specific performance is not available as a remedy
- a provision addressing the timing and effect of "changes of mind"
- a severability clause so that if one clause in an agreement is deemed unenforceable, it can be severed from the remainder of the agreement

POSTHUMOUSLY CONCEIVED CHILDREN

Given advances in assisted reproductive technology, it is now possible for children to be conceived after the death of one or both of their genetic parents through the use of cryopreserved gametes or embryos. (See Paralegal Application 7.6.) Section 707 of the Uniform Parentage Act of 2000 as revised in 2002 acknowledges this option, providing that:

> If an individual who consented in a record to be a parent by assisted reproduction dies before placement of eggs, sperm, or embryos, the deceased individual is not a parent of the resulting child unless the deceased spouse consented in a record that if assisted reproduction were to occur after death, the deceased individual would be a parent of the child.[69]

Most disputes regarding posthumously conceived children arise in connection with probate matters and claims for Social Security Benefits. Several states identify the intestate inheritance rights of posthumously conceived children by statute. For example, the applicable Florida statute requires that the intended parents and treating physician must have signed a written agreement regarding disposition of cryopreserved eggs, sperm, and preembryos in the event of the death of one of the spouses. The decedent also must have provided for the child in his or her will.[70] In Louisiana, a posthumously conceived child has inheritance rights, provided the child is born to the surviving spouse within three years of the death of the decedent.[71]

Paralegal **Application 7.6**

Life After Death—What Do You Think?

Do you think that people who are terminally ill, going off to combat, or participating in other inherently dangerous activities should be permitted to freeze gametes for use postdeath? What are the arguments for each side of the question? Would it make a difference in your opinion if the eggs or sperm are harvested postdeath? Without prior consent of the decedent? For use by parties other than the donors?

Posthumously conceived children may be eligible for Social Security Survivor Benefits if the child is entitled to inherit under the intestacy law in the state where the decedent was domiciled at death.[72] Courts in New Jersey[73] and Massachusetts have addressed this issue. In the Massachusetts case, a man who was dying from leukemia had some of his sperm cryopreserved so that his wife could conceive after his death. She was subsequently successfully inseminated and gave birth to twins about two years after he died. On appeal, the Supreme Judicial Court reversed the Social Security Administration's decision denying the children survivors' benefits on the basis that they were not the husband's children under the Social Security Act. The court held that posthumously conceived children can inherit in Massachusetts (and be eligible to receive survivor benefits) under certain conditions:

- The child's paternity is established.
- The decedent consented to posthumous reproduction and to support the child.
- All parties interested in the estate are given notice.
- An unreasonable period of time has not elapsed since the decedent's death.[74]

Children Born to Same-Sex Couples Through ART

When ART is utilized by same-sex couples to produce children, another dimension is added to the complex array of issues raised in parentage determination cases. In the past, courts in states such as Florida, Illinois, Michigan, New York, Ohio, and Tennessee[75] determined that only the birth parent was a legal parent to a child born to a lesbian couple that had a child together through artificial insemination. In effect, the other partner was considered a legal stranger, even if she lived in a committed relationship with the parent and child for several years, participated fully in the decision to have a child, supported the reproductive process and birth, helped to raise the child, provided financial support, and was referred to by the child as "mom."[76] The consequences for a child can be severe when such relationships are not acknowledged. In the extreme, the child may be sent to live with relatives or become a ward of the state. Even if the legal parent nominates the second parent as the child's guardian in his or her will, there is no guarantee that the courts will approve the nomination, especially if challenged by blood relatives.

PARALEGAL PRACTICE TIP

If the parties do not comply with statutory requirements in a given state, a donor may later be able to claim parental rights, particularly when the donor is known to the intended parents. For example, in a California case, *Jhordan C. v. Mary K.*,[77] a lesbian couple chose a sperm donor from among several potential donors. Contrary to a requirement of a state statute of which the couple was unaware, the sperm was supplied directly to the couple and not to a physician, which would have allowed the donor not to be treated as the father of the resulting child. The parties also acted without legal advice and did not execute a contract regarding their arrangement. As a result, the donor was eventually able to have the rights of a legal father, entitling him to visitation.

Not all courts have been unreceptive to recognizing joint parental rights for same-sex partners, however. In Chapter 14, the topic of co-parent adoption is discussed as an option available in an increasing number of states. In Chapter 8, the coverage of child custody includes a review of several of the legal theories being used by some courts to attribute parental rights and responsibilities to same-sex co-parents. The trend toward recognizing parental rights and responsibilities in such circumstances also is consistent with Section 2.03 of the ALI Principles,[78] which provides that a person who is not an adoptive or biological parent may be deemed a parent by estoppel with all the rights and responsibilities of a legal parent if he or she:

> . . .lived with the child since the child's birth, holding out and accepting full and permanent responsibilities as a parent, as part of a prior coparenting agreement with the child's legal parent . . . to raise a child together each with full parental rights and responsibilities, when the court finds that recognition of the individual as a parent is in the child's best interests.

Ethical and Liability Fallout From Assisted Reproductive Technology

ETHICAL ISSUES

The science of assisted reproductive technology evokes strong reactions from the general public, religious leaders, legislators, and legal and medical professionals, among others. Despite the attention, little regulatory legislation exists at either the federal or state level.[79] Absent clear boundaries, the science of ART continues to evolve and to generate considerable ethical concerns that tend to fall into two primary areas:

1. **Considerations that concern laboratory standards, procedures, and accountability** address the underlying question, "Is this technical process being performed according to acceptable standards?" Some of the issues that arise include the following:
   - How will gametes be collected, tested, maintained, and disposed of?
   - Should ART facilities be licensed and monitored and, if so, how and by whom?
   - What kinds of agreements should users execute?
   - Who will perform the procedures and under what conditions?
   - How will "success" be measured and by whom?
2. **Considerations that concern the application of ART** address the broad question, "Should a particular application of ART be undertaken at all and, if so, under what constraints or conditions?" For example:
   - Should people be able to select an embryo for implantation based on its physical and personal characteristics and/or its freedom from genetically transmitted diseases?
   - Should a parent be able to conceive, carry, and bear a child after the other parent's death, with or without the deceased's consent?
   - Should commercial surrogacy be permitted?
   - Should parents be able to use ART to select a genetically suitable embryo (a "savior sibling") for the primary purpose of having it serve as a bone marrow donor for an already existing sibling afflicted with a potentially terminal disease?
   - Should human cloning be permitted?
   - Should everyone be permitted to utilize ART? (See Paralegal Application 7.7.)

LIABILITY ISSUES

The eventual range and forms of liability associated with the availability and use of assisted reproductive technology are unknown. Thus far, courts have addressed liability issues primarily through the application of traditional tort, negligence,

Paralegal **Application 7.7**

Should ART Be Available to Everyone?

Procreation is a fundamental right that enjoys constitutional protection, but does that right extend only to reproduction through traditional means (sexual relations) or also to assisted methods as well? ART provides a valuable resource for a variety of individuals and couples seeking to have children: infertile couples, couples engaged in same-sex relationships, parties seeking to avoid transmission of disease (such as sickle cell anemia, Tay Sachs, or sexually transmitted diseases), or individuals wanting to produce a child with particular characteristics. Do you believe everyone should be able to make use of the technology available, or should access be restricted? Consider the following:

William Gerber is a forty-one-year-old inmate at Mule Creek State Prison in California serving a sentence of 100 years to life plus eleven years. Given the length of his sentence it is unlikely that he will ever be paroled. He and his wife want to have a child. To

that end, Mr. Gerber has requested that he be allowed to provide his wife with a sperm specimen she can use to be artificially inseminated. He argues that a refusal to permit him to do so would constitute cruel and unusual punishment and violate his fundamental right to procreate.

How do you think the warden should respond to this request? Why? A sharply divided opinion dealing with this fact pattern was rendered in *Gerber v. Hickman,* 291 F.3d 617 (9th Circ. Ct. of Appeals 2002).

PARALEGAL PRACTICE TIP

The opinion in *Gerber v. Hickman* can be accessed at *www.pearsonhighered.com/wilson* in the companion website material related to Chapter 7 under "Cases" and in the Case Resources Section of the MyLegalStudiesLab.

---

contract, criminal, and consumer protection law. A sampling of actual and potential areas of liability include the following:

Wrongful birth
an action brought by parents claiming that the defendant's negligent conduct resulted in the birth of a child with serious defects or disabilities, thereby causing the parents serious emotional distress and expense

Wrongful life
an action brought by a plaintiff who claims he or she was brought into the world with a disability that was foreseeable and that could have been prevented by a competent physician exercising due care

- **Wrongful birth**: This is an action brought by parents claiming that the defendant's conduct (negligence, failure to advise, etc.) resulted in the birth of a child with serious defects or disabilities, thereby causing the parents serious emotional distress and expense.
- **Wrongful life**: In an action for wrongful life, the plaintiff claims that the fact he or she was brought into the world with some form of physical, mental, or social disability is a compensable wrong that could have been prevented by the provision of competent medical advice to the mother prior to or during pregnancy. Courts do not favor wrongful life claims, given an inability to determine "what defects should prevent an embryo from being allowed life"[80] and a perception that "measuring the value of an impaired life as compared to non-existence is a task beyond mortals."[81] However, some courts are willing to award special damages for costs associated with the disability, such as extraordinary medical and educational costs.
- **Failure to warn:** There are risks associated with the various forms of assisted reproductive technology. For example, a physician or clinic may be held liable for a failure to warn patients about potential side effects of fertility-enhancing drugs, such as the possibility of multiple pregnancies and births, premature births, and higher risks of birth defects.[82]
- **Failure to properly screen donors for significant health risks:** The failure of a fertility clinic to properly screen a gamete donor that results in harm may give rise to a negligence action. For example, in a sixth circuit case, a surrogate mother sued a clinic for failing to test the man for whom she served as a surrogate for a particular sexually transmitted disease that resulted in her child being born with cytomeglic inclusion disease, a condition characterized by mental retardation and other defects.[83]

- **Wrongful implantation of gametes or embryos:** The state of California penalizes wrongful use or implantation of sperm, ova, or embryos as a felony punishable by three to five years in state prison and up to $50,000 in fines.[84] The statute was enacted following misappropriation of embryos at the In Vitro Fertilization Clinic at the University of California at Irvine. Embryos produced by and for some clients were used for research and use by other well-paying clients without consent of the owners.[85]

- **Negligent implantation of gametes or embryos:** A New York *in vitro* fertilization clinic accidentally implanted in a Caucasian woman an embryo of an African-American couple participating in the same program. The Caucasian woman subsequently gave birth to two children, one of whom was African-American. Four months after the birth, the Caucasian couple was required to transfer the child to the other couple and was denied visitation rights.[86] Both couples sued the physician responsible for the negligent implantation. The African-American couple's case was based on a theory of emotional distress due to the lost opportunity to experience pregnancy and the birth process and the loss of the companionship of their child during its first four months of life.[87] The Caucasian couple claimed both physical and emotional injury resulting from the necessity of a caesarian delivery and having to make the difficult decision to give up a child.[88]

- **Failure to obtain, update, or comply with consent:** Ideally, written consents should be obtained from all appropriate parties including donors, surrogates, and intended parents. The consent should clearly state the circumstances under which it can be withdrawn and whether it is a general consent or only a consent to an initial procedure, which needs to be renewed prior to any subsequent procedures.

- **Unauthorized disclosure of confidential information:** The potential for this problem to arise is especially great when gamete donors have been promised anonymity.

- **Deceptive advertising:** Assisted reproductive technology is a big, largely unregulated business. Among other forms of false advertising, clinics and physicians providing assisted reproduction services may artificially inflate success rates to attract clients.

- **Wrongful death:** Fertility clinics may be sued for wrongful death if they intentionally or negligently destroy frozen embryos and embryos are defined as persons under state law or a court elects to so treat them.

- **Breach of fiduciary duty and bailment contract:** Clinics that store and "lose" embryos have been held liable for breach of contract.[89]

- **Malpractice:** The potential scope of liability for attorneys who handle ART cases is unknown, but it presents a virtual minefield. Potential conflicts of interest are rampant; legal risks and obligations for clients are not fully known; "agreements" are not necessarily enforceable; and state statutes and case law vary, leaving no clear road maps for counsel to follow.

PARALEGAL PRACTICE TIP

Agreements that a donor will remain anonymous may not always be enforceable against a physician, clinic, or hospital. For example, it may be necessary to reveal the identity (or at least the characteristics) of the donor in the event of a medical emergency involving the child. It is also not outside the realm of possibility that even a posthumously conceived child of a deceased donor could discover the donor's identity and make a claim to his or her estate.

The Role of the Paralegal

The paralegal's role in this area will be determined largely by the prevailing law in the jurisdiction where the paralegal is employed and the degree to which the firm handles cases involving parentage determinations and assisted reproductive technology. Tasks performed are likely to include the following:

- locating controlling statutes and case law governing parentage determinations and/or techniques of assisted reproduction
- researching related jurisdictional issues, including the potential existence of multiple forums in which to execute an ART agreement or seek to establish or disestablish paternity
- gathering information in preparation for drafting pleadings and/or documents related to parentage issues
- maintaining a list of reputable test banks and arranging for DNA testing, if required
- drafting pleadings and/or agreements
- drafting discovery materials, such as proposed interrogatories, deposition questions, and requests for admission and production of documents and things
- drafting responses to discovery requests received from the opposition
- maintaining a file of experts on related topics
- coordinating communication with experts and other witnesses, if necessary
- preparing affidavits, exhibits, memoranda, correspondence, etc., as assigned
- assisting with preparation for hearings and/or a trial on the merits
- organizing materials for appeals, if necessary
- making sure the client is kept informed of progress and upcoming deadlines, hearings, discovery matters, etc.

CHAPTER **SUMMARY**

This chapter focuses on the concept of "parenthood" in an era in which scientific technology and the structure of the American family are undergoing dramatic change. Just when people began to believe that DNA testing would bring simplicity and near certainty to determinations of parentage, many courts have begun to recognize that biology is only one of several means of establishing parenthood and parental rights. Legal parenthood is increasingly being granted to individuals who have functioned as parents and to individuals (including same-sex partners) who have become "parents" as a result of advances in reproductive technology.

In this chapter, we began by identifying many kinds of "parents" recognized in contemporary society. We reviewed the traditional methods of making determinations of parenthood, including the marital presumption, voluntary acknowledgment of parentage, and adjudication of parentage with particular attention to the establishment and disestablishment of paternity. In the latter part of the chapter, we looked briefly at some of the legal and ethical implications of developments in the field of assisted reproductive technology, especially with respect to surrogacy, cryopreservation of embryos, and posthumous reproduction. The statutes and cases regarding determination of parentage referenced throughout the chapter mirror the controversy and tension currently permeating this rapidly evolving area of family law.

The content of this chapter reflects some of the moral, religious, ethical, and legal considerations that confront the courts as they struggle to fit cases into a legal system ill-equipped to accommodate fact patterns involving complex parentage determinations and reproductive technologies. Judges are compelled to draw from a patchwork quilt of contract, constitutional, criminal, property, adoption, probate, and family law to resolve disputes, all the while urging legislatures to step up to the plate and provide guidance. No matter what any of us may feel about how parenthood should be determined and about assisted reproductive technology in all its permutations, courts are going to continue to be called upon to determine the lawful parentage of children in increasingly diverse scenarios. Family law teams inevitably are going to continue to play a part in that process.

CONCEPT REVIEW AND REINFORCEMENT

KEY **TERMS**

Artificial insemination
Assisted reproductive technology (ART)

Best interests of the child test
Biological parent
Biology-plus approach

Co-parent
Cryopreservation
De facto parent

Disestablishment of paternity

Donor

Equitable parent doctrine

Filius nullius

Forum shopping

Genetic test

Gestational mother

Gestational test

Intended parent

Intent test

In vitro fertilization

Legal parent

Marital presumption

Parent by estoppel

Paternity fraud

Posthumous reproduction

Presumed father

Psychological parent

Putative father

Wrongful birth

Wrongful life

REVIEW **QUESTIONS**

1. Identify the three parties with the strongest interests in parentage determinations and describe the basic nature of those interests.
2. Identify and describe the three primary ways of establishing legal parentage.
3. Describe the basic process for adjudicating paternity.
4. Describe the equitable parent doctrine and explain how it was applied by the Wisconsin Supreme Court in *A.J. v. I.J.*
5. Explain what it means to "disestablish" paternity when a man has been the victim of paternity fraud. Identify some of the common arguments in favor of and against disestablishment.

6. Identify and describe the four tests most often applied by the courts to resolve disputes arising out of surrogacy arrangements.
7. Describe the trend with respect to resolution of disputes regarding disposition of cryopreserved embryos upon divorce.
8. Define posthumous reproduction and give an example of circumstances in which it might be utilized.
9. Describe the current trend with respect to recognition of same-sex partners as parents of children born through assisted reproductive technology.
10. Identify some of the ethical and liability issues that arise in the context of assisted reproductive technology.

DEVELOPING YOUR PARALEGAL SKILLS

FOCUS ON **THE JOB**

In this activity, students have an opportunity to consider with their classmates the relative merits of seven parties' claims to legal parenthood of a baby boy.

The Facts

Stephen and Mary recently married after dating each other for four years. They want to share a life together and have a child, but Stephen carries a rare genetic disease, and Mary has had a hysterectomy due to uterine cancer. They have decided to execute a surrogate parent agreement with their friends Carol and Chip. Chip feels he and Carol could use the money they would receive. Carol really doesn't care about the money and just loves having babies. She and Chip are raising their three daughters in their small five-room home, which they are hoping to remodel.

Carol signs a contract with Stephen and Mary in which Carol agrees to have an embryo implanted in her womb, to carry it full term (absent severe medical complications), and to release the child and execute a consent to adoption one week after the child's birth. Chip also signs a consent to the agreement in his capacity as Carol's husband.

The embryo will result from *in vitro* fertilization using egg and sperm from two unmarried donors identified by Stephen and Mary following exhaustive research concern-

ing their backgrounds and characteristics. The donors, Steve and Marta, each take great pride in their genetic heritage and are very honored to be selected as donors. Each is professionally successful and independently wealthy. Neither will accept payment for services as a donor. No formal, written contract is executed with the donors.

Over the course of the gestation period, several events occur:

1. Stephen and Mary develop marital problems when Stephen becomes intimately involved with his best friend, David. Mary and Stephen agree to separate and consider their respective options for the future. Each of them wants custody of the baby about to be born, and David is looking forward to co-parenting with Stephen.
2. Steve and Marta begin dating and decide they should get married and seek custody of the baby about to be born. They want to protect the product of their genes and ensure that the child has the best opportunity to develop his or her potential. They claim separate and joint rights to be declared the child's parents.
3. Chip gets a promotion at work and decides he can afford to move his family to a much nicer and more spacious home, spacious enough to accommodate a fourth child. He decides that if the baby his wife is carrying is a boy, he

wants to keep it. Carol also has had a change of heart. She has bonded with the fetus she is carrying and wants to keep it post birth with or without her husband's consent.

One week after Carol gives birth to a seven-pound, eight-ounce healthy baby boy (Baby B), each of the seven parties seeks a declaration of legal parentage, and the cases are consolidated.

The Assignment

The members of the class should be divided into seven groups, with each group working for an attorney represent-ing the interests of one of the parties in this case: Stephen, David, Mary, Carol, Chip, Steve, and Marta. Each group should research governing law (both statutory and case law) in their jurisdiction and develop an argument in support of their client's claim to legal parentage of Baby B. If completing this assignment in a group format is not feasible, each student should select one of the parties and research the merits of that party's claim in light of the law governing the case. Present the argument in a paper with the heading: "Argument in Support of the Claim of *client's name* to Parentage."

FOCUS ON **ETHICS**

In this exercise, the student addresses ethical issues that arise regarding "confidential" information, conflicts of in-terest, and dishonesty of a party in a hypothetical case.

The Assignment

Assume that you are a paralegal in the large firm where Attorney Jane Newton is employed. Attorney Newton rep-resents Carol in the above fact pattern. You work for Attorney Judie Woodford, who has represented Chip and Carol in the past on a variety of matters. An ethical wall presently insulates both Attorney Woodford and you from the present case. However, as you are riding down in the elevator to go to lunch, you realize that Carol and a friend of hers are also in the elevator. You say "hi" but Carol does not recognize you and continues to carry on a conversation with her friend. She "confides" to the friend that, even though there was a celibacy clause in the surrogacy agreement, she engaged in a "one-night stand" with a stranger around the time when she conceived. She says there is a slight chance that Baby B is the product of that incident, but she doesn't intend to risk Chip's and her chances for legal parenthood by admitting it. How should you address this situation? In preparing your response, refer to the canons of the National Association of Legal Assistants contained in Appendix A for guidance. Your response should be in the form of an inter-nal memorandum to your supervisor.

FOCUS ON **CASE LAW**

In this activity, the student is asked to brief a case involving establishment of parentage in one of three contexts.

The Assignment

All three cases are available at *www.pearsonhighered.com/ wilson* in the companion website material for Chapter 7 under "Cases" and in the Case Resources Section of the MyLegalStudiesLab.

Select one of the following cases to read and brief using the format provided on the companion website in the mate-rial related to Chapter 1 (unless your instructor directs you to use an alternative form):

1. *Kevin Q. v. Lauren W.,* 174 Cal. App. 4th 1557 (2009) This case involves a paternity contest between two men whose claims are based on two conflicting presump-tions: a presumption based on a voluntary declaration of paternity and a presumption of paternity based on a man's having received a child into his home and openly holding him out as his natural child.

2. *In the Matter of the Parentage of the Child of Kimberly Robinson,* 383 N.J. Super. 165, 890 A.2d 103 (2005) In this case, a same-sex partner of the biological mother of a child seeks to be designated as the child's other legal parent under New Jersey's Artificial Insemination Statute.

3. *Paternity of Cheryl,* 434 Mass. 23, 746 N.E.2d 488 (2001) This is a disestablishment case in which a man who had previously acknowledged paternity seeks to set aside a judgment of paternity when genetic tests establish that he is not the child's biological father.

FOCUS ON **STATE LAW AND PROCEDURE**

In this Focus exercise, the student is asked to draft a Complaint for Paternity based on a specific fact pattern us-ing a jurisdictionally appropriate format.

The Facts

Susan Westcott, your firm's client, wants to file an action to establish paternity of her one-year-old son, Christopher Westcott, born on May 28, 2011. She is certain the child's father is Peter Cann, who lives at 22 Surfer Lane in your city or town. He was born on May 5, 1988, in the capital city of your state and his social security number is 016-23-1947. Susan resides at 2 Woodbine Road in your city or town. She was born in that city or town on January 30, 1989, and her social security number is 106-23-1904. She and Peter had sexual relations every weekend between June 21, 2010, and September 30, 2010, at the Merromar Inn in your city or town, where they were registered guests. She got pregnant during that period and Christopher was born approximately nine months later. She was not intimately involved with any other man during that time frame and she has never been married. On his birth certificate, the child is identified as Christopher Westcott although the father is listed as unknown. The child's social security number is 092-23-9437. Susan intends to seek full custody and child support in an amount consistent with your state's child support guidelines.

Assignment

Locate the statute(s) governing paternity actions in your state, along with the form used in actions to establish paternity in contested cases. Complete the form tailoring it to the above fact pattern.

FOCUS ON **TECHNOLOGY**

In addition to the Links provided throughout the chapter, this Focus on Technology provides a series of websites for reference along with technology-related assignments for completion,

Websites of Interest

Links to all of the listed websites are provided at *http://www. pearsonhighered.com/wilson* in the companion website material for Chapter 7 under "Resources."

bioethics.gov

Sponsored by the President's Council on Bioethics, this user-friendly site offers a rich variety of resources, including transcripts, reports, background materials, and books on ethical issues related to ART. The reports may either be downloaded or ordered in print form.

cdc.gov/art

This is the Center for Disease Control's site on Assisted Reproductive Technology. It provides a wealth of information about ART, including reports on success rates.

family.findlaw.com/paternity

This site has links to state paternity laws. Many of the links provide access to forms related to establishment of parentage, including Voluntary Acknowledgments, Complaints, and Affidavits.

www.paternityfraud.com

This is the website of the New Jersey Citizens Against Paternity Fraud, an organization founded by Patrick McCarthy, a man who unsuccessfully sought to disestablish paternity after learning postdivorce that he was not the biological father of his fourteen-year-old daughter.

Assignments

1. Locate three sites on the Internet that market eggs and/ or sperm for ART purposes. Describe each of the sites. What quality control measures are in place, if any? How does one donate? How does one make a purchase? What costs are indicated?

2. Locate the website for the Title IV-D child support enforcement agency in your state. Describe the information and forms you find there regarding establishment of paternity. A directory of IV-D agencies in all states is available at *www.ocse.acf.hhs.gov/int/directories*.

3. Several states provide online user-friendly resources for individuals seeking to establish paternity. Check out:
   - Connecticut's site, which includes a booklet called "Establishing Paternity for Your Child. . . and For You." *www.ct.gov/dss* Select "Publications." Under "Publications and Brochures," select "Brochures." Then scroll down to the title of the booklet.
   - The California Courts Self Help Center, which provides information, forms, and instructions for parentage cases. *www.courtinfo.ca.gov* Select "Self Help." Then select "Families and Children" and "Parentage" as your topic.
   - New York's site, which provides a narrative that walks a person through a paternity case and includes a twenty-minute video with Spanish subtitles that illustrates the process in the child support context. *www. courts.state.ny.us* In the FAQs box in the top right-hand corner of the screen, insert "paternity" and you can then explore the various materials that are available. The link for the video is at the bottom of the page.

PORTFOLIO PRODUCTS

1. Paper on merits of a client's claim to parentage
2. Internal memorandum concerning ethical issues in a hypothetical case
3. Brief of a case on establishment of parentage
4. Complaint for Paternity

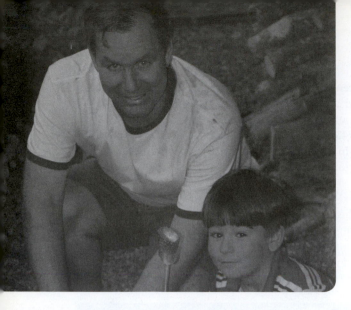

chapter 8

CHILD CUSTODY

LEARNING OBJECTIVES

After reading this chapter and completing related assignments, you should be able to:

- identify various types of child custody

- identify at least three jurisdictional issues that sometimes arise in child custody cases

- describe the primary standards that guide the courts when making child custody decisions, including the "best interests of the child"

- list some of the major factors courts consider when making decisions about custody and visitation

- describe the nature and purpose of parenting plans

- explain why parent education programs are important

- describe when and how custody and visitation orders may be modified

- explain how custody and visitation orders can be enforced

- describe the rights of third parties in the custody context

- explain who speaks for the child in custody matters

- describe the role of the paralegal in a custody case

> Diana and Ramon Acevedo are the grandparents of Melody and Paco, the children of their unmarried daughter, Christina, and Miguel Rodriguez, her former boyfriend. They believe they should be awarded visitation with their grandchildren so that they can at least temporarily rescue them from the harmful influence of their parents. Although Christina and Miguel are no longer a couple, they both say, "No way. . . . "

Introduction

Many married parents whose marriages fail get divorced, and unmarried parents whose relationships break down leave each other without ceremony. But married or divorced, together or apart, parents cannot change the fact they are parents. Custody issues do not simply involve parents battling over inanimate pieces of property. Custody is about live children who have interests in the outcome of the battle. They are what the battle is supposed to be about.

In the majority of divorces, there is no dispute with respect to which parent should have custody of the children or if custody should be shared. The parties establish an agreed-upon schedule and related provisions and present their agreement to the court for approval and incorporation in the decree dissolving their marriage. In some cases, however, before an agreement is reached, a considerable amount of negotiating may occur. One parent may even threaten the other parent with the loss of custody in an effort to obtain some unrelated advantage, such as a more favorable property division.[1] In a small minority of cases, there is such hostility and disagreement between the parties that they are unable to reach an agreement even with the assistance of mediation.

At considerable emotional and financial cost, these high-conflict cases will go to trial to be decided by a judge. Each party will present evidence and testimony and will have an opportunity to cross-examine the other party and his or her witnesses. Customarily, the parties will testify about their relationship with the child, relating anecdotes about involvement in as many aspects of the child's life as possible—health, education, recreation, daily routines, medical care, religious training, discipline, and the like. **Lay witnesses**, such as friends, neighbors, teachers, and counselors, may be called to buttress a parent's testimony, and occasionally a battle of experts may ensue—especially if the child or either or both of the parents have health, psychiatric, or behavioral problems impacting on their fitness as a parent or if there is evidence that either parent is abusing the child in some manner. The court may also appoint its own resources, including a **guardian *ad litem***, to provide a neutral assessment of the situation, and may interview the child **in camera** as to his or her feelings and parental preference. The court then has to make a decision about the course of action that will best serve the child's interests based on objective evidence and a weighing of the credibility of the various witnesses. States afford judges broad discretion, and a trial court's decision will customarily not be disturbed on appeal absent a showing of an abuse of discretion, insufficient evidence to support the court's conclusion, or an error in declaring or applying the law.

Types of Custody

In general, **physical custody** (called residential custody or physical placement in some states) refers to where the child will live, and **legal custody** refers to decision-making authority. A **sole award** is vested primarily in one parent. A **joint award** involves shared responsibility. The various types of custody described in traditional terms are as follows:

Sole legal custody One parent has the right and responsibility to make the major decisions regarding the child's welfare, including matters of education, medical care, and emotional, moral, and religious development.

Joint legal custody Both parents have continued mutual responsibility and involvement in the making of major decisions regarding the child's welfare. Absent an emergency, when legal custody is joint, neither parent should make a major decision related to the child without first consulting the other parent. Although this arrangement sounds fine in principle, conflicts frequently arise, especially with respect to what constitutes a "major" decision. For instance, is getting a tattoo or dyeing one's hair purple a major or a day-to-day decision?

PARALEGAL PRACTICE TIP

It is often the case that parents with shared legal custody cannot reach a decision on an issue. To avoid continual and costly trips back to court, judges may appoint a parenting coordinator or may designate one of the parents as the "final decision-making authority." See, for example, *Rembert v. Rembert,* 285 Ga. 260, 674 S.E.2d 892 (2009).

Sole physical custody The child resides with and is under the day-to-day supervision of one parent, subject to reasonable visitation with the other parent unless a court determines that visitation would not be in the best interests of the child. The parent with whom the child primarily resides is commonly called the "**custodial parent**" and the parent with visitation rights is the "**noncustodial parent**".

Joint or shared physical custody The child has periods of residing with and being under the day-to-day supervision of each parent. The custody is shared in such a way that the child has frequent and continuing contact with each parent.

Lay witness
a witness who is not an expert on a matter at issue in a legal proceeding who testifies as to opinions based on firsthand knowledge

Guardian *ad litem*
a person, usually a lawyer, appointed by the court to conduct an investigation and/or to represent a party who is a minor or otherwise unable to represent himself or herself in a legal proceeding; the guardian's role may be limited to a particular matter, such as custody

In camera
in the judge's chambers

Physical custody
custody relating to where and with whom the child resides; can be either sole or joint

Legal custody
custody relating to decision-making authority with respect to major issues affecting a child; may be sole or joint

Sole award
an award made to one parent only; may apply to legal or physical custody

Joint award
an award made to both parents; may apply to legal or physical custody

Custodial parent
the parent with whom the child primarily resides; the parent who has the right to have the child live with him or her

Noncustodial parent
a parent who does not have sole or physical custody of a child but who is still a legal parent with enforceable rights and responsibilities

Split custody Each parent has legal and/or physical custody of one or more of the parties' children. Strong public policy supports keeping siblings together. Absent an extraordinary emotional, medical, or educational need or some other compelling circumstance (such as a significant age gap or severe conflict between the siblings), **split custody** is not favored by the courts.

PARALEGAL PRACTICE TIP

One of the situations in which split custody may be awarded is when one parent has irreparably alienated one or more of the parties' children from the other parent but there is still potential to salvage the other children's relationship with the targeted parent. See, for example, *In re the Marriage of Noland Vance,* 321 S.W.3d 398 (Mo. App. 2010).

Although many still use traditional terms to refer to custody, several states have abandoned the old terms in favor of a new terminology that emphasizes allocation of parental responsibilities for the benefit of the child.[2] The "new" approach to custody-related terminology is reflected in the New Hampshire Parental Rights and Responsibilities Act, which replaces the term "custody" with the phrase "parental rights and responsibilities" and refers to legal custody as "decision-making responsibility" and physical custody as "residential responsibility."[3] The emphasis is on custody as a shared effort to meet the needs of children rather than as a battle between parents for possession and control.

PARALEGAL PRACTICE TIP

To see the New Hampshire Parental Rights and Responsibilities Act, go to *www.gencourt.state.nh.us.* You can find a link to this site at *www.pearsonhighered.com/wilson* in the companion website material for Chapter 8 under "Statutes."

Whatever terminology is used, there is no fixed formula for child custody determinations. Under the guidance of state statutes and case law, courts are free to create multiple forms of custody arrangements tailored to meet the unique needs and challenges of each family. This flexibility is especially useful in complex, interstate, or high-conflict cases.

The two most common forms of custodial awards are:

1. Joint legal custody and sole physical custody in one parent with reasonable rights of visitation in the other parent
2. Joint legal and physical custody

Prior to the 1970s, the first option was predominant and it continues to be common today. However, with the coming of no-fault divorce, gender-neutral custody laws, and equal rights movements in their many forms, joint physical and legal custody awards have become more common. Most states now provide by statute or case law that, absent a history of domestic violence, joint awards are in the best interest of children. However, joint awards have met with mixed success. The prospects for success are greatest when chosen by parties who are able to communicate effectively or when parents want to become or remain actively involved in their children's lives. They are less likely to be successful when imposed on disinterested parents, parties who cannot each afford to maintain a residence for the children, or parents who are unable to rise above hostility toward each other in order to commit to a shared role for the benefit of their children. Joint custody can also be difficult for children, particularly if they are forced to live in two different homes in two totally different communities.

Jurisdictional Issues in Child Custody Cases

A court's authority to issue a child custody order is based on statute. Personal jurisdiction over a parent or a child is not sufficient. Subject matter jurisdiction is required. The parties cannot confer subject matter jurisdiction by agreement, and therefore, a party must establish it by complying with governing statutes.

Jurisdictional problems are minimal in child custody cases when the parents' identities are known and both parties and the child reside in the same state. However, problems can arise when multiple states are involved, particularly in domestic violence cases or when variations in jurisdictional requirements exist. Interstate conflicts were especially prevalent prior to 1968, when courts based jurisdiction for custody decisions on the child's physical presence in a state at the time an action was filed. This sometimes led to **forum shopping** by parents, some of whom would abduct their children and go to another state where they might secure a more favorable custody award.

Forum shopping
seeking a court that will grant the most favorable ruling in a case

Four Acts have made a particular effort to address such issues in interstate child custody cases:

1. The Uniform Child Custody Jurisdiction Act (UCCJA)[4]
2. The Uniform Child Custody Jurisdiction and Enforcement Act (UCCJEA)[5]
3. The Federal Parental Kidnapping Prevention Act (PKPA)[6]
4. The Hague Convention on the Civil Aspects of International Child Abduction.[7]

UCCJA

The National Conference of Commissioners on Uniform State Laws (NCCUSL) promulgated the Uniform Child Custody Jurisdiction Act in 1968, and by 1981 it was adopted in all fifty states, the District of Colombia, and the Virgin Islands. The Act authorized four independent bases of jurisdiction for initial custody determinations: home state, significant connection, emergency, and last resort/vacuum. None of these required the presence of the child in the state at the time of filing, thus reducing the incentive to temporarily take a child to another state solely to file a custody action there. The Act also required states to enforce and not modify sister states' valid child custody and visitation orders.

The UCCJA was an improvement over pre-1968 law governing jurisdiction in child custody cases and helped to reduce the filing of competing custody actions in multiple states. However, some problems remained. For example, because priority was not given to home state jurisdiction, the potential still existed for multiple orders from different states to exist, with one based on home state and the other on significant connection jurisdiction.

UCCJEA

Like the UCCJA, the Uniform Child Custody Jurisdiction and Enforcement Act is a uniform law designed to reduce jurisdictional conflicts between states, deter child abductions for the purpose of obtaining jurisdiction in another state, avoid relitigation of decisions from other states, and ensure that custody matters are heard in the state that has the closest connection with the child and the family. Now enacted in all fifty states, the UCCJEA addresses weaknesses in the UCCJA that had continued to result in costly litigation and inconsistent decisions

PARALEGAL PRACTICE TIP

A copy of the Act can be accessed at *www.pearsonhighered.com/ wilson* in the companion website material related to Chapter 8 under "Resources."

Home state jurisdiction
jurisdiction in custody matters based on where the child has lived for a specified period of time

Significant connection jurisdiction
jurisdiction based on the existence of substantial evidence in a state concerning a child

Forum *non conveniens*
the forum in which an action is filed is not convenient for one or both of the parties, and the court, in its discretion, may find that justice would be better served if the matter is heard in another court

Last resort jurisdiction
jurisdiction based on the fact no other state is willing or able to exercise jurisdiction, and it is in the child's best interest for a state to do so

in interstate custody cases. It accomplishes this in part by tightening the four bases for initial jurisdiction under the UCCJA and preserving exclusive, continuing jurisdiction in the decree state if that state has a basis for continuing jurisdiction. The primary bases of initial jurisdiction under the UCCJEA are as follows:

a. **Home state** Home state jurisdiction exists when a child has lived with a parent or a person acting as a parent for at least six consecutive months immediately before the commencement of a child custody proceeding. In the case of a child less than six months of age, the term means the state in which the child has lived from birth. Periods of temporary absence from the state are included in the six-month period. Once the home state is established, if the child is removed from the state, a parent (or person acting as a parent) who remains there may bring a custody action within a six-month period. Consistent with federal law, the UCCJEA makes the child's home state the priority ground for original jurisdiction in interstate child custody cases. If the minor child has a home state, jurisdiction will be proper only in the home state unless that state declines jurisdiction.

b. **Significant connection** Sections 201(a)(2)(A) and (B) of the UCCJEA provide that significant connection jurisdiction exists when "(A) the child and the child's parents, or the child and at least one parent or a person acting as a parent, have a significant connection with a State other than mere physical presence; and (B) substantial evidence is available in that State concerning the child's care, protection, training, and personal relationships; . . ." Under the UCCJEA, a state can exercise "significant connection" jurisdiction only if the "home state" declines jurisdiction, there are **forum** *non conveniens* or parental misconduct grounds, or there is no home state. The potential exists for more than one state to have jurisdiction on this basis but only one may exercise it. The Act resolves the conflict in favor of the first-filed proceeding unless the courts agree otherwise after mandatory communication.

c. **More appropriate forum** This type of jurisdiction exists when both the home state and the significant connection state(s) decline jurisdiction in favor of a third more appropriate state based on inconvenient forum or parental misconduct grounds.

PARALEGAL PRACTICE TIP

Under section 207 of the UCCJEA, a court may, after taking into account specified factors, determine that a court in another state is better able to make a custody determination. The specified factors include whether domestic violence has occurred and, if so, which state can best protect the parties and child; how long the child has lived outside of the state; where the evidence is located; and which court is most familiar with the case.

d. **Vacuum/last resort jurisdiction** If no state has jurisdiction under options a, b, and c above, a court in another state may exercise jurisdiction over an initial custody proceeding.

PARALEGAL PRACTICE TIP

Vacuum jurisdiction would apply to cases involving migrant or homeless children who do not remain in any state for a period sufficient to establish any other type of jurisdiction. It may also apply to the children of military personnel who are frequently reassigned to new locations.

e. **Temporary emergency jurisdiction** Under Section 204 of the UCCJEA, courts can exercise temporary emergency jurisdiction when a child in the State has been abandoned or when emergency protection is necessary because a child, or a sibling or parent of the child, has been subjected to or is threatened with mistreatment or abuse. Courts may exercise emergency jurisdiction even if a custody proceeding has been initiated in another state but may only issue temporary orders. If there is no prior order and no proceeding has been initiated in a state with jurisdiction, the temporary order may become final once the issuing state becomes the child's home state.

Under the UCCJEA, exclusive, continuing jurisdiction will remain in the initial decree state until one of two events occurs: (a) a court in the decree state or another state determines that the child, the child's parents, and any person acting as a parent no longer resides in the decree state; or (b) the decree state determines that neither the child, the child's parents, nor any person acting as a parent still has a significant connection with the decree state and there is no longer substantial evidence in the state concerning the child.

> **Emergency jurisdiction** jurisdiction based on a child's physical presence in a state and need for emergency protection

PARALEGAL PRACTICE TIP

Jurisdiction cases can be heavily fact-intensive. For example, in an interstate modification case, the family law team may need to gather evidence to show that even though one of the parties in a custody case still resides in the decree state, his or her relationship with a child now in a new home state is so attenuated that the court that issued the initial custody order will no longer be able to find a significant connection or substantial evidence in that state. In such circumstances, the decree state may determine that continuing jurisdiction no longer exists.

Other major improvements in the UCCJEA as compared with the UCCJA include the following:

- The UCCJEA brought the UCCJA into compliance with more recent federal statutes, such as the Parental Kidnapping Prevention Act (PKPA) and the Violence Against Women Act (VAWA).
- It creates mechanisms for courts in different states to "communicate and cooperate" with one another.
- It provides procedures for interstate registration and enforcement of a child custody and visitation order, provided the order was issued in substantial conformity with the UCCJEA.
- It authorizes the issuing of warrants authorizing law enforcement officers to protect children at risk of being unlawfully removed from a state.
- Unlike the UCCJA, the UCCJEA is not applicable in adoption cases, but it does apply to tribal court proceedings.

PKPA

The major federal child custody jurisdiction act is the Parental Kidnapping Prevention Act (PKPA) enacted in 1980 to address interstate custody problems that continued to exist after the adoption of the UCCJA and before the UCCJEA was created. Its scope is not limited to "kidnapping" cases; rather, its primary purpose is to maintain jurisdiction in one court over custody orders pertaining to a given child in interstate cases. The PKPA has essentially the same primary jurisdictional bases as the UCCJEA and it, too, fills a major gap in the UCCJA by giving priority

PARALEGAL PRACTICE TIP

To see a variety of UCCJEA related forms, visit *www.nycourts.gov/forms*. You can find a link to this site at *www.pearsonhighered.com/wilson* in the companion website material for Chapter 8 under "Forms." (New York)

PARALEGAL PRACTICE TIP

To learn more about the PKPA and how it compares with other Acts, visit *www.vaw.umn.edu*. You can find a link to this site at *www.pearsonhighered. com/wilson* in the companion website material related to Chapter 8 under "Resources."

in initial child custody determinations to home state jurisdiction. By doing so, it prevents a "significant connection" state from exercising jurisdiction over a custody matter as long as the child involved has a "home state." If it does exercise jurisdiction, its order will not be entitled to recognition by other states.

To avoid the issuing of conflicting custody orders, the PKPA mandates that states give full faith and credit to other states' custody determinations as long as they are made in conformity with the provisions of the PKPA. Subject to the emergency jurisdiction provision, it also provides for exclusive continuing jurisdiction over modification of custody actions involving the child as long as the original decree state continues to have jurisdiction. Jurisdiction continues in the decree state until such time as (1) the initial state has lost jurisdiction because it is no longer the home state and it no longer has a significant connection to the case because significant evidence is not present there or (2) neither the child nor either parent continues to reside in the decree state.

Although the UCCJEA is designed for adoption by the states and the PKPA is a federal act, the goals and procedures of the two Acts largely mirror each other. When there is a conflict, the jurisdictional provisions of the PKPA will prevail, given the supremacy of federal law under the Constitution.

THE HAGUE CONVENTION ON THE CIVIL ASPECTS OF INTERNATIONAL CHILD ABDUCTION

International child custody disputes present highly complex, specialized, and challenging issues. The major challenge is that laws and court orders issued in the United States are not always recognized and enforceable internationally, and not all orders issued in foreign countries are necessarily enforceable in the United States.

PARALEGAL PRACTICE TIP

To learn more about the Hague Convention on the Civil Aspects of International Child Abduction, visit *http://www.hcch.net*, the site of the Hague Conference on Private International Law. You can find a link to this site at *www.pearsonhighered.com/wilson* in the companion website material for Chapter 8 under "Resources."

There are a number of federal laws in place concerning custody, parental child abduction, and missing children, such as the National Child Search Assistance Act,[8] the International Parental Kidnapping Crime Act (IPKCA),[9] and the Fugitive Felon Act.[10] One of the most effective resources in the area of international child abduction is The Hague Convention on the Civil Aspects of International Child Abduction (Hague Convention) endorsed by more than fifty nations and implemented as federal law in the United States in 1988 by the International Child Abduction Remedies Act (ICARA).[11] The Hague Convention establishes administrative and judicial procedures to expedite the return of children (usually to their "habitual residence") who have been abducted or wrongfully retained and to facilitate the exercise of visitation rights across international borders. (See Focus on Case Law at the end of this chapter.)

PARALEGAL PRACTICE TIP

The UCCJEA contains provisions addressing when foreign custody determinations from both Hague and non-Hague nations are entitled to enforcement and when U.S. courts must defer to the custody jurisdiction of a foreign court.

Paralegal Application 8.1

Which State Has Jurisdiction Under the UCCJEA?

Fact Pattern

Assume that the parties in this custody case are the unmarried parents of one son who was born in 2005 when they were living together in Hawaii. While there, the mother, Samantha, was the primary caretaker for the child. The relationship between Samantha and the father, Timothy, was abusive. On several occasions he threatened and assaulted her, sometimes in front of their son, who was traumatized and potentially endangered by the abuse. As a result of the domestic violence, Samantha (along with the parties' son) moved to Maine where several of her relatives, including her mother, resided. After the move, Timothy continued to threaten Samantha by telephone and she sought and was granted a protection-from-abuse order.

Sidebar

Assume that within a month after Samantha moved to Maine, Timothy filed a complaint for determination of paternal rights and responsibilities in Hawaii, and shortly thereafter, Samantha filed a complaint for determination of parental rights and responsibilities in Maine. Under the UCCJEA, on what basis might Hawaii have jurisdiction? On what basis might the state of Maine have jurisdiction? Read the opinion to see what the courts decided in *Rainbow v. Ransom,* 2010 ME 22, 990 A.2d 535 (2010).

PARALEGAL PRACTICE TIP

To see an example of a Complaint for Determination of Parental Rights and Responsibilities, visit *www.courts.state.me.us.* (Maine) You can find a link to this site at *www.pearsonhighered.com/wilson* in the companion website material for Chapter 8 under "Forms."

PARALEGAL PRACTICE TIP

The full opinion in *Rainbow v. Ransom* can be found at *www.pearsonhighered.com/wilson* in the companion website material related to Chapter 8 under "Cases" and in the Case Resources Section of the MyLegalStudiesLab.

Evolving Legal Standards for Making Custody Decisions

Once the appropriate jurisdiction for bringing a custody action is identified, the standard used for making custody decisions in that state can be ascertained. Over the years, a variety of approaches have existed, depending on the state of society, economic forces, gender stereotypes, and prevailing public policies with respect to children. Some approaches have been fairly cut-and-dried; others are more flexible and open-ended. The most prominent approaches have included the following:

- Paternal Preference
- Maternal Preference
- Tender Years Doctrine
- Best Interests of the Child
- Primary Caretaker Presumption
- American Law Institute's Approximation Rule

PATERNAL PREFERENCE

In the early history of child custody awards, a **paternal preference** was predominant. When the identity of the father was known, custody virtually always was granted to the father. Under the doctrine of *pater familias* (Latin: father of the family), he had an absolute legal right to custody (in effect, physical possession) of his offspring regardless of their welfare. In essence, custody was a matter of property law. The father had complete authority over his children and controlled all aspects

Paternal preference
the common law doctrine that fathers had an absolute right to the care and custody of their children

of their lives, their education, their training, and their labor. This "paternal preference," under which mothers had no legal authority with respect to their children, persisted in the United States until the late eighteenth century and is still evident in present-day patriarchal families and societies elsewhere in the world.

MATERNAL PREFERENCE

By the early nineteenth century, the Industrial Revolution, urbanization, and the decline of an agrarian way of life had brought about major societal changes and a redefining of roles within the family. Although the father remained the head of the family and the ultimate maker of major decisions, his primary role was that of breadwinner, and the mother's role was that of homemaker. She was viewed as the "heart" of the home and tended to all of the children's physical, emotional, and spiritual needs. Upon divorce, consistent with his role, the father was customarily ordered to pay spousal and child support for his dependent wife and children. However, given a **maternal preference** for the mother as caretaker, the mother was most often granted physical custody, even over the father's objection.

TENDER YEARS DOCTRINE

By the end of the nineteenth century, the common law doctrine of paternal rights had been firmly replaced by the **tender years doctrine**. Based on tradition and biological dependence, it was assumed that young children should be placed in the care of their mother as the natural custodian of the young and immature, provided she was fit to have custody. Occasionally, custody of older children, especially teenage boys, was awarded to fathers, particularly if the parties agreed and the children expressed a preference to that effect. The desire for "young men" to have "male role models" was commonly a factor in the decision.

The preference for awarding custody to mothers lasted until the 1960s and the onset of the various "rights" movements. It was inevitable that the effects of the "civil rights," "women's rights," "children's rights," and "equal rights" movements would spill over into the custody context. "Fathers' rights" came to the fore at the same time as many women were choosing the world of work over homemaking as their primary focus (sometimes out of necessity). The father was no longer necessarily the primary breadwinner, and the mother was no longer the undisputed choice for physical custody. Custody laws in most states became gender-neutral. Without a rule of gender preference to drive decision making, parents and the courts necessarily sought a more flexible standard that could accommodate diverse family models. Enter the "best interests of the child", which is now the dominant standard across the country.

BEST INTERESTS OF THE CHILD

Applying the "**best interests of the child**" standard, the custody determination ideally involves an analysis of the child's needs and an assessment of which parent can most effectively meet those needs. Whether the arrangement is established by the parties or by the court, it must serve the best interests of the child. States identify by statute and/or case law a series of "best interest" factors that courts should consider, among others, in making custody determinations. The factors are not prioritized and the court is free to assign weight to them based on the facts of each case. The New Jersey statute in Exhibit 8.1 contains an extensive, representative list

---

Maternal preference
the concept that custody should be awarded to a mother over a father, provided she is fit

Tender years doctrine
the doctrine holding that custody of very young children should be awarded to the mother rather than the father unless she is found to be unfit

Best interests of the child
the legal standard for resolving custody disputes that focuses on the needs of the child over the rights or wishes of the parents

of these factors. Others appearing in various state statutes include but are not limited to the following:

- the ability of each parent to provide the child with nurture, love, affection, and guidance; the emotional ties existing between the parties and the child; the relationship of the child with any other person who may significantly affect the child
- the mental and physical health of all individuals involved
- the child's adjustment to his or her home, school, and community; the length of time the child has lived in a stable, satisfactory environment and the desirability of maintaining continuity; the intention of either party to relocate the principal residence of the child
- the ability of each parent to ensure that the child receives adequate food, clothing, shelter, medical care, and a safe environment; the child's developmental needs and the ability of each parent to meet them, both in the present and in the future; if one parent, both parents, or neither parent has provided primary care of the child[12]
- the capacity and disposition of the parties to continue the education and raising of the child in his or her religion or creed, if any
- the wishes of the child's parents as to his or her custody; the nature and extent of coercion or duress used by a parent in obtaining an agreement regarding custody;[13] and which parent is more likely to allow the child frequent and meaningful continuing contact with the other parent
- the moral fitness of the parties involved;[14] if a parent is incarcerated, the reason for and length of the incarceration and any unique issues that arise as a result of the incarceration

Customarily, there is a final catchall provision allowing the court to consider any other factors it deems necessary and relevant.

PARALEGAL PRACTICE TIP

Take a look at some best interest statutes in addition to New Jersey's in Exhibit 8.1:

MICHIGAN *http://www.legislature.mi.gov*
TENNESSEE *http://www.michie.com*
UTAH *http://le.utah.gov*

Links to each of these sites can be found at *www.pearsonhighered.com/wilson* in the companion website material related to Chapter 8 under "Statutes."

EXHIBIT 8.1 New Jersey Statute Re: Custody of Child, Rights of Both Parents Considered N.J. Stat. § 9:2–4

FROM THE STATUTE

The Legislature finds and declares that it is in the public policy of this State to assure minor children of frequent and continuing contact with both parents after the parents have separated or dissolved their marriage and that it is in the public interest to encourage parents to share the rights and responsibilities of child rearing in order to effect this policy.

In any proceeding involving the custody of the minor child, the rights of both parents shall be equal and the court shall enter an order which may include:

a. Joint custody of a minor child to both parents, which is comprised of legal custody or physical custody which shall include: (1) provisions for residential arrangements so that a

(Continued)

EXHIBIT 8.1 (*Continued*)

child shall reside either solely with one parent or alternatively with each parent in accordance with the needs of the parents and the child; and (2) provisions for consultation between the parents in making major decisions regarding the child's health, education and general welfare;

b. Sole custody to one parent with appropriate parenting time for the noncustodial parent; or

c. Any other custody arrangement as the court may determine to be in the best interests of the child.

    In making an award of custody, the court shall consider but not be limited to the following factors:

- the parents' ability to agree, communicate and cooperate in matters relating to the child;
- the parents' willingness to accept custody and any history of unwillingness to allow parenting time not based on substantiated abuse;
- the interaction and relationship of the child with its parents and siblings;
- the history of domestic violence, if any;
- the safety of the child and the safety of either parent from physical abuse by the other parent;
- the preference of the child when of sufficient age and capacity to reason so as to form an intelligent decision;
- the needs of the child;
- the stability of the home environment offered;
- the quality and continuity of the child's education;
- the fitness of the parents;
- the geographical proximity of the parents' homes;
- the extent and quality of the time spent with the child prior to or subsequent to the separation;
- the parents' employment responsibilities; and
- the age and number of the children.

    A parent shall not be deemed unfit unless the parent's conduct has a substantial adverse effect on the child.

    The court, for good cause and upon its own motion, may appoint a guardian ad litem or an attorney or both to represent the minor child's interests. The court shall have the authority to award a counsel fee to the guardian ad litem and the attorney and to assess that cost between the parties to the litigation.

d. The court shall order any custody arrangement which is agreed to by both parents unless it is contrary to the best interests of the child.

e. In any case in which the parents cannot agree to a custody arrangement, the court may require each parent to submit a custody plan which the court shall consider in awarding custody.

f. The court shall specifically place on the record the factors which justify any custody arrangement not agreed to by both parents.

    The best interest test is child-centered and individualized. It affords courts maximum discretion and parents minimal predictability in custody decisions.[15] The child's best interests are supposed to be paramount.[16] However, the test clearly is subjective and inevitably forces judges to make qualitative judgments into which they may subtly project personal views of what constitutes a "good" or a "bad" parent. What is "best" varies by child, and what a court considers "best" is not always what a parent may consider "best." A judge sitting in one family court may emphasize and reward parenting that is firm and regimented and emphasizes rules, discipline, and control. Another family court judge sitting in an adjacent courtroom may look more favorably on parents who promote individuality, creativity, and self-actualization of their children.

THE PRIMARY CARETAKER PRESUMPTION

In an effort to refine the best interests standard into a manageable test capable of producing predictable results, in the 1980s some courts began applying a "primary caretaker presumption" in making custody determinations.[17] A child's **primary caretaker** is the individual who has performed most of the significant parenting tasks for the child since birth or in the years preceding the divorce. The presumption builds on a wealth of child development research that suggests a child is likely to form the closest bond with the individual who is most involved in meeting his or her daily needs and who is his or her secure base in times of stress. Child psychologists generally agree that maintenance of this relationship is essential to healthy development, supporting the presumption that custody should be awarded to the primary caretaker.

Rather than "custodial" and "noncustodial" parents, states applying this approach often refer to the parents as "the primary caretaker" and "the secondary caretaker."[18] Although both roles can be filled by either a father or a mother, many claim that the primary caretaker presumption is simply the maternal preference in disguise, as the determination focuses on activities traditionally performed by "moms." Paralegal Application 8.2 describes a sampling of the kinds of caretaking activities that are considered in attempts to identify a "primary caretaker."

Primary caretaker
the individual who has performed most of the significant parenting tasks for the child since birth or in the years preceding the divorce

PARALEGAL PRACTICE TIP
To read an interesting article about this presumption, Google "The Primary Caretaker Presumption: Are We Presuming Too Much?"

THE AMERICAN LAW INSTITUTE'S APPROXIMATION RULE

The ALI's **Approximation Rule** with respect to custody is that the custodial responsibilities of the parents at dissolution should be allocated in a manner that approximates the proportion of time each parent spent caring for the child when the family was intact.[19] Similar to the primary caretaker presumption, the focus of the ALI Rule is on concrete acts of parenting rather than on subjective judgments. It removes considerations of race, gender, religion, sexual preference, marital misconduct, and economic circumstances from the custody decision. As a result, to some extent it relieves judges of having to make subjective, relative judgments about parental fitness. The Rule assumes that after the divorce, each parent will be granted some level of access to the child, a level that will be comparable to his or her daily involvement with the child prior to the divorce. The Rule is not absolute, however. It allows for variation under certain circumstances, e.g., to keep siblings together, to accommodate reasonable child preferences, or to protect a child or parent from abuse.

Approximation Rule
the rule that the custodial responsibilities of the parents at dissolution should be allocated in a manner that approximates the proportion of time each parent spent caring for the child when the family was intact

The Rule is still essentially focused on the best interests of the child, but it provides parents the greater predictability and children the greater continuity in care afforded by the primary caretaker presumption. It has been cited favorably by courts in several states. West Virginia was the first state to adopt the ALI substantive custody standard over the primary caretaker rule, which it had adopted in 1981.

PARALEGAL PRACTICE TIP

To see relevant excerpts from the West Virginia child custody statutes, visit *www.pearsonhighered.com/wilson* and look in the companion website material related to Chapter 8 under "Statutes."

Paralegal Application 8.2

Caretaking Activities

Whether the standard applied is best interests, primary caretaker, or the ALI Approximation Rule, courts will consider the nature of each parent's relationship with the child in making custody determinations. Therefore, paralegals are often assigned to work with clients to gather information about the activities performed by each parent and the extent of his or her involvement with the child. Careful interviewing and preparation are critically important in preparing for a client's direct testimony and cross-examination at trial. For example, cross-examination can be very effective when a parent falsely claims to be the primary caretaker. The party might be asked when the child last went to the doctor, who took him or her, what the doctor's name was, how the child behaved, what the diagnosis was, what treatment was prescribed, who administered the treatment, etc. In relation to school, the party might be asked about the names of the child's teachers, the grades the child receives, the child's most and least favorite subjects, when the last parent-teacher conference was, who attended it, who the child's best friend at school is, etc. An uninvolved parent is very unlikely to be able to answer these questions.

The kinds of caretaking activities most commonly considered are listed below. The extent to which any single activity is likely to be exercised by a parent will vary according to the age and developmental needs of the child. The list is drawn in large part from Section 2.03 of the ALI Principles of Marital Dissolution.

- Attending to the basic nutritional needs of the child
- Managing wake-up and bedtime routines

- Taking care of the child's personal hygiene needs, such as bathing, washing, and brushing teeth
- Attending to dressing and grooming
- Facilitating toilet training
- Attending to the child's needs when sick or injured and arranging for medical care
- Playing with the child
- Arranging for recreational activities
- Providing transportation to and from recreational and educational activities
- Protecting the child's physical safety
- Meeting the child's motor, cognitive, and socioemotional development needs
- Providing discipline and promoting moral and ethical development and self-discipline
- Arranging for the child's education, including remedial or other special services, communicating with school personnel, and working on homework
- Building the child's self-confidence
- Maintaining appropriate relationships with peers, siblings, and extended family members
- Arranging for and monitoring alternative care arrangements, including day care, babysitters, or other childcare providers

PARALEGAL PRACTICE TIP

Nutrition can be an especially important topic when a child has special dietary problems or needs such as chronic deficiencies, allergies, or diabetes. Caretakers should document that they are alert to dietary concerns both at home and when the child is at school and visiting family and friends. In the way of evidence, a monthly menu may be prepared and copies of advisory letters sent to schools, etc., may be submitted to the court.

A Closer Look at Some of the Factors Courts Consider When Making Decisions About Custody and Visitation

AVAILABILITY

PARALEGAL PRACTICE TIP

A useful resource on this topic can be found at *www.americanbar.org*. A link to this site is located at *www.pearsonhighered.com/wilson* in the companion website material related to Chapter 8 under "Resources."

Although not usually articulated as a discrete factor in statutory codes, availability is a consideration in custody decisions by implication. For example, courts look at activities parents participate in with their children, routines they perform (getting up and going to bed, etc.), attendance at school and recreational events, attending to medical and dental appointments, doing homework with the child, and providing religious training. To do these things, a parent has to be available, and therefore custody determinations are likely to favor the parent who has more time to devote to the children. Availability may be reduced or enhanced by work schedule, and a flexible work schedule may be especially attractive.

PARALEGAL PRACTICE TIP

The paralegal may be asked to develop Exhibits that illustrate why the client is the better custodial choice. For example, if it works to the client's advantage, the paralegal can prepare one (or two) maps that illustrate the geographical proximity of each parent's residence to the child's school, church, recreational centers/parks, homes of relatives and friends, daycare providers, etc. Another potential Exhibit is a schedule illustrating where the child will be (who he or she will be with and what he or she will be doing) 24/7 if the client is designated primary caretaker.

In today's busy world, most parents need to arrange with third parties for child care. Courts may consider the nature and extent of such arrangements when making custody decisions. For example, in a 2006 Idaho case, an appellate court held that "consideration of a parent's work schedule and need for third-party child care is appropriate in a custody determination to the extent that these circumstances are shown to affect the well-being of the children."[20]

PARALEGAL PRACTICE TIP

The opinion in the Idaho case (*Silva v. Silva,* 136 P.3d 371 (Idaho App. 2006) is available at *www.pearsonhighered.com/wilson* in the companion website material related to Chapter 8 under "Cases" and in the Case Resources Section of the MyLegalStudiesLab.

PARALEGAL PRACTICE TIP

When working on a case in which child care is an issue, the paralegal should research case law in the jurisdiction to learn when the courts are likely to decide the child's "well-being" is affected and why. For example, does it matter who provides the child care and how regular, how frequent, or how costly it is?

STABILITY

Stability is an important factor in custody deliberations. Recognizing that children's lives are seriously disrupted by divorce, courts often strive to maintain as much stability and continuity for them as possible. When fashioning custody agreements, the model that is likely to provide the greatest degree of stability for the child is one based on caretaking patterns during the marriage. Essentially, this amounts to the ALI or primary caretaker approach.

Although the ALI Approximation Rule provides that custodial arrangements during a period of temporary custody will not be considered by the court, the parent who has temporary custody pending a final order often has a subtle advantage in a contested custody case. If the child is doing well with that parent, the court may be very reluctant to disturb the status quo. In relocation cases, the parent with primary physical custody is likely to have an advantage, and, in some states, there is a presumption to that effect.

GENDER

Gender-based presumptions have largely been abolished or declared unconstitutional as a violation of equal protection. The public policy of virtually all states is that fit parents have equal custody rights regardless of gender. Sometimes the policy is expressly referenced in court decisions, as in the following excerpt from a

South Carolina case: "When analyzing the right to custody as between a father and a mother, equanimity is mandated. . . . The parents stand in perfect equipoise as the custody analysis begins."[21]

Many states have codified a gender-neutral position as Missouri has in its child custody statute: "As between the parents of a child, no preference may be given to either parent in the awarding of custody because of that parent's age, sex, or financial status, nor because of the age or sex of the child."[22] Whatever the stated policy may be, however, the reality is that gender stereotypes persist in practice. The functions considered as evidence of caretaking of children involve activities still performed predominantly by mothers and over 80% of custody awards are made to women. Based on census data, only 2.2 million men in the United States have primary custody of their children. That represents one-sixth of the total number of custodial parents, a very modest increase over the one-ninth proportion in 1970.[23]

RACE

The U.S. Supreme Court made clear in the landmark case of *Palmore v. Sidoti* that the Equal Protection Clause of the Constitution prohibits the making of custody decisions based upon racial bias and a fear of potential harm to a child as a result of racial prejudice. (See Case 8.1.) Although special rules apply with Native American children, race of the parents or the child may not be used as the sole factor in determining what will be in the child's best interests. The issue remains open, however, as to what a court's proper course of action is if actual harm is occurring in response to a child's racial or ethnic heritage.

CASE 8.1 *Palmore v. Sidoti*, 466 U.S. 429, 104 S. Ct. 1879, 80 L. Ed. 2d 421 (1984)

PARALEGAL PRACTICE TIP

The opinion in *Palmore v. Sidoti* is available at *www.pearsonhighered. com/wilson* in the companion website material related to Chapter 8 under "Cases" and in the Case Resources Section of the MyLegalStudiesLab.

BACKGROUND

In this case, custody of the parties' minor daughter initially was granted to the Caucasian mother. The father (who also was Caucasian) subsequently petitioned for and was granted a modification of custody based on allegations of several instances of the mother's failure to properly care for the child and the fact that she was planning to marry an African-American man with whom she had been living. A lower court and the Florida District Court of Appeals affirmed that the change in custody would serve the best interests of the child. The mother appealed the decision to the U.S. Supreme Court.

The Supreme Court reversed and stated the following:

FROM THE OPINION

. . . The goal of granting custody based on the best interests of the child is indisputably a substantial governmental interest for purposes of the Equal Protection Clause.

. . . It would ignore reality to suggest that racial and ethnic prejudices do not exist, or that all manifestations of those prejudices have been eliminated. There is a risk that a child living with a stepparent of a different race may be subject to a variety of pressures and stresses not present if the child were living with parents of the same racial or ethnic origin.

. . . The question, however, is whether the reality of private biases and the possible injury they might inflict are permissible considerations for removal of an infant

(Continued)

child from the custody of its natural mother. We have little difficulty concluding that they are not. The Constitution cannot control such prejudices, but neither can it tolerate them. Private biases may be outside the reach of the law, but the law cannot directly or indirectly give them effect.

SIDEBAR

Do you agree with the decision given the basic fact pattern? Do you think that race should be considered in custody determinations?

PARALEGAL PRACTICE TIP

If two parents are equally qualified to parent a child, race can tip the balance in favor of one of the parents. In a 2006 Illinois case, an appellate court held that, given two such parents, the fact that the mother was African-American made her more qualified than the Caucasian father to parent their biracial child, as she was better prepared to help the child deal with hostility toward biracial individuals (*In re Marriage of Gambla*, 367 Ill. App. 3d 441, 853 N.E.2d 847 (2006)). To read the opinion in this case, go to *www.pearsonhighered.com/wilson* and the companion website material related to Chapter 8 under "Cases."

RELIGION

The majority of courts that have addressed custody conflicts between parents arising from religious differences have affirmed each parent's right to freedom of religion and to parent a child by providing religious exposure and instruction as he or she sees fit. Conflicts involving religious differences most frequently arise in situations in which there is a dispute regarding medical care or disciplinary measures (particularly excessive corporal punishment), when a religion promotes illegal activities (polygamy, animal sacrifice, use of illegal drugs, etc.), or when one parent has no religious affiliation. Although under the Establishment Clause of the U.S. Constitution, courts cannot favor one religion over another, they can properly consider which parent can best meet the religious needs of a child.

PARALEGAL PRACTICE TIP

Some states address this factor in their statutes governing custody decisions. For example, Michigan includes "the capacity and disposition of the parties involved to give the child love, affection, and guidance and to continue the education and raising of the child in his or her religion or creed, if any" as a statutory best interest factor.[24]

Given that loss of custody is a high price to pay for exercising one's freedom of religion, courts generally are reluctant to intervene, even in cases involving medical treatment. However, if the conduct of the parent or a challenged religious belief or practice presents a substantial threat of present or future physical or emotional harm to the child, courts have been willing to restrict parental custody or behavior in the least intrusive manner possible. In declining to deprive a mother of custody, the Nebraska Court of Appeals opined that the harm in such situations must be actual or highly likely and not simply speculative:

> . . . in order for Jeanne's religion to constitute a ground for awarding custody to Larry, we must be able to determine from the record that the Jehovah's Witness religion as practiced by Jeanne constitutes an immediate and substantial threat to the minor children's well-being. . . .

As evidence of an immediate and substantial threat,. . . Larry makes reference to the fact that even in a medical emergency, Jeanne would refuse to consent to any of the children's receiving a blood transfusion. . . .

No evidence was presented showing that any of the minor children were prone to accidents or plagued with any sort of affliction that might necessitate a blood transfusion in the future. We cannot decide this case based on some hypothetical future accident or illness that might necessitate such treatment.[25]

In a Pennsylvania case, the Superior Court opined that "For children of divorce in general, exposure to parents' conflicting values, lifestyles and religious beliefs may indeed cause doubts and stress. However, stress is not always harmful, nor is it always to be avoided and protected against. The key is not whether the child experiences stress, but whether the stress experienced is unproductively severe."[26] (See Paralegal Application 8.3.)

Paralegal Application 8.3

You Be the Judge . . .

Fact Pattern

Although such agreements are generally held to be unenforceable, a Jewish mother and a Catholic father agreed prior to marriage that their children would be raised in the Jewish faith. They subsequently had three children: Ari, ten, Moriah, six, and Rebekah, four, at the time of this action. Three years after the parents married, the father joined a Fundamentalist Christian church. The mother adopted Orthodox Judaism, the strictest of the Jewish movements. Ari was circumcised and was described as having a "Jewish identity," which is akin to having an ethnic identity as well as a religious faith. The two girls had traditional naming ceremonies, and all three children attended a Jewish school. The father testified at trial that he would never stop trying to save his children. His behavior toward them projected a negative image of the Jewish faith and culture, and he opposed their being taught about the Holocaust. The father told the children that all individuals who do not accept his faith are sinners and will burn in hell. In addition, he cut off his son's payes (sideburns with religious significance) and threatened to cut off his tzitzitz (clothing fringe). The guardian *ad litem* reported that Ari's motivation and academic performance were declining and that he was uncomfortable and unhappy when visiting his father when he had "to do stuff he's not supposed to do on shabbas." The elder of the two daughters was experiencing stress relating to the ongoing conflict between the two parents. The mother sought to limit the children's exposure to their father's religion and the father responded that any limitation would constitute a restriction of his right to freedom of religion under the state and U.S. Constitutions.

Sidebar

What do you think the Court should do given the facts of this case? Why? Read the court's opinion in *Kendall v. Kendall*, 426 Mass. 238, 687 N.E.2d 1228 (1997) and see if you agree with the result.

PARALEGAL PRACTICE TIP

The opinion in the *Kendall* case is available at *www.pearson-highered.com/wilson* in the companion website material related to Chapter 8 under "Cases" and in the Case Resources Section of the MyLegalStudiesLab.

PARENTAL HEALTH OR DISABILITY

Poor physical or mental health of a parent will not necessarily render that parent unfit as a custodial parent. The court will examine the "nexus" or connection between the condition and the parent's capacity to provide proper child care. Stereotypes are hard to overcome, but some courts have come a long way. For example:

- In an Illinois case, an appellate court upheld the decision of a trial court to reject a custody evaluator's advice and granted custody of a child to a mother with an IQ of sixty-seven. The court found that the mother had been the child's primary caregiver, was capable of protecting the child from harm, and, with assistance, was able to foster the child's intellectual development.[27]

- In a Massachusetts case, the appeals court upheld a lower court's award of custody to a mother suffering from debilitating multiple sclerosis, contrary to the recommendation of the guardian *ad litem*. The court found that the lower court had properly considered the best interests of the child and noted that the mother had a full-time personal care assistant.[28]

But cases involving health-related issues are fact-intensive, and the results are not always positive for a parent with a disability. For instance, in the Illinois case above, the outcome might have been different if the child had a serious medical condition that required administering oxygen, balancing medications, and maintaining complicated dietary restrictions. In the Massachusetts case, the mother might not have been granted custody if she had not had her personal care assistant. Some courts even consider the disability of a parent's partner. A Kentucky court found, for example, that cohabitation of a custodial parent with an HIV-infected partner is, taken alone, a sufficient ground for modifying custody in favor of the noncustodial parent.[29]

SEXUAL ACTIVITY

The majority view is that a parent's sexual behavior or cohabitation with a heterosexual or same-sex partner is a proper factor to be considered by a court in making a custody determination, but that it should not play a role in the custody decision unless there is a connection between the behavior and the health and welfare of the child. However, some courts have held that extramarital cohabitation in the presence of children is contrary to a public policy of maintaining a stable environment for children and that "a parent's unmarried cohabitation with a romantic partner, or a parent's promiscuous conduct or lifestyle, in the presence of a child cannot be abided."[30] Courts have also enforced agreements between parties prohibiting either party from having "overnight guests of the opposite sex in front of the children" even if no adverse impact is shown.[31]

PARALEGAL PRACTICE TIP

States vary with respect to treatment of sexual activity, and cases are heavily fact-based. In a 2009 case, for example, the Georgia Supreme Court upheld a lower court's decision naming the husband/father primary physical custodian and "final decision-maker" based at least in part on the fact that the wife/mother had been romantically involved with a married man before filing for divorce from her husband. See *Rembert v. Rembert*, 285 Ga. 260, 674 S.E.2d 892 (2009).

Historically, the level of tolerance has been higher for heterosexual relationships, but many states have applied a ***per se* rule** with regard to gay and lesbian parents. Harm was assumed to occur if a child were being raised by a gay or lesbian parent. Despite the legalization of homosexual behavior and authorization of same-sex marriage in six states and the District of Columbia as of January 2012, efforts sometimes still are made to argue that a parent's homosexuality has a detrimental impact on his or her children. Even if not expressly argued, old biases are hard to eliminate. Concern is expressed about the "stigma" of being raised by a gay or lesbian parent, particularly in a rural, conservative community where the parent may be perceived as immoral and the child is subjected to physical and psychological abuse as a result of the parent's sexual orientation. In affirming a lower court's decision

Per se rule
by itself, without reference to any additional facts or circumstances

conditioning visitation with a homosexual father on his not residing in the same house with his male partner during visits, the Idaho Supreme Court opined:

> . . . It is important to observe that last year's landmark United States Supreme Court decision in *Lawrence v. Texas*, 539 U.S. 558, 156 L. Ed. 2d 508, 123 S. Ct. 2472 (2003) legalized the practice of homosexuality and in essence made it a protected practice under the Due Process clause of the United States Constitution.
>
> . . . This decision also has at least some bearing on the degree to which homosexuality may play a part in child custody proceedings. . . .
>
> . . . Sexual orientation, in and of itself, cannot be the basis for awarding or removing custody; only when the parent's sexual orientation is shown to cause harm to the child, such that the child's best interests are not served, should sexual orientation be a factor in determining custody.[32]

PARALEGAL PRACTICE TIP

Depending on the facts of a case and the sympathies of the presiding justice, it may be useful to introduce legal research and/or expert testimony regarding the effects on children of being raised by gay and lesbian parents. Sites for organizations such as the American Psychological Association (*www.apa.org*) can be good starting points for researching this issue. Legal and psychological journal searches may also be productive. See, e.g., *www.rsu.edu*, the site for Rogers State University. Links to both these sites can be found at *www.pearsonhighered.com/wilson* in the companion website material for Chapter 8 under "Resources."

PARENTAL LIFESTYLE

Judges are expected to rise above their own prejudices and to base their decisions on an objective analysis of the needs of children and the course of action best suited to meet those needs. However, judges are human. They have their own views of the world, and their own biases, moral codes, and levels of tolerance for what might be called "nonmainstream" behaviors or unusual beliefs. Some behaviors clearly are simply lifestyle choices, such as the decision to have pets or to engage in social drinking. Others are sufficiently extreme or potentially harmful that they may be viewed by the courts as lifestyle choices that cross an invisible dividing line between moral conduct and immoral conduct that may be harmful to children.

It is apparent from judicial decisions and state statutes that moral character and conduct count under some circumstances. The Michigan "best interest statute," for example, lists as a factor for consideration the "moral fitness of the parties involved."[33] A Georgia court has held that a parent may be denied custody of a child by putting "her own desires and perceived needs ahead of and to the detriment of her children" and lacking "the moral fiber" to be a role model for her children.[34] On the other hand, an Illinois statute reflects the general rule regarding the relationship between conduct and custody decisions that the "court shall not consider the conduct of a present or proposed custodian that does not affect his relationship to the child."[35] The critical question is, "Does the behavior harm the child?" Even common lifestyle choices may be deemed harmful under certain circumstances. For example, a Florida court conditioned a father's right to visitation on his agreement to remove his cats from his home before his allergic sons would be allowed to stay overnight with him.[36] Courts in several states have either denied or conditioned custody on a smoking parent's agreement to not smoke in the presence or environment of a child suffering from respiratory problems. Often the parents both have problems, and some states reflect this possibility in the statutory factors to be considered in custody determinations. For example, the applicable

Wyoming statute calls for the court to consider the "relative competency and fitness of each parent."[37] However, the courts are often willing to grant considerable benefit of the doubt to parents who have had conduct issues such as drug or alcohol abuse, particularly if a parent is seeking treatment and making progress.

PARALEGAL PRACTICE TIP

Although smoking used to be considered a relatively harmless lifestyle choice, it is increasingly viewed as a behavior that puts both the smoker and others at risk. In the custody context, it is usually raised by a nonsmoking parent as a risk to the child. However, in a highly unusual action, an Ohio court raised the issue of the danger of secondhand smoke on behalf of a healthy child under the **parens patriae doctrine**. The court took **judicial notice** of the dangers of secondhand smoke, citing overwhelming authoritative scientific evidence. It then issued an order restraining a custodial mother and her significant other from smoking in the presence of the mother's healthy eight-year-old daughter to protect her from having her health compromised by being forced to breathe secondhand smoke. The court held that the parent's right to privacy did not include the right to inflict secondhand smoke on the child.[38]

Parens patriae doctrine
the doctrine holding that the government, as parent of the country, has standing to act on behalf of a citizen, particularly one who is a minor or under a disability

Judicial notice
a court's acceptance of a well-known fact without requiring proof

HISTORY OF ABUSE

Every state provides by statute or case law that a history of domestic abuse will be considered in custody determinations.[39] Although it has not always been the case, courts now take judicial notice of the research documenting the effect of being a victim of and witnessing domestic violence. Most especially, the courts recognize that children who have witnessed domestic abuse are at significantly greater risk of both becoming abusers and being abused in their intimate relationships as adults. Many states include a history of domestic violence as a statutory factor to be considered by the court when making custody determinations, as in the New Jersey Statute in Exhibit 8.1. Other states go further and establish a rebuttable presumption against granting custody to a parent who has been a documented perpetrator of domestic violence. (See Chapter 13.)

CHILD PREFERENCE

Historically, children's custodial preferences carried no weight, given their lack of legal status and the existence of strong paternal and maternal preferences. This situation has changed dramatically over the years, and today children's wishes may be considered to some extent in all states. Even though it is permitted, however, most courts, attorneys, and even parents oppose asking children to state a preference unless mandated by law. A small minority believes that children, even immature children, have a right to be heard, and, in some states, the child's preference will be determinative under certain circumstances. (See Exhibit 8.2.)

EXHIBIT 8.2 Statutory Provisions Re Child Preference in Custody Context—Ga. Code Ann. §19–9–3

FROM THE STATUTE

(a)(4) In all custody cases in which the child has reached the age of 14 years, the child shall have the right to select the parent with whom he or she desires to live. The child's selection for purposes of custody shall be presumptive unless the parent so selected is determined not to be in the best interests of the child.

(a)(4.1) In all custody cases in which the child has reached the age of 11 but not 14, the judge shall consider the desires and educational needs of the child in determining which parent shall have custody. . . .the child's desires shall not be controlling. . . .. The best interests of the child standard shall be controlling.

The South Carolina Code reflects the majority view with respect to parental preferences of minor children: "In determining the best interests of the child, the court must consider the child's reasonable preference for custody. The court shall place weight upon the preference based upon the child's age, experience, maturity, judgment, and ability to express a preference."[40] Usually, minimal weight is given to the preferences of children under the age of seven. However, once children reach the teenage years, most courts have taken the position that their preferences should be given serious consideration. If a child's preference is to be expressed, the challenge then becomes one of determining how to solicit it in a sensitive and age-appropriate manner: as a witness, through a guardian *ad litem,* through the child's attorney or some other advocate such as a CASA (Court Appointed Special Advocate) volunteer (if one has been appointed), or through an interview with the judge in chambers. (See Exhibit 8.3 and Paralegal Application 8.4.) Most commonly, the guardian *ad litem* testifies as to the child's preferences unless the court allows either party to call the child as a witness or the judge is asked or elects to take testimony on the issue.

EXHIBIT 8.3 Statutory Provisions Re Testimony in Custody Cases—Utah Code Ann. §30–3–10(1)(c)(d) and (e)

FROM THE STATUTE

c. The children may not be required by either party to testify unless the trier of fact determines that extenuating circumstances exist that would necessitate the testimony of the children be heard and there is no other reasonable method to present their testimony.

d. The court may inquire of the children and take into consideration the children's desires regarding future custody or parent-time schedules, but the expressed desires are not controlling. . . . The desires of a child 16 years of age or older shall be given added weight, but is not the single controlling factor.

e. If interviews with the children are conducted by the court . . . , they shall be conducted by the judge in camera. The prior consent of the parties may be obtained but is not necessary if the court finds that an interview with the children is the only method to ascertain the child's desires regarding custody.

Paralegal **Application 8.4**

Preparing Children for Court

One of the tasks paralegals are sometimes called upon to perform under the supervision of an attorney is to assist in preparing witnesses for court appearances. This does not involve telling the witness what to say, but rather explaining what is likely to happen in court and supporting the witness emotionally. Children, particularly young children, are rarely called as witnesses in custody proceedings because of the potential trauma it may cause them. Occasionally, however, judges do "interview" children in chambers or in the courtroom. Parents are rarely present, but counsel for the parties are.

If called upon to orient a child for an interview, the following excerpt from a handbook for children published by the American Bar Association may be especially helpful and could easily be adapted for a conversation between a paralegal and a child rather than between the judge and a child. A copy of the Handbook may also be given to the parent for possible sharing with the child.

From the Handbook

Your Talk with the Judge

When I talk with a child, I do not use the courtroom. Often we sit in my office, also called my "chambers"—which is an old English term for office. Most of the time parents will not be present. A court reporter may be

(Continued)

there to write down everything we say and type it up for me in what is called a "transcript." Lawyers for your parents may be present—as will your lawyer if you have one. While not exactly private, we try our best to provide a comfortable place for you to talk.

I never ask a child to choose with whom he or she wants to live. Divorce is hard enough on kids without that. My number one goal is to get to know you and what you are feeling so that I can make the best decision to help you grow into a healthy adult.

I may ask you lots of questions about your interests, school, and your living situation. I may ask about people in your life who matter to you, including your parents. I will ask you questions about the time you spend with your parents, before the divorce and now. I may ask who helps you when you have a problem or need help with school work or need a haircut or spending money. I may ask how you celebrate holidays and what you like to do on vacations. I will probably share some ideas I have about visiting schedules with your parents and get your ideas on the subject.

Sometimes a child tells me of a desire to live with one parent. Your wishes are very important for me to consider, particularly if you are older. . . . I must consider all the information I have heard. Sometimes I cannot honor a child's request to live with a parent because it is not the best decision for that child.

Not all judges will talk with the children in all cases. If the judge in your parents' case will not be talking with you, it is not because he or she does not care about you. Or the judge may decide that going to court would not be good for you. In that case, other witnesses will give the judge a good idea of what you think and feel.

Excerpted from "When Parents Can't . . . The Judge Decides" by Nancy J. Katz, published in *Family Advocate*, Volume 29, No. 1, Summer 2006. Copyright © 2006 by the American Bar Association. Reprinted with permission. This excerpt appeared in a special edition of *Family Advocate* entitled *My Parents Are Getting Divorced: A Handbook by and for Kids* (product code: 513-11002901) available for purchase through the ABA webstore at *http://www.abanet.org/abastore*.

Children's true feelings in custody conflicts are not always easy to discern. Their expressed preferences may be suspect, as they are often consciously or unconsciously influenced by a variety of factors and circumstances. Children may believe they are to blame for the breakup of the marriage and the ensuing conflict. They may be the pawns of one of the parents or subject to manipulation by both parents. They may be overtly angry in general or at one of the parties in particular. One of the parents may be viewed as more likely to "spoil" them with material benefits. One may be viewed as the more lax in setting and enforcing rules and administering discipline. The courts are especially cautious about expressed preferences in situations where there is a history of abuse, as a child may fear or identify with an aggressor who will not necessarily be the parent best suited to meet the child's needs. Whatever a child's preference, the overriding weight must be given to the best interests of the child.

PARENTAL ALIENATION SYNDROME

In assessing which parent would be the preferred custodial parent, the court will look at the extent to which each parent has the capacity to rise above his or her own desires and hostility to focus on the child's need to maintain a warm and positive relationship with both parents. For some parents, this is an impossible challenge, and such a parent will do everything within his or her power to disrupt visitation, denigrate the other parent in front of the child, and alienate the child from the other parent. In the extreme, some experts believe that a child who was close to both parents before the divorce will come to idealize one parent and demonize the other as a result of the former's pressure and manipulation. Some psychologists label this condition the **parental alienation syndrome**.

Parental alienation syndrome a condition in which a child involved in a custody dispute comes to idealize one parent and demonize the other parent as a result of the former parent's pressure and manipulation

Visitation Rights and Parenting Schedules

Although it is generally acknowledged that children benefit most when they have the sustained physical and emotional support of both parents, divorce often makes this ideal an impossible one to realize.

> Like Humpty Dumpty, a family, once broken by divorce, cannot be put together in precisely the same way. The relationship between the parents and the children is necessarily different after a divorce and, accordingly, it may be unrealistic in some cases to try to preserve the noncustodial parent's accustomed close involvement in the children's everyday life. . . .[41]

When joint custody is not desirable or feasible, visitation will customarily be awarded to a fit noncustodial parent, unless it would pose a threat to the child's health and welfare. There are no fixed formulas for visitation provisions. They assume a variety of forms, depending in large part on the degree to which the parents are able to communicate with one another regarding the children's needs and schedules and the extent to which they share a common vision as to appropriate parenting behaviors and goals for the children's welfare. The overriding goal is to provide a sufficient amount of time to enable the noncustodial parent to remain a significant part of the child's life. Schedules are tailored to a number of variables, most especially the relative availability of the parents, the proximity of the parents' residences to one another, and the ages, activities, and developmental needs of the children.

The schedule will ideally be agreed on by the parties and may reflect the results of consultation with the children, depending on their ages and levels of maturity. It will customarily be laid out in a "**Separation Agreement**" or a "**Parenting Plan**." If the parties cannot agree, the court will determine the schedule and include it in its order or decree. Some courts rely heavily on model parenting schedules prepared by legal and mental health professionals that take developmental needs and milestones into account. Assuming the parents live near each other and the children are in elementary school, a common schedule would be to have visitation Wednesdays after school, one to two weekends a month (or one day each weekend with an occasional overnight), alternating holidays, shared school vacation weeks, and an extended period during the summer months (at least one month). This schedule amounts to the child being with the noncustodial parent approximately 20% of the time.

Separation agreement
an agreement made between spouses in anticipation of a divorce or legal separation, concerning the terms of the divorce or separation and any continuing obligations of the parties to each other

Parenting plan
a written agreement in which parents lay out plans for taking care of their children postseparation or postdivorce

PARALEGAL PRACTICE TIP

In Minnesota, a court-appointed task force has promulgated reasonable visitation schedules for consultation by parties and use by the courts when parents are unable to agree on their own terms. It is called "A Parental Guide to Making Child-Focused Parenting Time Decisions." An excellent manual has been produced in Massachusetts called "Planning for Shared Parenting: A Guide for Parents Living Apart." It combines research about children and the impact of divorce with strategies for addressing the practical needs of parents and children postdivorce. Sponsored by the Association of Family and Conciliation Courts and the Chief Justice of the Probate and Family Court, it can be accessed at *www.mass.gov/courts/courtsandjudges*. You can find a link to this site at *www.pearsonhighered.com/wilson* in the companion website material for Chapter 8 under "Resources."

DEFINED VERSUS FLEXIBLE VISITATION SCHEDULES

Visitation schedules range from those described in flexible, open-ended terms, such as "visitation as the parties may reasonably agree," to highly detailed provisions, such as the one contained in the Sample Separation Agreement in Chapter 12. Open-ended schedules tend to work best when parents have been separated for an extended period and already have worked out a mutually satisfactory plan. Defined schedules usually address weekly/monthly visitation, holidays and vacations, pickup and delivery times and places, out-of-state travel with the children, illness and medical treatment of a child, transportation arrangements and costs (if incurred), telephone contact, guidelines for handling cancellations and other deviations from the schedule, provision of clothing and other supplies for the children during visitation, any conditions with respect to third parties being present during visitation, dispute resolution measures, etc.

Most visitation provisions fall somewhere between the two extremes. Some degree of structure is preferred by a majority of family law practitioners to minimize potential misunderstandings and disputes between the parties. The basic parameters are provided and provision is made for alterations as mutually agreed upon. This approach offers each parent a desirable degree of flexibility, while guaranteeing a basic level of involvement of the noncustodial parent that each parent and the children can plan on.

PARALEGAL PRACTICE TIP

The Arizona Court site provides a "Planning for Parenting Time: Guide for Parents Living Apart." It offers ideas for various scheduling options based on children's needs. Color-coded options are available. To see the Guide, visit *www.azcourts.gov.* You can find a link to this site at *www.pearsonhighered.com/wilson* in the companion website material for Chapter 8 under "Resources."

Although detailed visitation plans often are useful, they may also give rise to or be unable to prevent disagreements in high-conflict cases. Disputes may focus on technical violations (such as arriving late, failing to return the children exactly on time, or making disparaging remarks about the other parent) or major issues (concealing the child's whereabouts or engaging in inappropriate behavior with a new sexual partner in front of the children). These cases are costly and burdensome to everyone involved—parents, attorneys, and the court—and they can be very stressful for children. Courts make every effort to provide for traditional and innovative dispute resolution strategies to avoid repeated return trips to court.[42] A visitation monitor or parenting coordinator may be appointed to oversee visitation on an ongoing basis, with the cost to be divided between the parties. In the extreme, if the actions of one of the parents deprive the child of having any kind of relationship with the other parent, the court may remove the child from the custody of the uncooperative parent as a last resort, even if such an action is contrary to the preference of the child.[43]

PARALEGAL PRACTICE TIP

To see an example of a Stipulated Parent Coordination Order, visit *www.vermontjudiciary.org/eforms.* You can find a link to this site at *www.pearsonhighered.com/wilson* in the companion website material related to Chapter 8 under "Forms."

SUPERVISED AND UNSUPERVISED VISITATION

Unsupervised visitation occurs when a parent is free to spend visitation time with children as he or she wishes without additional persons being present or being subject to conditions imposed by the court or the other parent. Most visitation is unsupervised.

Supervised visitation may be ordered in a variety of circumstances in which a question exists as to the fitness or competency of the noncustodial parent to appropriately or adequately care for his or her child. In extreme cases, there are situations in which a parent may be deemed unfit to parent, and his or her parental rights may be terminated. Even without a termination of rights, courts may deny not only custody but also visitation if such an action is in the best interest of the child. The most common reasons why a court might order supervised visitation are that a parent has a history of substance abuse problems, mental illness, domestic violence, or failure to properly supervise and care for a child while in his or her custody, or when there is a reasonable fear that the noncustodial parent may try to abduct the child. The visitation may take place in an informal setting with supervision being by a friend or family member, or it may be in a facility that is equipped to monitor visitation in a controlled environment and that charges a fee for services, such as a YMCA or Domestic Violence Center. A parent who has been denied unsupervised visitation may eventually ask the court to consider elimination of restrictions, a request that may or may not be granted, depending on the circumstances.

PARALEGAL PRACTICE TIP

To see an example of a "Supervised Order of Visitation," visit *www.cookcountyclerkofcourt.org*. (Illinois) You can find a link to this site at *www.pearsonhighered.com/wilson* in the companion website material related to Chapter 8 under "Forms."

In some problematic situations, a court will not necessarily order that visitation be supervised, but rather will condition the right to visitation on a parent's agreeing to abstain from or engage in a particular behavior or activity. A parent may be ordered to attend parenting classes or participate in family counseling or treatment programs for anger management or substance abuse problems. A parent with a substance abuse problem may be required to agree to abstain from the use of drugs or alcohol as a condition of having visitation with his or her child.[44] Restrictions may also be placed on the kinds of activities the children can participate in while in the noncustodial parent's care, on the third parties who may be present during visitation, or on activities the parent may participate in with his or her child present.

VIRTUAL VISITATION

The potential of technology for promoting communication between parents and children during periods of absence seems boundless. Technology offers benefits for parents who are separated from their children by blocks, counties, states or national boundaries. Video- or text-based e-mails, instant messaging, and interactive online games are just the beginning. A host of social networking sites, such as Facebook, My Space, and blogs, provide virtual journals and scrapbooks. Whether across town or separated by thousands of miles, many parents and children can now have real-time auditory, vocal, and visual interaction on a daily basis, if desired. The technology needed to support this form of virtual visitation is currently widely available and increasingly less expensive. Many households already have the basics: a computer with built-in webcam and microphone, and a video software program such as Skype, which can be downloaded for free.

PARALEGAL PRACTICE TIP

Provisions may be very basic, such as the following from a Connecticut case:

The Husband shall have "virtual visitation" with the children twice per week, on Tuesdays and Thursdays, from 6:00 p.m. to 7:00 p.m. and at such additional times as the parties may agree. To facilitate the virtual visitation each party shall forthwith purchase and install a video camera attachment and the related software for his or her computer.[45]

Recognizing its potential, some states, including Utah, Florida, Illinois, North Carolina, Texas and Wisconsin, have passed legislation authorizing judges to include virtual visitation provisions in court decrees. Courts in other states have begun on their own initiative to include **virtual visitation** provisions in the parenting provisions of their initial decrees without statutory authorization. The trend is most apparent in the context of relocation cases. For example, in the *McCoy* case in 2001, a New Jersey appellate court granted a mother permission to relocate from New Jersey to California with her nine-year-old disabled daughter over the objection of the child's father. The court praised the mother's "virtual visitation" proposal to develop an interactive website to facilitate the child's communication with her father as "creative and innovative." Through the use of camera-computer technology, the site would give the father and others the ability to communicate face-to-face with the daughter daily and to review her schoolwork and records on an ongoing basis.[46]

PARALEGAL PRACTICE TIP

To see the North Carolina Statute, visit *www.ncga.state.nc.us*. You can find a link to this site at *www.pearsonhighered.com/wilson* in the companion website material related to Chapter 8 under "Statutes."

Virtual visitation is a particularly valuable resource in cases involving parents residing in different nations or in international relocation requests. For example, in what was a leading-edge case in 1997, a New York court included the following provision in its order granting a mother's request to relocate to Saudi Arabia with her six-year-old son:

> . . .Respondent shall hire, at her expense, a computer consultant in both New York and Dhahran to select, purchase and set up compatible computer systems with laser printers in both Petitioner's residence in New York and in Adrian's new residence in Dhahran to enable petitioner and son to communicate on the dedicated phone line. In addition, Adrian's room shall have a telephone with answering machine also with a separate dedicated phone line for Petitioner and Adrian to utilize. In the order to be settled, Respondent shall propose a reasonable schedule of communication by telephone, internet and fax and shall provide proof that the aforesaid systems and telephone have been installed, are fully operational, and that the dedicated phone lines are in place.[47]

PARALEGAL PRACTICE TIP

When drafting documents relating to custody, consideration should be given to including virtual visitation provisions in parenting agreements for incorporation in court orders. A variety of techniques can be proposed that will allow parents and children who are physically separated to share information daily about what is happening in their respective lives, discuss problems, and work on projects or plans together.

Virtual visitation
communication between parents and children through the use of technology

Parenting Plans

A parenting plan is now a critical component of a child custody case. In some states, parents are encouraged to develop plans covering their children's remaining childhood years. In other states, they are required to do so. The court may waive the requirement in a limited number of cases, such as those involving a history of domestic violence. When required, if custody is a contested issue, each parent must submit a proposed custody implementation plan at trial. The court may issue an order that tracks the proposal of one or the other of the parties' plans in whole or part or may reject both and create its own order.

A primary goal of a parenting plan is to promote cooperative parenting and minimize disputes and continued hostility around parenting issues after dissolution of the marriage. Ideally, plans should reflect children's developmental needs at the time of the divorce and going forward into the future. By statute, the state of Washington has identified the following objectives of a parenting plan:

a. Provide for the child's physical care;
b. Maintain the child's emotional stability;
c. Provide for the child's changing needs as the child grows and matures, in a way that minimizes the need for future modifications to the permanent parenting plan;
d. Set forth the authority and responsibilities of each parent with respect to the child. . .;
e. Minimize the child's exposure to harmful parental conflict;
f. Encourage the parents,. . . to meet their responsibilities to their minor children through agreements in the permanent parenting plan, rather than by relying on judicial intervention; and
g. To otherwise protect the best interests of the child.[48]

The range of topics covered in plans is reflected in the Wisconsin Proposed Parenting Plan. The topics are similar to those contained in detailed child-related provisions of separation agreements. The essential differences are in process and focus rather than specific terms. The focus in a separation agreement is on contractual terms binding the adversarial parents with respect to each other. At least in spirit, a parenting plan is focused more on the children and on the importance of shared involvement and cooperation in meeting their ongoing needs.

Several states now make parenting plan formats available online, generally through court-sponsored websites. A number of computer programs also are available to help parties and counsel establish parenting schedules and courts to more easily and quickly review their nature and scope. Some programs generate color-coded calendar graphics to help parties and children visualize the schedule and plan ahead. These programs are especially useful in complex cases involving multiple children and frequent visitation.

Parent Education Programs

Parents struggling with their own needs, conflicts, and stress during divorce proceedings often forget that it is not all about them. Parenting programs are designed to sensitize parents to the needs and feelings of their children, who are frequently victims of their parents' anger, frustration, and bitterness.

Many states require parents who are getting divorced to complete a parent education program, and virtually all of the rest recommend it. Some states also recommend that the parties' children in a certain age range also participate. The programs for children are designed to help them cope with divorce and share their feelings with others in their age group. Courts make available information about approved program providers in pamphlets or Q&A sheets, and many do so online, including the names and locations of various programs by city and town. Some states grant waivers of participation in a limited number of circumstances, such as institutionalization or other unavailability of a party, chronic and severe abuse that negates safe parental communication, or when there are language barriers.

PARALEGAL PRACTICE TIP

To see an example of a motion to waive attendance at a parent education program, visit *www.lawlib. state.ma.us.* You can find a link to this site at *www.pearsonhighered. com/wilson* in the companion website material related to Chapter 8 under "Forms." (Massachusetts)

PARALEGAL PRACTICE TIP

To see an example of a "Parenting Education Program—Order, Certificate and Results" go to *www.jud. ct.gov.* (Connecticut) You can find a link to this site at *www.pearsonhighered.com/wilson* in the companion website material related to Chapter 8 under "Forms."

The primary purposes of parent education programs are to

- encourage parents to work cooperatively for the benefit of their children
- help children through the difficult period of divorce and separation
- reduce postdivorce litigation and court appearances

The curriculum of parent education programs varies from state to state and program to program, but commonly includes topics such as the following:

- the emotional effects of divorce or separation on parents and children
- what parents can do to help their children adjust
- harmful effects of parental conflict on children and how to avoid them
- communication and co-parenting skills
- developmental stages and needs of children
- factors that contribute to a child's healthy adjustment
- the function and value of parenting plans
- techniques of problem solving and conflict resolution

- warning signs that children are having problems
- community resources

In jurisdictions where participation in parent education programs is mandatory, failure to complete a program may have serious consequences. Among other options, the court may:

- refuse to move the case forward
- dismiss the case
- hold one or both parties in contempt

Modification of Custody Orders

At some time after the court issues its initial order, either parent may come to believe that a change in custody and/or visitation is warranted. Customarily, courts will not allow the parents to agree in advance to self-executing grounds for modification, as custody decisions are supposed to be based on a determination of the best interests of the child at the time of the modification. However, occasionally parties accomplish changes informally, and this may work as long as the parties are in agreement. However, an informal approach can be a problem if child support is an issue or if one of the parties later files for contempt, claiming he or she never agreed to a change.

The usual process for obtaining a modification involves filing a Motion (Petition/Complaint) for Modification of Custody (commonly accompanied by an affidavit in support of the Motion) in the court that has continuing jurisdiction, followed by service of notice on the other party, possible filing of an affidavit in opposition to the Motion by the other party, and then a hearing before the court, at which time the parties each have an opportunity to testify, call witnesses, and present documentation in support of their respective positions.

PARALEGAL PRACTICE TIP

To see an example of a Motion for Modification that can be used to request modifications in both custody and support in Connecticut, visit *www.jud.ct.gov*. You can find a link to this site at *www.pearsonhighered.com/wilson* in the companion website material related to Chapter 8 under "Forms."

A party seeking to modify a custody order generally must show that:

- there has been a substantial and material change of circumstances that affects the child's welfare,
- the change has occurred since entry of the decree and was not foreseeable,
- the change warrants a modification in custody, and
- the change will be in the child's best interests.

PARALEGAL PRACTICE TIP

To learn more about the Uniform Marriage and Divorce Act, visit *www.ncusl.org*. You can find a link to this site at *www.pearsonhighered.com/wilson* in the companion website material related to Chapter 8 under "Resources."

Although theoretically a Motion for Modification can be brought whenever a substantial change occurs that impacts the child's best interests, in states that have adopted the Uniform Marriage and Divorce Act (UMDA),[49] absent an emergency, a modification cannot be sought for at least two years from the date the decree or prior order was issued. The rationale for the rule is that children need stability in their lives, and changes in primary custody should be discouraged because they disrupt the child's life.

Motions will usually be granted if the parties agree to the modification; if it is apparent that an initial allocation of parental rights and responsibilities is not working; if there is clear and convincing evidence that the child's present environment is harming his or her physical, mental, or emotional health; or if the court finds that there is repeated, intentional, and unwarranted interference by one parent with the rights and responsibilities of the other parent. Commonly, the request for modification relates to a change in the circumstances of the custodial parent, but occasionally it results from a change in the noncustodial parent's circumstances that significantly alters his or her relative fitness and/or availability as a parent. Case 8.2 illustrates a situation in which changes had occurred in the lives of both parents.

CASE **8.2** *Jackson v. Jackson,* 2004 WY 99, 96 P.3d 21 (Wyo. 2004)

DISCUSSION OF THE CASE

In this case, the mother had been awarded primary physical custody of the parties' two children at the time of divorce. From September to December 2002, the mother changed jobs five times. In February 2003, after being unemployed for over two months, she enrolled in cosmetology school. She subsequently dropped out of that program and enrolled in a different school a few months later. While she was at school the children attended day care.

During essentially the same time period, the father remained in the town where he had been living and continued working for a cable company. He made significant improvements in his lifestyle, including quitting drinking and smoking, and ended his association with "bad influences." He received a promotion at work and was able to provide health insurance for the children. He also developed a stable relationship with a woman whom he married shortly before the hearing on his request for modification of custody.

The court found that the balance had shifted in favor of the father and awarded him primary physical custody of the children. The Wyoming Supreme Court affirmed the change.

SIDEBAR

Read the case available on the companion website. Do you agree with the court's decision? Explain your response.

PARALEGAL PRACTICE TIP

The opinion in the *Jackson* case is available at *www.pearsonhighered.com/wilson* in the companion website material related to Chapter 8 under "Cases" and in the Case Resources Section of the MyLegalStudiesLab.

RELOCATIONS

Inevitably following divorce, at least one of the parents establishes a new place of residence. In today's mobile world, this initial relocation is often the first of several moves due to job changes, remarriages, economic conditions, extended family needs, and other life changes. Although courts have held that a parent has a constitutional right to travel and cannot be required to live in a particular place,[50] a problem often arises when a custodial parent wants to relocate with a minor child against the wishes of the noncustodial parent.

PARALEGAL PRACTICE TIP

To see an example of a "Notice of Intent to Move," visit *http://courts.mt.gov.* You can find a link to this site at *www.pearsonhighered.com/wilson* in the companion website material for Chapter 8 under "Forms."

Although the constitutional right to travel is customarily raised in interstate cases, the Montana Supreme Court addressed a situation in which a trial court had amended a parenting plan to make a father primary custodial parent on the grounds that the mother should be the one to pay the price for reduced parental contact due to her moving a substantial distance within the state of Montana. The state's high court reversed. "It is difficult to conceive that the right to travel protected by the United States Constitution does not include a right to freely travel within each of the states. The right to travel between states would mean little if a person did not also have the right to travel within a state after crossing its borders. We hold, therefore, that the right to travel guaranteed by the United States Constitution includes the right to travel within Montana." *Griffen v. Plaisted-Harmon*, 2009 MT 169, 350 Mont. 489 (2009).

Relocation cases present a particular challenge for the courts, as they involve seemingly "irreconcilable conflicts in which the custodial parent's interest in building a new life with the children is often pitted against the noncustodial parent's interest in maintaining a close relationship with the children." They implicate "two legitimate interests—the custodial parent's interest in making unfettered decisions for the benefit of the new nuclear family and the noncustodial parent's interest in maintaining a close bond with the children."[51] The balancing act the court must perform occurs under the umbrella of the best interests of the child. The trend in family law is "generally to allow the residential parent to move away with the child so long as satisfactory alternative parenting time arrangements with the nonresidential parent can be achieved and there are no bad faith motives for the geographical move."[52]

States usually identify by statute and/or case law the factors to be considered in relocation cases. Although the child's best interests are paramount, courts will commonly also assess the following:

- Each party's reasons for seeking or opposing the move;
- The nature, extent, duration, and quality of the relationship of each parent and other significant persons with the child;
- The age, developmental stage, and needs of the child;
- The child's preference;
- The current employment and economic circumstances of each parent;
- The extent to which the objecting parent has fulfilled his or her financial obligations to the other parent and the child;
- Any history of substance abuse or violence by either parent;
- The feasibility of preserving the relationship between the noncustodial parent and the child through suitable visitation arrangements; and
- The degree to which the custodial parent's and the child's life may be enhanced economically, socially, emotionally, and educationally by the move.

Although the trend is toward allowing relocation and basic continuity in care, there is no uniform position among the states. Approaches run the gamut. In California, the custodial parent has a presumptive right to relocate with a minor child, subject to a court restraining a change on the ground that it would prejudice the rights or welfare of the child. In Minnesota, if a custodial parent seeks to move permanently to another state with the minor children over the noncustodial parent's objection, an evidentiary hearing is not required absent a prima facie case of endangerment to the child or a showing that the move was intended to deprive the noncustodial parent of visitation. The relevant Missouri statute presently provides that a person entitled to custody of a child shall not relocate the residence of the child for a period of more than ninety days except upon order of the court or with the written consent of the parties with custody or visitation rights. The applicable Colorado statute reflects a compromise approach in which the geographical extent of the relocation is critical. In determining whether to grant a custodial parent's relocation motion, the paramount concern is the best interests of the child. In effect, a parent may be forced to choose between custody and relocation.[53]

Enforcement of Custody and Visitation Orders

When a parent fails to comply with court-ordered custody and visitation provisions, the other parent may be forced to return to court to enforce the order. The parent in violation may be found in contempt and be ordered to pay a fine, go to jail, or both. In especially egregious cases, the court may deny custodial rights or impose a plan for supervised visitation.

PARALEGAL PRACTICE TIP

To see an example of an Affidavit for Citation for Contempt of Court (for use by noncustodial parent), visit *www.judicial.state.sc.us/forms.* (South Carolina) A link to this site can be found at *www.pearsonhighered.com/wilson* in the companion website material for Chapter 8 under "Forms."

Two especially difficult situations in this context occur when:

1. A parent who is failing to pay court-ordered child support insists on exercising his or her visitation rights. It is difficult for an attorney to explain to a client who is not receiving child support payments ordered by the court that he or she cannot refuse visitation and must comply with the court's order regarding custody and visitation. However unfair it may seem, the two orders are independent of one another, and each party's remedy is to pursue enforcement relief through the court.
2. A parent harbors a strong belief that the other parent is sexually abusing the child and refuses visitation or, in the extreme, flees with the child or conceals the minor's whereabouts, as in the high-profile case of Dr. Elizabeth Morgan, who at one point was incarcerated for more than two years for contempt of court because she refused to produce her daughter based on her fears of further abuse.[54]

Third Parties in the Custody Context

Thus far in this chapter it may have seemed as if custody issues occur only in traditional families in the context of divorces between married biological or adoptive parents. However, a basic theme of this text is that the "traditional American family" has become the exception rather than the rule. Approximately one-third of families in this country have no father living in the home (in some urban areas, the figure is considerably higher). Nearly 14 million children live with parties other than their parents, and that number continues to grow.[55] We have more stepparents than ever before. We have same-sex marriage, civil unions, and domestic partnerships. We have surrogate parents, co-parents, and **psychological parents,** among other parental variations. Although a custody action commonly is part of

PARALEGAL PRACTICE TIP

The Colorado relocation statute can be seen at *www.pearsonhighered. com/wilson* in the companion website material related to Chapter 8 under "Statutes."

PARALEGAL PRACTICE TIP

To see an example of a Petition for Enforcement of Custody/Visitation, visit *http://www.nycourts.gov/forms.* You can find a link to this site at *www.pearsonhighered.com/wilson* in the companion website material for Chapter 8 under "Forms."

PARALEGAL PRACTICE TIP

To see an example of a Petition for Third Party Visitation, visit *www.courts. delaware.gov.* A link to this site can be found at *www.pearsonhighered.com/ wilson* in the companion website material for Chapter 8 under "Forms."

psychological parent
the individual who has the strongest "parental" bond with the child, who has provided the most significant care for the child in quality and quantity, and whom the child often regards as the "parent"

an action for divorce or legal separation, it may be brought by an unmarried parent or by a third party in a separate action, such as a Complaint for Custody or for Grandparent Visitation. Who are these individuals and what rights, if any, do or should they have?

"Third parties" generally fall into a limited number of categories:

- unmarried fathers whose legal status as parents is not established
- step-parents
- grandparents
- co-parents
- others, such as foster parents or extended-family members

There are two primary and competing views regarding the custodial and visitation rights of third parties:

1. One school of thought holds that a biological parent has a presumptive right to custody of his or her child. This approach focuses on the fundamental rights of a fit parent to the care, custody, and control of his or her children and to direct the upbringing and education of those children.
2. The other school of thought believes it is in the best interests of a child to be placed in the custody of whichever adult will provide the healthiest and most stable environment. This approach focuses on the needs of the child and the nature and strength of the emotional bond between the child and the third party.

When a third party seeks custody or visitation rights, the court must engage in a two-part inquiry:

1. Does the third party have standing to seek custody or visitation?
2. If the third party does have standing, would an award to that party be in the best interest of the child?

STANDING

Standing
an individual's right to bring a matter before the court and seek relief based on a claim that he or she has a stake in the outcome of the case

Equitable parenthood
parenthood established on the basis of equitable principles of fairness rather than on biological connection

Standing is a jurisdictional concept that refers to an individual's right to bring a matter before the court and seek relief based on a claim that he or she has a stake in the outcome of the case. Standing is usually based on statute (see Exhibits 8.4 and 8.5) but may be grounded in case law. Hawaii has one of the most liberal rules with respect to third-party standing to seek custody and visitation, extending it to "persons other than the father or mother whenever the award serves the best interests of the child."[56] Legislatures and the courts have relied on a variety of theories of **equitable parenthood** to enable third parties to be granted rights to custody, visitation, and guardianship. The ALI Principles give the legal parents priority if they are able to care for their children, but state that custody ought to be available to individuals in addition to biological parents whose continued caregiving is presumed beneficial to a child. Specifically included are adults who have functioned in good faith as parents, believing they were legal parents;

parents by estoppel; and *de facto* **parents**. Some jurisdictions recognize the concept of the "psychological parent," the individual who has the strongest "parental" bond with the child, who has provided the most significant care for the child in quality and quantity, and whom the child often regards as the "parent." Some states extend standing to third parties when the child has been in their custody for a certain minimum period. In extreme cases involving abuse and neglect, the state has third-party standing to seek custody of a child.[57]

Parent by estoppel
an individual who has functioned as a parent with the approval of the legal parents

De facto **parent**
an individual who performs a caretaking role without compensation for an extended period, knowing he or she is not a child's legal parent, often with the consent of the legal parents

EXHIBIT 8.4 Kentucky Statute KRS § 403.270 (2006) Pertaining to Custody Issues—Best Interests of Child Shall Determine—Joint Custody Permitted—De Facto Custodian

FROM THE STATUTE

(1) (a) As used in this chapter and KRS 405.020, unless the context requires otherwise, "de facto custodian" means a person who has been shown by clear and convincing evidence to have been the primary caregiver for, and financial supporter of, a child who has resided with the person for a period of six (6) months or more if the child is under three (3) years of age and for a period of one (1) year or more if the child is three (3) years or older or has been placed by the Department for Community Based Services. . . .

   (b) A person shall not be a de facto custodian until a court determines by clear and convincing evidence that the person meets the definition of de facto custodian established in paragraph (a) of this subsection. Once a court determines that a person meets the definition of de facto custodian, the court shall give the person the same standing in custody matters that is given to each parent under this section. . . .

Unmarried Fathers

Over the last four decades, increasing numbers of children have been born out of wedlock or to married women as a result of extramarital affairs. As a result, fathers might be legal fathers, biological fathers, or psychosocial/de facto fathers. Some fathers are "thwarted" fathers who are unaware they even are fathers or have been deceived as to their children's existence. They have, for all practical purposes, become third parties.

PARALEGAL PRACTICE TIP

A review of case law based on both federal and state statutes reveals that courts are far more ready to establish parentage of unmarried fathers for purposes of ordering child support than for purposes of establishing parental rights.

In theory, unmarried fathers should have the same rights and obligations as married fathers and be entitled to petition the court for custody or visitation. However, that is not always the case. Biological fathers have some constitutionally protected rights to establish a connection with their offspring, but those rights do not necessarily extend to fathers who knowingly fail to acknowledge paternity in a timely manner.[58] The states vary in their approach to such situations, ranging from establishing a fixed window within which fathers must establish paternity to an approach tailored to the facts of individual cases, in hopes of reaching a fair result in each instance. The law also may impose obligations and extend rights to men who acknowledge paternity but who are ultimately determined to not be the biological father of a child. Under the Welfare Reform Act of 1996, with limited exceptions states are required to treat acknowledgments of paternity signed by mothers and "putative" fathers as establishing legal paternity. Issues related to such situations, including the establishment of putative father registries, are discussed more fully in Chapters 7 and 14.

Step-Parents

It is estimated that one in every four children will live with a step-parent before reaching the age of majority.[59] Although step-parents have become part of American family life and are often as important in children's lives as (or even more important than) biological or legal parents, the law is unclear and inconsistent with respect to their rights and obligations. The majority view is that a step-parent's rights flow from marriage to the child's parent and do not survive dissolution of that marriage. A minority of states impose financial child support obligations on step-parents upon divorce in limited circumstances, such as when the step-parent voluntarily assumed a parental obligation to the child while married to the child's mother.[60] Step-parents who want to continue their relationship with their step-children often face considerable obstacles. Although a limited number of states afford them standing to petition for custody and visitation in some circumstances (see Exhibit 8.5), many do not.

Absent statutory authority, courts sometimes struggle to find legal theories to support the good-faith desires of step-parents to continue to play a meaningful role in the lives of children they have lived with and cared for. Equitable estoppel, *de facto* parenthood, the concept of the psychological parent, and the doctrine of *in loco parentis* have each been utilized on a limited basis to recognize a step-parent's history of parenting a child who is "not their own."[61] (See Case 8.3.)

CASE **8.3** *McAllister v. McAllister,* 2010 ND 40, 779 N.W.2d 652 (2010)

PARALEGAL PRACTICE TIP

The *McAllister* opinion is available at *www.pearsonhighered.com/wilson* in the companion website material related to Chapter 8 under "Cases" and in the Case Resources Section of the MyLegalStudiesLab.

DISCUSSION OF THE CASE

In this case, the North Dakota Supreme Court upheld a lower court order finding that a stepfather, Mark, was a "psychological parent" to his stepchild and that exceptional circumstances existed justifying granting him reasonable visitation rights under North Dakota law. Mark had married the child's mother, Robin, in 2004. Robin had a son, E.M., born in 2002, and fathered by another man whose parental rights had not been terminated. Mark and Robin subsequently had two children. The parties raised E.M. together until 2008, when Robin left and moved in with a third man with whom she had had a prior relationship. She took E.M. with her and left the other two children with Mark. It was not until she left that Robin told E.M. that Mark was not his biological father. Mark testified that he loved E.M. as he did his two biological children, had been there for the child essentially since birth, and functioned as a parent to the child, who called him "dad" or "daddy." The custody investigator found that E.M. considered Mark his father and she was confident that Mark could consistently maintain a strong bond with the child. The investigator did not find Robin unfit but, given a history of depression, questioned her ability to consistently provide a strong, nurturing relationship to her son. She testified that it was important for E.M. to maintain regular contact with both Robin and Mark because "that's his family." In its findings, the court described Mark's role in E.M.'s life as that of a psychological parent who provides a child's daily care, develops a close bond to the child, and is the one a child looks to for love, guidance, and security. Mark had requested decision-making and primary residential responsibility. He

(Continued)

was granted "stepfather visitation" every other weekend, every Thursday, two weeks in the summer, and part of Christmas Day.

SIDEBAR

Do you agree with the outcome in this case? In your opinion should step-parents have standing to seek custodial rights with respect to their step-children? Explain your response.

EXHIBIT 8.5 Illinois Statute 750 ILCS 5/601(b)(3) (2006) Pertaining to Jurisdiction; Commencement of [Custody] Proceeding

FROM THE STATUTE

(b) A child custody proceeding is commenced in the court: . . .

(3) by a stepparent, by filing a petition, if all of the following circumstances are met:

A. the child is at least 12 years old;

B. the custodial parent and stepparent were married for at least 5 years during which the child resided with the parent and stepparent;

C. the custodial parent is deceased or is disabled and cannot perform the duties of a parent to the child;

D. the stepparent provided for the care, control, and welfare of the child prior to the initiation of custody proceedings;

E. the child wishes to live with the stepparent; and

F. it is alleged to be in the best interests and welfare of the child to live with the stepparent as provided in Section 602 of this Act [750 ILCS 5/602].

PARALEGAL PRACTICE TIP

A federal law called the Service Members Civil Relief Act[62] is designed to protect military personnel on active duty by staying civil court actions or administrative proceedings during periods of military activation. Although child custody proceedings are civil in nature, some family court judges have held that in custody actions, state law must trump federal law. They argue that custody disputes are not comparable to civil property disputes, and such cases must proceed in the best interests of children. In effect, this means that parents may be forced to decide between custody and service to the country, unless they can regain custody once they are no longer deployed.

Courts sometimes find ways to accomplish a desired end even if it stretches basic legal principles. For example, in a 2002 Kansas case, the Supreme Court of Kansas affirmed a lower court's denial of a noncustodial mother's motion for temporary custody for a one-year period, during which the custodial father would be on a tour of duty in Korea and would be unable to take his current wife and children with him. The children had been living with the father and his new wife, the children's step-mother, for four years. The mother claimed that under the parental preference doctrine, she should be granted custody during the father's extended absence. The father argued that the children had resided with him and their step-mother for an extended period, during which they had thrived and established a strong bond with their step-mother. The court denied the mother's motion for a temporary one-year change in custody stating that it was in the children's best interests to remain in the primary residential custody of the father. The court essentially reasoned that the custody contest was between the mother and the father, not the mother and the step-mother, and that cases involving military families must be decided on a case-by-case basis.[63]

PARALEGAL PRACTICE TIP

To see an example of a Petition for Grandparent Visitation used in New Hampshire, visit *www.courts.state. nh.us*. A link to this site can be found at *www.pearsonhighered. com/wilson* in the companion website material for Chapter 8 under "Forms."

Grandparents

In 2009, 7.8 million children (11.8% of all children in the country) were living in households with at least one grandparent present.[64] Although under common law grandparents had no right of access to their grandchildren, legislatures in every state now have provided standing for grandparents to petition for custody and/or visitation rights under certain circumstances.[65]

In most states grandparents will have standing only under certain limited conditions, such as when the child's parents never married, the parents are divorced, one or both of the parents have died, or the parental rights of one or both of the parents have been terminated. Most states also provide that in order to have standing, there must have been a significant preexisting relationship between the child and the grandparents.

Once a grandparent establishes standing to seek visitation over the objection of a parent, he or she must satisfy the standard set out by the state for resolving visitation disputes between legal parents and grandparents. Based on the Supreme Court's decision in *Troxel v. Granville* (see Case 8.4), the grandparent must establish something more than that visitation would be in the child's best interest. A number of states interpreting *Troxel* have held that the courts must give presumptive validity to a fit parent's decision, and in order to rebut that presumption, the grandparents must show by a preponderance of the evidence that failure to grant visitation to the grandparents will cause the child significant harm by adversely affecting his or her health, safety, and welfare.[66]

CASE **8.4** *Troxel v. Granville,* 530 U.S. 57, 120 S. Ct. 2054, 147 L. Ed. 2d 49 (2000)

PARALEGAL PRACTICE TIP

The lengthy and convoluted decision in this case can be accessed in its entirety at *www.pearsonhighered.com/wilson* in the companion website material related to Chapter 8 under "Cases" and in the Case Resources Section of the MyLegalStudiesLab.

DISCUSSION OF THE CASE

This decision represents one of the rare instances in which the federal government has intervened in a family law matter traditionally left to regulation by the states. "The opinion marks an evolution in parental autonomy protection. . . . By balancing the State's interest in protecting the child with the parent's interest in making child-rearing decisions free from unnecessary State interference, the Court no longer accords blind unquestioning deference to the decisions of presumptively fit parents."[67] At issue in the case was the state of Washington's third-party visitation statute that provided "Any person may petition the court for visitation rights at any time including but not limited to, custody proceedings." The U.S. Supreme Court described this language as being "breathtakingly broad." The case involved the two minor daughters of an unmarried couple, Tommie Granville and Brad Troxel, whose relationship ended in 1991. Brad committed suicide in 1993, but before doing so had established a relationship between his daughters and his parents. After the father's death, the mother had not entirely denied the grandparents visitation but wanted to limit it and not permit any overnight visits. The grandparents petitioned to continue their relationship with the children on a more extensive basis than the mother was willing to allow. On the mother's second appeal of a lower court's ruling allowing the visitation, the appeals court reversed the lower court's order on the grounds that the grandparents lacked standing to petition for visitation absent a pending custody action. The Washington Supreme Court reviewed the case at the request of the grandparents. It held that the Troxels did have standing but that visitation should not be ordered over the mother's objection, as such an

(Continued)

action would infringe on the mother's fundamental right to parent her children as she sees fit. The grandparents then sought certiorari and the U.S. Supreme Court agreed to hear the case. The Court subsequently held that the statute was unconstitutional as applied to the facts of the case.

In a decision that many say raises as many questions as it answers, the Court at the least held the following:

- Parents have a fundamental liberty interest in the care, custody, and control of their children, which previously has been deemed by the Court to be protected by the Due Process Clause of the Fourteenth Amendment. The Washington statute was held to deprive the mother of this liberty interest without due process of law.
- Given this liberty interest, any decision made by a fit parent should be given "special weight." There was no allegation that the mother in this case was unfit, yet the Washington statute contained no requirement that her decision be given any weight whatsoever.
- Courts should presume that a fit parent will act in his or her child's best interest. The Court did not indicate what kind of evidence is required to overcome this presumption.
- The courts are not free to simply substitute their view of what is in a child's best interest for that of the parent. The Washington statute placed the best interest determination solely in the hands of the judge rather than the parents.

The nine-justice court was divided four/two/three as to the specifics of the case. The majority opinion, written by Justice O'Connor was joined by Justices Rehnquist, Ginsburg, and Breyer. Separate concurring opinions were written by Justices Souter and Thomas. Dissenting opinions were written by Justices Stevens, Scalia, and Kennedy.

SIDEBAR

Do you think grandparents should be granted visitation when it is against the wishes of the children's parent(s)?

Paralegal **Application 8.5**

You Be the Judge

Fact Pattern

In this 2005 case, contrary to the custody evaluator's recommendation, an Oregon court awarded custody to a father over a maternal grandmother with whom the children had lived, with his consent, for virtually their entire lives. The record indicated that during their marriage, the mother and father used illegal drugs and the father used alcohol. The father had been emotionally and physically abusive and had shown no interest in caring for the children. He had been convicted of two felonies and three misdemeanors and had been incarcerated on four occasions for periods ranging from thirty days to eighteen months. After his most recent release in 2002, the father had additional contact with the police and was convicted of improperly using 911 while he was intoxicated. While in prison and following his release, he completed counseling and treatment programs focusing on domestic violence, anger management, parenting, drugs and alcohol, and Bible studies. He earned his GED and had completed two terms at a community college. Although he had a job after his release from prison, he had been laid off for approximately a year prior to the custody trial. He has been diagnosed with attention deficit hyperactivity disorder (ADHD) and "possible alcohol dependency." For the three years prior to the trial, he had been living with a woman and her four children between the ages of five and thirteen; they were planning to marry. On most weekdays, the

(Continued)

child's mother was living at the grandmother's. She also had been convicted of crimes in the past, including forgery and theft, and was undergoing drug counseling at the time of trial. Her coping skills were described as poor. The father and grandmother had not gotten along well over the years, but the father told the court he wanted to improve that situation and maintain contact between the children and their grandmother on a regular basis.

In Oregon, to rebut the presumption that a legal parent's objection to custody or visitation by a grandparent is in the child's best interests, the court may consider factors including, but not limited to, the following:

A. The legal parent is unwilling or unable to care adequately for the child.
B. The petitioner is or recently has been the child's primary caretaker.
C. Circumstances detrimental to the child exist if relief is denied.

D. The legal parent fostered or consented to the relationship between the child and the petitioner.
E. The legal parent has unreasonably denied or limited contact between the child and the petitioner.

Sidebar

In light of the applicable statute, how would you have decided this case? Read the opinion in *Dennis v. Dennis,* 199 Ore. App. 90, 110 P.3d 607 (2005) and see if you and the appeals court reached the same conclusion.

PARALEGAL PRACTICE TIP

The opinion in the *Dennis* case can be accessed at *www.pearson-highered.com/wilson* in the companion website material related to Chapter 8 under "Cases" and in the Case Resources Section of the MyLegalStudiesLab.

Co-Parents

Co-parent
a person who is engaged in a nonmarital relationship with the legal parent of a child and who regards himself or herself as a parent rather than as a legal stranger to the child

A **co-parent** is a person who is engaged in a nonmarital relationship with the legal parent of a child and who regards himself or herself as a parent rather than as a legal stranger to the child. The perception is usually based on a mutual intent to parent a child together, the performance of a variety of caretaking functions, and the provision of some degree of financial support for the child for an extended period of time. As with step-parents, co-parents have relied on a variety of legal constructs in an effort to maintain a relationship with a child they have helped to raise after the relationship with the child's legal parent has terminated.

PARALEGAL PRACTICE TIP

Courts addressing these cases typically look at the following factors articulated in *Holtzman v. Knott (In re H.S.H.–K)* 193 Wis.2d 649, 533 N.W.2d 419 (1995):

• The relationship existed with the consent of or was fostered by the biological or adoptive parent;
• The parties lived in the same household;
• The petitioner assumed the obligations of care, custody, education, and development of the child without accepting compensation;
• The petitioner functioned in the parental role long enough to create a bonded and dependent relationship with the child that was parental in nature.

Decisions are mixed in cases involving same-sex co-parents in particular. (See related discussion in Chapter 7.) Many states deny them "parental" status but may afford them third-party standing as persons such as grandparents and step-parents who bear a significant relationship to the child. Other courts claim that recognizing co-parents' rights in the absence of statute, precedent, or well-established legal principle constitutes judicial lawmaking that denigrates fundamental parental rights and infringes on the province of the legislature. Despite such reservations, as this area of the law evolves, co-parents are likely to see an expansion of their rights, not only to visitation, but also to custody. (See Case 8.5.)

CASE 8.5 *Mullins v. Picklesmeier,* 317 S.W.3d 569 (Ky. 2010)

DISCUSSION OF THE CASE

In this case, the Kentucky Supreme Court considered the appeal of a woman seeking joint custody of a child, Zachary, conceived through artificial insemination and born to her former same-sex partner. Phyllis Picklesmeier and Arminta Mullins had lived together as a couple for nearly five years. During that time they decided they wanted to have a baby. Together they found a sperm donor and Mullins was then artificially inseminated and became pregnant. Zachary was born in May 2005. Although the parties had a troubled relationship they continued with their plan to raise the child as a family and did so until their relationship ended and Arminta allegedly refused to allow Phyllis to visit Zachary. A series of motions ensued, with Phyllis seeking joint care, custody and control of Zachary and requesting to be his primary residential custodian, and Arminta opposing those efforts.

Under Kentucky law, there were basically two routes available to Phyllis to obtain standing to seek custody:

1. She could try to establish standing as a *de facto* custodian. To qualify as a *de facto* custodian in Kentucky, one must be "the primary caregiver for, and financial supporter of, a child who has resided with the person for a period of six (6) months or more if the child is under three years of age." The nonparent must "literally stand in the place of the natural parent." Parenting alongside the natural parent does not meet the standard. Since Phyllis lacked *de facto* status, she could not pursue custody on that ground.

2. The court reaffirmed the constitutionally protected right of parents to raise, care for, and control their own children. To prevail, a nonparent pursuing custody must establish one of two exceptions to a parent's superior right to custody:

   a. The parent is shown by clear and convincing evidence to be an unfit custodian, or

   b. The parent has waived his or her superior right to custody by clear and convincing evidence.

The Kentucky Supreme Court affirmed the Court of Appeals' and trial court's determination that Phyllis did not qualify as a *de facto* custodian even though the parties had previously obtained an agreed judgment to that effect (based on a joint false allegation by the parties that Phyllis satisfied the statutory requirements). However, it reversed the Court of Appeals and reinstated the trial court's finding that Arminta had waived her superior right to custody, thereby giving Phyllis standing to seek custody.

The state's high court accepted the trial court's findings that Arminta had waived her superior right to custody by acknowledging on a continuous basis that Phyllis was a parent to the child. The parties had decided jointly to start a family and they had

(Continued)

selected a sperm donor based on Phyllis's characteristics. Zachary was given a hyphenated surname combining the parties' last names, and that name appeared on the child's birth certificate. Phyllis was present at the insemination, during the difficult pregnancy, and at the delivery, and cared for the baby while he remained in the neonatal unit postbirth. They functioned as a family unit for more than a year and for a few months after the parties separated. Zachary looked to both of the parties as parents and referred to Phyllis as "momma" and Arminta as "mommy." It was undisputed that Arminta had fostered and facilitated an emotional and psychological bond between Phyllis and the child and that Phyllis had provided for the child's care and support when the parties lived together and after they separated. Even though it was eventually found to be invalid, the parties' attempt to enter a formal written agreement granting Phyllis custody status was further evidence of Arminta's waiver.

The Court distinguished Phyllis from a grandparent, babysitter, or friend who watches a child for a parent but is never intended to be doing so in the capacity of a "parent." Based on the facts of this case, the Kentucky Supreme Court held that there was substantial clear and convincing evidence to support the trial court's finding that Arminta had waived her superior custody rights for the purpose of co-parenting Zachary with Phyllis as joint custodians.

SIDEBAR

Do you agree with the outcome in this case? Why? The dissent asserts that the majority ruling is precariously close to running afoul of the U.S. Supreme Court's decision in *Troxel* by infringing on the fundamental right of parents to make childrearing decisions. Do you agree? Explain your response.

PARALEGAL PRACTICE TIP

Third-party cases involving nonparents are heavily fact-based. As between an unrelated nonparent and a biological parent, the parent will usually have the superior right to custody unless the nonparent is able to establish that the parent has relinquished that right due to surrender, abandonment, neglect, unfitness, or some other "extraordinary circumstance," which may include an involuntary disruption of custody over an extended period of time. See, e.g., *Holmes v. Glover*, 2009 NY Slip Op 9228, 68 A.D.3d 868, 890 N.Y.S.2d 629 (2009).

Others

Occasionally the third party is someone such as a foster parent, aunt or uncle, or friend of the family who has established a parentlike relationship with a child. These cases tend to particularly rely on the psychological parent doctrine. Courts in several states have recognized the importance of a psychological bond between a child and a third party. As the Pennsylvania Superior Court has put it:

> . . . the need to guard the family from intrusions by third parties and to protect the rights of the natural parent must be tempered by the paramount need to protect the child's best interest. Thus, while it is presumed that a child's best interest is served by maintaining the family's privacy and autonomy, that presumption must give way where the child has established strong psychological bonds with a person who, although not a biological parent, has lived with the child and provided care, nurture, and affection, assuming in the child's eye a stature like that of a parent. Where such a relationship is shown, our courts recognize that the child's best interest requires that the third party be granted standing so as to have the opportunity to litigate fully the issue of whether that relationship should be maintained even over a natural parent's objections.[68]

New Jersey has established that when there is a conflict between a legal parent and a psychological parent, the case will be decided as if it involved two legal parents and the standard to be applied is the best interest of the child.[69]

Who Speaks for the Child in Custody Matters?

When minor children are involved in a legal matter, the law generally presumes that their interests will be represented by their parents, guardians, or others acting **in loco parentis** (Latin: in the place of a parent) on their behalf. Until children have the knowledge and maturity to act on their own, parents act and speak for them in virtually all contexts.[70] In custody cases, however, parents are often so wrapped up in their own concerns that they lose sight of their children's interests.

In loco parentis
taking on some or all of the responsibilities of a parent

A guardian *ad litem* (GAL) is a neutral evaluator appointed by the court (often at the request of one or both of the parents) to attend to the interests of the children whose custody is in dispute (although GALs may be appointed in any matter involving children). Depending on the state, the guardian may be an attorney, a licensed social worker, a psychologist, or, in some instances, a volunteer trained and appointed by the court to assist with child-related issues.

PARALEGAL PRACTICE TIP

To see an example of an Order Appointing Guardian Ad Litem on Behalf of Minor in the state of Washington, visit *www.courts.wa.gov/forms*. A link to this site can be found at *www.pearsonhighered.com/wilson* in the companion website material related to Chapter 8 under "Forms."

PARALEGAL PRACTICE TIP

Sometimes parties will make an effort to keep GAL costs down by completing comprehensive questionnaires, drafting position summaries, and encouraging the GAL to focus on particular areas relevant to the case.

The primary role of the GAL is to objectively examine the child's situation as fully as possible, with special attention to the nature and quality of the child's relationship with each parent. At a minimum, the GAL usually will visit the parties' homes and interview each of the parents, the children, and any other individuals who may be able to contribute helpful information, such as schoolteachers, counselors, neighbors, or members of the clergy.

The GAL will present the court with his or her opinion in a written report as to the needs of the children, the strengths and weaknesses of each party as a parent, and the course of action most likely to serve the best interests of the children. The court considers, but is not necessarily bound by, the GAL's report, and the parties may cross-examine the GAL on issues related to the report and the basis for the recommendations made. The cost of the GAL is usually fully paid or heavily subsidized by one or both of the parties. However, the GAL is not intended to represent the interests of either of the parties, nor is the GAL technically an advocate for the child unless so designated by the state and/or the court. There are those who regard this as a flaw in the process and who believe that in especially complex cases involving parental manipulation, concealing of information, or allegations of abuse or parental unfitness, an attorney should be appointed to represent the child. The "child ought to be a player and not the football."[71]

PARALEGAL PRACTICE TIP

It is often difficult for clients who are convinced that their position is the only valid position, that the results of a custody evaluation or the content of a GAL's report may not support their perspective in whole or part. Attorneys often need to prepare their clients carefully for both the custody evaluation process and its potential consequences.

The court may assign or approve additional responsibilities for a GAL as well. For example, a Wisconsin court approved a provision in a marital settlement agreement (later rejected by the mother) that a GAL and a family counselor would have the right to break any impasse between the parties regarding decisions pertaining to their son's schooling.[72] In a Massachusetts case, a trial court judge provided in the parties' judgment of divorce that, in the event of a dispute concerning whether or not a particular religious belief or practice is harmful to the children, a GAL named by the court would be retained at the expense of the parties to investigate and evaluate the dispute.[73]

Because of the complexity of custody decisions, the courts may look to multiple resources for guidance over and above the GAL. Customarily, when custody is at issue on a contested or uncontested basis, the parties will be required to meet with a representative of a family services division located right at the courthouse. Family service personnel are usually not attorneys, but they generally are individuals with strong backgrounds in social work and developmental psychology who are trained in working through the maze created by disputing adults to come up with custody recommendations for the court. Although their recommendations are not binding, they are usually accorded considerable respect by judges.

Another important resource for children and the courts in every state is the CASA Program. **CASA (Court Appointed Special Advocates)** is an organization that trains court-appointed volunteer advocates to work one-on-one with abused and endangered children. Much like GALs, CASA volunteers gather information in child abuse and neglect cases, assess each child's situation, and make objective recommendations to the court concerning the environment that will best ensure a particular child's safety and well-being.

CASA Program

a national program that trains court-appointed volunteer advocates to work one-on-one with abused and endangered children; CASA volunteers provide objective recommendations to the court concerning the environment that will best ensure a particular child's safety and well-being. Although CASA has nearly 1,000 programs across the country and a presence in every state, it is not an available resource in every county

PARALEGAL PRACTICE TIP

For information on CASA Programs across the country, visit *www.casaforchildren.org*. You can find a link to this site at *www.pearsonhighered.com/wilson* in the companion website material related to Chapter 8 under "Resources."

The judge may also hear testimony from a variety of expert witnesses called by the parties on a variety of topics. In some states the court may designate a neutral court-appointed psychologist (sometimes called a "custody evaluator" or "custody investigator") and order that the parties and children cooperate with that individual by participating in interviews, producing relevant documents and records, and potentially submitting to psychological testing if deemed warranted. The parties must each waive their confidentiality rights in this context, thereby allowing the psychologist to reveal and discuss information that might otherwise be privileged.

What Is the Paralegal's Role in a Custody Case?

The most common tasks a paralegal performs in a child custody case are the following:

- researching the law governing custody actions in the jurisdiction
- preparing related memoranda based on research as requested
- gathering information and documentation essential to successful negotiation and resolution of custody cases (See Paralegal Application 8.6.)

Paralegal **Application 8.6**

Information Gathering in a Contested Custody Case

Contested custody cases are fact-intensive, and considerable information needs to be gathered about the relationship of the child or children with *each* of the parents. This is accomplished through client interviews and questionnaires; traditional discovery vehicles such as interrogatories, depositions, and examination of documents and audiovisual materials; and interviews with individuals familiar with the child and the parents. In addition, the court may be gathering its own information through the use of a court-appointed psychologist, a GAL, or other resources. The paralegal often plays a key role in the information-gathering effort as an integral member of the family law team.

Some of the kinds of information to be gathered include the following:

- The various caretaking functions performed by each parent need to be identified. Which parent has been primarily responsible for meeting the child's daily needs?
- Although clients are not always cooperative with the effort, the parenting strengths and weaknesses of each party need to be identified.
- Does either of the parents have any special problems or limitations that may interfere with his or her capacity to parent effectively? For example, does either parent have a mental health or substance abuse problem?
- The client's motivation for seeking custody needs to be assessed. Is it realistic? Is it based on revenge, a need to prove oneself, or some other unhealthy motive?
- Descriptions of the children need to be provided. What are they like? What are their favorite and least favorite activities? How are they doing in school? What are their parental preferences, if known?
- Any special needs, medical issues, or behavior problems of a child need to be identified, along with an explanation of how they are being handled and by whom.
- It is useful to know if there are any major areas of disagreement between the parents with respect to the raising of the children, such as disciplinary measures, religious practices, or activities the children should be allowed to engage in.
- If there are siblings, step- or otherwise, the relationships between the child and those individuals should be explored.
- The nature of the relationship each parent has with the child needs to be described.
- In addition to basic parenting activities, what kinds of activities does each parent engage in with the child?
- Questions should be asked about the child's friendships, role models, and involvement in community activities and organizations.
- It is important to know whether either parent has intentions to remarry or reside with another romantic partner (of either gender) and whether there will be any additional nonbiological children in that parent's home.
- If the parties have not already established new "permanent" residences, does either parent plan to relocate in the near future and, if so, how far away? The potential impact of any relocation on proposed custody plans needs to be considered.
- The work schedules and relative availability of the parents need to be determined. Does either party's job require him or her to travel or be called out on emergencies at irregular hours? Will child care need to be provided by a third party when the child is with either parent? Does either party have a support system, such as parents, grandparents, friends, or neighbors?
- Potential witnesses should be identified, including friends and relatives but more importantly, teachers, neighbors, childcare providers, coaches, medical professionals, clergy, probation officers, mental health professionals, etc. Issues of privileged communications may be raised, depending on the type of professional.
- Available documents should be identified and copies gathered, such as photos, videos, written reports of professionals, correspondence relevant to parental fitness and cooperation (attempts to visit, etc.), and materials produced by the child (with the child's knowledge and consent), such as e-mails, letters, creative work, and journals.

- scheduling and participating in interviews as assigned
- drafting correspondence, complaints/petitions, supporting affidavits, and proposed orders or responsive pleadings to complaints/petitions involving custody matters
- drafting discovery materials such as interrogatories, requests for admissions, and questions for depositions

- drafting parenting plans/child custody provisions for inclusion in agreements
- assisting in preparation for temporary hearings or trials on the merits, including drafting pretrial memoranda for review and preparing subpoenas for potential witnesses if needed
- helping to prepare witnesses under the supervision of the attorney
- tracking the progress on the case to be certain timelines are met
- coordinating communication with the GAL, CASA volunteer, etc.
- making sure the client is kept informed of progress and upcoming deadlines, hearings, discovery matters, etc.

CHAPTER **SUMMARY**

Although children are no longer deemed the "property" of either parent, this is not always apparent in contested custody battles in which parents duel with each other over their respective rights to physical custody and decision-making authority. In most cases, the parents themselves are able, with or without assistance of counsel or mediators, to arrive at an agreed-upon custodial arrangement and parenting plan. When they cannot, the courts are left to deal with the agonizing task of allocating responsibility between two very fit and committed parents, two parents who are not unfit but who have serious inadequacies, or two parents who both have parental strengths and weaknesses. The relative fitness of parents usually turns on the extent to which either parent has been the primary caretaker of the child and whether or not either parent has engaged in conduct that would negatively affect the welfare of the child.

The controlling consideration in a child custody case, be it an initial award or a modification, is the child's best interests. How will living with one parent and/or the other impact all aspects of the child's life: physical, psychological, cognitive, emotional, spiritual, familial, educational, and recreational? In order to make that decision, the court must examine and assess each parent's "fitness," character, parenting skills, and bond with the child. The court considers the weight of the evidence, the credibility of witnesses, and the recommendations of experts, GALs, and other resources. Each case must be decided on its own facts and the totality of the circumstances as perceived and interpreted by individual judges.

The consideration and weighing of the factors in a custody dispute is essentially factual. . . . Cases with very similar facts may be decided in divergent ways by courts of different states, and even by courts within the same state. The differing results often come from the hearts and emotions of judges, rather than from the facts of the case.[74]

In this chapter, the focus is primarily on custody decisions in the context of divorce. However, the nuclear family is no longer the dominant norm. It is reasonable to anticipate that in our rapidly evolving society with its multiplicity of "family" models, state courts will continue to explore creative ways of extending custodial and visitation rights to third parties as well as to biological parents. Some of these situations are discussed at greater length in Chapter 7. Although there are logic and justice to the results in such cases, there is a fear among advocates of family autonomy that they "open the door to virtually unfathomable exercises of judicial discretion, all in derogation of the constitutionally protected interests of natural parents with respect to their children."[75]

We have treated child custody in this chapter as if it were a discrete topic, but it is important to keep in mind the extent to which it is intertwined with other areas, such as support and tax issues; property division and who remains in the marital home, if anyone; conflict of law when multiple states are involved; paternity questions; adoption; reproductive technology; domestic violence, abuse, and neglect; and constitutional rights of children and parents.

CONCEPT REVIEW AND REINFORCEMENT

KEY **TERMS**

ALI Approximation Rule	Emergency jurisdiction	Home state jurisdiction
Best interests of the child	Equitable parenthood	In camera
CASA Program	Forum *non conveniens*	*In loco parentis*
Co-parent	Forum shopping	Joint award
De facto parent	Guardian *ad litem*	Last resort jurisdiction

Legal custody
Maternal preference
Noncustodial parent
Parens patriae doctrine
Parental alienation syndrome
Parent by estoppel

Parenting plan
Paternal preference
Physical custody
Primary caretaker
Psychological parent
Significant connection jurisdiction

Sole award
Split custody
Standing
Tender years doctrine
Virtual visitation

REVIEW **QUESTIONS**

1. Identify the various types of custody and describe the two most common kinds of custodial awards.
2. Identify the primary purposes of the UCCJEA and the PKPA and describe their bases for jurisdiction.
3. Identify the major purpose of The Hague Convention in custody cases.
4. Describe how standards for making custody awards have evolved.
5. Describe the best interest standard and give examples of factors considered by the courts in applying it.
6. Explain what a "gender-neutral standard" is in the context of custody decisions. Do you believe that custody decisions are, in fact, gender-neutral? Why or why not?
7. Describe the primary caretaker presumption and explain how the courts determine the identity of a child's primary caretaker.
8. Identify the majority position with respect to each of the following in the making of custodial decisions: availability, stability, gender, race, religion, parental health/disability, sexual activity, parental lifestyle, child preference, and a history of abuse.

9. Define visitation (supervised and unsupervised) and describe a common schedule including a suggested virtual visitation component.
10. Describe the nature and purpose of a parenting plan.
11. Describe the nature and purposes of a parent education program.
12. Describe the circumstances under which a modification in custody is likely to be sought and granted.
13. Identify the important interests that must be balanced in relocation disputes.
14. Describe the majority position with respect to each of the following categories of third parties seeking custodial and/or visitation rights: step-parents, grandparents, and co-parents.
15. Explain what a guardian *ad litem* (GAL) is. What role do GALs play in custody cases? What other kinds of individuals may advocate for the child in a custody dispute?
16. Describe the potential role of the paralegal in a custody case.

DEVELOPING YOUR PARALEGAL SKILLS

FOCUS ON **THE JOB**

This activity requires the student to assess the relative strengths and weaknesses of the custody claims of two parents and to draft a recommended parenting plan.

The Facts

Miguel Rodriguez and Christina Acevedo are the unmarried parents of a daughter, named Melody, who was born on September 4, 2007, and a son, Paco, born on November 26, 2010. They lived together for a four-year period from 2007 to 2010, at which time they separated, largely due to arguments over Christina's drug use and Miguel's suspicion that she was abusing their daughter. The daughter had experienced a series of unexplained broken bones and bruises, and on one occasion, the emergency room physician filed a report with the state's Social Services Agency, which is responsible for investigating complaints of suspected abuse. An investigation was conducted, but no

conclusive finding was issued. The case has remained open, but no complaints have been filed for eighteen months since Christina completed a recommended parenting-skills course.

Christina has lived with her parents, Diana and Ramon Acevedo, on and off after she and Miguel separated. She recently moved out of their home because she had grown tired of their constant preaching to her about what an evil person they think she is. They are deeply religious and have been trying to "heal" and "save" their daughter from the life she has been living. They also want to "save" the children who they believe are the fruit of immoral unions. They are quite wealthy and have a lovely farmhouse in the country with animals, including horses and rabbits. There is also a swimming pool, a pond for skating in the winter, and an extensive exercise/play gym on the property. Christina has taken the children to visit her parents on several occasions (accompanied by Miguel as a "supervisor"), and the children have enjoyed participating in all the activities available at the farm. They like going there as long as their grandparents don't lecture them about "sin and all that stuff." Neither Miguel nor Christina wants to allow the grandparents to visit with the children without one of them being present.

Christina has had a series of jobs over the past few years but until recently has rarely managed to keep one for more than three months at a time. She has been waitressing at a local restaurant and playing the organ in a nearby church, where she has become a regular member. She is also volunteering at a shelter for abused women and children. Although she had participated in a number of treatment programs, she was still drinking heavily and using cocaine and heroin on a regular basis until about a year ago, when she seemed to get her act together. Shortly thereafter she was diagnosed as HIV-positive but shows no signs of full-blown AIDS. She continues to smoke cigarettes but is trying to give them up.

Miguel works full time as a conductor on a commuter train. His regular shift is Wednesday through Sunday each week, ten hours a day. He recently married a woman who is a native of Uruguay. He met her when he began taking courses at a local community college where she was enrolled in an English-as-a-second-language program. She hopes eventually to master English and become a nurse. In the meantime she is working as an aide in a local nursing home.

When Miguel and Christina split up, Miguel took the children with him and refused to let Christina visit them for the first two years. She went to court and, over Miguel's objection, obtained an order granting her supervised visitation at the local shelter where she is now volunteering. Her lawyer is reasonably confident that Christine will be able to successfully pursue primary custody of the children, now that her life has changed dramatically. The staff at the shelter say she is a very attentive and sensitive parent.

The children have been doing well living with Miguel and his wife, Remigia. They have no health problems, with the exception of Melody's asthma, which is reasonably well controlled with medication and inhalers. Melody says that she would like to live with her mother because she can talk with her, as she understands English. She also feels sorry for her because "everyone has been so mean to her." Paco does not seem to have bonded with his mother and appears largely indifferent toward her. He adores his dad and follows him around like a shadow. Miguel is close to and very involved with both children. He enjoys taking care of and playing with them. He especially likes teaching them new games and skills.

The Assignment

Assume that both Miguel and Christina are seeking custody of the children. They are in agreement that they should share the responsibility of making major decisions affecting the children, but they cannot agree on which parent the children should live with. Miguel does not want Christina to have anything more than supervised visitation, given her history. Christina doesn't want Miguel to have visitation because she believes he will take the children away from her, as he did when they split up years before. Assume that you are working for the judge who is hearing this case, Judge Solomon Stevens.

a. Outline in a memorandum to the judge the relative strengths and weaknesses of each of the parties' positions based on prevailing governing law in your state.

b. Draft a recommended parenting plan tailored to this case in a format used in your state.

Courts in many states provide parenting-plan forms online. As a default, you may use the Permanent Parenting Plan Order form available online for use in the state of Tennessee or the Wisconsin Proposed Parenting Plan format.

PARALEGAL PRACTICE TIP

A Tennessee Parenting Plan Form can be found at *www.tncourts.gov*. A link to this site is available at *www.pearsonhighered.com* in the companion website material for Chapter 8 under "Forms."

To locate the State of Wisconsin's Proposed Parenting Plan, go to *www.pearsonhighered.com/wilson* and look in the companion website material related to Chapter 8 under "Forms."

FOCUS ON **ETHICS**

In this activity, the student is required to consider the ethical issues raised when a client tells a paralegal that she intends to remove her child from the country and the paralegal shares this information with her parents.

The Assignment

Assume that you are a paralegal in the law office of Attorney Sofia Hidalgo, who is representing Christina Acevedo in the above comprehensive fact pattern. While you were interviewing Christina recently about her parenting skills at your supervisor's request, she shared with you that she is quite certain that the court will not grant her custody of her two children. She says the only way she will ever be able to be with them is to take them to Canada, where her older sister and her husband live. They would welcome them and be able to provide for Christina and the children. She believes she could do this at the time of one of her visits with the children, as supervision has become very informal. This conversation is troubling you, and over dinner, you tell your parents about what she said. Your father says he doesn't blame you for being concerned and that you should go to the police about this woman, who must be mentally unstable and a danger to the children if she would even think of doing such a thing. Your mother says she thinks you should keep your reservations to yourself and just do

your job. Analyze this situation, applying the ethical canons for paralegals promulgated by the National Association of Legal Assistants contained in Appendix A. Include in your analysis a description of what, if anything, you plan to do about this situation.

FOCUS ON **CASE LAW**

In this activity the student reviews two cases to learn more about international custody disputes and the role played by the Hague Convention.

The Assignment

Read the opinions in the two cases below and then respond to the questions which follow. The instructor may ask students to answer the questions orally in class or in a one- to three-page paper.

Blanc v. Morgan, 721 F. Supp. 2d 749 (2010)
Castillo v. Castillo, 597 F. Supp. 2d 432 (2009)

1. Briefly summarize the facts in *Blanc v. Morgan*.
2. Briefly describe the facts in *Castillo v. Castillo*.
3. The courts reached opposite results in these two cases. Explain the courts' reasoning in each case.

PARALEGAL PRACTICE TIP

The opinions in *Blanc v. Morgan* and *Castillo v. Castillo* are available at *www.pearsonhighered.com/wilson* in the "companion website" material related to Chapter 8 under "Cases" and in the Case Resources Section of the MyLegalStudiesLab.

FOCUS ON **STATE LAW AND PROCEDURE**

In this activity, the student assesses the claim of maternal grandparents seeking visitation with their grandchildren against the wishes of both of the children's parents.

The Assignment

Assume that you are a paralegal working in the law firm of Wilson and Tauson, LLP, and your supervisor is Attorney Tauson. Your firm represents Ramon and Diana Acevedo in the comprehensive Focus on the Job fact pattern above. They are seeking visitation with their grandchildren, Melody and Paco, against the wishes of the children's parents, Miguel and Christina. Your supervisor has asked you to research the law governing grandparent visitation in your jurisdiction and assess the likelihood of the Acevedos prevailing given the facts of their case. Present your findings in a memorandum and include your conclusion with respect to the clients' prospects, given the facts of this case and the governing law. Use the following format unless directed otherwise by your instructor.

Memorandum

TO: *Your supervisor*

FROM: *Your name and title*

RE: *Assessment of Diana and Ramon Acevedo's Petition for Grandparent Visitation*

DATE:

Brief description of assignment: *What is it that you have been asked to do?*

Brief description of facts: *Describe the basic facts of the case.*

Results of research: *Describe the applicable statute(s)/case law.*

Discussion: *Apply the governing law to the facts of this case.*

Conclusion: *What is your opinion about the prospect of the grandparents being granted visitation?*

FOCUS ON **TECHNOLOGY**

In addition to the links provided throughout the chapter, this activity provides a series of useful websites for reference, along with technology-related assignments for completion.

Websites of Interest

Links to all of the listed websites are provided at *www.pearsonhighered.com/wilson* in the companion website material for Chapter 8 under "Resources.

www.abanet.org

This is the website for the American Bar Association. Go to the site and search for "Family Law in the Fifty States Tables." Review chart 2 on custody criteria and chart 6 on third-party visitation to learn more about state variations with respect to these topics.

www.childcustody.org

This site contains information about child custody organizations nationwide with links to state codes, topic- or state-specific discussion forums, and "friendly" websites.

www.courts.state.nh.us

Family-law-related forms for New Hampshire are available at this website, including a parenting plan.

www.dadsdivorce.com

This site has the flavor of a support system and contains a variety of tools and guides useful to those involved in custody disputes, including a newsletter and links to divorce laws by state.

deltabravo.net

This is the site of the Separated Parenting Access and Resource Center (SPARC). The stated goal of this site is to ensure that children of divorce have access to both parents—regardless of marital status. It offers links to a rich variety of resources, including an online parenting plan generator.

www.divorceinfo.com/kidsacrossmiles.htm

This site is offered by a rather upbeat divorce attorney/mediator who limits his work to people who want a divorce and are prepared to interact reasonably. The site offers guidance and tools to minimize difficulty and stress. It also includes links to state-specific information.

www.divorcenet.com

This site is similar to dadsdivorce.com but is broader in scope. It contains information on all aspects of divorce. It also provides a guide to finding resources and professional support by geographical area. Specific attention is given to the impact on divorce procedures of being in the military.

www.findlaw.com

This site provides links to the child custody laws of all states and the District of Columbia. Some of the links include forms. Findlaw also provides some judicial opinions, particularly U.S. Supreme Court decisions and a selection of opinions from courts in California, Texas, New York, and Florida.

www.internetvisitation.org

The purpose of this site is to educate and provide information on virtual visitation and to promote and track related legislation. It provides access to helpful articles and other resources on this topic.

www.kidmate.com

This is the site of the Custody X Change, a resource for joint custody software.

Assignments

1. Assume that the mother in this chapter's Focus on the Job fact pattern is willing to agree at this point to virtual visitation between the grandparents and the children. Draft a provision for inclusion in an agreement between the parties that addresses this topic. *www.internetvisitation.org* may be a useful resource when completing this assignment.

2. Locate three websites providing support to fathers seeking custody of their minor children. In a brief report, describe the kinds of information available at each site.

3. Go to the following website for the Oregon Judicial Department: *www.ojd.state.or.us/familylaw*. Select the Parenting Plan Information link. Access and review the Basic Parenting Plan Packet for Parents containing information about parenting plans and the Oregon Parenting Plan Form and Instructions. Complete the form as if your client is Christina in the Focus on the Job fact pattern.

4. Working with another student in your class, locate the Permanent Parenting Plan Order Form for the State of Tennessee (available online). Each student should independently complete the form, with one student representing Miguel and the other representing Christina in the comprehensive fact pattern above. After completing the form, each student should meet with his or her partner and identify any differences between the two proposed plans. The students should then negotiate a resolution to the differences. If the differences cannot be resolved, solicit the assistance of another classmate to function as a "mediator" (albeit untrained!).

5. Locate the CASA Program contact in your jurisdiction.

6. Locate the most current information in your state regarding parent education programs. Is participation required? Do minor children have to attend a program? Where is the nearest/most accessible program for you? Is there an online program option?

7. Locate the statutes addressing virtual visitation in the states of Utah and Wisconsin.

PORTFOLIO PRODUCTS

1. Parenting Plan
2. Analysis involving application of ethical canons to a hypothetical situation
3. Memorandum on the merits of a custody claim
4. Paper on two Hague Convention custody cases
5. Memorandum assessing a petition for grandparents' visitation

chapter 9
CHILD SUPPORT

William and Betty married three years ago after having had three daughters together. An accountant for ten years, William now has "found himself," quit his job, and decided to head to Africa to be a missionary. He says God will provide for Betty and the girls, since he will not be able to, and, besides, if he won't be seeing them, why should he have to pay child support?

What Is Child Support and When, How, and to Whom Is It Awarded?

Child support refers to a parent's legal obligation to contribute to the economic maintenance of his or her child. It is usually in the form of a payment made by a **noncustodial parent** to a **custodial parent** for the benefit of a minor child for whom the parent is deemed legally responsible, including, for example, biological and adopted children. Historically, mothers were awarded custody of children, and **child support** was deemed to be the father's moral obligation—sometimes enforced under the **doctrine of "necessaries."** The duty of support was eventually codified as a legal duty, and nonsupport was made a crime in all states. Based on legislation in each of the states, the duty now is imposed on both parents regardless of who has legal or physical custody.

PARALEGAL PRACTICE TIP

In child support cases, the custodial parent is customarily the recipient of child support paid by the noncustodial parent. However, in some circumstances, the argument may be made that the custodial parent should be the payor of child support when the other parent has custody of the child a significant portion of the time and is on the short end of a major disparity in income and assets. See, e.g., *Colonna v. Colonna,* 581 Pa. 1, 855 A.2d 648 (2004).

LEARNING OBJECTIVES

After reading this chapter and completing related assignments, you should be able to:

- explain what child support is and when, how, and to whom it is awarded

- distinguish between child support and spousal support

- list primary initiatives the federal government has undertaken in the area of child support

- identify major jurisdictional issues that arise in child support cases

- explain what child support guidelines are and how they are applied

- list factors courts consider when establishing child support orders

- explain when and how a child support order can be modified

- list ways of enforcing child support orders

- identify the primary tax implications of child support

- identify the kinds of tasks paralegals perform in child support cases

Noncustodial parent
a parent who does not have sole or primary physical custody of a child but who is still a legal parent with enforceable rights and responsibilities

Custodial parent
the parent with whom the child primarily resides

IN WHAT CONTEXTS DO CHILD SUPPORT ISSUES ARISE?

Child support issues arise in several contexts: Temporary and permanent child support are commonly sought in divorce or separate support actions. Support is also frequently an issue in abuse prevention actions, as well as in guardianship and paternity matters or cases in which a child is removed from a parent's home. When child support is ordered, subsequent modifications may be sought. Single or multiple states, even nations, and both state and federal law may be involved.

PARALEGAL PRACTICE TIP

A parent may be ordered to pay child support to a third party, such as a state agency or a grandparent acting as a custodian or guardian of a child.[1]

Temporary Child Support

Temporary child support is designed to provide for children while an underlying action is pending. Temporary orders are usually issued after brief hearings with limited testimony. The court will customarily review the parties' financial affidavits, their child support guideline worksheets (which often differ from each other), the pleadings, and any supporting affidavits. In some jurisdictions, courts will issue temporary orders without a hearing based on the documents submitted. Requests for temporary child support orders must be taken seriously, as they often lay the groundwork and set a precedent for permanent orders.

"Permanent" Child Support

In a contested case, a trial on the merits of a support issue is considerably more in-depth than a hearing on temporary orders. Counsel usually will address issues such as the reasons for any proposed deviation from the guidelines, unique needs of the children, and potential tax consequences related to the child support order. The case will be decided on the basis of the sworn testimony of the parties and witnesses (sometimes including experts), along with exhibits (including financial affidavits and documentation of expenses, work history, needs of the children, standard of living, etc.).

PARALEGAL PRACTICE TIP

Although often called "permanent" orders, the characterization really is not accurate, as child support orders remain subject to the continuing jurisdiction of the court and may be modified or terminated in a variety of circumstances.

PARALEGAL PRACTICE TIP

To see an example of a Complaint for Support used in Massachusetts visit *www.lawlib.state.ma.us.* You can find a link to this site at *www.pearsonhighered.com/wilson* in the companion website material for Chapter 9 under "Forms."

WHO HAS A DUTY OF SUPPORT?

In an era in which the concept of "family" is evolving and scientific technology is expanding, the answer to the question of who has a duty of child support is becoming increasingly complex. For example, some states impose a duty to pay support on a third party who is not the child's biological or adoptive parent, but who acts *in loco parentis* (Latin: in the place of a parent). A person such as a step-parent may perform the role of a parent even if he or she has not formally adopted the child. However, the majority rule is that a step-parent will not have a legal duty to support the child absent an agreement or a court order. In some instances, a support duty may be imposed on a man who has voluntarily acknowledged paternity but who is later proven by DNA evidence not to be a parent.[2]

The parents' duty to support their child may continue even if the child is in the custody of a government agency (a residential treatment program, a juvenile justice department, a department of social services, etc.) rather than in the custody of one of the parents. The agency that has custody may initiate an action for support.[3]

WHEN DOES THE CHILD SUPPORT DUTY END?

The duty to support a child most often continues until the child's emancipation. **Emancipation** usually means that the child has reached the **age of majority** (age eighteen in most states). However, it can also refer to some other statutory, judicial, or agreed-upon indicator that the child should no longer be considered a minor, such as entering military service, getting married, moving out of the custodial parent's home, or becoming self-supporting. The award will also end if the obligor's parental rights are terminated or upon the death of the obligor, absent agreement or order to the contrary. The court may order, or the parties may agree, that the **obligor** will maintain a life insurance policy for the benefit of the child or establish a trust or some other vehicle to help ensure the child continues to receive an appropriate level of support during his or her minority in the event the obligor dies.

PARALEGAL PRACTICE TIP

Paralegals should be alert to applicable jurisdictional variations in procedure. For example, in 2006, Pennsylvania amended its rule regarding termination of a child support award upon emancipation and established a requirement that the court conduct an "emancipation inquiry" within one year of the date a child who is the subject of a support order reaches age eighteen. If there is an order in place that applies to more than one child, the obligor may want, or be required, to file a petition for modification or a petition to terminate child support for a specific child upon emancipation if there would be a reduction in the current support amount as a result. The obligor should not just start paying a reduced child support amount absent court authorization.

PARALEGAL PRACTICE TIP

To view an example of a "Verified Petition to Reduce Child Support Due to Emancipation of Minor Child," visit *www.in.gov/judiciary/forms*. (Indiana) You can find a link to this site at *www.pearsonhighered.com/wilson* in the companion website material related to Chapter 9 under "Forms."

PARALEGAL PRACTICE TIP

Variations exist among the states with respect to how long parents remain responsible for the support of their disabled children. For example, in a 2009 decision, a Kansas Appellate Court held that Kansas common law no longer required a parent to support a disabled son with cerebral palsy beyond the end of the school year in which the child turned nineteen. Under Arizona law, however, the family court can order either or both parents to provide support for mentally or physically disabled adult children after they reach the age of majority.[4]

In loco parentis
Latin: in the place of the parent; taking on some or all of the responsibilities of a parent

Emancipation
the age, act, or occasion that frees a child from the control of a parent and usually the parent from a child support obligation unless otherwise ordered or agreed

Age of majority
the age, usually eighteen, at which a person attains adulthood and associated legal rights. The age varies from state to state. As of January 2011, for example, the age of majority was twenty-one in Mississippi and nineteen in Alabama and Nebraska.

Obligor
a person who owes a legal duty; in the child support context, the parent who owes the duty of support

Public charge
a person dependent on public assistance programs for necessaries

In some circumstances, the court has the discretion to order continuation of support beyond the age of majority, such as when a child is disabled and would otherwise become a **public charge**. Several states also provide by statute that the duty of support may continue provided the youth remains in a qualifying program of higher education.

EXHIBIT 9.1 Child Support and Spousal Support (Alimony)—A Comparison

Child Support	Spousal Support (Alimony)
Child support is a right of the child.	Alimony involves a spousal duty at the time of divorce or legal separation. It is based on a showing of need by one spouse and an ability to pay on the part of the other spouse.
Child support obligations cannot be permanently waived in premarital or separation agreements between the parties.	In most states, rights to spousal support can be waived in valid premarital and separation agreements between the parties.
Child support is calculated using federally mandated child support guidelines developed in each state.	In the majority of jurisdictions, there are no guidelines for courts to use when establishing amounts and duration of alimony awards.
Child support awards remain under the continuing jurisdiction of the court and can be modified upon a substantial change in circumstances or based on periodic reviews.	Alimony awards may be modified upon a material change in the parties' circumstances unless otherwise provided by statute, court decree, or a surviving agreement of the parties.
Child support obligations are not terminated as a result of the remarriage of either spouse.	In most jurisdictions, remarriage of the recipient spouse customarily will terminate an alimony award.
Child support is neither deductible by the obligor nor includable in the income of the recipient.	Alimony is usually tax-deductible to the obligor and taxable income to the recipient.
Child support obligations are not discharged in bankruptcy and are entitled to priority in payment.[5]	Spousal support obligations usually are not dischargeable in bankruptcy.

Initiatives the Federal Government Has Undertaken in the Area of Child Support

In order to understand the operation of child support procedures in the individual states, it helps to be aware of how they are in many respects shaped by federal law. Historically, the federal government has largely left regulation of family law matters to the states. However, since the 1970s, it has assumed a powerful leadership role in an effort to accomplish several important objectives related to the establishment and enforcement of child support obligations:

Public assistance programs
government programs providing financial and other forms of assistance to poor and low-income families

- In order to contain the costs of **public assistance programs,** the federal government now holds both mothers and fathers accountable for support of their children.

- In an effort to address historical inadequacies and inconsistencies in child support awards from state to state, county to county, and judge to judge, it has taken dramatic steps to promote uniformity in procedures used by the states to determine child support awards.
- Given the high rate of noncompliance with child support orders, particular emphasis is placed on strengthening and streamlining enforcement of child support obligations, especially when multiple jurisdictions are involved.

It is impossible to cover the many initiatives undertaken by Congress over the past four decades, but reference to some of them is appropriate to convey a sense of the nature and scope of federal involvement in the child support arena. Although these efforts have had a significant impact, support generally still remains inadequate to meet the daily needs of many American children, predominantly those in female-headed households.

- **The Child Support Enforcement and Establishment of Paternity Act of 1974**[6] (added Title IV-D to the Social Security Act).
  a. This Act established the Office of Child Support Enforcement (OCSE), the federal agency now responsible for monitoring and helping states develop and manage their child support programs in accordance with federal law.
  b. It required each state to develop a comprehensive child support program to be run by a single state agency (designated the state's **IV-D agency**) charged with facilitating parents' efforts to obtain and enforce child support awards. Currently, the primary tasks of a IV-D agency are to:
     1. when necessary, assist in establishing paternity through testing of **putative fathers**
     2. assist with location of noncustodial parents through state and federal parent locator services empowered by statute to search records of state and federal agencies
     3. facilitate entry of support orders after paternity is established and noncustodial fathers are located
     4. periodically review child support awards
     5. enforce existing orders through an arsenal of resources
- **The Child Support Enforcement Amendments of 1984 (CSEA)**[7]
  a. This Act required states to establish advisory numeric, formula-based child support guidelines for reference by judges and other officials who set child support amounts in separation, divorce, and paternity cases.
  b. It required each state to have a law addressing procedures for establishing paternity of a child at any time before the child attains eighteen years of age.[8]
  c. It required state child support agencies to seek medical support as part of any petition to establish or modify support whenever health care coverage is available at a reasonable cost.
  d. It strengthened Title IV-D enforcement efforts by requiring the states to implement income withholding, state and federal tax intercepts, and liens against the property of obligors in default.
  e. It mandated that states receiving public assistance funds make the full range of parent locator and child support services available to all custodial parents and not solely to those receiving public assistance.
- **The Family Support Act of 1988** This Act mandated that by 1994, the states implement **presumptive** rather than advisory child support guidelines to be

PARALEGAL PRACTICE TIP

www.acf.hhs.gov/programs/cse is the website for the federal Office of Child Support Enforcement. On the home page you will find links to information about many topics, including Parent Locator Services, Directories of New Hires, and Case Registries. A link to this site can be found at *www.pearsonhighered. com/wilson* in the companion website material for Chapter 9 under "Resources."

IV-D agency
the state agency charged with responsibility for enforcing child support obligations

Putative father
a man who is reputed or believed to be the father of a child but who was not married to the mother when the child was born and whose paternity has not yet been established by legal process

Presumptive child support guidelines
guidelines that are presumed to generate an appropriate amount of child support, given a particular set of assumptions and circumstances

Uniform Interstate Family Support Act (UIFSA)
a model act designed to facilitate establishment and enforcement of interstate child support orders. In 1996, the federal government mandated that all states adopt the 1996 version of UIFSA by 1998 in order to continue to receive federal funding. The Act was subsequently amended in 2001. The amendments clarified and extended the Act without making any fundamental changes in the earlier policies and procedures. As of January 2011, twenty-one states and the District of Columbia had enacted the 2001 version. A 2008 version has been drafted and adopted in seven states as of 2010 (Maine, Nevada, New Mexico, North Dakota, Tennessee, Utah, and Wisconsin). A primary addition to the 2008 UIFSA is the expansion of international child support enforcement initiatives consistent with the tenets of the new Hague Convention on the Enforcement of Child Support and Other Forms of Family Maintenance signed in 2007.

Long-arm jurisdiction
jurisdiction over a nonresident defendant on the basis of his or her contacts with the state that is seeking to exercise personal jurisdiction

Transitional Assistance to Needy Families Program (TANF)
the welfare system that replaced the former Aid to Families with Dependent Children Program

State Case Registry (SCR)
a federally mandated statewide database containing basic information on all child support orders entered by courts within the state

State Directory of New Hires (SDNH)
a federally mandated statewide database containing basic information from employers regarding all newly hired employees and applicants for unemployment compensation within the state

used in establishing initial awards and for any subsequent modifications.[9] The Act called for the National Conference of Commissioners on Uniform State Laws (NCCUSL) to create a new Uniform Act designed to improve the interstate collection of child support by replacing and addressing problem areas in the prior Uniform Reciprocal Enforcement of Support Act (URESA) drafted in the 1950s and revised several times. The "new" Act, eventually called the **Uniform Interstate Family Support Act (UIFSA)**,[10] was designed to promote uniformity in the processing of interstate cases; eliminate the potential for multiple, conflicting support orders; and expand **long-arm jurisdiction** to make it easier for a custodial parent to prosecute a child support case in his or her own state.[11]

- **The Personal Responsibility and Work Opportunity Reconciliation Act of 1996 (PRWORA)**[12]
  a. This Act abolished the former Aid to Families with Dependent Children program (AFDC) and replaced it with the **Transitional Assistance to Needy Families program (TANF)**.
  b. The Act called for creation and maintenance of a **State Case Registry** containing basic information regarding all child support orders within the state and the creation and maintenance of state and national **Directories of New Hires**. The act required all states to adopt UIFSA by 1998 in order to remain eligible to receive federal child support funds, thereby creating a powerful incentive for states to comply with federal mandates.
  c. The Act provides a mechanism for dealing with international child support cases.

The Major Jurisdictional Issues in Child Support Cases

SUBJECT MATTER JURISDICTION

The processes by which child support awards are established, modified, and enforced all involve jurisdictional issues. The court issuing, modifying, or enforcing an order must have **subject matter jurisdiction** over child support actions and also **personal jurisdiction** over the obligor. Based on state statutes governing subject matter jurisdiction, child support actions are usually filed in family courts, particularly if child support is an issue in a pending divorce action. However, they may also be heard in juvenile courts or the equivalent of district or county courts dealing with protective orders and other matters pertaining to children and their parents.

OBTAINING PERSONAL JURISDICTION OVER A RESIDENT DEFENDANT

Each state has its own statutes governing the ways in which personal jurisdiction can be obtained over a defendant. If the defendant in a child support action resides in the state where the action is brought, most often a copy of the complaint/petition and court summons will be personally served on the defendant. This is called

actual service of process. If the defendant is believed to be in the state, but his or her precise whereabouts are unknown, the court may authorize an alternative mode of service, such as mailing the complaint to the defendant's last known address or service by publication in area newspapers. A defendant may also consent to the court's jurisdiction by voluntarily accepting service at the courthouse or filing a responsive pleading to a complaint.

OBTAINING PERSONAL JURISDICTION OVER A NONRESIDENT DEFENDANT IN THE PETITIONER'S OWN STATE

Approximately one-third of child support orders involve parents living in different states. Obtaining jurisdiction over a nonresident defendant and enforcing support orders across state lines can be challenging. If the defendant is a nonresident, a court may be able to obtain personal jurisdiction over the defendant in the petitioner's own state under the state's long-arm statute or under one of UIFSA's long-arm provisions. Under UIFSA, which now has been adopted in every state, if a defendant has one or more of the following eight kinds of "purposeful minimal contacts" with another state, it is considered fair and reasonable for a court in that other state to exercise personal jurisdiction over the individual and to adjudicate a child or spousal support dispute:

1. The nonresident is personally served in the state.
2. The nonresident submits to the jurisdiction of the state by consent, by entering a general appearance, or by filing a responsive document having the effect of waiving any contest to personal jurisdiction.
3. The nonresident once resided with the child in the state.
4. The nonresident once resided in the state and provided prenatal expenses or support for the child.
5. The child resides in the state as a result of the acts or directives of the nonresident.
6. The nonresident engaged in sexual intercourse in the state and the child may have been conceived by that act of intercourse.
7. The nonresident asserted parentage in the state such as through a **putative father registry**.
8. Any other basis consistent with the constitutions of the state and the United States for the exercise of personal jurisdiction.

(See Paralegal Application 9.1.)

Subject matter jurisdiction
the authority of a court to hear and decide a particular type of claim or controversy

Actual service of process
actual delivery of notice to the person for whom it is intended

Personal jurisdiction
the authority of the court to issue and enforce orders binding a particular individual; sometimes called *in personam* jurisdiction

Putative father registry
a vehicle available in several states that is designed to protect a putative father's parental rights by giving him notice of a pending adoption proceeding without his having to rely on the birth mother or prospective adoptive parents for information

PARALEGAL PRACTICE TIP

For examples of long-arm statutes in the states of Florida and Ohio, visit *www.leg.state.fl.us/Statutes/index.cfm* and *www.codes.ohio.gov*. Links to both of these sites can be found at *www.pearsonhighered.com/wilson* in the companion website material for Chapter 9 under "Statutes."

PARALEGAL PRACTICE TIP

To read the full text of UIFSA visit *www.nccusl.org*. A link to this site can be found at *www.pearsonhighered.com/wilson* in the companion website material for Chapter 9 under "Resources."

Paralegal Application 9.1

Jurisdiction Under UIFSA

Fact Pattern

Susan and her husband were married in Texas, by operation of common law, in 1997. Throughout their marriage, her husband (a known gang member) abused her both physically and psychologically. Susan also believed her husband was sexually abusing her daughter from a previous relationship. He threatened to kill her if she turned him in. Despite his threats, she contacted the police and reported both the death threats and the abuse, but the police did not investigate because she had not personally witnessed the abuse. She eventually left her husband and moved into a friend's trailer, but her husband continued to stalk her and slashed the tires on her car at work. She again reported the incidents to the police, and they told her she should move to a women's shelter. After that, her husband and a friend were seen armed with guns breaking into the trailer where she used to live. Her husband also made threatening phone calls to her father, who lived in Colorado. Early in January of 1999, pregnant by her husband and fearing for her life, she fled to her father's home in Colorado, where she gave birth to a son. In April of 2000, she filed for divorce in Colorado and sought child support, maintenance, and division of property and debt. After being personally served in Texas, her husband filed a motion to dismiss for lack of personal jurisdiction.

Sidebar

Should the Colorado court be able to exercise personal jurisdiction over Susan's husband under UIFSA? On what basis? To learn how the Colorado Supreme Court resolved this question, read the opinion in the case, *In re Marriage of Malwitz*, 99 P.3d 56 (Colo. 2004).

PARALEGAL PRACTICE TIP

The opinion in the *Malwitz* case can be found at *www.pearson-highered.com/wilson* in the companion website material related to Chapter 9 under "Cases" and in the Case Resources Section of the MyLegalStudiesLab.

OBTAINING PERSONAL JURISDICTION OVER A NONRESIDENT DEFENDANT IN HIS OR HER OWN STATE

If the court cannot obtain personal jurisdiction in the petitioner's state, the matter cannot be adjudicated in that state. However, another avenue remains open to the petitioner working through the state's IV-D agency with the agency acting on the petitioner's behalf with or without the assistance of counsel.

PARALEGAL PRACTICE TIP

Forms relating to interstate cases can be viewed at *www.acf.hhs.gov/programs/cse*. A link to this site can be found at *www.pearsonhighered.com/wilson* in the companion website material for Chapter 9 under "Forms."

- The petitioner files a petition for child support in his or her own state.
- The IV-D agency in that state forwards the petition to the IV-D agency in the nonresident defendant's state.
- The appropriate court in the nonresident defendant's state obtains personal jurisdiction over the defendant and conducts an administrative or judicial hearing on the child support issue.
- The IV-D agency in the nonresident defendant's state then uses its enforcement powers to collect the child support amount from the defendant.

CONTINUING EXCLUSIVE JURISDICTION UNDER UIFSA

Under UIFSA, there should be only one valid support order between the parties that is enforceable in all states, and the states are required, under the Full Faith and Credit for Child Support Orders Act (FFCCSOA),[13] to respect properly issued support orders from other states (including orders issued by tribal courts).

Once a court issues a valid child support order, under UIFSA that court will have continuing exclusive jurisdiction over the case for purposes of modification, and no court in any other state can modify the order as long as either parent or the child continues to reside in that state or the parties file written consents that another state assume jurisdiction. If neither of the parents nor the child continues to reside in the state that issued the initial order, that state loses its continuing exclusive jurisdiction and a court in another state can acquire it. It is conceivable that the parties may then simultaneously seek orders in different states, resulting in multiple and potentially conflicting orders. In this situation, under UIFSA, preference will be given to the child's **home state**. If neither state is the child's home state, the more recent order will control.

Home state
under UIFSA, the state where the child has lived for six consecutive months prior to the filing or since birth if the child is less than six months old

PARALEGAL PRACTICE TIP

It is possible for jurisdiction over child custody and child support to be in two different states. For example, a state that has issued custody and support orders may cede custody jurisdiction to another state when one parent and the child relocate to that other state for an extended period. However, under UIFSA, jurisdiction over child support will continue to be in the initial state as long as the other parent resides there (unless the parties execute written consents that another state assume jurisdiction). See, e.g., *In the Matter of Jeffrey M. Gray and Janette L. Gray*, 160 N.H. 62, 993 A.2d 203 (2010).

Child Support Guidelines: What Are They and How Are They Applied?

Once the proper jurisdiction for a child support action is determined, the paralegal can locate the appropriate child support guidelines and forms to utilize.

THE ORIGIN AND PURPOSE OF THE GUIDELINES

In response to federal mandate, every state has put in place a system of child support guidelines designed to help parents and judges determine how much child support should be ordered in a given case. The basic requirements for each state's child support guidelines under federal law are as follows:[14]

- Application of the guidelines will produce a **rebuttable presumption** of the appropriate amount of support to be ordered.
- The guidelines must consider all earnings and income of the noncustodial parent.
- The guidelines must incorporate specific descriptive and numeric criteria.
- They must provide for children's health care needs.
- They must apply to all child support orders, whether at establishment or modification.
- Any order that deviates from the guidelines must include written findings of what the order would have been under the guidelines and why a deviation is warranted.
- Every four years each state's guidelines must be reviewed and revised, if necessary, to ensure that their application results in appropriate child support awards. The review must consider economic data on the cost of raising children and must analyze the application of the guidelines to ensure that awards are consistent and deviations limited.

PARALEGAL PRACTICE TIP

To see examples of child support guidelines and instructions in Massachusetts, Utah, and Virginia, visit the following: *www.lawlib.state.ma.us* (Massachusetts); *www.utcourts.gov/howto/Family/#Child_Support* (Utah); and *www.courts.state.va.us* (Virginia) You can find links to these three sites at *www.pearsonhighered.com/Wilson* in the companion website material related to Chapter 9 under "Forms."

Rebuttable presumption
an inference drawn from certain facts that can be overcome by the introduction of additional or contradictory evidence

THE NATURE OF STATE GUIDELINES

Although the federal government mandated their creation, it left the design of child support guidelines up to the individual states. As a result, no two states' guidelines are identical.

State guidelines vary with respect to the income basis for the determination of support; the estimate of spending on children upon which the guidelines are based; the treatment of child care costs; the treatment of medical insurance and out-of-pocket expenditures for medical care; provisions for other children to whom the parent owes a duty of support; adjustments for parenting time; and provisions for adjusting support when the obligor is low-income.[15]

Paralegal **Application 9.2**

Child Support Guideline Worksheets

Paralegals in a family law practice are frequently asked to draft child support guideline worksheets. A copy of the worksheet for the state of Missouri is contained in Exhibit 9.2. Depending on the guidelines formula, a Worksheet may need to be completed for each child for whom support is an issue. Many firms have purchased software packages that can be used to calculate the amount of child support due under a given state's guidelines. The guidelines for virtually all states are available online, and most states post worksheets on the Web pages of their courts or IV-D agencies.

When preparing child support guideline worksheets, it is important to know what kinds of income will be considered includable for purposes of calculating child support in a given state and to identify and document all sources of income. When any source of income is likely to be challenged or when income may be imputed, appropriate research needs to be done with respect to the issue in an effort to support the client's position.

Because of the potential value of child support awards, it is important for the family law team to conduct adequate discovery with respect to the parties' respective incomes and any factors that may be used to argue for a deviation from the guidelines. If a deviation is going to be sought, the paralegal will very likely be asked to gather the information necessary to support or oppose that deviation, based on the facts of the case.

EXHIBIT 9.2 Child Support Amount Calculation Worksheet for the State of Missouri

Courtesy of the State of Missouri

IN THE CIRCUIT COURT OF _____ COUNTY, MISSOURI
CASE NO. _____ DIV/CT ROOM _____

FORM 14 CHILD SUPPORT AMOUNT CALCULATION WORKSHEET

In re the Matter of: _____ and _____
Petitioner   Respondent

CHILDREN	AGE	CHILDREN	AGE
Child One		Child Four	
Child Two		Child Five	
Child Three		Child Six	

	Parent Receiving Support	Parent Paying Support	Combined
1. MONTHLY GROSS INCOME	$	$	
a. Court ordered maintenance being received.	$	$	
2. ADJUSTMENTS (per month) a. Other court or administratively ordered child support being paid.	($)	($)	
b. Court ordered maintenance being paid.	($)	($)	
c. Support obligation for other children in parent's custody.	($)	($)	
3. ADJUSTED MONTHLY GROSS INCOME (Sum of lines 1 and 1a, minus lines 2a, 2b and 2c).	$	$	$
4. PROPORTIONATE SHARE OF COMBINED ADJUSTED MONTHLY GROSS INCOME (Each parent's line 3 income divided by combined line 3 income).	%	%	
5. BASIC CHILD SUPPORT AMOUNT (From support chart using combined line 3 income).			$
6. ADDITIONAL CHILD-REARING COSTS (per month) a. Reasonable work-related child care costs of the parent receiving support ($) less any child care tax credit ($).	$		
b. Reasonable work-related child care costs of the parent paying support.		$	
c. Health insurance costs for the children who are subjects of this proceeding.	$	$	
d. Uninsured extraordinary medical costs. (Agreed by parents or ordered by court).	$	$	
e. Other extraordinary child rearing costs. (Agreed by parents or ordered by court)	$	$	
7. TOTAL ADDITIONAL CHILD-REARING COSTS (Sum of lines 6a, 6b, 6c, 6d and 6e).	$	$	$
8. TOTAL COMBINED CHILD SUPPORT COSTS (Sum of line 5 and combined line 7).			$
9. EACH PARENT'S SUPPORT OBLIGATION (Multiply line 8 by each parent's line 4)	$	$	
10. CREDIT FOR ADDITIONAL CHILD-REARING COSTS (Line 7 of parent paying support).		($)	
11. ADJUSTMENT FOR A PORTION OF THE AMOUNTS EXPENDED DURING PERIODS OF OVERNIGHT VISITATION OR CUSTODY (Multiply line 5 by _____ %).		($)	
12. PRESUMED CHILD SUPPORT AMOUNT (Line 9 minus lines 10 and 11).		$	
PREPARED BY:			

Net income
total income from all sources minus voluntary and nonvoluntary deductions

Adjusted gross income
income after nonvoluntary deductions are taken out, such as federal and state tax obligations, social security withholding, union dues, and wage assignments related to prior support orders

Gross income
total income from all sources before any deductions are made

DEFINITION AND PROOF OF INCOME

Guidelines are generally designed to calculate child support obligations when the parties' total combined income (**net**, **adjusted**, or **gross**, depending on the state) is under a certain maximum. For example, the maximum in January 2011 was $187,200 in New Jersey, and $80,000 in New York. States vary with respect to treatment of parental income above the maximum. Most states leave the matter to the discretion of the court and some consider a percentage approach.[16]

If not controlled by federal law, the question of what should be included in income for purposes of calculating child support obligations will be determined by state statutes, administrative regulations, and case law. Most states define income broadly as "income from whatever source." All states include income from employment, including commissions, and virtually all include income from investment earnings, unemployment compensation, pensions, social security, and veterans' benefits. Treatment of occasional income (odd jobs, overtime, tips, bonuses, etc.) varies.

PARALEGAL PRACTICE TIP

In determining whether income from investments will be included in income for the purpose of calculating child support, courts usually consider whether the income is realized (actually received by the party) or unrealized (a paper-only increase in the value of an investment to which a party may not even have access). Courts will also consider whether a corporation's earnings are undistributed in an effort to serve a legitimate business purpose or to shield income.

PARALEGAL PRACTICE TIP

Some states will impute income to affluent parents who have sufficient income-producing assets to support themselves and their child support obligations without working. They may also factor in the value of non-income-producing assets such as boats, cars, and collections of such items as jewelry or artwork. If not considered by the formula, such assets may be used to justify a deviation from the guidelines if it appears a parent is deliberately trying to tie up funds that would otherwise be available to meet family obligations.[17]

PARALEGAL PRACTICE TIP

Gifts are not usually considered income for federal tax purposes, but the states are divided on whether they should be included as income in child support calculations. Those that decline to do so refer to federal tax law and also to the fact that the donor of a gift has no legal obligation to continue giving. Other states include gifts when they are recurring cash gifts of predictable amounts from dependable persons.

Proof of income is often a central issue in a child support case. There are few types of income that continue totally unchanged from year to year. People lose or change their jobs, bonuses may be variable, interest rates rise and fall, and business conditions can result in inconsistent profits and losses, especially in cases where one or both of the parties are self-employed. The more something resembles a steady source of annual income that one can reasonably expect to receive in the future, the more likely it will be considered income for purposes of calculating a child support obligation. Questions occasionally arise with respect to the following sources of income, among others:

- **Spousal or child support from a person not a party to the order** Spousal support is usually considered income. Child support received by either party for children other than the child for whom support is being determined is not usually considered income.
- **Cash and gifts from family members** An occasional modest gift may not be included, but if every year a party receives substantial gifts from his or her parents directly or from a family trust and does not have to repay or pay taxes on those sums, the amounts are likely to be included in income.[18]

Loans from friends, family, employers, and others that are forgiven are usually considered income. See, e.g., *In the Matter of Timothy and Dorothy Sullivan*, 159 N.H. 251, 982 A.2d 959 (2009).

- **Lump-sum severance pay** Payments associated with compensation for employment are generally included in income. The same reasoning applies to severance pay and settlement amounts in suits for wrongful termination of employment that include compensation for lost pay.
- **Bonuses** When bonuses are reasonably certain in the sense that they are awarded each year, even if in varying amounts, they are likely to be included in income. If a bonus is an occasional and uncertain event, a court may be reluctant to include it, depending on the circumstances.

Some states, such as California, expressly include bonuses as part of a parent's annual gross income. In states that do not address the matter by statute, courts tend to hold that if a bonus is speculative, completely discretionary, or dependent on performance or the success of an industry (such as residential housing in a sluggish economy), it may not be included as income in the child support calculation. But if it is predictable, such as annual bonuses from a parent's tribe, it may be included. See, e.g., *M.S. v. O.S.*, 176 Cal. App. 4th 548, 97 Cal. Rptr. 3d 812 (2009).

- **Lump-sum personal injury settlements:** Although lump-sum personal injury settlements are often not considered assets subject to property division between the parties, they are usually considered income in the child support context. The court may choose to prorate an award over a number of years.[19]
- **Lottery or gambling winnings, prizes, and awards** Even though these are not customarily "continuing" sources of income, they are usually included.
- **Social Security Disability Benefits (SSD/SSDI)** Because SSD benefits derive from prior employment, they are usually deemed includable in income.[20] Although the benefit will be included in his or her income, a disabled parent is ordinarily entitled to have Social Security Disability Benefits paid to a child (because of that parent's disability) credited against his or her child support obligation for that child.[21]

A person becomes eligible to receive SSD/SSDI benefits if he or she meets certain disability requirements and an employer has paid into the social security retirement system for his or her benefit. SSD is essentially an insurance policy intended to replace lost income when the employee is disabled and unable to work.

- **Means-tested sources of benefits, such as Pell grants, TANF benefits, food stamps, and Supplemental Social Security Income (SSI)** These usually are not considered income. Means-tested benefits are essentially social welfare programs designed to meet the basic needs of low-income persons. Congress has expressly exempted SSI from child support payments.[22]
- **Military allowances for housing (BAH) and subsistence (BAS)** Although these subsidies are not included in income for income tax purposes, several states (including New York,[23] Pennsylvania, Ohio, and Minnesota) have held them includable in gross income for purposes of calculating child support.

- **Military retirement benefits** These benefits are includable as income, although under federal law there are limitations on the maximum percentage of the benefit that can be distributed pursuant to orders for property distribution, alimony, or child support.[24]
- **Reimbursements received in the course of employment** When the reimbursements are significant and reduce personal living expenses, such as free housing, use of a company car, and meals, they may be included. Louisiana, for example, specifically includes such reimbursements in income by statute.[25]

IMPUTED INCOME

Imputed income

income that is attributed to a party based upon his or her earning capacity rather than on actual earnings

Imputed income is income that is attributed to a party based upon his or her earning capacity rather than on actual earnings. Most states will impute income to one or both of the parties if appropriate. (See Paralegal Application 9.3.) This practice is designed to prevent a party from avoiding a child or spousal support obligation by manipulating his or her income, for example, by voluntarily retiring early or remaining unemployed or underemployed. Many states will impute income when a party's wrongdoing results in the loss of gainful employment. Most states will not impute income if there is a good-faith reason for unemployment, such as physical disability or remaining at home for child-related reasons.

Some states establish by statute a formula for imputation of income. For example, in New Hampshire, RSA 458-C:2, IV(a) provides that, in cases in which a parent is determined to be voluntarily unemployed or underemployed, a trial court "in its discretion, may consider as gross income the difference between the amount a parent is earning and the amount a parent has earned." The court is also free to impute a lesser amount.[26] The amount set may depend in part on the noncustodial parent's educational background and job skills, as well as work history and job opportunities in the area. If the individual is unemployed and has no recent work history, the amount will be left to the court's discretion, absent governing statutory or case law.

Most courts will also consider averaging the income of a parent over a period of years, especially if the individual is self-employed in a highly volatile profession that is subject to market trends or when he or she has a windfall year that is totally inconsistent with an overall employment history. Income averaging imputes consistency in income rather than the income itself. In some jurisdictions, income averaging is specifically authorized by statute or court rule (for example, Alaska, Ohio, and Nebraska). New Hampshire expressly prohibits income averaging based on case law rather than statute.

Paralegal **Application 9.3**

Imputed Income Cases—What Do You Think?

PARALEGAL PRACTICE TIP

The four cases referenced in this Paralegal Application are available at *www.pearsonhighered.com/wilson* on the companion website in the material related to Chapter 9 under "Cases" and in the Case Resources Section of the MyLegalStudiesLab.

Case 1: *McKenzie v. McKenzie, 709 N.W.2d 528 (Iowa 2006)*

The noncustodial parent in this case, Tim, voluntarily left his employment in Iowa to move to South Carolina to be with his girlfriend, whom he subsequently married. At the time he quit his job he was earning $45,260 a year and was paying court-ordered child support for his daughter, Kilie, in the amount of $495 per month. In South Carolina he had to take a job that paid less than his prior employment and he sought a modification of child support based on that change in circumstances. An Iowa district court denied his petition for modification finding that he was voluntarily underemployed, and the appellate court reversed. The mother appealed to the Iowa Supreme Court. Whose best interests do you think that court will find more important: Tim's or Kilie's? Read the opinion available on the companion website to find out how the court ruled.

Case 2: *Lisa Lauderman v. State of Wyoming Department of Family Services ex rel. Jen, a minor child, and Russell Nomura, 2010 Wyo. 70, 232 P.3d 604 (2010)*

Lisa and Russell never wed but they had one child together. Lisa had physical custody and Russell, a drywaller, was ordered to pay child support of $263 a week. Despite accumulating a significant arrearage at one point, Russell struggled to meet his obligation. With the collapse of the construction industry, he fell on particularly hard times despite good-faith efforts to find work. When the Department of Family Services filed a petition for modification, the district court reduced his child support obligation after imputing income to both parents. With reference to Lisa, the court found that she had been employed for seven months in 2007 as a welder earning $16.00 an hour until she was terminated from her employment in the late stages of a second pregnancy. She subsequently decided to be a stay-at-home mother. In calculating Russell's child support amount, the court imputed a net monthly income to Lisa of $2,562 based on the wage she was earning in 2007. Lisa acknowledged there were welding jobs available at her former rate but claimed she could not work full-time because she was unable to arrange adequate child care for her second child because welders work twelve-hour shifts. She appealed the district court's decision, objecting to the amount of income imputed to her. Do you think Lisa had a good argument with respect to this issue on appeal? Read the case on the companion website to see what the Wyoming Supreme Court held.

Case 3: *J.M. v. D.A., 935 N.E.2d 1235 (Ind. Ct. App. 2010)*

In this case, a father of four children unsuccessfully sought a modification of child support. He had lost his job "either by being fired for absenteeism or by not appearing" and at the time of the hearing was enrolled as a full-time student. An Indiana Circuit Court concluded that he was voluntarily unemployed and that he should be attributed a weekly gross income of $480, his last gross weekly wage. He claimed that even if he previously was voluntarily unemployed, that status ended when he became a full-time student. On appeal, in support of his argument that he should not be considered unemployed or underemployed, he relied on another Indiana Court of Appeals decision that characterized pursuit of higher education as follows:

> . . . we believe that it is a parent's responsibility to continually try to better herself and to create more and better opportunities for the child and the family unit. We are hard-pressed to come up with a better example of a way to do just that than by pursuing education. . . . A parent who finds within herself the diligence and ambition to obtain a degree will be rewarded not only with better job prospects and increased earning potential, but also with a child who has learned by example that education is essential and valuable. *Thomas v. Orlando,* 834 N.E.2d 1055 (Ind. Ct. App. 2005)

J.M.'s appeal was denied. The courts in these two cases reached different conclusions based on the fact patterns presented. Do you think enrolling in a program of higher education should constitute voluntary unemployment?

DEVIATIONS FROM THE GUIDELINES

PARALEGAL PRACTICE TIP

A copy of a Massachusetts form for documenting a deviation from the guidelines is available at *www.pearsonhighered.com/wilson* in the companion website material for Chapter 9 under "Forms." The form provides a record of the trial court's reasoning for reference if the deviation is appealed.

Child Support Guidelines set a base from which a judge can then exercise discretion in a manner consistent with governing statutes, regulations, and case law. In addition, federal regulations specifically require that any deviation from the guidelines' amount be in the best interests of the child.[27] The presumption that application of the guidelines will result in an appropriate amount of child support is rebuttable. A court may deviate from the guidelines' amount if it is unjust, unreasonable, or inappropriate under the circumstances or not in the best interests of the child, provided the court issues findings regarding the reason(s) for the deviation. Some of the factors or circumstances that may justify a deviation include the following:

Extraordinary Expenses

Extraordinary expense
an unusual, unanticipated childrearing expense that is substantial in cost and/or duration

In general, it is assumed that the custodial parent is responsible for payment of a child's ordinary day-to-day living expenses. These are costs that are reasonably predictable and consistent from child to child. On occasion, an unusual, unanticipated childrearing expense may arise that is substantial in cost and/or duration. Such **extraordinary expenses** are often medical in nature. For example, a child may require either physical or psychological therapy on an ongoing basis or have a chronic medical condition, such as diabetes or cystic fibrosis. Such situations can involve costly medical care and medications, some of which may not be covered by insurance. Some conditions may require a custodial parent to make physical accommodations in the child's residence. Extraordinary expenses may be of other kinds as well. States vary with respect to how such costs will be treated. Most commonly, they are handled as a deviation from the guidelines for a temporary or extended period. A prorated amount may be added onto the child support obligation based on the respective incomes of the parties.

PARALEGAL PRACTICE TIP

The cost of higher education usually is not considered an extraordinary expense in the sense that it can be anticipated and is not viewed by some as a "necessary." However special education programs for gifted or disabled children are treated by some courts as extraordinary expenses.

Multiple Families

PARALEGAL PRACTICE TIP

Some states address this situation by statute. For example, in New Hampshire, RSA 458-C:4 provides, "When considering a request for an original support order or modification of a support order under this chapter, the court shall take into account any stepchildren for which either parent may be responsible."

According to the U.S. Department of Health and Human Services, almost 75% of people who divorce remarry.[28] A new marriage often results in a his, hers, and ours situation when it comes to children, frequently resulting in both emotional and financial stress.

Although a new partner generally has no legal obligation to support his or her spouse's children from prior marriages or relationships, states may give consideration to such circumstances within their guidelines. The contemporary view is that there is no precise, mathematical formula for calculating child support when multiple families are involved. The determination is left to the discretion of the court. However, the traditional rule is that "first families come first" in child support calculations, and an obligor usually cannot request a downward modification in support due a first family based upon his or her new obligations to a second family. Some states deduct the amount of support due to "first" or prior families from the income available to support potential obligations flowing from the more recent relationship. The obligor also may be able to use obligations to a new family as a defense to a claim by a former spouse for an upward modification in child support to a prior family. For example, in 2002, the rules for the Nebraska Guidelines were amended to include the following provision:

> Limitation on Decrease: An obligor shall not be allowed a reduction in an existing support order solely because of the birth, adoption, or acknowledgement of subsequent children of the obligor; however, a duty to provide regular support for subsequent children may be raised as a defense to an action for an upward modification of such existing support order.[29]

PARALEGAL PRACTICE TIP

Even if support obligations to a prior family can be deducted from income, a deviation from the guidelines amount will generally not be permitted on the sole basis that the noncustodial parent has a child from a prior relationship living with him or her. See, e.g., *Beck v. Beck,* 165 Md. App. 445, 885 A.2d 887 (Md. Spec. App. 2005).

Educational Needs of the Children

In the preschool, elementary, middle, and high school years, educational needs of the minor children may include enrollment in a private or alternative school, participation in extracurricular activities, tutoring and other forms of compensatory education for a child with disabilities, or special lessons for a gifted child who demonstrates unusual potential in a particular field such as music or athletics.

Several states that set the age of emancipation and termination of child support at eighteen years provide that if the child continues his or her high school education past age eighteen, the court, in its discretion, may order the continuation of support until the child finishes high school or reaches the age of nineteen. This is the approach taken in Idaho, for example. The Idaho Supreme Court has described the rationale behind the policy as follows:

> There is a strong public policy in favor of providing support to students. A large population of educated persons greatly benefits society. All students should be encouraged to finish high school, regardless of whether they have reached the age of eighteen, and the absence of child support should not influence the decision to stay in school.[30]

The current trend with respect to higher education is away from requiring parents to pay for college expenses absent an agreement, but there is a range among the states that address the issue by statute. At one end is New Hampshire, which revised its statute in 2004 to provide that "No child support order shall require a parent to contribute to an adult child's college expenses or other educational expenses beyond the completion of high school."[31] In 1997, Colorado also completely reversed its earlier position and terminated the court's authority to order postsecondary education support absent an agreement of the parties.[32] Massachusetts is at the other end of the spectrum. By statute, it provides that a court may order support "for any child who has attained age twenty-one but who has not attained age twenty-three, if such child is domiciled in the home of a parent, and is principally dependent on said parent for maintenance due to the enrollment of such child in an educational program, excluding educational costs beyond an undergraduate degree."[33]

Iowa is an example of a state that falls in the middle. Iowa Code section 598.21(F) authorizes courts to order a postsecondary education subsidy under certain conditions for good cause shown. However, the amount to be paid by each parent cannot exceed one-third of the total cost of postsecondary education. The court determines "the cost of postsecondary education based on the cost of attending an in-state public institution for a course of instruction leading to an undergraduate degree and shall include the reasonable costs for only necessary postsecondary education expenses." By case law, the Iowa courts have expanded the nature of what will be considered necessary educational expenses: "We recognized the reasonable and necessary costs of attending college surpass the costs of tuition, books, room, board, and supplies. A college education is not limited to what is learned in the classroom; it includes social, cultural, and educational experiences outside the classroom."[34]

Custodial and Visitation Arrangements

Most early versions of state child support guidelines were based on a traditional custody model, with one parent having primary physical custody and the other parent having "reasonable visitation rights" approximately 20% of the time. Deviations were sometimes allowed to accommodate infrequent **joint** or **split** custody arrangements. As the concept of family has evolved, and parents have adopted new custodial models, legislatures and courts have gradually recognized the need to calculate child support awards tailored to those models.

Child support amounts now may be adjusted based on variations in visitation patterns or degrees of shared custody, etc. In more than half the states, the deviation is left to the discretion of the court, but several states (such as Wisconsin,[35] Arizona,[36] Colorado,[37] Maine,[38] and New Jersey[39]) apply a different formula once visitation or shared custody reaches a certain level. (See Exhibit 9.3.) The relevant Oklahoma statute provides for an adjustment in the base amount of child support when "shared parenting" time has been ordered by the court or agreed to by the parents. Shared parenting time means that each parent has physical custody of the child or children overnight for more than one hundred twenty (120) nights each year.[40] In determining what constitutes parenting, the courts may look beyond the quantitative number of days a child is technically in the custody of each parent, to qualitative factors such as participating in school activities and arranging for and attending extracurricular activities in which the child is involved, etc.

Joint physical custody
a custody arrangement in which a child spends a more-or-less equal amount of time living with each parent

Split custody
a custody arrangement in which each parent has legal and/or physical custody of one or more of the parties' children

PARALEGAL PRACTICE TIP

Visit *www.alaska.gov* to see examples of forms and calculators of child support tailored to a variety of custody arrangements. You can find a link to this site at *www.pearson-highered.com/wilson* in the companion website material for Chapter 9 under "Forms."

PARALEGAL PRACTICE TIP

Given the considerable variety of approaches among the states, paralegals need to be familiar with the current formula applicable to the child support cases they work on. If unique custodial models are not addressed in the applicable guideline formula, arguments may need to be made for a deviation. For example, what if a parent spends only the summer months with the child or has to travel across the country monthly at considerable expense to exercise visitation rights?

PARALEGAL PRACTICE TIP

Occasionally, a custodial parent relinquishes possession and control of a child to a noncustodial parent without a formal change in custody. In doing so, the custodial parent may well lose a right to child support previously ordered by the court. Texas addresses this situation by statute and provides that an obligor may plead the obligee's actions as an affirmative defense (in whole or in part) to a motion for enforcement of child support. In such situations, the most appropriate course of action is to seek an order of the court formally modifying both child custody and support based on the change in circumstances.[41]

EXHIBIT 9.3 North Dakota Formula for Child Support with Equal Physical Custody

---

FROM THE ADMINISTRATIVE CODE

Equal physical custody—Determination of child support obligation. A child support obligation must be determined as described in this section in all cases in which a court orders each parent to have equal physical custody of their child or children. Equal physical custody means each parent has physical custody of the child, or if there are multiple children, all of the children, exactly 50% of the time. A child support obligation for each parent must be calculated under this chapter, assuming the other parent is the custodial parent of the child or children subject to the equal physical custody order. The lesser obligation is then subtracted from the greater. The difference is the child support amount owed by the parent with the greater obligation.[42]

Cost of Living in a Geographical Area

The states vary with respect to whether or not cost of living will warrant a deviation from the guidelines when the parents live in different geographical localities. For example, an individual living in New York City is likely to have a considerably higher cost of living than one living in Littleton, New Hampshire. The Maryland Court of Appeals has held that "a lower cost of living in the child's locality is not a proper basis for deviating from the guidelines."[43] However, other courts have held that a noncustodial parent's higher cost of living may be an acceptable reason for deviating from the guidelines if substantiated by concrete evidence.

Standard of Living

The primary purpose of child support is to provide for a child's basic survival "needs." However, when substantial resources are available, an effort is made to provide the child with the standard of living he or she would have had if the family had remained intact. The higher the parents' income, the more likely a court will consider standard of living—the country club life, overseas travel, pedigree pets, private school, summer camp, etc. In effect, a child's needs are viewed as relative and directly related to the parents' incomes, and therefore, support awards may vary accordingly. "To be sure, many people, adults and children alike, have far more than they truly 'need' to survive, or even to live comfortably. . . . Even among middle class populations, there is a range of tastes with varying costs. . . . Simply put, given a choice between rhinestones and rubies, many people opt for the latter if they can afford to do so."[44]

PARALEGAL PRACTICE TIP

Courts have broad discretion when calculating child support obligations in cases where the parties' income(s) exceed the maximum guidelines amount. However, they may exercise restraint in high-income cases when unrestrained child support awards unrelated to the characteristics or needs of the children appear to serve more as disguised alimony or property division awards than as child support. In a 2010 case, the Connecticut Supreme Court took the position that an affluent noncustodial parent should not have to contribute more than 15.89% of his income over the maximum guideline amount as additional child support (the maximum percentage at the upper limit of the state's guidelines). See *Maturo v. Maturo*, 296 Conn. 80, 995 A.2d 1 (2010)

Additional examples of circumstances that may justify a deviation include, but are not limited to, the following:

- **Number and ages of the children** This information may be considered if not already factored into the guidelines formula.
- **The financial resources of the child(ren)** A child may receive governmental benefits (such as social security disability income), be a beneficiary of a trust

established by a grandparent, or be employed and earning limited or substantial income.

- **Needs, liabilities, and resources of the custodial and the noncustodial parents** Income from a new partner may need to be considered if it frees up parental income and makes it available for child support purposes. For example, the new partner may be covering the rent or mortgage payment and other household expenses. The child support amount may also include adjustments for substantial liabilities such as student loans.

- **Financial misconduct of either parent** The court may consider whether either parent has failed to comply with discovery requests, made excessive expenditures, or fraudulently concealed or disposed of property in an effort to reduce a child support obligation. Under such circumstances a court may order child support in an amount that deviates from the guidelines and at a level substantially disproportionate to the guidelines amount or to the obligor's alleged ability to pay. (See Case 9.1.)

- **Existence of an agreement between the parties** Based on the strong public policy in favor of protecting the rights and needs of children, the courts retain jurisdiction over child-related issues, including child support. Parents cannot totally waive or relinquish support obligations by agreement, because the right to support is the child's right. However, an agreement of the parties containing provisions relating to child support may be given considerable weight by the court if the terms are reasonable and beneficial to the child, and do not provide for a level of child support below the minimum called for by the child support guidelines as applied to the parties. Courts in many states have enforced provisions in agreements in which noncustodial parents agree to pay child support amounts far in excess of the guidelines amount. For example, in the *Pursley* case, the Kentucky Supreme Court observed that parties to divorce frequently have valid motives for making what may appear to others to be "bad bargains." (See Case 9.2.)

CASE **9.1** *Farish v. Farish*, 279 Ga. 551, 615 S.E.2d 510 (2005)

DISCUSSION OF THE CASE

In this case, the Georgia Supreme Court affirmed a district court's order that a noncustodial parent of five children with a gross monthly income of $10,374 be required to pay $3,000 per month for support of the three minor children and $2,000 per month in alimony to his wife of twenty-six years. The court stated that, in determining the obligor's ability to pay, the district court had:

> . . . properly considered appellant's income, property in his possession, the fact that he appropriated for his own use $55,000 of joint or marital assets after the parties' separation for which he had not accounted at the time of trial, and the fact that the appellant accumulated substantial debt after the separation by providing monetary support for his paramour and her family to the detriment of his own children and wife.

SIDEBAR

Do you think parental misconduct should factor into child support decisions? Explain your response.

CASE **9.2** *Pursley v. Pursley*, 144 S.W.3d 820 (Ky. 2004)

BACKGROUND

Under the parties' agreement in this case, the wife was awarded custody of the parties' two children. The husband agreed to pay 30% of all of his income from salaries and bonuses as child support until such time as the children turned eighteen or graduated from college or graduate school, whichever was latest. He also agreed to pay the cost of undergraduate and graduate educations for the children at any school that they chose in the United States. Additionally, he agreed to maintain the children's medical and health insurance and to pay any medical and dental expenses not covered by insurance.

In finding the agreement was not "unconscionable," the court noted the husband was "an educated and sophisticated businessman" with a strong moral desire to meet his obligations and that he was advised by counsel during extensive negotiations.

FROM THE OPINION

. . . One of the primary goals in enacting child support guidelines was to "increase the adequacy of child support awards." Unquestionably, Kentucky took a giant step towards this goal when it enacted the Guidelines. And the purpose of the Guidelines is not offended, but rather is aided by allowing divorcing parents to agree to provide greater support for their children. The Guidelines do not constitute the maximum support that a parent may agree to provide for his or her children. Although, as a rule, it is not in the best interests of the children when their parents agree to an amount of child support below the Guidelines, no one can convincingly argue that the best interests of children are not served when their parents agree to support in excess of the amount established by the Guidelines. Although a court is not bound by such agreements, . . . the Guidelines should not act as a barrier.

PARALEGAL PRACTICE TIP

The full opinion in the *Pursley* case is available at *www.pearsonhighered.com/wilson* in the companion website material related to Chapter 9 under "Cases" and in the Case Resources Section of the MyLegalStudiesLab.

PARALEGAL PRACTICE TIP

Visit *www.vermontjudiciary.org/eforms* to view a child support order form that contains information about parentage, parental responsibilities, medical support, child support (current and arrearages), duration of payment, and method of payment (including a wage-withholding option). You can find a link to this site at *www.pearsonhighered.com/wilson* in the companion website material related to Chapter 9 under "Forms."

When and How Can a Child Support Award Be Modified?

Modification of child support awards is governed by federal and state statutes, case law, and specific court rules. There are three primary bases for modification of a child support award:

1. modification triggered by a self-executing provision in an agreement of the parties that has been incorporated into a court's decree
2. modification based on proof of a substantial change in circumstances
3. modification based on a periodic review and adjustment of orders by the state's IV-D agency

MODIFICATION BY AGREEMENT

Although the courts generally encourage settlements, parental agreements that prohibit or limit the power of a court to establish or modify future child support are usually held invalid based on public policy. (See Case 9.3.) However modifications by agreement sometimes are accepted by the courts when they do not waive the child's right to a reasonable level of support consistent with the guidelines and they are in the best interests of the child. Modification provisions in agreements should be tied to actual financial circumstances such as a greater than 20% increase or decrease in the income of one of the parties. Courts have rejected provisions that call for a simple pro rata adjustment in the child support amount as each child reaches age eighteen.[45]

CASE **9.3** *Lee v. Lee,* 2005 ND 129, 699 N.W.2d 842 (2005)

PARALEGAL PRACTICE TIP

The full opinion in the *Lee* case is available at *www.pearsonhighered.com/wilson* in the companion website material related to Chapter 9 under "Cases" and in the Case Resources Section of the MyLegalStudiesLab.

BACKGROUND

In this case, the Supreme Court of North Dakota awarded a custodial father child support despite a provision in his divorce agreement that he would receive primary physical custody of the child and pay a reduced amount of spousal support to his spouse in exchange for her not having to pay child support.

FROM THE OPINION

"The best interests of the children require child support obligors to provide adequate support and maintenance for their minor children." *Smith v. Smith*, 538 N.W.2d 222 (N.D. 1995). . . . For this reason, the court has said, . . . Trial courts should not accept parental stipulations regarding child support if the court determines the stipulation is not in the child's best interests.

SIDEBAR

Do you think parents should be able to determine their child support responsibilities rather than the courts? Explain your response.

MODIFICATION BASED ON PROOF OF A SUBSTANTIAL CHANGE IN CIRCUMSTANCES

PARALEGAL PRACTICE TIP

To see a Massachusetts "Complaint for Modification of Child Support," and a "Joint Petition for Modification of Child Support" Form, visit *www.lawlib.state.ma.us*. You can find a link to this site at *www.pearsonhighered.com/wilson* in the companion website material for Chapter 9 under "Forms."

PARALEGAL PRACTICE TIP

Visit *www.vermontjudiciary.org/eforms* to find an example of a form that can be used by a party proceeding *pro se* to request modification of child support or spousal support. A link to this site can be found at *www.pearsonhighered.com/wilson* in the companion website material for Chapter 9 under "Forms."

Because children's needs and parents' resources can change unpredictably over the life of a support order, states provide for periodic review and modification—up or down as changed circumstances dictate. Either parent can bring a modification action based on a substantial change in circumstances. The moving parent has the burden of proving by a preponderance of the evidence that the requested modification is warranted. State IV-D agencies also can initiate requests for modification on a client's behalf. Although there is no guarantee that a motion for modification will be granted, it is likely to be if the court is persuaded that the change is substantial enough to make the prior award inequitable and the change is in the best interests of the child. In most states, the burden of showing a substantial change in circumstances will be satisfied if there is a given level of difference between the current presumptive guideline amount and the amount of the order then in force. The difference is usually expressed in a percentage. As of January 2011, in Iowa, for example, the amount was 10%; in Tennessee, 15% (if the current support is $100 or greater per month); and, in Indiana, 20%.

Many states require the change to have been "unforeseeable" at the time the initial order was entered. The claims raised most often relate to unanticipated changes in the employment or financial resources of one or both of the parties, a serious injury or illness of a parent or child, the impact of a subsequent family on either party's resources, a change in custody, a major change in the law governing some aspect of child support, or a change in a child's level of need. Generally, a parent may not rely on a claim of decreased income to obtain a modification of support if the parent's reduced earning capacity and inability to pay child support is voluntary. (See Paralegal Application 9.4.) Parents who intentionally try to avoid payment of support or who do not consider their children's needs when changing employment, etc., may not be entitled to a change in child support.

Paralegal **Application 9.4**

Does Incarceration Constitute a Substantial Change of Circumstances in the Child Support Context? Yes? No?

Yerkes v. Yerkes, 573 Pa. 294, 824 A.2d 1169 (2003)

In this case of first impression in that state, Pennsylvania's high court, answered "No" given the facts presented. The father/obligor, Keith, was incarcerated in 1994 after being convicted of sexually assaulting his then eleven-year-old daughter. In 1997, he petitioned the court for a modification or termination of the child support order entered when he and the child's mother separated in 1992. The basis for his argument was that he was unable to pay because he was incarcerated and earned an inadequate wage. The court reviewed cases in other jurisdictions and identified three primary approaches to assessing the impact of incarceration on child support obligations:

- No justification rule: Incarceration does not justify a modification of child support.
- Complete justification rule: Incarceration alone is sufficient to warrant a termination or reduction in child support.

- One factor rule: Incarceration should be considered along with other relevant factors when making decisions regarding modification of child support.

The court adopted the "no justification" rule based on three underlying considerations:

- It is not in the child's best interest to terminate the award because even if not paid during the period of incarceration, the door to reimbursement in the future remains open.
- It is unfair to allow the obligor to benefit from criminal conduct by allowing him to use incarceration as a means of escaping child support obligations.
- It is not appropriate to treat incarceration in the same manner as other forms of voluntary unemployment.

Clark v. Clark, 902 N.E.2d 813 (Ind. 2009)

In this case, the Indiana Supreme Court considered an incarcerated man's motion to reduce, revoke or

(Continued)

abate his child support obligation until his release from prison. Prior to his incarceration, the man, Todd, was ordered to pay child support in the amount of $53 per week based on the minimum wage. Once incarcerated, he was unable to meet his obligation because he was making less than $21 per month at his prison job. The trial court had denied his motion and the Indiana Court of Appeals reversed. The state Supreme Court vacated the trial court's denial of the petition and remanded the case.

The court held that Todd's incarceration created a continuing and substantial change in circumstance, making the current order unreasonable and justifying a modification. It reasoned that its decision served the best interest of the child primarily based on the following:

- Child support orders should reflect current earning capacity even if earnings are below minimum wage. It is error to set support based on income that is not there during incarceration.
- Imposing high child support payments on incarcerated parents is a punitive measure that can potentially damage the parent-child relationship.
- Incarceration should be distinguished from voluntary unemployment and underemployment. Unlike

incarceration, the latter two require not only a conscious choice to reduce income but also an ability to earn more income.

- Studies show that unsustainable support orders make it statistically more likely the child will not receive adequate support over the long term.
- When prisoners are released and face the twin barriers of substantial child support arrearages and problems finding employment, they are more likely to face jail time for nonpayment and to enter the "underground economy."

Sidebar

Which position do you think is most appropriate? Why? What if it is not the obligor who is incarcerated but rather the child for whom support is being paid? See *Baumgartner v. Baumgartner,* 237 Ill.2d 468, 930 N.E.2d 1024 (2010).

PARALEGAL PRACTICE TIP

The full opinions in the *Yerkes, Clark,* and *Baumgartner* cases referenced in Paralegal Application 9.4 are available at *www. pearsonhighered.com/wilson* in the companion website material related to Chapter 9 under "Cases" and in the Case Resources Section of the MyLegalStudiesLab.

MODIFICATION BASED ON A PERIODIC REVIEW AND ADJUSTMENT OF ORDERS BY THE STATE'S IV-D AGENCY

Under federal law,[46] without having to show a change in circumstances, the parties to a child support order may request a review every three years to determine whether the child support order in force continues to comply with the state's child support guidelines. States are free to institute shorter review cycles but cannot extend the period beyond three years.

How and by Whom Are Child Support Orders Enforced?

An action to enforce a support order may be brought by a custodial parent, a custodian or guardian of a child, a IV-D agency on behalf of a client, or an agency substantially contributing to the support of the child. There are three primary approaches to enforcement of child support orders:

- The custodial parent may proceed on his or her own with or without counsel, using the resources available through the court system.
- The custodial parent may retain the services of a private child support agency that charges a fee for helping the parent recover the amount of child support owed.
- The custodial parent may use the services of the state's IV-D agency, which has a broad array of available resources and enforcement tools.

Paralegal Application 9.5

An Ethical Issue

The services of a state's IV-D agency are available to every parent with a child support issue at little or potentially no cost and without the need to have legal counsel. An attorney has an ethical duty to advise clients of the availability of free IV-D services before undertaking a child support enforcement matter on behalf of a client so that the client can make an informed decision with respect to the need for representation. The IV-D agency is not intended to eliminate the need for counsel but rather to complement it. If a client chooses to retain counsel, the family law team may explain IV-D procedures and assist the client in locating necessary information and completing required paperwork. It is not the paralegal's role to provide legal advice, but the paralegal should be aware of the policy in this area at the firm where he or she works. Some firms have information sheets that can be provided to clients, describing various enforcement and representation options available.[47]

WHEREABOUTS OF THE NONCUSTODIAL PARENT

Often, the first major obstacle to enforcing a child support order is that the whereabouts of the obligor are concealed or unknown. In such cases, counsel and the custodial parent can potentially benefit from the availability of a wide range of centralized databases that can be accessed through the state-sponsored IV-D agency or through a private company engaged in the business of collecting delinquent child support payments. As one of its mandated services, each state's IV-D agency provides a **State Parent Locator Service (SPLS)** that connects a variety of data sources at the federal, state, and local levels. The sources include vital statistics, state and local tax records, real and personal property records, records of occupational and professional licenses, employment security, and public assistance records. SPLS also has access to records of other state agencies, such as the Division of Motor Vehicles, Unemployment Commission, Department of Revenue, and Bureau of Prisons. It also maintains the federally mandated State Case Registry (containing information about all support cases within the state's jurisdiction) and the State Directory of New Hires.

State Parent Locator Service (SPLS) a federally mandated service provided by each state for the purpose of helping to locate parents who are delinquent in meeting their child support obligations

If unsuccessful in locating addresses and information about income and assets at the state level, the state's IV-D agency can seek assistance from the **Federal Parent Locator Service (FPLS)** operated by the OCSE. The FPLS, in turn, can draw on the records of other federal agencies such as the Internal Revenue Service, Social Security Administration, Selective Service System, and the Departments of Defense and Labor, as well as the Federal Case Registry of Child Support Orders (FCR) and the National Directory of New Hires

Federal Parent Locator Service (FPLS) a service operated by the OCSE for the purpose of locating parents delinquent in meeting their child support obligations when multiple states are involved

THE BASIC TITLE IV-D PROCESS

When a custodial parent applies for public assistance, he or she is automatically referred to the state's designated IV-D agency for child support services. As a condition of receiving assistance, the parent must assign his or her rights to support to the state and must agree to cooperate with the state in identifying and locating the other parent unless a good cause for noncooperation can be established, such as a prior history of abuse that continues to pose a threat of serious violence. Once a support order is issued, the support obligation runs directly from the noncustodial parent to the state. Any support collected is then used to reimburse the state and federal governments for public assistance payments made to the custodial parent. Under federal law, states may elect to "pass through" to the custodial parent a modest portion of the amount collected, usually not more than fifty dollars.

PARALEGAL PRACTICE TIP

Applications for IV-D services are fairly consistent state to state. The form for New Jersey can be viewed at *www.njchildsupport.org*. The "Application for Services of Child Support Services Division" used in the state of Alaska can be seen at *www.courts.alaska.gov*. Links to both of these sites can be found at *www.pearsonhighered.com/wilson* in the companion website material for Chapter 9 under "Forms."

Paralegal Application 9.6

Alert Re Victims of Domestic Violence

Sometimes the resources of state and federal locator services are misused by individuals who have abused a former partner who has fled in order to protect himself or herself from further abuse. When a client is initiating a search, it is sometimes difficult to assess whether or not the search is being made in good faith. If the client is a victim and IV-D services will be used, it is important that the IV-D agency be advised of the history of abuse so that appropriate protective steps can be initiated at both the state and federal levels. In order to protect victims of domestic violence, a family violence indicator (FVI) is placed on the at-risk individual's name and the names of the children, indicating a restriction on disclosure of data. States are prohibited from releasing information on the whereabouts of "flagged" parents and children to anyone who has committed or threatened domestic violence. The address of the victim(s) will be blocked out in paperwork pertaining to both initial and enforcement actions.

Many custodial parents not applying for or receiving public assistance elect, but are not required, to receive assistance from the state's IV-D agency. At the time a child support order is obtained, the custodial parent, on his or her own or with the assistance of counsel, can ask the court to order that the payments be made through the state's designated IV-D child support enforcement agency. When the agency accepts the application, it assumes responsibility for collecting and disbursing payments, for monitoring compliance, and for initiating appropriate enforcement measures if a delinquency occurs. The underlying rationale for providing this service is that, if parents receive their child support payments, their need for public assistance will be reduced.

PARALEGAL PRACTICE TIP

Under federal law, all child support orders must include an income-withholding provision, but only IV-D cases are subject to an immediate withholding requirement absent good cause shown or an alternative agreement. If a custodial parent does not initially accept IV-D services but later wants to, he or she can apply for them by completing the appropriate application. Although a payor may not initially favor income withholding, it does have practical advantages. For example, it ensures that payments will be made regularly and that there will be a written record of payments made. Although the employer may be somewhat inconvenienced by the order, it is illegal to fire someone because of an income assignment order. In addition, failure to comply with an order can subject an employer to sanctions, including fines. The employer also may be held responsible for the amount of any support that should have been but was not withheld due to the employer's omission.

Arrearage
a payment that is due but has not been made

When an **arrearage** arises, the custodial parent may provide, by request or on his or her own, the following kinds of information about the obligor to the IV-D agency in an effort to facilitate enforcement efforts:

- social security number
- place of birth
- last known residential address
- current marital status
- responsibility for additional children
- current and past employers' names and addresses
- nature, sources, and location of assets and income
- names and addresses of relatives and friends
- clubs and organizations the obligor has belonged to
- licenses held (driver's, professional, etc.)
- local banks, public utilities, and other creditors of the obligor

ENFORCEMENT OF AN ORDER AGAINST A NONRESIDENT DEFENDANT

Once a child support order is made, it can be enforced in any state where the obligor or his or her assets are located. However, traveling to the nonresident defendant's state, retaining counsel, and asking the court in that state to enforce the child support order can be time-consuming, costly, and inconvenient. In the alternative, under UIFSA, the petitioner can use the IV-D agency in his or her state to send the court order to an appropriate court in the state where the obligor resides. This is called "registering" the order with the second state, which can then enforce (but not modify) it as if it were an order of that state's court. The petitioner's state is called the "initiating state" and the defendant's state is called the "responding state." Once the order is registered, it is important to keep track of when the nonregistering party receives notice of the order. Generally, if the nonregistering party fails to contest the validity, enforcement, or modification of the registered order, or to seek to vacate the registration within twenty days after notice of registration, the order will be conformed (considered a legal copy) by **operation of law**.[48]

ENFORCEMENT METHODS

There are several mechanisms available to help the **obligee** enforce a child support order. Some flow from federal law and some from state law. Most can be initiated by a state's IV-D agency on behalf of a client, and some can be pursued privately without agency assistance and with or without the assistance of an attorney. The strongest and most comprehensive arsenal is available to the state's IV-D agency. The IV-D process is especially helpful in dealing with nonpayment of support by obligors whose identity or whereabouts are unknown or who have moved to another state or are traveling from state to state to avoid paying support.

A brief description of various enforcement methods is provided below. The success of many of these measures is possible because of the extensive linkages between various state and federal agencies that allow for sharing of data at an unprecedented level.

Operation of law
a result that occurs automatically because the law mandates it regardless of whether or not a party agrees or intends that result; a party does not need to take any further action to bring about the result

Obligee
a person to whom a debt is owed

PARALEGAL PRACTICE TIP

In several states, failure to pay child support is viewed as a "continuing" offense. However, actions to enforce child support orders usually are subject to **statutes of limitations**. For example, in Michigan, in a civil context the statute of limitations for bringing an enforcement action for failure to pay support "is ten (10) years from the date that the last support payment is due under the support order regardless of whether or not the last payment is made."[49] On the other hand, the crime of felony nonsupport is subject to a six-year period of limitations.[50] Such statutes protect defendants from having to defend against stale claims long after witnesses and evidence may have been lost through the passage of time.

Statute of limitations
a statute that bars a certain type of claim after a specified period of time

Criminal Prosecution

In virtually all states, intentional failure to pay child support is a crime that can be prosecuted and punished by probation, fine, and/or incarceration. An intentional failure to pay is distinguished from an involuntary inability to pay. Before a delinquent obligor can be prosecuted at either the state or federal level, the obligor must be financially able to pay the overdue child support.

Under the federal Deadbeat Parents Punishment Act,[51] criminal nonsupport is a federal felony offense that can result in imposition of a sentence of from six months to two years. The nonsupport must have persisted for at least a year and be in an amount greater than $5,000. To trigger federal involvement, multiple states must be involved.[52] For example, the obligor and the child may reside in different states or the obligor may have left the child's home state to avoid paying his or her support obligations. Sometimes criticized as an unwarranted intrusion into matters best left to the states, this option is usually pursued only in the most egregious cases and, generally, when other federal offenses are involved, such as use of a false social security number. An action can be initiated by the state, the IV-D agency, or the individual.

Contempt Action

Civil contempt
a sanction for failure to obey a court order issued for another's benefit; a civil contempt proceeding is remedial in nature and its purpose is to promote compliance with the order

Criminal contempt
a punishment for failure to comply with a court order; a criminal contempt proceeding is punitive in nature and designed to punish an attack on the integrity of the court

An action may be brought against the delinquent obligor for civil or criminal contempt or both, depending on the circumstances. Although both potentially can result in fines, probation, or jail sentences, the purposes they serve are distinctly different. The purpose of **civil contempt** is remedial in nature. It is designed to encourage the obligor to comply with the child support order and catch up on payment of child support arrearages and thereby purge the contempt and avoid jail. The purpose of **criminal contempt** is punitive. It is designed to punish an individual for willfully disobeying an order of the court. The former serves the needs of the recipient of child support. The latter serves the dignity of the criminal justice system.

PARALEGAL PRACTICE TIP

Although some courts have linked child support and custody/visitation orders, the majority view is that support and custody are independent issues and should not be linked. If the custodial parent denies the noncustodial parent visitation in retaliation for a failure to pay child support, he or she may be subject to a contempt action. If the interference is sufficiently extreme, such as concealing the child's whereabouts, the parent may even lose physical custody of the child. The better course of action for the obligee is to seek enforcement of the support order and not risk contempt.

Income Withholding

Income withholding
an automatic deduction of child support from an obligor's paycheck

The most effective enforcement tool is **income (wage) withholding,** an automatic deduction from the paycheck of an obligor. All child support orders must include a wage-withholding provision, and an income-withholding order can be sent to an employer in any state. If it is a Title IV-D public assistance case, the wage withholding will take effect immediately absent good cause to suspend it or an alternative arrangement agreed to by the parties. If there is an arrearage, the income-withholding order may be increased on a percentage basis until the arrearage is paid off. If income withholding initially is suspended, it will go into effect when a month of support arrearages has accrued. Prior to this happening, the obligor is entitled to notice and a hearing.

PARALEGAL PRACTICE TIP

To see an example of an income-withholding form, visit *www.acf.hhs.gov/programs/cse*. Note that the form includes information with respect to limitations on the total amount that may be withheld under federal law. You can find a link to this site at *www.pearsonhighered.com/wilson* in the companion website material for Chapter 9 under "Forms."

More than half of all child support orders are enforced through this method. There are few defenses to income withholding other than a mistake in the amount of the support or arrearage due or a claim that the amount will exceed the maximum amount that can be withheld from the obligor's disposable earnings under the Federal Consumer Protection Act.

The income-withholding notice can also include a requirement that the employer enroll the obligor's children in the group health insurance program available to the obligor, without the necessity of formally petitioning the court for a **Qualified Medical Child Support Order (QMCSO)**. Prior to federal legislation in this area, many insurance companies denied coverage unless the employee was the custodial parent or claimed the child as a dependent.

Qualified Medical Child Support Order (QMCSO)
a court order requiring provision of medical support or health benefits for the child of a parent covered by a group insurance plan

Seizure of Assets

Under federal law, states are required to create administrative procedures designed to automatically create a **lien** on the real or personal property of an obligor located within the state in the amount of unpaid child support. The lien arises by "operation of law" without any action having to be taken by the custodial parent. Under federal law, states must give full faith and credit to liens arising in another state.[53] The lien on the property restricts the ability of the obligor to sell, transfer, or borrow against the property until the arrearage is paid. The custodial parent may need to "perfect" the lien under some circumstances. For example, a lien against real estate should be recorded in the appropriate registry for public records of deeds in order for it to be effective against third parties. This measure is especially effective in cases in which the obligor lacks any income subject to withholding but does own property.

Lien
an encumbrance on the property of another that operates as a cloud against clear title to the property

To see a Notice of Lien Form, visit *www.acf.hhs.gov/programs/cse*. A link to this site can be found at *www.pearsonhighered.com/wilson* in the companion website material for Chapter 9 under "Forms."

Title IV-D agencies can also attach and seize accounts of a delinquent obligor in financial institutions that operate in more than one state. The seizure can cover several kinds of accounts, such as checking and savings accounts, certificates of deposit, and mutual funds. The obligor will have a limited ability to sell or otherwise transfer those funds until the child support arrearage is satisfied.

Tax Refund Intercepts

Both state and federal tax refunds due to obligors can be intercepted and offset up to the amount of an obligor's child support arrearage. State IV-D agencies submit to the Internal Revenue Service and state Departments of Revenue the names, social security numbers, and amounts of past-due child support arrearages. The Tax Refund Offset Program can collect past-due child support payments from the refund after the obligor has received notice of the pending action and been given an opportunity to correct possible errors in a hearing. Only the IV-D agency has access to the federal intercept.

Unemployment Compensation Intercepts

A state's IV-D agency can arrange to intercept social security or unemployment compensation benefits to meet both past-due and continuing child support obligations. Needs-based benefits, such as Social Security Supplemental Income (SSI), are not subject to interception or withholding.

To view an example of an "Order Suspending License (Child Support or Parenting Time)," visit *www.courts.Michigan.gov*. You can find a link to this site at *www.pearsonhighered.com/wilson* in the companion website material for Chapter 9 under "Forms."

License Denials or Revocations

Under federal law, IV-D agencies can arrange to have a delinquent obligor's vehicle registration and/or driver's license suspended. They may be reinstated once the child support arrearage is paid. The agency can also seek denial or revocation of professional, recreational, or occupational licenses required by states to practice in a variety of professions, such as real estate, plumbing, and teaching. Virtually every state's Bar Association provides that the licenses to practice law of attorneys in contempt for failure to pay child support may be suspended. In particularly egregious cases, an attorney may be disbarred.

Passport Denial

Under federal law, an individual owing over $5,000 in child support may be denied a passport or have an existing passport restricted or revoked.

Credit Reporting

Under federal law, IV-D agencies must periodically report to credit bureaus the names of delinquent obligors whose support arrearages have reached a specific dollar amount.[54] Prior to the report being made, the obligor must receive notice and have an opportunity for an administrative review. The reporting of child support debts creates a "cloud" on the obligor's credit and alerts potential creditors that an obligor may be a poor risk.

PARALEGAL PRACTICE TIP

Some enforcement measures raise issues of constitutional dimension. For instance, according to the U.S. Supreme Court, a state cannot deny a marriage license to a delinquent obligor.[55] However, in 2001, the Wisconsin Court of Appeals held, as a condition of probation, that a father who intentionally failed to pay child support for the nine children he'd fathered by four different women could be prevented from having additional children until he made sufficient efforts to support his current children. The dissent expressed deep concern that a dangerous precedent had been set in the area of reproductive rights as the decision in effect established a state-sponsored court-enforced financial test for future parenthood.[56]

To encourage compliance with support orders, Title IV-D agencies use a variety of additional, less onerous preliminary techniques, such as frequent delinquency notices and telephone reminders. Occasionally, states also implement creative measures such as intercepts of lottery winnings. Many states publish "wanted" posters in public buildings, such as town halls and courthouses, containing photographs of the state's most serious offenders for whom arrest warrants have been issued. Some states have had "amnesty days" when a delinquent obligor can pay arrearages and avoid penalties. The threat of prosecution and public humiliation sometimes provides a sufficient incentive to a delinquent obligor to pay arrearages.

Tax Implications of Child Support

TAX TREATMENT OF CHILD SUPPORT PAYMENTS

Unlike spousal support payments, child support is a tax-neutral event. Child support payments are not deductible by the payor and are not includable as income to the recipient for income tax purposes. However, when spousal and child support payments are lumped together in a single payment without any designation as to what portion, if any, constitutes child support, the entire unallocated support amount will be treated as alimony by the Internal Revenue Service (IRS). The full amount paid will then be deductible from the payor's gross income and will be includable in the recipient's income. As tempting as it may be to use this approach (assuming the recipient is in a lower tax bracket and unallocated payments result in a net tax gain for the parties), there may be costly consequences in the long run. As of 2011, the federal tax code retained specific provisions governing unallocated support payments. If, for example, any portion of the unallocated amount is associated in the parties' agreement with a child-related contingency such as a child's reaching the age of majority, getting married, or enlisting in the armed services, there is a rebuttable presumption that a portion of the amount is child support. The IRS may then disallow a previously claimed deduction for that portion and require the obligor to pay taxes, interest, and penalties on it. The obligee, in turn, should be entitled to a refund of the tax paid on that amount.

THE DEPENDENCY EXEMPTION

The general rule is that the custodial parent is entitled to claim the children as dependents for tax purposes, resulting in an adjustment to that party's gross income.[57] The amount of the exemption is subtracted from gross income before the tax is calculated. Because of the potential value of the exemption, parties to a divorce frequently negotiate other arrangements. The parties may agree, for example, to alternate years for claiming the exemption(s), or to divide the exemptions if there is more than one child. In any tax year in which the custodial parent agrees that the other parent may claim one or more of the minor children as dependents, the custodial parent must sign a written release, which must be submitted with the tax return of the parent claiming the deduction (IRS Form 8332).

THE CHILD TAX CREDIT

Since 1997, the parent claiming the exemption is also entitled to a child tax credit. This benefit provides the parent with a credit against his or her tax liability rather than an adjustment to gross income.[58] The amount of the credit in 2010 was $1,000. The basic rules and a worksheet for calculating eligibility to claim the credit are explained in IRS publication 972.

The Role of the Paralegal in Child Support Cases

GENERAL RESPONSIBILITIES

The most common tasks a paralegal performs with respect to child support cases are the following:

- Identifying and gathering information concerning any related jurisdictional questions
- Researching the law governing child support actions in the applicable jurisdiction(s)
- Gathering financial and other kinds of documentation necessary to complete appropriate forms and prepare necessary documents and pleadings
- Drafting complaints/petitions, supporting affidavits and proposed orders for child support, or responsive pleadings to complaints/petitions
- Assisting with completion of child support guideline worksheets and drafting related memoranda if a deviation is at issue
- Assisting with preparation of the client's financial affidavit

- Recommending and drafting discovery materials such as interrogatories and deposition questions, and drafting responses to discovery requests received from the opposition
- Drafting child support provisions for inclusion in separation agreements or parenting plans (See Paralegal Application 9.7)
- Assisting with preparation for temporary hearings or trials on the merits
- Tracking the progress of the case to be certain timelines are met
- Drafting Title IV-D correspondence and forms
- Making sure the client is kept informed of progress and upcoming deadlines, hearings, discovery matters, etc.

PARALEGAL PRACTICE TIP

One of the most fundamental task a paralegal performs in a child support case is to organize and monitor workflow and timelines in the office. An attorney has an ethical duty to carry out contracts to provide legal services and not to neglect or cause damage or prejudice to clients. A failure to file the documents necessary to secure child support for a client that results in a loss of payments to which that client would otherwise be entitled may result in a suspension from the practice of law.[59]

SPECIFIC TASKS PERTAINING TO SEPARATION AGREEMENTS

Child support is frequently a hotly debated issue in a divorce case. Even though the guidelines provide some direction and are intended to be fair to both parents, the issue is not always simple enough to be distilled into a set formula. If the divorcing parties are able—either on their own or with the assistance of counsel and/or a mediator—to negotiate child support terms, they may develop a child support component for inclusion in their separation or parenting agreement. (See Paralegal Application 9.7 and the child support provision in the sample separation agreement in Chapter 12.)

Prior to drafting a child support provision or a proposal to be submitted to the court, information needs to be gathered regarding several preliminary questions:

- What are the financial resources of each of the parties? What is the presumptive figure when child support is calculated according to the guidelines? How long will support last? Is a deviation warranted?
- Do the children have any special needs? Will child support cover expenses like orthodontia, summer camp, clothing for when the child is with the non-custodial parent, dance lessons, private school or college expenses, and uninsured therapy for psychological problems?
- Does either of the parents have any limitations with respect to being able to provide for the children?
- What was the family's standard of living before the parties' separation? Will each of the parties be able to maintain that standard following the divorce, or will the child's standard of living be negatively impacted by living with one parent or the other?
- What is the anticipated parenting plan? Will physical custody be shared or split? Will the children be with the noncustodial parent for significant portions of time? Do the parties live at a considerable distance from each other?
- What are the expectations and motivations of the parties? Is there any chance that a client feels threatened and is agreeing to a low amount of child support because of a fear that if he or she does not comply, custody will not be awarded in the manner desired?

Paralegal **Application 9.7**

Drafting Pointers for a Child Support Provision in a Separation Agreement or Parenting Plan

PARALEGAL PRACTICE TIP

Increasingly states are providing standardized agreement forms that address all issues related to dissolution of a marriage including child support. The parties fill in the blanks on the form to reflect their facts, circumstances, and mutual agreements. To see one such form used in Minnesota, visit *www.mncourts.gov.* You can find a link to this site at *www.pearsonhighered.com* in the companion website material for Chapter 9 under "Forms."

A child support provision should address the following:

Amount of child support. The agreement may state that "child support will be in an amount consistent with the child support guidelines," or it may set an amount. If the parties want to deviate from the guidelines in their agreement, the child support amount must first be calculated according to the guidelines. Counsel must be prepared to provide evidence to show that application of the guidelines amount would be unjust, inappropriate, or not in the best interests of the child. If lower than the guidelines amount, it should be shown that the deviation was bargained for in exchange for some other benefit for the child under the agreement.

Timing of support payments. Will there be one or more payments per month, and when are they due?

Method of payments. If neither the child nor the custodial parent is receiving public assistance, will payments be made directly to the recipient? In person? By mail? By direct deposit? If none of these, will payments be made through the state's IV-D agency?

Termination of child support. The agreement should specify the circumstances that will constitute emancipation and be sufficient to trigger termination of child support, such as a child moving away from home or getting a job and covering his or her own living expenses.

Escalation clause. Sometimes the parties build in an automatic-increase clause by tying increases in the child support amount to an official indicator, such as the Consumer Price Index. Some courts do not favor or permit this approach, because it is not sufficiently related to the parties' specific financial circumstances or to the best interests of the child. Another option is to provide that the parties will exchange basic financial information annually and recalculate the child

support amount based on the guidelines. This approach takes into account fluctuations in the income of the respective parties but requires continuing contact and may be difficult to implement if the parties' relationship is especially strained.

Income of the child. Will payments be influenced by resources that may become available to the child as a result of employment, trust income, inheritances, etc.?

Visitation/time with the noncustodial parent. Will any adjustment be made in child support payments during periods when the child is with the noncustodial parent? This is an especially important consideration if physical custody is shared or if a child will be spending extended periods (such as the entire summer) with the noncustodial parent.

Extended absences from the custodial parent's home. Will any adjustments be made in the child support amount if, for example, a child will be away at a private school for much of the year or at a summer camp for two months in the summer?

Costs of higher education. Although not permitted in an increasing number of states, the parties may agree on coverage of the costs of higher education. The sample separation agreement provided in Chapter 12 contains a detailed provision addressing this issue. Consideration needs to be given to the resources of the parties, where the children will go to college, their special needs or abilities, the resources that may be available to them through scholarships and financial aid, and the costs associated with a basic program of study. For instance, will "college expenses" cover tuition, room, board, books, computers, uniforms, fees, etc.? Will payments for educational expenses go to the custodial parent or directly to the educational institution?

Extracurricular activities. There are a host of activities available to children today, such as music, dance, art or drama lessons, computer camps, and athletic activities, including sports clinics, etc., but not without cost. The parties need to spell out how decisions will be made with respect to participation in these activities as well as how associated costs will be covered.

Medical insurance. Which party will pay for the coverage and how will uninsured medical expenses be handled? "Medical" should be broadly defined to include dental and eye care (glasses, etc.).

(Continued)

Income tax treatment of the child support payments. Assuming there will not be an unallocated support amount, the parties should indicate that child support payments will be nondeductible to the payor and nonincludable in the income of the recipient.

Dependency exemption. The parties should set forth their understanding regarding who will claim the exemption. If the noncustodial parent is going to claim the exemption for one or more of the children, the agreement should provide that the custodial parent agrees to cooperate by executing IRS Form 8332 in a timely manner so that it can be filed with the obligor's return.

Security for child support payments. The parties may agree on some form of security for child support, such as a trust or insurance policy with the child as the named beneficiary.

Dispute resolution. The general provisions of the parties' separation agreement usually include a dispute resolution provision, but if not, it is useful to indicate how the parties intend to resolve disputes pertaining to child support.

CHAPTER **SUMMARY**

As much as the concept of family has evolved over the past four decades, one feature has remained constant: the belief that parents have a duty to provide for the children they adopt or bring into the world until such time as those children reach the age of majority or are otherwise emancipated. The economic impact of a parental failure to do so is sufficiently costly to society at large that the federal government has assumed a dramatic leadership role in an area historically left to regulation by the states. It has taken giant steps in a national effort to hold parents accountable by mandating the designation of Title IV-D agencies in each state and facilitating interstate cooperation through UIFSA.

In order to establish and enforce child support awards, the courts must have subject matter jurisdiction over matters relating to the financial needs of children and personal jurisdiction over potential obligors. These requirements are not always easily satisfied. The child may have been moved from state to state. The identity of a child's father or the whereabouts of a noncustodial parent may be unknown. To help address this challenge, the federal government has required the states to have expedited procedures for establishing legal paternity, mandated the adoption of the Uniform Interstate Family Support Act, and created massive interrelated databases such as parent locator services, child support case registries, and new hire directories.

At the heart of a child support case is the establishment of a child support award through application of guidelines mandated by the federal government and designed by the states to promote efficiency and fairness. Each state chooses its own underlying model and identifies the kinds of factors the courts can consider when establishing and modifying child support awards, taking into account special circumstances such as the existence of multiple families, shared parenting arrangements, and educational needs. However, whether dealing with an initial order or a modification, an order is essentially worthless if it cannot be enforced. Once again, the federal government has stepped into the arena, creating the federal crime of criminal nonsupport and mandating that the states put in place a variety of other enforcement strategies, such as income withholding, tax intercepts, and denial of professional and driver's licenses, in addition to the more traditional methods of civil and criminal contempt.

Because of the complexity and fact-intensive nature of child support cases and the considerable variation in approaches from one state to another, the content of this chapter includes many illustrative examples. When working with a specific child support issue, it is important for paralegals to be aware of, and to research as necessary, the governing law in the jurisdiction where the case arises. Statistics suggest that progress is being made, but that there is still much to be done to ensure that parents meet their legal obligations and adequately provide for their children.

CONCEPT REVIEW AND REINFORCEMENT

KEY **TERMS**

IV-D agency	Case registry (federal and state)	Criminal contempt
Age of majority	Child support	Custodial parent
Arrearage	Civil contempt	Directory of New Hires

Emancipation

Extraordinary expense

Home state

Imputed income

Income withholding

In loco parentis

Joint physical custody

Lien

Long-arm jurisdiction

Noncustodial parent

Obligee

Obligor

Parent Locator Service (state and federal)

Personal jurisdiction

Presumptive child support guidelines

Public assistance programs

Public charge

Qualified Medical Child Support Order (QMCSO)

Rebuttable presumption

Statute of limitations

Transitional Assistance to Needy Families Program (TANF)

Uniform Interstate Family Support Act (UIFSA)

REVIEW **QUESTIONS**

1. Define "child support" and explain the public policy behind requiring parents to pay child support.
2. Identify conditions under which the duty to pay child support commonly terminates. Under what kinds of circumstances might the duty of support continue?
3. Distinguish between child support and spousal support.
4. Describe the origin and purposes of Title IV-D agencies.
5. Describe the origin and primary purposes of the Uniform Interstate Family Support Act, and identify three bases on which a court might obtain personal jurisdiction over a nonresident defendant under UIFSA's long-arm provisions.
6. Identify the primary purposes child support guidelines serve.
7. Define income. Identify three types of "income" that are usually not considered income in the child support context.
8. Define the term "imputed income." Give two examples of circumstances in which income might be imputed to a party.

9. Identify three circumstances in which a court might consider deviating from a child support amount that is presumptively appropriate under the guidelines.
10. Identify three ways in which a parent may obtain a modification of child support.
11. Describe the potential impact of incarceration on child support obligations.
12. Define and give two examples of "extraordinary expenses." How do the courts generally deal with such expenses?
13. Describe how the majority of courts treat the existence of multiple families when making decisions about child support.
14. Identify some of the ways in which courts address parental responsibility for the cost of their children's higher education.
15. Identify at least five methods of enforcing child support obligations.
16. Identify and describe the major tax implications of child support.

DEVELOPING YOUR PARALEGAL SKILLS

FOCUS ON **THE JOB**

In this activity, the student is asked to draft a Motion for Temporary Child Support, a supporting affidavit, and a proposed order tailored to a comprehensive fact pattern.

The Facts

William Pelletier and Betty Kelley began living together in the month of September nine years ago and got married three years ago on Valentine's Day. They have three daughters, Jennifer, Judie, and Jessica. Jennifer was born on June 26, 2002; Judie was born on June 24, 2004; and Jessica was born on July 4, 2007. William voluntarily acknowledged paternity at the time of each child's birth and has been a consistently adequate provider for Betty and the children. The three children are presently living with their mother in the home she inherited outright from her mother. The home is assessed at $375,000. Betty's father also has been very generous to her throughout her life. Over the past nine years, he has given her gifts of furniture, clothing, an automobile, several vacations with William and the children, and occasional cash gifts of up to $10,000 a year to help out with expenses, including special activities for the children. Betty hopes that he will continue to help her out when William is gone. She is aware that when her father dies, he plans to leave his fortune to a cancer research facility.

William has been working as an accountant for the entire period the parties have been together. His income has varied from a low of $24,000 in 2006 to a high of $97,000 in 2003. His income for last year was $62,000. Betty was a nurse before the children were born, and in her last year of full-time work, 2001, she earned about $42,000. She has occasionally worked night shifts since then but last year earned only $2,000. William and Betty agreed when Jennifer was born that Betty should stay home and care for the baby, and they have maintained that arrangement until the present time. Recently William decided to leave his job as an accountant working for wealthy people whose values and business ethics he found offensive. He has developed a fervent desire to become a missionary in Africa, where he will be receiving a token stipend of $5,000 a year. He will not have to pay for his food or housing, and his primary means of transportation will be a bicycle. He has not left the state yet but plans to leave before next Christmas. For now, he is living with a friend at 120 Bay Road in your town and state. Betty's address is around the corner at 250 Harrison Avenue, your town and state.

Betty is not certain what William has in the way of assets, as he has managed all the finances and paid all the bills during their relationship, saying it was "the least I can do, given that you take care of the kids all day." She knows at the very least that he has an investment portfolio valued at about $500,000, which generates interest and dividends of a minimum of $25,000 a year. They had a joint bank account with $17,000 in it, but William closed it out without notice to Betty. About $10,000 of that amount was a gift to Betty from her dad. Neither of the parties has any debts.

Betty says she doesn't care about herself but anticipates that she will continue to require the basic necessities for the children's benefit, such as food, clothing, and housing costs (taxes, insurance, utilities, etc.), medical expenses, and education-related expenses. In addition, Jennifer shows

considerable promise as a figure skater, and Betty hopes she can continue to keep up with her lessons and practice time, which cost about $250 a month. All three children are likely to require orthodontia work at some point down the road. Although he plans to stay in Africa for an indefinite period of time, William intends to retain his citizenship and residency in the state by using his sister's address. Although he realizes there are some negatives to this arrangement, such as having to pay taxes, he is a patriotic American citizen and wants to be able to complete absentee ballots and vote in each election.

William has filed a Complaint for Divorce in your local jurisdiction. He says that, since he will be in Africa and unable to visit the children, he doesn't think he should have to pay child support. Betty says the two of them brought the children into the world and each of them has a duty to support them.

The Assignment

Betty has contacted your supervisor, Attorney Howell, and wants to seek child support. She feels she should at least get the amount she would receive under the state's child support guidelines but isn't sure she can do that given the circumstances. Attorney Howell has asked you to draft the appropriate documents for your jurisdiction to accomplish this end, including a Motion for Temporary Child Support, a supporting affidavit for Betty's review and signature, and a proposed order. You should locate the statute in your jurisdiction that allows the court to order William to pay temporary child support. Locate models of all three documents, but be sure to tailor your documents to the facts of this particular case, applying the material covered in this chapter as appropriate.

FOCUS ON **ETHICS**

In this activity the student is asked to prepare an internal memorandum to his or her supervisor regarding the unethical conduct of a paralegal in the context of a meeting with a client.

The Assignment

Assume that you are a paralegal in the law office of Christopher Riggs, Esquire, a solo family law practitioner who represents William Pelletier in the above fact pattern. You are impressed with William and the personal sacrifice and commitment he intends to make as a missionary. While sitting with you in your lovely private office, William tells you that he expects Attorney Riggs to represent him on a *pro bono* basis. In response, you tell him that Attorney Riggs never accepts *pro bono* cases. William also tells you that he realizes that, because he has some substantial assets, he probably will be ordered to pay child support, but doesn't think he should have to under the circumstances.

You sympathize with him and suggest that if he can get Betty to agree to let him satisfy his child support obligation in the form of "alimony" rather than "child support," he will be able to deduct it from his income and at least receive that advantage. You also suggest that he should try to get the dependency exemptions for the three children. You later tell Attorney Riggs about this conversation and he is very concerned. He gives you a copy of the ethical canons for paralegals promulgated by the National Association of Legal Assistants (contained in Appendix A) and directs you to prepare a memorandum to him in which you (a) describe the ethical issues the incident raises, (b) explain how you have violated the canons, and (c) recommend an appropriate course of action given your conduct. For example, should you be fired or reprimanded? Should you be required to enroll in an ethics course for paralegals? Should you be required to draft a letter to the client, and if so, what should it say?

FOCUS ON **CASE LAW**

In this Focus on Case Law, the student is asked to respond to a series of questions regarding a case that involves several of the issues addressed in this chapter.

The Assignment

Read the New Hampshire case *Donovan v. Donovan, Jr.,* 152 N.H. 55, 871 A.2d 30 (2005) and then respond to the following questions:

1. What is the legal history of the case: Where was it brought prior to reaching the New Hampshire Supreme Court and with what result?
2. What were the issues being appealed and by whom?

PARALEGAL PRACTICE TIP

The opinion in the *Donovan* case can be accessed at *www.pearson-highered.com/wilson* in the companion website material related to Chapter 9 under "Cases" and in the Case Resources Section of the MyLegalStudiesLab.

3. On what authority did the trial court impute income to the mother? How was the figure for imputed income determined and by whom? What did the New Hampshire Supreme Court decide with respect to this issue and why? Do you agree with the trial court's or the supreme court's decision? Explain your reasoning.
4. Describe the respective positions of the parties regarding whether or not the basic support award covered the cost of extracurricular activities. What did the New Hampshire Supreme Court decide with respect to this issue, and do you agree with that position?
5. What was the state of the law in New Hampshire regarding the court's ability to order parents to pay for the college education of their children at the time the case was tried? What was the parties' agreement with respect to coverage of college expenses? Did the New Hampshire Supreme Court modify the parties' agreement? Why? What was the position of the dissent? Do you agree with the majority or the dissent? On what grounds?
6. What did the parties' agreement provide with respect to an annual increase in child support? Did the New Hampshire Supreme Court agree with this position? Why?

FOCUS ON **STATE LAW AND PROCEDURE**

This activity requires the student to complete a jurisdictionally appropriate child-support-guidelines worksheet based on a specific set of facts.

The Assignment

Assume that the firm where you are employed represents William in the above Focus on the Job exercise. On his behalf, locate and complete the child support guidelines form/worksheet used in your state. Two websites may be of particular assistance with this task: *www.findlaw.com* and *www.supportguidelines.com*. For purposes of the guidelines calculation, assume that the parties have agreed on the following:

- The three children will live with their mother and the father will have no visitation for the foreseeable future, given his unique circumstances.

- Betty is caring for the children a majority of the time, and childcare expenses should amount to no more than $250 per month.
- Betty's annual gross income is $2,000 and her adjusted gross income is $1,850.
- William's annual gross income is $59,000 and his adjusted gross income is $ $49,000 (Federal taxes $7,500, social security tax $2,500).
- William has agreed to maintain health insurance coverage for Betty and the children at a cost of $320 per month. He will not carry insurance for himself, as he will be in a remote African village where medical services are minimal and available at no cost to missionaries.
- Betty's dad has agreed to make arrangements to cover Jennifer's ice skating program for as long as she remains involved.

FOCUS ON **TECHNOLOGY**

In addition to the many links included throughout the chapter, this activity provides a series of useful websites for reference, along with technology-related assignments for completion.

Websites of Interest

Links to all of the listed websites are provided at *www.pearsonhighered.com/wilson* in the companion website material for Chapter 9 under "Resources."

www.abanet.org

This is the website for the American Bar Association. The Home page provides a search option where you can search for child support, child support guidelines, etc. You should be able to locate a number of excellent resources, including a chart that indicates the type of child support model used in each state (and the District of Columbia) and whether each state's guidelines address extraordinary medical expenses, child care expenses, college support, and shared parenting. See "Chart #3 Child Support Guidelines" at *www.americanbar.org/groups/family_law/resources/family_law_in_the_50_states.html*.

www.acf.hhs.gov

This is the site for the Administration for Children and Families (ACF), the federal agency that assists the states, territories, and tribal organizations through programs in support of children and families. It contains links to a number of topics related to family law, including child support. A useful *Handbook of Child Support Enforcement* is available at this site.

www.acf.hhs.gov/programs/cse

This is the website for the federal Office of Child Support Enforcement. There is a wealth of material available on this website, including the publication "Essentials for Attorneys in Child Support Enforcement" (3rd edition, 2002) and a listing of and links to child support (IV-D) agencies in each state.

www.alllaw.com

This site offers a feature called child support calculators for all states. Care must be taken to verify that appropriate and current guidelines are used.

www.ancpr.org

This is the website of the Alliance for Noncustodial Parents' Rights. It is both an informational and advocacy site, particularly for noncustodial fathers. Cases relating to various child support issues are identified.

www.census.gov

This site provides a number of statistical reports related to the topic of child support. Visit *www.census.gov/hhes/www/childsupport/childsupport.html*. One of the most informative reports available at this site is by T. Grail, "Custodial Mothers and Fathers and Their Child Support."

divorcenet.com

This site provides advice on family-law-related issues, including child support.

www.findlaw.com

Click on "Legal Professionals" and then "Family Law" under "Practice Areas," and then search for child support guidelines. Relevant links are provided to information about child support in all states and the District of Columbia.

www.supportguidelines.com

This is a comprehensive resource on child support guidelines in the United States. It provides a number of useful resources and links. Child support guideline worksheets for most states can be accessed via links on this site.

Assignments

1. Visit the following three websites, which are designed to help custodial parents receive the child support to which they are entitled. Explore the sites, summarize the kinds of information available, and indicate which site you think is most helpful.

   www.jfs.ohio.gov/ocs This is the site for the Office of Child Support in the Ohio Department of Jobs and Family Services.

   www.judiciary.state.nj.us This is the Home Page of the New Jersey Judiciary. Scroll to the bottom of the page to the "Quick Site Index." Open the dropdown menu in the box and select "Child Support." Click on "Go." Check out the resources "Guide to Applying for Child Support and Application," "Guide to Court Enforcement of Child Support," etc.

   www.dss.virginia.gov//Family/dcse/index.cgi This is the site for the Virginia Department of Social Services. Select "Child Support" on the top banner of the Home Page.

2. Go to *www.supportguidelines.com*. Click on "Resources and Links" and then on "Child Support Guidelines on the Web." Find your state and see what information and forms you are able to find.

3. Locate online information about your local IV-D agency and the services it provides. In particular, search for an Application to receive services.

PORTFOLIO PRODUCTS

1. Motion for temporary child support with an affidavit and a proposed order
2. Memorandum on ethics issues in a hypothetical case
3. Questions on New Hampshire child support case
4. Child Support Guidelines Worksheet

chapter 10
SPOUSAL SUPPORT

Jim, thirty, has been married to Julie, twenty-nine, for seven years. They have two children, ages four and six. When they married, Jim was going to college to become a teacher, but he dropped out, took care of the kids during the day, and waited on tables at night to support the family while Julie went to law school. Julie is now working at a large urban law firm and has decided that it is time to move on. Jim says, "That's okay, but now you can support me." Julie laughs and says, "You have got to be kidding!"

LEARNING OBJECTIVES

After reading this chapter and completing related assignments, you should be able to:

- define spousal support and describe how it has evolved

- distinguish between spousal support and property division

- identify various types of spousal support

- identify the kinds of factors courts consider when making spousal support determinations

- list at least five terms a spousal support provision in a separation agreement should contain

- explain when and how spousal support awards can be modified, terminated, and enforced

- identify the primary tax and bankruptcy implications of spousal support

- describe the role of the paralegal in a spousal support case

What Is Spousal Support?

Spousal support is an allowance for support and maintenance that one spouse may be ordered by a court to pay to the other spouse while they are divorced or living apart. If the parties are divorced, it is usually called **alimony,** maintenance, or spousal support. If they are legally separated, it is customarily called separate support or separate maintenance. Each state has developed its own approach to if and when spousal support will be awarded, what it will be called, what its purpose is, who will receive it, how much will be received, and for how long.

Spousal support is distinct from child support. (See Exhibit 9.1 in chapter 9.) Parents have a legal duty to support their children that cannot be waived or bargained away. Spousal support, on the other hand, is a duty that flows from one spouse to the other. However, marriage does not create an "entitlement" to spousal support upon divorce or separation. It generally can be waived and bargained away, and it may not be awarded absent one spouse's demonstrated need and the other spouse's ability to pay. It may also be subject to other restrictions based on state law.

PARALEGAL PRACTICE TIP

Paralegals need to be familiar with the approach to alimony/spousal support in their jurisdiction. For example, absent exceptional circumstances, Utah does not permit an alimony award to last longer than the length of the parties' marriage, and a minority of states, including Louisiana, allow alimony only to a party who is "free of fault" prior to the filing of a divorce action.

Spousal support/alimony
an allowance for support and maintenance that one spouse may be ordered by a court to pay to the other spouse while they are divorced or living apart; also called alimony, maintenance, or separate support depending on the circumstances and the jurisdiction

How Has Spousal Support Evolved?

AN HISTORICAL PERSPECTIVE

The origins of alimony in the United States can be traced to the English legal system. In England, ecclesiastical or church courts initially had exclusive jurisdiction over family-related legal matters. The church courts applied **canon law**, the church's body of law. Ecclesiastical courts granted two kinds of "divorces": **divorce *a mensa et thoro***, a divorce from bed and board that allowed the parties to live separate and apart but not remarry (as in a present-day **legal separation**), and in rare instances **divorce *a vinculo matrimonii***, essentially an **annulment** of an invalid marriage based on a canonical disability existing before the marriage (e.g., bigamy). Upon a divorce *a mensa et thoro*, an ecclesiastical court could require a husband to pay support to his wife (provided she was an innocent spouse) based on the belief that he had a lifelong duty to provide for her, even if they ceased living together.

The Divorce Act of 1857[1] (the Matrimonial Causes Act) relieved the ecclesiastical courts of their divorce jurisdiction and established **absolute divorce** by judicial decree under English common law, allowing the courts to terminate valid marriages. The Act also granted judges jurisdiction to order a husband to provide for an innocent wife after the marriage ended. The amount he was required to provide was based on her wealth, his means, and their respective conduct during the marriage. The assumption was that innocent women who were abandoned by or separated from their husbands should be awarded alimony because they lacked the ability to provide for themselves. That assumption was reasonable, given that, upon marriage, women gave up their rights to enter into contracts, own property in their own names, and possess and control their earnings. The English common law system eventually adopted by the states brought with it this dual emphasis on fault and the economic dependence of wives on their husbands. Prior to the 1970s, men still tended to hold title to the majority of assets obtained during the marriage. Upon divorce, they kept their assets, and "innocent" wives often received substantial long-term alimony awards with which to support themselves. The courts continued to retain the remnants of a husband's duty of support into the early no-fault era, although **Married Women's Property Acts**, eventually passed in all fifty states, eliminated many of the economic legal disabilities that made it impossible for women to earn money or own property in their own names while married.

A CONTEMPORARY PERSPECTIVE

Since the onset of no-fault divorce in the 1970s and the revision of property division laws allowing women to be awarded a "fair" or equal share of the marital assets, alimony awards have decreased in number and generally become limited in duration. Today, a reasonable estimate of the frequency of alimony awards granted upon divorce is 10% to 15%, and the vast majority of these awards are to women. They are primarily designed to enable a dependent spouse to develop skills, enter or reenter the workforce, and become self-sufficient. The ultimate goal is, in a relatively short time, to cut permanently the economic cord between the husband and wife.

The general rule is that, even if marital fault is sometimes factored into alimony determinations, the purpose of alimony is no longer to punish an obligor for some alleged misconduct or to reward an "innocent" spouse. The *Mani* case in New Jersey reflects the challenge faced by a court in a heavily "no-fault" state struggling with the question of what role, if any, fault should play in alimony determinations. (See Case 10.1.)

Canon law
church law; the body of law developed within a particular religious tradition

Divorce *a mensa et thoro*
a divorce from bed and board only; a legal separation

Legal separation
a judicial decree that allows the parties to live separate and apart without dissolving their legal relationship as husband and wife; sometimes called a limited divorce

Divorce *a vinculo matrimonii*
literally, a divorce from the chains or bonds of matrimony; a divorce that frees the parties to remarry

Annulment
the legal procedure for declaring that a marriage is null and void because of an impediment existing at its inception

Absolute divorce
a total divorce of husband and wife that dissolves the marital bond; frees the parties to remarry

Married Women's Property Acts
state statutes that extended to women various property rights that were denied to them under common law, including ownership and control of property. The majority of states passed such acts in the 1850s.[2]

CASE **10.1** *Mani v. Mani*, 183 N.J. 70, 869 A.2d 904 (2005)

DISCUSSION OF THE CASE

Unusual for several reasons, this case involved an alimony award to a husband. After a twenty-seven-year marriage, the wife was ordered to pay her spouse $610 per week in spousal support. She had well over $2 million in assets, and her spouse had assets totaling a few hundred thousand dollars and a minimum earning capacity of about $25,000 per year. Both parties appealed. The husband sought more alimony, claiming he would otherwise be unable to meet his monthly expenses, and the wife argued he should receive no alimony whatsoever based on his "indolence" in meeting his own needs and his lack of noneconomic contribution to the marriage. The appeals court refused to eliminate the alimony award but also refused to raise it, based on the husband's alleged adulterous and abusive conduct during the marriage (which was not taken into account by the trial court). Both parties appealed to the New Jersey Supreme Court.

The New Jersey Supreme Court's opinion includes a thoughtful review of the history of alimony in general and specifically in New Jersey. It describes alimony as an economic right arising out of marriage that is designed to provide a dependent spouse with a standard of living generally commensurate with the quality of economic life that existed during the marriage. While noting that New Jersey can be characterized as a "no-fault" state in most respects, the court addressed the issue of what consideration, if any, should be given to marital misconduct in alimony determinations. The court ruled that marital fault is irrelevant except in two narrow instances:

1. when the fault affects the couple's economic life, as when one spouse gambles away the parties' assets
2. when the fault "so violates societal norms that continuing the economic bonds between the parties would confound notions of simple justice." Hiring someone to murder a spouse would constitute such a fault

A dependent husband's extramarital affair standing alone was not viewed as a sufficiently shocking violation of social norms to deny him alimony in the context of a divorce.

SIDEBAR

Do you agree with the court's decision? To what extent, if at all, do you believe marital fault should factor into the alimony equation?

PARALEGAL PRACTICE TIP

The full opinion in the *Mani* case is available at *www.pearsonhighered. com/wilson* in the companion website material related to Chapter 10 under "Cases" and in the Case Resources Section of the MyLegal-StudiesLab.

PARALEGAL PRACTICE TIP

The South Carolina alimony statute can be found at *www.judicial.state.sc.us*. Note that under the statute marital fault can be considered in alimony determinations if it affected the economic circumstances of the parties or contributed to the breakup of the marriage, and that no alimony will be awarded to a spouse who commits adultery prior to execution of a separation agreement or entry of an order of separate maintenance. A link to this site can be found at *www.pearsonhighered.com/wilson* in the companion website material for Chapter 10 under "Statutes."

In the current no-fault environment, the primary focus is on spousal support as an economic event flowing from the marital partnership, and either the husband or the wife may be ordered to pay alimony. Most states gender-neutralized their alimony statutes on their own initiative in the 1970s. The issue was settled for the remainder of the states by the U.S. Supreme Court's 1979 decision in *Orr v. Orr.* In *Orr*, the Court declared an Alabama statute that imposed alimony obligations only on husbands unconstitutional as a violation of the Fourteenth Amendment's Equal Protection Clause.[3]

What Are the Differences Between Alimony and Property Division?

In states where it is allowed, decisions about alimony are generally not made until after the court has determined a suitable division of marital property. If each party is allocated sufficient property to maintain the standard of living that characterized their marriage, alimony may not be even become an issue. It is also unlikely to become an issue in many divorces because the parties have more liabilities than assets, and there is rarely sufficient income for an alimony award to even be considered.

Although an order for alimony cannot realistically be viewed apart from a division of marital assets, the considerations involved in each decision are different. The primary distinctions between alimony and property division are briefly summarized in Exhibit 10.1.

EXHIBIT 10.1 Alimony and Property Division—A Comparison

Alimony	Property Division
Alimony originated in the common law duty of a husband to support his wife, a duty now deemed gender-neutral.	Property division evolved with no-fault divorce and its emphasis on marriage as a partnership.
At the time of divorce, alimony focuses on what each party will need going forward into the future.	At the time of divorce, property division looks back to identify assets accumulated by the parties during the marriage that should be divided upon divorce.
Alimony awards are based on need and ability to pay, along with other factors considered relevant by statute and/or case law.	Division of property is based on the concept that both parties contribute to the marital enterprise, and thus each party is entitled to a share of the partnership upon divorce according to community property or equitable distribution principles.
The court must have personal jurisdiction over the defendant, who must be provided with notice in order for an alimony order to be issued and be enforceable.	The court must have jurisdiction over the parties and the property to be divided.
Alimony is usually in the form of cash payments payable on a periodic basis (e.g., monthly).	Property division usually involves transfers of property at the time of the divorce, such as an interest in a marital residence or a bank account.
Although lump-sum alimony is occasionally awarded, alimony is usually payable over a period of time. Payments **vest** as they fall due.	A property division order is effective as of the date of divorce, at which time the rights to property are vested and enforceable against the other party's estate as a debt.

Vest
to give a person an immediate, fixed right of ownership and present or future enjoyment; this right usually cannot be taken away by subsequent events or circumstances

EXHIBIT 10.1   *(Continued)*

Alimony is usually modifiable upon a material change of circumstances that significantly affects the payee's need or the payor's ability to pay, although some jurisdictions consider alimony awards final absent a specific reservation of jurisdiction.	Absent fraud, etc., property division is rarely modifiable.
Alimony is tax-deductible to the payor and income to the payee.	Payments or transfers made pursuant to a property division are not taxable events.
Alimony is generally not dischargeable in bankruptcy.	Property division settlements in the nature of "support" are generally not dischargeable
Death usually terminates alimony obligations (with the exception of arrearages) absent a judgment or agreement to the contrary.	Property division is not affected by the death of a party after the court has rendered a judgment. A property division is enforceable against the estate of a decedent
Alimony obligations usually terminate on the recipient's remarriage, absent a statute, court order, or agreement to the contrary.	Property division is not affected by the remarriage of either party.
Alimony is no longer primarily punitive in nature, although in some states, the courts consider misconduct during the marriage, particularly economic misconduct, as a factor in calculating an alimony award.	In a divorce granted on fault grounds (still available in many states), a court may award a larger portion of the marital assets to the aggrieved party. Even in states where fault grounds are unavailable, serious misconduct during the marriage (particularly misconduct with economic consequences) may influence the division of property in both community property and equitable division jurisdictions.

How Does a Party Obtain an Alimony Award?

PROCEDURE

Customarily, the procedure for obtaining spousal support is for the parties to exchange proposals, negotiate, and agree to an alimony provision in a separation agreement, or for one or both of the parties to petition the court for a suitable award given the facts of the case. In rare instances, however, a court will make an alimony award on its own initiative.[4]

Requests for temporary alimony may be made while a divorce action is pending.

PARALEGAL PRACTICE TIP

To see an example of a Motion and Declaration for Temporary Order (including alimony), visit *www.courts.wa.gov/forms*. (Washington) A link to this site can be found at *www.pearsonhighered.com/wilson* in the companion website material for Chapter 10 under "Statutes."

INITIAL STEPS TOWARD AN ALIMONY AWARD

Initial efforts of the family law team on behalf of a client in an alimony case usually focus on answering the following five questions:

PARALEGAL PRACTICE TIP

The 2005 *Thornley* case (*In re Marriage of Thornley,* 361 Ill. App.3d 1067, 838 N.E. 2d 981 (2005)), in which the Illinois appellate court ordered alimony on its own initiative, can be found at *www.pearsonhighered.com/wilson* in the material related to Chapter 10 under "Cases."

1. What is the governing law in the jurisdiction with respect to alimony awards?
2. Have the parties executed a premarital agreement, and if so, what does it provide with regard to alimony?
3. Does one party have a need for alimony that the other party has the ability to pay?
4. What factors will the court consider when making an alimony decision?
5. Is one or both of the parties likely to file for bankruptcy at some point in the future?

What Is the Governing Law in the Jurisdiction With Respect to Alimony Awards?

It is important to identify the current statutes, rules, and case law that govern alimony in the jurisdiction given the tremendous variation among the states and even among counties and individual judges within states. The kinds of questions needing to be answered include the following:

- Are alimony awards allowed in the jurisdiction?
- If alimony is allowed, what kinds of alimony awards are made? (See Exhibit 10.2.)
- Are waivers of alimony permitted?
- Are awards of limited duration?
- Are there guidelines in place that need to be considered with respect to setting the amount of alimony to be paid?
- Is marital fault a bar to receiving alimony or a factor to be considered in the amount of the award?
- What other factors does the court consider important in the alimony context?

Based on the governing law, counsel will consult with the client about the merits of a potential alimony claim, the form or forms of alimony that may be available, and an appropriate amount and duration.

Have the Parties Executed a Premarital Agreement and, If So, What Does It Provide With Regard to Alimony?

Premarital agreement
an agreement made by two persons about to be married defining for themselves their respective rights, duties, and responsibilities in the event their marriage terminates by death, annulment, separation, or divorce

Waiver
the giving up of a right or privilege

If the parties have executed a **premarital agreement,** a copy needs to be obtained for review by the attorney. If the agreement contains a **waiver** of alimony, research may need to be done on the enforceability of such waivers in the jurisdiction. A majority of the states that have considered premarital agreements waiving spousal support have upheld them,[5] but a limited number of states (such as South Dakota) exclude alimony waivers from premarital agreements by statute or case law. (See Case 10.2.) The Uniform Premarital Agreement Act, adopted in some form or another in just over half of the states, allows provisions in premarital agreements that establish or eliminate spousal support unless enforcement would bring about an unconscionable result, such as cause a spouse to become eligible for public assistance at the time of separation or divorce.

PARALEGAL PRACTICE TIP

The full text of the Uniform Premarital Agreement Act is accessible at *www. nccusl.org.* A link to this site can be found at *www.pearsonhighered.com/ wilson* in the companion website material for Chapter 10 under "Resources."

PARALEGAL PRACTICE TIP

If the parties did waive their alimony rights in a premarital agreement but later wish to agree to an award, there is case law (in New York, for example) to the effect that they may be able to do so.[6] The general rule appears to be that "No public policy is violated by permitting enforcement of a waiver of spousal support executed by intelligent, well-educated persons, each of whom appears to be self-sufficient in property and earning ability, and both of whom had the advice of counsel regarding their rights and obligations as marital partners at the time they executed the agreement."[7]

CASE 10.2 *Sanford v. Sanford*, 2005 SD 34, 694 N.W.2d 283 (2005)

DISCUSSION OF THE CASE

The premarital agreement executed by the parties in this case included a single unallocated payment structure for alimony, support, and property division. The husband claimed that this provision not only protected his $55-million net worth, but also constituted a waiver of alimony by his wife.

Although the state of South Dakota had adopted the Uniform Premarital Agreement Act, it did not include the provisions allowing parties to contract regarding elimination or modification of spousal support. The legislature chose instead to exclude alimony waivers from prenuptial agreements by statute (SDCL 25–2–18), thereby protecting the rights of both men and women asked to sign away these rights.

The court noted that the agreement in question did not include specific reference to alimony and support, but that even if it had, a waiver would be of no effect. The Court held that provisions in a premarital agreement purporting to waive spousal support are void and unenforceable, as they are contrary to public policy and may be severed from valid portions of the agreement without invalidating the agreement in its entirety.

SIDEBAR

Do you think spouses should be able to waive alimony in premarital agreements?

PARALEGAL PRACTICE TIP

The full opinion in the *Sanford* case is available at *www.pearsonhighered. com/wilson* in the companion website material related to Chapter 10 under "Cases" and in the Case Resources Section of the MyLegalStudiesLab.

Even if there is no premarital agreement, the parties may choose to waive their respective rights to alimony in their **separation agreement.** Notwithstanding the parties' freedom to contract to this effect, many judges will not incorporate such a waiver in a divorce decree in the case of a long-term marriage unless there has been a sufficient **quid pro quo.** For example, a spouse might be awarded a greater share of the marital assets in lieu of alimony.

Does One Party Have a Need for Alimony That the Other Party Has the Ability to Pay?

Whether or not alimony will be sought depends in large part on the respective needs of the parties and their relative abilities to pay. Before making the decision to pursue an alimony claim, the client must prepare a complete and realistic budget of his or her needs, and a thorough review of the financial assets and liabilities of each of the parties should take place. An assessment can then be made as to whether after the marital property is divided, one of the parties will have a need for alimony that the other party will be able to pay. In short-term marriages involving few assets, alimony awards are rarely made. There simply are not enough resources "to go around," or the resources are limited in terms of how they can reasonably be divided. In marriages involving substantial assets, need will be determined relative to the standard of living the parties maintained during the marriage.

What Factors Will the Court Consider When Making the Alimony Decision?

If it appears that alimony is needed and should be sought, information needs to be gathered regarding all of the factors potentially considered by the court in the jurisdiction to assess the strengths and weaknesses of the client's case. Although need and ability to pay are threshold factors, courts usually consider a number of

Separation agreement
an agreement made between spouses in anticipation of divorce or a legal separation concerning the terms of the divorce or separation and any continuing obligations of the parties to each other

Quid pro quo
an action or thing exchanged for another action or thing of relatively equal value

additional factors as well, such as duration of the marriage, the ages and health of the parties, the education and employment history of each spouse, and their reasonably anticipated future income and earning potential.

Is One or Both of the Parties Likely to File for Bankruptcy at Some Point in the Future?

If bankruptcy looms in the future of either or both of the parties, counsel will discuss with the client its potential impact. Particularly relevant is the fact that property division settlements in a divorce that are not in the nature of "support" may possibly be discharged in bankruptcy, whereas spousal and child support generally are not. A client needing alimony may choose to settle for less in the way of an unprotected property award and seek a higher and potentially more secure award of alimony.

After these questions are addressed, negotiations with the opposing party/counsel will begin or continue if already begun. If negotiation does not lead to an agreement, the parties may attempt to mediate their dispute. If that fails, a proposed alimony provision will be drafted by each party for the court's consideration. Later in this chapter, Paralegal Application 10.2 provides basic drafting suggestions for alimony provisions.

What Are the Various Types of Alimony?

Although alimony is legally recognized to some degree in virtually every jurisdiction, there is no consensus regarding its purpose, amount, or duration. Some states, such as Texas, are reluctant to make any awards at all and allow only short-term, limited-purpose maintenance except in certain circumstances. Others, like South Carolina, are flexible and creative and define a number of alimony options by statute. A brief summary of the most common types of alimony is provided in Exhibit 10.2.

EXHIBIT 10.2 Types of Alimony/Spousal Support[8]

Temporary Alimony/Alimony *Pendente Lite*	Interim alimony ordered by the court pending an action for divorce or separation in which a party has made a claim for alimony
Permanent/Traditional Alimony	Alimony usually payable in weekly or monthly payments, either indefinitely or until a time or circumstance specified in a court order
Term Alimony	Alimony payable in weekly or monthly payments for a specified period of time
Rehabilitative Alimony (sometimes called limited or transitional alimony)	Alimony found necessary to assist a divorced person in acquiring the education or training required to find employment outside the home or to reenter the labor force
Restitution/Reimbursement Alimony	Alimony designed to repay a spouse who during the marriage made financial contributions that directly enhanced the earning capacity of the other spouse
Separate Maintenance	Money paid by one married person to the other for support if they are not divorced but are no longer living together as husband and wife
Lump-Sum Alimony/Alimony in Gross	Alimony in the form of a single and definite sum usually not subject to modification

PARALEGAL PRACTICE TIP

The cases and statutes referenced in this chapter reflect the considerable variation that exists across the states in terms of the types of alimony awards permitted in different jurisdictions and favored by particular judges. An understanding of the legal environment in which the client's case is filed will help guide interviewing, discovery, and drafting efforts.

PARALEGAL PRACTICE TIP

A copy of the relevant section of the Texas Family Code is accessible at *www.pearsonhighered.com/wilson* in the companion website material related to Chapter 10 under "Statutes."

PARALEGAL PRACTICE TIP

A copy of the Act reforming Alimony in Massachusetts effective March 2012 can be found at *www.lawlib.state.ma.us*. You can find a link to this site in the companion website material for Chapter 10 under "Resources."

TEMPORARY ALIMONY / ALIMONY *PENDENTE LITE*

Temporary alimony or **alimony *pendente lite*** is support awarded to a dependent spouse in order to maintain the status quo as to financial circumstances while a marital action is pending. The action could be one seeking an annulment, a legal separation, or a divorce. Temporary alimony generally continues until the matter is settled on the merits (i.e., an annulment, legal separation, or divorce is granted).

Temporary alimony/alimony pendente lite

support awarded to a dependent spouse in order to maintain the status quo as to financial circumstances while a marital action is pending.

PARALEGAL PRACTICE TIP

The general rule is that temporary alimony will not continue beyond the voluntary dismissal or abandonment of the underlying action or entry of the judgment and exhaustion of all appeals. In some jurisdictions, resumption of sexual relations between the parties will constitute a reconciliation warranting termination of the divorce action and the temporary alimony order.

The timing and procedure governing a filing for temporary support are established by statute or court rules. The request for alimony is usually made in the initial complaint for divorce or by separate motion. Notice will be given to the other party, and a hearing will customarily be held. The burden is on the requesting party to establish that the parties are married; that a petition has been filed for divorce, legal separation, or annulment; and that facts exist justifying an award. The appropriate facts often are laid out in a supporting affidavit addressing the factors considered by the court in making alimony determinations. The respondent has the right to submit an affidavit in opposition to the motion for temporary alimony, and sometimes courts will make temporary alimony decisions based on the parties' affidavits without holding a hearing.

PARALEGAL PRACTICE TIP

Motions for temporary alimony need to be taken seriously as they often set the stage for permanent orders. If there is an urgent need, the request will be made early in the proceedings. However, if there are substantial assets, counsel may want to wait at least until initial discovery is conducted. In a limited number of jurisdictions, the amount of a temporary alimony award is based on guidelines similar to the guidelines used to calculate child support awards according to a basic formula.

PARALEGAL PRACTICE TIP

A sample Motion for Temporary Orders with a Supporting Affidavit can be accessed at *www.pearsonhighered.com/wilson* in the companion website material related to Chapter 5 under "Forms."

Motions for temporary alimony are not always granted. If the petitioning spouse has sufficient means to support himself or herself according to the parties' accustomed lifestyle and to prosecute or defend the pending action, that party's motion for temporary alimony may not be granted. There are also some specific circumstances that may bar alimony *pendente lite*, such as a voluntary departure from the household and abandonment of the other spouse, unless it can be shown that the other spouse's conduct justified the departure (abuse, threats, etc.). A defendant spouse may also raise as a defense a provision in a premarital agreement in which the parties both waived their respective rights to any form of alimony upon the filing of an action for divorce or legal separation. The agreement may bar a claim for temporary alimony unless the petitioning party has no other source or reasonable means of support.

Permanent alimony

alimony usually payable in weekly or monthly payments either indefinitely or until a time or circumstance specified in a court order

Surviving agreement

an agreement of the parties incorporated in a court's divorce decree that also retains its existence as an independent contract enforceable under basic principles of contract law

PARALEGAL PRACTICE TIP

Some states, such as Louisiana, do not permit waivers of temporary alimony in premarital agreements. See, e.g., *Barber v. Barber,* 38 So. 3d 1046 (2010).

PERMANENT ALIMONY

Permanent alimony is somewhat of a misnomer, given that in most jurisdictions, a court-ordered award is not truly permanent, but rather customarily remains modifiable given a change in circumstances, unless the order incorporates a **surviving agreement** of the parties that specifically addresses duration. For example, the parties may agree that alimony payments will continue until either party dies or the recipient spouse remarries, cohabits with another, or attains a certain age. Absent an agreement to the contrary, permanent alimony usually terminates upon remarriage of the recipient or death of either party.

PARALEGAL PRACTICE TIP

It is important that terms be clearly defined in agreements. For example, what exactly does "cohabitation" mean to the parties? Cohabiting with either a man or a woman? Living with an adult or a child? Sharing a residence and its expenses? Living together with someone in a relationship that has a romantic or sexual component? For a case that explicitly addresses this issue, see *Remillard v. Remillard,* 297 Conn. 345, 999 A.2d 713 (2010).

The primary purpose of permanent alimony is to provide financial assistance to the spouse who is in an economically weaker position. No duty is imposed on the dependent party to obtain employment and achieve economic self-sufficiency. When a permanent alimony award is granted, it is most likely to occur in a case involving a long-term marriage and a spouse who was a homemaker and primary caretaker of the parties' children for the bulk, if not all, of the marriage. The underlying premise is that, absent some extenuating circumstance, it would be unfair for one party's standard of living to remain high following divorce, while the other party's quality of life markedly declines as a result of mutual choices made during the marriage.

Although substantial permanent alimony awards were once common, they are relatively rare today. They are viewed as inconsistent with current assumptions about female economic independence. In addition, obligors, understandably, do not welcome permanent awards by which they will remain economically tied to a former spouse, and courts usually prefer to facilitate a clean break.

TERM ALIMONY

Term alimony

alimony payable in weekly or monthly payments that continue for a set period of time or until a condition specified in a court order or agreement

Term alimony continues for a set period of time or until a condition specified in a court order or agreement. It is customarily payable in weekly or monthly payments and usually remains modifiable upon a change in circumstances. In some states, the duration of term alimony will be limited by statute to no more than the length or some percentage of the length of the marriage.

LUMP-SUM ALIMONY/ALIMONY IN GROSS

PARALEGAL PRACTICE TIP

Lump-sum alimony may be particularly appropriate in some situations. For example, assume that a wife, fifty-five years old, has a demonstrated need for alimony and that her eighty-year-old spouse has an ability to pay it. Assume also that the husband is suffering from a terminal illness and is near death. A spousal support award of $5,000 a month for seven years is illusory, given that it is unlikely the husband will live more than a matter of months. Assuming the resources exist, an equivalent lump-sum award of $420,000 (perhaps adjusted for interest) may be more appropriate. See, e.g., *Schwartz v. Schwartz,* 225 P. 3d 1273 (2010).

Lump-sum alimony, sometimes called **alimony in gross**, is alimony ordered payable in the form of a definite sum, usually in a single or limited number of installments. It has distinct advantages to each party. It may appear to be more in the nature of a component of a comprehensive property division settlement. However, because it is characterized as alimony, if structured properly, it usually will be deductible by the payor for income tax purposes. From the recipient's perspective, although it will be taxable as income, it vests in the recipient when awarded and thus may be recovered from the obligor's estate if necessary. It is also generally not subject to modification, to elimination upon remarriage or cohabitation, or to discharge should the obligor declare bankruptcy. It also has the added advantage of "cutting the cord" and not dragging out the financial connection between the parties.

> **Lump-sum alimony/alimony in gross** alimony ordered payable in the form of a definite sum, usually in a single or limited number of installments; usually not subject to modification

PARALEGAL PRACTICE TIP

In some states, such as Florida, courts have awarded what they term "bridge the gap" alimony. It is generally short term in length and designed to help a party make the transition from married life to single life. For instance, the recipient may need to find a job and a new place to live, triggering one-time related costs (job search, moving, new furniture, etc.). The Florida alimony statute can be found at *www. leg.state.fl.us/Statutes.* You can find a link to this site at *www.pearsonhighered.com/wilson* in the companion website material for Chapter 10 under "Statutes." Note the heavy emphasis in the statute on the duration of the marriage. A short-term marriage is described as no more than seven years, and alimony is granted in short-term marriages only in exceptional circumstances. Note also that "durational" alimony is not to exceed the length of the marriage.

REHABILITATIVE ALIMONY

Rehabilitative alimony is usually awarded in situations in which one spouse has delayed or given up education or a career in order to remain at home and care for the children and the household. It is customarily awarded for a period sufficient in length to allow the dependent spouse to obtain education and training that will enable him or her to acquire greater earning power, reenter the workforce, and become self-sufficient with the exercise of reasonable effort. It is usually awarded for a fixed period and is generally not modifiable. Ideally, the recipient spouse proposes a plan for rehabilitation along with a timeline and an estimate of related costs. Some states, such as Florida, specifically require by statute that a detailed plan be provided to the court.

> **Rehabilitative alimony** alimony designed to assist a divorced person in acquiring the education or training required to find employment outside the home or to reenter the labor force; sometimes called limited or transitional alimony

In some states, a limit on the length of rehabilitative alimony is established by statute. More often, the court will set a time period within which the recipient is expected to make a realistic good-faith effort to complete a rehabilitative program and attain self-sufficiency. If either of the parties wants the award to be reviewable, the parties' agreement or the court order should include language to that effect. Circumstances in which a review might be warranted are, for example, when an educational program is interrupted due to a chronic illness or when the recipient fails to pursue an agreed-upon "rehabilitation" plan.

Consistent with no-fault reform, rehabilitative alimony represents a departure from the historical view of alimony as being fault-based and unlimited in duration. The preferred approach in many jurisdictions, it accomplishes the dual purposes of (1) affording an economically dependent spouse an opportunity to build his or her job skills, obtain employment, and become economically self-sufficient and (2) setting a predictable end to the ongoing obligations of the parties to each other. Despite these advantages, some courts are reluctant to make rehabilitative alimony awards, particularly in cases of long-term marriages in which one party has a dramatically reduced earning capacity due to the allocation of responsibilities during the marriage. It may also be denied if the planned rehabilitation is unrealistic or if the petitioner is already employed or employable and does not plan to change jobs.

In the *Anliker* case, the Iowa Supreme Court considered that state's alimony statute and weighed the relative merits of permanent "traditional" alimony awarded by the trial court against the appeals court position that rehabilitative alimony was more appropriate. (See Case 10.3.)

PARALEGAL PRACTICE TIP

The opinion in the *Anliker* case is available at *www.pearsonhighered.com/wilson* in the companion website material related to Chapter 10 under "Cases" and in the Case Resources Section of the MyLegalStudiesLab.

CASE **10.3** *In Re Marriage of Anliker,* 694 N.W.2d 535 (Iowa 2005)

FROM THE OPINION

The factors in section 598.21(3) pertinent to this case include (1) the length of the marriage; (2) the age and physical and emotional health of the parties; (3) the property distribution; (4) the educational level of each party at the time of the marriage and at the time the action is commenced; (5) the earning capacity of the party seeking alimony, including educational background, training, employment skills, work experience, length of absence from the job market; (6) the feasibility of the party seeking alimony becoming self-supporting at a standard of living reasonably comparable to that enjoyed during the marriage, and the length of time necessary to achieve this goal; and (7) other factors the court may determine to be relevant in an individual case. Iowa Code § 598.21(3) (a)-(f), (j) (Supp. 2001). . . .

The district court considered these factors in deciding to award Donna traditional alimony as an appropriate form of spousal support. In applying these factors, we think the district court had it exactly right when it made the following findings:

In this case, neither party is receiving a substantial amount of property. The property being divided relates to minimal household goods and furnishings as well as Donna's basic transportation. The debts being assigned to Scott are no more onerous to him than the debts being assigned to Donna pursuant to this decree. . . .

While Donna is only 51 years of age, the record supports a finding that her health has deteriorated since 1996 and is not likely to improve. She suffers ongoing pain and incapacity, and even Scott does not believe that she has exaggerated her testimony regarding her physical health. She is currently on several medications and is limited in her ability to alleviate her pain due to her loss of a kidney several years ago. Donna has been determined to be disabled by the Social Security Administration and her sole source of income at this point is her disability benefits, which net her $309 per month. Although Scott feels that any alimony award should be for rehabilitative purposes only, the record does not support such a conclusion. Due

(Continued)

to her physical infirmities, Donna is an unlikely candidate for further education or training. She has never been able to put what training and experience she has accrued in 51 years to practical use in the job market. The Court does not find it to be realistic to think that Donna is employable in her current condition. . . .

This is a long-term marriage of nearly 20 years. Scott has a substantially better earning capacity than Donna, who is permanently disabled. Donna's earning capacity appears limited to her social security disability benefits. Scott continues to have an earning capacity of $50,000 annually or more. Scott will have far greater social security retirement benefits than Donna. Additionally, Scott receives use of a vehicle as an employment benefit and does not currently have the expense of car payments. . . . the Court takes note that the settlements she received for her injuries and future disabilities were invested in the marriage and are no longer available to Donna at the very time she needs the money.

In view of these findings, which are fully supported in the record and which we adopt, we think the spousal support award of $1,250 per month in traditional alimony until Donna attains the age of sixty-five or either party dies was equitable and should not be disturbed.

SIDEBAR

Do you agree with the court's decision? Why would the court have the award terminate at age sixty-five? Would any other form of alimony have been more appropriate?

RESTITUTION ALIMONY

Restitution or reimbursement alimony is designed to repay a spouse who made financial contributions during the marriage that directly increased the future earning capacity of the other spouse. It is not based on need but rather on equitable considerations—considerations of fairness. The recipient spouse may have interrupted his or her education and earned and expended resources for the other party's benefit in the belief that the marital enterprise and the parties' future lifestyle would be enhanced in the long term. If the marriage is terminated, it is considered fair that the contributing spouse be paid or reimbursed for the investment he or she made in the marriage. When permitted, it is most likely to be awarded when there is a short-term marriage, no children, limited assets, and one spouse has delayed or interrupted his or her education or career and worked to allow the other spouse to pursue graduate studies. Some courts may choose to use restitution alimony for the purposes served by rehabilitation alimony. Such an approach avoids the stigma that there is somehow something deficient or unhealthy in the recipient spouse that needs to be "rehabilitated."

Because it runs counter to traditional alimony principles, which base alimony on need, ability to pay, and standard of living of the parties during the marriage, restitution or reimbursement alimony is viewed with disfavor in some states and by some individual judges. It may be denied if the petitioner is self-sufficient, even if only as a result of receiving disability benefits. It also may be deemed unwarranted if the requesting party already has a degree, does not require additional training, or is already employed in a good job and his or her earning capacity did not suffer as a result of contributions to the marriage.

The landmark decision of the New Jersey Supreme Court in the *Mahoney* case in 1982 illustrates a set of circumstances in which restitution or "reimbursement"

Restitution or reimbursement alimony
alimony designed to repay a spouse who made financial contributions during the marriage that directly enhanced the future earning capacity of the other spouse; sometimes called reimbursement alimony

PARALEGAL PRACTICE TIP

The Utah alimony statute can be found at *www.utah.gov*. You can find a link to this site at *www.pearsonhighered.com/wilson* in the companion website material for Chapter 10 under "Statutes." Note that in determining alimony, the courts in Utah may consider fault and also whether a spouse paid for or "allowed" his or her spouse to attend school during the marriage. Although alimony cannot be ordered for longer than the duration of the marriage (absent extenuating circumstances), the court may use it in an attempt to equalize the parties' standards of living. By statute, the court also may factor into the alimony calculation a subsequent spouse's ability to share living expenses.

alimony was considered appropriate to the facts of the case. (See Case 10.4.) In *Mahoney*, the husband left the marriage shortly after attaining an advanced degree that he had earned with the wife's support. The court held that she was entitled to reimbursement for household expenses, educational costs, school travel expenses, and any other contribution she made enabling her husband to attain his degree.

CASE 10.4 *Mahoney v. Mahoney,* 91 N.J. 488, 453 A.2d 527 (1982)

FROM THE OPINION

In this case, the supporting spouse made financial contributions towards her husband's professional education with the expectation that both parties would enjoy material benefits flowing from the professional license or degree. It is therefore patently unfair that the supporting spouse be denied the mutually anticipated benefit while the supported spouse keeps not only the degree, but also all of the material benefits and rewards flowing from it.

. . . Also the wife has presumably made personal financial sacrifices, resulting in a reduced or lowered standard of living. Additionally, her husband, by pursuing preparations for a future career, has foregone gainful employment and financial contributions to the marriage. . . . She has postponed, as it were, present consumption and a higher standard of living, for the future prospect of greater support and material benefits. . . . The unredressed sacrifices . . . coupled with the unfairness attendant upon the defeat of the supporting spouse's shared expectation of future advantages, further justify a remedial reward. . . .

SIDEBAR

Do you agree with the court's decision? Which form(s) of alimony do you think are appropriate in such cases?

PARALEGAL PRACTICE TIP

The opinion in the *Mahoney* case is accessible at *www.pearsonhighered. com/wilson* in the companion website material related to Chapter 10 under "Cases" and in the Case Resources Section of the MyLegalStudiesLab.

What Factors Will a Court Consider When Making an Alimony Determination?

PARALEGAL PRACTICE TIP

Copies of the California and New Hampshire alimony statutes are accessible at *www.pearsonhighered. com/wilson* in the companion website material related to Chapter 10 under "Statutes."

The power to award spousal support is statutory, but unlike child support awards, which are essentially formula-based, alimony decisions usually are left to the discretion of judges. The threshold question asked is "Does one of the parties have a need for financial support that the other party has the ability to meet?" Virtually all states, whether by statute or judicial decision, have identified additional economic and noneconomic factors to be considered by the courts. These factors afford judges considerable flexibility in tailoring their decisions to the unique facts of each case. They also help guide the information-gathering efforts of the family law team on behalf of the client. The Uniform Marriage and Divorce Act (UMDA)[9] lists the following factors as appropriate for consideration in the making of alimony determinations:

- the financial resources of the party seeking alimony, including marital property apportioned to him or her; the party's ability to meet his or her needs independently; and the extent to which a provision for support of a child living with that party includes a sum for that party as custodian
- the time necessary to acquire sufficient education or training to enable the party seeking alimony to find appropriate employment
- the standard of living during the marriage

- the duration of the marriage
- the age and physical and emotional condition of the spouse seeking alimony
- the ability of the spouse from whom alimony is sought to meet his or her needs while meeting those of the spouse seeking alimony

Additional kinds of factors that may appear in a given state's spousal support statute include the following:

- the relative needs of the parties and ability to pay
- the earned and unearned income of each party, including, but not limited to, earnings, dividends, and benefits such as medical, disability, retirement, or Social Security
- the relative current and future earning capacities of the spouses
- the respective liabilities of the parties
- the backgrounds of the parties in terms of education and training and the prospects of the spouse seeking alimony to become self-supporting within a reasonable period of time
- contribution of each of the parties to appreciation of the marital estate or to the education, training, career, and increased earning power of the other party
- contribution as a homemaker
- the misconduct/fault of either or both of the parties up to the time of the separation—most particularly fault with financial consequences
- the property brought to the marriage by the parties (or their families)
- the federal, state, and local tax ramifications of the alimony award
- a final catchall provision allowing the court to consider any additional factors it may consider relevant

PARALEGAL PRACTICE TIP

The full text of the Uniform Marriage and Divorce Act can be found at *www.nccusl.org*. You can find a link to this site at *www.pearsonhighered.com/wilson* in the companion website material for Chapter 10 under "Resources."

A judge usually is required to consider and make findings with respect to each of the statutorily defined factors in the jurisdiction but customarily may assign whatever weight he or she believes is appropriate to any particular factor in light of the facts of each case. Absent an abuse of discretion, an alimony decision will generally not be disturbed on appeal. Although this approach maximizes flexibility for the courts, it provides little predictability for clients and often escalates the cost of a divorce.

In a contested alimony case, the family law team may be presented with a monumental information-gathering challenge. The effort to meet that challenge usually begins with a review of controlling law in the jurisdiction. An effort then is made through interviews, formal discovery, and other information-gathering activities to identify and assess the strengths and weaknesses of the client's case. It is not enough simply to identify the relevant factors. Each must be addressed and supported by provable facts backed by admissible evidence. It is also important to identify the merits of the opposing party's case. For example, if one party is seeking alimony, can the potential obligor raise any defenses to the claim?

Alimony cases are fact-intensive. THERE ARE NO SUBSTITUTES FOR CAREFUL LISTENING AND THOROUGH PREPARATION! The decision of the Supreme Court of Oklahoma in the *Ray* case illustrates the potential consequences of failing to provide sufficient facts on the client's behalf for the court's consideration. (See Case 10.5.)

PARALEGAL PRACTICE TIP

Attorneys have an ethical duty to provide competent representation and to advocate zealously on the client's behalf. A well-trained paralegal who is aware of inadequate preparation may discuss the case with the supervisor or even send an unsolicited internal memorandum courteously bringing facts and documentation in support of the client's case to the attention of the supervisor "in case it might be helpful."

PARALEGAL PRACTICE TIP

The opinion in the *Ray* case is available at *www.pearsonhighered.com/ wilson* in the companion website material related to Chapter 10 under "Cases" and in the Case Resources Section of the MyLegalStudiesLab.

CASE 10.5 *Ray v. Ray,* 2006 OK 30, 136 P.3d 634 (Okla. 2006)

FROM THE OPINION

The trial court's "quasi summary" dissolution hearing produced a paucity of facts serving as a basis for the alimony award. . . . There is here no evidence of (a) the amount of money wife reasonably needs for readjustment of her lifestyle to a new economic situation, (b) her income-producing capacity, such as the number of hours she works per week and her monthly income; (c) her monthly expenses and future living plans and expenses, (d) her physical condition, (e) the cost of her desired education, (f) whether her station in life or standard of living has changed since the separation; (g) how much her cohabiting partner contributes to her monthly needs. Neither is there any evidence of (a) the husband's ability to pay support alimony, (b) the value of his home, (c) his net worth, (d) his physical condition, (e) his living standard based on monthly income and expenses. . . .

. . . Because the wife has failed to meet, before the trial court, her burden of affirmatively demonstrating the amount of needed support, if any, during the period of her economic readjustment, the trial court's alimony award is reversed and the cause remanded for further proceedings to be consistent with today's pronouncement.

SIDEBAR

Do you agree with the court's decision? Why? Do you think the wife may have a malpractice claim against her attorney? Explain your response.

Paralegal **Application 10.1**

The Fact-Finding Mission in an Alimony Case

Length of Marriage

How long have the parties been married? This is the customary starting point when assessing the potential of an alimony claim. There is consensus among the majority of states that marriages of different lengths should have different consequences with respect to alimony. For example, absent unusual circumstances, alimony is generally not an option in a short-term marriage of less than five years and may not last longer than the length of the marriage. The premise is that the parties have not as yet built up substantial economic reliance on one another or changed their premarital work patterns for a sufficiently extended period. In a marriage of more than fifteen years, many courts agree that long-term support may be warranted if necessary to enable both spouses to maintain as closely as possible the standard of living that characterized their married life. Most litigation and inconsistencies in outcome occur with intermediate-length marriages of between five and fifteen years in duration.

The answer to the question "How long have the parties been married?" is not always as simple as it might seem. Look behind the answer. Although it technically "doesn't count," how long were the parties together prior to marriage? Were they simply dating or living together? Were there periods during the marriage when the parties were separated due to problems in the marriage or factors such as military deployment or other substantial work-related travel (as an entertainer, merchant mariner, etc.)?

Don't let "general rules" restrict thinking given the facts of a specific case. If it is a short-term marriage and the client is seeking alimony, what unusual factors are present that argue for an award when it normally would not be granted? Illness? Abuse? If it is a long-term marriage and the client is fighting alimony, what distinguishes the case at hand from others in which permanent alimony would likely be awarded based on precedent?

Examples of Proof: Certificate of Marriage, leases in either party's name, employment records, military service,

(Continued)

counseling or court records documenting periods of separation, medical records.

Income

A complete employment history should be compiled for each of the parties, including job titles, hours worked, salaries, job skills, and responsibilities. With respect to current employment, if any, is each party bringing in income to his or her full capacity, or is he or she intentionally decreasing income to an artificially low figure; refusing to seek gainful employment; quitting second jobs and part-time work performed while married; falsely claiming to be disabled; not reporting "under the table" income; postponing taking raises, bonuses, or commissions; or otherwise manipulating income? Under such circumstances, income may be imputed to the party who is deliberately reducing his or her earnings. On the other hand, is one party's income inflated in a given year by, for example, receipt of a substantial contingent fee, making it appropriate to average that party's income over a period of years? Is either party holding an unreasonable number of assets in a low or non-income-bearing form to the detriment of the potential recipient? If either spouse is cohabiting with another person, does that other person contribute to support of the household, so that more funds are available to the spouse to meet an alimony obligation or fewer funds are needed by the recipient?

Examples of Proof: Resumes, tax returns, employment records, pay stubs, mortgage applications, documentation that the payor spouse will receive or has received appreciating assets in the property division, evidence of transfers made to third parties, evidence of purchases of luxury/non-income-producing items, logs of efforts to find work.

Needs

What are the *reasonable* needs of the parties as reflected in food, clothing, housing, and other basic living expenses as well as debts? Is either party living beyond his or her needs? The client should prepare a realistic budget of his or her living expenses for careful review. Keep in mind that "need" is a relative concept and cannot be considered apart from the parties' standard of living. What Madonna or your state senator "needs" is likely very different from what a laborer, teacher, or unemployed person needs.

Examples of Proof: Financial statements, tax returns, credit card statements, bank statements, mortgage statements, bills, car payments.

Standard of Living During the Marriage

In most cases, the level of assets in a marriage is such that it is simply not possible for both parties to maintain the marital standard of living post divorce. The issue is more one of how the negative impact of divorce on lifestyle can be equally or equitably shared. However, in cases involving substantial assets, it is important to establish the nature of the parties' lifestyle during the marriage. What was the marital home like? Did it have a pool, tennis courts, or game room? What kind of neighborhood was it in? How did the parties spend their free time? Did they belong to golf, tennis, or yacht clubs? Did they take vacations and, if so, where? Did they own or have access to vacation homes? How often and in what manner did they entertain company? Did they make many charitable donations and attend prestigious fundraising events? What kind of a clothing budget did they have? Where did they shop? How did they pay their bills (cash, credit, loans, employment bonuses, gifts from parents, etc.)? How sustained was their lifestyle (were there a couple of good years and a decade of poor ones, or the reverse)? Was there a considerable amount of readily available cash that was put into savings for a later date rather than spent? Did they spend their funds on property, on tangible assets, or on events like lavish celebrations of birthdays and anniversaries? Were the parties unusually frugal?[10]

Examples of Proof: Photographs, receipts, credit card statements, bank statements, newspaper articles (society columns), membership records, invitations, employment records, deeds, titles to boats and RVs, expense accounts.

Contribution

Identify and document to the fullest extent possible the financial and nonfinancial contributions of each of the parties to the marriage, including homemaking, home maintenance and improvement, childrearing, entertaining in support of one of the parties' careers, and/or vacations at retreats owned by the family of one of the spouses. Financial contributions should be broadly defined and may include trust income, inheritances, accident settlements, and gifts from family members that were spent on marital expenses, etc.

Examples of Proof: Bank statements, credit card statements, appraisals, receipts, copies of trust instruments, photographs, deeds, titles.

Fault

Much to the consternation of wronged clients, approximately half the states do not consider fault when making alimony determinations. With those that do, the fault generally must have resulted in some form of economic loss. For example, the mere existence of an adulterous relationship usually is not enough. The family law team should research how the adultery impacted the marital relationship and estate. Were significant funds spent on gifts, travel, lodging, etc., that would otherwise have been available to support the marriage? Was the aggrieved spouse's emotional and physical health injured by the conduct?

(Continued)

Other types of fault also should be explored: criminal conduct; abusive behavior (physical and/or psychological); reckless spending, dissipation (such as through gambling), or diversion/concealment of assets; excessive use of alcohol or drugs; willful failure to provide essential support to the spouse and children. An isolated incident normally is not enough (unless especially egregious), so search for patterns in misconduct.

Examples of Proof: The type of supporting documentation needed will depend on the specific type of misconduct but is likely to include admissions, statements of the co-respondent or witnesses, photographs/videos, bank and credit card statements, reports of private investigators, police and court records, phone records, e-mails and other forms of correspondence, hotel/motel records, medical and rehabilitation facility records.

Education

Compile histories for each of the spouses, covering all kinds of education and training received along with information about each party's career goals.

Examples of Proof: Resumes, college transcripts, job applications, certificates of completion, on-the-job training records, college applications.

Employability

A party may have an impressive educational history and yet have obsolete job skills and be unemployable. What are the employment prospects for each party? Are there any factors that limit employment options, such as age, physical capacities, or chronic health problems? Has the party been terminated for cause at prior places of employment due to poor performance or misconduct in the workplace? Is the party's level of employability the result of his or her own efforts, or of market forces?

Examples of Proof: Labor market forecasts produced by reputable sources, medical records, job descriptions listing required skills, testimony from employment counselors.

Age

The age factor seems to be straightforward, but its importance stems less from the number of years a person has lived than it does from how age influences employment prospects, health issues, capacity to acquire additional assets to improve living standard, etc. For example, a seventy-year-old attorney or stockbroker may be at the height of his or her career, whereas a professional football player may be barely hanging onto employment at age thirty-five.

Examples of Proof: Medical records, employment records, tax returns.

Health

PARALEGAL PRACTICE TIP

An illness doesn't have to be manifest at the time of dissolution. It can be enough that a party has a condition that goes through periods of active symptoms and periods of remission. See *Moore v. Moore,* 858 So.2d 1168 (2003), a case in which the alimony recipient suffered from Crohn's disease.

Does either party suffer or allegedly suffer from any illnesses or injuries that impede earning potential and result in additional uninsured medical costs?

Examples of Proof: Work absence records, medical records.

Paralegal Application 10.2

Drafting Pointers for an Alimony Provision in a Separation Agreement

This Application highlights the major topics that need to be addressed in an alimony provision of a separation agreement. The precise content needs to be tailored to specific client needs, given the facts of each case.

- **Goal** The goal of the alimony award should be stated. For example, if the award is in the nature of rehabilitative alimony, ideally a plan should be provided that includes a description of the program, a timeline for completion, and the associated costs. If the award will be in the form of restitution/reimbursement alimony, the expenses being reimbursed should be specified.

- **Designation of the payment as alimony** The designation of the payment to be made as "alimony" should be clearly spelled out, along with a statement of the parties' intentions as to whether or not it will be includable in the taxable income of the recipient and deductible to the obligor.

- **Amount** The amount should be established. Usually a fixed dollar amount is stated, which facilitates wage assignments, if warranted. However, if the payor's income fluctuates seasonally or otherwise, the amount may be set in the form of a percentage of that income. This approach has the disadvantages of uncertainty for the recipient and the need for periodic documentation and review of the payor's financial status.

- **Duration** The duration of the alimony should be established. Under what conditions will the obligation terminate? Some jurisdictions have specific limitations regarding the duration of alimony awarded by the court. The parties may agree on events that

(Continued)

will terminate the alimony obligation, such as remarriage, cohabitation with another person for longer than a specified period, completion of an educational program, or obtaining full-time employment at a particular wage or higher.

- **Frequency and timing of payments** The frequency and timing of payments should be laid out. Will there be a lump sum or periodic payments? Will payments be made weekly or monthly?

- **Form of payments** The form of payments may be agreed on. For example, alimony may be paid by check payable to the recipient spouse and sent by mail or by direct deposit. Each party should be required to notify the other of any change in address or applicable accounts. Payment can be made to a third party for the recipient's benefit to meet an obligation such as a mortgage on the marital residence. Another option is to have a court-ordered payroll deduction by the payor's employer (wage assignment or income withholding). Some states require payment through a state IV-D agency in a variety of circumstances. Whatever the method of payment, a party with an obligation to pay alimony should be advised by his or her attorney to keep detailed records and corroborative evidence of all payments to protect against a potential claim of contempt for nonpayment.

- **Modification of alimony** The modifiability of the alimony award should be addressed in the agreement if modification is permitted in the jurisdiction. The courts generally link changes to actual financial circumstances. However, the parties may agree on self-executing provisions that will result in an automatic modification based on an annual cost-of-living increase, a certain percentage increase or decrease in the payor's income, or receipt of an anticipated inheritance by either party. The triggering events should not be child-related, in order to protect deductibility of the alimony payment for income tax purposes.

PARALEGAL PRACTICE TIP

Several states provide that when making an alimony order, the court "shall" as in "must" determine if the obligor has health insurance available at a reasonable cost that can be extended to cover the spouse. The obligor can exercise the option, obtain comparable coverage, or reimburse the spouse for health insurance (without any adjustment in the alimony award amount).

- **Health care costs** It is important for the client to be aware of any potential health insurance coverage issues prior to or upon divorce. If the client is insured through his or her employer, the state, or a private policy, there should be no interruption in coverage. However, if the client is covered through the spouse's

PARALEGAL PRACTICE TIP

The Consolidated Omnibus Budget Reconciliation Act (COBRA) codified as 26 U.S.C. section 4980B(f) enables a nonemployee spouse to continue health insurance coverage provided by the spouse's employer for as long as three years postdivorce at his or her own expense unless otherwise ordered.

employer, proactive steps may need to be taken. Some plans allow employees to remove someone from their health plan, including a spouse. Although the removed spouse may be eligible for COBRA extension coverage postdivorce, there may be a gap in coverage between the date of removal and the date of divorce, when COBRA eligibility commences. The topic of health insurance needs to be addressed in the agreement at some point. It should be expressly indicated if alimony is at least partly designed to cover medical, dental, and/or mental health expenses. If the employee spouse is required by the divorce decree to pay COBRA premiums for his or her spouse, the employer should be promptly notified of the divorce.[11]

- **Security for alimony payments** The recipient spouse will want to include security for the payment of alimony. Most states authorize courts to order the obligor spouse to maintain life insurance or some other form of security such as a trust for the recipient's benefit. Life insurance policies for the benefit of the recipient are the most common form of security for alimony payments.

- **Survival or merger of the alimony provision** If alimony will be waived or paid pursuant to the terms of the parties' separation agreement, the attorney will consider with the client the issue of survival or merger of the alimony provision. If the agreement is incorporated in the divorce decree but also survives as an independent contract, the provision will generally not be able to be modified by the family court, absent a showing of something more than a change in circumstances (such as the likelihood the recipient will become a **public charge** absent modification). This is a difficult choice, but given the uncertainties in life, many practitioners believe it wisest to have alimony provisions merge in the decree. This way, in the event of a later economic downturn or windfall or the serious illness of either party, the option to modify the alimony award upon a material change in circumstances usually remains open to both parties. The concepts of survival and merger are discussed more fully in Chapter 12. Exhibit A in the Separation Agreement in that chapter provides an example of a provision in which the parties to a divorce both waived alimony.

Public charge
a person dependent on public assistance programs for necessaries

When and How Can Alimony Awards Be Modified or Terminated?

The decision as to whether or not alimony can be modified or terminated is made on a case-by-case basis and is driven by statute, court order, case law, and/or the language of the agreement executed by the parties. Many of the cases addressing this issue demonstrate the importance of careful drafting.

MODIFICATION

PARALEGAL PRACTICE TIP

To see an example of a Motion to Modify or Terminate Maintenance/Alimony, visit *www.courts.state.co.us.* (Colorado) You can find a link to this site at *www.pearsonhighered.com/wilson* in the companion website material for Chapter 10 under "Forms."

Material change in circumstances
a change in the physical, emotional, or financial condition of one or both of the parties sufficient to warrant a change in a support order; a change that, if known at the time of the divorce decree, would have resulted in a different outcome

If permanent or term alimony was awarded in the parties' divorce decree, most states allow a party to later file a Complaint or Petition for Modification based on a **material change in circumstances.** However, in most jurisdictions, absent agreement, extraordinary circumstances, or extreme hardship, a lump-sum, rehabilitative, or restitution alimony award will not be modifiable. In some states, if alimony was not addressed in the divorce judgment, an alimony claim may not be pursued at a later date unless the right to pursue alimony was preserved by a nominal award (e.g., $1.00 per year) at the time of the divorce.

PARALEGAL PRACTICE TIP

Florida is one of the states that permits a party to preserve a right to alimony by making an award of $1.00 in permanent periodic alimony. See, e.g., *Blanchard v. Blanchard,* 793 So.2d 989 (Fla. App. 2001). Some states (including Alaska) allow a Complaint for Alimony to be filed subsequent to the divorce, given an unanticipated change in the parties' circumstances since the time of divorce.

The complaint for modification is usually filed in the court that issued the original order if it retains continuing jurisdiction over the matter. The burden of proving the change of circumstances rests with the party seeking the modification. The kinds of changes in circumstances that might justify an up or down adjustment in alimony include forced unemployment or early retirement, a windfall increase in income or assets, the onset of a serious medical condition resulting in permanent disability and increased uninsured medical expenses, a third-party mortgagee's exercising its option to accelerate payment of a mortgage loan on the marital home, or cohabitation with a person who assumes responsibility for many of the dependent spouse's living expenses. The court will examine the nature of the change and assess whether or not the request is made in good faith. For example, if it is based on a reduction in the payor's income, is the reduction the fault of that individual? Has he or she engineered circumstances so that it appears there is a reduction in income or an increase in liabilities when there is not? Or is the increase in liabilities the result of spendthrift spending or an extravagant lifestyle? There are no fixed rules for determining what meets the threshold, and each case is decided in the context of the surrounding circumstances.

In about half of the states, misconduct on the part of the recipient may constitute a sufficient change in circumstances to support a modification. For example, in the *Miller*[12] case in Massachusetts, the wife openly and intentionally conducted herself in a "scandalous" manner that embarrassed the husband, injured his reputation, and adversely affected his business. In response to the husband's motion for modification, the court reduced his alimony obligation to his former wife. The reduction was upheld on appeal. However, the courts are reluctant to modify payments when the change in circumstances underlying the request is the consequence of the petitioner's own wrongful acts, such as criminal behavior resulting in incarceration.

PARALEGAL PRACTICE TIP

When the obligor claims incarceration as a change in circumstances warranting modification, some courts agree and some consider it as one factor among others. However, most courts have adopted a "no justification rule" that being in prison standing alone is not sufficient to justify modification of an alimony obligation. The reasoning behind the rule is that criminal activity that could lead to incarceration is seen as being within the control of the individual, as distinguished from other obstacles to payment such as injury, illness, job loss, or other involuntary obstacles. Even if the alimony payments are not made while the obligor is incarcerated, the obligor is unlikely to be relieved of his duty to pay the accrued arrearages upon release. See, e.g., *Willoughby v. Willoughby,* 2004 PA. Super. 439, 862 A.2d 654 (2004). The opinion in this case is available in its entirety at *www.pearsonhighered.com/wilson* in the companion website material related to Chapter 10 under "Cases" and in the Case Resources Section of the MyLegalStudiesLab. See also Paralegal Application 9.4 in Chapter 9 addressing the effect of incarceration on child support orders.

PARALEGAL PRACTICE TIP

A modification may also be based on mistake or fraud at the time an alimony award was made. For example, if the obligor accidentally or intentionally failed to include a substantial asset on his or her financial statement at the time of the divorce proceeding, the court may be willing to modify the award at a later date when the mistake or fraud is discovered.

If the parties have executed a separation agreement, it may provide that they will initially attempt to resolve modification issues through mediation prior to resorting to litigation. If the agreement is incorporated in the judgment of divorce and that agreement provides that alimony shall be unmodifiable or modifiable only under certain limited circumstances, the courts will usually hold the parties to their agreement absent extraordinary circumstances. The *Williams* case in Connecticut addresses a situation of this kind. It illustrates the potential impact of language in the parties' agreement; the interplay among statutes, case law, and agreements; and the importance of maintaining a complete case file. (See Case 10.6.) The court may also be constrained by provisions of a surviving agreement of the parties. In a few states, a court will have no power to modify spousal support unless the parties' agreement allows the court to do so. Other courts may refuse to honor a "no modification" clause in an agreement on public policy grounds if, for example, a spouse will be forced into dependence on public assistance as a result.

CASE 10.6 *Williams v. Williams,* 276 Conn. 491, 886 A.2d 817 (2005)

DISCUSSION OF THE CASE

In this case, the parties executed an agreement that provided for weekly alimony to the wife for approximately ten years. The parties' agreement incorporated in the judgment stated the following with respect to modification:

> Husband shall not be entitled to receive a decrease in his alimony obligation unless he satisfactorily demonstrates to the court that he has suffered a substantial and significant decrease in income, such decrease was not due in any way to his voluntary change in lifestyle, career choice, place of residence or new responsibilities, and that he has taken affirmative steps and used his best efforts

(Continued)

PARALEGAL PRACTICE TIP

The opinion in the *Williams* case can be found at *www.pearsonhighered.com/wilson* in the companion website material related to Chapter 10 under "Cases" and in the Case Resources Section of the MyLegalStudiesLab.

to maintain his income. Pursuant to General Statutes § 46b-86 (b), husband's alimony may be modifiable upon wife's remarriage or cohabitation.

The statute at issue provides as follows:

> In an action for divorce, dissolution of marriage, legal separation or annulment brought by a husband or wife, in which a final judgment has been entered providing for the payment of periodic alimony by one party to the other, the Superior Court may, in its discretion and upon notice and hearing, modify such judgment and suspend, reduce or terminate the payment of periodic alimony upon a showing that the party receiving the periodic alimony is living with another person under circumstances which the court finds should result in the modification, suspension, reduction or termination of alimony because the living arrangements cause such a change in circumstances as to alter the financial needs of that party.

When the husband's motion to modify the alimony terms of the dissolution judgment was denied, he appealed, claiming that the trial court improperly placed a burden on him to prove that the defendant's financial circumstances had been altered as a result of her remarriage. He claimed that the statute pertained only to cohabitation and that there was a presumption based on Connecticut case law that the alimony obligation should terminate because every marriage alters the financial needs of the party.

The husband relied on *Cary*, 112 Conn. 256, 152 A. 302 (1930), in which the Connecticut Supreme Court stated:

> The remarriage of the wife should relieve the husband from the obligation of supporting the wife of another man. To permit her to have alimony from the first husband as an equivalent for her support after she had secured the legal obligation from the second husband to support her would give her support from her present and her former husband and . . . would offend public policy and good morals. . . . Two husbands should not be liable for the obligation of support for a woman who is the divorced spouse of one and the wife of the other. Id. At 261.

The Connecticut Supreme Court took the position that *Cary* and subsequent cases did not deprive it of authority to award nonmodifiable alimony or, in its equitable powers, to award alimony that does not terminate even in the event of remarriage.

In a footnote, the court dealt with the obligor's assertion that the reference to the statute may have been a drafting error. It observed that the record was clear that the settlement agreement had undergone considerable scrutiny. The parties were represented by counsel when it was drafted, and the agreement itself indicated numerous handwritten changes, deletions, and substitutions, including several within the section at issue.

The state supreme court affirmed the lower court's decision.

> . . . in the absence of compelling reason to disregard the clear and unequivocal language set forth in the parties' settlement agreement, as incorporated into the judgment of dissolution. There is nothing inherently improper about requiring the plaintiff under the facts of this case, as the party with the alimony obligation, to demonstrate that remarriage of the defendant had a financial impact that should warrant a modification in his alimony obligation. . . . In the present case, the parties' decision to use the standard set forth in the statute as a basis for determining whether alimony should be modified was reasonable and clearly expressed. Therefore the trial court's decision was not improper as a matter of law.

SIDEBAR

Do you agree with the court's decision? Explain your response.

TERMINATION

Unless otherwise provided in a final divorce decree, or by its nature as in alimony in gross, an alimony obligation will usually terminate upon the earliest to occur of the following events:

- death of the recipient
- death of the payor
- expiration of a stated period of time
- remarriage of the recipient
- cohabitation of the recipient with another

The court frequently sets a termination date in the decree or incorporates one or more self-executing termination dates that the parties set forth in their agreement. For example, they may agree that cohabitation with another adult in an intimate relationship for greater than one month, recovery from a serious illness, retirement on or before a certain age, completion of a specific educational program, or obtaining full-time employment will trigger a cessation of alimony. Regardless of how the alimony obligation terminates, the payor (or his or her estate in the case of death) generally remains liable for arrearages (i.e., unpaid back payments) unless otherwise ordered by the court.

Termination Upon Remarriage

The general rule is that "permanent" alimony will terminate upon remarriage of the recipient or on whatever date or condition the parties agree to in their agreement. Some states, such as New Jersey and North Carolina, have automatic-termination-on-remarriage rules. Some, such as Illinois, Maryland and Washington, recognize an exception to automatic termination when the parties have expressly agreed to continue alimony upon remarriage. Provisions to that effect must expressly state that alimony survives the statutory presumption. Parties who know they want to remarry sometimes elect to choose this route and provide for a reduction in the amount of alimony to be paid upon remarriage. In this essentially win-win situation, the former spouse who wants to remarry can do so without a total loss of alimony and the paying spouse is relieved of a portion of the full alimony obligation.

PARALEGAL PRACTICE TIP

Paralegals should be familiar with the approach to termination of alimony upon remarriage in their respective jurisdictions. Is termination of alimony on the recipient's remarriage automatic or is court action required? If the latter, obligors may be subject to contempt if they just stop paying without court authorization.

In states such as South Dakota and Massachusetts, remarriage establishes a ***prima facie*** **showing** supporting termination of alimony on remarriage unless the recipient is able to show the existence of extraordinary circumstances that require the continuation of alimony. If the obligor remarries, his or her alimony obligation will continue, absent a court order to the contrary. However, a court may entertain a complaint for downward modification if children are born to the subsequent marriage or for an upward modification if the recipient can show that the paying spouse has more of his or her income available as a result of a new spouse's contributions to his or her customary living expenses.

Prima facie showing
a legally rebuttable showing

Termination Upon Death

If either of the parties dies, alimony payments customarily cease unless the parties' separation agreement or the court expressly provides otherwise. For example, the parties may agree that payments will continue to be paid from the decedent's estate or from a trust. The American Law Institute's Principles of the Law of Family Dissolution provide that the alimony obligation may survive the obligor's death if the court makes written findings establishing that the termination of the award would work a substantial injustice because of facts not present in most cases. A more common approach is for the divorce decree to include an order requiring the obligor to maintain an insurance policy for the recipient's benefit.

Termination Upon Cohabitation

The majority rule with respect to cohabitation in jurisdictions without a specific statute on point is that cohabitation can result in the reduction or elimination of a spousal support award only if it improves the financial circumstances of the recipient spouse enough to substantially reduce the need for support. This requirement of proof of a substantial change in need level rather than an automatic termination reflects the fact that cohabitation, unlike marriage, does not create a reciprocal and continuing support obligation between the cohabiting parties. The court will look at facts such as the following:

1. Does the cohabitant provide housing for the recipient?
2. Does the cohabitant contribute financially to rent/mortgage and household operating expenses? Is the contribution consistent?
3. Was the benefit received unanticipated at the time of the divorce decree?
4. Has the recipient made substantial purchases, such as vehicles, a boat, or property, since the period of cohabitation began?

How Are Alimony Awards Enforced?

In most jurisdictions, the primary enforcement vehicle for nonpayment of alimony is a **contempt** action, **civil** or **criminal,** depending on the circumstances. When court-ordered alimony is not paid, the aggrieved recipient is entitled to file appropriate papers in the applicable court (usually a Motion or Complaint for Contempt or a Citation with an **Order to Show Cause**) to enforce the order. If the obligor is found to be in civil contempt of an alimony order, the court will usually order payment of the overdue amount according to a schedule tailored to the obligor's ability to pay. Although the court has the authority to impose a jail sentence for an indefinite period to compel payment, usually the defendant in a civil contempt case will be given the opportunity to pay the arrearages and thereby purge the contempt and avoid jail. Usually the obligor will not be found in contempt if there was an inability to pay at the time the delinquent payments were due or if the recipient contributed to the nonpayment, for example, by failing to provide the obligor with notice of a change of address. In a criminal contempt case, a sentence may be imposed for a fixed period, and the contempt cannot be purged by payment.

If the alimony recipient is also receiving court-ordered child support, he or she may also seek assistance from the state's Title IV-D agency and its arsenal of enforcement measures, such as income withholding and tax refund intercepts. States may also provide additional enforcement support for individuals not eligible for IV-D assistance. If the obligor presently resides in another state, the recipient can also seek enforcement across state lines under the Uniform Interstate Family Support Act.

PARALEGAL PRACTICE TIP

In some states, such as Mississippi, cohabitation creates a presumption that a material change in circumstances has occurred. The alimony recipient has to rebut a presumption of "mutual support." See, e.g., *Rester v. Rester,* 5 So.3d 1132 (2008).

Civil contempt

a sanction for failure to obey a court order issued for another's benefit; a civil contempt proceeding is remedial in nature and is designed to promote compliance with the order

Criminal contempt

a punishment for failure to comply with a court order; a criminal contempt proceeding is punitive in nature and is designed to punish an attack on the integrity of the court

Order to Show Cause

an order directing a party to appear in court and explain why he or she took, or failed to take, some action and why relief should not be granted

PARALEGAL PRACTICE TIP

Visit *www.acf.hhs.gov/programs/cse* to see an example of a "Uniform Support Order" under UIFSA. The order addresses all forms of support. You can find a link to this site at *www.pearsonhighered.com/wilson* in the companion website material for Chapter 10 under "Forms."

In some circumstances, the recipient may seek to place a lien on property owned by a defendant found in contempt. In many states, statutes that protect property from legal process for collection of debts (attachment, etc.) do not apply to alimony or support claims. Another, more extreme measure, abolished in many states, is for the aggrieved party to file for a **writ *ne exeat***, a court order restraining a person from leaving the jurisdiction until the petitioner's claim has been satisfied.

The general rule is that when the alimony obligation is based on an agreement of the parties not merged in the divorce judgment, the agreement continues to exist as an independent contract, which the family court has no power to modify. If, given unusual circumstances, the family court imposes or varies the alimony obligation notwithstanding the agreement, the aggrieved party can pursue traditional breach-of-contract remedies, such as a suit for damages in a court with equity jurisdiction (to recover the difference between the alimony to be paid under the court order and the amount, if any, provided for in the parties' agreement).

If the obligor dies while there are outstanding alimony payments due, the recipient can seek to recover the accrued amount of arrearages from the decedent's estate if payment has not otherwise been secured by agreement of the parties or by order of the court.

Writ *ne exeat*
a court order restraining a person from leaving the jurisdiction until the petitioner's claim has been satisfied

What Are the Tax and Bankruptcy Implications of Alimony?

The material that follows provides a very basic description of the relationship between alimony or spousal support obligations and tax and bankruptcy law. Each of these areas is a complex and specialized area of law, and determinations made by the Internal Revenue Service and Bankruptcy Courts will depend on the facts of each individual case.

TAX IMPLICATIONS

PARALEGAL PRACTICE TIP

Visit *www.irs.gov* to learn about tax concerns of divorced or separated individuals, including alimony. You can find a link to this site at *www.pearsonhighered.com/wilson* in the companion website material for Chapter 10 under "Resources."

In general, the parties cannot come up with their own private agreement dictating the deductibility and includability of alimony payments unless the agreement satisfies applicable tax regulations. Under federal and state tax law, alimony is deductible from gross income by the payor and is income to the payee provided the following criteria are satisfied:[13]

1. The payments are made to a spouse or former spouse incident to a divorce decree or separation agreement. (An order for temporary alimony *pendente lite* will also qualify.)
2. The parties do not file a joint tax return for the period during which alimony payments are made.
3. The parties are not living in the same household when the payment is made.
4. The payments are made in cash (bank check, money order, etc.) and not in-kind (services rendered).
5. The payor has no liability for payments after death.
6. The payment is not improperly disguised child support (as when there are children but no child support is agreed to, and reductions in alimony amounts

are tied to child-related events such as a child reaching the age of eighteen, graduating from high school, moving out of the custodial parent's home, or entering the military service).

7. The parties have not designated the payments as nonincludable in the recipient's income.

When alimony payments are made to a third party for the recipient's benefit (typically for payment of a mortgage), to be deductible the payment to the third party must be at the written request of the recipient to the payor. The writing must specify that the payments are in lieu of alimony payments directly to the recipient and that both spouses intend the payments to be treated as alimony.

The IRS requires the payor deducting alimony to provide on his or her tax return the social security number of the recipient spouse. This information allows the IRS to verify that the recipient is including alimony received as income. Failure to provide the number can result in a disallowance of the deduction and/or a penalty.

Alimony recapture rule
the IRS rule that the government can recover a tax benefit (such as the prior claiming of a deduction for payment of alimony) by taxing the income that no longer qualifies for the benefit

The **alimony recapture rule** found in Section 71(f) of the Internal Revenue Service Code is designed to prevent parties to divorce from disguising what is actually part of a property division settlement as alimony in order to obtain the benefit of a tax deduction. It applies when there appears to be a front-loading of alimony payments that decrease substantially or end during the first three calendar years following the divorce. The determination of whether or not the rule will apply is based on a formula. If the Internal Revenue Service determines that the alleged support payments are actually in the nature of a property settlement, the negative consequences can be especially dramatic for the payor. Any claimed deduction on previously filed tax returns in the applicable period is disallowed, and the amount of "alimony" previously deducted is "recaptured" and subject to taxes, interest, and penalties. The recipient spouse becomes entitled to a corresponding refund for taxes previously paid on "alimony" declared as income.

PARALEGAL PRACTICE TIP

Essentially, "front-loading" of alimony is deemed to occur when the alimony payments made in the first year following the divorce (year one) are significantly higher than the payments in years two and three and there is more than a $15,000 decrease in alimony payments between years two and three.

BANKRUPTCY

Discharge
to extinguish a legal obligation; a discharge relieves an obligor of the legal obligation to pay a debt

In general, individuals who are deeply in debt have the right to file for bankruptcy in federal bankruptcy court in an effort to be relieved of full or partial payment of as many of their debts as possible. In the event that a bankruptcy petition is successfully filed, the Bankruptcy Court has the authority to **discharge** some debts, but other debts cannot be discharged, based largely on public policy grounds. For example, the Bankruptcy Abuse Prevention and Consumer Protection Act (BAPCPA) has made it more difficult to avoid domestic support obligations (DSOs) to former spouses. In the bankruptcy context, a DSO is a debt incurred before or after a bankruptcy filing that is owed to or recoverable by a spouse, former spouse, child, or governmental unit, in the nature of alimony, maintenance, or support established in a court decree, a separation agreement, a property settlement agreement, or an administrative determination.

Bankruptcy actions are governed primarily by federal law. Divorce is governed by state law. Although a family court can enter a divorce decree, it has no authority to determine whether or not a debt addressed in that decree is dischargeable in bankruptcy. However, if a debt is discharged (such as the responsibility to pay joint credit card bills), the injured spouse can go to family court and seek an increase in alimony or child support based on changed circumstances.

The extent to which DSOs will be dischargeable depends to some degree on whether the obligor files a Chapter 7 (liquidation) or Chapter 13 (reorganization) bankruptcy. In general, "support payments" pursuant to a divorce cannot be discharged under either Chapter 7 or 13. Under Chapter 7, domestic relations obligations are not dischargeable whether they are in the nature of "support," or property or hold harmless provisions if they are incurred as a result of a divorce. The potential discharge is broader under Chapter 13 because it can include debts arising from a property division settlement unless the debt constitutes "support." Every provision in a judgment of divorce or separation made solely for the purpose of "support" will be considered support whether it is expressly labeled as such or not, and irrespective of whether it is paid in a lump sum or in intervals. The Bankruptcy Court looks at a number of factors in determining whether or not an award is in the nature of support. The bottom line is ". . . if it looks like a duck, walks like a duck, and quacks like a duck, then it probably is a duck,"[14] and a party cannot avoid paying alimony simply by filing bankruptcy.

PARALEGAL PRACTICE TIP

In a Chapter 7 bankruptcy action, the petitioner seeks a determination that he or she cannot pay unsecured debts (debts not secured by collateral). Under Chapter 13, the petitioner has a regular but insufficient income and seeks to reorganize or adjust payment of his or her debts.

PARALEGAL PRACTICE TIP

There is no hard-and-fast rule about what will be discharged. The nonfiling spouse may need to file a Complaint in the bankruptcy court objecting to discharge of a particular debt. For example, an argument can be made that certain debts payable to third parties are in the nature of support obligations: educational and uninsured medical expenses of minor children, payment of the mortgage on the former marital home, a QDRO, a life insurance policy for the benefit of the minor children, etc. Even if considered support, the debtor may still try to be relieved of such debts by claiming that the discharge will be a significant benefit and will do no or minimal harm to the ex-spouse and/or minor children.

Trends

As the content of this chapter indicates, approaches to spousal support are evolving and vary considerably from state to state and court to court. Clearly, alimony is awarded far less frequently than it was prior to 1970. While some believe it has lost its rationale in a no-fault era, others continue to believe it still has a role to play at the dissolution of a marriage. Some of the general trends commentators have identified with respect to the future of spousal support include the following:

1. **A decreased emphasis on fault in the alimony equation.** About half the states continue to consider marital fault relevant to an alimony determination. However, Section 308 of the Uniform Marriage and Divorce Act provides that maintenance awards should be set "without regard to marital misconduct." Although adopted in only a minority of states to date,[15] the Act has been cited as persuasive authority in many jurisdictions, and the trend is generally away from a consideration of "moral fault" of either partner. Even among the states that still consider marital fault as a factor, the primary focus is on economic fault. The basic inquiry to be made is "Did the misconduct

have financial consequences that took resources away that would otherwise have been available to the spouse and children?"

PARALEGAL PRACTICE TIP

If fault is considered in alimony determinations, it will usually appear in the state statute listing factors to be weighed by the court. For example, Virginia is among the states that still specifically include adultery in their statutes governing maintenance and support as a factor to be considered.[16] In 1995, the Utah Legislature amended the Utah Code to include a subsection allowing trial courts to consider fault in determining alimony awards.[17]

PARALEGAL PRACTICE TIP

In North Carolina, a party can request a jury trial on the issue of marital misconduct. The North Carolina statute can be found at *www.nc.courts.org*. You can find a link to this site at *www.pearsonhighered.com/ wilson* in the companion website material for Chapter 10 under "Statutes."

2. **The use of guidelines in alimony determinations.** Unlike child support awards, there is no federal requirement that states adopt guidelines for the calculation of spousal support. To address the resulting lack of consistency and predictability in awards, the American Law Institute recommends the adoption of computational guidelines, and an increasing number of states, counties within states, and individual judges[18] have experimented with and implemented guidelines in an effort to improve efficiency, decrease litigation, and provide predictability in this area.[19]

3. **A potential shift toward "compensatory alimony."** In the early 1970s at the outset of no-fault reform, the assumption was that if a wife received an equal or equitable share of the marital property and was employed, she should be able to be self-supporting. If not, the most she should require would be short-term transitional support allowing her to strengthen her job skills and reenter the workforce. On the surface, reliance on short-term rehabilitative alimony made sense. Today, the reality is that despite the women's movement and the constitutional mandate that alimony statutes be gender-neutral, traditional ways of thinking still persist. Even though women have made great strides, on average they still earn less than men, receive the overwhelming majority of alimony awards, and are disproportionately represented on the welfare rolls. They continue to be more likely than men in the context of marriage and the family to make sacrifices that reduce their earning potential and standard of living if and when they exit the marriage. Consistent with these observations, legislators in some states have begun to reexamine their statutes. As one court has put it, "This has nothing to do with feminism, sexism, male chauvinism or any other trendy social ideology. It is ordinary common sense, basic decency and simple justice."[20]

The view of alimony as compensation is reflected in an Illinois maintenance statute that requires a court to consider, among other factors, "any impairment of the present and future earning capacity of the party seeking maintenance due to that party devoting time to domestic duties or having forgone or delayed education, training, employment, or career opportunities due to the marriage."[21] The *Sutphin* case in Ohio (see Case 10.7) falls short of actually endorsing a loss-of-income-production-capacity method to determine a maintenance obligation, but the trial court clearly took such an approach, labeling the award to the wife "compensatory spousal support."

CASE 10.7 *Sutphin v. Sutphin,* 2004 Ohio 6844 (Ohio App. 2004)

DISCUSSION OF THE CASE

Prior to the parties' marriage in 1987, they had signed a premarital agreement in which the wife, Susan, agreed to be a stay-at-home parent. Per the agreement, the wife quit her job and did not work outside the home until their one minor child graduated from high school. Based on evidence presented, the trial court found that the parties had maintained an "opulent" lifestyle during their marriage with income and expenditures of nearly $500,000 a year. After they separated in 1998, the husband, Stuart, continued to support Susan in a comfortable lifestyle.

At trial, the court heard testimony from Ann Crittenden, author of the book *The Price of Motherhood* (which was admitted into evidence), regarding lost income opportunities of stay-at-home mothers. Crittenden had received a master's degree in economics and had worked as a financial writer for *Fortune* magazine, *Newsweek,* and the *New York Times.* She was also an economics commentator for CBS News and had authored three books. Based in part on her testimony and that of Dr. Louis Noyd, an economist, about the value of the wife's total projected earnings, the trial court ordered Stuart to pay Susan spousal support in the amount of $1,415,620 in monthly installments of $9,000 and to contribute $100,000 toward her legal fees. In determining the amount of spousal support (which it referred to as "compensatory spousal support"), the trial court took the total projected earnings of the wife, subtracted the projected earnings for the period after the minor child graduated from high school, and subtracted an amount attributable to the duration of the parties' marriage.

The husband appealed, claiming that his substantial rights were affected by Crittenden's testimony and that her book should not have been admitted in evidence. The Ohio intermediate appellate court affirmed the lower court's decision. The appellate court held that Stuart was not prejudiced by Crittenden's testimony as the trial court was required by statute to consider "the lost income capacity of either party that resulted from that party's marital responsibilities," and he was also not prejudiced by admission of the book because the author testified and was available for cross-examination.

The court did express reservations about the characterization of the award as "compensatory," but that reservation was based on the fact that the phrase "compensatory spousal support" was not found anywhere in the state's maintenance statute.

SIDEBAR

Do you agree with the court's decision? Explain your response.

PARALEGAL PRACTICE TIP

The opinion in the *Sutphin* case can be found at *www.pearsonhighered.com/wilson* in the companion website material related to Chapter 10 under "Cases" and in the Case Resources Section of the MyLegalStudiesLab.

The Role of the Paralegal in a Spousal Support Case

The tasks most commonly performed by a paralegal in a spousal support case are:

- researching current governing law (statutes, court rules, and case law) regarding spousal support in the applicable jurisdiction
- scheduling and participating in interviews as assigned

- making discovery-related recommendations and drafting discovery requests as instructed, with particular attention to the factors the court will consider when making the spousal support decision
- drafting complaints, motions, supporting affidavits, and proposed orders (including motions for temporary support)
- drafting spousal support provisions for inclusion in separation agreements
- assisting in identification and preparation of prospective witnesses
- drafting a pretrial memorandum, if required, advising the court of the merits of the client's request for or opposition to alimony
- assisting with gathering and preparation of exhibits related to spousal support requests for use in negotiations and at hearings and trial
- drafting proposed findings of fact and conclusions of law addressing each of the factors to be considered by the court
- tracking progress on the case to be sure all deadlines are met
- making sure the client is kept informed about progress on the case, upcoming deadlines, hearings, etc.

CHAPTER **SUMMARY**

Alimony awards are allowances ordered by a court for support and maintenance of one spouse payable by the other spouse upon separation and divorce. Parties to a marriage now frequently create their own agreements with respect to spousal support and often waive their respective rights to alimony in those agreements. Since the onset of the no-fault era, the primary vehicle for allocating marital resources upon divorce is property division, and only a small percentage of divorce decrees provide for alimony. The majority of those awards are made to wives, although women are now generally viewed as capable of providing for their own needs. At least by law, alimony has become gender-neutral based on the U.S. Supreme Court ruling in the 1979 case *Orr v. Orr.*

Although there is considerable variation across the country, it appears that most state legislatures and courts are willing to explore creative ways of providing for dependent spouses and especially for those who would otherwise end up on public assistance. The most common types of alimony are temporary, permanent, term, lump-sum, rehabilitative, and restitution. The types vary primarily with respect to purpose, duration, and conditions governing termination and modification.

Unlike child support awards, which are based on guidelines established in each state, there are few guidelines for determining when alimony will be awarded, in what amount, and for what purpose or duration. Alimony decisions are largely left to the discretion of individual judges, and awards are seldom overturned absent an abuse of discretion. In making alimony determinations, courts consider a variety of factors established by statute and case law and assign weights to the factors according to the facts of each case. Given the limited assets in most marriages, the initial focus is usually on relative need and ability to pay. Other commonly considered factors include the length of the marriage, the age of the parties, the employability and earning capacity of each spouse, and the standard of living that characterized the marriage. Some states still consider marital fault, particularly misconduct with economic consequences.

Given the complexity of this topic and the diversity in its treatment among the states, this chapter initially describes a generic approach to the issue of alimony and then references a number of jurisdictional variations and cases. Because alimony cases are fact-intensive, the paralegal applications focus on locating governing law and procedure and gathering and organizing information to support the client's position in the context of that law. A limited number of tax and bankruptcy issues related to alimony are briefly described, although the family law paralegal's role in these complex areas is likely to be limited.

PARALEGAL PRACTICE TIP

It is important to remember that when a marriage dissolves, the courts have multiple tools to work with in effecting a fair termination that will allow the parties to move forward. Alimony, child support, and property division are the three primary tools. Decisions about one should not be made in a vacuum, without consideration of the other two.

This chapter began by tracing the evolution of spousal support from its origins under ecclesiastical and common law as a lifetime duty of a husband to support his wife. It concludes with a view to future trends with respect to alimony, including less consideration of moral fault, increased interest in the development of guidelines for calculating awards, and a potential move toward alimony as compensation in appropriate cases.

CONCEPT REVIEW AND REINFORCEMENT

KEY **TERMS**

Absolute divorce

Alimony/spousal support

Alimony recapture rule

Annulment

Canon law

Civil contempt

Criminal contempt

Discharge

Divorce *a mensa et thoro*

Divorce *a vinculo matrimonii*

Legal separation

Lump-sum alimony/alimony in gross

Married Women's Property Acts

Material change in circumstances

Permanent alimony

Premarital agreement

Public charge

Rehabilitative alimony

Restitution/reimbursement alimony

Separation agreement

Surviving agreement

Temporary alimony/alimony
    pendente lite

Term alimony

Vest

Waiver

REVIEW **QUESTIONS**

1. Define spousal support/alimony and identify its purpose.
2. Describe how a premarital agreement might influence whether or not a spouse obtains alimony.
3. Describe the significance of the *Orr* decision.
4. Distinguish between alimony and property division.
5. Describe the nature and purpose of each of the following types of alimony: separate support, temporary, "permanent," lump-sum, rehabilitative, and restitution.
6. Identify the type or types of alimony that might be granted to a spouse who supported his or her spouse while the latter pursued a graduate degree during the marriage.
7. Identify the kinds of factors courts will consider when making alimony determinations.
8. Describe the kinds of evidence that need to be gathered to document the parties' standard of living during the marriage when significant assets are involved.
9. Identify the general rule governing modification of alimony awards.
10. Identify a minimum of three events that commonly result in the termination of an alimony obligation.
11. Describe the basic tax rule applicable to alimony awards with respect to includability and deductibility.
12. Describe how bankruptcy law treats property division and spousal support awards.

DEVELOPING YOUR PARALEGAL SKILLS

FOCUS ON **THE JOB**

This activity provides students with an opportunity to apply the content of this chapter by drafting a proposed alimony provision for inclusion in a separation agreement based on a comprehensive fact pattern.

The Facts

Jim Jones, thirty, has been married to Julie Jones, twenty-nine, for seven years. They have two children, Morgan, age four, and Freeman, age six. When they got married, Jim was in his senior year of college and planning to graduate the following June and go on to get his master's degree in education. His lifelong dream has been to be a teacher. However, Julie got pregnant right after they were married and stopped working for a year. As a result, Jim dropped out of college and went to work in a local steak house. He continues to work part-time waiting tables and earns about $500 per week. He gets no employment benefits.

Morgan was born on September 15 six years ago and Freeman was born on January 12 four years ago. Right after Morgan was born, Julie enrolled in law school. She received some financial aid and took out substantial student loans to support the cost of most of her tuition and books. Jim paid the remainder of her educational expenses as well as the household expenses for the three years she was in law school. Julie did not work at all during those years because she wanted to put all her energy into her studies. She graduated with high honors and was promptly hired at a major urban law firm where she had interned for a semester. Her supervisor was Marcus Tye, a senior partner in the firm. She and Mr. Tye became very close and Jim has reason to believe that he and Julie are having an affair, given that Attorney Tye's wife recently filed for divorce. Although he doesn't know for sure, Jim believes Tye's wife is claiming that her husband is having an affair with "some new employee at the office."

While Julie was going to school and for the couple of years she has been working, the parties agreed that Jim would stay home and manage the household and be primary caretaker for the children. He really didn't mind, because he loves the children and always figured that his turn would come once Julie got settled in her $170,000-a-year job, where she receives bonuses of varying amounts each year and benefits including medical insurance and a pension plan. Jim and the children are presently covered by her insurance.

The parties' only asset is the marital home, which is valued at $350,000, and they are carrying a $150,000 mortgage. Jim's parents gave them the $50,000 for the down payment when Jim and Julie bought it. They have been very generous to the couple and have frequently picked up the slack when debts piled up and upset Jim. They figured he had enough stress. The way Jim dealt with his stress (to no one's knowledge) was to gamble, and his gambling often ate up his paychecks. He also ran up substantial credit card debt taking cash advances. He did have a few big hits, though, and has hidden away about $70,000, which no one knows about.

Jim recently told Julie that he feels the time has come for him to go back to school and resume his career goals. He said she is making plenty of money now and could support their expenses along with day care for the kids. In response, Julie said she had been meaning to talk with him about her desire to get a divorce and move on. It was nothing personal, she said, just that their individual lives have evolved in different directions. The life they had shared was too "low-end" for her. She said she wants to start living "the good life." He can plod along watching DVDs and going to amusement parks with the kids for vacations, but she wants more. Jim is very hurt and angry but said he will make the best of a bad deal, and she can pay him support so that he can get his life back on track. She told him that he had to be kidding and then left the house and hasn't come home since. He is not sure where she is.

The Assignment

Jim has decided to file for divorce and is hoping to negotiate an agreement with Julie, who will be representing herself in the divorce. Anticipating the likely outcome of the negotiations, your supervisor, Attorney Purdie, has asked you to draft a reasonable alimony provision for inclusion in a potential separation agreement. The provision should be tailored to the facts of the case and be sufficiently defensible that a court in your state would approve it. You should research some models and be sure to reflect what you have learned reading this chapter about the nature of alimony provisions and the various types of alimony that may be available.

FOCUS ON **ETHICS**

This focus on ethics asks the student to consider some of the ethical issues that arise when the client in the Focus on the Job fact pattern asks a paralegal to engage in a potentially illegal act.

The Assignment

The family law firm where you are employed represents Jim in the above fact pattern. You have been interviewing Jim and gathering information from him regarding his divorce and claim for alimony. You and Jim have become quite friendly, and he apparently trusts you. Today, when the two of you met regarding the case, Jim asked if you could "grab a bite to eat" with him at the local delicatessen. It was lunchtime and you needed to eat, so you decided to go and insisted on paying for your own lunch so that Jim would not get the wrong impression. While eating lunch, Jim shared with you the fact that as a result of his gambling, he has accumulated nearly $70,000 in cash, which he has kept at home in a bureau drawer. He told you that Julie doesn't know about the cash and he doesn't plan to tell her about it or declare it on his financial statement, because he doesn't want her to get any of it. He is going to move to a small apartment in a tough neighborhood and doesn't want to take the money with him. He asked if you would be willing to hold it in safekeeping for him and said that he will give you 10% of it if you do. He told you not to answer right away and to think about it. You told him that if you do not agree to hold the cash, your supervisor probably will. In a 1-2 page paper respond to the following questions. What are you going to do? Why? What do you think will happen if and when you report the details of this incident to your supervisor? Relate your response to the ethical canons for paralegals promulgated by the National Association of Legal Assistants contained in Appendix A.

FOCUS ON **CASE LAW**

This activity requires the student to respond to a series of questions about an alimony case that addresses several topics covered in this chapter.

The Assignment

Read the Iowa Supreme Court case *In re the Marriage of Olson,* 705 N.W.2d 312 (Iowa 2005), and then respond to the following questions:

1. Describe the legal history of the case.
2. What issue is addressed in the appeal to the Iowa Supreme Court?
3. Briefly describe the facts of the case.
4. How did the district court treat the husband's overtime income? Was it included in his income for purposes of calculating alimony? Did the state's high court agree with this approach?

5. What factors do the Iowa courts consider when determining whether or not an award of alimony is appropriate? Where are those factors set forth?

6. Describe the types of alimony considered by the court in this case.

7. Which type of alimony did the court conclude was appropriate and why?

8. Explain how the court factored the wife's gambling into the alimony decision, if at all.

9. What was the decision of the Iowa Supreme Court in this case?

10. What was the essence of Justice Carter's concurring opinion?

PARALEGAL PRACTICE TIP

The opinion in the *Olson* case can be found at *www.pearsonhighered. com/wilson* in the companion website material related to Chapter 10 under "Cases" and in the Case Resources Section of the MyLegalStudiesLab.

FOCUS ON **STATE LAW AND PROCEDURE**

This activity requires the student to locate the rules governing spousal support in his or her state and apply them to the Focus on the Job fact pattern by assessing the potential of the client's claim for alimony.

The Assignment

Locate the statute(s) and/or case law in your jurisdiction governing initial alimony awards. Identify the factors considered by the courts in making alimony determinations. Assume that in your capacity as a paralegal, you have been asked by your supervisor, Attorney Purdie, to assess Jim Jones's prospects for receiving an alimony award in your state based on those factors. Present your findings in an internal memorandum using the format below. Be sure to include a list of the factors. Is marital fault relevant and, if so, under what circumstances? Do any of the sources you located specify the kinds of support that

can be awarded? If yes, which kind would be appropriate in this case, if any?

Memorandum

To: *Your Supervisor*

From: *Your name, paralegal*

Re: *Assessment of James Jones's Claim for Alimony*

Date:

Description of assignment: *What is it that you have been asked to do?*

Results of research: *Describe the applicable statute(s)/ case law.*

Discussion: *Apply the governing law to the specific facts of Jim's case.*

Conclusion: *What is your opinion about the client's likelihood of success with respect to his claim for alimony?*

FOCUS ON **TECHNOLOGY**

In addition to the links provided throughout the chapter, this activity provides a series of useful websites for reference along with technology-related assignments for completion.

Websites of Interest

Links to all of the listed websites are provided at *www. pearsonhighered.com/wilson* in the companion website material for Chapter 10 under "Resources."

www.divorceonline.com

This site provides a wide range of articles and information on various aspects of divorce. It includes links to state divorce laws. Click on "Professional Resources" and then on "State Divorce Laws."

www.divorcehelp.com

This site is operated by a lawyer. One of the resources it provides is a copy of "A Short Divorce Course" for people considering and/or going through a divorce.

www.divorcelinks.com

This site provides direct links to state and federal divorce law by topic.

www.divorcenet.com

This site offers family law advice on divorce. It provides links to state resource pages that contain a wealth of articles and links on a variety of topics, including alimony.

www.findlaw.com

A search on "spousal support" will prove fruitful. The site offers alimony information by state along with articles on types of alimony and criteria for awards. Primary sources should be checked to verify information when appropriate.

www.irs.gov

This is the website for the Internal Revenue Service. In addition to provisions of the federal tax code, many useful publications are available at this site, including Publication 504 containing tax information for Divorced and Separated Individuals.

www.totalbankruptcy.com/state—laws

This site provides a wealth of information about bankruptcy, including links to state laws. The information provided should be verified to be sure it reflects current law.

Assignments

1. Using online resources, locate the factors considered by the court when making alimony determinations in your state.
2. Go to the website for the U.S. Department of Labor (*www.dol.gov*) and locate information about COBRA health insurance coverage post divorce.
3. Go to *www.abanet.org*, the website for the American Bar Association. Search for the table on alimony/spousal support factors (Table 1), which contains a state-by-state summary indicating:

- which states have a statutory list of factors for courts to consider when making alimony decisions
- which states consider marital fault
- which states consider standard of living
- which states consider a party's status as a custodial parent

To locate the table at the site, search for "Family Law in the 50 States Tables" in resources available to the public. This table also appears annually in the *Family Law Quarterly* published by the ABA. What did you learn about your state from this resource? Is the information you found current?

PORTFOLIO PRODUCTS

1. Alimony provision for a separation agreement
2. 1-2 page paper on ethical issues in a hypothetical fact pattern
3. Responses to questions regarding an alimony case
4. Memorandum: Assessment of a client's claim for alimony

chapter 11
PROPERTY DIVISION

Jimmy and Alice had been married for ten years and lived a comfortable life with their three children—that was until Alice had an affair with her boss and Jimmy found out about it. He says he will make her pay for hurting the family like that. He tells his lawyer he wants to file for divorce on the grounds of adultery and that he intends to win at all costs. She will walk away with nothing.

LEARNING OBJECTIVES

After reading this chapter and completing related assignments, you should be able to:

- identify the five phases of the property division process

- distinguish between separate and marital property

- identify kinds of property subject to division when a marriage dissolves

- distinguish between the community property and equitable distribution approaches to property division

- list factors the courts consider when dividing property and liabilities upon divorce

- describe the paralegal's role in the property division process

Introduction

Jimmy makes a naïve assumption in the opening scenario. It is naïve in the sense that no one really "wins" in a divorce. Each party ends up materially with less than he or she had during the marriage and is often emotionally bankrupt as well. The old idea that a wronged spouse can somehow punish his or her former partner, "get everything," and make him or her pay forever largely passed from the legal scene four decades ago with the coming of no-fault divorce.

Complaints for divorce on the grounds of irreconcilable differences are rarely denied, and marriages often are dissolved as if they were business partnerships. Marital property is divided between the spouses based on an assumption that, since marriage is a partnership, when it dissolves both parties have an interest in the marital assets and should be held accountable for the liabilities incurred during the marriage. Generally, courts first divide the marital estate and then, if allowed in the jurisdiction, make a determination with respect to whether or not an alimony award is also appropriate. A comprehensive comparison of property division and alimony was provided in Chapter 10 in Exhibit 10.1.

PARALEGAL PRACTICE TIP

Although the parties may not appreciate the distinction between alimony and property division, it is especially significant in the tax or bankruptcy context. In most circumstances it is best to label payments or transfers as either alimony or property division to avoid confusion and postdivorce litigation. However, language in the parties' agreements or labels in family court orders are not necessarily determinative in every context. The IRS and bankruptcy courts make their own determinations as to the character of each transaction.

The Five Phases of the Property Division Process

Property division is a complex and often emotionally charged topic. Although specific approaches, procedural rules, and case law vary from state to state, the basic process remains constant. It essentially involves five phases, each of which addresses a specific task:

1. Definition of property: What is "property" and what property do the parties have?
2. Classification of property: Is the property "separate" or "marital" property?
3. Identification of property subject to division upon divorce: Which property can the courts reach to effectuate a division of property?
4. Valuation of property: What is the property worth—how and when is it valued?
5. Division of property: How is property divided—what approaches do the courts apply?

PARALEGAL PRACTICE TIP

Given state variations, it may help readers to identify at the start of this chapter the basic terminology applied in their respective jurisdictions. For example, in a community property state, marital property will be referred to as "community property."

DEFINITION OF PROPERTY

The threshold question in a property division case is, "Does a particular asset fall within a definition of 'property'?" In most cases, this question does not even arise because the parties' only assets are clearly property, such as automobiles, household furnishings, bank accounts, or a marital home, but some cases involve assets that are less clearly "property." Assets that are mere expectancies (such as possible inheritances or future earning capacity) or that have no presently determinable value (such as a patent on an obscure engine part) will generally not be considered property subject to division.

It is important that all actual and potential assets and liabilities be identified. Before even filing for divorce, counsel will usually ask the client to identify (and document where possible) the **tangible** and **intangible** "property" the parties may have. Clients often initially fail to recognize the nature and extent of property they and/or their spouses may own that has value. They need to be encouraged to think in broad terms. Exhibit 11.1 provides some examples of "property" that may be subject to division upon divorce. Some of the types of property listed are not necessarily considered property in every state, but a sound and creative legal argument can often be persuasive.

PARALEGAL PRACTICE TIP

A failure to identify, value, and seek distribution of property for the client may amount to malpractice if significant assets or liabilities are overlooked.

Tangible property
property that has a physical form, capable of being touched and seen

Intangible property
property that has no physical presence or form such as legal claims, patents, and trademarks

PARALEGAL PRACTICE TIP

This process can be facilitated by the completion of a client questionnaire, such as the sample provided at *www.pearsonhighered.com/wilson* in the companion website material related to Chapter 5 under "Resources."

PARALEGAL PRACTICE TIP

For readers seeking an introduction to or a review of basic property concepts, a list of definitions relating to types of property (real and personal, tangible and intangible, etc.) and forms of ownership is available at *www. pearsonhighered.com/wilson* in the companion website material related to Chapter 11 under "Resources."

EXHIBIT 11.1 Property Potentially Subject to Division

- annuity contracts
- antiques, heirlooms
- appreciation in the value of property during the marriage, depending on whether it relates to separate or marital property and active or passive appreciation
- artwork
- bank accounts (checking, savings, credit union, etc.)
- boats
- bonuses
- business interests (sole proprietorships, corporations, partnerships, etc.)
- cash
- certificates of deposit
- clothing (including furs, etc.)
- club memberships (social, golf, tennis, yacht, etc.)[1]
- collectibles (guns, china, figurines, stamps, coins, baseball cards, etc.)[2]
- contingent fee agreements[3]
- contracts (such as a professional athlete's contract)[4]
- copyrights, patents, and trademarks
- deferred compensation
- disability awards
- employment "perks" (housing, car, parking space, etc.)
- frequent-flier miles
- furniture and appliances
- gifts
- goodwill of a business
- governmental benefits
- inheritances
- insurance policies with cash-surrender values
- jewelry
- licenses (e.g., pilot's license or a taxi medallion)
- lottery winnings[5]
- motor vehicles, including cars, trucks, recreational vehicles, motorcycles, trailers, etc.
- mutual funds
- pending lawsuits and judgments
- pension plans (IRAs, 401(k)s, etc.)
- personal injury awards
- pets/companion animals[6]
- professional degrees
- profit-sharing plans
- real estate (residence, vacation homes, rental property, time-shares, cemetery lots, deeded rights to parking spaces, etc.)
- season tickets to athletic events, theaters, concerts, and other cultural events
- silverware
- Social Security benefits[7]
- stocks and bonds
- stock options (vested and unvested)[8]
- tax refunds and overpayment of state and federal taxes
- trusts (beneficial interests)
- accrued vacation or sick leave time
- worker's compensation benefits[9]

PARALEGAL PRACTICE TIP

Sometimes it may be necessary to determine if a gift being claimed as separate property is truly a gift. For example, during the marriage, an elderly aunt gives a "gift" of $50,000 to a niece who has been her primary caretaker for a year. It might be argued that the cash is not in fact a gift but rather compensation paid for the niece's services and that it is therefore marital property.

PARALEGAL PRACTICE TIP

Occasionally, despite the best efforts of a client and the family law team, an asset concealed by the other party will not be discovered until after entry of the judgment dissolving the parties' marriage and dividing their assets. Although property distributions are generally held to be final and not subject to modification, courts will sometimes reopen a case based on discovery of additional assets concealed at the time of the divorce.[10]

Paralegal Application 11.1

To Be or Not to Be Property

There are some things listed in Exhibit 11.1 that look like property but that may or may not be considered property, depending on the jurisdiction: Consider, for example, the following:

The Professional Goodwill of a Business

Goodwill has been defined as "the favor which the management of a business has won from the public and probability that old customers will continue their patronage."[11] The financial value of goodwill sometimes can be determined by an expert. When goodwill is based on personal characteristics of a party or is intrinsically tied to the attributes and skills of a particular individual, most states do not consider it to be property subject to division, because the value of the goodwill cannot be sold—it does not survive the disassociation of the individual from the business. However, goodwill that is wholly attributable to a commercial business, such as a hardware store, the business itself, its location and customer lists, etc., may be considered property subject to valuation and division upon divorce.[12] (See Case 11.1.)

Pets

We have pet adoption and foster care and we have societies to protect animals from abuse that generate more funds annually than societies to protect children. It is estimated that pets or "companion animals" are present as treasured additions in more than 50% of American households. So it is not surprising that what happens to Spike, Pumpkin, Mittens, and Kaspar can present a challenging issue for divorcing spouses and the courts. Some couples provide for "custody and visitation" with cherished pets by formal agreement, and others do so by informal cooperative arrangements. When disputed, the courts grapple with whether they should consider the animal's best interests and make custody awards or deem them personal property and distribute them along with the dishes, iPods, cars, and bank accounts. Most of the courts that have considered this issue have determined that they are personal property subject to division.[13] (See Case 11.2.)

PARALEGAL PRACTICE TIP

When researching this issue, paralegals should look at journal articles as well as case law. Consider, for example, Heidi Stroh, *Puppy Love: Providing for the Legal Protection of Animals When Their Owners Get Divorced*, 2 J. ANIMAL L. & ETHICS 231 (2007), arguing for a best interests standard, and *Juelfs v. Gough*, 41 P.3d 593 (Alaska 2002), in which the court considered the parties' dog, Coho, in the context of a property settlement but ultimately granted sole "custody" to the husband believing it to be in the dog's "best interests."

A Professional Degree or License

A majority of jurisdictions hold that a professional degree (J.D., M.D., Ph.D., etc.) does not possess the basic characteristics of marital property. "It is personal to the holder; it cannot be sold, transferred, pledged, or inherited. It does not have an assignable value, . . ."[14] "A degree only gives the owner a speculative increase in future earnings, which is affected by so many other influences and factors that it can hardly be considered more than a future expectancy."[15] Even if the degree was earned during the marriage and marital funds were used to pay for related expenses, the degree is still not necessarily a marital asset. Most states choose to consider degrees earned during marriage in the spousal support context. For example, a court may choose to award reimbursement or restitution alimony to a spouse who worked to support the family unit while the other spouse earned a degree. Case 11.3 presents the minority view that professional degrees constitute marital property that should be assigned a value based on evidence offered through an expert witness if not agreed upon by the parties.

PARALEGAL PRACTICE TIP

The opinion in the *Traczyk* case is available at *www.pearsonhighered.com/wilson* on the companion website in the material related to Chapter 11 under "Cases" and in the Case Resources Section of the MyLegalStudiesLab.

CASE 11.1 *Traczyk v. Traczyk,* 1995 OK 22, 891 P.2d 1277 (1995)

BACKGROUND

In this case, a husband appealed a trial court's consideration of the goodwill of his medical practice as an element of the marital property to be divided between the parties. He testified that the reason clients came to the clinic was because of him and that few would remain as patients if he sold his foot clinic practice. He claimed that such goodwill could not be valued and sold as part of the business, because it was personal

(Continued)

to him. The Oklahoma Supreme Court affirmed the decision of the trial court. This case also addresses the distinctions and interplay among property division, alimony, and alimony in lieu of property division.

FROM THE OPINION

The professional practice of one spouse is an appropriate element of the marital property to be divided between the parties where it is jointly acquired property. *Ford v. Ford*, 766 P.2d 950 (Okla. 1988); . . . The issue before us is whether goodwill of Husband's podiatry practice may be considered in determining the value of the practice.

Pursuant to 60 O.S. 1991 §§ 315 and 316, goodwill of a business is defined as "the expectation of continued public patronage," and is considered property transferable like any other property. . . .

In determining the value of the Bethany Foot Clinic, the expert witness consulted the Goodwill Registry, "an accumulation of information concerning sales of medical related practices by experts." From this publication, the expert determined that of the most recent purchases of podiatry clinics, an average of thirty-two percent (32%) of the podiatry patients stay with the clinic after it is sold to a new doctor. The range from which he obtained the average was 21% to 44% of clients staying.

Noting that the traditional method used in valuing a medical practice is the previous year's gross income, the expert then took the previous year's gross income at the clinic ($324,201.51) and multiplied it by the 32% figure to arrive at a goodwill value of $103,744.00. Adding this to the value of the remaining business assets, the expert found the total value of the Bethany Foot Clinic to be $152,605.44. The trial court accepted this valuation and used it in determining how much alimony in lieu of property division to award.

We find that the trial court did not err in considering the goodwill of the Bethany Foot Clinic as a factor in determining the value of the clinic as marital property. The goodwill of the Bethany Foot Clinic is distinct from the personal reputation of Dr. Traczyk. Although many of Dr. Traczyk's patients would not continue to patronize the Bethany Foot Clinic were Dr. Traczyk to sell to another podiatrist, competent evidence indicates that many would stay. Indeed, Dr. Traczyk may use the goodwill as a selling point to potential purchasers.

> If goodwill is to be divided as an asset, its value should be determined either by an agreement or by its fair market value. Both of these methods are widely accepted for valuing goodwill. See annotation, 78 A.L.R.4th 853, 860–71 (1987). Mocnik, 838 P.2d at 505.

The goodwill of the Bethany Foot Clinic was valued as an asset and was a factor in determining the total value of the business for property division purposes. This goodwill was part of the property which should be divided between the parties; Wife had a right to receive her share of the property. 43 O.S. 1991, §121. On the other hand, the award of support alimony was a separate determination based upon Husband's ability to pay and Wife's demonstrated need. . . . Although the property division is permanent and irrevocable, the award of support alimony is subject to modification upon a showing of substantial change in circumstances, i.e. Husband's ability and/or Wife's demonstrated need. 43 O.S. 1991, §134; *Clifton v. Clifton*, 801 P.2d 693 (Okla. 1990).

By awarding support alimony and including goodwill in the value of the business for property division purposes, the trial court did not "double dip" into Husband's future income. Both awards, one for support alimony and one for alimony in lieu of property division were proper and distinct from the other. . . .

SIDEBAR

Do you agree with the court's decision? Explain your response.

PARALEGAL PRACTICE TIP

The opinion in the *Bennett* case is available at *www.pearsonhighered. com/wilson* in the companion website material related to Chapter 11 under "Cases" and in the Case Resources Section of the MyLegalStudiesLab.

CASE **11.2** *Bennett v. Bennett,* 655 So.2d 109 (Fla. App. 1995)

BACKGROUND

In this case, a Florida appellate court considered a husband's appeal of a trial court's decision to award his wife visitation with the parties' dog.

FROM THE OPINION

. . . [T]he trial court's ruling . . . reads:

7. *Dog. Roddy:* The former husband . . . shall have custody of the parties' dog "Roddy" and the former wife . . . shall have visitation every other month beginning October 1, 1993. The visitation shall begin on the first day of the month and end on the last day of the month.

Based on the history of this case, there is every reason to believe that there will be continued squabbling between the parties concerning the dog.

While a dog may be considered by many to be a member of the family, under Florida law, animals are considered to be personal property. . . . There is no authority which provides for a trial court to grant custody or visitation pertaining to personal property. . . .

While several states have given family pets special status within dissolution proceedings (for example, see *Arrington v. Arrington,* 613 S.W.2d 565 (Tex. App. 1981)), we think such a course is unwise. Determinations as to custody and visitation lead to continuing enforcement and supervision problems (as evidenced by the proceedings in the instant case). Our courts are overwhelmed with the supervision of custody, visitation, and support matters related to the protection of our children. We cannot undertake the same responsibility as to animals.

While the trial judge was endeavoring to reach a fair solution under difficult circumstances, we must reverse the order relating to the custody of "Roddy," and remand for the trial court to award the animal pursuant to the dictates of the equitable division statute.

SIDEBAR

In the family law context, do you believe pets should be treated as personal property and distributed like other assets or treated more like children for whom custody and visitation determinations need to be made? Explain your answer.

CASE **11.3** *Woodworth v. Woodworth,* 126 Mich. App. 258, 337 N.W.2d 332 (1983)

PARALEGAL PRACTICE TIP

The opinion in the *Woodworth* case is available at *www.pearsonhighered. com/wilson* in the companion website material related to Chapter 11 under "Cases" and in the Case Resources Section of the MyLegalStudiesLab.

BACKGROUND

In this case, a Michigan appeals court considered the issue of whether a law degree is subject to distribution and adopted the minority view that it is. During their marriage, the plaintiff, Michael Woodworth, and his wife, Ann, had relocated their family to Detroit so that Michael would be able to attend law school and increase his earning capacity for the benefit of the family. He subsequently graduated, passed the bar, and practiced law, first as an attorney with the court of appeals and later as a partner in a Lansing law firm. The trial court held that the law degree was property valued at $20,000 and awarded this amount to the wife in payments of $2,000 over ten years, the length of the period between the parties' wedding and date of separation. The husband appealed the order, contending that the degree was not a marital asset subject to division.

(Continued)

FROM THE OPINION

The basic issue in this case is whether or not plaintiff's law degree is marital property subject to distribution. . . .

The facts reveal that plaintiff's law degree was the end product of a concerted family effort. Both parties planned their family life around the effort to attain plaintiff's degree. Toward this end, the family divided the daily tasks encountered in living. While the law degree did not pre-empt all other facets of their lives, it did become the main focus and goal of their activities. . . .

We conclude, therefore, that plaintiff's law degree was the result of mutual sacrifice and effort by both plaintiff and defendant. While plaintiff studied and attended classes, defendant carried her share of the burden as well as sharing vicariously in the stress of the experience known as the "paper chase."

We believe that fairness dictates that the spouse who did not earn an advanced degree be compensated whenever the advanced degree is the product of such concerted family investment. The degree holder has expended great effort to obtain the degree not only for himself or herself, but also to benefit the family as a whole. The other spouse has shared in this effort and contributed in other ways as well, not merely as a gift to the student spouse nor merely to share individually in the benefits but to help the marital unit as a whole.

. . . a marriage is not intrinsically a commercial enterprise. Instead it is a relationship sanctioned by law governed at its essence by fidelity and troth. Neither partner usually expects to be compensated for his or her efforts. But that consideration does not end the discussion. We are not presently concerned with how best to characterize a marriage while it endures. Instead, we are concerned with how best to distribute between the parties what they have once the marriage has for all intents and purposes dissolved. In other words:

> "To allow a student spouse *** to leave a marriage with all the benefits of additional education and a professional license without compensation to the spouse who bore much of the burdens incident to procuring these would be unfair***." O'Brien, supra, 452 NYS2d 805.

. . . Defendant is not asking us to compensate for a failed expectation that her husband would become a wealthy lawyer and subsequently support her for the rest of her life. Instead, she is merely seeking her share of the fruits of a degree which she helped him earn. We fail to see the difference between compensating her for a degree which she helped him earn and compensating her for a house in his name which her earnings helped him buy.

. . . Clearly, in this case, the degree was a family investment, rather than a gift or a benefit to the degree holder alone. Treating the degree as such a gift would unjustly enrich the degree holder to the extent that the degree's value exceeds its cost. . . .

SIDEBAR

The holding reflects the minority position on the question of whether or not professional degrees earned during a marriage constitute marital property subject to division. The award in this instance was rather modest. In the *O'Brien* case cited in this opinion, the trial court held the value of the husband's medical license at the time of divorce was $472,000 and awarded the wife 40% of that amount ($188,000) payable over an eleven-year period. Do you agree that degrees should be considered marital property? Why? If they are deemed property, what factors should a court consider when placing a value on the degree? How else might they be handled?

CLASSIFICATION OF PROPERTY AS SEPARATE OR MARITAL

Marital property
property that is acquired by either or
both parties during the marriage,
other than by gift or inheritance, that
is subject to division at the time of
dissolution

Separate property
property that a spouse owned before marriage or acquired during the
marriage by inheritance or gift from
a third party; may include property
acquired during marriage in exchange for separate property

PARALEGAL PRACTICE TIP

The section of the West Virginia
Code defining marital and separate
property can be seen at *www.
pearsonhighered.com/wilson* in the
companion website material related
to Chapter 11 under "Statutes."

Generally, the parties begin acquiring **marital property** at the commencement
of the marriage and cease to do so at the time of separation, the filing of the
complaint for divorce, or as of the date of the divorce decree. Many states have
legislatively established statutory definitions of marital and separate property.
For example, the South Carolina legislature has defined marital property as "all
real and personal property which has been acquired by the parties during the
marriage and which is owned as of the date of filing or commencement of marital
litigation. . . ."[16] It usually includes property classified as marital regardless of
how title to that property is held. For example, the deed to the marital home may
be in the name of both parties as tenants by the entirety, joint tenants with rights
of survivorship, or solely in the name of one spouse. Marital property excludes
separate property, property owned by a party prior to marriage although in some
states it may include appreciation in the value of separate property during the
course of the marriage. Most states also exempt from marital property gifts and
inheritances received by either of the parties from third parties during the marriage,
but some consider interspousal gifts purchased with joint funds to be marital property. Some states distinguish between segregated separate property and separate
property supported, maintained, and improved with marital funds, time and effort.
Sometimes classification of property as separate or marital is especially challenging.
(See Paralegal Application 11.2.)

Paralegal Application 11.2

Separate or Marital Property?

Disability Awards

The majority of courts that have considered the proper classification of disability benefits have adopted an approach which focuses on the underlying purpose of the specific disability benefits at issue, separating awards into retirement and true disability components when appropriate. Where justified by the particular facts of a case, the retirement component is considered marital property and the disability component separate property because it is personal to the spouse who receives it.[18] In determining the character of disability benefits in a specific case, courts usually will look at several factors:

- Does a state statute specifically exclude them from marital property?
- Are the benefits the result of a private disability policy paid for with marital funds?
- Are the benefits compensation for past services rendered during the marriage?
- Did the right to receive benefits result from employment during the marriage?
- Do the benefits replace future income?
- Does the benefit compensate for lost earning capacity?
- Does the benefit represent retirement pay earned during the marriage?
- Did the parties discuss the benefit and view it as a joint investment to secure their future?

Personal Injury Awards

As with disability payments, the courts will customarily look at the purpose(s) served by the award. The West Virginia Supreme Court of Appeals expressed it this way: ". . . to the extent that its purpose is to compensate an individual for pain, suffering, disability, disfigurement, or other debilitation of the mind or body, a personal injury award constitutes the separate nonmarital property of an injured spouse. However, . . . economic losses, such as past wages and medical expenses, which diminish the marital estate are distributable as marital property when recovered in a personal injury award or settlement."[19]

Appreciation in the Value of Separate Property

Property owned by one of the parties prior to marriage often appreciates in value during the marriage. For example, assume that the husband had a stock portfolio worth $10,000 prior to the marriage. He knew little about managing stocks and had essentially let the market take its course. During the marriage, the wife read several books and enrolled in two workshops addressing investment strategies. The husband let her "play" with the account and over the course of their ten-year marriage, the account increased in value to $100,000. Thirty percent of that increase ($30,000) was attributable to market trends and would have occurred had the parties taken no action whatsoever (known as **passive appreciation**). However, $60,000 of the increase was a direct result of the wife's effective management of the account (known as **active appreciation**). Although the stocks are not registered in the wife's name, the increase in value (particularly the $60,000) derived during the marriage may well be considered marital property subject to division. In most jurisdictions, the husband's share of the account would be $70,000 (his initial $10,000, the $30,000 passive appreciation, and half of the $60,000 active appreciation during the marriage). The wife's share would be $30,000 (half of the active appreciation during the marriage). A minority of jurisdictions would consider the full amount of appreciation to be separate property based on the nature of the underlying asset as separate.

Accrued Vacation or Sick Leave Time

The courts that have considered these assets are divided. If an employee will be paid the value of accrued vacation or sick leave time at some point, courts may construe time credits that accrued during the marriage as a marital asset divisible upon divorce or at a later date when actually received by the employee spouse such as on retirement. However, if accrued sick time cannot be cashed in or can only be applied toward the employee's postretirement health insurance premiums, it may not be deemed marital property because it is personal, intangible, difficult to value, and impossible to transfer.[20]

Passive appreciation
increase in the value of an asset that results without effort and as a result of market forces and the passage of time

Active appreciation
increase in the value of an asset that results from effort rather than simply market forces or the passage of time

Classifying a property as marital rather than separate does not mean that the particular property must be divided or that the holder of title to the property will not be permitted to keep it. It just means that the family court has the authority to divide it if necessary to effect an equal or equitable division. The paralegal may be involved in gathering the information necessary to support the classification and the distribution most favorable to the client.

Transmutation

a change in the classification of an asset from separate to marital or marital to separate

An argument is sometimes made that separate property has lost its identity as separate and has become marital property during the course of a marriage, that a **transmutation** or change has taken place in the character of the property due to certain circumstances:

Postmarital agreement

an agreement made by two people already married to each other who want both to continue their marriage and also to define their respective rights upon separation, divorce, or death of one of them

- After ten years of "a wonderful marriage," in a state that permits them to do so, the parties may decide to execute a **postmarital agreement** in which they mutually designate their separate property as marital.
- For estate-planning purposes, they may decide to jointly title the marital home or certain other property.
- The parties may use or treat a separate asset as a marital asset by spending both marital time and funds on the asset. For example, the husband may own a home in his name prior to marriage. After marriage, he and his wife live in the home for twenty years. During the marriage they both participate in remodeling, redecorating, and landscaping initiatives paid for with marital funds, and they warmly refer to the residence as "our home."

Commingling

mixing together a spouse's separate property with marital property, or mixing together the separate property of both spouses

- The transmutation may result from a **commingling** of separate resources with marital resources. For example, the wife sells a condominium she owned prior to the marriage for $250,000, and the parties then buy a new marital residence with that amount plus $10,000 from the husband's savings account that he held prior to the marriage, $100,000 in marital funds, and a mortgage in both their names.

Given such fact patterns, the majority of courts are likely to assume that basic fairness requires the property involved be treated as marital property available for division upon divorce.

One spouse may add the other spouse's name to a deed to separate property for a variety of reasons. In determining whether that property should be considered separate or marital at the time of divorce, in most states, courts will look to the intent of the spouse who added the name. Did he or she intend to convey a half interest in the property or was he or she merely trying to accomplish some other purpose such as obtaining a mortgage on the property? See e.g. *Barrett v. Barrett,* 232 P.3d 799 (Idaho 2010).

Inception of title theory

a theory that fixes ownership of property at the time it is acquired and holds that postmarital contributions are of no effect

Source of funds/*pro rata* theory

a theory that bases ownership of property on contribution; an asset may be characterized as both separate and marital in proportion to the respective contributions of the parties

Courts have adopted a variety of approaches to establish ownership of commingled property. The two most prominent theories are **inception of title** and **source of funds/*pro rata*.** Inception of title theory bases ownership on whichever spouse first acquired title to the property: A party acquires property at the time of initial purchase, and postmarital contributions are of no effect. The preferred approach to establishing ownership, source of funds theory, bases ownership on contribution toward acquisition of the property. The two theories can lead to opposite results in the same situation. For example, if the marital home cost $150,000 and was initially titled in the wife's name but the husband paid the down payment and all of the mortgage payments, under inception of title theory, the property is viewed as owned by the wife despite her lack of financial contribution. Under source of funds theory, it belongs to both of them according to their respective contributions. If the wife contributed 40% of the down payment and mortgage payments, the property would be considered 40% hers and 60% his. Courts may even consider the contributions of third parties when relevant to determining each party's interest in the marital property. For instance, if in the above fact pattern the entire down payment came from the wife's parents, then the wife's share may be greater.[21]

If either party seeks to establish that he or she did not intend for his or her separate property to lose its identity as separate, that party must be able to **trace** his or her contribution to what appears to be marital property back to separate property. The property may retain its separate identity even if it is refinanced and the proceeds of the refinancing become marital property.[22] If all or part of the transmuted property can be retraced to separate property, the burden usually shifts to the other party to establish that there was an intention to make a gift of the separate property to the marital estate.

Tracing
the process of tracking ownership of a property from the time of inception to the present

Paralegal Application 11.3

Separate or Marital? What Do You Think?

The Facts

The parties in this case were divorced in 2003 after fifteen years of marriage. The wife, Violeta, was a mother and homemaker during much of the marriage, and the husband, Chad, worked as an electrician and occasionally for his family's business. There was a dispute during the divorce concerning the characterization of two assets as separate or marital: the marital home and an investment account.

The Marital Home

During their marriage, the parties lived in a home given to Chad by his mother one week before the wedding. Over the thirteen years they lived there, the taxes, insurance, and maintenance expenses were paid from marital funds. Violeta cleaned and maintained the house during the marriage and Chad made no attempts to maintain the separate character of this property. However, at the time of the divorce, he claimed that the home remained his separate property because "the parties always viewed it as such."

The Investment Account

In 1998, Chad's mother, Molly Miller, gave him a cash gift of $230,000. He initially placed this money in an investment account bearing his name alone but listed Violeta and his children as beneficiaries of equal shares in the event of his death. Approximately one year later, these funds were transferred to a joint account in the names of both Chad and Violeta. Under this account the parties were joint tenants with rights of survivorship, so if one party died before the other, the surviving spouse would receive the entire account balance. The investment account grew from an initial investment of $230,000 in 1998 to $290,000 in 2000, but the balance had dropped to $173,729 by the time the parties separated in March 2001. Chad claimed that this decline was due to market losses. However, after the parties had separated, he began to spend vast sums of money on personal items, living expenses, gifts (some to Violeta), and Internet gambling, depleting the account by more than $94,000 by the end of May 2001, the month he filed for divorce. He said he didn't think he had done anything wrong because he believed the account was his, an advance on his inheritance, and that he maintained full control over it. Violeta explained that she never attempted to access funds from the joint account because Chad was unwilling to let her participate in major decisions or to exercise any control over the parties' finances. However, she said she considered the account to be marital property because her name was on it, and she and Chad used the account for ongoing household expenses such as taxes.

Sidebar

In your opinion, how do you think each of these assets should be classified: separate or marital? Explain your

(Continued)

reasoning for each decision. What kinds of additional information might it have been useful to have? Check the opinion in this case to see if the court agreed with you. *Miller v. Miller,* 105 P.3d 1136 (Alaska 2005).

IDENTIFICATION OF THE PROPERTY SUBJECT TO DIVISION

When parties to a marriage sever their relationship, they (or the courts) necessarily must divide their property. The general rule is that only the property acquired during the marriage is subject to division by the court. Property belonging to a spouse prior to marriage usually remains the property of that spouse unless the parties otherwise agree (as in a premarital agreement or separation agreement) or the property has undergone a transmutation from separate to marital property as described above. Jurisdictions that classify property as separate or marital and allow only marital property to be distributed at divorce are called **dual property** jurisdictions. The limited number of states, such as Massachusetts and Connecticut, in which the court may assign any of a spouse's property to the other spouse are called **all property states**. If necessary to accomplish an equitable division in these states, the courts are permitted to disregard the distinction between separate and marital property and to reach all of the parties' assets regardless of when, how, and by whom they were acquired.

Dual property states
states that distinguish between marital and separate property for distribution purposes and permit only marital property to be divided and distributed at divorce

All property states
states in which divorce courts may reach all property however acquired without distinguishing between separate and marital property if necessary to achieve an equitable distribution. Some describe to this approach as "dipping into" separate property to achieve a fair division of property. It has been argued that equitable distribution statutes deprive an individual of property without due process of law, but such statutes have been upheld as constitutional.[23]

Valuation
the process of assessing the financial worth of property, real or personal

Real property
land and anything growing on, attached to, or erected on it, excluding anything that may be severed without injury to the land

Personal property
any movable or intangible thing that is subject to ownership and is not classified as real property

VALUATION OF PROPERTY

When dividing marital property, courts seek to allocate the parties' property, with each spouse receiving a portion of an equal and/or equitable value depending on the jurisdiction and the facts of the case. In order for the court to do so, ideally the value of each major piece of property to be divided needs to be determined. **Valuation** is the process of assessing the financial worth of property, **real** or **personal**. If contested, the value of a particular piece of property is a question of fact to be determined by the judge based on testimony and evidence presented by the parties. Few statutes specify how a particular asset is to be valued, and a wide variety of approaches are used. If opposing parties use different approaches or propose conflicting values using the same method, the court has the discretion to accept the valuation of either of the parties or to establish its own. Technically, it may constitute reversible error for a trial court to order a division of property without first determining values. However, if a party fails to present evidence as to the value of a contested asset, he or she may waive a right of appeal on the issue. Thorough preparation is essential!

PARALEGAL PRACTICE TIP

Usually there is no "right" answer to a valuation question, but rather a range of possible answers, each supported by a rationale and documentation whenever possible. Attorneys will often generate multiple valuations and first present the one most favorable to the client in negotiations or to the court. If that one is rejected, the alternatives are ready for backup.

There are three basic issues in valuation cases:

1. Which property of the parties should be valued?
2. What is the appropriate date for valuation?
3. Who will conduct the valuation and how?

Which Property of the Parties Should Be Valued?

In some cases, the parties have few if any assets, and valuation is not an issue. In other cases, the parties may be able to agree on a division of property without engaging in valuation. If so, they can avoid a costly and time-consuming process, but they will have no way of knowing whether the agreed-upon settlement really is fair. Absent agreement on a fair allocation of assets and liabilities that a court will be willing to approve, property subject to division may need to be valued. This includes, but is not necessarily limited to, all of the property identified at the beginning of this chapter in Exhibit 11.1. Sometimes the parties will agree that only property above a certain threshold amount will be valued. That amount may be $500, $5,000, or even $50,000 or more, depending on the nature and extent of the marital estate.

The kinds of property most commonly warranting valuation are retirement plans (**vested** or unvested), business interests, and the marital home (and any other real estate such as a rental or vacation property). If there is a mortgage and/or a loan secured by the real estate, the amount of **equity** in the property needs to be determined. Equity is the **fair market value** of the property less any encumbrances (mortgages, loans, tax liens, etc.).

What Is the Appropriate Date of Valuation?

Some states establish by statute or case law the date as of which marital assets are to be valued, but most prefer a flexible approach. Common options include the date when the parties separate, the date on which the divorce complaint (or action for division of property) is filed, the date when discovery is completed, the trial or final hearing date, or the date when the decree of dissolution is entered. The issue can be critical, for example when:

- there is a long period between the date of separation and the filing for divorce;
- the marriage is terminated in one proceeding and other issues (such as custody, support, and division of property) are decided at a later date in the same or a different state;
- the value of an asset is highly volatile and likely to change during the pendency of the divorce litigation due to rapid shifts in the market or broader economic climate; and/or
- one of the parties dissipates or increases the value of assets while the case is pending.

When there is flexibility regarding the date for valuation, multiple alternative dates should be explored so that the attorney can determine which will work to the client's best advantage.

Vest
gives a person an immediate, fixed right of ownership and present or future enjoyment; a vested interest is fixed or accrued and is usually unable to be taken away by subsequent events or circumstances

Equity
in real estate law, the fair market value of a property less any encumbrances (mortgages, loans, tax liens, etc.)

Fair market value
the price a willing buyer would pay a willing seller in an arm's-length transaction (e.g., not between friends or family members) when neither party is under any compulsion to buy or sell

Paralegal Application 11.4

Does Cohabitation Count—What Do You Think?

The paralegal should be alert to the fact that, in some states, contribution to property during a period of premarital cohabitation may be considered by the court when fashioning a division of marital assets, particularly if the contribution was made in contemplation of marriage.

Fact Pattern

This case involves an eight-year marriage preceded by a ten-year period during which the parties lived together. They had no children. When the parties first met, the husband had a small jewelry business with an inventory of approximately $5,800 and gross annual sales of $62,769. The wife learned and worked in the business on a full-time basis for the nine years preceding the marriage. Through their joint efforts, the business thrived, and by the time they married it had an inventory of nearly $100,000 and gross annual sales of over $400,000. Each party had accumulated considerable savings and retirement benefits. Notwithstanding their success in business both before and during the marriage, their personal relationship deteriorated. The husband was verbally and physically abusive to the wife, and she, in retaliation, engaged in an extramarital affair. At the time of the divorce, the trial court awarded the wife approximately one-third of the marital assets. In calculating the award, the judge included, within the assignable estate, the parties' premarital pension and retirement benefits. The husband appealed.

Sidebar

Do you think that premarital contributions to marital assets should be considered as marital property upon dissolution and, if so, under what circumstances? Should it make a difference if a prospective spouse purchases property during a period of cohabitation in anticipation of marriage such as a home for the couple to eventually live in post marriage? Read the opinion in *Moriarty v. Stone,* 41 Mass. App. Ct. 151, 668 N.E.2d 1338 (1996), to see if you agree with the decision of the Massachusetts Court of Appeals. Explain your answer.

PARALEGAL PRACTICE TIP

The opinion in the *Moriarty v. Stone* case is available at *www.pearsonhighered.com/wilson* in the companion website material related to Chapter 11 under "Cases" and in the Case Resources Section of the MyLegalStudiesLab.

Who Will Conduct the Valuation and How?

Valuation of assets such as bank accounts is reasonably straightforward and can usually be accomplished by the client, who often is in a position to obtain account statements directly. Paralegals can research the value of several kinds of property such as automobiles, recreational vehicles, stock values, and the like, by checking "blue book" values and stock listings online or in the business section of the newspaper. Some family law practitioners and paralegals are skilled at other kinds of valuation, but because valuation issues may sometimes be beyond their expertise, most maintain lists of **experts,** including their respective areas of expertise, fee schedules, and current resumes. The task of maintaining these resource lists may be assigned to the paralegal. Experts may include, among others, appraisers, accountants, **actuaries,** financial planners, and investment counselors able to assess the values of such things as real estate, jewelry, pensions, degrees, a party's interest in a professional practice or ongoing business, a pending lawsuit, a copyright, or a spouse's contribution as homemaker and caretaker for the children.

Expert
a person who, through education or experience, has developed special skill or knowledge in a particular subject

Actuary
a statistician who determines the present value of a future event; one who calculates insurance and pension values on the basis of empirically based tables

PARALEGAL PRACTICE TIP

Available at *www.pearsonhighered.com/wilson* in the companion website for this text in the material related to Chapter 6 is a Guide to Documenting Asset Values. It provides a list of several common types of assets, some of the kinds of documentation and resources that are available with respect to valuation of those assets, and the basic data elements regarding them that may be useful in preparing financial statements, conducting negotiations, or preparing exhibits for hearings or trial.

Paralegal Application 11.5 _____

Protecting the Firm

The standard approach to a property division case is to identify assets and liabilities, value them, factor in the client's goals, and then propose an appropriate allocation. Throughout the process, the family law team works in consultation with the client, always mindful of an ethical obligation to provide competent and zealous representation. In turn, the client needs to understand the strengths and weaknesses of his or her case in order to make informed decisions after reviewing with counsel the risks and benefits of various courses of action.

Sometimes a client will not agree to follow the legal advice provided. He or she may direct that the firm not search for concealed property or value a significant asset or may insist on settling for less than he or she reasonably would be entitled to in order to avoid a trial or as a trade-off for some other objective. Under such circumstances, the client should be sent a letter reiterating the recommendations made and noting that, notwithstanding that advice, the attorney has been explicitly directed by the client not to pursue the recommended course of action.

DIVISION OF PROPERTY

In cases involving few if any assets or liabilities, property division is a relatively simple matter often settled by the parties without advice of counsel. Agreements are usually based on the parties' relative needs, personal preferences, and emotional attachments to particular possessions. The primary task of attorneys in such cases is to advise clients with respect to whether or not they have settled for the shares to which they may be legally entitled. Sometimes this is a challenge, as clients often exaggerate or deflate the values of property based on their own subjective appraisals. For example, in exchange for getting to keep the family pet, a client may "give away" all of the household appliances and furnishings.

If the parties are unable to agree on how their property should be divided, it falls on the courts to determine the distribution. In the current no-fault era, an equal division of the marital estate is implicit in the community property approach and strongly favored in equitable distribution jurisdictions. This is particularly the case given a long-term, traditional marriage in which the husband contributed primarily as the "breadwinner" and the wife as the homemaker, and there is a reasonably conventional mix of assets. However, the courts may deviate based on the facts of an individual case and one can never predict a certain outcome.

There are three primary ways in which the property of parties to a divorce may be divided:

1. The parties may have executed a **premarital agreement,** a contract in which they mutually agree as to how their property will be divided in the event of divorce, annulment, or death. The court hearing the divorce case will first determine the validity of the agreement, which should be brought to its attention at the outset of the divorce proceeding. If an agreement is held to be valid, property will be distributed according to its terms.

2. If there is no premarital agreement or it is held to be invalid, the parties may negotiate a mutually agreeable property division for inclusion in a settlement or **separation agreement** (see Chapter 12) and submission to the court for approval. A court will usually accept the parties' agreement, provided its terms are consistent with governing law, do not violate public policy, and are not unconscionable.

3. Judges strongly urge attorneys and counsel to settle cases in order to save costs and conserve judicial resources. However, if the parties are unable to

Premarital agreement
an agreement made by two persons about to be married defining for themselves their respective rights, duties, and responsibilities in the event their marriage terminates by death, annulment, separation, or divorce

Separation agreement
an agreement made between spouses in anticipation of divorce or a legal separation concerning the terms of the divorce or separation and any continuing obligations of the parties to each other

Community property

assets owned in common by a husband and wife as a result of having been acquired during the marriage by a means other than an inheritance or a gift to one spouse, each spouse generally holding a one-half interest in the property no matter in whose name it is held; usually divided equally between the parties upon dissolution of the marriage absent an agreement to the contrary

Equitable distribution

the legal concept that upon divorce property accumulated during a marriage should be divided between the parties equitably, but not necessarily equally, based upon principles of fairness

Error of law

a mistake made by a court in applying the law to the facts of a case

Abuse of discretion

the failure of a court to exercise sound, reasonable, and legal decision making

reach an agreement with respect to the distribution of their assets and liabilities, the matter will be tried before the court. Guided by case law and either **community property** or **equitable distribution** statutes, trial courts have considerable discretion in resolving property division disputes on a case-by-case basis, given the evidence and testimony presented by the parties. A trial court's decision regarding property distribution generally will not be reversed on appeal absent an **error of law** or an **abuse of discretion.**

EXHIBIT 11.2 Overview: Equitable Distribution and Community Property Approaches

Equitable Distribution Approach	When this approach is used, property accumulated during a marriage is divided between the parties based upon principles of fairness. • The majority of states apply this approach to property division upon dissolution of a marriage. • Each state adopts by statute and/or case law a series of factors to be considered by the court when making a property distribution.
Community Property Approach	The premise of the community property approach is that property acquired during the marriage, with the exception of gifts and inheritances, belongs equally to the spouses and therefore should be divided equally upon divorce. Community property generally includes all earnings, assets, and liabilities accumulated during the marriage by either or both of the parties. • This approach is applied by a minority of the states: Arizona, California, Idaho, Louisiana, New Mexico, Nevada, Texas, and Washington. Wisconsin[24] and Alaska[25] are also sometimes characterized as community property states. • Community property statutes may allow for unequal divisions under some circumstances such as when the parties otherwise agree or when there has been "economic misconduct."

The Equitable Distribution Approach

A majority of the states are equitable distribution jurisdictions, in which the courts apportion marital property between the parties in a manner that is fair and "equitable" (albeit not necessarily equal) based on a consideration of factors laid out in case law and/or statutes. (See the Illinois statute in Exhibit 11.4.) The courts are not required to give equal weight to each factor but rather to consider them in light of the facts of each case, recognizing that both parties contributed to the marriage in a variety of ways (financially, maintaining and improving the home, raising the children, etc.). In some equitable distribution states there is a presumption that the division will be equal; but the presumption is rebuttable.

PARALEGAL PRACTICE TIP

The applicable equitable distribution statute for the state of Mississippi can be seen at *www.pearsonhighered.com/wilson* in the companion website material related to Chapter 11 under "Statutes." The Mississippi property division guidelines were initially established in case law and are now codified.

EXHIBIT 11.3 Community Property and Equitable Distribution States

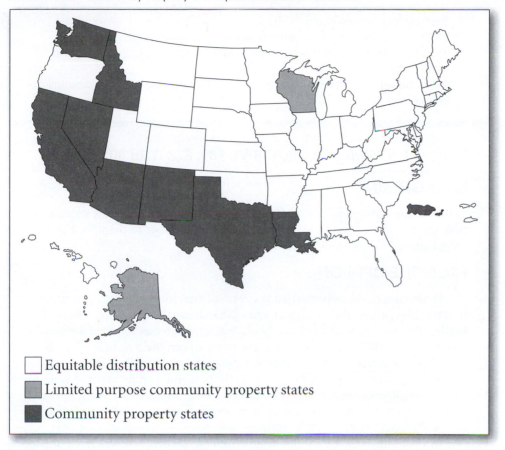

☐ Equitable distribution states

▨ Limited purpose community property states

■ Community property states

EXHIBIT 11.4 Illinois—An Equitable Division Jurisdiction—750 ILCS 5/503 (8)(d)

FROM THE STATUTE

(d) In a proceeding for dissolution of marriage or declaration of invalidity of marriage, or in a proceeding for disposition of property following dissolution of marriage by a court which lacked personal jurisdiction over the absent spouse or lacked jurisdiction to dispose of the property, the court shall assign each spouse's non-marital property to that spouse. It shall also divide the marital property without regard to marital misconduct in just proportions considering all the relevant factors, including:

1. the contribution of each party to the acquisition, preservation, or increase or decrease in value of the marital or non-marital property, including (i) any such decrease attributable to a payment deemed to have been an advance from the parties' marital estate . . . and (ii) the contribution of a spouse as a homemaker or to the family unit;
2. the dissipation by each party of the marital or non-marital property;
3. the value of the property assigned to each spouse;
4. the duration of the marriage;
5. the relevant economic circumstances of each spouse when the division of property is to become effective, including the desirability of awarding the family home, or the right to live therein for reasonable periods, to the spouse having custody of the children;
6. any obligations and rights arising from a prior marriage of either party;
7. any antenuptial agreement of the parties;
8. the age, health, station, occupation, amounts and sources of income, vocational skills, employability, estate, liabilities, and needs of each of the parties;

(Continued)

EXHIBIT 11.4 *(Continued)*

9. the custodial provisions for any children;
10. whether the apportionment is in lieu of or in addition to maintenance;
11. the reasonable opportunity of each spouse for future acquisition of capital assets and income; and
12. the tax consequences of the property division upon the respective economic circumstances of the parties.

CASE 11.4 *Wade v. Wade,* 178 Vt. 189, 878 A.2d 303 (2005)

BACKGROUND

In this case, a Vermont family court applied the factors set forth in the state's equitable division statute and awarded 90% of the marital estate to the wife. The Vermont Supreme Court upheld the award.

FROM THE OPINION

Husband and wife were married in 1991, had one child together, and separated in 2002. The parties, their daughter and husband's son from a prior relationship lived in the town of Waitsfield in a home that wife purchased before the parties married. Since 1985, wife used part of the home to run the Sunshine Montessori School, Inc., a nursery school she founded and continues to operate. Husband has a landscaping business. During the marriage, the husband took on seasonal work in the restaurant, construction and ski industries. Over the last four years, husband earned between $13,000 and $23,000 annually. Wife's income from the Sunshine School averaged $21,824 in 2000–2002.

In 1996, wife received a series of gifts from her mother. She was given title to her mother's home, which wife rented out until 2002 when she sold the property. Wife also received $22,000 in cash and put $40,000 from her mother into a VUGMA account for the parties' minor daughter. The $22,000 went into an account in her name only. Wife subsequently exhausted the money in the account by using it to pay for various family expenses. . . .

After wife sold the home her mother gave her in 2002, the parties each received $10,000 from the proceeds. The remaining proceeds of $59,000 were placed into escrow pending distribution in the divorce proceeding. After her mother died, wife used some of her inheritance to purchase a twenty-nine foot sailboat and a catamaran for the family. Husband spent time repairing and maintaining the boats for the family, and used his carpentry and other handyman skills to maintain and improve the parties' residence. The family also owned a camper, and husband held a half interest in a seasonal camp in Rochester, Vermont.

Throughout the marriage, wife paid the mortgage on the marital residence and most of the household expenses. Husband paid half of the utilities and charged many of his own expenses, and those of his landscaping business to credit cards. At the time the parties separated, husband had over $23,000 in personal and business credit card debt. Wife's credit card debt was a fraction of the husband's. After separating, wife remained in the marital home, and husband moved into a friend's home where he acts as a caretaker.

Wife filed for divorce in October 2002. She sought primary custody of the parties' daughter and most of the parties' property. . . . Husband . . . asked the court to split their property roughly fifty-fifty. Both parties hired expert witnesses to testify about the value of the Sunshine School. It was undisputed that the husband's business had no value.

(Continued)

The court issued a written order following a hearing in December 2003. Wife received approximately ninety percent of the marital property, including the parties' home and all of its equity, the catamaran, the camper, and the escrowed proceeds from the sale of her mother's home. The court awarded husband the sailboat, $10,000 from the sale proceeds that he had already received, his interest in the Rochester camp, and his tools. Crediting wife's expert witness, the court found that the Sunshine School, while valuable to the wife personally, had no market value. . . .

In support of the property award, the court explained that wife had lived in the parties' home since 1985, six years before the parties married. Wife paid the mortgage and property taxes. She also paid for the parties' two boats and contributed all of her income to other household expenses. The court acknowledged that what money husband earned was spent primarily on the household, but it noted that husband "never earned much in any year." The court found that the husband had not "followed a conventional career; instead he has enjoyed the freedom of working on a seasonal basis and taking time when he wishes to work on his own business." The court found that husband could earn more money working a full-time job in construction or some other business if he chose.

Husband . . . argues that the court awarded a disproportionate share of the marital property to wife by ignoring some of the statutory factors in 15 V.S.A. §751 and giving too much weight to others. Section 751 of Title 15 directs the family court to divide the marital estate in an equitable manner after considering several factors:

1. the length of the marriage
2. the age and health of the parties
3. the occupation, source and amount of income of each of the parties
4. vocational skills and employability
5. the contribution by one spouse to the education, training, or increased earning power of the other
6. the value of all property interests, liabilities and needs of each party
7. whether the property settlement is in lieu of or in addition to maintenance
8. the opportunity of each for future acquisition of capital assets and income
9. the desirability of awarding the family home or the right to live there for reasonable periods to the spouse having custody of the children
10. the party through whom the property was acquired
11. the contribution of each spouse in the acquisition, preservation, and depreciation or appreciation in value of the respective estates, including the nonmonetary contribution of a spouse as a homemaker
12. the respective merits of the parties

. . . The family court has broad discretion when analyzing and weighing the statutory factors in light of the record evidence. . . . When fashioning an equitable award, the court must explain the underlying rationale for its decision . . . , which we will not disturb absent a showing that the court abused its discretion. . . .

Husband asserts that the property division lacks equity because the court did not consider the length of the marriage; husband's lack of a college education and his contribution to wife's business; husband's inability to acquire capital assets or additional income; husband's sweat equity in maintaining and improving the marital home and the rental property acquired from wife's mother; and the lack of a proper home for their daughter when she spends time with husband. We find no merit to husband's contention because the text of the court's decision reflects that it considered all of those factors.

The court found that the parties were married for twelve years. It determined that in light of all the factors the length of marriage did not weigh in favor of either party. The court acknowledged husband's lack of a college degree, but it found that

(Continued)

husband could increase his annual income by taking a full-time position in the construction industry or in another industry in the Mad River Valley. Husband is healthy and his age—forty-eight-years old—at the time of the divorce did not preclude him from acquiring his own home or other assets in the future. On the issue of maintenance, husband did not request maintenance in lieu of property, and cannot now fault the family court for not considering this factor.

As for husband's suggestion that the property award left him without an ability to obtain a suitable residence where his daughter can stay when she is in his care, there is no factor in §751 that directly addresses this issue. . . . the court must consider the "desirability of awarding the family home . . . to the spouse having custody of the children." . . . The court considered that factor when it determined the child's best interests were served by allowing her to remain in the marital residence—the only home the child has ever known—under wife's primary care.

According to the family court, the statutory factors that weighed most heavily in its decision were numbers (10) and (11): through whom the assets were acquired, and which party contributed more to their preservation. . . . All of the assets in this case came through wife, either because she acquired them before marriage or purchased them after marriage with money wife's mother provided. All of wife's income, as well as her inheritance, went to support the family and the family's recreational interests. She paid the mortgage and property taxes on the marital home. Husband's financial contribution was recognized through the $10,000 he received from the sale of the wife's mother's home and the sailboat court awarded husband. The court declined to allocate the parties' debt because it found that husband's larger share of credit card debt was due to the relatively low income he earned by choice. In light of the wife's substantial monetary contribution to the family's expenses, the court determined that it would be unfair to saddle her with a portion of husband's personal and business debt. . . .

We recognize that wife received ninety percent of the parties' assets. Had the family court failed to explain in detail the reasons for the facially, disproportionate property distribution, the outcome of this case would likely be different. But the family court carefully explained why it weighed factors (10) and (11) more heavily in reaching its decision. As trier of fact, the family court was in the best position to assess the merits of the parties' contentions, and its decision addresses the relevant statutory factors. Therefore we cannot say that the court abused its discretion in fashioning the property award in this case. . . .

SIDEBAR

Do you agree with the Vermont Supreme Court's holding? Read the entire case including the strong dissent by Justice Skoglund, in which he states his belief that the "lopsided award" in this case would not have been affirmed "if it had been the wife and not the husband who received the paltry ten percent share of the parties' marital estate." Do you agree with the majority or with the dissenting justice? How would you have decided the case? Explain your response.

PARALEGAL PRACTICE TIP

Whether employed in an equitable distribution or community property jurisdiction, the family law team needs to be aware of any community property states in which the parties have resided and in which they have purchased property, given the potential consequences for clients during marriage, upon divorce, and at death.

The Community Property Approach

A minority of the states are community property jurisdictions in which property acquired during the marriage is viewed as belonging equally to the spouses and, therefore, as rightfully divided equally between them upon divorce. Predominantly located in the American Southwest, most community property states were originally settled by Spanish colonists and adopted a system of law rooted in

Spanish (or French, in the case of Louisiana) civil law rather than English common law. Although only about one-fifth of the states are community property states, approximately one-quarter to one-third of the population of the United States lives in those states (which include both Texas and California).

The contemporary community property approach is based on a view of marriage as a partnership and an assumption that both the husband and the wife contribute to the acquisition and accumulation of marital assets and liabilities. It assumes that each spouse acts for the benefit of the marital unit and is, therefore, entitled to an interest in half of the property acquired during the marriage through the expenditure of marital funds or the efforts of either or both spouses. Separate property remains separate property in community property jurisdictions, and it generally includes assets brought into the marriage, property acquired in exchange for separate property, and gifts and inheritances received by a spouse during the marriage.

EXHIBIT 11.5 Community Property—Ten Commonly Asked Questions

QUESTION 1: What are the community property states?

ANSWER: The traditional community property states are Arizona, California, Idaho, Louisiana, Nevada, New Mexico, Texas, and Washington. Wisconsin is also sometimes classified as a community property state and is recognized by the federal government for tax purposes as such. Alaska is technically not a community property state; however, under Alaska's Community Property Act, ". . . property of the spouses is community property . . . only to the extent provided in a community property agreement or a community property trust."[26]

QUESTION 2: Is the law governing community property the same in all the community property states?

ANSWER: No. The marital property laws of the community property states differ significantly, not only from the marital property laws in **common law property states**, but also from one another's laws. Although the federal government recognizes community property for tax purposes, it has established no mandatory definition of community property for use by all of the states. There are variations among the community property states, for example, in terms of how they define community property, how they treat income from separate property, and when they hold that the "marital community" terminates for purposes of accumulation of community property.

PARALEGAL PRACTICE TIP

To fully appreciate the impact of these differences, compare the Texas and California community property laws. As with its spousal support laws, Texas is conservative in the sense that its rules lead to a smaller community estate and greater protection for separate assets. For example, with the exception of Louisiana, Texas is the only community property state that does not consider personal goodwill to be community property. The California rules tend to result in a larger community estate for division. See J. Thomas Oldham, *Everything Is Bigger in Texas, Except the Community Property Estate: Must Texas Remain a Divorce Haven for the Rich?* 44 FAM. L. Q. No.3 (Fall 2010).

QUESTION 3: How is community property treated upon divorce?

ANSWER: Under community property theory, when the parties marry, they form a "marital community." Absent an agreement of the parties to the contrary, upon dissolution, the courts start with a presumption that all property acquired (and liabilities incurred) during the marriage and still existing at the time of divorce is community property and subject to a fifty-fifty division regardless of the relative contributions made by each of the parties. In Wisconsin, for example, by statute, "An obligation incurred by a spouse during marriage, including one attributable to an act or omission during the marriage, is presumed to be incurred in the interest of the marriage or the family."[27] The time period in which the debt was incurred is more relevant than the name on the account under which the debt was created.

(Continued)

PARALEGAL PRACTICE TIP

A copy of the Nevada community property statute is provided at *www.pearsonhighered.com/wilson* in the companion website material related to Chapter 11 under "Statutes."

PARALEGAL PRACTICE TIP

To see a California Property Declaration Form, visit *www.courtinfo.ca.gov/forms.* You can find a link to this site at *www.pearsonhighered.com/wilson* in the companion website material for Chapter 11 under "Forms."

PARALEGAL PRACTICE TIP

To see the Alaska Community Property Act, visit *www.legis.state.ak.us.* You can find a link to this site at *www.pearsonhighered.com/wilson* in the companion website material for Chapter 11 under "Statutes."

Common law property state
a state in which property is generally owned by the party who acquired it during the marriage; with limited exceptions, property acquired during the marriage is divided equitably upon divorce in common law property states

Basis
the value assigned by the IRS to a taxpayer's investment in property

EXHIBIT 11.5 (*Continued*)

QUESTION 4: How is community property treated at death?

ANSWER: The primary advantage of the community property system is evident, upon the death of one of the spouses, in the form of a "double step-up" in **basis** for the surviving spouse. Basis is defined as the value assigned to a taxpayer's investment in property. It is the reference point used for calculating a gain or a loss when the property is transferred to another. Assuming assets increase in value while they are owned, there is a tax incentive to hold property as community property because when one spouse dies, the shares of both spouses receive a "step-up" in basis, and not solely the share of the decedent. A higher basis translates to a smaller capital gain (or greater loss) if the surviving spouse sells the property. If the asset is depreciable, larger depreciation reductions will be available. These advantages are lost if the property has decreased in value between the date it was acquired and the date of death of the first spouse to die.[28]

QUESTION 5: Does conduct have any impact on the division of community property?

ANSWER: The general rule is that conduct will not play a role in a no-fault divorce. However, in most community property states, the courts may consider conduct when dividing the marital estate, particularly economic misconduct. For example, if a party has committed "community waste" by concealing assets or disposing of them in a fraudulent or irresponsible manner (such as through excessive gambling), that party's share of the community property upon divorce may be reduced.

QUESTION 6: What are the primary disadvantages of holding property as community property?

ANSWER: The two primary disadvantages are:

- The former/surviving spouse may receive a larger share of the assets upon divorce or death than desired or intended by the other spouse.
- A spouse does not have complete management or control over the community property. Some of the kinds of restraints that may be imposed include prohibitions against:
  - Devising or bequeathing by will more than one-half of the community property
  - Gifting community property without the express or implied consent of the other spouse
  - Selling, conveying, or encumbering community real property without the other spouse's participation and acknowledgment
  - Purchasing or contracting to purchase community real property without the other spouse joining.[29]

QUESTION 7: What happens if spouses move from a common law property state to a community property state and later divorce?

ANSWER: In some community property states (such as Arizona and California), if the parties are both residents of the community property state at the time of the divorce, the court will treat property acquired during the marriage in a common law property state as if it were acquired in the community property state and apply the concept of quasi-community property.

QUESTION 8: What happens to community property if spouses move from a community property state to a common law property state?

ANSWER: The general rule is that property acquired with, or traceable to, community funds will continue to maintain its character as community property in most states. However, if an asset (such as a vacation home) is actually located in the common law property state, the common law state may decline to treat that particular asset as community property, based on public policy.[30]

The Restatement (Second) of Conflicts of Laws rule[31] is that, absent an effective choice of law by the parties, the law of the spouses' domicile at the time of acquisition will usually determine the rights of each spouse in tangible and intangible personal property.

(*Continued*)

PARALEGAL PRACTICE TIP

An illustration may help to clarify what may happen when spouses move from a community property state to a common law property state. In an Iowa case in which the parties had made no agreement regarding governing law, an appellate court held that Texas community property law should govern disposition of a brokerage account created and funded when the spouses lived in Texas, a community property state. The court held that greater weight should be given to the law of the state where the spouses were domiciled when the movable property was acquired.[32]

EXHIBIT 11.5 (*Continued*)

> **QUESTION 9: Can the parties change the nature of property from separate to community or community to separate during their marriage?**
>
> **ANSWER:** Yes, in most states. Spouses often choose to change the characterization of property by means of agreements (e.g., a pre- or postmarital agreement where permitted) or by gifting an interest in property to the community or to the other spouse in his or her sole name. The spouses may also, intentionally or unintentionally, convert a separate asset to community property by commingling separate property with community assets such that the separate property loses its identity. The burden of tracing the asset is on the spouse who claims a separate interest.
>
> **QUESTION 10: Can the parties influence the division of community property upon divorce?**
>
> **ANSWER:** Yes, by executing a separation agreement or a premarital agreement, or by proposing a division to the court in contested cases.

The Role of Conduct in the Context of Property Division

A majority of the states have adopted the position advocated in section 307 of the Uniform Marriage and Divorce Act, which provides that decisions about property division should be made "without regard to marital misconduct." In general, the courts have little patience with a party rambling on about how his or her spouse "cheated and lied." However, many states still consider misconduct—particularly extreme instances of abuse or economic misconduct, which can come in many forms:

- Incurring excessive credit card debt for unnecessary expenses that do not support the family unit
- Failing to make a contribution of any kind (financial or otherwise) to the marital partnership over an extended period
- Using marital funds or assets to entertain or support an adulterous relationship
- Gambling excessively during the course of the marriage
- Making sham loans and transfers of property for less than fair market value to friends and family members, etc., in anticipation of divorce[33]
- Transferring *or* concealing assets after being served with notice of an impending divorce and while under a court order not to do so

PARALEGAL PRACTICE TIP

Upon filing and serving of a divorce complaint, many states automatically restrain the parties from disposing of assets subject to division during the pendency of a divorce action unless otherwise agreed by the parties or ordered by the court.

- Intentionally destroying marital or the other spouse's separate property
- Making high-risk or speculative investments during the marriage
- Cashing out joint accounts without the consent of the other party

PARALEGAL PRACTICE TIP

Cashing out accounts may be especially tempting when one of the spouses is in the military overseas and is unable to monitor property and income deposits at home. See e.g. *Leininger v. Leininger, 766 N.W.2d 649* (Iowa 2009).

PARALEGAL PRACTICE TIP

To learn more about the Uniform (Model) Marriage and Divorce Law, visit *www.nccusl.org*. You can find a link to this site at *www.pearsonhighered.com/wilson* in the companion website material for Chapter 11 under "Resources."

- Engaging in criminal conduct that results in the imposition of fines that must be paid during the course of the marriage[34]
- Refusing to cooperate in the discovery process

Dissipation
the use of an asset for an illegal or inequitable purpose, such as when a spouse uses or expends marital property for personal benefit when a divorce is pending

When **dissipation** of assets is demonstrated at trial based on evidence and testimony, the court in its discretion may choose, among other options, to award a greater percentage of the assets to the innocent spouse and/or assign the bulk of the liabilities to the offending spouse. In some situations, the court may require that it be shown only that assets disappeared and not necessarily how they were spent. A Kentucky appeals court took this position when it held that a wife "did not have any information as to how the dissipated funds were spent, or the means to discover such information. It would be inequitable to require the party claiming dissipation to show exactly what use was made of the marital assets, because this information is not as readily available to the complaining party as it is to the dissipating party."[35] (See Case 11.5.)

CASE **11.5** *Szesny v. Szesny*, 197 Ill. App.3d 966, 557 N.E.2d 222 (1990)

PARALEGAL PRACTICE TIP

The full opinion in the *Szesny* case is available at *www.pearsonhighered. com/wilson* in the companion website material related to Chapter 11 under "Cases" and in the Case Resources Section of the MyLegal-StudiesLab.

FROM THE OPINION

. . . [I]n the case here the trial court specifically found that respondent was solely responsible for the over $82,000 in debt. There was testimony that after they purchased the marital home, petitioner drastically reduced her expenditures while respondent maintained or increased his. The trial court noted that respondent would go out at night without his wife and child; that he belonged to a health club; that respondent opened charge accounts without petitioner's knowledge or permission; that respondent spent money on clothing for himself and at fine restaurants; that he gave money to his mother; that respondent borrowed money but he did not use it to reduce marital debt; and that he "in effect kited his account in consumer debt." The trial court also found that petitioner spent minimal amounts on clothing, ate in fast food restaurants, and in one year was responsible for less than one-twelfth of their total expenses.

Dissipation can occur prior to dissolution. . . . The key is whether one spouse uses marital property for his or her own benefit for a purpose unrelated to the marriage. . . . When one party is charged with dissipation, he must prove by clear and convincing evidence that the questioned expenditures were made for a marital purpose. . . .

The trial court here noted that respondent claimed to have spent the money for family expenses but that he could produce only a few credit card statements for insignificant amounts. The court also noted that respondent opened credit card accounts without petitioner's permission, even though her name was used, and that respondent retained total control of these accounts, having the statements sent to his mother's house. Where one spouse has sole access to funds or incurs debt without the knowledge of the other, that spouse can be held to have dissipated marital assets and can be held responsible for the entire debt. . . .

. . . We affirm the distribution of marital debt as ordered by the trial court. . . .

Division of Major Assets

It is virtually impossible to divide each piece of marital property equally, and it is seldom practical to liquidate all of the parties' assets so that the proceeds can be equally divided. Rather, the courts try to assign property of an appropriate value and type to each party. If there are sufficient assets, the court will assign to each party a variety of different properties up to a determined value. For example, one party may be awarded the marital home and the other a vacation property; each party may retain his or her pension; a stock portfolio may be divided; joint bank accounts might be split; etc.

Marital estate

the property acquired during the marriage other than by gift or inheritance that is subject to division at the time of marital dissolution

THE MARITAL RESIDENCE

Given the fact that it is often the parties' only major asset, many emotionally charged property disputes focus on the marital residence. Disposition is especially complicated when minor children are involved. Some statutes specifically require consideration of custodial issues when effecting a property division. The most common options for dispositional treatment of the marital residence are the following:

- If neither spouse wishes to keep the house, the residence may be sold and the proceeds divided equally or in some other agreed-upon or court-ordered proportion.
- When the marital home is the only asset the parties have, the court may be forced to order the sale of the residence and division of the proceeds so that the parties can receive cash awards and move forward with their respective lives.
- One spouse may buy out the other spouse's interest (often refinancing the property) and keep the home.
- One spouse may be awarded the marital home, while the other spouse is awarded offsetting assets such as a bank account or pension.
- The house may continue to be held jointly, with one party having the right to exclusive use and occupancy until a future date (usually connected with a child-related contingency), at which time the property will be sold and the proceeds divided. The precise terms of such an arrangement need to be laid out carefully in the parties' agreement or the court's order (i.e., who is responsible for payment of the mortgage, taxes, insurance, maintenance, and repairs; what will be deducted from the proceeds prior to distribution; how will the proceeds eventually be divided; and how will appreciation and depreciation be treated?).

Paralegal **Application 11.6**

Who Gets the House?

Once the value of the marital home has been established, additional information may be needed to develop a compelling rationale for why the home ought to be awarded to the client. For example, assume it is valued at $250,000. There is a $50,000 first mortgage and a $20,000 second mortgage. The equity in the home is therefore $180,000. The parties obtained the second mortgage in order to pay off gambling debts the husband incurred during the marriage. The parties purchased the property in 1990 for $125,000 and took title as tenants by the entirety. The wife provided a down payment of $40,000 out of funds she had accumulated prior to marriage. She paid the mortgage and taxes throughout the marriage, landscaped the property, and redecorated the interior, making it a virtual showplace. She is emotionally very attached to the home and both of the parties' two children were home-birthed there. She is seeking custody of the children and wants to continue to raise them in the only home they have ever known. This scenario provides a strong case for awarding the home to the wife and illustrates that property division decisions are not always just about dollars and cents.

PENSIONS, RETIREMENT BENEFITS, AND QUALIFIED DOMESTIC RELATIONS ORDERS (QDROs)

PARALEGAL PRACTICE TIP

Visit *www.courts.alaska.gov* to learn more about a variety of pensions including federal and military. Notice in the information provided that a QDRO must be approved by the Plan Administrator in addition to the court. You can find a link to this site at *www.pearsonhighered.com/wilson* in the companion website material related to Chapter 11 under "Forms."

Individuals in a position to do so usually anticipate and plan for eventual retirement from the world of work. Acquired either individually or through an employer, retirement plans come in a variety of forms such as pensions, individual retirement accounts (IRAs), 401(k) plans, deferred compensation, profit sharing, and stock option plans. Retirement plans are generally tax-deferred, which means that the income produced will not be taxed until the income is paid during retirement. Along with the marital home, retirement plans are commonly one of the only large assets available for division upon divorce.

A **pension** is a job-related retirement benefit acquired by an employee and funded through contributions by the employer, the employee, or a combination of both. It is a form of deferred compensation. There are two primary types of pension plans:

- In a **defined-benefit plan**, the amount of the benefit is usually determined according to a formula based on the participant's earnings, length of service, or a target monthly benefit. The value of a defined-benefit plan (a "traditional" pension) is usually established by an actuary, who determines the total benefits the employee is likely to receive based on his or her life expectancy and then calculates the present cash value of the right to receive that amount in the future. Upon retirement, the employee is entitled to receive the defined benefit in a lump sum or in periodic payments (depending on the definition of the benefit).

- In a **defined-contribution plan,** each employee has his or her own separate account, such as a 401(k) plan. Such plans may involve purchase money arrangements, profit sharing, stock bonuses, etc. The eventual benefit is based on the amount of contributions and investment earnings in the years during which the employee is covered by the plan. The value of a defined contribution plan is based on its current value without any adjustment for income taxes and/or penalties if the balance were withdrawn early. Upon retirement, the employee is entitled to withdraw the pension funds as he or she sees fit (subject to certain constraints imposed by the government). Because a defined-contribution plan has an account value in the participant's name, its value can be determined without actuarial assistance in property division deliberations.

In either plan, the employee is entitled to receive the pension funds that he or she contributed. In addition, the employee is entitled to receive those contributed by the employer, provided the pension is vested. A pension vests when an employee has met certain threshold requirements—for example, being employed for a certain period of time such as ten years. If an employee has not satisfied the minimal threshold requirements, the pension is unvested. When employees leave employment prior to vesting of their pensions, they generally are entitled to receive only the funds contributed personally and none of the funds contributed by the employer.

Pension
a job-related retirement benefit acquired by an employee and funded through contributions by the employer, the employee, or a combination of both

Defined-benefit plan
a retirement plan in which the amount of the benefit is usually determined according to a formula based on the participant's earnings, length of service, or a target monthly benefit

Defined-contribution plan
a retirement plan funded by the employee's contributions and the employer's contributions (usually in a preset amount) in which the eventual benefit is based on the amount of contributions and investment earnings in the years during which the employee is covered by the plan

A vested pension is customarily considered marital property although the general rule is that only that portion of the pension attributable to the period of the marriage is subject to division upon divorce. For example, if the husband's pension is based on twenty-five years of employment and he was married to his wife for ten of those years, 10/25 or 2/5 (40%) of his pension constitutes marital property. His spouse may be awarded half of that amount (20% of the total pension [2/5 × 1/2 = 1/5 = 20%]), especially if the pension is the parties' only major asset. If there are other assets, the pension may be left intact and the wife may be awarded other property equivalent in value to 20% of the pension. Courts vary in their treatment of unvested pensions. Some consider them future expectancy interests not subject to division. Others consider the amount of the contribution made by a party to the pension fund during the marriage to be marital property.[36]

State law generally establishes how property will be divided upon divorce, but federal law largely controls retirement benefits. Most employers must comply with the Employee Retirement Income Security Act (ERISA), a federal statute passed in 1974 and amended by the Retirement Equity Act (REA) of 1984. The Act is designed to protect employee pensions in the event an employer goes out of business or declares bankruptcy. Under ERISA, a qualified retirement plan is one that does not discriminate in favor of highly compensated employees. Although most are, not all retirement plans are subject to ERISA. For example, some governmental and church-offered plans are not. Military pensions are also subject to their own rules and regulations at the state and federal levels. Generally, the federal government will honor domestic relations orders dividing military pensions if the parties have been married for at least ten years and the award to the alternate payee does not exceed 50% of the net pension.

When one or both of the parties are participants in pension plans, it is necessary to obtain from each plan administrator (through the client or during the discovery process) copies of the plan and a record of contributions. The plan should then be valued. As indicated above, depending on the nature of the plan, valuation may require the assistance of a pension valuation expert/service. If a client waives valuation, the waiver should be in writing and preferably expressly stated in the parties' separation agreement to avoid a later malpractice claim against the attorney advising the client.

Pension plans can pose complex challenges for the family law team including, but not limited to, the following:

- As noted above, the value of a participant's interest in a retirement plan may not be ascertainable without expert advice. For example, it is hard to predict a specific retirement date, the life expectancy of the participant, the amount of the contributions that eventually will be made by the employer and the participant, or the ultimate value of the account at some future date.
- The participant may choose not to retire at his or her earliest retirement age unless required to do so. Continued employment beyond the age projected at the time an agreement is negotiated may result in the other party receiving less of a benefit than he or she bargained for![37]
- Pensions of various kinds (e.g., the military and public and private employers) are governed by an array of federal, state, and employer rules and regulations. The rules governing distribution of pensions are complex and must be followed scrupulously.
- As indicated earlier in this chapter, questions may be raised as to whether disability retirement pensions constitute property divisible as marital property.[38]

Pensions may be divided in a variety of ways depending on the parties' preferences, assets, needs, and circumstances. Commonly employed options include the following:

- Assume that a wife has a pension presently valued at $120,000, which she does not wish to have divided. She has other assets totaling $60,000 that she is willing to liquidate and use to "buy out" her husband's share and thereby leave the pension intact.
- Assume the husband has a pension presently valued at $300,000. He and his spouse own a marital home as tenants by the entirety. The home is valued at $300,000 and is owned outright. He does not wish to divide his pension and is willing to offset the pension by transferring his interest in the marital home to his wife. She, in turn, is pleased with this arrangement, as she wants to remain in the home and sell it at a later date after the children have graduated from high school.
- Assume the parties met when they began teaching at a Midwestern, state-funded community college, where they have continued to teach for the last twenty years. Each has been contributing to the state retirement system for the full period. Although their contributions have not been exactly equal, the parties are willing to waive valuation and their respective potential rights in each other's pensions.
- Applying an "if, as, and when" approach, a nonemployee spouse may be awarded a share of an employee spouse's pension funds if, as, and when the employee spouse receives them. The share is most often determined according to a "marital fraction" formula based on the ratio of the years of marriage to the number of years of employment at the time of distribution. The present value of the pension does not need to be determined and no offsetting award is required.
- Assume the parties have been married for over twenty years and that the husband's General Electric pension is their only major asset. The nonemployee spouse may seek to directly reach the pension funds by obtaining a **Qualified Domestic Relations Order (QDRO)**. A QDRO is a court order directing the administrator of a pension plan to pay a specified portion of the pension to an alternate payee, the nonemployee spouse.[39] Considerable care must be taken to specify whether the QDRO includes only the retirement benefit or also the death benefit as well.[40] The QDRO must be approved by counsel for each party, the Plan Administrator, and the court in order to be effective.

Qualified Domestic Relations Order (QDRO)

a court order directing the administrator of a pension plan to pay a specified portion of the pension to an alternate payee

PARALEGAL PRACTICE TIP

Under federal law, the employee is required to designate the non-employee spouse as the beneficiary of his or her retirement benefits. If there is no QDRO upon divorce, the employee should be advised to change the designee following dissolution, assuming he or she wishes to do so. A certified copy of the judgment should be filed with the additional paperwork required by the plan.

Division of Liabilities

Although we have primarily focused in this chapter on the division of assets when a marriage terminates, it is equally (and sometimes more) important to consider personal and business debts. Often substantial debt has contributed to the breakdown of the relationship between the parties, and they have come to view divorce as the only way to bring an end to an escalating debt that is spiraling out of control.

The parties' debts should be classified as separate and marital. **Marital debt,** like marital property, is usually specifically identified, valued, and apportioned between the parties. The general rule is that debt incurred prior to marriage is a separate debt, as it was presumably not incurred for the benefit of the marriage, although that assumption may be rebutted by the facts and circumstances. Debts for **necessaries** for the family unit (such as shelter, food, clothing, and medical care, for example) are considered marital debts. For purposes of equitable distribution, the South Carolina courts have defined a marital debt as a debt incurred for the joint benefit of the parties regardless of who incurred the obligation.[41]

Marital debt
debt incurred during the marriage for the benefit of the marital enterprise regardless of which party incurred the obligation

Necessaries
things that are indispensable to living, such as food, clothing, and shelter

Paralegal **Application 11.7**

Identification of Debts

The paralegal may be asked to work with the client in an effort to compile a summary of the parties' debts, both individual and joint. For each debt, the summary should indicate:

- the amount of the debt
- the amount and frequency of payments
- who is making the payments and out of what source of funds
- who incurred the debt

- why the debt was incurred (i.e., for what purpose)
- when the debt was incurred (before the marriage, during the marriage, post separation, or after commencement of the divorce proceeding)
- whether or not the debt is secured (for example, a mortgage secured by the marital home, a car loan secured by the vehicle, etc.)
- the duration of the obligation

As with marital assets, there are three primary ways in which separate and marital debts are divided.

1. The parties may have executed a premarital agreement that addresses responsibility for separate and marital debt.
2. The parties may allocate responsibility for debt in their separation agreement.
3. Absent an agreement of the parties, the issue may be presented to the court for resolution.

The courts use a variety of approaches to allocating responsibility for debt, such as the following:

- The court may require payment of the parties' debt out of existing assets and then allocate the remaining assets, if any.
- The debt may be factored into the overall property division. For example, rather than awarding a wife $15,000 of property, the court may order the husband to pay $15,000 of the wife's outstanding student loans.
- The court may make an equal allocation of debt.
- The court may decide to assign all or a disproportionate amount of the debt to one of the parties. (See Case 11.5.)

Although a divorce decree may allocate responsibility for marital debt between the parties, the family court does not have the power to limit the rights of third-party creditors. For example, if both parties took out a car loan and the divorce decree provides that the wife will pay the balance of the loan and she fails to do so, the lender is free to try to collect from either spouse individually or both spouses jointly. To help protect against such situations, it is important to include a

Hold harmless provision
a provision specifying that a particular spouse will be solely responsible for payment of certain debts and that the other spouse shall be free and clear of any obligation regarding those debts and will be indemnified by the debtor spouse if forced to pay them

hold harmless provision in the parties' separation agreement. A hold harmless provision specifies that a particular spouse will be solely responsible for payment of certain debts and that the other spouse shall be free and clear of any obligation regarding those debts and will be indemnified by the debtor spouse if forced to pay them.

Sometimes the debt burden is so extensive and overwhelming that, subsequent to divorce, one of the parties declares personal bankruptcy. Bankruptcy involves complex issues and procedures usually handled by attorneys who specialize in this area of the law, but there are two basic points of particular relevance to the topic of property division:

- With the exception of debts in the nature of child support and spousal maintenance, bankruptcy law may provide for discharge of the bulk of a petitioner's debts. If a jointly held debt is discharged in this context, the creditor is still free to pursue the other spouse to collect on the remainder of the debt.
- Although child support and alimony generally are not dischargeable in bankruptcy, payments due to a former spouse under a court-ordered division of property may be dischargeable under some circumstances.

Tax Consequences of Property Division

Under current federal tax law, transfers of real or personal property between spouses during a marriage or at dissolution as incidents of divorce are not taxable events.[42] A transfer is "incident to a divorce" if it occurs within one year after the date on which the marriage ends or if it is related to the ending of the marriage. However, this does not mean that there are no tax issues to be considered. In fact, several jurisdictions require that the court consider the tax implications of a property division for each of the parties.[43] An attorney's failure to advise a client regarding related tax issues may give rise to a malpractice claim in some circumstances. For example, assume that a wife is awarded a substantial number of shares of Starbucks stock worth $150,000 at the time of the divorce. If and when she elects to sell the stock, she may receive a rude awakening when she learns that she is liable for payment of a significant **capital gains tax** because the stock was initially purchased at a mere fraction of its current worth. She will actually realize much less than the $150,000 she thought she'd bargained for and would receive. Of course, if the stock sells for less than its purchase price, a loss may be claimed.

Capital gains tax
a tax on income derived from the sale of a capital asset (a long-term asset) as defined by the Internal Revenue Code

PARALEGAL PRACTICE TIP

Attorneys have an ethical duty to advise clients of the tax consequences of divorce. In complex cases, accountants may be retained to calculate costs and benefits for the client. Although attorneys' fees in general are not tax-deductible for income tax purposes, the portion of fees attributable to services pertaining to tax matters is tax-deductible, and the client should be advised in writing as to that amount.

Some other tax-related issues that may arise include:

- If the property division is such that a party must withdraw funds from a retirement plan before he or she is entitled to in order to "pay off" the other spouse, the value of the retirement plan is reduced, and the participant also is likely to face an early-withdrawal tax penalty.
- The parties may attempt to disguise as alimony a portion of the property division in order for one party to receive a tax deduction for the transfer. This is

usually accomplished by "front-loading" the first two or three years of "alimony" payments, i.e., making them significantly larger than in subsequent years. The IRS will determine whether the transfer is alimony or property division based on its own criteria, not on others' labels or titles. If the IRS determines that the "alimony" paid was in fact property division, it will **recapture** the tax deduction claimed by the payor, who will then have to pay taxes, interest, and penalties on the improperly deducted amount. The recipient, on the other hand, will now be able to deduct the amount on which he or she previously paid taxes as alimony income.

- Sometimes, part or all of a division of property is paid to a third party. For example, a husband may pay off his wife's mortgage on her condominium. The Internal Revenue Service will still allow the transfer between the spouses to be a nontaxable event between them if:

1. the transfer is made pursuant to a divorce or separation agreement,
2. the transfer is made pursuant to a written request of the beneficiary spouse, and
3. the transferring spouse receives a written acceptance of the property after it has been transferred.

Alimony recapture rule
the IRS rule that the government can recover a tax benefit (such as the prior taking of a deduction for payment of alimony) by taxing the income that no longer qualifies for the benefit

Paralegal **Application 11.8**

Additional Property-Related Tax Issues

There are several additional tax issues related to division of property, debt, and spousal support. Of particular importance is the designation of who will be obligated to pay any taxes due and who will be eligible to claim tax benefits. For example, the following issues should be addressed in the parties' separation agreement:

- Have the parties failed to file any required state or federal tax returns for any year(s) during their marriage?
- Who will be responsible for paying any tax deficiencies, interest, and penalties should the Internal Revenue Service or a state department of revenue impose them for any prior years during which the parties filed joint tax returns?
- If both parties signed joint tax returns in the past, but only one of the parties prepared the forms, controlled the information that went into them, and is responsible for errors, omissions, and/or fraud committed, resulting in significant penalties, Congress now provides some relief for an **innocent spouse** under certain circumstances. The spouse must be able to prove that at the time the return was signed, he or she did not know and had no reason to know that the spouse understated taxes that were due. Otherwise, the parties will be jointly and individually liable for the deficiency, meaning that the IRS

can collect from one or both of them. An "innocent spouse" will want to include language in the agreement that the spouse who prepared the returns will indemnify the innocent spouse against any taxes and penalties arising out of any joint returns filed during the marriage.

- Will the parties file joint or separate tax returns for the year in which they separate and sign their agreement, and who will pay the taxes due, if any? Who will be entitled to any tax refund that may be due to the parties?
- If the parties are going to continue to jointly own the marital home post divorce, who will be responsible for paying property taxes, and who will be entitled to claim any related mortgage interest and taxes as deductions?
- If the marital home is subsequently sold, how will the capital gains tax be handled should any be due?

Innocent spouse
a spouse who may be relieved of liability incurred if the other spouse prepared the tax forms, controlled the information that went into them, and is solely responsible for errors, omissions, and/or fraud that resulted in imposition of significant taxes, interest, and penalties

EXHIBIT 11.6 A Property Division Illustration

Hugh and Nancy are divorcing after fifteen years of marriage. It is an "amicable" divorce and they have worked out what they believe is a fair division of their major assets. They will now "run it by" their respective attorneys. In the way of basic background: Hugh has owned (individually) and operated a sub shop for the past thirteen years (which he is about to sell for $125,000) and Nancy has been a probation officer for ten years. Hugh has been contributing to an IRA for eighteen years ($20,000 during the marriage) and Nancy has contributed $30,000 to a state pension fund (now vested) over the past ten years. Hugh inherited $120,000 from his mother fourteen years ago. He used $75,000 to buy the sub shop and put the balance in a checking account in his name only. He used $10,000 of it (along with $10,000 from Nancy) to purchase a boat. The two of them have shared the expenses for the boat and worked on it in free time. They own a condo which they bought for $175,000. Although Nancy paid the $40,000 down payment, they have shared all other related expenses over the years. They purchased a time-share together five years ago for $11,000 that is in both their names. They have a joint bank account to which they have both contributed. They own two cars and household furnishings and they have two pets. They have agreed to divide their debts equally and to sell the condo.

Asset/Liability	Separate (S) and/or Marital (M)	Hugh (H)	Nancy (N)
Marital home To be listed at $240,000 and sold at fair market value	S/M	50% net proceeds after deduction of N's down payment	50% net proceeds (postdeduction) plus $40,000 down payment
Sub shop Under agreement for sale at $125,000	S/M	50% net proceeds (post deduction for down payment) $25,000 plus $75,000 = $100,000	50% net proceeds after deduction of H's $75,000 down payment = $25,000
Checking account at Pilot's National Bank $14,000	S (balance of Hugh's inheritance)	$14,000	0
Checking account at compass rose savings and loan balance $8,992	M (both parties contributed; no record of deposit histories)	$4,496.00 = 50%	$4,496.00 = 50%
IRA	S/M $20,000 deposited during marriage	$73,000. Full value ($20,000 contributed during marriage)	0 Offset by contributions to N's pension ($30,000 during marriage)
State pension	M	0	N will keep her pension but pay H $5,000 over 5 years to reimburse remaining half of the contributions during marriage. N will retain H as survivor beneficiary on account until paid
Vehicles	M	Avalon	Solara convertible
30-foot Marine Trader trawler	M	50% owner; will pay 50% expenses; use of boat Jan. to June	50% owner; will pay 50% expenses; use of boat July to Dec.

EXHIBIT 11.6 *(Continued)*

Asset/Liability	Separate (S) and/ or Marital (M)	Hugh (H)	Nancy (N)
Time-share—Aruba	M	Week 12; expenses divided equally	Week 13; expenses divided equally
Household furnishings	M	@50% (items agreed on)	@50% (items agreed on)
Debts (credit card)	M	Liable for 50% as of date of divorce	Liable for 50% as of date of divorce

The Paralegal's Role in a Property Division Case

The tasks most commonly performed by a paralegal in a property division case are:

- compiling a list of the parties' assets indicating how the property is titled, its value, and how the value was calculated
- scheduling and participating in interviews as assigned
- drafting complaints/petitions, motions, supporting affidavits, and proposed orders, as well as correspondence related to the case
- making discovery-related recommendations and drafting interrogatories, depositions, and requests for production of documents as directed to assist in identifying and valuing assets and the parties' respective contributions to those assets; in equitable distribution jurisdictions, discovery efforts may also be designed to gather information relating to factors to be considered by the court when making property distributions
- researching current law (statutes, case law, and secondary sources) to support the client's position with respect to contested assets so that the court will have a rationale on which to base a decision.[44] In some cases, this may mean both state and federal law need to be considered.[45]
- suggesting issues on which expert testimony may be necessary, such as valuation of pensions, and maintaining lists of experts qualified to assist with and potentially testify as to specific issues, such as valuation of a business interest or the marital home
- drafting a pretrial memorandum, if required, informing the court of the nature and extent of the marital estate and the merits of the client's claim as to property distribution
- assisting in preparation for motion hearings
- drafting a property article/paragraph/exhibit for inclusion in a separation agreement if the parties negotiate a mutually agreed-upon division

PARALEGAL PRACTICE TIP

Examples of property division provisions addressing real property, personal property, and debts and liabilities in a separation agreement are contained in the sample agreement provided in Chapter 12.

- assisting with gathering and preparing evidentiary exhibits related to each of the property-related issues for trial, including, where applicable, statutory factors to be considered by the court

- helping to identify prospective witnesses
- drafting proposed conclusions of law and findings of fact, which, in an equitable distribution jurisdiction, should address each of the factors to be considered by the court
- making sure the client is kept informed of progress and upcoming deadlines, hearings, discovery matters, etc.
- tracking progress on the case to be certain timelines are met
- if within scope of expertise, preparing preliminary draft of a QDRO

PARALEGAL PRACTICE TIP

ETHICS ALERT: A paralegal should not undertake a task beyond his or her expertise. There is no shame in acknowledging a need for guidance and supervision. A failure to do so does a disservice to the client and, in the extreme, may give rise to a malpractice claim against the firm if an assignment is not thoroughly researched and properly prepared. Even a supervising family law attorney may choose to consult with an expert on a particularly complex issue beyond his or her level of competence.

CHAPTER SUMMARY

The division of marital property upon divorce is one of the most hotly contested and emotionally charged issues addressed in a family law practice. The discussion in this chapter reflects the contemporary view of marriage as a partnership to which each party is presumed to make both economic and noneconomic contributions. When that partnership dissolves, both assets and liabilities need to be allocated between the parties. This may be accomplished via an enforceable premarital agreement, a separation agreement negotiated by the parties and approved by the court, or a court order following a trial on the merits of the parties' respective proposals.

In this chapter, we review the five basic phases of the property division process:

1. Definition and identification of the parties' "property"
2. Classification of the property as separate, marital, or both
3. Identification of the property subject to division upon divorce
4. Valuation of major assets and liabilities
5. Division of the parties' property according to the appropriate jurisdictional standard: community property or equitable distribution

Particular attention is given to some of the more challenging issues confronted in the property division context. For instance, are assets such as a professional degree or the goodwill of a business actually property on which a dollar value can be placed, and, if so, do they constitute separate or marital property? Does separate property lose its identity as separate when it becomes commingled with marital property? Should the conduct of the parties (such as dissipation of assets) be considered when allocating marital property? Should one party be permitted to access the other party's pension? What are some of the potential tax issues related to property division?

This is an area in which the role played by a paralegal will vary considerably based on training, skills, and experience. A property division case provides an opportunity for the paralegal to do some creative thinking about assets, development of arguments and theories to support a request for division, and organization of materials (exhibits, charts, PowerPoint presentations, etc.) to persuade a court to adopt the client's position at trial.

The chapter text and endnotes reference a broad array of statutes and case references illustrating the various topics covered. It must be emphasized that states and courts vary considerably in their approaches, and the paralegal needs to be attentive to the current governing law in his or her jurisdiction and in other jurisdictions, when appropriate. There simply are no guidelines a family law attorney can use with a client to predict the precise outcome of a property distribution upon divorce. Particularly in equitable distribution jurisdictions, even though judges may be required to consider certain factors in reaching a decision, no specific formula applies, and they are free to exercise broad discretion and weigh the various factors as they see fit in each individual case. Their decisions are rarely overturned absent an abuse of discretion or an error in application of the law.

CONCEPT REVIEW AND REINFORCEMENT

KEY TERMS

Active appreciation	Expert	Premarital agreement
Actuary	Fair market value	Qualified Domestic Relations Order
Alimony recapture rule	Hold harmless (indemnity) clause	(QDRO)
All property state	Inception of title theory	Separate property
Commingling	Innocent spouse	Separation agreement
Common law property states	Marital debt	Source of funds/*pro rata* theory
Community property	Marital property	Tracing
Dissipation	Passive appreciation	Transmutation
Dual property state	Pension	Valuation
Equitable distribution	Postmarital agreement	Vested

REVIEW QUESTIONS

1. Identify the five phases of the property division process.
2. Distinguish between separate and marital property. Give an example of each.
3. Describe three ways in which an asset may change from separate to marital (or marital to separate) property.
4. Identify the majority view regarding treatment of each of the following in the property division context: professional degrees; disability and personal injury awards; and pets.
5. Define valuation and indicate why it is important and when it occurs.
6. Identify the three most common ways in which property will be divided upon dissolution of a marriage.

7. Distinguish between a community property approach and an equitable division approach to property division.
8. Identify a minimum of six factors generally considered by courts dividing property in equitable distribution jurisdictions.
9. Describe the nature and purpose of a QDRO.
10. Describe how the courts generally treat debt in a property distribution.
11. Identify three tax issues related to property division cases.
12. Describe the paralegal's role in a property division case.

DEVELOPING YOUR PARALEGAL SKILLS

FOCUS ON THE JOB

In this activity the student will have an opportunity to propose an appropriate division of property based on a specific fact pattern in a community property or equitable distribution jurisdiction.

The Facts

Jimmy and Alice have been married for ten years and have three children. They appeared to have a good life and a decent marriage until recently, when Alice had an affair with her boss and Jimmy found out about it. He is filing for divorce and says he wants to "take Alice to the cleaners so she walks away with nothing." His lawyer appreciates his feelings, but has told him that that's just not the way it works anymore.

The assets involved in this case include the following:

- When the parties married, the wife had a jewelry collection valued at approximately $10,000. During the marriage she received as gifts from her relatives an additional $15,000 worth of jewelry. The collection is now valued at $35,000, $10,000 of which is attributable to appreciation in the value of the rings, watches, and necklaces included in the collection.
- Before marriage, the husband had a baseball card collection valued at $7,300 that is now worth approximately $29,100. Half of the increase is the result of the purchase of new cards with marital funds and the balance is due to appreciation in the value of the cards owned prior to the marriage.

- The parties have resided in the marital home since their marriage ten years ago. The property has been appraised at $225,000. The down payment of $40,000 came from the wife's mother and father, who insisted that the home be titled solely in their daughter's name. The purchase price was $170,000 and there is a mortgage on the property with a remaining balance of $72,000. The husband added a den to the property through his own labor over a six-month period. It is estimated that this increased the value of the home by approximately $15,000. The remainder of the increase in value is attributable to market forces. The parties have contributed equally throughout the marriage to payment of the mortgage, insurance, property taxes, and household expenses. The wife wants to remain in the marital home for the next five years until the parties' youngest child graduates from high school, and she doesn't figure this is any problem because the house is in her name.

- The wife is a nurse and the husband is a physical therapist. They have each worked throughout the marriage and contributed to their respective pension plans. Both plans are vested but neither has been valued. The parties believe they are relatively equal in value and do not want to go to the expense of having them valued. They have each advised their respective attorneys to this effect. They each want to keep their own pension intact.

- The parties bought two pets during their marriage: a seven-year-old beagle named "Spike" and a five-year-old cat named "Kaspar." They both adore the pets and have contributed to their care throughout their marriage. Both pets were obtained from a local pet shelter at no cost other than the cost of an initial medical examination and shots.

- The parties have an investment portfolio that they opened together and have funded equally in the total amount of $60,000. The account is presently worth $92,000; $12,000 of this amount is due to market trends (passive appreciation), and the balance appears to be the result of the husband's sound management of the asset (active appreciation).

- The parties have a joint bank account used for necessaries. The balance in the account is presently $2,632.18. They have contributed equally to the account.

- The parties have a joint savings account to which they have both contributed, but neither has maintained any records regarding their respective contributions to the account over the years. They each acknowledge that this account was established to support the marital enterprise in the event of an emergency or a special opportunity. The account presently contains $16,234.

- The wife has credit card debt in the amount of $1,368, and the husband has credit card debt in the amount of $4,786.

- Although they each had their educational degrees prior to marriage, the wife has been paying back student loans throughout the marriage. The balance on the loans is now only $924. She has paid off approximately $7,000 during the marriage out of joint marital funds.

The Assignment

Working with another student in your class, negotiate an appropriate division of the property given the above fact pattern. You will need to:

1. Determine whether you are in an equitable distribution or community property jurisdiction.
2. Create a chart depicting what you believe to be marital property and the separate property of each of the spouses. The chart should reflect the value of each asset (and the amount attributable to each spouse). Note that some assets may be part separate and part marital/community property.
3. Create a chart indicating the results of your negotiation with respect to how the property should be divided between the parties, given the standard in your state and the facts of this case. Remember to factor the parties' liabilities into your deliberations.

FOCUS ON **ETHICS**

In this activity, students address a situation in which a supervisor essentially directs a paralegal to engage in negotiation of a property settlement with opposing counsel.

The Assignment

Assume that you are a paralegal in the law office of Attorney Karen Goldberg. Attorney Goldberg represents Alice in the above hypothetical but is presently away on her honeymoon with her fourth husband. She has told you that the client just wants what is fair. Alice feels bad about the affair but does not think it should be held against her. Attorney Goldberg has directed you to negotiate a property settlement with representatives of the law firm representing Jimmy. As a paralegal, what course of action should you take, and how should the situation be addressed? Which of the ethical canons for paralegals promulgated by the National Association of Legal Assistants, contained in Appendix A, are applicable in this context? Present your responses to these questions in a 1-2 page paper.

FOCUS ON **CASE LAW**

In this Focus on Case Law, the student responds to a series of questions about a case in which a state's highest court addressed the treatment of several assets in the property division context.

The Assignment

Read the opinion in *Edelman v. Edelman*, 3 P.3d 348 (Alas. 2000), a case decided by the Supreme Court of Alaska and then respond to the following questions orally or in writing as directed by your instructor.

1. What is the legal history of the case: Where was it brought prior to reaching the Alaska Supreme Court and with what result?
2. What are the issues being appealed and by whom?
3. What is the Alaska Supreme Court's standard of review of a lower court's ruling of this nature?
4. According to the opinion, what are the three steps the lower courts take when making decisions about property division?
5. Based on this case, would you conclude that Alaska is an equitable distribution or a community property state?
6. What factors did the Supreme Court indicate should be considered by the superior court when making decisions concerning property division? What is the source of those factors?

7. Identify the assets in dispute in this case.
8. What did the court decide with respect to the "set net permit"? Was it deemed to be separate or marital property? Why?
9. What was the primary issue with respect to valuation of the marital home?
10. How did the court deal with the wife's post separation payments of the mortgage on the marital home?
11. What was the nature of the tort claim in this case? Did the Court consider this claim to be in the nature of separate or marital property or both?
12. What did the Alaska Supreme Court decide with respect to the superior court's ruling regarding the husband's pension?
13. What did the court decide with respect to the wife's claim for alimony?
14. Although the court remanded the issue of attorneys' fees to the superior court, how did it view the wife's appeal on this issue in particular?

PARALEGAL PRACTICE TIP

The *Edelman* opinion can be found at *www.pearsonhighered.com/ wilson* in the companion website material related to Chapter 11 under "Cases" and in the Case Resources Section of the MyLegalStudiesLab.

FOCUS ON **STATE LAW AND PROCEDURE**

In this activity, the student is asked to research basic property division topics in a single jurisdiction.

The Assignment

Locate the primary property distribution statute(s) in your jurisdiction and then respond to the following questions:

1. Is your state an equitable distribution or a community property jurisdiction?

2. How is marital/community property defined? How is separate property defined?
3. If you are in an equitable distribution state, do the courts apply a dual or all property approach?
4. What factors does a court consider when dividing marital property?
5. Are the nonfinancial contributions of spouses considered?

FOCUS ON **TECHNOLOGY**

In addition to the links provided throughout the chapter, this Focus segment provides a series of useful websites for reference along with related assignments for completion.

Websites of Interest

Links to all of the listed websites are provided at *www. pearsonhighered.com/wilson* in the companion website material for Chapter 11 under "Resources."

www.abanet.org

This is the site of the family law section of the American Bar Association. At this site you can search "Family Law in the Fifty States" and find a Chart (Chart 5) which provides a state-by-state survey of approaches to property division. To locate the Table, search for "Family Law in the Fifty States Tables" in "Resources Available to the Public." This chart also appears in the *Family Law Quarterly* published by the ABA on an annual basis.

www.dol.gov/ebsa

The U.S. Department of Labor provides a wealth of information at this site about insurance and retirement benefits including informative publications regarding QDROs.

www.findlaw.com

This site provides links to articles and state laws concerning a variety of divorce-related topics including property division. It also includes links to a checklist for dividing property and a settlement agreement form.

Assignments

1. Locate online an example of a property division provision/exhibit for a separation agreement.

2. Locate online an example of a QDRO.
3. Locate online information about a firm/company that values pensions and prepares QDROs.
4. Of what use are the following websites with respect to the topic of property division, if any?
   a. *www.divorceinfo.com*
   b. *divorcelinks.com*
   c. *www.divorcenet.com*
   d. *divorcesource.com*

PORTFOLIO PRODUCTS

1. Property division proposal
2. 1-2 page paper concerning ethical issues in a hypothetical case

3. Responses to questions on a property division case
4. Responses to questions about property division statute(s) in the student's jurisdiction

chapter 12

SEPARATION AGREEMENTS

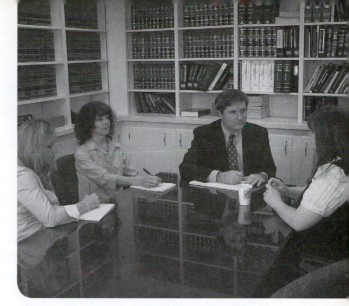

Herman, an elderly multimillionaire, and Anna, a relatively young model, have been married for twelve years and have a minor son, Theodore. The couple has decided to seek a no-fault divorce because they no longer seem to have anything in common. Anna believes she is getting a pretty good settlement, given that she came into the marriage with little more than good looks. She figures she recognizes a good deal when she sees it and doesn't need some high-priced attorney telling her what she already knows.

LEARNING OBJECTIVES

After reading this chapter and completing related assignments, you should be able to:

- explain the nature and purpose of a separation agreement

- identify the characteristics of an effective separation agreement

- describe how a separation agreement is developed

- describe the role of a paralegal in preparing a separation agreement

- list the basic components of a separation agreement

- describe the role the courts play in approving, modifying, and enforcing separation agreements

- explain the difference between a merged and a surviving agreement

What Is a Separation Agreement?

Separation agreements are relative newcomers to the family law legal scene. For centuries, and even after the passage of married women's property acts, a husband and wife could not execute a valid contract with each other. Separation agreements, in particular, were considered contrary to public policy favoring the preservation of marriage, because they appeared to promote divorce by providing financial incentives for terminating the marital relationship. As late as the 1960s, state legislatures and courts were still in the process of lifting such restrictions.

A **separation agreement** is a contract that sets forth the understanding reached by parties to a divorce or **legal separation** regarding their individual rights and obligations with respect to matters relating primarily to finances, property, and minor children, if any. The name given to the document varies by jurisdiction. For example, it may be called, among other options, a marital agreement, marital dissolution agreement, marital property settlement, or a permanent stipulation of the parties. In theory, a separation agreement addresses any and all rights and obligations arising out of the marital status. In an increasing number of states, the agreement is divided into two parts: a parenting plan that addresses child-related provisions and a stipulation/property settlement agreement that covers all other issues.

Separation agreement
an agreement made between spouses in anticipation of divorce or legal separation concerning the terms of the divorce or separation and any continuing obligations of the parties to each other

Legal separation
a judicial decree that allows the parties to live separate and apart without dissolving their legal relationship as husband and wife; sometimes called a limited divorce

You can review the sample *pro se* parenting plan and separation agreement forms provided by the Colorado courts at *www.courts.state.co.us*. A link to this site can be found at *www.pearsonhighered. com/wilson* in the companion website material for Chapter 12 under "Forms."

Since the agreement is a contract, it must meet all the requirements of a valid contract:

- The parties must have the legal capacity to contract—they must be able to understand the nature and effect of the agreement.
- The parties must enter the contract of their own free will—they must not be acting under duress.
- There must be an offer and an acceptance—there must be a **meeting of the minds** with respect to the terms of the agreement.
- There must be **consideration** for the agreement—a separation agreement is a bilateral contract in which the parties have reciprocal obligations, and the consideration is the mutual promises of the parties contained within the agreement.

Meeting of the minds
a shared understanding with respect to the terms and conditions of a contract

Consideration
a bargained-for exchange or mutual promises underlying the formation of a contract

PARALEGAL PRACTICE TIP

Sometimes it is difficult to assess "capacity" and "meeting of the minds," but the Virginia Court of Appeals had little trouble doing so when it affirmed a trial court's judgment in a 2009 case. In the *Bailey* case (54 Va. App. 209, 677 S.E.2d 56 (2009)), a wife presented her husband a marital property agreement to sign while he was on a weekend furlough from a psychiatric hospital. She told him that he would not be able to come home unless he signed. Under the "agreement," he transferred all marital property to his wife and all debts incurred during the marriage were assigned to him. The husband had suffered from serious psychiatric problems for more than a decade.

In an uncontested divorce, the parties' agreement must customarily be filed with the divorce petition or shortly thereafter. Timing of the submission is based on procedural rules or local practice in each state. In a contested case, the parties may file no agreement or may file a partial agreement that addresses the issues they agree on and separate proposed agreements with respect to the remaining issues. The contested issues are left for the court to determine following a trial. For example, the parties may agree on custody, visitation, and child support but be at loggerheads when it comes to division of their property.

What Are the Characteristics of an Effective Separation Agreement?

The primary characteristics of an effective separation agreement are as follows:

- **The agreement is comprehensive.** In order to minimize disputes and avoid costly post-divorce litigation, the agreement should address all of the rights and obligations that arise out of the marital status including, for example, property division, spousal support, insurance, taxes, and matters pertaining to minor children, if any.

PARALEGAL PRACTICE TIP

In *Brennenstuhl v. Brennenstuhl,* 169 N.C. App. 433, 610 S.E.2d 301 (2005), a section of the parties' property division settlement provided as follows:
   F. Retirement Benefits: Issues of retirement will be addressed at a later date.

The husband subsequently retired from the military and the wife filed a motion requesting the trial court to award her a share of his military retirement pay. The husband tried unsuccessfully to assert that the provision was too vague to establish a right in his former wife to seek a portion of his military retirement pay subsequent to the divorce. Had he anticipated this result, he might not have agreed to the other terms of the initial agreement. The opinion in this case can be found at *www.pearsonhighered.com/wilson* in the companion website material related to Chapter 12 under "Cases" and in the Case Resources Section of the MyLegalStudiesLab.

- **The terms of the agreement are clearly defined and reflect the parties' intentions.** For example, if a provision of the agreement will vary with a party's income, does "income" include both earned and **unearned income**? Does a reference to a party's "pension" include both the pension and any related death benefit? If spousal support will terminate upon remarriage or cohabitation, does "cohabitation" mean with an intimate partner or with anyone who subsidizes the recipient's living expenses, including roommates or even adult children?

Unearned income
income derived from investment rather than labor

PARALEGAL PRACTICE TIP

To read a case dealing with a failure to clearly define "income," see *Larson v. Larson*, 37 Mass. App. Ct. 106, 636 N.E.2d 1365 (1994), available at *www.pearsonhighered.com/wilson* in the companion website material related to Chapter 12 under "Cases." See also *Isham v. Isham,* 292 Conn. 170, 972 A.2d 228 (2009), a case in which the parties' settlement agreement required the husband to pay alimony. The alimony provisions were described using both "income" and "salary" and the terms were not defined. The wife filed a motion for contempt because her husband was paying alimony based only on his "salary" rather than on his "income," which would include bonuses. The Connecticut Supreme Court reversed the trial court's judgment finding that the terms were unambiguous and remanded the case for further proceedings, during which extrinsic evidence should be permitted to clarify the parties' intent at the time the agreement was made.

- **The terms of the agreement are stated fully so that the parties know what is expected of each of them.** For example, if one party will continue to reside in the jointly owned marital home, the agreement should specify who will be responsible for payment of the mortgage (if any), property taxes, insurance, utilities, and maintenance expenses such as repairs, landscaping, painting, or snow removal, if warranted. Each attorney must carefully review the agreement with his or her client to be certain it reflects what the parties actually have agreed to and that there are no misunderstandings or extraneous oral or written agreements between the parties.

PARALEGAL PRACTICE TIP

When an agreement is intended to embody the parties' entire understanding, the **parol evidence rule** provides that its terms cannot later be varied or contradicted by evidence of earlier or contemporaneous agreements.

Parol evidence rule
the rule that when a writing is intended to embody the entire agreement between the parties, its terms cannot later be varied or contradicted by evidence of earlier or contemporaneous agreements

- **Although the parties are free to settle for less than they might be entitled to under the law, the agreement still should be fair and freely entered** (although it inevitably reflects considerable compromise on both sides). When courts assess whether or not an agreement is fair and reasonable at the time of separation, divorce, or post-divorce litigation, they consider both **procedural** and **substantive fairness**. They may look at several factors including the following:[1]
  - Are the financial provisions fair and reasonable when the agreement is viewed as a whole? For example, is one party left nearly destitute while the other receives substantial assets?
  - Is the agreement consistent with the statutory or case law factors governing alimony, property division, and custody issues in the jurisdiction? Does it appear to relieve one parent of his or her statutory duty to support a child?

Procedural fairness
fairness in the negotiation and execution of the agreement

Substantive fairness
fairness in the specific terms of an agreement

- Under what circumstances did negotiations take place? Was one party under considerable duress, such as a threat of abuse or loss of custody of the children?
- How complex are the issues? Were experts consulted to assist with complicated valuation problems?
- How legally sophisticated are the parties? What kinds of education and professional background do they each have?
- Was each party represented by separate counsel competent in family law matters? Was one party not represented? Did both parties believe themselves to be represented by the same attorney?

PARALEGAL PRACTICE TIP

Sometimes it is difficult to assess fairness and other times it is not. The North Dakota Supreme Court granted "relief from judgment" in the *Eberle* case (2010 ND 107 (2010)) finding that the parties' settlement agreement was "so one-sided no rational, undeluded person" would make the agreement and "no honest and fair person would accept it." The court found that the facts suggested there was some duress or undue influence in the "negotiation" and execution of the agreement. The wife was not represented by counsel, the agreement was rushed, and there was little discussion of its terms. The wife said she had a chance to read the agreement and knew what she was signing but that she was on medication that "affected her ability to think" and resist her husband's demands.

How Is a Separation Agreement Developed?

In the majority of cases, the parties to a divorce or separation reach an agreement with or without the assistance of counsel and/or mediation. This may be accomplished in a variety of ways including the following:

Pro se
the condition under which a person represents himself or herself in a legal proceeding without the assistance of an attorney

- The parties may reach an agreement on their own and proceed ***pro se*** or present it to their respective attorneys for review and submission to the court.

PARALEGAL PRACTICE TIP

To see a Connecticut *pro se* agreement, visit *www.jud.ct.gov.* You can find a link to this site at *www.pearsonhighered.com/wilson* in the companion website material for Chapter 12 under "Forms."

Bottom line
the limit beyond which a party will not go in a negotiation

- The parties may retain counsel and discuss with their respective attorneys what each considers his or her goals and **bottom line** terms. Financial information will be exchanged, and necessary documents, such as bank statements, deeds, and mortgages, will be gathered. If there is no need for formal discovery, counsel may negotiate an agreement via telephone, correspondence, and four-way conferences. In relatively uncomplicated cases, one attorney will prepare a draft reducing the agreement to writing for the other's review and input. Successive drafts will be exchanged until an agreement is reached that reflects a "meeting of the minds."

PARALEGAL PRACTICE TIP

Many family law attorneys prefer to prepare the first draft, as it provides them with the sometimes subtle opportunity to shape the negotiations in a particular direction.

- In more complex cases, drafts will not be prepared until discovery is completed, the value of major assets is established, and each party has an opportunity to consider his or her options after carefully examining the full nature and extent of the **marital estate.** In high-conflict cases, the attorneys often draft and exchange initial proposals outlining their clients' respective positions on issues such as child custody, visitation, support, alimony, health insurance, property division, distribution of debts, and attorneys' fees. Areas of agreement, if any, will be identified, and negotiation will proceed with respect to the remaining issues. Once the agreed-upon terms are framed, a partial or full agreement is prepared. If the agreement does not address all of the issues, the remaining topics may be referred for mediation. The issues that remain unresolved after exhaustive efforts will be presented to the court for resolution. More often than not, even those issues may be settled "on the courthouse steps" by parties not wishing to incur the risk or expense of a trial.

Marital estate
the property acquired during the marriage other than by gift or inheritance that is subject to division at the time of marital dissolution

PARALEGAL PRACTICE TIP

Successive editions of the agreement, including copies of those marked up by counsel for the other party, should be retained in the client file. Occasionally, questions arise later as to whether the opposing party knew about or had input into a particular provision. **Forensic** material can help establish that he or she clearly was aware of the challenged provision and may even have proposed it.

Forensic
gathered as potential evidence in a lawsuit

The client ultimately controls the case in the sense that he or she has the final word on terms, on the scope of discovery, and on whether or not a case will proceed to trial. With respect to agreements, the client must have input and approve all proposals communicated to the other party and also must have an opportunity to review and consider all counterproposals.

Paralegal Application 12.1

Information Gathering for Separation Agreements

Except in cases involving few if any assets, before an agreement is actually drafted a considerable amount of information should be gathered from the client, the other party, and third parties as well, if appropriate. The parties should have a comprehensive picture of their circumstances before negotiating an agreement or agreeing to a single term in isolation. For example, a party initially opposed to paying spousal support eventually may prefer to pay tax-deductible alimony over time if it means his or her pension will remain intact.

What follows is a summary of the kinds of documents and information that should be collected and compiled in summary form for easy reference when drafting an agreement. The paralegal generally plays an active role in gathering this information through informal and formal discovery, if necessary.

- Personal data:
  - Names
  - Addresses (home and business)
  - parties' dates of birth
- Social security numbers
- Home, business, and cell phone numbers
- E-mail address (for communication purposes)
- Details regarding the date and location of the marriage
- Names and birthdates of children born to both and/or either of the parties
- Contact information for all attorneys involved in the divorce and any other potentially related matters, such as abuse complaints and pending claims
- Summary of all property owned by the parties indicating how it is held (by husband, wife, jointly, with third parties, in trust, etc.), when it was acquired (before or during the marriage, before or after the date of separation), the value of the property, and the means by which the value was established
- Income from all sources of both parties

(Continued)

- Liabilities of both parties: identity (and relationship) of each creditor, amount of debt, who incurred the debt and for what purpose, whose name the debt is in, etc.
- Documents to collect (not intended as an exhaustive list):
  - Pre- or postmarital agreements
  - Deeds
  - Leases
  - Titles
  - Contracts for purchase or sale of property
  - Mortgage/loan applications
  - Insurance policies
  - Wills and trusts
- Tax documents
- Financial statements (current and past)
- Business and professional licenses
- Pension/retirement account plans, statements, etc.
- Bank account statements
- Appraisals
- Medical reports
- Pending claims (personal injury, etc.)
- Court orders or judgments affecting the rights and liabilities of either or both of the parties (including decrees from previous divorces, if any)
- Credit card statements
- Royalty statements
- Articles of Incorporation, corporate by-laws, etc.

The Form of the Separation Agreement

The actual document is usually in one of three formats:

1. **A two-part format.** Two part formats generally consist of:
   A. A main body containing:
      - a recital of pertinent facts (names and addresses of the parties; names and ages of the parties' children, if any; date and place where the parties were married; and when and where they last lived together)
      - several general provisions/articles common to most agreements (clauses relating to waivers, disclosure, interpretation, implementation, modification, severability, nonmolestation, and enforcement of the agreement)

   Incorporation by reference
   adoption by reference; made a part of the agreement by including a statement in the agreement that the Exhibits are to be treated as if they are part of the agreement

   B. A series of "exhibits" that are **incorporated by reference,** each of which addresses a specific topic (such as spousal support, child custody and visitation, or property division) (See Exhibit 12.2.)

2. **An integrated document.** Integrated documents customarily have numbered sections (Articles I, II, III, etc.) following the introductory "recitals" of pertinent facts. Each Article is customarily labeled, for example, General Provisions, Custody and Visitation, Personal Property, etc.

3. **A format recommended or prescribed in the jurisdiction.** Several states provide forms online on state/court-sponsored websites. For example, the New Hampshire courts provide standard forms online for parenting plans and permanent stipulations, which contain numbered paragraphs on all major topics. Several options are provided under each main topic, with boxes for the parties to check indicating their choices. This approach vastly simplifies the process for parties proceeding *pro se*, who lack knowledge about the nature and scope of issues that need to be resolved when their marriage dissolves. If the parties are represented by counsel who choose to develop their own agreements, those agreements must use the same topical numbering system as is used in the court's format. This requirement facilitates review by judges so that they do not have to struggle with the organization of each individual agreement to locate the terms (such as custody, spousal support, or health insurance) that most concern them.

PARALEGAL PRACTICE TIP

To see the New Hampshire forms, visit *www.courts.state.nh.us.* You can find a link to this site at *www.pearsonhighered.com/wilson* in the companion website material related to Chapter 12 under "Forms."

Whatever the basic format, there is considerable similarity agreement to agreement. However, each separation or divorce involves two parties, each with his or her own unique goals, needs, and circumstances. Therefore, considerable care must be taken to ensure that the agreement is tailored to those circumstances and meets the client's specific goals and needs to the greatest extent possible (understanding that there are rarely any fully satisfied customers in the divorce context).

The Paralegal's Role in Drafting the Separation Agreement

Paralegals are often asked to draft separation agreements based on the specific terms provided by the supervising attorney after consultation with the client. A basic approach generally includes the following steps:

- The supervising attorney will first review the client's priorities and expectations as well as his or her rights and responsibilities under governing law. In order to establish the basis for an agreement, the attorney must identify the client's position on fundamental issues, such as child custody, pensions, and the division of any real property, including the marital residence. After discovery is completed, if the basic terms are negotiated and agreed upon (or formulated as proposals), an outline of the agreement is prepared. The paralegal is sometimes present for these initial discussions and may be asked to take notes and develop an outline for review.
- The paralegal should review (or already have knowledge of) basic laws (case or statutory), rules, and procedures governing the content and format of agreements. For example, does the court mandate specific numbered paragraphs and topics? Are child-related provisions addressed in the agreement or in a separate parenting plan?
- The paralegal will examine available "model agreements" in firm files, both paper and electronic. Form books, state practice manuals, and other resources may also be consulted. Previously drafted agreements in closed divorce files may be especially useful when cases present similar fact patterns (for example, a high-conflict child custody and visitation situation or cases in which bankruptcy or tax audit issues are looming in the immediate future). There are many online resources for agreements—some are helpful, but all need to be carefully assessed, adapted to reflect jurisdictional terminology and formats, and tailored to the facts of the case.
- The paralegal carefully drafts an agreement for review based on the outline provided/approved by the supervising attorney. Drafting generally involves considerably more than filling in the blanks or simple cut-and-paste activity. Although there is no need to reinvent the wheel, the content must reflect the facts and intentions of the parties in the particular case and comply with

current governing law and procedure. Caution always must be exercised when duplicating or using **boilerplate** provisions. For example, there may be a recent change in the state's treatment of some issue in agreements, such as whether or not the court will approve a provision pertaining to responsibility for college expenses.

- The paralegal may be asked to review a proposed agreement or feedback received from the opposing party. Generally the paralegal will check to be sure all of the appropriate terms are included, identify any differences from the client's position, and, if necessary, recommend potential additions, deletions, and/or alternative language for review by the supervising attorney.
- The complete Final Draft must be carefully reviewed prior to signature and submission to the court for incorporation into the judgment. Before signing, counsel should walk through the entire document with the client and address any questions that may arise.

EXHIBIT 12.1 Checklist of Basic Topics Covered in Separation Agreements

Identification Clause/Opening Paragraph

    Date of execution

    Names and addresses of the parties and names used to refer to the parties in the agreement

Recitals/Statement of Facts

    Date and place of marriage and the number of the marriage for each party

    Names and birthdates of all children born to or adopted by the parties

    Date of separation and location where the parties last resided together

    Reason for separation (e.g., irreconcilable differences)

    Current living status (usually separate and apart)

    Identification of any pending action for divorce or legal separation (separate maintenance) with name of court and docket number

    Purpose of the agreement and parties' intent with respect to its effect

    Confirmation of participation in negotiation of agreement and knowledge of rights and liabilities

    Confirmation agreement is signed freely and voluntarily

    Consideration for agreement (mutual promises)

General Provisions

    Separation

        Intention to live separate and apart

        Nonmolestation provision (an agreement not to restrain or interfere with each other)

    Mutual/General Release (acceptance of the agreement in full satisfaction of all claims against each other except those arising from the agreement and subsequent divorce)

    Waiver of Estate claim (a waiver of any rights in the other's estate upon death)

    Execution of Documents necessary to implement agreement (deeds, QDROs, etc.)

    Acknowledgments

        Independent representation of choice (or opportunity for it or an acknowledgment that one or both of the parties proceeded *pro se*)

        Full disclosure made or opportunity to do so

        Parties have read and understood terms of the agreement

        Agreement is free from fraud or coercion

        Agreement is fair and reasonable

(Continued)

EXHIBIT 12.1 *(Continued)*

Situs/Governing Law (designation of the state's law that will govern interpretation and enforceability of the agreement)

Validity/Severability/Savings Clause (a clause stating that if any provision of the agreement is declared void, the remaining provisions will continue to be valid)

Entire Agreement (statement that the agreement embodies the parties' complete understanding with respect to resolution of the rights and responsibilities flowing from their marital relationship)

Effective Date

Binding Effect on heirs, assigns, etc.

Intention with respect to merger or survival of agreement (whether the agreement will merge in the divorce decree or survive as an independent contract)

Modification (under what circumstances, if any, the agreement can be modified)

Strict Performance (whether a party can waive an occasional "breach" by the other party without waiving other breaches or whether strict performance of the terms of the agreement will be required)

Dispute Resolution (method; process for selection of mediator, arbitrator, etc.; coverage of costs; binding effect)

Breach of Agreement

Attorneys' Fees

Number of counterparts executed, each constituting an original

Signature and Acknowledgment/Certification

Specific Exhibits

Alimony
   Waiver(s) OR
   Payment of alimony

      Type (permanent, lump sum, restitution, etc.)
      Amount and form of payment
      Payment schedule and duration
      Termination contingencies—cohabitation, death, remarriage, etc.
      Modifications/cost-of-living adjustments
      Intended income tax consequences (intention that payments will be tax-deductible to the payor and includable in the income of the recipient)
      Security (insurance policy, trust, etc.)
      Interest on unpaid balance (arrearages)

Child Custody and Visitation ("parenting time") (may be covered in a parenting plan)
   Physical and legal custody—joint/sole
      Allocation of decision-making responsibility (major and day-to-day)
      Identification of topics considered "major" and requiring consultation (e.g., religious upbringing, education, major surgery, and participation in hazardous activities)
      Parental cooperation
      Access to school, medical, and dental records, etc.
      Visitation/parenting time schedule
         Reasonable rights based on mutual agreement
         Structured
            Days, weekends, weeks
            Holidays
            Birthdays, Mother's Day, and Father's Day
            Transportation arrangements and cost

(Continued)

EXHIBIT 12.1 *(Continued)*

Illness—emergency medical treatment
Removal/absence from the state—temporary, long term
Contact by phone, e-mail—virtual visitation
Visitation with extended family
Adjustments to schedule—cancellation provisions
Supervised visitation, if warranted
Agreement with respect to children's surname(s)

Child Support (may be covered in a parenting plan)

Amount—relationship to guidelines
Payment schedule
Form of payment—wage assignment, if appropriate
Duration—definition of emancipation
Child care (built into child support formula in several states)
Modification
Expenses related to special activities
Education—elementary, secondary, postsecondary, if permitted
Public, private
Costs covered
Allocation of responsibility
Use of children's assets, scholarships, etc.
Decision-making process and cooperation in seeking financial assistance
Access to records
Security for obligation (trust fund, etc.)
Extracurricular activities (sports, music, etc.)

Dependency exemption
Treatment for tax purposes, execution of necessary tax forms
Effect of bankruptcy (not dischargeable)
Security for child support (insurance, trust for benefit of children, etc.)

Property Division

Personal property
Waiver of any rights to each other's property
Delivery of documents evidencing ownership
Vehicles
Schedule of property already divided, if appropriate
Property remaining to be divided—time frame and process for division
Retirement funds—Qualified Domestic Relations Order(s)

Real property
Identification/description of all real property
Disposition of each parcel—timing of conveyances, treatment of proceeds, closing costs, commissions, fees, encumbrances, shares to parties, etc.
Assumption and/or payment of mortgages and operating expenses
Marital home—exclusive right to occupy, responsibility for related expenses, mortgage, right of inspection, etc.
Rights to purchase/agreements to sell
Execution of deeds
Tax treatment and capital gains distribution

Liabilities

Allocation of joint debt

Hold harmless provisions for past and future debts

Responsibility for individual debt

(Continued)

EXHIBIT 12.1 *(Continued)*

Insurance
- Medical insurance
  - Medical insurance for parties
  - Medical insurance for children
  - Name of insurer—policy number(s)
  - Notice of changes
  - Payment obligations
  - Duration of coverage
  - Release from obligation (remarriage, change of employment, emancipation, etc.)
  - Responsibility for uninsured medical costs of spouses
  - Responsibility for uninsured medical costs of children
    - Scope of expenses included (dental, orthodontic, psychological, optical, prescriptions, etc.)
  - Agreement regarding elective and cosmetic surgery
  - Claim and reimbursement procedures
  - Rights under state/federal law (COBRA, etc.)
- Other kinds of insurance
  - Life
    - Identify policy(ies) and ownership
    - Amount
    - Beneficiaries
    - Responsibility for payment
    - Proof of policy
    - Changes
      - Right to provide alternative coverage
  - Property
  - Liability
  - Automobile
  - Other

Taxes
- Status of all prior returns (state and federal)
- Allocation of refunds
- Liability for past-due taxes, interest, and penalties
- Notification of audits or assessments, etc.
- Innocent spouse language, if appropriate
- Cooperation in preparation, etc.

Bankruptcy Filing (if appropriate)
- Notice of intention to file
- Support obligations not dischargeable

Sample Separation Agreement

The following sample separation agreement is based almost entirely on an agreement executed and filed in a divorce case in the Commonwealth of Massachusetts. The names of the parties have been changed and other identifying information is omitted. Some brief additions have also been made to the actual text for instructional purposes. Specific terms of the agreement are tailored to the needs of a middle-income couple married for twelve years who have two minor children. They have been separated for approximately eighteen months. The parties have filed a joint petition for divorce on the grounds that irreconcilable differences have caused an irremediable breakdown of their marriage. They have reached agreement on all issues after an extended period of negotiation, initially in the context of mediation without counsel present and then with counsel. The most challenging issues for these parties involved the specific provisions concerning custody and visitation, disposition of the marital home, payment of substantial joint debt, and the parties' respective retirement funds.

The content of the sample agreement is written in "plain English" and avoids excessive use of "legalese" wherever possible. Some of the language is common boilerplate. Note that after the initial statement of facts/recitals, headings are used for each major topic. Each Article is designated with a Roman numeral and each Exhibit with a letter. Whatever system is used, it should afford easy reference for the parties, counsel, and the court. Exhibit 12.1 provided a summary of the basic elements that should be considered for inclusion in the agreement. Drafting Tips appear throughout the agreement to indicate some possible variations, explanations, cautions, etc. Places in the agreement where specifics (name of the court, county, state, etc.) need to be filled in are indicated by blanks and italicized lettering.

EXHIBIT 12.2 Sample Separation Agreement

NAME OF STATE
NAME OF COURT

NAME OF COUNTY   Docket No. *11D-xxxx-DVI*

SEPARATION AGREEMENT

DRAFTING TIP

The title of the agreement will vary according to local custom, practice, and procedure.

This Agreement ("Agreement") is made this *date* day of January 2012 by and between **Stephen Morgan** (hereinafter referred to as **"Stephen"**) of *address* and **Juliana W. Morgan** (hereinafter referred to as **"Julie"**), of *address*. The term "parties," as used in this Agreement, refers to Stephen and Julie.

DRAFTING TIP

This is the "Identification Clause" of the Agreement. The date is often filled in by hand on the specific date of signing. The parties' names and current addresses are included, along with the names that will be used to refer to each of the parties throughout the agreement. The two most common approaches are to use the first names by which the parties are commonly known or to use "husband" and "wife." In the case of same-sex marriages, the parties may be referred to as "spouse A" and "spouse B." The use of "plaintiff" and "defendant" has fallen into disfavor with the institution of no-fault divorce, and given the potential for confusion when multiple actions are filed involving the parties.

(Continued)

EXHIBIT 12.2 *(Continued)*

DRAFTING TIP

If there is a history of serious abuse and/or a restraining order in force against one of the parties, the address of the other party may not appear in the agreement and also may be **impounded** in court records.

DRAFTING TIP

Some attorneys include the parties' social security numbers in the agreement. Most no longer do so, however, because of the potential for identity theft, given that agreements filed in divorce actions are part of a public record.

Impounded
kept in the custody of the court and not available to the public, and, in some instances, to other parties

STATEMENT OF FACTS

The parties were married on May 16, 1999, in Fort Lauderdale, Florida. This was the first marriage for both parties.

Two children have been born of this marriage, both minors: Robert G. Morgan, born 1/14/2002, and Jennifer Ruth Morgan, born 04/10/2005. Julie has borne no other children during the marriage.

Due to serious and irreconcilable differences that have arisen between the parties, causing the irretrievable breakdown of their marriage, Stephen and Julie separated on January 16, 2010. They continue to live separate and apart, and it is their wish and intent to remain living apart from each other.

The parties have filed a Joint Petition for Divorce (Docket No. # *number*), which is currently pending in the *name of court*.

The parties have decided to confirm their separation and effect this Agreement to settle between themselves all of the issues relating to their respective property and estate rights, spousal support, care and custody of their minor children, and all other claims and demands each might have against the other by reason of their marital relationship.

Each of them fully understands the facts, each has been fully informed of his or her legal rights and liabilities, and each signs this Agreement freely and voluntarily.

NOW, THEREFORE, in consideration of the mutual promises and covenants contained herein, the parties agree as follows:

PARALEGAL PRACTICE TIP

Remember the "marital presumption" discussed in Chapter 5? Under the presumption, a husband is presumed to be the father of any children born to a woman while she is married or within a certain period thereafter.

DRAFTING TIP

This above section is often referred to as the "Recitals." It includes the basic facts of the case. In some models, the section begins with the heading "Witnesseth," and each paragraph begins with "Whereas. . . ."

DRAFTING TIP

One of the recitals confirms that the parties have separated. Historically the courts looked with disfavor on agreements negotiated while the parties were still living together, particularly when the agreement provided that if one party subsequently filed a complaint for divorce, the other party would not appear or defend against that action (even if he or she had a valid defense). Such promises constituted a form of **collusion** or fraud on the court in order to obtain a divorce. Courts have been less concerned about such provisions since the arrival of no-fault divorce.

(Continued)

Collusion
an agreement by the parties to a divorce action to jointly deceive the court as to the true nature and purpose of the action

PARALEGAL PRACTICE TIP

In *In re Marriage of Grossman*, 338 Ore. 99, 106 P.3d 618 (2005), the parties executed a marital settlement agreement, separated briefly, and then reconciled and lived together for another ten years before seeking to dissolve their marriage. The husband then sought to enforce the agreement that the parties had already made. The wife successfully argued that the court should divide their property in a "just and proper" manner under the applicable state statute without enforcing the earlier agreement, given the long period of time since the "agreement" was signed. The opinion in this case can be found at *www.pearsonhighered. com/wilson* in the companion website material related to Chapter 12 under "Cases" and in the Case Resources Section of the MyLegalStudiesLab.

EXHIBIT 12.2 *(Continued)*

DRAFTING TIP

If no complaint for divorce has yet been filed, the agreement should indicate what effect, if any, a subsequent filing will have on the validity of the agreement. If the complaint has been filed, the agreement may indicate the effect of a reconciliation between the parties.

DRAFTING TIP

The fact that one of the recitals states that the agreement was signed freely and voluntarily is evidence that it was so signed, but is not necessarily dispositive. Abused spouses frequently sign agreements out of fear and a desire to escape a threatening situation, but may later challenge them once in a safe environment.

ARTICLE I SEPARATION

From this date forward, Stephen and Julie will continue to live separate and apart from each other, as if sole and unmarried, and free from the authority of or interference by the other. Each agrees to respect the other's privacy. However, the parties do not intend to create a restraining order or intend that either of them be entered on the computer tracking system for restraining orders on account of this provision or any other provision hereof.

DRAFTING TIP

This provision is sometimes called a "Nonmolestation Clause." It does not constitute a restraining order and is not designed to prevent all contact between the parties. Rather, it serves as a confirmation that each party is free to live his or her individual life as if never married, without interference from or unwanted contact with the other party. If there is a restraining order in place, the language in this paragraph would be modified to reflect that fact.

ARTICLE II MUTUAL RELEASES

Subject to other provisions of this Agreement, each party, individually, and for his or her heirs, legal representatives, executors, administrators, and assigns, releases and discharges the other of and from all causes of action, all claims, rights, or demands in either law or in equity, which either of the parties ever had or now has against the other or which may hereafter arise by reason of their marriage. This does not apply to any or all causes of action for this divorce, and such liabilities as may accrue or any payments due under the terms of this agreement.

DRAFTING TIP

This general mutual release is designed to prevent post-decree litigation between the spouses for any cause of action arising out of or occurring during the marriage. For example, this provision could foreclose a wife who was physically abused during the marriage and never raised the abuse as an issue during the divorce proceeding from filing a post-divorce civil complaint seeking damages for assault and battery and intentional infliction of emotional distress. Although this may serve the interests of judicial economy and bring some closure to the parties, it does not take into consideration the dynamics of an abusive relationship. Until free and clear of the marriage, an abused spouse may not dare risk raising such an issue, and may later claim that he or she signed the agreement under duress.

(Continued)

EXHIBIT 12.2 *(Continued)*

ARTICLE III WAIVER OF ESTATE CLAIM

Except as otherwise provided in this Agreement, each party hereby waives and releases any and all rights that she or he may now have or hereafter acquire as spouse under the present or future laws of any jurisdiction:

   a. To elect to take against any will or codicil of the other party now or hereafter in force;
   b. To share in the other party's estate in case of intestacy; and
   c. To act as executor or administrator of the other party's estate.

    Both parties intend that their respective estates shall be administered as though no marriage between them ever existed. However, each is specifically not waiving any rights he or she may have in: (1) claims against the other's estate by reason of a breach of this Agreement; (2) any testamentary provisions that are voluntarily made for his or her benefit by the other; and/or (3) any rights either may have to social security benefits by virtue of their marriage to the other.

DRAFTING TIP

Generally, a divorce automatically revokes bequests to a former spouse unless otherwise provided in a will. However, the revocation is not effective until the divorce is granted and the parties are no longer "spouses." It is therefore wise for the parties to cover the time period between the date of separation and the date of divorce in their agreement, especially if there will be an extended period of separation.

DRAFTING TIP

The personal representative of a decedent (executor, administrator, etc.) may be required to satisfy remaining alimony, child support, and property division obligations under the agreement from the assets of the estate.

ARTICLE IV EXECUTION OF IMPLEMENTING DOCUMENTS

Within a reasonable time after this Agreement has been signed, each party will execute, seal, deliver, file, or record such bills of sale, deeds, leases, waivers, or other instruments or documents as the other party requests and may reasonably require to effectuate the terms of this Agreement.

DRAFTING TIP

Some agreements expressly provide that if either party fails to comply with the provisions of this paragraph, the agreement itself will constitute a satisfactory substitute for the unexecuted document. However, third parties may not be satisfied with this alternative to an executed deed or transfer of title of a vehicle or boat, etc. A party's failure to comply with this Article that results in damages to the other party may constitute a breach of the agreement.

ARTICLE V ACKNOWLEDGMENT OF THE PARTIES

Each party to this Agreement acknowledges and agrees:

   a. that each is represented by a competent attorney of her or his own choosing or has freely chosen not to be represented;
   b. that each of the parties has made full disclosure of his or her respective assets and liabilities and that this Agreement is entered into with knowledge of the financial circumstances and needs of the other party;

(Continued)

EXHIBIT 12.2 *(Continued)*

c. that each has carefully read this Agreement, has discussed it with his or her respective counsel, understands the provisions contained within it, and considers the Agreement to be fair and reasonable;

d. that this Agreement is not the product of fraud or coercion; and

e. that this Agreement is fair and reasonable at the time it is being signed and at the time it is being submitted to the court as part of the parties' divorce proceedings.

DRAFTING TIP

The "acknowledgments" in this Article are sometimes called "representations" and may appear in separate Articles to highlight their importance.

DRAFTING TIP

When only one party is represented by counsel, courts may be reluctant to approve or enforce an agreement if it appears that the unrepresented party did not understand the effect of the agreement or was pressured to sign it under duress. In such circumstances, it is wise to include language such as the following: "Husband acknowledges that this agreement was drafted by wife's attorney, that he has been advised to seek independent counsel, and that he has declined to do so of his own volition."

DRAFTING TIP

Occasionally, when one party is represented by counsel and the other is not, the agreement is lopsided in favor of the represented party. Before issuing a decree, the court may require the unrepresented party to seek counsel for the limited purpose of reviewing the agreement and ensuring that he or she understands its terms and the impact of any rights that may be waived, etc.

DRAFTING TIP

Article V b) provides an example of when boilerplate might be dangerous. In this case, the parties believed there was full disclosure. However, if a party has been concealing assets that have not been located despite due diligence or if a client has refused to permit adequate discovery despite counsel's recommendation, this language may be modified to provide for later discovered assets presently "unknown" to either party. For example, "The parties further agree that any intentional material misrepresentation by either of them in his or her financial statement shall be grounds to seek **rescission** or other equitable relief. In the alternative, it will constitute grounds for seeking modification of any court order or judgment incorporating the terms of this agreement or for objecting to consideration of the agreement in any subsequent legal proceeding between the parties or their personal representatives, heirs, or assigns."

DRAFTING TIP

Either here or elsewhere in the agreement, there usually is a reference to attorneys' fees, e.g., "Except as herein otherwise provided, each party agrees to pay his or her own attorney's fees incurred in negotiation, preparation, and execution of this agreement." (See Article XIV.)

(Continued)

Rescission
the cancellation or unmaking of a contract for a legally sufficient reason

EXHIBIT 12.2 *(Continued)*

ARTICLE VI SITUS

This Agreement shall be construed, governed, and enforced in accordance with the applicable laws of the state of *name of state*.

ARTICLE VII VALIDITY

In the event that any provision of this Agreement is held to be invalid and unenforceable, such invalidity shall not invalidate the whole agreement, but the remaining provisions of this Agreement shall continue to be valid and binding to the extent that such provisions reflect fairly the intent and understanding of the parties at the time of execution.

DRAFTING TIP

This clause is a "severability" or "savings" provision. It provides, for example, that if the Exhibit pertaining to alimony is held to be invalid as violating public policy, the rest of the Agreement will still be valid and effective.

ARTICLE VIII ENTIRE AGREEMENT

There are no representations, warrantees, conditions, promises, or undertakings other than those set forth in this Agreement, which contains the entire agreement of the parties.

DRAFTING TIP

Any "side" agreements between the parties are unenforceable and in the extreme may invalidate the entire agreement if they appear to constitute a fraud upon the court.

ARTICLE IX EFFECTIVE DATE

This Agreement shall be effective upon execution by the parties.

ARTICLE X BINDING EFFECT

Except as otherwise stated herein, all the provisions of this Agreement shall be binding upon the respective heirs, next of kin, trustees in bankruptcy, personal representatives, executors, administrators, and assigns of the parties.

ARTICLE XI INDEPENDENT CONTRACT

This Agreement may be submitted to any court before which any Complaint or proceeding for divorce or dissolution of marriage shall be tried, and in the event that a Judgment of Divorce shall be entered, the same shall incorporate in full or in substance the provisions of this Agreement and the Agreement shall be incorporated and not merged but shall survive as a document having independent legal significance, and the property settlement and any alimony provisions herein shall forever be binding upon the parties. Notwithstanding the foregoing, any provisions of this Agreement relating to children who are not emancipated shall remain modifiable by the court upon a change in governing law, a material change in circumstances of a party or a child, or if a modification is consistent with the best interests of the child.

DRAFTING TIP

The parents cannot bargain away the rights of their children, and all child-related provisions remain subject to the continuing jurisdiction of the court.

(Continued)

PARALEGAL PRACTICE TIP

"Side agreements" can cause problems for both clients and attorneys. In *Reaser v. Reaser*, 2004 S.D. 116, 688 N.W.2d 429 (2004), for example, the husband initiated divorce proceedings against his wife in January of 1999. He was represented by counsel, but she was not. The parties entered a stipulation prepared by the husband's attorney that addressed child custody, child support, alimony, and property division. Under the agreement, he was to have custody of the children and she waived any claim to alimony. He relieved her of any claim for child support. The judge refused to grant the divorce because the stipulation did not provide for child support. The parties then modified the stipulation to establish a child support obligation for the wife, but prior to submitting it to the court, the husband's attorney drafted a "document of private agreement" in which the wife "was to have no duty to pay ongoing [child] support despite the language of the Divorce Decree." This "private agreement" was kept in the lawyer's office and was not disclosed to the judge, who subsequently approved the second stipulation. In 2002, the wife sought a change in custody and child support. During the course of the hearing, the "private agreement" came to light! The South Dakota Supreme Court affirmed a trial court's decision to set aside the divorce decree by reason of fraud upon the court. The Court described the conduct of the parties and the attorney as "egregious conduct involving corruption of the judicial process itself." It also opined that it may have violated a criminal statute and clearly constituted a violation of the attorney's professional duty of candor before the court. The opinion in this case can be found at *www.pearsonhighered.com/wilson* in the companion website material related to Chapter 12 under "Cases" and in the Case Resources Section of the MyLegalStudiesLab.

EXHIBIT 12.2 (*Continued*)

ARTICLE XII MODIFICATION

A modification or waiver of any of the provisions of this Agreement shall be effective only if made in writing and executed with the same formality as this Agreement or by order of a court of competent jurisdiction.

DRAFTING TIP

If the agreement merges in the decree, this paragraph will reflect that distinction. For example, "After approval of this agreement it shall be incorporated and merge in the final judgment of divorce and may not be altered or modified except pursuant to the court's order."

ARTICLE XIII STRICT PERFORMANCE

The failure of either party to insist upon strict performance of any of the provisions of this Agreement shall not be construed as a waiver of any subsequent default of the same or a similar nature.

DRAFTING TIP

This paragraph provides that if, for example, Julie chooses to excuse Stephen's failure to pay child support for the month of December because he is experiencing a temporary financial crisis, she is not agreeing to excuse his failure to pay support in any other past or future months. Rather, she can insist that the agreement be enforced with respect to those other periods. Such "informal" waivers of breach do not deprive the court of its ultimate jurisdiction over child-related issues and may occur at the risk of either or both parties.

ARTICLE XIV RESOLUTION OF DISPUTES, BREACH OF AGREEMENT, AND ATTORNEYS' FEES

Except as herein otherwise provided, Stephen and Julie will each pay their own attorneys' fees incurred in connection with negotiation of this Agreement and the pending Joint Petition for Divorce.

In the event that a dispute arises between the parties regarding any of the provisions of this Agreement that Stephen and Julie are unable to resolve on their own or with the assistance of counsel, they agree that prior to filing any legal action in court, they will make an effort to resolve the dispute through mediation at Thomas Kelley and Associates or another similar agency mutually agreed upon. The fees and costs of the mediation shall be borne equally by the parties unless the court later determines that the actions of one party were so unreasonable as to require such mediation, in which case, the party responsible for the unreasonable action shall be responsible for that portion of the fees and costs that the court deems equitable. Nothing in this paragraph shall prevent either party from proceeding directly to court or pursuing any other legal remedy if either party defaults on a financial obligation under this Agreement.

If either party commits a breach of any provisions of this Agreement and legal action is reasonably required to enforce such provisions and is instituted by the nonbreaching party, the party in breach shall be liable to the party who prevails in the court action for all statutory interest from the date of breach and for all court costs and reasonable attorneys' fees incurred in instituting and prosecuting such action. If either party brings legal action against the other on frivolous, insubstantial grounds or in bad faith, and does not prevail in that action, then the prevailing party shall be awarded reasonable attorneys' fees and other costs and expenses incurred in defending against such action.

(*Continued*)

EXHIBIT 12.2 *(Continued)*

DRAFTING TIP

If one of the parties promises in the agreement to pay the fees of the other party, the attorney for that other party becomes a creditor of, and can seek to recover fees directly from, the promisor as a **third-party beneficiary** of the contract between the parties.

DRAFTING TIP

Another common option for conflict resolution is arbitration. The provision should state who the arbitrator will be (or how she or he will be selected) and how the related costs will be paid.

Third-party beneficiary
a person who, though not a party to a contract, benefits from performance of the contract

ARTICLE XV ARTICLE HEADINGS OF NO EFFECT

The headings at the beginning of each Article and Exhibit of this Agreement are included for convenience and reference purposes only and do not constitute terms or conditions of the Agreement.

ARTICLE XVI EXHIBITS

There are annexed hereto and incorporated by reference Exhibits A through K. Stephen and Julie agree to be bound by and to perform and carry out all of the terms contained in said Exhibits to the same extent as if each Exhibit was fully set forth in the text of this Agreement.

Exhibits A through K are enforceable and may not be discharged in any bankruptcy action brought by or against either of the parties, as they are necessary provisions for the support and maintenance of the other as a consequence of possible disparities in income, the special needs of the parties, and the allocation of resources.

IN WITNESS WHEREOF the parties have signed, sealed, and acknowledged this Agreement in three (3) counterparts, each of which shall constitute an original.

Witnesses to Husband's Signature

_____

_____

Witnesses to Wife's Signature

_____

_____

_____
Stephen Morgan
Date:_____

_____
Juliana W. Morgan
Date:_____

DRAFTING TIP

The signature section should comply with any governing procedural requirements. For example, some states require each signature to be witnessed by two disinterested parties. Others require counsel to sign the agreement as well as the client. The names used by the parties should conform to the names used in the underlying action for divorce or legal separation.

(Continued)

EXHIBIT 12.2 (*Continued*)

CERTIFICATION

STATE

COUNTY_____

On this _____ day of January 2012, personally appeared JULIANA W. MORGAN, known to me to be the person whose name is subscribed to the within instrument and acknowledged that she executed the same for the purposes therein set forth, as her own free act and deed, before me.

    IN WITNESS WHEREOF, I hereunto set my hand and official seal.

                                                 _____

                                               Notary/Justice of the Peace
                                               (Seal)

STATE

COUNTY_____

On this _____ day of January 2012, personally appeared STEPHEN MORGAN, known to me to be the person whose name is subscribed to the within instrument and acknowledged that he executed the same for the purposes therein set forth, as his own free act and deed, before me.

    IN WITNESS WHEREOF, I hereunto set my hand and official seal.

                                                 _____

                                               Notary/Justice of the Peace
                                               (Seal)

EXHIBIT A

ALIMONY

A.1 Each party currently receives income and incurs expenses at a level consistent with the financial statements filed at the time of the final hearing on this matter, which statements are incorporated herein.

A.2 Each party is able to provide for his or her own needs without any support or contribution from the other party.

A.3 Julie waives any and all right to alimony, past, present, and future from Stephen.

A.4 Stephen waives any and all right to alimony, past, present, and future from Julie.

A.5 Each party understands that this waiver of alimony can be forever binding and intends that his/her waiver be so binding on him/her even if the circumstances of either party change with the passage of time.

DRAFTING TIP

Depending on the jurisdiction, alimony may be referred to as spousal support, separate maintenance, or by some other designation.

DRAFTING TIP

Because of the parties' limited resources and the fact that each of them is presently employed and able to be self-supporting if necessary, Stephen and Julie have chosen to permanently waive alimony. Assuming they remain healthy and employed, this may not present a problem, but what if one of them should hit the lottery and

(*Continued*)

EXHIBIT 12.2 *(Continued)*

the other become indigent? Some courts do not look favorably on permanent waivers even if they are "voluntary, knowing, and intelligent." Counsel must make every effort to ensure that the parties understand the potential consequences of such waivers and, in the alternative, that ultimately they may be unenforceable under certain conditions (extreme hardship, debilitating illness, the likelihood of one of the parties becoming a public charge, etc.).

DRAFTING TIP

For a discussion of terms commonly included in alimony provisions in separation agreements when a party will be granted alimony, see Chapter 10.

DRAFTING TIP

In some situations, the parties may agree to a flexible approach to alimony payments. For example, if the obligor's sole income is from an ice cream stand he owns and operates twelve hours a day from April 1 through October 1 each year, the parties may agree that alimony will be paid only during that six-month period when there is a steady flow of income.

DRAFTING TIP

Some jurisdictions hold that if alimony is not awarded in the final decree, it cannot be sought at a later date. In such circumstances, the parties may agree to a nominal alimony award of $1.00 simply to preserve their options.

DRAFTING TIP

Largely depending on the jurisdiction, an alimony provision may designate the type of alimony to be paid (rehabilitative, permanent, restitution, etc.).

EXHIBIT B

CHILD CUSTODY AND VISITATION

B.1   Stephen and Julie shall have joint legal custody of the children. Julie shall have physical custody of the children. The parents agree that it is of paramount importance for each of them to remain involved in the major parental decisions and guidance of the children, for the children to feel deep affection for each parent, and for each parent to foster and nurture in the children respect and affection for the other parent, to the end that each parent's relationship with the children will remain as close as possible. Accordingly, each parent agrees to keep the other well and promptly informed of the academic, physical, emotional, and social status and activities of each child. Each parent may, without further permission of the other, review all school, medical, dental, and other reports or written

(Continued)

EXHIBIT 12.2 (*Continued*)

communications concerning the welfare of the children, and consult with individuals providing medical, psychological, dental, educational, or other services for the children. Each may give authorization for provision of emergency services for the children. Each also may exercise sole authority and responsibility for decisions concerning the daily living needs and activities of a child while in his or her physical custody.

B.2 The parties shall consult on significant issues concerning the welfare of each child, including, but not limited to, medical, mental health, and dental treatment; religious education; educational choices and alternatives; social and recreational activities, including participation in any inherently dangerous or unusual activities; and the time spent with each of the parties. The parties agree that in all such matters, the interests and the desires of the children shall be determined and given primary consideration.

B.3 Stephen's visitation rights shall remain open and liberal at all reasonable times and places as agreed between the parties, subject to reasonable advance notice to Julie and the school schedule and activities of the children. However, in the event that the parties are unable to agree as to reasonable visitation rights, the following schedule will define minimum visitation rights.

 a. Stephen will pick up the children at Julie's residence at 6:00 p.m. on the second and fourth Fridays of each month (unless otherwise agreed) for the weekend, and will return them on Sunday afternoon at 4:00 p.m.

 b. On each Wednesday evening, Stephen will pick up the children at Julie's residence at 5:30 p.m. and return them at 8:30 p.m.

 c. The parties agree to alternate the major holidays such that if the children spend Christmas Day of 2012 with one parent, they will spend Christmas Day of 2013 with the other parent and so on. This provision will affect the following holidays:
 Christmas Eve
 Christmas Day
 Thanksgiving
 Easter
 Independence Day
 Halloween

 d. In 2012, the children will be with Julie on Easter, Thanksgiving Day and Christmas Eve 5 p.m. to 9 a.m. Christmas morning and with Stephen on Independence Day, Halloween and Christmas Day from 9:00 a.m. to 9:00 p.m. In 2013, they will be with Julie on Independence Day, Halloween, and Christmas Day and with Stephen on Easter, Thanksgiving, and Christmas Eve from 5:00 p.m. to 9:00 a.m. Christmas morning.

 e. The children will spend Father's Day with Stephen and Mother's Day with Julie (from 10:00 a.m. to 8:00 p.m. if there is a conflict with another visitation provision). Stephen and Julie will make arrangements such that the children are able to spend some portion of each parent's birthday with that parent.

 f. Stephen and Julie agree that they each should be able to spend time with them on the children's birthdays. They agree that each child should have a single birthday party at which both parents will be present. The parent who has physical custody of the child on the day of the birthday will be responsible for planning and paying for the costs of the party.

 g. The children shall spend a total of four weeks with Stephen during the summer months (July and August) in two uninterrupted two-week periods in addition to the full week of the February school vacation.

 h. Unless otherwise agreed, Stephen will be responsible for any transportation of the children necessary to implement the visitation provisions of this Agreement.

B.4 During any period when a child is in the physical custody of the other parent, the absent parent shall have the right to communicate with the child by telephone and/or electronic

(Continued)

EXHIBIT 12.2 (*Continued*)

     means at all reasonable times. The parties agree that they will not use the children as the means of communicating with each other and that they will communicate directly.

B.5   Stephen and Julie acknowledge that at some future time, either or both of them may marry again. Until that time, when the children are present, neither parent will entertain overnight guests with whom he or she has an intimate sexual relationship.

B.6   In the event of any serious illness of a child, the parent with whom the child is then staying shall immediately notify the other parent and, under such circumstances, shall permit the other party to visit the sick child upon reasonable notice and request.

B.7   Neither party shall permanently remove the children from the state or change the children's principal residence more than twenty-five miles from the children's current residence in *location* without obtaining prior written consent of the other party, or, if said consent is denied, the permission of the *name of court* pursuant to applicable state law.

B.8   Both parties shall have the right to take trips with the children, including the right to take the children out-of-state for trips and vacations that are temporary in nature, but shall notify the other parent in advance of such trips and vacations. This provision shall include the making of a "safe call" after arrival at the destination, advising the other parent of the arrival, where the children will be staying, and how the other parent may reach the children by telephone or other means.

B.9   The parties agree that it is important for the children to maintain an ongoing relationship with each of their extended families, including, among others, grandparents, aunts, uncles, and cousins, and each will seek to foster and support those relationships.

B.10 The parties acknowledge that there will be occasions when something occurs that may require an adjustment in the visitation schedule, such as illness, a school trip, or a major work-related commitment. When such situations arise, Stephen and Julie agree to make every effort to accommodate them and ensure that Stephen does not experience any loss in overall visitation time.

DRAFTING TIP

The agreement should use the appropriate terminology pertaining to custody in the jurisdiction, for example, primary/secondary parent, custodial/noncustodial parent, or residential/nonresidential parent. Many states require that a primary caretaker be designated.

DRAFTING TIP

Any agreement made by the parties concerning child custody remains subject to the continuing jurisdiction of the court and is modifiable based upon a change in circumstances and what will serve the best interests of the child.

DRAFTING TIP

Although the courts cannot realistically enforce parental cooperation clauses, they may penalize a parent who actively seeks to alienate a child from the other parent or who obstructs the other parent's custodial or visitation privileges. Some states, such as Tennessee, require that Marital Dissolution Agreements and Parenting Plans include a list of the statutorily guaranteed rights of noncustodial parents.

(*Continued*)

EXHIBIT 12.2 *(Continued)*

DRAFTING TIP

The nature of a custody and visitation provision depends heavily on the extent to which the parties are able to communicate with each other. The provisions in this particular agreement are quite specific, in an effort to minimize questions and misunderstandings between parties who have a history of conflict on child-related issues.

DRAFTING TIP

When the parties have been separated for an extended period and communicate effectively with each other, they may already have in place an acceptable custody and visitation plan. In such situations, the Custody and Visitation Exhibit may simply state that the noncustodial parent shall have reasonable visitation with the child at all times mutually agreed upon by the parties.

DRAFTING TIP

The right to access medical and school records in B.1, etc., may be restricted if an abuse order is in effect or to otherwise protect a parent or the children.

DRAFTING TIP

This sample agreement involves a situation in which the parties reside within ten miles of each other. Significant variations necessarily occur when parents reside at a considerable geographical distance. Although the noncustodial parent may have as much visitation in real time as he or she would have if the parents lived in close proximity, it is likely to occur in large blocks of time. In such situations, provisions may also address telephone access, virtual visitation, and transportation costs, if not already factored into child support.

EXHIBIT C

CHILD SUPPORT

C.1 Commencing the first month after execution of this Agreement and continuing each month thereafter until the children are emancipated, as hereinafter defined, Stephen will pay $_____ per week to Julie as child support, said amount being consistent with the state's child support guidelines. The payment should be sent or delivered so that it is received by Julie no later than the first day of each month.

C.2 Currently, the child support obligation is based on the parties having two children who are not emancipated. The parties agree that, when either child becomes emancipated, as defined below, the amount of child support Stephen pays will be adjusted accordingly without need for intervention from the *name of court*. The adjusted Child Support obligation shall be consistent with the amount for the remaining one minor child under the state's Child Support Guidelines in effect at the time of the first child's emancipation.

(Continued)

EXHIBIT 12.2 *(Continued)*

C.3 Emancipation with respect to each minor child shall occur on the earliest to happen of the following:

    a. At age eighteen (18) or graduation from high school, but not later than at age 20, whichever occurs later, unless the child is pursuing postsecondary schooling as a full-time student as defined in b) below.

    b. At age twenty-three (23), if a child is attending an accredited postsecondary educational training school or a two-year or four-year college program as a full-time student, such schooling has not been completed, and the child is still a dependent of the parents;

    c. At the completion of schooling as it is defined in b) above;

    d. Death or marriage of the child;

    e. Permanent residency away from the custodial parent's home. (Residency at boarding school, camp, or college is not to be deemed a permanent residence away from the custodial parent's home if the child is engaged in activities pursuant to a) and b) above);

    f. Engaging in full-time employment, including the military, after the age of eighteen (18), except that full-time employment during vacation and summer periods shall not be deemed emancipation. Such emancipation shall be deemed to terminate upon cessation by the child for any reason of full-time employment, including the military, provided the child thereafter becomes engaged in activities pursuant to a) or b) above, or other applicable provisions of this paragraph.

C.4 Any payment of support as required by this Agreement may be made in cash or by check or money order payable to Julie. Child support shall not be paid by wage assignment, except as may hereafter be required by a court of competent jurisdiction or any applicable federal or state statute, rule, or regulation, or in the event that Stephen breaches this provision of the Agreement. If Stephen falls behind in child support payments by three or more months, Julie will utilize the services of the state's IV-D agency to secure payment of past-due and future payments.

C.5 Upon request of either party, before February 15 in any year in which Stephen is obligated to pay child support, the parties agree to exchange W-2 forms. Either party may seek a change in the amount of the child support obligation upon a material change in circumstances.

C.6 The parties agree that they will consult with each other regarding extracurricular activities and agree to share equally the mutually agreed-upon expenses of said activities for the children, which shall include but not be limited to music and dance lessons, sports and sports-related equipment and clothing, and summer camp.

C.7 The parties agree that their children should receive the best education available to them, including education at the college level. They further agree that choices of educational institutions for the children shall be made on the basis of joint consultation with due regard for the parties' financial circumstances and the children's aptitudes and interests. It shall be the children's and the custodial parent's obligation to consult with the other parent and come to an agreement regarding reasonable and affordable postsecondary schooling for the children. To the extent that they are then financially able to do so, the parties shall contribute equally to the net expenses of postsecondary education for their children who are not emancipated to the extent that educational expenses are not otherwise covered by scholarships, grants, loans, and the children's savings and earnings. For purposes of this Exhibit, the term "expenses" shall include application fees and related before-college expenses, tuition, board, room, books, uniforms (if required), basic computer equipment, usual and normal student activity fees and other expenses normally charged on college or university bills, and a reasonable allowance for transportation to and from such institution. The parties agree to cooperate with each other in applying for financial aid. However, it shall be the children's obligation to pursue scholarships, grants, loans, and other financial aid, as well as to contribute earnings from summer jobs and other part-time employment. The parents' obligation shall extend only to those costs not

(Continued)

EXHIBIT 12.2 *(Continued)*

> covered by the foregoing and shall be capped at the tuition level of the highest-cost in-state public university. The obligation to contribute to schooling shall terminate upon a child's emancipation.
>
> C.8   The parties hereby agree that all payments designated for the support and maintenance of the minor children under the terms of this Agreement are exclusively for child support and maintenance, and further agree that such payments shall be excludable from Julie's gross income and nondeductible by Stephen subject to the law governing such deductions on any future federal or state income tax returns.
>
> C.9   The parties agree that for the tax year beginning on January 1, 2012, and as to any tax year thereafter, Julie shall be entitled to claim the dependency exemption for Robert, and Stephen shall be entitled to claim the exemption for Jennifer, subject to applicable federal and state laws. When Robert becomes emancipated, the parties will claim the exemption for Jennifer in alternate years with Julie taking the exemption in the first tax year. Julie agrees to execute any tax forms necessary to enable Stephen to claim an exemption under the terms of this Agreement.
>
> C.10   Stephen's obligation to make payments for the support and maintenance of the minor children under this section of the Agreement is an obligation in the nature of support as defined under the relevant provisions of the United States Bankruptcy Code, as amended, and the said obligation shall not be dischargeable in bankruptcy. In the event that any arrearages for support due to Julie under this Exhibit, or any obligation to make future payments due under the Agreement, shall be discharged in bankruptcy, Julie shall have the unrestricted right to seek appropriate relief in any court of competent jurisdiction to obtain further orders of support.

DRAFTING TIP

Because of the circumstances and conflict between the parties in this case, this is an extensive and detailed child support provision.

DRAFTING TIP

Although it is not necessarily stated in an agreement, clients paying child or spousal support are usually advised to make all payments by check or money order (NOT in cash) so that their payments are documented.

DRAFTING TIP

Child support provisions remain subject to the continuing jurisdiction of the court. Modifications are governed by state law. If permitted in the jurisdiction, some parties build an annual review process into the agreement. Even if the parties agree to a change, child support is an order of the court, and any changes should be approved by the court to avoid a later contempt claim.

DRAFTING TIP

Occasionally, child support and alimony/spousal support payments are lumped together ("unallocated"). To minimize potential tax problems, it is often better to differentiate between them. For tax purposes, alimony is deductible to the payor and income to the recipient, and child support is neither.

(Continued)

EXHIBIT 12.2 *(Continued)*

DRAFTING TIP

Many agreements provide that the obligor will maintain a life insurance policy in a set amount for the benefit of the minor children. It is designed to guarantee an income source for the children in case the parent with the child support obligation should die prematurely. Another option is to establish a trust fund as in Exhibit H of this agreement.

DRAFTING TIP

Courts in several states will no longer order a parent to pay a child's college expenses. This particular agreement reflects the law in Massachusetts (as of 2011), a state that still strongly supports a parental duty to provide the costs of a child's basic college expenses, up to the age of twenty-three under some circumstances. Although the agreement references educational contributions by the children, it does not bind them to those obligations because they are not parties to the agreement.

DRAFTING TIP

If the minor children are enrolled in private school, related expenses should be addressed in the agreement.

DRAFTING TIP

In some states, childcare costs are factored into the child support formula. If not, they should be addressed in the agreement.

PARALEGAL PRACTICE TIP

In *Milark v. Meigher,* 17 A.D.3d 844, 793 N.Y.S.2d 581 (2005), the parties' agreement provided that "the parties shall equally divide all primary and secondary school tuition, the cost of all school supplies, all mutually acceptable extracurricular activities,. . ." At the time the agreement was executed, the children were enrolled in private school. After two years, the wife failed to pay her share of the private school tuition, claiming unsuccessfully, among other things, that she should not be compelled to pay private school tuition when the community makes available a public school. The court reasoned that if private school were not contemplated, the agreement would not have referred to "tuition." This case can be accessed at *www. pearsonhighered.com/wilson* in the companion website material related to Chapter 12 under "Cases" and in the Case Resources Section of the MyLegalStudiesLab.

EXHIBIT D

DIVISION OF PERSONAL PROPERTY

D.1 Except as otherwise specifically provided in this Agreement, Stephen and Julie have already divided their personal property. Each agrees that from now on each shall continue to possess, own, have, and enjoy independently of any claim of right of the other, all of his or her personal property of every kind, nature, and description with full power to dispose of the same as fully and with such effect in all respects and for all purposes as though he or she were unmarried.

D.2 Julie specifically waives any right, title, interest, or claim she may have to the proceeds, if any, of a settlement or judgment obtained by Stephen in connection with a pending personal injury action filed by him relating to a motorcycle accident on January 1, 2009, in which he received extensive injuries.

D.3 The parties agree that all of the personal property (books, records, tools, etc.) currently stored in the shed in the yard at the marital home located at *location* presently belongs to Stephen. With reasonable notice to Julie, he will remove the property within thirty (30) days of the execution of this Agreement. If not removed within thirty (30) days, the property will belong to Julie, who will be free to keep, sell, or destroy it as she sees fit.

D.4 Each party shall deliver to the other all property or documents evidencing ownership of property that, by the terms of the Agreement, is to remain or become the property of the other. All property acquired from now on by either Stephen or Julie and all income and

(Continued)

EXHIBIT 12.2 *(Continued)*

earnings of each party shall constitute and be the sole and separate property of the person by whom the said property is acquired or earned.

D.5 Each party shall retain as his or her sole property free of any claim of right of the other the vehicle in his (the Dodge truck) or her (the Toyota Camry) possession and shall be solely obligated for payment of any expenses incurred for use, operation, maintenance, and financing thereof. Each shall indemnify and hold the other harmless from any liens or debts in connection with the vehicle he or she is retaining.

DRAFTING TIP

Depending on the nature and extent of the parties' personal property, the various items assigned to each party may be listed to avoid confusion (e.g., husband receives his Roth IRA account *identifying information*; the joint savings account at First Third Bank, account # *number*; his General Electric pension *identifying information*; and his baseball card collection. Wife receives her 401(k) account *identifying information*; her pension *identifying information*, her china collection, her jewelry, bank CD *identifying information*, and three checking accounts: bank account # *number*, bank account # *number*, and bank account # *number)*. When the assets are specified in such a manner, it makes it more difficult for a party to claim later that a particular asset on the list was not disclosed and distributed at the time of divorce.

DRAFTING TIP

Ideally, the parties should divide their personal property prior to executing the agreement in order to avoid problems post divorce. Paragraph D.3 gives the husband the opportunity to collect his possessions that are still stored on the marital property where the wife now resides. However, by establishing a reasonable time frame, it does not grant him an unlimited opportunity to do so. If the property remaining to change hands is not all conveniently located in one place (the shed, in this instance), the items should be specifically listed, if possible, to avoid disputes and misunderstandings. In extremely high-conflict cases in which a restraining order is in force, the agreement may set a particular time for the pickup and require that a police officer be present.

DRAFTING TIP

The personal property of most divorcing couples is of modest value. However, parties in some divorce actions own substantial assets such as business interests; valuable antiques and artworks; stock portfolios; rights to receive funds in the future, such as royalties on works created during the marriage or contingent fees for work performed during the marriage. To avoid confusion and subsequent litigation, these assets should be specifically addressed in the agreement. A schedule reflecting the division of property also may be appended to the agreement.

EXHIBIT E

REAL ESTATE

E.1 Stephen and Julie own real property, the marital home, located at *location*, as tenants by the entirety, having taken title by deed dated May 18, 1999, recorded in the *name of county* Registry of Deeds in Book 7539, page 031. The property is encumbered by two

(Continued)

EXHIBIT 12.2 (*Continued*)

mortgages on which Stephen and Julie are co-signors and co-mortgagors, dated May 18, 1999, and June 13, 2006, both to Berger Mortgage, Inc., and each secured by the marital home. The first is a purchase money mortgage with a remaining principal balance of $124,000 and recorded at the above-referenced Registry in Book 7539, page 045. The second mortgage was obtained in order to pay jointly incurred marital debt of the parties. It is in the principal amount of $21,900 and is recorded in Book 9887, page 331.

E.2   The parties agree that Julie shall have exclusive possession, use, and control of the marital home effective upon the execution of this Agreement.

E.3   Within ninety (90) days of execution of this Agreement, Stephen shall convey his interest in the above property to Julie by quitclaim deed.

E.4   Julie agrees that within ninety (90) days of execution of this Agreement, she shall obtain financing sufficient to:

a. pay off both of the outstanding mortgages referenced in E.1 above; and

b. pay Stephen the sum of thirty thousand dollars ($30,000) for his equity interest in the marital home, which the parties agree is currently valued at $270,000 based on the appraisal completed by Marjorie Anderson, a mutually agreed-upon licensed appraiser.

E.5   Julie further agrees that from the time of her receipt of the deed from Stephen, she shall indemnify and hold him harmless from any responsibility for all sums due, and that may become due in the future, on the two outstanding mortgages.

E.6   Both Stephen and Julie understand that Sections 1041(a) and (b) of the U.S. Internal Revenue Code of 1980, as amended, are applicable to the conveyance and transfer described in E.3 above; that no gain or loss will be recognized by Stephen upon his conveyance or transfer of any property interest to Julie; and that Julie will have a carryover basis in said property and receive Stephen's interest at his adjusted cost basis. Each party will provide the other with any and all documentation in his or her possession and control establishing the cost basis of the property.

DRAFTING TIP

In this case, the wife was able (with assistance from a "friend") to buy out the other party's interest in the property. If resources had been more limited and the marital home was the only major asset, the agreement may have provided that the custodial parent continue to remain in the home with the parties' children until the youngest reached the age of emancipation. At that time, the house would be sold, with the parent in residence having a "right of first refusal" to buy the home at fair market value. The net proceeds then would be divided between the parties in agreed-upon percentages.

DRAFTING TIP

All kinds of "real property" should be covered in the agreement including residences, vacation homes, business properties, leases, time-shares, contracts to purchase or sell property that may impact the nature and extent of the marital estate, etc.

DRAFTING TIP

Part of this provision spells out the tax consequences of the transfer so that the party receiving the property cannot later claim she was unaware of a related capital gains tax possibly being due.

(*Continued*)

EXHIBIT 12.2 *(Continued)*

EXHIBIT F

JOINT AND SEVERAL DEBTS

F.1   Stephen and Julie have four (4) jointly held credit card accounts on which they are co-signors with balances that remain outstanding. Each party acknowledges that they are equally responsible for incurring this debt and that the balances owed constitute joint marital debt. The following is a complete list of the joint credit card accounts that remain outstanding, in the amounts owed at the time of execution of this Agreement:

Creditor	Indebtedness
a) MBNA America	$21,000.
b) Citizens	$22,300.
c) AT&T Universal	$ 7,500.
d) Discover Card	$ 2,350.
	$53,150.

F.2   Julie agrees that from the date of this Agreement forward, she will hold Stephen harmless for these four debts and she will indemnify Stephen for all sums remaining to be paid on these four unsecured credit card accounts.

F.3   Julie agrees that she shall assume the indebtedness for all four of the above jointly held credit cards and that, as soon as practicable after the execution of this Agreement, she will obtain sufficient financing to pay off the remaining balances on all four cards and close the accounts. Julie has agreed to these terms because in January of 2008, Stephen liquidated his entire retirement annuity from his employer in order to pay off part of the joint marital debt the parties had incurred. At that time, Julie had a retirement account through her employer that was approximately equal in value to Stephen's. Julie did not then, and has not since, withdrawn any of her retirement funds—her account remains entirely intact and has since grown in value and become vested due to her years of service. The parties acknowledge that they jointly agreed that Stephen's retirement annuity should be used to pay down the joint marital debt and that Julie could have contributed one-half of that amount from her own funds but did not do so per their agreement. Julie's assumption of the remaining credit card debt will fairly compensate Stephen for liquidating his retirement savings in 2008. Assumption of the debt by Julie will allow Stephen to make a fresh start and continue to prepare for his future retirement needs.

F.4   Neither Stephen nor Julie may hereafter incur any debts or obligations on the credit of the other, and shall indemnify and hold the other harmless from any such debt or obligation incurred.

F.5   Except as provided in paragraph F.1 above, and as may be otherwise provided herein, and as set forth on each party's Financial Statement filed at the time of the final hearing on this matter, each of the parties represents to the other that he or she knows of no other debts for which the other may be liable, and each shall be responsible for and hold the other harmless for any liability incurred as a result of the breaching party's nondisclosure. If either party violates this Agreement and the other party becomes obligated to make payment to any third party as a result of such breach, then the nonbreaching party shall have the right to be indemnified by the breaching party and the breaching party shall pay all of the nonbreaching party's costs and attorneys' fees in connection therewith.

F.6   Except as provided in paragraph F.1 of this Exhibit and as may be otherwise provided herein, Stephen shall be solely responsible for and indemnify Julie for all of the debts set forth on his financial statement filed with the Court at the time of the final hearing on this matter.

F.7   Except as provided in paragraph F.1 of this Exhibit and as may be otherwise provided herein, Julie shall be solely responsible for and indemnify Stephen for all of the debts set forth on her financial statement filed with the Court at the time of the final hearing on this matter.

(Continued)

EXHIBIT 12.2 (*Continued*)

> **DRAFTING TIP**
>
> The heading of this section may vary, but whatever it is called, it addresses liabilities of the parties.

> **DRAFTING TIP**
>
> It is important to include **"hold harmless" provisions** in this Exhibit. (See F.4, F.5, F.6, and F.7.)

> **DRAFTING TIP**
>
> Paragraph F.3 is somewhat unusual. However, in this case, the judge specifically required that the agreement address the rationale for why the wife was assuming a seemingly disproportionate percentage of the marital debt.

EXHIBIT G

MEDICAL INSURANCE AND UNINSURED MEDICAL EXPENSE

G.1 For the benefit of the children, Julie shall maintain in full force and effect her current health insurance coverage, or its equivalent, as long as it is available through her employer, and as long as each child is not emancipated as that term is defined herein.

G.2 For the benefit of Stephen, Julie shall maintain in full force and effect her current health insurance coverage, or its equivalent, as long as it is available through her employer, and as long as the cost or premium is not in excess of that which Julie is required to pay to maintain such coverage for herself and the children who are not emancipated.

G.3 Stephen agrees that maintaining health insurance coverage for the children is a duty that he bears equally with Julie. Therefore, as long as Julie maintains family health insurance coverage through her own employer for the benefit of the children, or for the benefit of both Stephen and the children, Stephen agrees that if not otherwise addressed in the governing Child Support Guidelines, he shall pay Julie a sum equal to one-half the difference between what Julie would pay for individual health insurance coverage and what she must pay for family health insurance coverage. Upon Stephen's request, Julie shall provide him with evidence of the cost of the premiums for coverage.

G.4 In the event that Julie remarries and thereby affects Stephen's eligibility for continued coverage, or in the event that Stephen can no longer be covered by Julie on her plan without additional cost to her, Stephen shall have the right, pursuant to state and other applicable law, to continue to receive benefits as are available to Julie by any means then existing, including by rider to the existing policy or conversion to an individual policy. If Stephen elects to continue such coverage, Julie shall cooperate with him in making the necessary arrangements for, and shall execute any documents necessary to effectuate, the continuation of said coverage. If such coverage results in an additional cost or premium to Julie and Stephen elects to continue such coverage, then Stephen shall pay to Julie the additional cost or premium incurred as a result of his election as such payment comes due. In addition to any obligation imposed by applicable law upon the insurer to notify Stephen of cancellation of coverage, Julie shall forthwith notify Stephen as soon as she becomes aware of any circumstance that would affect his eligibility for, the availability of, or the nature of his continued health insurance coverage.

G.5 Each party shall be responsible for payment of his or her own uninsured medical, dental, psychiatric, prescription, hospital, and other expenses of a medical nature.

(*Continued*)

Hold harmless provision
a provision specifying that a particular spouse will be solely responsible for payment of certain debts and that the other spouse shall be free and clear of any obligation regarding those debts and will be indemnified by the debtor spouse if forced to pay the debt

PARALEGAL PRACTICE TIP

Care must be taken throughout the agreement to be sure there is a "meeting of the minds" and that the document clearly says what is mutually intended. For example, in *In re Marriage of Wassom,* 352 Ill. App. 3d 327, 815 N.E.2d 1251 (2004), the parties divorced in 1997 and they had one son. They executed a marital settlement agreement that was incorporated in the judgment. Article III of that agreement titled "Support of Children and Related Matters" provided in part:

> WIFE will carry the child on her health insurance, and the parties will equally divide any uncovered medical, dental, or orthodontic expenses on a 50/50 basis. . . . In addition to child support in Article III, paragraph 1, the HUSBAND will reimburse the WIFE for 50 percent of the health insurance premiums currently being paid by the WIFE.

The husband claimed he should only be responsible for 50% of the health insurance premiums paid for the child and not for those paid for the former wife's benefit. The court agreed with the wife, given the language of the agreement. The opinion in this case can be accessed at *www.pearsonhighered.com/wilson* in the companion website material related to Chapter 12 under "Cases" and in the Case Resources Section of the MyLegalStudiesLab.

EXHIBIT 12.2 *(Continued)*

G.6 The parties shall share equally the payment of the reasonable and necessary uninsured medical and dental expenses of the minor children. Each party shall consult with the other in advance about any need for uninsured medical expenses of the children beyond a total of $500 per year, per child, and shall obtain the other party's prior consent for any such expenditure, which consent shall not be unreasonably withheld.

G.7 In the event that individual or family insurance coverage is no longer available through Julie's current employer or that she is no longer eligible, insurance coverage for the children will be secured through Stephen's employer or Julie's subsequent employer as mutually agreed upon by the parties. If said insurance incurs a cost, the cost will be borne equally by the parties.

DRAFTING TIP

This Exhibit should cover medical insurance for both the parties and the children and should address insured and uninsured expenses. If a parent and/or child has any extraordinary medical needs, these should be considered (e.g., physical therapy, counseling, home care, etc.). In circumstances in which the parties are unemployed and have few assets, consistent with governing federal and state law, the parties may go without medical insurance or apply for government benefits.

DRAFTING TIP

The courts tend to be especially interested in this provision, particularly as applied to any minor children. In some states, including Massachusetts, the cost of medical insurance for the children now is factored into the child support formula.

EXHIBIT H

LIFE INSURANCE

H.1 Stephen shall maintain a total of $250,000 of term insurance on his life ($125,000 for the benefit of each of the minor children). Stephen shall maintain said insurance for the benefit of each child until such time as that child becomes emancipated and Stephen is no longer obligated to pay child support for the benefit of that child.

H.2 At Stephen's option, the life insurance provided for the benefit of the minor children in paragraph H.1 above shall be held in trust by a trustee of his choosing selected by him in a form of trust to be approved by Julie, whose approval shall not be unreasonably withheld.

H.3 Stephen will, from time to time, and as requested by Julie, furnish her with satisfactory evidence that said insurance policies are in full force and effect.

H.4 Except as otherwise provided in H.1 and H.2 above, after execution of the Agreement, Julie and Stephen shall each have the right to make any changes in his or her respective insurance policies including, but not limited to, changing his or her beneficiaries, increasing or decreasing coverage, or canceling such policies.

DRAFTING TIP

This provision is designed to guarantee an income stream for the benefit of the minor children and often appears in the Exhibit pertaining to child support. The designation of the children as beneficiaries should be irrevocable as long as the child support obligation continues.

(Continued)

EXHIBIT 12.2 *(Continued)*

> ### DRAFTING TIP
>
> The parties often have several kinds of insurance in addition to life insurance, such as health, homeowners', automobile, and liability in connection with a business or professional practice, that may be covered in one Exhibit or separately.

EXHIBIT I

RETIREMENT ACCOUNTS

Except as otherwise herein provided, from the date of this Agreement forward, all 401(k), IRA, and other retirement-type accounts and state and federal retirement plans standing individually in a party's own name shall be retained by that party as his or her sole property free of any claim of any right of the other, with full power in that party to dispose of the same as fully and with such effect in all respects and for all purposes as though he or she were unmarried. However, either party may voluntarily name or retain the other as a beneficiary, or as trustee of said funds for the benefit of the parties' children.

EXHIBIT J

BANKRUPTCY FILING

J.1 In the event that either party to this Agreement decides to petition for bankruptcy under the provisions of the United States Code, that party must notify the other of his or her intention to file such a petition. Such notice shall be in writing and shall be given to the other party at least ninety (90) days prior to the filing of such petition. The notice shall be given by certified first-class mail, return receipt requested. The notice must include, but is not limited to, the name, address, and telephone number of the attorney, if any, who has been retained to represent the petitioning party in the bankruptcy action and must identify the court in which the petition will be filed. The receipt of such notice shall not in any way limit, restrict, or prevent the right of the party receiving notice from seeking any appropriate remedy or relief available to him or her under existing law or this Agreement prior to the filing of the petition in bankruptcy, nor shall the receipt of such notice limit, restrict, or prevent the party receiving the notice from asserting any claim available to him or her under law after such petition has been filed.

J.2 In the event that a party to this Agreement petitions for bankruptcy under the United States Code, that party shall be liable for attorneys' fees incurred by the other party in protecting his or her rights under this Agreement to the extent that they are incurred as a consequence of the filing.

> ### DRAFTING TIP
>
> This is not a common provision in most agreements, but in this case, one of the spouses was seriously considering filing for bankruptcy.

> ### DRAFTING TIP
>
> Although bankruptcy court rulings will ultimately control in the event that a bankruptcy action is subsequently filed, an effort should be made to protect as many of the obligations created under this agreement as possible by designating them as being in the nature of "support" and thus generally not dischargeable in bankruptcy.

(Continued)

EXHIBIT 12.2 (Continued)

EXHIBIT K

TAXES

K.1 Stephen and Julie agree that they will file a joint tax return for the 2011 tax year.

K.2 Stephen and Julie hereby warrant to each other that all income taxes, local, state, and federal, on all joint returns filed by the parties have been paid, and that to their knowledge, no interest or penalties are due and owing, and no tax deficiency proceeding or audit is pending or threatened.

K.3 If there is a deficiency assessment in connection with any of the joint returns, the party receiving notice of such deficiency shall notify the other party immediately in writing. The party responsible for the act or omission that caused the deficiency assessment shall be solely liable for any deficiency assessment, penalty, and interest, and shall hold the other harmless against any loss or liability in connection therewith. In the event that neither party is responsible for the act or omission that caused the deficiency assessment, then the parties shall pay the assessment in proportion to their income in the tax year for which the assessment is due.

K.4 In the event that there is a refund, the parties shall divide the amount of the refund equally.

The Court's Role

The courts encourage the parties to resolve their differences and negotiate agreements whenever possible. However, this does not mean that courts play no role. In fact, the courts play a variety of roles with respect to separation agreements. The most common are the following:

- Reviewing the agreement at the time of the final hearing or trial for possible incorporation into the decree
- Modifying the agreement
- Enforcing the agreement
- Vacating/setting aside the agreement

REVIEW OF THE AGREEMENT AT THE TIME OF TRIAL OR FINAL HEARING

Merger
the process by which a separation agreement is incorporated in a divorce judgment and does not survive but rather loses its identity as a separate and independent contract

Independent legal significance
a contract that is legally binding in its own right

Surviving agreement
an agreement of the parties incorporated in a court's divorce decree that also retains its existence as an independent contract enforceable under basic principles of contract law

When a complete or partial separation agreement is presented for approval, the court generally exercises one of three options (the first two at the choice of the parties):

- It may incorporate and **merge** the terms of the agreement into the decree; or
- It may incorporate the terms of the agreement into the decree, including the provision that it will not merge but rather survive as a separate contract with **independent legal significance** (thereby making it a **surviving agreement**); or
- It may reject the agreement in whole or in part because it violates the law or a strong public policy. In contrast to negotiation of a commercial contract, the parties' freedom to contract the terms of the dissolution of their marriage is not unlimited.

In an uncontested case, neither spouse objects to the granting of the divorce, and the parties execute a mutually agreed-upon separation agreement. However, even in an uncontested case, the court customarily holds a brief hearing with one or both of the parties present. The judge/magistrate does not simply rubber-stamp the agreement (even if it resulted from arbitration) but rather reviews and occasionally asks questions about it. Particular attention is usually given to the conditions for payment of child support (e.g., will there be a wage assignment?); the arrangements made for continuing health insurance; the presence of waivers of alimony, if any; and whether the agreement will merge with the divorce or separation decree or survive as an independent contract. (See Exhibit 12.3.) Usually each of the parties is asked whether he or she has read, understood, and freely signed the agreement; whether each has exchanged and reviewed relevant financial information and agrees that there has been full disclosure of assets and liabilities; and whether each believes the agreement is fair.

In a contested case, if a partial agreement is submitted, the court may approve it and incorporate its terms into the divorce decree along with determinations regarding the contested issues following a trial. As in an uncontested case, the partial agreement

EXHIBIT 12.3 Distinction Between Merger and Survival as an Independent Contract

A separation agreement is a contract that is effective upon signing unless otherwise provided. If a judge eventually approves the agreement at the request of the parties, it is either incorporated and merged into the court's decree OR it is incorporated by reference in the decree but does not merge. Rather, it continues to survive and retain its independent legal significance as a contract separate and apart from the divorce decree. Often, the distinction between merger and survival is confusing for clients, but its consequences can be dramatic. Counsel needs to explain the options clearly to the client so that he or she can make an informed decision about which route to pursue. The two options are represented graphically below.

The Separation Agreement
is presented to the court
with one of the following two results:

The Agreement is incorporated and merged into the divorce decree

OR

The Agreement is incorporated into the divorce decree and also survives as an independent contract

DECREE
The decree includes the terms of the agreement that are incorporated by reference and merged into the decree, making it an order of the court. The terms are enforceable only by the family court.

DECREE
The decree includes the terms of the agreement that are incorporated by reference and made part of the decree, making it an order of the court. The decree is enforceable by the family court according to its terms and applicable law.

AND

NO INDEPENDENT CONTRACT/AGREEMENT
The agreement has merged into the decree and no longer exists as an independent contract.

INDEPENDENT CONTRACT/AGREEMENT
The agreement continues to exist as a contract with independent legal significance separate from the decree and is enforceable as a contract in a court of equity.

may be incorporated and merged into the decree or survive as an independent contract.

It is important that the parties understand what the terms of the agreement mean and what they have agreed to. Occasionally, a judge will address a question directly to a party in a hearing. It is a poor reflection on counsel if the client is able only to stare blankly at the court or look helplessly to the attorney in response! Given that no one "wins" in a divorce and that agreements invariably reflect compromises between what a party wants and what she or he can reasonably expect to have, clients are rarely 100 percent satisfied with agreements. Given a chance to speak, inadequately prepared clients occasionally vent such dissatisfaction, to the end that a court may send the parties back to the drawing board. When helping to prepare a client for court, the paralegal must be careful to leave explanations of the legal effect of various provisions to the attorney, but the paralegal can be a source of moral support to the client.

MODIFICATION OF THE AGREEMENT

If the agreement is incorporated and merged into the divorce decree, the court retains the authority to modify it based on a substantial change in circumstances. If the agreement is incorporated but survives as an independent contract, the general rule is that it can be modified in only a limited number of circumstances:

- The agreement itself may provide for modification under certain circumstances, such as cohabitation or remarriage of one of the parties or a substantial increase or reduction in income.
- Since the court retains jurisdiction over child-related matters, provisions relating to the parties' children remain modifiable, given a substantial change in circumstances that affects the welfare of the children.
- If there has been a more-than-substantial change in circumstances such that one of the parties will become a public charge if a modification is not granted, many courts will order a modification rather than have the indigent person be supported by the taxpayers.

ENFORCEMENT OF THE AGREEMENT

PARALEGAL PRACTICE TIP

To see a "Motion to Enforce" (Maine), visit *www.courts.state.me.us.* You can find a link to this site at *www.pearsonhighered.com/wilson* in the companion website material for Chapter 12 under "Forms."

If the agreement is incorporated and merged into the divorce decree, then enforcement is pursued in the family court because the "breach" is a violation of an order of that court. The aggrieved party generally files a contempt action or a motion to enforce the judgment.

If the agreement is incorporated into the decree and also survives as an independent contract, the courts generally make every effort to enforce the terms of the agreement, unless doing so would violate the law or contravene a strong public policy. With a surviving agreement, the aggrieved party has two routes to use to obtain relief. As with a merged agreement, he or she may file a contempt action in the court that issued the decree. In addition, however, because the agreement retains its existence as an independent contract, contract remedies are also available. For example, the aggrieved party may sue for breach of contract, seeking damages or specific enforcement of a term of the agreement.

A confusing situation can develop when a family court modifies an agreement that was incorporated into its decree but also survived as an independent contract. For example, assume the parties' agreement provides that wife will pay husband $500 per month in spousal support. She does so for the first two years following the divorce but then stops paying after losing her job. She seeks and is granted a modification by the family court based on a more-than-substantial change of circumstances. The court reduces her payment to $100 a month and she resumes making payments. Since the original agreement survives, technically the husband can sue in contract to recover the $400 difference between the new amount of court-ordered alimony ($100) and the contractually agreed-on amount ($500).

The agreement may also be enforced in the context of other kinds of actions. For example, a party to a divorce who has been ordered to transfer property to a former spouse and to pay child support and alimony may try to avoid these obligations by filing for bankruptcy. The bankruptcy court will determine which of the obligations are in the nature of "support" and not **dischargeable** in bankruptcy. Agreements may also be considered in probate proceedings. For example, a spouse who has remarried may have been ordered to maintain an insurance policy for the benefit of his children but changes the beneficiary to his new wife. Upon his death, the children may seek to recover from the estate the amount they should have received from the policy.[2]

Discharge
the method by which a legal duty to pay a debt is extinguished

ACTION TO VACATE THE AGREEMENT

After the divorce is "final," a party may seek (in an appeal, new trial, or other action) to have the court vacate or set aside the judgment incorporating the agreement. For example, six months after the decree has issued, one of the parties may discover that, despite his or her best efforts to obtain full disclosure before negotiating their agreement, the other party successfully concealed a substantial asset. Had the asset been brought to light in a timely manner, the property settlement would have been significantly different. Another scenario involves the situation in which an agreement was executed under duress. For example, an abusive husband may have threatened physical harm to both his wife and their children if she did not sign an agreement granting him custody of the children and a disproportionate share of the marital assets. Several months after the divorce, when the wife feels more confident and safe from harm, she may seek a settlement that is truly fair and reasonable, including custody of the children and a greater portion of the marital assets.

PARALEGAL PRACTICE TIP

More than one kind of relief may be sought. For example, in a 2009 South Dakota case, the husband filed three alternative motions: a motion for a new trial, a motion to vacate the judgment, and a motion to enforce a personal property provision of the property settlement agreement. He contended that the parties' property settlement agreement was procedurally unfair because it was drafted by his wife's attorney, he did not read it and was not represented by counsel, and he was suffering from alcoholism, depression, and anxiety at the time he signed it. He also contended it was substantively unfair because the wife was awarded approximately 90% of the marital assets. The court rejected his arguments, finding that he had had the time and opportunity to read it and to obtain legal advice. It also opined that the division of assets was fair in light of the property the parties brought into the marriage and their conduct during the marriage. See *Vann v. Vann,* 2009 ND 118, 767 N.W.2d 855 (2009).

PARALEGAL PRACTICE TIP

Decrees issued by trial courts may be appealed to higher courts within the state and may be affirmed or set aside. In a 2009 case, for example, the Virginia Court of Appeals set aside a property settlement agreement which awarded all the marital assets with the exception of an automobile and a few personal possessions to the husband. The assets included the marital residence valued at $300,000. Although the wife acknowledged reading the agreement, she had a third-grade education and numerous health problems and claimed she didn't really understand its legal effect. She just knew if she signed it she would "be able to get a divorce." The initial decree left her on public assistance after thirty-eight years of marriage. The court found the agreement unconscionable and observed how divorce creates a situation which is "particularly susceptible to overreaching and oppression."

CHAPTER **SUMMARY**

We devote an entire chapter to the nature, purpose, modification, and enforcement of agreements in the context of divorce and separation because of their importance in bringing closure to a couple's marriage and shaping the parties' future. In a sense, this chapter brings together many of the other chapters in the text given the topics covered in agreements such as marital rights and responsibilities, child custody, child support, spousal support, and division of property both real and personal. The primary focus of the chapter is on the structure and components of agreements that must be tailored to the facts of each individual case. Attention is given to preparing paralegals for the important role they play in drafting effective separation agreements.

In today's legal climate, separation agreements are welcome. From the court's perspective, they conserve judicial resources by eliminating the need for lengthy, costly, and bitter trials. From the clients' perspective, they allow the parties to privately negotiate the terms of their separation or divorce without governmental interference. The separation agreement provides a blueprint for them to follow as their marriage terminates. A carefully drafted agreement, which the parties negotiate, review, and understand, not only allows the case to proceed on an uncontested basis, but also helps minimize post-divorce confusion, aggravation, disagreements, and litigation. It is a win-win for the parties and the judicial system.

CONCEPT REVIEW AND REINFORCEMENT

KEY TERMS

Boilerplate

Bottom line

Consideration

Discharge

Forensic

Hold harmless provision

Impounded

Incorporation by reference

Independent legal significance

Legal separation

Meeting of the minds

Merger

Parol evidence rule

Pro se

Separation agreement

Surviving agreement

Third-party beneficiary

REVIEW QUESTIONS

1. Describe what a separation agreement is and identify the purposes it serves.
2. Identify the characteristics of an effective separation agreement.
3. Describe how most separation agreements are developed and identify the role commonly played by the paralegal.
4. Define "boilerplate." Identify at least five sections of a separation agreement that generally consist of boilerplate.
5. Identify the major topics commonly addressed in separation agreements.
6. Describe the nature and purpose of a severability clause.
7. Distinguish between a separation agreement that is incorporated and merges into a divorce decree and one that is incorporated and survives as an independent contract. Explain the significance of the distinction.
8. Identify the various ways in which the courts become involved with separation agreements.

DEVELOPING YOUR PARALEGAL SKILLS

FOCUS ON THE JOB

In this activity, the student drafts a separation agreement tailored to a specific fact pattern involving a divorcing couple and their minor son.

The Facts

Anna and Herman Nicole were married on August 16, 1998, in San Diego, California. It was the first marriage for Anna and the fourth for Herman. At the time of their marriage, Anna was twenty-seven years old and Herman was eighty-two. The parties have one minor child, Theodore Carleton Nicole, born on November 16, 1999. Anna presently lives at 23 Chandler Street in Chicago, Illinois, and Herman lives at 1102 Country Club Drive in your city and state. They separated on Christmas Day 2011 after opening gifts at the Country Club Drive residence and intend to continue to live separately for the rest of their lives. On January 2 of this year, they filed jointly for a no-fault divorce because of the irreconcilable differences that have arisen between them. The action has been filed in your county in the appropriate court.

Both parties want to remain actively involved in their son's life but agree that Anna will be his primary caretaker, particularly during the school year so that there will at least be continuity in that aspect of his life. He is presently enrolled in a private school and is very active in a variety of sports. He is taking trumpet lessons and shows considerable musical talent. Herman will pay reasonable child support in an amount consistent with the state's child support guidelines (if they apply) based on an unearned income of $400,000 a year. It will be payable monthly.

The parties have exchanged financial statements but have engaged in no additional discovery. Anna earns approximately $125,000 a year as a model, and intends to continue her career. She has no retirement fund. Herman has been retired for some time but is independently wealthy. His assets are valued at approximately $5.5 million. Herman has managed all of the couple's financial affairs, and his accountant has prepared all of the joint tax returns submitted during the marriage based on the information Herman provided.

Herman was both physically and emotionally abusive to Anna during their twelve-year marriage, but she is willing to forget all that if he pays her alimony of $10,000 per month for the rest of his life and lets her have their apartment in New York City, their summer home in Newport, Rhode Island, and the condo where she is presently residing. All of the properties are owned outright by Herman. (Anna owns no real estate in her own name.) He has also agreed to split his General Electric pension with her (requiring preparation of a QDRO) and to make her the sole beneficiary of a $500,000 Prudential life insurance policy. She will receive the Rolls-Royce and he will keep his collection of vintage automobiles. For understandable reasons, Herman is willing to waive any rights to ever claim alimony and wants the alimony provisions of the agreement to be nonmodifiable by any court under any circumstances. He has no objection to paying his own debts but refuses to pay Anna's credit card debts, which have been a constant source of tension between them. (Anna is somewhat of a shopaholic.) Anna figures he will end up paying some of the debt anyway, because two of her three cards are in their joint names. The accounts are a Bank of America account numbered 1772-2356-7631-8976 (balance $7,980), a Jet Green Master charge account numbered 028-3456-93 (balance $13,569), and an American Express account numbered 1357-2468-0864 (balance $22,567).

The parties have already divided their personal property, except that Herman needs to remove from the New York and Newport properties all the works of art he has collected over the years.

Herman says he feels sort of bad about the divorce and that he may decide to provide for Anna in his will, but she is not counting on that. However, she is happy that he will pay for comprehensive medical insurance for her until his death and for Theodore until his emancipation. That is important to her because she has heavy bills for psychiatric treatment and medications. Anna figures that she is "making out like a bandit" and has chosen not to obtain legal advice because she doesn't want to waste any of the funds she is receiving on an attorney.

The Assignment

Assume that you are a paralegal in the family law firm representing Herman in this matter. Draft a separation agreement tailored to the above fact pattern. Use a format that is appropriate in the jurisdiction where you are studying family law. This may mean that, instead of an integrated separation agreement, you will be preparing a parenting plan and a marital property settlement/stipulation. You should also be sure to use the appropriate terminology in your jurisdiction for child-related and spousal support matters.

FOCUS ON **ETHICS**

In this activity, the student explores ethical issues involving billing, conflict of interest, and the unauthorized practice of law among others in the context of a specific case.

The Assignment

Edward E. Edwards III is the attorney who represents Herman in the above fact pattern. His office is located at 12 Beacon Street in your city and state. You are his paralegal. Edward is thrilled to be handling this case and has told you to prepare monthly invoices for as long as the case continues; he figures he will be able to "drag it out for a while." He tells you to keep track of your hours as well as his and to bill them all at his regular hourly rate of $250. He says he is happy to split the fee with you because you are such a good employee. You are uneasy about this—it just doesn't feel right but you really need the money. Besides, you are aware that Herman has abused all of his wives and you figure he deserves to pay. As a matter of fact, when you saw Anna at a local club recently, you told her she really ought to get a lawyer because she could probably "do better."

Discuss this situation from an ethical perspective in a one-to two-page paper. Relate your response to the ethical canons for paralegals promulgated by the National Association of Legal Assistants, which are contained in Appendix A of this text.

FOCUS ON **CASE LAW**

This activity allows the student to address questions about a case involving the enforceability of a separation agreement, particularly with respect to an alimony provision.

The Assignment

Read the opinion in *In re Marriage of McInnis*, 199 Ore. App. 223, 110 P.3 639 (2005), and then respond to the following questions.

1. Describe the legal history of the case. Where was it first brought and with what result?
2. What were the issues on appeal?
3. Was the parties' agreement approved by the trial court? Did it merge into the judgment or did it survive as an independent contract?
4. What did the agreement provide with respect to spousal support?

5. What was the basis of the trial court's decision not to enforce the agreement with respect to modification of spousal support?

6. What was the basis of the appellate court's decision to enforce the agreement with respect to modification of spousal support?

7. What remedies do the courts in Oregon provide to support the enforceability of marital agreements?

8. Do the courts in Oregon always enforce marital settlement agreements?

9. What did the appellate court decide regarding both the requested modification and the trial court's

award of attorneys' fees, and do you agree with the decision?

If needed, a format for briefing a case can be found on the companion website at in the material related to Chapter 1 under "Resources."

PARALEGAL PRACTICE TIP

The *In re Marriage of McInnis* opinion is available at *www.pearson-highered.com/wilson* in the companion website material related to Chapter 12 under "Cases" and in the Case Resources Section of the MyLegalStudiesLab.

FOCUS ON **STATE LAW AND PROCEDURE**

This activity requires students to locate and brief a case involving a separation agreement in the jurisdiction where they are studying family law.

The Assignment

Locate and brief a recent case in the state where you are studying family law regarding the enforceability of separation agreements.

FOCUS ON **TECHNOLOGY**

In addition to the links in the chapter, this activity provides a series of useful websites for reference along with a technology-related assignment for completion.

Websites of Interest

Links to all of the listed websites are provided at *www.pearsonhighered.com/wilson* in the companion website material for Chapter 7 under "Resources."

www.divorcelawinfo.com

This is the website for a commercial service that provides, for sale, online interactive preparation of a variety of forms having to do with divorce. The service comes in two forms, a do-it-yourself format and a paralegal-assisted format. Forms and services are purportedly state-specific. The site also has a frequently asked questions feature.

www.divorcesupport.com

This site provides material related to a broad range of divorce-related topics. For separation agreements, there are generic informational features such as Frequently Asked Questions (FAQ), online discussion forums, and state-specific

separation agreement preparation services. The site also provides links to state divorce law information.

www.findlaw.com

This site provides a sample separation agreement (which is not state-specific) for a short-term marriage with no children. It also provides links to divorce forms by state. Several of the state links contain sample separation agreements and parenting plans.

www.uslegalforms.com

This is the website for a service that provides, for sale, either downloadable or hard-copy forms for a variety of legal situations that are purportedly state-specific. For each state, it offers a number of different separation agreement forms that are tailored to the requirements of various general separation situations.

Note: Caution needs to be exercised when considering using commercial packages.

Assignments

1. Locate three online resources that provide information about separation agreements in your state.

PORTFOLIO PRODUCTS

1. Separation agreement tailored to a hypothetical fact pattern

2. One- to two-page discussion of ethical issues in the context of a specific case

3. Responses to questions regarding a case involving the enforceability of a separation agreement

4. Brief of a case on the enforceability of a separation agreement in a specific state

chapter 13
FAMILY VIOLENCE

Joe has been served with a Complaint for Divorce, and he is furious. His rage is apparent to the paralegal in his attorney's office, who has suspected for some time that Joe abuses his wife. Fearful for the wife's safety, the paralegal speaks with the supervising attorney, and they both struggle with the question of what they should do.

After years of studying family and intimate violence, by the 1990s Richard Gelles wondered aloud how we had ever come to characterize the family as "warm, intimate, stress reducing, and the place that people flee for safety."[1] His research had shown that the family was one of society's most violent institutions, in that people were "more likely to be killed, physically assaulted, hit, beat up, slapped, or spanked in their own homes by other family members than anywhere else, or by anyone else."[2]

Introduction

The history of family violence in this country has long been colored by the old common law right of a husband to treat both his wife and his children as property and to maintain domestic order through the use of physical force. **Interspousal immunity** and the law of **coverture,** which gave men control over their wives' bodies and property, created a climate that essentially fostered and condoned violence in the home environment. Although there were isolated efforts to address this problem prior to the 1900s, it was not until the 1960s and 1970s that advocates for the rights of women and children galvanized public and legislative support for victims of family violence. Initially, the focus was on abuse as a problem to be dealt with privately through treatment aimed primarily at maintenance of the family unit. In more recent years, the shift has been toward a focus on protection of victims and the treatment of abuse as a crime.

This chapter focuses on the deeply troubling topic of family violence, first with respect to adult intimate partners and then in the

LEARNING OBJECTIVES

After reading this chapter and completing related assignments, you should be able to:

- explain what family violence is, and who the victims and perpetrators are

- identify remedies available to adult victims of family violence, including criminal actions, civil actions, protective orders, and guardianships

- explain how to recognize and respond when a client is a victim or perpetrator of abuse

- identify various kinds of child abuse and neglect

- describe who is required to report abuse and to whom, and how the state responds

- explain how abuse and neglect influence custody decisions

- discuss the ethical duty of members of the family law team in the family violence context

Interspousal immunity
a doctrine preventing spouses from suing each other in civil actions

Coverture
the legal doctrine that upon marriage, a husband and wife become one person (the husband), and the wife loses many of the legal rights she possessed prior to marriage

context of parent-child relationships. In each instance, we examine the nature and extent of the abuse, the federal government's recognition of the problem, and some of the remedies available to victims. We also consider how intimate partner violence and child abuse and neglect impact custody determinations. Finally, we explore the duty of members of the family law team in cases involving family violence and the ethical challenges it presents.

PARALEGAL PRACTICE TIP

Most family law textbooks treat family violence as two separate chapters, one focusing on domestic violence and one focusing on child abuse and neglect. To some extent, the two are treated separately in this chapter for purposes of organizational convenience. However, the reader should be aware that there is a significant overlap between the two. A majority of studies find that both forms of abuse occur in 30% to 60% of violent families.[3] From a family systems perspective, one form of violence in the family cannot be understood in isolation from the other.

Family violence
a pattern of coercive behavior designed to exert power and control over a person in a familial relationship

Stalking
a knowing and willful course of conduct intended to cause another substantial emotional distress or fear for his or her safety; includes behaviors such as following, telephoning, or watching a person's place of residence or employment

Cyberstalking
repeated use of the Internet, text messaging, e-mail, or other forms of electronic communication with the intent to harass, intimidate, torment, or embarrass another person

PARALEGAL PRACTICE TIP

To learn more about the demographics of intimate partner violence and crime in domestic settings, visit the website of the Bureau of Justice Statistics *www.bjs. ojp.us.doj.gov*. You can find a link to this site at *www.pearsonhighered. com/wilson* in the companion website material for Chapter 13 under "Resources."

PARALEGAL PRACTICE TIP

Because the victims of intimate partner violence are predominantly female, in this chapter we will generally refer to victims as females.

Defining Family Violence

Family violence goes by many names, most commonly domestic violence, domestic abuse, intimate partner violence, and spousal and child abuse. Generally, it involves a pattern of coercive behavior designed to exert power and control over a person in a familial relationship. It comes in no single form, but rather may involve any combination of behaviors such as threatening, intimidating, belittling, harassing, and outright physical attacks. Legal definitions of various kinds of abuse differ from state to state. Most focus on the infliction of physical abuse that causes bodily injury, compelled sexual activity, and fear of physical assault. Some definitions encompass abuse inflicted through neglect, **stalking** (including **cyberstalking**), and other psychological tactics and behaviors.

PARALEGAL PRACTICE TIP

To see the Missouri statute defining "abuse" and the Georgia statute defining "stalking," visit *www.pearsonhighered.com/wilson* and look in the companion website material related to Chapter 13 under "Statutes."

Family Violence Against Adult Victims

THE SCOPE OF THE PROBLEM

"Domestic violence crosses all geographic, socioeconomic, racial, cultural, religious, educational, and occupational boundaries. The overwhelming majority of domestic violence is committed by men against women, although some women are abusive to their male or female partners. It occurs with about the same statistical frequency in heterosexual and homosexual relationships, . . ."[4] Although domestic violence appears disproportionately to impact minorities, immigrants, and individuals on welfare, the reader should not be misled by popular statistics into thinking that domestic violence is a problem solely in low-income families. Victims with financial resources have options that may allow them to conceal or escape abuse and avoid becoming public statistics. For example, the victim may be able to relocate to a new residence and/or file for divorce without ever having to seek public assistance. However, while having money may increase options for these victims, it does not necessarily insulate them from abuse.

EXHIBIT 13.1 Family Violence—A Statistical Profile

- One in every four women will experience domestic violence in her lifetime.[5] Although both men and women are victims, about 85% of domestic violence victims are women.[6]
- An estimated 1.3 million women are victims of physical assault by an intimate partner each year.[7] Domestic violence occurs in same-sex as well as in heterosexual relationships. Based on a National Violence Against Women Survey, 11% of lesbians and 15% of gay men who had lived with a same-sex partner reported being victimized.[8]
- In a study of adolescent mothers, approximately one of every eight pregnant adolescents reported having been physically assaulted by the father of her baby during the preceding twelve months.[9]
- In a National Center on Elder Abuse Survey of Adult Protective Services (APS), based on reports from states that separated out data on elder abuse, 89.3% of the incidents of alleged elder abuse were reported to have occurred in a domestic setting.[10]

PARALEGAL PRACTICE TIP

Definitions of elder abuse vary. According to the National Center on Elder Abuse (NCEA), "elder abuse is a term referring to any knowing, intentional, or negligent act by a caregiver or any other person that causes harm or a serious risk of harm to a vulnerable adult." Despite persistent efforts of some legislative leaders, there still is no federal legislation that focuses exclusively on elder abuse, there is no official source of national data or uniform reporting system, and laws protecting elders vary from state to state.

PARALEGAL PRACTICE TIP

Research has uncovered several key perpetrator characteristics associated with abuse of elders: (1) drug and/or alcohol abuse, (2) impairments such as mental illness and developmental disabilities, (3) financial dependence on the elder, and (4) a bad past relationship with the elder.[11]

PARALEGAL PRACTICE TIP

To learn more about elder abuse visit *www.ncea.aoa.gov.* You can find a link to this site at *www.pearsonhighered.com/wilson* in the companion website material related to Chapter 13 under "Resources."

- Incidence of domestic violence varies considerably by race and ethnicity.[12] For example, Department of Justice statistics indicate that, averaged over the interval 1993 to 2004, African-American females were victims of intimate partner violence at a rate 30% higher than that of white females.[13] A survey of immigrant Korean women found that 60% had been battered by their husbands.[14]
- Approximately 60% of the incidents of nonfatal intimate partner violence are unreported, and the primary reasons given for nonreporting include a preference for treating the incident as a private or family matter, a desire to protect the offender, a fear of reprisal, and a belief that the crime was minor, and that, if contacted, the police would be biased, ineffective, or unresponsive.[15]

PARALEGAL PRACTICE TIP

Intimate partner violence is by no means unique to the United States. It is especially prevalent in patriarchal societies such as Egypt, India, Jordan, Pakistan, and Uganda, in which women have few, if any, rights. In the extreme, "honor killings" of women are still perpetrated for a wide range of alleged "offenses," such as marital infidelity, engaging in premarital sex, flirting, being a rape victim, or participating in any behavior that is perceived as impugning family honor. Such killings often occur with the full support of both male and female family members and are usually punished, if at all, with lenient sentences.[16]

Federal Recognition of the Problem: The Violence Against Women Act

PARALEGAL PRACTICE TIP

To learn more about VAWA and the initiatives it sponsors, visit *www.ovw.usdoj.gov.* You can find a link to this site at *www.pearsonhighered.com/wilson* in the companion website material for Chapter 13 under "Resources."

At the federal level the most dramatic illustration of the legislative attention brought to bear on the problem of family violence is the Violence Against Women Act, a comprehensive, landmark piece of legislation designed to improve criminal justice- and community-based responses to domestic violence, dating violence, sexual assault, stalking, and trafficking. It was initially passed in 1994 (VAWA I) and reauthorized in 2000 (VAWA II), and the Violence Against Women and Department of Justice Reauthorization Act of 2005 was signed into law in January 2006, reauthorizing the Act for fiscal years 2007 through 2011 (VAWA III).[17]

It is administered by the Department of Health and Human Services and the Department of Justice. Since VAWA was signed into law, the following (among others) have become federal crimes: cyberstalking; crossing state or tribal boundary lines in order to injure, intimidate, or stalk an intimate partner or to violate a protective order; and stalking on Indian Reservations or military bases. VAWA has provided crucial services by funding twenty-four-hour emergency hotlines, emergency shelters, rape crisis centers, and child advocacy centers, among other initiatives. Culturally and linguistically diverse programs are designed to meet the needs of all women and not just those of one race, cultural background, or income level. Special efforts are made to meet the needs of many vulnerable target populations: victims with disabilities, the elderly, youth under the age of eighteen, those who live in rural communities, Native Americans, immigrants, and the homeless.

PARALEGAL PRACTICE TIP

VAWA includes provisions expanding transitional housing options for the homeless and ensures victims' confidentiality within the homeless services system. It also forbids domestic violence discrimination in public housing to prevent landlords from denying housing or evicting tenants based on their status of being victims of domestic violence.

PARALEGAL PRACTICE TIP

Successive versions of the Act have provided increased protections for immigrant victims of domestic violence. Immigrant spouses and children have access to alternative procedures for obtaining visas without the cooperation of the abusive spouse by permitting them to self-petition for legal permanent resident status. Additional protections are afforded immigrants who divorce their abusers or whose marriages are invalid because the citizen spouse was already married. In recognition of the fact that immigrants often lack access to shelters, professionals, court interpreters, hotlines, and 911 services due to language barriers, VAWA legislation has required the Secretary of Homeland Security to develop a pamphlet (translated into at least fourteen languages) containing information on the illegality of domestic violence and the rights of an abused immigrant.

You can see an Application for Cancellation of Removal and Adjustment of Status for Certain Non-permanent Residents (including victims of abuse) at *www.ovw.usdoj.gov.* You can find a link to this site at *www.pearsonhighered.com/wilson* in the companion website material for Chapter 13 under "Forms."

Remedies Available to Adult Victims

In addition to the kinds of social services and assistance provided by VAWA, other remedies available to victims of abuse include criminal prosecution, civil actions, protective orders, and guardianship.

CRIMINAL PROSECUTION

Involvement of the criminal justice system most often begins when the police receive and respond to a 911 call reporting a "domestic incident." In general, when responding to such calls, an officer must use all reasonable means to prevent further abuse whenever there is reason to believe that a "family member" has been abused or is in danger of being abused. The officer usually is required by statute and/or department policy to do the following:

- provide protection for the victim at the scene
- assist the victim in obtaining medical treatment, if appropriate
- assist the victim in relocating to a safe location, if warranted
- provide oral and written instructions to the victim (preferably in the victim's native language) about how to apply for a protective order

PARALEGAL PRACTICE TIP

Many states print applications for restraining orders in several languages. For example, applications for restraining orders and civil stalking protective orders are available online in Korean, Russian, Spanish, and Vietnamese in Oregon. See *www.ojd.state.or.us/familylaw*. You can find a link to this site at *www.pearsonhighered.com/wilson* in the companion website material for Chapter 13 under "Forms."

- assist the victim in accessing emergency judicial help if the courts are closed (on a weekend or holiday, etc.)

PARALEGAL PRACTICE TIP

States have in place procedures allowing plaintiffs to obtain emergency orders on weekends, holidays, and any other nonbusiness days. This is generally accomplished by having local judges/magistrates serve twenty-four-hour on-call shifts on a rotating basis. Any orders issued on an emergency basis are usually effective only until the next business day, when a hearing can be held.

- arrest the perpetrator of the abuse if the officer witnesses or has probable cause to believe that he or she has committed a felony assault and battery, or has violated a temporary or permanent restraining, vacate, or no-contact order. (In some states or localities, arrest is mandatory regardless of the victim's wishes. In others, it is discretionary.)

PARALEGAL PRACTICE TIP

To learn about domestic violence arrest policies in each of the states, visit *www.americanbar.org*. You can find a link to this site at *www.pearsonhighered.com/wilson* in the companion website material for Chapter 13 under "Resources."

- advise the victim that if the abuser is arrested, he or she will likely be eligible for bail or release

The role of the police in investigation and documentation of abuse incidents is critically important because in many cases, the victim will refuse to participate as a complaining witness for a variety of reasons. However, today many prosecutors have adopted "no-drop" policies and will proceed with **evidence-based prosecutions** using photographs, medical records, incident reports, and the testimony of police officers and other witnesses to establish a case. Supporters of mandatory arrest and "no-drop" policies assert that victims often are too helpless and/or too fearful to make appropriate decisions about arrest and prosecution. Opponents

Evidence-based prosecution
prosecution of a defendant that relies on physical evidence and testimony of persons other than the victim, such as police officers; formerly called "victimless" prosecutions

supportive of victims' rights argue that such policies disempower victims by depriving them of the opportunity to realize strength and power by making decisions about how the abuser should be treated.[18]

PARALEGAL PRACTICE TIP

In many states, police officers are required to complete supplemental incident reports in domestic violence cases. To see the form used in New Jersey, visit *www.state.nj.us.* You can find a link to this site at *www.pearsonhighered.com/wilson* in the companion website material for Chapter 13 under "Forms."

Paralegal **Application 13.1**

"Why Do They Stay? If Anyone Ever Hit Me, I Would Be Out the Door in a Minute"

It is often difficult for people who have never been in such a situation to comprehend why a person would remain in an abusive relationship and/or not prosecute or testify against his or her abuser. As an unfortunate result, courts, juries, and members of the legal profession often do not find claims of abuse to be credible. Research indicates that victims (primarily women) protect their abuser and stay in such relationships for several reasons:

- Fear of retaliation against themselves and/or their children
- Isolation from friends and extended family, resulting in the lack of a social and emotional support system
- Fear of loss of social status and professional associations
- Economic dependence, lack of marketable skills, or lack of adequate public assistance
- Desire to keep the family together and fear of losing custody of children
- Cultural and religious beliefs about the permanence of marriage
- Sense of responsibility for or loyalty to the abuser
- Belief that they love their abuser and that he or she will change
- Fear that the abuser will reveal information pertaining to sexual preference, immigration, HIV status, etc.[19]

- Chronic depression and exhaustion to the point of being unable to make decisions or major life changes
- Guilt and self-blame when the abuser convinces the victim the abuse is his or her fault
- Low self-esteem and feelings of failure as a spouse, partner, and/or person
- Conviction that no one other than the abuser would ever want or love them and that a bad relationship is better than no relationship at all
- Learned helplessness, a condition in which the victim comes to believe that all avenues of escape are closed and that she or he is powerless to leave
- Traumatic bonding, a psychological adaptive response in which the victim actually becomes attached to or bonded with his or her abuser (as in the "Stockholm syndrome" when kidnapped victims bond with their kidnappers)
- Lack of information about options for escape and resources available such as shelters and hotlines
- Inability to make use of support services due to language or cultural barriers, disabilities, lifestyle issues, or substance abuse problems
- Lack of effective responses to prior efforts to seek assistance

PARALEGAL PRACTICE TIP

According to research figures, family violence accounted for 11% of all reported violent crime between 1998 and 2002 in the United States. Approximately 49% of the offenses were committed against a spouse, 11% against a child by a parent, and 41% against another family member. Approximately 12% of persons killed in 2005 were killed by a family member. See Matthew R. Durose et al., U.S. Dep't. of Justice, NCJ 207846, *Family Violence Statistics,* June 2005.

Abusive conduct may be prosecuted under a variety of criminal statutes, ranging from murder and manslaughter in cases involving deaths, to assault, battery, aggravated assault, rape/sexual assault, stalking, and cyberstalking, among others. Many states have criminalized domestic battery specifically and provide for heightened penalties when other crimes are committed against family members.

Stalking

According to the Stalking Resource Center of the National Center for Victims of Crime, based on the results of a National Violence Against Women Survey (NVAW), 1 out of every 12 women and 1 out of 45 men will be stalked during their lifetime. Overall, 87% of stalkers are men. 59% of female victims and 30% of male victims are stalked by an intimate partner wanting to control, frighten, or keep them in a relationship. Of the female victims, 81% are also physically assaulted and 31% are sexually assaulted by their intimate partner; 55% of female victims and 48% of male victims reported the stalking to the police and 28% of the females and 10% of the males were granted orders of protection. More than 65% of those orders were violated. The average length of stalking of intimate partners was 2.2 years.[20]

Every state has enacted one or more antistalking measures that provide protection for victims of this specific form of abuse with or without the existence of a "special relationship." Most stalking statutes provide for enhanced penalties for aggravated stalking, such as when the stalking occurs in violation of a protective order or involves a repeated offense or the use of a weapon. Several states have enacted statutes that specifically address cyberstalking.

PARALEGAL PRACTICE TIP

Technology provides a wealth of tools cyberstalkers can use to terrorize their victims. GPS, cell phones and other devices can be used to track targets. If stalkers can access their victims' computers, they can use spyware software, sometimes sent through e-mail, to track keystrokes (including passwords), e-mails sent, and websites visited. They can verbally attack by posts on message boards or in discussion forums and on a host of social networking sites. Visit *www.ncvc.org* to learn more about the use of technology by stalkers and protective measures victims can take. Also available at this site is a "Handbook for Stalking Victims."

PARALEGAL PRACTICE TIP

To see forms used by South Dakota courts in Stalking Cases, visit *www.sdjudicial.com*. You can find a link to this site at *www.pearsonhighered.com/wilson* in the companion website material for Chapter 13 under "Forms."

PARALEGAL PRACTICE TIP

As of January 2012, the NVAW report can be accessed at *www.ncjrs.gov/pdffiles/169592.pdf*. To learn more about federal and state-by-state stalking laws, and stalking under tribal codes and the Uniform Code of Military Justice, visit the National Center for Victims of Crime site at *www.ncvc.org*. A link to this site can be found at *www.pearsonhighered.com/wilson* in the companion website material for Chapter 13 under "Resources."

PARALEGAL PRACTICE TIP

See the state of Washington's cyberstalking statute at *www.pearsonhighered.com/wilson* in the companion website material related to Chapter 13 under "Statutes."

Paralegal **Application 13.2**

Battered Woman's Syndrome—A Viable Defense?

Many states permit evidence of a history of abuse to be raised as a defense when a victim finally retaliates and causes injury or death to the abuser. What has come to be known as **battered woman's syndrome** is usually not a complete defense to a crime, but rather may serve to reduce the degree of the crime with which the defendant/victim is charged (from first-degree murder, for example, to second-degree murder or manslaughter) or to mitigate the sentence imposed.

This defense is by no means universally accepted. Many in the criminal justice system agree with commentators who contend it is just one of dozens of potential "abuse excuses" by means of which criminals fail to accept responsibility for their conduct. These critics assert that no prior acts of abuse justify killing or injuring an abuser absent an immediate act of provocation.

Sidebar

Do you believe that evidence of a history of abuse should be admissible as a defense to the killing or assaulting one's abuser? Should it be a complete defense (resulting in a not guilty verdict) or only reduce the severity of the crime or the sentence? Are there circumstances in which the defense is more appropriate than others?

Battered woman's syndrome
the psychological condition of a woman who has been abused for a sustained period of time; sometimes used as a defense to justify the act or mitigate the penalty when the woman attacks her abuser

CIVIL ACTIONS

Historically, the doctrine of interspousal immunity prevented spouses from suing each other in civil actions. The doctrine was designed to serve strong public policies favoring the preservation of marriage and family harmony and the prevention of fraudulent claims between spouses with liability insurance. The doctrine has eroded to a considerable extent, such that most states now permit one spouse to sue the other spouse for intentional or negligent injury to property and for intentional (but not negligent) injury to the person (e.g., assault, battery), especially if the parties are not living together. If a divorce is pending, the courts may require that such claims be raised in the context of that action. The premise is that, if a party receives a greater share of the marital property based on the other party's abusive conduct during the marriage, that party should not be permitted to file a post-divorce tort claim for battery or intentional infliction of emotional distress for injuries that occurred during the course of the marriage, thereby getting a "second bite of the apple."[21]

PROTECTIVE ORDERS

Under civil domestic violence laws of all fifty states and the District of Columbia, a victim of family violence can seek an order of protection if he or she satisfies the threshold requirements regarding standing and qualifying conduct laid out in applicable statutes, which vary considerably from state to state.

PARALEGAL PRACTICE TIP

A valuable resource regarding state-by-state statutory definitions of domestic violence and civil protection order (CPO) statutes (addressing who has standing to file and kinds of relief that can be granted, etc.) can be found at *www.americanbar.org,* the site of the American Bar Association. Note that there are also CPO summary charts relating to sexual assault and stalking/harassment. There is also an overview of CPO protections for lesbian, gay, bisexual or transgendered (LGBT) victims. You can find a link to this site at *www.pearsonhighered.com/wilson* in the companion website material for Chapter 13 under "Resources."

Standing

Standing to seek protective orders is generally available to individuals involved in spousal, intimate, or other "special" relationships. Depending on the state, this may include individuals who:

- are or were married to each other
- have a child in common or a child *in utero*
- are related by blood or marriage
- are or have been in a substantial dating relationship
- are or have lived together in the same household (this may include couples, parents and children, roommates, etc.)

A limited number of states expressly extend standing to individuals involved in same-sex as well as heterosexual intimate relationships. The decision with respect to who has standing often is ultimately a matter of judicial discretion. For example, under what circumstances will a couple be deemed to be in a "substantial" dating relationship? Will standing be extended to same-sex couples in states that ban extension of the rights and benefits of marriage to same-sex couples?

Qualifying Conduct

Some states require that the petitioner have suffered actual or attempted physical harm or have been caused to engage in sexual relations as a result of force or threat of force. In several states, a threat of serious physical harm is sufficient. A limited number of states extend standing when there is serious emotional or verbal abuse or malicious destruction of property, particularly when there is a history of violence on the perpetrator's part clearly evidencing a potential for harm. (See Case 13.1.) Typical examples of violent and controlling abusive behaviors considered by the courts include:

- slaps, punches, bites, or "head butts"
- grabbing, choking, pulling hair
- display or use of weapons in an intimidating manner
- intimidation by use of threatening gestures, shouting, driving recklessly, or refusing to allow entry to or exit from a location
- destruction of furniture or other property
- ripping out phone lines, slashing tires, etc.
- threatening to harm the victim's children or take them away to another state or country
- injuring or threatening to injure pets

CASE **13.1** *Lefebre v. Lefebre,* 165 Ore. App. 297, 996 P.2d 518 (2000)

BACKGROUND

In this case, the defendant challenged the legal sufficiency of the allegations and evidence underlying a restraining order that had been entered against him. The petitioner had alleged that after their separation, her husband persistently harassed and frightened her, barricaded her out of her house, telephoned many of her friends telling them a "disparaging" story about her, and engaged in a number of other threatening acts. She said her fear was intensified because of an episode nine years earlier in which he was obsessed for six months with the idea of killing his former employer. She also indicated that he lived with his brother, who was a police officer, and that he had easy access to guns. She did not allege that there had been any actual or overtly threatened harm. Her husband claimed that the restraining order should not be issued because there was no overt threat and only a "minimal level" of physical contact.

FROM THE OPINION

An overt threat is not required in order to authorize the issuance of an abuse prevention restraining order. Instead, FAPA requires that the respondent has "intentionally, knowingly or recklessly" placed the petitioner in fear of "imminent serious bodily injury." ORS 107.705(1); ORS 107.710(1). In addition, the petitioner must be in immediate danger of further abuse. Id. As to the latter requirement, respondent correctly points out that our previous reported decisions upholding FAPA orders have generally involved more overtly threatening conduct than that present here. . . .

In Cottongim, we held that the respondent's behavior fulfilled the statutory definition of abuse because it "deviated considerably from that which a reasonable person would exhibit under similar circumstances [,] and a reasonable person faced with such behavior would be placed in fear of imminent serious bodily harm." Cottongim, 145

(Continued)

PARALEGAL PRACTICE TIP

The opinion in the *Lefebre* case can be found at *www.pearsonhighered. com/wilson* in the companion website material related to Chapter 13 under "Cases" and in the Case Resources Section of the MyLegalStudiesLab.

PARALEGAL PRACTICE TIP

The victim may request in the Complaint or separately that his or her address be impounded. The U.S. Postal Service will also keep an address confidential when the victim presents a copy of his or her protective order to the appropriate postal office employee, although the address will still be provided to agents of the state or federal government. To see a form used in Connecticut to request nondisclosure of information in a case, visit *www.jud.ct.gov*. You can find a link to this site at *www.pearsonhighered.com/wilson* in the companion website material for Chapter 13 under "Forms."

Protective order
in the context of family violence cases, a court order directing a person to refrain from harming or harassing another person

Affidavit
a written statement of facts based on firsthand knowledge, information, or belief and signed by the affiant under pain and penalty of perjury

Concurrent jurisdiction
two or more courts having simultaneous jurisdiction over the same subject matter

Ore. App. at 45. The same reasoning applies here as well. Respondent's conduct was erratic, intrusive, volatile, and persistent. He screamed obscenities in petitioner's face, unrestrained by the presence of their child, made numerous hang-up phone calls, and rummaged through her possessions. Notably, respondent's late night call describing the sleeping clothes petitioner was wearing put her on notice that he was lurking about her house, watching her, and that she was vulnerable. Moreover, petitioner knew that respondent had previously been obsessed with the idea of killing another person. Despite the lack of an explicit threat, the totality of the circumstances supports the petitioner's assertion that respondent at least recklessly placed her in fear of imminent serious bodily injury and in immediate danger of further abuse.

SIDEBAR

Do you agree with the court's decision? Explain your response.

Procedure for Obtaining a Protective Order

The procedure for obtaining a **protective order** varies somewhat from state to state, but is invariably relatively simple:

- The plaintiff files a Complaint or Petition for a Protective Order requesting a variety of forms of relief. The Complaint usually includes or is accompanied by an **affidavit** in which the plaintiff describes the nature of the abuse that has led to the filing. In some states, such as Indiana, if the petition is made on the basis of the petitioner's information and belief rather than on personal knowledge, the petitioner also must attach affidavits by one or more persons who have personal knowledge of the facts stated within the petition.

PARALEGAL PRACTICE TIP

A helpful resource for locating Domestic Violence state forms is *www.findlaw.com*. Copies of a California Request for a Temporary Restraining Order and an Indiana Petition for an Order for Protection and Request for a Hearing are available at *www.pearsonhighered.com/wilson* in the companion website material related to Chapter 13 under "Forms."

PARALEGAL PRACTICE TIP

Visit *www.vermontjudiciary.org/eforms* to see a Complaint for Relief from Abuse and an Affidavit in Support of a Request for Emergency Relief from Abuse used in that state. You can find a link to this site at *www.pearsonhighered.com/wilson* in the companion website material for Chapter 13 under "Forms."

- The Complaint is filed in a court with jurisdiction over such matters. Usually several types of courts have **concurrent jurisdiction,** including courts that hear criminal, juvenile, and family matters. Most states do not require a filing fee, and those that do allow the fee to be waived upon proof of inability to pay.

PARALEGAL PRACTICE TIP

In some states, such as Massachusetts, when a complaint for a protective order is filed, the court is required to search a statewide computerized database to determine if the defendant has been charged with a crime, been involved in domestic or other violence, or has an outstanding arrest warrant. Depending on the circumstances, the court may be required to take further action, which might result in the arrest of the alleged abuser.

- At the petitioner's request, the Complaint often is considered by the court initially on an ***ex parte*** basis (without notice to the defendant).

PARALEGAL PRACTICE TIP

Defending a client in an action for a protective order can be a challenge. Initial orders are frequently issued *ex parte* and become a matter of record; the rules of evidence are often not strictly observed; little discovery is usually available; and courts often err on the side of caution and grant extensive relief to petitioners. Despite an attorney's best efforts, a defendant in such actions may feel, sometimes justifiably so, that he or she is being denied due process.

- A temporary order will be issued if the court believes there is reason to believe that abuse has occurred or is threatened. The extent of relief granted at this initial stage may be limited to **restraining**, **stay away**, or **no-contact orders**.
- The defendant is served with the Complaint and any *ex parte* orders in a manner consistent with local procedure.

PARALEGAL PRACTICE TIP

To see a Domestic Violence No-Contact Order and a Protected Person's Motion to Modify/Rescind a Domestic Violence No Contact Order, visit *www.courts.wa.gov/forms*. (Washington) You can find a link to this site at *www.pearsonhighered.com/wilson* in the companion website material related to Chapter 13 under "Forms."

- A second hearing is held within a statutorily prescribed period (commonly ten days), at which both the plaintiff and defendant have an opportunity to be heard, and the court decides whether to extend, modify, or vacate the initial order. In some states, this second hearing must be requested by the defendant, and a failure of the plaintiff to appear may result in automatic dismissal.
- An extended order will contain an expiration date. When that date approaches, if the plaintiff wants the order extended for an additional period, he or she usually must petition the court for an extension.

Because the procedure for obtaining a restraining order is relatively uncomplicated, it can be completed by the plaintiff on his or her own or with minimal technical assistance from court personnel. In some cases there is merit to proceeding *pro se,* as filing often represents the first time the victim has ever asserted his or her rights against the abuser. That psychological advantage aside, it may be helpful for the client to have assistance, particularly with completion of the affidavit, identification of potential forms of relief that may be available based on the parties' circumstances, and representation at court hearings when the defendant may be present.

Types of Relief Available in Protective Orders

Courts may grant a variety of forms of relief tailored to the facts and circumstances of each case. For example, the court may order that the defendant:

- stay away from the plaintiff at home, work, school, or any other place he or she may be (The stay away order may also extend to locations where the plaintiff's child or children may be)
- have no contact with the plaintiff by any means, including telephone, text messaging, e-mail, U.S. mail, notes on vehicle doors and windows, etc.

Ex parte
without advance notice to the opposing party; a matter considered and initially ruled on by the court without hearing from both parties

Restraining order
a court order, most commonly issued in domestic violence cases, restricting an individual from threatening and/or harassing another individual or individuals

Stay away order
a court order requiring a person to keep away from another individual wherever he or she may be (home, work, school, etc.)

No-contact order
a court order prohibiting an individual from having contact of any kind with a person he or she has threatened and/or abused in some manner

- refrain from abusing, injuring, or harassing the plaintiff either directly and/or with the assistance of third parties

PARALEGAL PRACTICE TIP

Paralegals should not contact the opposing party without supervisor approval when a no-contact order against the firm's client is in force. A 2004 New Hampshire case involving a protective order with a no-contact provision illustrates the potential consequences of unauthorized contact in such circumstances. The New Hampshire Supreme Court held that, regardless of the purpose of the contact, the state could prosecute a defendant who, through his attorney, knowingly contacted the alleged victim. See *State v. Kidder,* 150 N.H. 600, 843 A.2d 312 (2004).

- vacate the household (if the parties live together) regardless of who holds title to the property or is responsible for the lease (The court may permit the defendant to collect his or her personal belongings from the property—usually with police supervision)
- surrender guns, license to carry a gun, and Firearm Identification Card (FID) (Exceptions may be available for individuals such as police officers and military personnel, who are required to carry a weapon as a condition of employment, but the exception applies only while the individual is on duty)[22]
- pay compensation to the plaintiff for damages, losses, or expenses incurred as a direct result of the abuse (e.g., for repair of destroyed property, installation of new locks, uninsured medical and counseling expenses, loss of time from work, relocation and moving expenses, costs of staying in a hotel, motel, or shelter, etc.)

PARALEGAL PRACTICE TIP

If requested, judges are customarily authorized to make temporary child custody and support awards in the context of protective order cases. Local procedural rules will dictate how custody and child support orders will be handled if there are already existing or pending orders and/or if one or both of the parties subsequently files for divorce, separation, or custody.

PARALEGAL PRACTICE TIP

In some states, such as Illinois, offenders convicted of domestic violence are liable by statute for the cost of counseling for children who witnessed their crimes. 720 ILCS 5/12–3.2.

In addition to other specific forms of relief, a majority of state statutes include a catchall provision authorizing courts to provide whatever relief is appropriate to stop the abuse and protect the victim in a given set of circumstances. For example, in a case in which a defendant is threatening to expose the plaintiff's HIV status, the court may order the defendant not to "directly or indirectly reveal any information about the Petitioner's health status to Petitioner's employer . . . with intent to cause emotional distress or harass the Petitioner. . . ."[23] Although on the surface such a provision may appear to restrain free speech, such orders have been granted.

PARALEGAL PRACTICE TIP

Approximately 20% of the 1.5 million people who annually experience intimate partner violence obtain civil protection orders.

Approximately one-half of the orders obtained by women against intimate partners who physically assaulted them were violated.

More than two-thirds of the restraining orders against intimate partners who raped or stalked the victim were violated.[24]

Police usually play a major role in serving and enforcing protective orders. Although protective orders are initially civil in nature, violations constitute contempt of court as well as independent criminal offenses potentially punishable by jail sentences and/or fines. In order to prove a violation, a valid order must have issued (counsel should have a certified copy of the order); the defendant must have been served with the order; the order must have been in effect at the time of the violation; and the defendant must have violated the order.

Occasionally a client will intentionally create a situation in which a violation of a protective order is inevitable. The potential for problems is especially great when the parties have a child in common. For example, assume both parents want to attend their child's basketball game, dance concert, or school play. Further assume that a protective order is in force requiring the defendant to stay at least 500 feet away from the plaintiff. The defendant arrives at the event after the other parent, and the school auditorium is so small that it is impossible to be present without being within 500 feet of the plaintiff. Technically there is a violation even if the defendant makes no effort whatsoever to approach, threaten, or otherwise communicate with the plaintiff, and the defendant may be subject to arrest in front of the child and others present if the plaintiff contacts the police. Absent a pattern of such behavior, there may be little that can be done other than to suggest to the client that such confrontations harm the innocent child most of all.

Most advocates argue that "mutual restraining orders" should be discouraged, particularly in cases where one of the parties strikes out only in self-defense. To issue a restraining order in such circumstances in effect relieves the real abuser of responsibility. In addition, when mutual restraining orders are issued, they may create confusion for police trying to enforce them and for judges trying to make custody orders when a prior history of abuse is a relevant factor to be considered. Some states have addressed this topic by statute. Wisconsin's mandatory arrest statute provides that when an officer has reasonable grounds to believe that spouses, former spouses, or other persons who reside together or formerly resided together are committing or have committed domestic abuse against each other, the officer does not have to arrest both persons but should arrest the person whom the officer believes to be the primary aggressor.[25]

Some states also provide for issuance of "domestic relations restraining orders" in the context of divorce and other family law proceedings. However, these orders are not technically protective orders, and the safety of victims is not their primary intended purpose. They may be included routinely in marital agreements or may issue at the discretion of the court. There is no requirement for abuse to have occurred to obtain a domestic relations restraining order. Essentially, they are designed to serve as reminders to parties that they are not to interfere in each other's lives.

GUARDIANSHIP

Guardian

an individual appointed by the court to have legal authority for another's person and/or property during a period of minority or incapacitation

Forms of relief such as protective orders reflect what has been termed an "empowerment model of domestic violence," which presumes that a victim of abuse is capable of deciding to leave an abusive relationship, hold the abuser accountable, and move on making use of available resources such as shelters and support groups. However, for some women, these resources are not genuine options. There are cases in which "a battered woman can become coercively controlled—so incapacitated by repeated abuse that she cannot protect herself or escape from her abuser."[26] She has lost her autonomy and must be empowered by forcible removal from the control of an abuser.

"In extreme cases . . . , the state-sanctioned intervention of guardianship is necessary because an abuser has brutally and systematically deprived a woman of her ability to exercise independent judgment."[27] Guardianship has the potential to bridge the gap between being totally subject to the control of the abuser and independence. The **guardian** is appointed by the court and is granted the authority to act on behalf of the "ward" for some or all purposes until such time as the court determines the ward has the capacity to act on his or her own behalf. The guardian can, for example, make housing arrangements for the ward, pay bills, make decisions regarding counseling and medical treatment, and represent the client in legal matters.

Recognizing and Responding When Intimate Partner Violence Is an Issue in a Case

Many victims are afraid, ashamed, or embarrassed about the abuse they experience and have never reported it to the police or discussed it with counselors, physicians, family, friends, or attorneys. Many perpetrators are aware that their conduct is criminal but they are unwilling to face the consequences of their actions by acknowledging it to others. As surprising as it may seem, some abusers do not even recognize that they are perpetrators, especially when their conduct is culturally condoned, and many victims, particularly those who believe they are responsible for the abuse they suffer, do not perceive themselves as victims. Some clients will directly acknowledge that they are victims or perpetrators, particularly if the abuse is already a matter of public record, documented in police reports, and substantiated by medical records and other evidence such as photographs. More often, however, the abuse will not be revealed by the client at the outset of a case. Members of the family law team need to listen carefully to the client's language and also be sensitive to cues in behavior that suggest the existence of unacknowledged abuse.

PARALEGAL PRACTICE TIP

Given the potential that a client is either a perpetrator or a victim of family violence, materials often are made available in family law office reception areas regarding resources designed to assist both victims of abuse and perpetrators who might conceivably be motivated to change their behavior or be forced to accept the consequences. Such materials include, among others, hotline numbers, emergency shelter contacts, law enforcement agency numbers, names of victim advocates, instructions and forms for obtaining protective orders, and locations of resource centers, support groups, and batterers' programs. They may also include educational and consciousness-raising materials about what constitutes abuse and techniques for recognizing when someone is a victim or an abuser.

In addition to whatever impact spousal abuse may have on property division or spousal support awards, it is important for family law teams to be aware of additional forms of relief that may be available in a particular jurisdiction to a client who has been abused. For example, the California legislature has created a tort of domestic violence, and if a divorce is pending the court can enforce a judgment by deducting the amount of any related award from the abusive spouse's share of community property. See Cal. Civ. Code 1708.6 (b)-(c) and Cal. Fam. Code 2603.5.

WHEN THE CLIENT IS A VICTIM

The most important issue to address when the client is a victim of family violence is her safety. This is particularly the case if she has made the decision to leave the relationship and, if married, divorce the abusive spouse. She needs to have a plan of action and a supportive safety net in place when the departure occurs and/or the Complaint is served.

> When an abusive partner realizes that the victim truly has made affirmative efforts to leave him, he may feel emasculated. His threats, protestations of love, and domestic terrorism have all proved futile in his efforts to retain control over her. It is at this time that many batterers turn to other devices to exert domination over the fleeing partner. It is at this time that the risk of serious violence in intimate relationships is at its h[e]ight. After the victim has made efforts to escape, the batterer is most likely to seek to retaliate against her by sabotaging the independent life she tries to establish for herself. . . . Victims constantly relay stories of the batterer's false reports to child protective services; false "anonymous" tip-offs to employers about the victim's disloyalty or dishonesty; and calls to employers or family members revealing damaging, . . . information about the victim.[28]

If the client is not yet committed to leaving the relationship, members of the family law team should listen to her patiently, allow her to freely express her feelings, and be sensitive to the many reasons why people remain in such relationships. Team members need to communicate the message that no one deserves to be threatened or beaten, but also be prepared to let the client make her own decision, even if it means not yet being ready to leave the relationship.

One of the reasons why the client may not be prepared to terminate the abusive relationship may be a sense of helplessness and inability to escape the situation. A common tool for helping clients who are victims develop a sense of control is a Safety Plan. Safety plans may be prepared by the victim independently or with the assistance of a family law team member. There are many models of safety plans and they typically address topics such as the following:

- Contact numbers for resources such as the police, hotlines, and shelters
- Locations where the victim can go if forced to leave home
- Suggestions for increasing safety at home, work, and in the community
- Items and documents to take when leaving home
- Strategies for protecting children

One model of a Safety Plan is accessible at *www.pearsonhighered.com/wilson* in the companion website material related to Chapter 13 under "Resources." Two additional resources for safety planning can be found at *www.ncvc.org* and *www.ncadv.org*, the site for the National Coalition of Domestic Violence. Links to these two sites may also be found at *www.pearsonhighered.com/wilson* in the companion website material for Chapter 13 under "Resources."

WHEN THE CLIENT IS A PERPETRATOR

Abusers rarely self-identify, and, therefore, members of the family law team may never learn of their conduct or, worse, may be taken by surprise by it! Abusers come in all forms and from all backgrounds, and there is no one mold into which they all fit. There are, however, some red flags to watch for, a cluster of characteristics that batterers in particular commonly share. The team should be alert to these indicators. (See Exhibit 13.2.)

EXHIBIT 13.2 Profile of an Abuser

Technically, there is no such thing as a profile of an abuser. However, there are certain traits, attitudes, and behaviors that may be strong indicators. They typically include the following:

- He believes in traditional, rigid, hierarchical sex roles.
- He engages in jealous, possessive, and controlling behaviors.
- He has a two-sided personality—one mild and gentle, the other mean and abusive.
- He believes he is a victim.
- He is hypersensitive to criticism.
- He has a distorted self-image. (It may be in the form of low self-esteem and feelings of inadequacy or an inflated positive self-image.)
- He is self-centered.
- He is manipulative.
- He engages in minimization, denial, blame, and criticism.
- He is overly dependent on his partner and unable to see her as a separate person.
- He has an explosive temper and breaks or throws things when angry and hits, shoves, and kicks his partner and/or children.
- He is cruel to animals.
- He has difficulty expressing feelings.
- He has a history of bad relationships.
- He was abused as a child in his family of origin (physically, emotionally, and/or sexually).[29]

If the client is an abuser, alleged or proven, the ethical challenges of representation are magnified. Members of the family law team need to remain as non-judgmental and emotionally uninvolved as possible in order to serve as zealous advocates. The legal system in this country is based on the premise that every client is entitled to competent representation, no matter how offensive or illegal his or her behavior may be. Perhaps the greatest challenge to the team is to balance the duty to maintain client confidentiality with the responsibility to prevent the commission of a crime that could cause serious physical injury or death to another individual. This sensitive question is discussed in greater depth at the end of this chapter.

Child Victims of Family Violence

THE SCOPE OF THE PROBLEM

The most comprehensive and authoritative source of data on child abuse and neglect in the United States is generated through the National Child Abuse and Neglect Data System (NCANDS) by the Children's Bureau in the Administration for Children and Families in the U.S. Department of Health and Human Services (HHS). The Bureau collects and analyzes data submitted by the states, the District of Columbia, and Puerto Rico on an annual basis. The data is presented in an annual report, "Child Maltreatment," published each spring since 1990. Major findings of the report for fiscal year 2009 include the following:

- Approximately 3.3 million referrals involving about 6 million children were made to child protective service (CPS) agencies. Of this number, approximately 25% were substantiated. Less than 1% of the reports were determined to be intentionally false.
- About 60% of the reports were made by professionals (police, teachers, medical and social services personnel, etc.), 9% by anonymous reporters, and the remainder by nonprofessionals (relatives, neighbors, friends, etc.).
- With respect to types of abuse experienced by confirmed victims, 78.3% suffered neglect; 17.8% physical abuse; 9.5% sexual abuse; 7.6% psychological maltreatment; and 2.4% medical neglect. 1,676 children reportedly died as a result of child abuse or neglect.
- More than half of the victims were seven years old or younger, and the highest rate of victimization was of children younger than one year old.
- Of the child victims, 51.7% were female and 48.3% were male.
- 44% of the victims of abuse were white, 22% African-American, and 20.7% Hispanic.
- Approximately 80% of the perpetrators of child maltreatment were parents (40% mother, 20% father, and 18% both parents).[30]

PARALEGAL PRACTICE TIP

The annual "Child Maltreatment" report can be accessed at *www.acf.hhs.gov/programs/cb*. You can find a link to this site at *www.pearsonhighered.com/wilson* in the companion website material related to Chapter 13 under "Resources."

Federal Recognition of the Problem

In 1974, Congress passed the first comprehensive federal legislation to address the problem of child abuse and neglect in the United States, the Child Abuse Prevention and Treatment Act (CAPTA),[31] establishing, among other initiatives, the National Center of Child Abuse and Neglect (NCCAN) to serve as a clearinghouse for information on child protection programs and research. Largely in response to CAPTA, all states now have in place child-abuse-reporting laws and comprehensive child protection systems vesting centralized responsibility in a single designated child protection agency, typically a department of child and family or social services.

Types of Child Abuse

As indicated in the summary "Child Maltreatment" report, children in the United States suffer a variety of forms of abuse in the family environment, ranging from, in the extreme, death at the hands of their parents, siblings, or caretakers, to emotional abuse and the potentially devastating effects witnessing the abuse of other family members. Types of child abuse are defined by both federal and state law. Under CAPTA, child abuse and neglect is defined as:

> . . . at a minimum, any recent act or failure to act on the part of a parent or caretaker, which results in death, serious physical or emotional harm, sexual abuse, or exploitation, or an act or failure to act which presents an imminent risk of serious harm.[32]

PARALEGAL PRACTICE TIP

To learn more about federal definitions and search for definitions of various kinds of abuse in your state, visit *www.childwelfare.gov.* You can find a link to this site at *www.pearsonhighered.com/wilson* in the companion website material related to Chapter 13 under "Resources."

The forms of abuse most commonly identified and further defined by the states are:

Neglect

Physical abuse

Emotional abuse

Sexual abuse

Substance abuse

The states vary with respect to their treatment of **abandonment** as a category of child abuse and neglect. Several states (including Connecticut, Illinois, Kentucky, Louisiana, New Jersey, Texas, and Virginia) include abandonment in the definition of neglect. More than a dozen states (including Indiana, Kansas, Maine, Massachusetts, New Mexico, New York, Ohio, and South Carolina) establish a separate definition of abandonment.

> In general, it is considered abandonment of the child when the parent's identity or whereabouts are unknown, the child has been left by the parent in circumstances where the child suffers serious harm, or the parent has failed to maintain contact with the child or to provide reasonable support for a specified period of time.[33]

NEGLECT

At the federal level, **neglect** is defined as "a type of maltreatment that refers to the failure by the caregiver to provide needed, age appropriate care although financially able to do so, or offered financial or other means to do so."[34] A distinction is made between an inability to provide for a child and a deliberate failure to provide with or without any apparent reason. Neglect usually involves an ongoing pattern of inadequate care falling into one or more categories: physical, emotional, medical, and educational.

- **Physical neglect** is the form most commonly reported. It generally involves inadequate supervision and/or a failure to provide adequate food, shelter, and clothing such that the child's health, safety, growth, and development are endangered.
- **Emotional neglect** generally includes a pattern of rejecting, isolating, and ignoring the child's needs for nurturance, stimulation, and social contact.
- **Medical neglect** involves the failure of a parent or caretaker to provide appropriate health care for a child. Although medical neglect cases tend to be

Abandonment
occurs when the whereabouts of a child's parent are unknown, the parent has left the child in unsafe circumstances, and/or has failed to maintain contact with or provide support for the child for an extended period of time

Neglect
failure by the caregiver to provide needed, age-appropriate care although financially able to do so, or offered financial or other means to do so

Physical neglect
inadequate supervision and/or a failure to provide adequate food, shelter, and clothing such that the child's health, safety, growth, and development are endangered

Emotional neglect
a pattern of rejecting, isolating, and ignoring a child's needs for nurturance, stimulation, and social contact

Medical neglect
the failure of a parent or caretaker to provide appropriate health care for a child

high-profile, they commonly make up less than 5% of cases of child maltreatment. Medical neglect ranges from situations in which caretakers ignore medical advice in nonemergency situations to circumstances in which a parent refuses medical care for a seriously ill child due to religious beliefs, cultural traditions, or financial limitations. The state will usually intervene in an emergency or when the child has a life-threatening or chronic condition.

PARALEGAL PRACTICE TIP

The CAPTA Amendments of 1996 added a provision specifying that the Act does not establish a federal requirement that "a parent or legal guardian provide a child any medical service or treatment against the religious beliefs of the parent or legal guardian."[35] Approximately thirty states and the District of Columbia exempt from the definition of neglect those parents who do not seek medical care for their children on the basis of religious beliefs, and three states (Arizona, Connecticut, and Washington) specifically exempt Christian Scientists. About half of the thirty states authorize the court to intervene and order treatment when warranted by the circumstances.[36]

- **Educational neglect** refers to a parent's failure to use his or her best efforts to ensure that a child of mandatory school age attends a legally recognized public or private school or participates in a state-monitored program of home schooling. A distinction is usually made when the child is a chronic truant through no apparent lack of supervision or effort on the parent's part.

Educational neglect
a parent's failure to use his or her best efforts to ensure that a child of mandatory school age attends a legally recognized school or program of home schooling

PHYSICAL ABUSE

In general at the federal level, physical abuse is defined as "non-accidental physical injury to the child"[37] that may be caused by behaviors such as punching, striking, kicking, biting, or burning. Although the most visible form of abuse, it is not as common as neglect. Physical abuse cases reflect varying degrees of culpability and involve:

- parents who deliberately and maliciously physically abuse their children
- parents who administer severe punishment to their children in the good-faith belief that they are acting in the children's best interests
- parents who have never developed effective parenting skills and who, as a result, are poor disciplinarians
- parents who accidentally injure their children

Investigations of physical abuse reports often reveal that alcohol and drug abuse as well as other forms of domestic violence are evident in a physically abused child's home environment.

Child Abuse or Discipline?

Common law recognized a parental privilege to use reasonable force in disciplining children. In describing the privilege, Blackstone commented that a parent "may lawfully correct his child, being under age, in a reasonable manner," and that "battery is, in some cases, justifiable or lawful; as where one who hath authority, a parent or a master, gives moderate correction to his child, his scholar, or his apprentice."[38] The U.S. Supreme Court has also held that parents have a constitutionally protected fundamental liberty interest in directing their children's upbringing.[39] However, the parental right to discipline is not unlimited, and the states have the right to restrict it to protect children from cruel and excessive punishment. (See Case 13.2.)

Although the Supreme Court has not set a fixed rule defining what constitutes unreasonable or excessive corporal punishment under all circumstances, a majority of states have adopted the common law standard of "reasonableness and moderation." For example, Ohio requires a parent's use of force to be "proper and reasonable under the circumstances."[40] In Washington State, "A parent has a right to use reasonable and timely punishment to discipline a minor child within the bounds of moderation and for the best interests of the child."[41] In Rhode Island, "[t]he test of unreasonableness is met at the point at which a parent ceases to act in good faith and with parental affection and acts immoderately, cruelly, or mercilessly with a malicious desire to inflict pain, rather than make a genuine effort to correct the child by proper means."[42] In Wisconsin, "the accepted degree of force must vary according to the age, sex, physical and mental condition and disposition of the child, the conduct of the child, the nature of the discipline, and all the surrounding circumstances."[43]

PARALEGAL PRACTICE TIP

Shaken baby syndrome
a condition that results from repeated, vigorous shaking of a baby that causes brain damage and sometimes death and that can result from a single incident or a more prolonged pattern of abuse

First identified in the early 1970s, **shaken baby syndrome** is a condition that results from repeated, vigorous shaking of a baby that causes brain damage and sometimes death. It can result from a single incident or a more prolonged pattern of abuse. "Violent shaking is especially dangerous to infants and young children because their neck muscles are not fully developed and their brain tissue is exceptionally fragile."[44]

Caretakers who abuse very young children in this manner often claim that the babies fell but "The force of shaking a child in anger and frustration is five to 10 times greater than if the child were simply to trip and fall."[45] Initially, the condition can be difficult to diagnose because the resulting injuries are not always the same and are frequently not externally observable. They usually include brain damage and swelling, mental retardation or developmental delays, loss of sensory functions such as sight and hearing, and sometimes death. Because of its nature and the lack of a national database addressing this specific form of physical abuse, the number of children who are victims of shaken baby syndrome is unknown.

CASE 13.2 *State of New Mexico v. Lefevre,* 138 N.M. 174, 2005 NMCA 101, 117 P.3d 980 (2005)

PARALEGAL PRACTICE TIP

The opinion in the *Lefevre* case is available at *www.pearsonhighered. com/wilson* in the companion website material related to Chapter 13 under "Cases" and in the Case Resources Section of the MyLegalStudiesLab.

BACKGROUND

This case involved the father of a twelve-year-old daughter and her younger brother. The father had been divorced from his wife for several years, and their relationship was still contentious at the time of the incident addressed in this case. He visited regularly with their children (the daughter once a month and the son every other weekend and Wednesdays). He had become concerned that he was not receiving copies of "Wednesday Notes," which advised parents of school schedules and special activities. He had told his daughter that her brother had told him that she was removing the "Notes" from his backpack and that was why he was not seeing them. When the father went to school to pick up the children he approached them from the back, and it appeared that the daughter was removing something from her brother's backpack, which the father presumed were the notes he needed to see. He allegedly grabbed and squeezed her hand "really hard" and said, "That's not your backpack." When she said, "Dad, that's not fair," he replied, "I'm sick of you." The daughter continued to a sports tryout and only later told her mother about the incident. The mother asked if she wanted to speak to the guardian *ad litem*, go to the hospital, or speak to the police about it. The guardian was unavailable and she declined to see a doctor. She did, however, speak with the police. At the father's trial on a battery charge, a police officer testified that he saw a dime-sized bruise on the daughter's hand.

(Continued)

The father was convicted of battery and then appealed the conviction, arguing that the act of grabbing his daughter's hand was privileged under a parental control justification. He argued that: "(1) federal law recognizes a fundamental right of parents to make decisions concerning care, custody, and control of their children; (2) state law recognizes the common law parental control justification as an affirmative defense for offensive acts which would otherwise be punishable under the battery statute; (3) and the district court erred in finding that the touching was unlawful, . . ."

FROM THE OPINION

We hold that, in New Mexico, a parent has a privilege to use moderate or reasonable physical force, without criminal liability, when engaged in the discipline of his or her child. Discipline involves controlling behavior and correcting misbehavior for the betterment and welfare of the child. The physical force cannot be cruel or excessive if it is to be justified. . . .

2. Defendant's Act Fell Within The Parental Privilege

The battery offense of which the Defendant was convicted proscribes "the unlawful, intentional touching or application of force to the person of another, when done in a rude, insolent or angry manner." § 30–3–4. The State had the burden to prove beyond a reasonable doubt all elements of the offense, including unlawfulness. . . . When a parent's behavior falls within the parental privilege, the act is not unlawful. . . . Thus, when a question of parental privilege exists, the State must prove beyond a reasonable doubt that the parent's conduct did not come within the privilege. . . .

In considering whether the State has disproved the justification, the court or jury is entitled to consider such factors as "the age, physical condition, and other characteristics of a child as well as with the gravity of the misconduct." Arnold, 543 N.W.2d at 603; . . . there must exist some threshold at which parental physical force in the discipline of children is justified even though, technically, the elements of the battery offense can be proven. . . .

. . . there must exist for parents a harbor safe from prosecutorial interference in parental judgment. See Model Penal Code and Commentaries § 3.08, cmt. 2 (1985) ("So long as a parent uses moderate force for permissible purposes, the criminal law should not provide for review of the reasonableness of the parent's judgment."). In our view, an isolated instance of moderate or reasonable physical force as that in the present case that results in nothing more than transient pain or temporary marks or bruises is protected under the parental discipline privilege. . . .

This protection for parents should exist even if the parent acts out of frustration or short temper. Parents do not always act with calmness of mind or considered judgment when upset with, or concerned about, their children's behavior. . . . A reaction often occurs from behavior a parent deems inappropriate that irritates or angers the parent, causing a reactive, demonstrative act. Heat of the moment must not result in immoderate physical force and must be managed; however, an angry moment driving moderate or reasonable discipline is often part and parcel of the real world of parenting with which prosecutors and courts should not interfere. What parent among us can say he or she has not been angered to some degree from a child's defiant, impudent, or insolent conduct, sufficient to call for spontaneous, stern, and meaningful discipline?

In the present case, no reasonable minds could differ on the legal consequence of Defendant's acts. The district court did not find or determine that Defendant had no

(Continued)

legitimate disciplinary purpose whatsoever in mind. Even were a disciplinary purpose questionable or obscure, Defendant's act was an isolated one. He reacted when he saw Daughter with her hand in Son's pack. His demonstrative act, even if an angry touching, resulted in only a temporary dime-sized bruise on Daughter's hand and transient pain. The force was relatively inconsequential; the injury was marginal. Defendant's conduct was not cruel or excessive, and considering the totality of the circumstances, it was moderate and reasonable. "If such acts, . . . with no apparent evidence of any aggravating factors, are sufficient to support an assault charge, then any physical contact by a parent with a child that hurts the child may support an assault conviction if the State elects to prosecute." Wilder, 748 A.2d at 456.

We determine that Defendant's conduct did not reach beyond the point of departure from justified parental discipline and was privileged, and that, as a matter of law, the evidence in this case was insufficient to support a determination of guilt on the charge of battery beyond a reasonable doubt.

Conclusion

We reverse Defendant's conviction of battery and remand with instructions to enter a judgment of acquittal.

SIDEBAR

Do you agree with the decision of the appellate court in this case? Explain your response.

EMOTIONAL ABUSE

All states and territories except Georgia and Washington include emotional maltreatment in their statutory definitions of types of abuse, sometimes referring to it as psychological abuse. As of January 2012, more than twenty states specifically define emotional abuse.

> Typical language used in these definitions is "injury to the psychological capacity or emotional stability of the child as evidenced by an observable or substantial change in behavior, emotional response, or cognition," or as evidenced by "anxiety, depression, withdrawal, or aggressive behavior."[46]

Caretaker behavior that rises to the level of emotional abuse generally encompasses a persistent pattern of the behaviors described earlier under emotional neglect, along with more overt behaviors including verbally assaulting and belittling children, terrorizing them with threats of punishment and abandonment, humiliating and embarrassing them, and exploiting them by involving them in illegal behavior such as theft. It does not include occasional and unintentionally hurtful outbursts that can occur with even well-intentioned parents. It is more likely to occur among parents who were themselves abused as children, who have never had an opportunity to learn or develop effective parenting skills, and who have unrealistic expectations for their children. Whatever the cause, many researchers believe that emotional abuse is a stronger predictor of developmental problems than is physical abuse.

> Although the visible signs of emotional abuse in children can be difficult to detect, the hidden scars of this type of abuse manifest in numerous behavioral ways, including insecurity, poor self-esteem, destructive behavior, angry acts (such as fire-setting and animal cruelty), withdrawal, poor development of basic skills, alcohol or drug abuse, suicide, difficulty forming relationships, and unstable job histories.[47]

SEXUAL ABUSE

Under CAPTA's "minimum definition," sexual abuse includes:

- the employment, use, persuasion, inducement, enticement, or coercion of any child to engage in, or assist any other person to engage in, any sexually explicit conduct or simulation of such conduct for the purpose of producing a visual depiction of such conduct; or
- the rape, and in cases of caretaker or interfamilial relationships, statutory rape, molestation, prostitution, or other form of sexual exploitation of children, or incest with children.[48]

The states define sexual abuse in various ways, but they generally include both touching offenses (such as fondling the child's genitals, penetrating a child's vagina or anus to any extent directly or with an object, or having the child touch the caretaker's sex organs) and nontouching offenses such as exposing a child to sexual acts (masturbation, sexual relations, etc.) or to pornographic materials. They may also include sexual exploitation of children such as engaging them in acts of prostitution or using them as subjects of pornographic materials.

SUBSTANCE ABUSE

CAPTA requires states to have policies and procedures to notify children's protective services of substance-exposed newborns (SENs) and to establish a plan of safe care for those affected by illegal substance abuse or withdrawal symptoms as a result of prenatal drug exposure. The states have chosen to address this requirement in a variety of ways. Some have placed priority on making drug treatment more accessible for pregnant women. For example, Illinois and Minnesota require mandated reporters to report pregnant women they suspect are abusing drugs so that they can be referred for treatment. California, Maryland, and Missouri, among other states, require that when a substance-exposed newborn is identified, an assessment must be done of both the newborn and the child's family so that appropriate services can be arranged.[49]

Some states have attempted to criminalize prenatal substance abuse, using a variety of existing statutes such as delivering drugs to a minor (through the umbilical cord), assault with a deadly weapon, corruption of a minor, criminal abuse and neglect of a child, and manslaughter. Still others treat it under civil child abuse laws and view it as a ground for terminating or suspending parental rights. For example, the Wisconsin children's code as amended in 1998 grants that state's juvenile court exclusive jurisdiction over an unborn child when the pregnant mother "habitually lacks self-control" with regard to drugs or alcohol. The statute defines an unborn child as a "human being from the time of fertilization to the time of birth."[50] In the case *In re Baby Boy Blackshear*,[51] the Ohio Supreme Court interpreted that state's civil child abuse law to mean that if a newborn baby tests positive for drug exposure, it constitutes *per se* child abuse even though the civil child abuse law made no reference to prenatal abuse.

Some states address by statute the harm caused to a child of any age as a result of exposure to illegal drug activity. Approximately half the states do so in their criminal statutes and some (such as Alaska, Kansas, Minnesota, and Missouri) do so in their child endangerment statutes. Some states (California, Mississippi, Montana, North Carolina, and Washington, for example) impose enhanced penalties for the manufacturing of illegal drugs in the presence of a child. Idaho, Louisiana, and Ohio prosecute the manufacture or possession of any controlled substance in the presence of a child as a felony, and others (such as Illinois, Pennsylvania, and Virginia) specifically target the manufacture of methamphetamine in the presence of a child.

PARALEGAL PRACTICE TIP

To see an example of a Petition for Care and Protection of an Unborn Child, visit *www.wicourts.gov.* (Wisconsin) You can find a link to this site at *www.pearsonhighered.com/wilson* in the companion website material for Chapter 13 under "Forms."

PARALEGAL PRACTICE TIP

To learn more about how the states address prenatal substance abuse visit *www.childwelfare.gov.* You can find a link to this site at *www.pearsonhighered.com/wilson* in the companion website material related to Chapter 13 under "Resources."

Reporting of Child Abuse

Mandatory reporter

an individual who, by virtue of his or her employment as a police officer, nurse, etc., is required to report suspected child abuse and neglect

Permissive reporter

an individual who may, but is not required to, report suspected child abuse

Every state identifies individuals who are required to report suspected child abuse or neglect to a designated child protective services agency (usually a state social or human services agency). **Mandatory reporters** customarily include, at a minimum, law enforcement personnel, individuals in the health professions, social workers, teachers, and day care providers. Mandatory reporters are required to report suspected abuse and neglect or face civil and sometimes criminal penalties. **Permissive reporters** are individuals who may, but are not required to, report suspected abuse. These individuals include, among others, friends, family members, neighbors, store employees, and strangers, who most commonly witness incidents of abuse in public areas, such as playgrounds, malls, and parking lots. Permissive reporters are not liable for reports filed in good faith. However, some states provide a penalty (usually a fine) for knowingly filing a false report. Some states require "all persons" to report child abuse, by implication including attorneys and their employees. For example, the applicable New Jersey statute requires "Any person having reasonable cause to believe that a child has been subjected to child abuse or acts of child abuse shall report the same immediately to the Division of Youth and Family Services by telephone or otherwise."[52] The Act provides statutory immunity to those who file reports.[53] A failure to report constitutes a disorderly person's offense and may constitute evidence of negligence.[54]

PARALEGAL PRACTICE TIP

To learn more about reporting abuse in your state, visit *www.childwelfare.gov*. Reporting Forms for several states can be accessed at this site including, for example, Connecticut, Delaware, Florida, Iowa. Illinois, Massachusetts, and North Dakota. You can find a link to the site at *www.pearsonhighered.com/wilson* in the companion website material for Chapter 13 under "Resources."

PARALEGAL PRACTICE TIP

States provide notice of reports of abuse to both accused and nonaccused parents and sometimes provide guidance with respect to the nature of the process and the parents' rights. See, for example, forms used for this purpose in New Hampshire at *www.courts.state.nh.us*. You can find a link to this site at *www.pearsonhighered.com/wilson* in the companion website material for Chapter 13 under "Forms."

Reports are usually made to the state's designated child protection agency. The agency is responsible for:

- receiving reports of abuse or neglect
- promptly investigating reports, usually by making a home visit, interviewing relevant parties, and evaluating the child's living arrangements (An initial visit customarily must be made within twenty-four hours if a child is in imminent danger or, if not, within three to seven days)
- developing plans for families in need of services
- providing a wide range of services directly or through third parties (counseling, parent education, educational assessments, homemaker services, etc.)
- removing children from homes where they are at risk of immediate serious harm with or without a court order or prior notice to the parent(s)
- scheduling court hearings before or immediately after removal so that parents are given an opportunity to challenge the agency's actions
- arranging for and monitoring appropriate foster care placements in homes or group facilities

- initiating proceedings to terminate parental rights where appropriate and facilitating adoptions or other long-term care
- referring cases involving serious physical injury or child rape to law enforcement authorities for investigation and possible criminal prosecution

PARALEGAL PRACTICE TIP

In some cases, parents will voluntarily seek the assistance of the state with a child who, despite their best efforts, persistently runs away from home, willfully fails to attend school, and refuses to obey reasonable parental rules. When the parents believe they can no longer adequately care for or protect such a child, they may seek to have him or her designated by the court as a child in need of services (CHINS), thereby triggering a host of alternative placement and treatment options under the supervision of the state.

To see one state's description of the CHINS process, visit *www.vermontjudiciary.org/eforms* and read "Form 116 Booklet for Parents in CHINS Cases" and "Form 117 Youth in CHINS Cases: Understanding the Court Process." You can find a link to this site at *www.pearsonhighered.com/wilson* in the companion website material related to Chapter 13 under "Resources."

PARALEGAL PRACTICE TIP

In the late 1800s and early 1900s, societies for the prevention of cruelty to children in various states carried out many of the functions now performed by publicly funded child protective agencies. Many, if not all, states still have private, nonprofit societies whose mission is to strengthen families and prevent child abuse through programs, services, and strong public advocacy. They are generally licensed by the state to provide community-based services such as intervention programs, mental health treatment, day care, home visitation programs, and adoption services.

When a report of abuse or neglect is received and processed by a child protection agency, the case customarily proceeds along one of four paths:

1. When the report is determined to be false or frivolous, it is deemed invalid.
2. When the agency determines that the report was made in good faith but finds no reasonable cause to believe the child is at risk, the case is designated unsubstantiated and is closed, although the record remains in the department's files.
3. When the report is substantiated, the agency develops a service plan with the parent(s)/caretaker(s). If the abuse is not serious and services are accepted and effectively implemented, the child may remain with the family. If the services are not accepted or successfully implemented, the agency may file a **care and protection petition** seeking temporary removal or removal and termination of parental rights, if appropriate.
4. When the agency has reasonable cause to believe that removal is necessary to ensure the child's safety, the agency may immediately remove the child and file a dependency action/care and protection petition for hearing usually within seventy-two hours. The court will determine whether a service plan should be developed and a reunification sought, or the agency should seek to terminate parental rights in anticipation of adoption or some other permanent placement in the best interests of the child.

Care and protection/dependency proceeding
a court proceeding in which the state seeks custody of a child and termination of parental rights if warranted

The U.S. Supreme Court has long recognized the preservation of the family as a priority. It has also afforded constitutional protection to the right of parents to raise their children as they see fit. However, it has also recognized that parental rights must be balanced with the duty of the state to protect children. Removal of a child from his or her home is clearly an extreme measure, but the state has the authority to initiate such action under the legal doctrine of ***parens patriae***, the Latin term for "parent of the country." However, it cannot do so arbitrarily, but rather only for good cause, and parents must be afforded due process to protect their parental rights.

Parens patriae
[Latin for "parent of the country"]
the authority of a state to protect those within its boundaries who cannot protect themselves

PARALEGAL PRACTICE TIP

To see an example of an Application and Order for Temporary Removal of Child, visit *www.nycourts.gov/forms*. You can find a link to this site at *www.pearsonhighered.com/wilson* in the companion website material related to Chapter 13 under "Forms."

PARALEGAL PRACTICE TIP

Whenever abuse and neglect, removal, or termination of parental rights is at issue in a case, discovery should include a search of child protection agency records with respect to reports and service plans, etc.

PARALEGAL PRACTICE TIP

To see an example of a Petition for Termination of Parental Rights, visit *www.courts.delaware.gov*. You can find a link to this site at *www.pearsonhighered.com/wilson* in the companion website material related to Chapter 13 under "Forms."

Termination of parental rights
a judicial severing of the legal relationship between a parent and child

Reasonable efforts
the effort a child protective agency must make to prevent removal of a child from his or her home, or, if removed, to reunify the family within a specified period of time

Permanency planning
planning for the return home of a child following removal or for termination of parental rights within a legally specified period of time in an effort to promote stability for the child

The removal of a child from his or her home may be temporary or permanent. Temporary removal may be appropriate in situations where a report of abuse is substantiated and reasonable steps have been taken to keep the child at home, but the child remains at risk because the parents are "temporarily" unable to provide appropriate care. To remove the child on a temporary basis, the agency files a care and protection/dependency action in which it asks a court to find the child dependent or in need of care and protection. The court also must determine that remaining in the home is contrary to the child's best interests, and that the agency has made reasonable efforts to prevent removal. If successful, the agency is granted temporary custody, assumes primary responsibility for the child, and can make an appropriate placement in foster care while the parents complete the requirements of a service plan. If the removal will be permanent, the agency may convince the parents to voluntarily surrender their parental rights or, if that effort fails, may file a petition for involuntary **termination of parental rights.** A termination of parental rights severs the legal relationship between a parent and his or her biological or adopted child. Given that parental rights enjoy a high degree of constitutional protection, they cannot be terminated without clear and convincing evidence of parental unfitness.

Since the passage of the federal Adoption Assistance and Child Welfare Act of 1980 (CWA),[55] child protective agencies have had a duty to make "**reasonable efforts**" to keep families together before removing children and, if removal is necessary, to make a reasonable effort to eventually reunite the family. This requirement sometimes has resulted in the premature return of children to high-risk family environments or, in the alternative, to lengthy stays in foster care. Partly to address these problems, in 1997 Congress passed the Adoption and Safe Families Act (ASFA), which retained the reasonable efforts requirement but gave considerable discretion to the states with respect to implementing it. The Act gave priority to the child's "health and safety" and also took steps to limit the time children spend in foster care.[56]

ASFA requires that a **permanency planning** hearing be held no later than twelve months after a child has been placed in foster care (or sooner in cases in which reunification is an impossible or inappropriate goal, such as when the child has been abandoned, the parent has subjected the child to serious abuse, or the parent has murdered another family member).

PARALEGAL PRACTICE TIP

To see an example of a Petition for Permanency Planning Hearing, visit *www.courts.state.va.us*. (Virginia) You can find a link to this site at *www.pearsonhighered.com/wilson* in the companion website material related to Chapter 13 under "Forms."

Child protection litigation can be costly, dehumanizing, disempowering, and traumatic for the parties and particularly for children who have been removed from their homes and separated from their parents, siblings, and extended families for reasons usually not of their own making. An alternative to litigation is child protection mediation, which may be used at any stage of a child protection case. It is usually initiated by a child protection worker or an attorney. The goal is to jointly develop a case plan to reunify the family or, if necessary, to find the most suitable permanent placement. "Mediated issues often include the services the parents will use, conditions that must be satisfied before the child may return home, alternative options for child care, and parenting practices, including alternative nonviolent approaches."[59] Statistics indicate that 60% to 85% of such mediations end in agreements and that they promote family progress and increased compliance with court orders.[60]

Abuse and Custody Disputes

The Model Code of the National Council of Juvenile and Family Court Judges recommends that in every proceeding where there is a dispute as to the custody of a child, a determination by the court that domestic or family violence has occurred should raise a rebuttable presumption that "it is detrimental to the child and not in the best interests of the child, to be placed in sole custody, joint legal custody, or joint physical custody with the perpetrator of family violence."[63] A report to the American Bar Association has also recommended that, where there is proof of domestic violence, "batterers should be presumed by law to be unfit custodians for their children."[64] Many of the states have adopted such provisions in one form or another. Some statutes require the courts to consider a history of domestic violence before joint custody can be awarded; some require the court to factor domestic violence into the best interests test; and some mandate that the courts not award joint custody where abuse has been demonstrated.

In addition to guardians *ad litem,* judges often make use of Court Appointed Special Advocates (CASA volunteers) in cases involving severely abused, abandoned, or neglected children. CASA is part of a national volunteer movement that began about three decades ago. It was initiated by a judge in Seattle, Washington, who sought a "voice in court" for abused and neglected children. There are now more than 900 CASA programs nationwide with at least one in every state. CASA volunteers serve as both mentors and advocates. They work with children who have been removed from their homes and placed in foster care. The one-on-one relationship formed with the child is often the only stable relationship he or she has in a world of social workers, attorneys, therapists, and caregivers. It positions the volunteer to provide the judge with information that will help safeguard the child's best interests and facilitate placement in a safe, permanent home.

To see a comprehensive state-by-state picture of the relationship between domestic violence and custody in applicable state statutes, visit *www.americanbar.org.* You can find a link to this site at *www.pearsonhighered.com/wilson* in the companion website material related to Chapter 13 under "Resources."

When the abuse has been interspousal and not actively directed at the parties' children, judges (and sometimes clients and attorneys as well) may fail to appreciate the impact that witnessing a parent's abusive behavior has on a child. Even if the children have not been the direct recipients of this violence, they are victims as a result of exposure to it. "According to reports by battered mothers, 87% to 90% of their children witnessed the mothers' abuse."[65] They may actually see the physical, sexual, and emotional attacks; overhear them; experience the emotional tension in the residence; and/or be exposed to the aftermath, including both the mother's physical injuries and the destruction of property (phones ripped from the wall, dishes and chairs broken, etc.).

> Children who live in a battering relationship experience the most insidious form of child abuse. Whether or not they are physically abused by either parent is less important than the psychological scars they bear from watching their fathers beat their mothers. They learn to become part of a dishonest conspiracy of silence. . . .
>
> The effects of witnessing domestic violence are often severe and multifaceted. Certainly, not all children are affected by exposure to domestic violence in the same manner or to the same degree. Numerous factors influence the extent to which a child is affected. These factors include: age, gender, race, frequency and severity of the violence witnessed, and the degree of maternal impairment. Nonetheless, all children exposed to domestic violence are affected in some way. Witnessing domestic violence can affect children behaviorally, cognitively, emotionally, physically and socially.[66]

The Utah statute on "Commission of Domestic Violence in the Presence of a Child" can be seen at *www.pearsonhighered.com/wilson* in the companion website material related to Chapter 13 under "Statutes."

A mother who has been abused by her partner is "damned if she does and damned if she doesn't" fight for custody of her children. Her abuser may threaten to harm her and/or the children, take the children where she "will never find them," or, if the circumstances fit, expose her to some kind of criminal liability or embarrassment as a result of her drug use or immigration status. The court may not believe her allegations of abuse, particularly if they are undocumented, or if her chameleon

Paralegal **Application 13.3**

Making the Case for Custody of a Child Who Has Witnessed Family Violence

Parents in abusive relationships do not come into court with equal power and ability to advocate for themselves and their children. The abusive parent's goal is to depict the victimized parent as unfit, immoral, and incapable of having the children.[67] Abusive parents frequently seek custody of their children, and they are often successful.[68] A client who has been abused and who makes a decision to pursue custody of her children usually faces an uphill battle, especially when those children have been exposed to her victimization. The family law team and client will need to work together to establish a solid case and to do so in a manner that does not expose the mother to liability and the children to further trauma. Depending on the judge's background and experience dealing with family violence issues, the family law team may need to research the effects on children of exposure to domestic violence. The client will need to assist by suggesting witnesses, documents, and other evidence that will establish how the children have been, or are likely to be, affected by continued exposure to the abuser's violent conduct. Examples of demonstrated effects of children's exposure to domestic violence that may be evident include, but are not necessarily limited to, the following:[69]

- Aggressiveness, acting out, and antisocial conduct, including behaviors such as bullying, assaults, and destruction of property

- Generally lower levels of social competence
- Poor problem-solving skills
- Lower levels of empathy
- Depression, suicidal behaviors, anxieties, fears, and phobias
- Feelings that they are helpless and powerless
- Low self-esteem
- Guilt and self-blaming for the violence or their inability to prevent or stop it
- Anger at both the abuser and the victim
- A pervasive attitude that the use of violence is an appropriate means of expressing anger, solving problems, and intimidating and gaining control over others
- Greater likelihood of abusing a spouse or partner as an adult[70]
- Abuse of drugs and alcohol
- Running away
- Sexual acting out
- Fear for their lives and/or the lives of their parents and siblings
- Lower levels of cognitive and academic functioning
- Poor health, including colds, elevated blood pressure, insomnia, and bed-wetting
- Post-traumatic stress disorder[71]
- Injuries suffered as a result of trying to intervene and protect the abused parent

spouse persuades the judge that her claims are unfounded or grossly exaggerated. In a state that criminalizes exposing a child to domestic violence, the mother may open herself to criminal liability if she fights back in self-defense against her abuser. In some states, permitting one's child to witness spousal abuse itself may constitute grounds for removing the child from the care and custody of both parents.[72]

In abuse cases, a court's custody order ideally should reflect a thoughtful assessment of the particular nature of the abuse experienced and its likely causes and effects. Based on the facts of the individual case, appropriate actions may range from termination of an abuser's parental rights to a plan in which visitation is permitted and a focus is placed on building the parties' skills in effective parenting, problem solving, and conflict management.

In general, when seeking custody on behalf of an abused mother, a proposed custody order needs to be carefully tailored to the facts of the case and designed to protect the safety and welfare of both the children and the mother. It may ask that the court order any one or more of the following conditions, which may be eased over time if the abusive parent remains in compliance and if it is in the best interests of the children.

- Sole legal and physical custody to the mother without visitation, because joint custody fosters continual conflict and gives the abuser an opportunity to continue his abuse, OR sole legal and physical custody to the mother with supervised visitation, preferably at a supervised visitation center that provides a safe location and trained personnel able to intervene if problems arise.

- A restraint on the abusive parent's communication with or proximity to the children except in the context of authorized visitation
- A requirement that the abuser not be granted, or not be permitted to continue, visitation unless he participates in and successfully completes a batterer's program or some other long-term treatment option that addresses anger, battering, and control issues in depth
- A requirement that the abusive parent not use alcohol or drugs during and/or within a specified time period prior to a visit
- Designation of a neutral location such as a social services agency, resource center, or police station for drop-off and pickup of the children for visitation
- Impounding of any information revealing the address and phone numbers of the mother and children
- Denial of access to school and other records containing information regarding the residence of the mother and children
- Exemption for the mother from any required state parenting program or, in the alternative, a requirement that the parents attend separate sessions where appropriate safety precautions can be arranged
- A requirement that the batterer be required to pay for counseling/therapy if needed for the mother and/or the children
- An appropriate recourse to address related disputes. Mediation should not be an option for dispute resolution, especially in cases where the dominant form of abuse is coercive control
- Appointment of a parenting coordinator or master to manage recurring child custody disputes (an approach presently in place in several states)
- Exclusion of any "boilerplate" parental cooperation or "friendly parent" language in separation agreements

Parent coordinator
an individual, usually appointed by the court, who assists with creation and implementation of parenting agreements and enforcement of decrees in high-conflict cases involving minor children

In high-conflict child custody cases, **parent coordinators** can "assist parents in creating, implementing, and monitoring parenting plans. . . . typically parent coordinators make decisions or recommendations about day-to-day matters such as scheduling, activities, transportation, child care, discipline, education, and health care. They generally cannot modify custody, allow relocation, or make any other major changes to court orders."[73]

> In those cases of domestic violence where one parent seeks to obtain and maintain power and control over the other, the role of the PC [parent coordinator] changes to an almost purely enforcement function. Here the PC is likely to be dealing with a court order, the more detailed the better, rather than a mutually agreed upon parenting plan; and the role is to ensure compliance with the details of the order and to test each request for variance from its terms with an eye to protecting the custodial parent's autonomy to make decisions based on the children's best interests and guarding against manipulation by the abusing parent.[74]

The coordinator in some situations may also have an opportunity to model conflict resolution skills.

Criminal Actions Against Abusive Parents

There has been a long-standing, albeit somewhat fading, tradition in this country of viewing family violence and abuse against children as a private family matter in which the state should intervene only when absolutely necessary. And there has been a parallel reluctance to prosecute family members and parents who harm their children except in particularly egregious cases.

> In the context of parenthood and the criminal justice system, family members are still far more likely to be excused for behavior that would be considered criminal if committed by third parties. Examples abound: the extraordinary difficulties prosecutors face in convicting parents on homicide charges in child abuse cases, the lighter sentences imposed on defendants who kill family members, the preferential treatment in some states given to sex offenders who victimize their own children rather than a stranger, and the outcry over prosecuting negligent parents. . . . This preferential treatment for parents persists even though young children in particular face far greater risk of danger from their relatives at home than they do from strangers in public places.[75]

PARALEGAL PRACTICE TIP

Overall, parents generally receive more favorable treatment by the criminal justice system than nonparents. However, research suggests that parents from various socioeconomic groups are treated differently. Parents in blue-collar professions and parents who are unemployed are four times more likely to be prosecuted than parents from wealthier socioeconomic groups.[76]

When parents are prosecuted for abusive conduct toward their children, they may be prosecuted under a variety of criminal statutes:

- Statutes ranging from murder and manslaughter in cases involving deaths, to assault, battery, aggravated assault, rape/sexual assault, etc., with imposition of heightened penalties when the crime is committed against a child
- Statutes that address intentional crimes committed against children in particular, such as rape of a child, incest, child endangerment, or use of a child to commit a crime such as production of child pornography
- Statutes that criminalize parental/caretaker neglect

PARALEGAL PRACTICE TIP

Prosecutions for criminal offenses are subject to applicable statutes of limitations, which may vary from crime to crime and state to state. They may also vary in terms of when they begin to run. For example, statutes for crimes relating to sexual abuse of minors usually begin to run when the abuse is first discovered (or recalled) rather than when the injury first occurred.

The same offense may be treated differently in different states. For example, some states, such as Utah, treat the commission of an act of domestic violence in the presence of a child as a distinct criminal offense, and others treat it as a more serious degree of assault resulting in an enhanced penalty.

Tort Actions

Under early common law, parents were immune from liability in **tort** for failure to prevent harm to their minor children resulting from the actions of third parties, and there still is little legislation or case law recognizing that parents who have not created the risk of harm have an affirmative duty to intervene to rescue a minor child from actual or potential harm caused by others. But what about situations in which the parents' child hurts others?

Although this is not technically abuse of a child, parents are sometimes sued by third parties, under a theory of negligent supervision, for damages caused by their children. "Under common law, parents can be liable for their children's acts 'where the parents' [own] negligence has made it possible for the child to cause the injury complained of and probable that the child would do so."[77] Section 316 of the Restatement (Second) of Torts provides that the duty of a parent to take reasonable measures to control a child arises when the parent knows or should

Tort

a civil wrong (other than breach of contract) for which a court provides a remedy, usually in the form of money damages; the wrong must involve harm resulting from breach of a legal duty owed to another

Negligent supervision
a cause of action based on parents' duty to society to exercise reasonable care in the supervision of their minor children in order to prevent them from intentionally causing injury to others

know of the need to control the child and has both the ability and the opportunity to do so. The cause of action commonly known as **negligent supervision** is based on the premise that parents have a duty to society at large to exercise reasonable care in the supervision of their minor children in order to prevent them from intentionally causing injury to others.

Although parents will not necessarily be held liable for the intentional or malicious acts of their minor children, a majority of states have enacted statutes making parents liable in certain circumstances. Some states legislate parental responsibility laws in specific areas of conduct. For example, a Mississippi statute[78] provides that, subject to some exceptions, a parent may be found guilty of knowingly permitting a child under eighteen to have, own, or carry a concealed weapon, the carrying of which is prohibited by law. (See Paralegal Application 13.4.)

Paralegal **Application 13.4**

Was Mom to Blame?

The Facts

At home one evening at 8:00 p.m., Mavis Daniels received a phone call from her employer. While she was on the phone, her fifteen-year-old son, Eddie Smith, left the house without her knowledge. At the time, he was subject to a 7:30 p.m. curfew Sunday through Thursday imposed by the youth court after he'd struck a boy at school. After Eddie left the house, he and two of his friends activated the alarm on a girl's car by hitting it with a ball. When the girl's boyfriend, Johnny Lee Williamson Jr., came out to investigate, Eddie confronted him and, after a verbal exchange, pulled out a gun and shot the unarmed Williamson, leaving him paralyzed from the waist down. Williamson subsequently filed a complaint alleging Eddie's mother was negligent in her supervision of Eddie and that her negligence was the proximate cause of his injuries.

Eddie had been in trouble on several occasions prior to this particular incident: He wounded his uncle in a fight with a knife, knocked a boy unconscious at school, dropped out of school, and was accused of threatening a ten-year-old girl with a pellet gun and being the lookout for a robbery committed by some of his friends. Without his mother's knowledge, he obtained a handgun. Ms. Daniels testified that she had tried to enforce the curfew and attempted to discipline her son by grounding him, taking away his video games, and applying corporal punishment. When he dropped out of school, she took him to work with her at the Head Start agency and had him clean up around the school, where she could keep an eye on him. She also took him to a mental health center for counseling.

In a negligent supervision action, the plaintiff, Williamson, must establish that the mother had a duty of care, that she breached that duty, that her breach was the proximate cause of his injuries, and that damages are warranted to compensate him for his loss. He must show

not only that there was negligence and an injury, but also that the injury was reasonably foreseeable.

Sidebar

In this Paralegal Application, Mavis Daniels appears to be a single mother, and the case makes no reference to the existence or identity of the youth's father. If there are two parents in the picture, each of whom plays a considerable role in the child's life, a question may arise as to whether both parents should be liable for negligent supervision or only the parent with primary custody. A Florida appellate court considered this question as a matter of first impression in that state. The majority held that only the mother (who had primary residential custody) was liable to a school district for her son's malicious destruction of school property. A strong dissent argued that "On the one hand, the father in this case has successfully sought and procured an equal voice and equal participation in all of the major decision-making process involving the rearing of this minor child. . . ." but on the other hand, was not being held accountable for his son's conduct. See *Canida v. Canida,* 751 So. 2d 647 at 652 (Fla. App. 1999).

In this case, do you think Mavis Daniels should be held liable for the injury to Williamson? What are the arguments for both sides of the question? Read the case *Johnny Lee Williamson, Jr. v. Mavis C. Daniels*, 748 So. 2d 754 (Miss. 1999), decided by the Mississippi Supreme Court to see if you agree with the court's decision.

PARALEGAL PRACTICE TIP

The opinion in *Williamson v. Daniels* is available at *www. pearsonhighered.com/wilson* in the companion website material related to Chapter 13 under "Cases" and in the Case Resources Section of the MyLegalStudiesLab.

To Know or Not to Know . . . to Tell or Not to Tell

Domestic violence often permeates many family law cases, whether or not it is revealed to or detected by counsel or other members of the family law team. If the issue does arise, it is often difficult, even frightening, to address. What can be done when a battered spouse is being bullied into a poor property settlement in order to protect her children and herself or when counsel or the paralegal begins to suspect the client is abusing his or her children or partner and will very likely continue to do so? How can the attorney reconcile the ethical duties to maintain client confidentiality and advocate zealously for the client with the duties to prevent a fraud on the court and prevent the commission of a crime that could result in serious physical injury or death?

Clearly, family violence poses ethical issues of monumental dimensions for attorneys and their employees, including paralegals. The legal community itself is split between those who believe lawyers should disclose serious threats to third parties and those who believe they should not. For example, some argue that

> in the context of domestic violence cases, lawyers have an affirmative duty to (1) screen battering clients who have indicated a likelihood of harming others, (2) attempt to dissuade them from carrying out planned violent crimes, and (3) warn identifiable abuse victims whom their clients have threatened.[79]

On the other side, it is argued that mandatory child abuse reporting in the context of representing domestic violence victims interferes with confidentiality and open communication, exposes domestic violence victims and their children to harm, subjects victims to state intervention and potential criminal prosecution for abuse or neglect, and discourages victims from seeking legal assistance.[80]

CAPTA essentially leaves confidentiality and disclosure requirements to the discretion of the states. Little clear guidance is provided to attorneys in this area in state reporting requirements, statutes governing the attorney-client privilege, rules of professional responsibility, or occasional guidelines from bar associations and ethics opinions. Rule 1.6 of the American Bar Association Model Rules of Professional Conduct (Model Rules), adopted in several states, provides in part that a lawyer shall not reveal information relating to the representation of a client unless the client gives informed consent, the disclosure is impliedly authorized in order to carry out the representation, or the lawyer believes the disclosure is reasonably necessary to prevent death or substantial bodily harm or to comply with a law or court order.

The ABA Model Rules are not binding, however, and the states are not uniform in their disclosure requirements.

- Some states specifically exclude attorneys from mandatory child-abuse-reporting requirements. The applicable Missouri statute provides: Any legally recognized privileged communication, except that between attorney and client or involving communications made to a minister or clergyperson, shall not apply to situations involving known or suspected child abuse or neglect and shall not constitute grounds for failure to report as required or permitted by sections 210.110 to 210.165, to cooperate with the division in any of its activities pursuant to sections 210.110 to 210.165, or to give or accept evidence in any judicial proceeding relating to child abuse or neglect.[81]
- The Model Rules for attorneys in Texas provide that "When a lawyer has confidential information clearly establishing that a client is likely to commit a criminal or fraudulent act that is likely to result in death or substantial bodily

harm to a person, the lawyer shall reveal confidential information to the extent revelation reasonably appears necessary to prevent the client from committing the criminal or fraudulent act."[82]

- The relevant Georgia rule is permissive. Georgia Rule 1.6(b)(3) provides: "Before using or disclosing information pursuant to Subsection (1), if feasible, the lawyer must make a good faith effort to persuade the client either not to act or, if the client has already acted, to warn the victim."
- In one of the few ethics opinions on the subject of the attorney's role in reporting abuse, the Ethics Committee in New Jersey stated that an attorney is not required to report past child abuse in a custody action. However, in a supplement to the opinion, the Committee clarified that the privilege does not apply when the client demonstrates a "continued propensity" for abuse.[83]
- In Wisconsin, attorneys are permitted to use discretion with respect to reporting or not reporting child abuse.[84]

Rules that leave disclosure to the discretion of the attorney are perhaps the least helpful of all.

> Discretionary disclosure may . . . place lawyers in the untenable position of choosing preservation of their bar licenses over victim safety as well as expose them to liability in tort. None of the state professional rules protect the attorney from tort liability in the decision to disclose. Mandatory disclosure rules provide greater protection to practitioners, yet most state rules employ permissive language."[85]

PARALEGAL PRACTICE TIP

To learn about mandatory reporters in your state, visit *www.americanbar.org*. The report identifies applicable statutes and mandatory reporters in each state as of the report date. The chart also specifically references the apparent treatment of legal professionals in this context. You can find a link to this site at *www.pearsonhighered.com/wilson* in the companion website material related to Chapter 13 under "Resources."

Paralegal Application 13.5

What Is Your Opinion?

Do you believe members of the family law team should be mandated reporters? Explain your response. What is the attorney's duty in your state? What do you think the paralegal should do if his or her supervising attorney is a mandated reporter who fails to report?

CHAPTER **SUMMARY**

Family violence is a painful reality in our society, as the statistics provided in this chapter indicate. Despite its significance, many members of family law teams have a very limited knowledge about family violence: its causes, manifestations, and effects. This chapter provides prospective paralegals with a very basic introduction to this multifaceted topic. It considers it in the contexts of both intimate partner and parent-child relationships. It introduces definitions and cold, hard statistics. It identifies a variety of legal remedies available to victims and their advocates. It reviews some of the subtle psychological and sociological dimensions of this complex topic. And finally, it raises troubling ethical questions confronting practitioners.

Child abuse and neglect cases clearly involve the balancing of critical and often competing public policies: a parent's right to raise his or her children free from governmental interference and the state's interest in protecting children. Everyone weighs in: parents, children, offenders, victims, judges, social workers, therapists, attorneys, and, of course, the general public. Paralegals may find themselves in the middle of wrenching situations, troubled deeply by what they see parents do to their children but also recognizing that the police and social service agencies sometimes cross constitutional lines based on "good intentions" and insufficient information. Parents, even parents suspected of harming their children, are protected by constitutional rights. Family violence cases are minefields that challenge members of the family law team. They compel us to examine and control our personal biases and our cultural and religious beliefs about what constitutes appropriate behavior. They strain our emotions, our legal skills, and our ethics, and they remind many of us why we have chosen to specialize in family law.

CONCEPT REVIEW AND REINFORCEMENT

KEY TERMS

Abandonment

Affidavit

Battered woman's syndrome

Care and protection/dependency
   proceeding

Concurrent jurisdiction

Cyberstalking

Educational neglect

Emotional neglect

Evidence-based prosecution

Ex parte

Family violence

Guardian

Interspousal immunity

Mandatory reporter

Medical neglect

Neglect

Negligent supervision

No-contact order

Parens patriae

Parent coordinator

Permanency planning

Permissive reporter

Physical neglect

Protective order

Reasonable efforts

Restraining order

Shaken baby syndrome

Stalking

Stay away order

Termination of parental rights

Tort

REVIEW QUESTIONS

1. Discuss the nature and scope of family violence against adults: Who are the victims? Who are the perpetrators?
2. Identify five services supported by the Violence Against Women Act (VAWA).
3. Identify the four primary remedies available to adult victims of family violence.
4. Identify a minimum of five reasons why victims stay in abusive relationships.
5. Define stalking and cyberstalking and give at least three examples of how a perpetrator might stalk and/or cyberstalk a victim.
6. Describe the basic procedure for obtaining a protective order, including who can commonly seek one and what kinds of relief can be sought.
7. Explain when it may be appropriate to seek a guardianship in a family violence case.
8. Describe the nature and purpose of a personal safety plan.
9. Identify at least five common characteristics of abusers.
10. Identify and distinguish among the five forms of child abuse most commonly identified and defined by the states.
11. Distinguish between mandatory and permissive reporters of child abuse.
12. Describe the nature and purpose of "reasonable efforts" and "permanency planning" in the context of child abuse and neglect actions.
13. Explain how abuse and neglect influence decisions about custody and visitation.
14. Explain whether or not members of the family law team have a duty to report suspected child abuse or other forms of family violence.

DEVELOPING YOUR PARALEGAL SKILLS

FOCUS ON **THE JOB**

In this Focus on the Job, students have an opportunity to explore common characteristics of perpetrators and victims of abuse as evidenced in the context of a family law case.

The Facts

You are a paralegal working for Attorney Sabrina Cann, a private practitioner who specializes in family law. She has asked you to conduct a series of information-gathering meetings with a client, Sara Frazier, who is seeking a divorce from her husband, Joseph. During the course of your meetings, you have developed a suspicion that Sara is being abused by her husband. There have been several clues:

- She has insisted that she initiate all contact with the office and that no one contact her at home or leave e-mail or phone messages for her.
- As the date for filing has approached, she has become increasingly more anxious.
- She has told you that "everyone" says she must "get out of the marriage."
- She is insistent that she "must" have custody of the children and is fearful that she will lose them.
- She does not want to fight for a fair share of the marital property.

- She says she does not know what her husband will do when he is served with the Complaint for divorce and wants to be certain she knows exactly when that will take place.
- She has said that she thinks she must be responsible for the failure of the marriage because she is not a good wife. She does not always have the meals prepared on time or have her husband's shirts ironed. Her husband says she is a bad mother as well because she "lets the kids get away with murder" and never disciplines them effectively.
- She says that her husband loves her so much that he worries about her every minute of the day. She and the children are so important to him that he wants them to spend all their time together, to the exclusion of other people.
- She always wears sunglasses and high-collared, long-sleeved shirts even when the weather is quite warm.

The Assignment

You have shared your concerns with your supervisor, and she has asked that you prepare a memo explaining why you believe the client is being abused and recommending a course of action.

FOCUS ON **ETHICS**

In this activity, the student will explore the duty of members of the family law team in cases involving domestic violence in his or her jurisdiction.

The Assignment

Assume that you are a female paralegal working for the attorney who represents Sara's husband, Joe, in the above fact pattern, and that Joe has recently been served with Sara's Complaint for Divorce on no-fault grounds. You are not comfortable working with Joe and have repeatedly expressed your discomfort to your supervisor, Attorney Jules Sanchez. Joe never misses an opportunity to make a sexist remark and always tells you that female paralegals should be home, where women belong, making and raising babies. He never wants to meet with a female paralegal and always says he wants to talk with the boss and get a few things straight. He has told you that up until now, he has kept his wife in line and that she will pay in more ways than one for thinking that she can do this to him. He comments that raising children is "woman's work" and that he isn't much of a parent. However, he says he will get the kids anyway. Besides, he says, "A bad father is better than no father at all." When encouraged, Joe admits that he has hit his wife on several

occasions and that he believes he has a right to do whatever he wants in the privacy of his own home. He tells you not to worry, though, because there is no record of any abuse. He has "a friend on the force" who makes sure of that, and he never lets Sara seek medical attention for any injury she claims to have. He says she has gone too far challenging his authority this time. He is "the man of the house" and he intends to make her understand that fact or else. . . .

Based on what you have learned about family violence, you strongly believe that Joe is abusing Sara and that she is presently at greater risk than ever before of being seriously injured or perhaps worse. You have shared your concern with your supervisor, Attorney Sanchez, who finds it all hard to believe. He wants to approach the matter cautiously and asks you to research his legal and ethical duties in this situation. What ethical issues does it raise? What is the attorney's duty in your state, given the facts of this case? Does the paralegal have a role to play? Do you find any guidance in the ethical canons for paralegals promulgated by the National Association of Legal Assistants contained in Appendix A or in any other code of ethics that may govern your conduct? Record your conclusions in a one- to two-page paper.

FOCUS ON **CASE LAW**

In this activity, the student will analyze a case involving child abuse and neglect using an IRAC format.

The Assignment

Find a case decided in your jurisdiction within the past five (5) years involving some aspect of child abuse and neglect such as termination of parental rights, prenatal substance abuse, or the parental privilege. Read and analyze the case using an IRAC format.

FOCUS ON **STATE LAW AND PROCEDURE**

In this activity, the student researches the law and procedure governing protective/restraining orders in her or his own state/county.

The Assignment

Describe the procedure used in your jurisdiction to obtain a protective order against an abusive partner. Who is

If you are unable to locate a case, use the opinion in *State of Hawaii v. Aiwohi,* 109 Haw. 115, 123 P.3d 1210 (2005), a case involving a criminal conviction of a mother for recklessly causing the death of her newborn son by ingesting crystal meth.

PARALEGAL PRACTICE TIP

The opinion in the *Aiwohi* case can be found at *www.pearsonhighered.com/wilson* in the companion website material related to Chapter 13 under "Cases" and in the Case Resources Section of the MyLegalStudiesLab.

eligible to petition for an order? What forms of relief may be requested? Obtain copies of any documents that must be filed. Information regarding state variations is available on websites identified in this chapter and may be of assistance with this assignment.

FOCUS ON **TECHNOLOGY**

In addition to the links provided throughout the chapter, this activity provides a series of useful websites for reference along with technology-related assignments for completion.

Websites of Interest

Links to all of the listed websites are provided at *www.pearsonhighered.com/wilson* in the companion website material for Chapter 13 under "Resources."

www.aardvarc.org

"AARDVARC" stands for Abuse, Rape, and Domestic Violence Aid and Resource Collection. The site contains links to many resources by state, statistical data, and information about warning signs of abuse, safety plans, related immigration issues, etc.

www.abanet.org/domviol

This is the site for the American Bar Association's Commission on Domestic Violence. Among other services, it provides links to statistical reports on the prevalence of various forms of domestic violence, articles, and links to statutory summary charts on topics such as civil protection orders, advocate confidentiality laws, prohibition of mutual protective orders, etc.

www.acf.hhs.gov

This is the website for his Administration for Children and Families. It is a rich source of information about children and families in general. From its home page you can link (via drop-down menu) to the Administration's programs, including the

Children's Bureau. There you will find, among other resources, the full text of the most recent Child Maltreatment report.

www.afccnet.org

This is the website for the Association of Family and Conciliation Courts (AFCC). AFCC promotes collaborative approaches to dealing with family matters in general and those pertaining to the well-being of children in particular. The organization sponsors conferences, training, projects, task forces, and practice standards, all of which appear on the website. It provides resources for parents as well as professionals.

www.ama-assn.org

AMA is the American Medical Association. Its home page provides a search function. Searches on family violence, child abuse, and elder abuse each yield a number of resources including journal articles relevant to the medical community's roles, responsibilities, practices, and liabilities in these areas.

www.avahealth.org

This is the website for the Academy on Violence and Abuse (AVA). AVA is an educational organization intended for health care professionals and dedicated to "making violence and abuse a core component of medical and related professional education." The website features online educational materials, including video presentations, written articles, literature searches, and links to other sites with relevant information.

www.bwjp.org

This is the site for the Battered Women's Justice Project's Criminal and Civil Justice Office. The Project aims to promote change within community organizations and governmental agencies engaged in responding to domestic violence. It serves as a national clearinghouse for information about domestic violence and the policing, prosecuting, sentencing, and monitoring of domestic violence offenders.

www.cdc.gov

This site for the national Centers for Disease Control (CDC) provides links to a wide range of resources in response to a search for information on intimate partner violence.

www.childwelfare.gov

This is the site for the Child Information Gateway, a service of the Children's Bureau of the Administration for Children and Families. It provides a wealth of information on adoption, child abuse and neglect, and child welfare issues. Of particular value are links to statistical information and state laws on many related topics, such as definitions of abuse, grounds for termination of parental rights, infant safe haven laws, and parental drug use as child abuse.

www.findlaw.com

This site provides links to state laws that then can be searched by specific topic.

www.fvpf.org

This is the website for the Family Violence Prevention Fund. Its mission is to prevent violence in the home and in the community. It seeks to "transform" the way health care providers, police, judges, employers, and others address violence. A number of fact sheets are available on domestic violence and its relationship to topics such as children, teens, guns, housing, immigrants, and the military. Every month, its personal stories section showcases someone who has triumphed over violence in his or her life or who has made a significant contribution toward preventing violence against women and children.

www.gmdvp.org

This is the site of the Gay Men's Domestic Violence Project, a grassroots, nonprofit initiative supporting men in relationships with men who are victims and survivors of abuse. It offers education, advocacy, and direct services.

www.lrcvaw.org

This is the site for the Legal Resource Center on Violence Against Women, funded by a Violence Against Women grant. The primary focus of the Center is on improving legal representation for domestic violence survivors in interstate custody cases and providing technical assistance in such cases. It features links to other national and state resources on topics including crisis lines, abuse later in life,

and assistance in battered immigrant cases. It also provides state-by-state links to child custody jurisdictional statutes (UCCJEA), long-arm statutes, and relocation statutes.

www.ncadv.org

The National Coalition Against Domestic Violence is accessed at this site. Among its other resources, it provides both topic- and state-specific fact sheets on domestic violence.

www.ncea.aoa.gov

This is the website for the National Center on Elder Abuse, a national center dedicated to preventing the mistreatment of elders. It is the major source of available statistics on elder abuse, neglect, and exploitation, including abuse in domestic settings. It provides links to resources for locating state statutes, codes, Supreme Court opinions, and case law. It also provides a directory of state resources on elder abuse prevention.

www.ncvc.org/dvrc

This is the site for the National Center for Victims of Crime. A Stalking Resource Center is available at this site that provides information about federal stalking laws as well as links to state civil and criminal stalking laws. It also provides a wealth of statistical information and a digest of both federal and state stalking cases. A dating violence resource center is also accessible at this site.

www.ndvh.org

This is the website for the National Domestic Violence Hotline (1-800-799-7233 or 1-800-787-3224), which provides 24/7 access to calls from all states. Translation services are available in 140 languages. Advocates at the Hotline provide intervention, safety planning information, and referrals to agencies in all states.

www.ojp.usdoj.gov/bjs

This is an excellent source for "official" crime data. Many reports on topics related to the content of this chapter are available at this site, including Shannon Catalano, *Intimate Partner Violence in the United States* (2006).

Assignments

1. Go to *www.childwelfare.gov* and locate the definitions for various kinds of abuse in your state.
2. Using one or more of the sites listed above, learn what you can about civil protective orders in your state.
3. Using one or more of the above sites, locate the stalking/cyberstalking laws in your state and at least one case addressing the issue of stalking.

PORTFOLIO PRODUCTS

1. Memorandum on signs of an abusive relationship evident in a family law setting.
2. One- to two-page paper on the legal and ethical duties of members of the family law team in a case involving family violence
3. IRAC of case on child abuse and neglect
4. Description of protective order forms and procedures in a specific jurisdiction

chapter 14
ADOPTION

Scott and Hayley Martinelli want Scott's son, Mike, to be a part of their family, and so they plan to have Hayley adopt him.... Mike's mother, Jessica Olivio, doesn't feel that she can handle the responsibility of raising Mike and sees adoption as a good solution, as long as she can maintain enough contact to watch him grow up....

Adoption is a fundamental family relationship and not simply a privilege created by state law.... Adoption has been a part of human society since prehistoric days and fulfills a key function in knitting together the fabric of parent-child relationships, especially in times of need.... Like marriage, adoption is a means of family formation that is no less fundamental because it is characterized by choice and commitment rather than blood ties and procreation.... Adoption is as crucial to children seeking parents as marriage is to adults seeking partners.[1]

Introduction

HISTORICAL PERSPECTIVE AND PURPOSE OF ADOPTION

Adoption has existed in one form or another for centuries and has served a variety of purposes. In other times and cultures, it primarily served the needs of adults seeking to maintain political power, ensure heirs, and transfer wealth. Historically, the primary purpose of adoption in this country has been to protect children and ensure their futures within the context of a family unit. Although Mississippi and Texas recognized informal adoptions prior to the 1850s, Massachusetts passed the nation's first comprehensive adoption statute in 1851, and other states promptly followed suit. These early acts essentially formalized the parent-child relationship for children already living in *de facto* family relationships. They also advanced welfare reforms targeted at

LEARNING OBJECTIVES

After reading this chapter and completing related assignments, you should be able to:

- explain what adoption is and the purposes it serves

- identify various types of adoption

- distinguish between an open and a closed adoption

- list the major steps in the adoption process

- discuss the rights of wed and unwed biological parents in the adoption context

- explain what a putative father registry is and the purposes it serves

- identify circumstances in which parental rights may be terminated

- identify who must consent to an adoption and what the characteristics of an effective consent are

- explain what a safe haven law is

- explain when an adoption may be challenged and by whom

- describe the role of the paralegal in an adoption case

De facto **adoption**
an adoption that does not meet formal statutory requirements but is considered an adoption based on the conduct of the parties and the surrounding circumstances; sometimes called an equitable adoption or adoption by estoppel

abandoned and orphaned children living in institutions and providing a source of cheap labor as apprentices.

DEFINITION OF ADOPTION

Adoption is the judicial process by which a new parent-child relationship is created. It constitutes, in effect, a birth by legal process in which an adoptive parent assumes the legal rights and duties of a biological parent. Adoption is essentially a two-step process in which an existing parent-child relationship (usually between the child and one or both of his or her birth parents) is terminated and a new parent-child relationship is judicially created. The birth parents may voluntarily surrender their rights and consent to the adoption, or their parental rights may be involuntarily terminated by the court. An adoptive parent may be a stranger to the child, a relative, a step-parent, or a known but unrelated adult, as is usually the case in an adult adoption. The adoption may and in some states must be coordinated by a state-approved public or private agency and, in the assisted reproductive technology context, may be facilitated by a contractual agreement enforceable in the courts. According to U.S. Census Bureau estimates, there are more than 2 million adopted children in the United States.[2]

LEGAL EFFECT OF ADOPTION

Once an adoption is finalized, the relationship between the **adoptee** (the child who is adopted) and his or her adoptive parents is as permanent as the relationship between a child and a biological parent in the sense that it does not end with divorce or the death of a parent. Only the court can end the relationship by invalidating or revoking the adoption or terminating the parental rights and responsibilities of the adoptive parent for cause. Adoption brings to the child the wide range of benefits that flow from the parent-child relationship, including, for example, the right to be supported by the adoptive parent(s) while a minor, to inherit by and through the adoptive parent(s), to be entitled to adoptive parents' worker's compensation benefits, for dependents, and to have **standing** to bring a wrongful death action on the death of an adoptive parent.

Types of Adoption

The five major types of adoption are:

> Agency adoption
> Independent adoption
> International adoption
> Equitable adoption/adoption by estoppel
> Illegal/black market adoption

AGENCY ADOPTION

Each state has a designated state agency responsible for regulating adoptions within its borders. In an **agency adoption**, a public or private agency licensed by the state takes temporary custody of a child for subsequent placement in a permanent adoptive home. Children come into the custody of an agency through two primary

---

routes: (1) The parent(s) voluntarily transfer custody of the child to the agency by executing a written surrender relinquishing their parental rights, or (2) a court terminates parental rights for cause, based on clear and convincing evidence of parental unfitness, and places the child in the temporary custody of an agency pending an adoption.

All states permit agency adoptions, and in some states, all adoptions must be facilitated by an agency except when the adoption is by a step-parent or close family member. The agency is essentially responsible for all phases of the adoption process, including, among other tasks, recruiting foster care and adoptive homes, screening prospective parents, conducting comprehensive home studies, locating potential adoptees, and securing proper consents/**terminations of parental rights**.

Termination of parental rights
the judicial severing of the legal relationship between a parent and child and associated rights; may be voluntary or involuntary, based on clear and convincing evidence

INDEPENDENT ADOPTION

In an **independent adoption** or private adoption, the biological parent(s) transfer custody of the child directly to the adoptive parents. The process is usually facilitated by a third party—such as a physician, a member of the clergy, and/or an attorney specializing in adoption law—who performs most of the tasks usually handled by an agency. This type of adoption generally allows biological parents to designate adoptive parents or to prescribe more fully the characteristics they would like prospective adoptive parents to possess. Sometimes the parents are brought together as a result of ads or by adoption exchange organizations and entrepreneurs listed in the yellow pages or posted on the Internet. Although privately arranged, independent adoptions still must be approved by the court.

Although a majority of the states permit independent adoptions, some states do not, due to concerns that they are not regulated and screened as carefully as agency adoptions. Birth parents usually do not receive counseling regarding their options, and preplacement home studies are not necessarily required. As a result, even in states where they are permitted, independent adoptions may be subject to regulations regarding the fees that may be charged by intermediaries, and adoptive parents may need to be approved or certified by the state.

Independent adoption
an adoption usually facilitated by a third party such as a physician or attorney, rather than by a licensed state agency; sometimes called private, designated, or identified adoption

PARALEGAL PRACTICE TIP

Although many adoptions are by relatives and step-parents, adoption has become a big (nearly $2-billion-a-year) business.[3] Competition is stiffening for traditional facilitators of adoptions, as profit-making adoption entrepreneurs enter the scene and use the Internet extensively to find and bring together financially and emotionally challenged pregnant women and prospective adoptive parents. Birth mothers under stress are prime targets of adoption brokers seeking to satisfy the needs of paying customers. For pregnant women with deeply held religious and moral beliefs, adoption is promoted as a morally acceptable alternative to abortion, one that achieves a positive result for children who are "unwanted" for any of a host of reasons.

PARALEGAL PRACTICE TIP

To learn more about advertising and payment of facilitators in adoption, visit www.childwelfare.gov. Look at Alabama to see an example of a state statute that prohibits payment for facilitating an adoption. You can find a link to this site at www.pearsonhighered.com/wilson in the companion website material for Chapter 14 under "Resources."

INTERNATIONAL ADOPTION

International adoption
an adoption in which a child residing in one country is adopted by a resident of another country

An **international adoption** takes place when a child residing in one country is adopted by a resident of another country. This is a highly specialized area of practice and usually involves a costly and protracted process. In some instances, the adoptive parents may be required to live in the child's birth country for a requisite period of time. Careful attention must be given to complying with the laws of both countries, including any applicable Immigration and Naturalization Service regulations. (See Paralegal Application 14.1.)

EQUITABLE ADOPTION/ADOPTION BY ESTOPPEL

Equitable adoption/adoption by estoppel
refers to a situation in which prospective adoptive parents accept a child into their home and raise the child as their own without ever formally finalizing the adoption; treated by some courts as an adoption to promote fairness and serve the ends of justice

An **equitable adoption,** sometimes called an **adoption by estoppel,** is not technically an adoption. It refers to a situation in which prospective adoptive parents accept a child into their home and raise the child as their own without ever formally finalizing an adoption. Some states allow a child in such circumstances to inherit from the "adoptive" parents should they die intestate (without a will) even though the adoption process was never completed. The adoption is treated by the court as if it took place, and the "adoptive" parents' estates are estopped (prevented) from denying the child's claim.

ILLEGAL/BLACK MARKET ADOPTION

Illegal/black market adoption
an adoption brokered by an individual who collects a substantial fee for locating a child who is transferred from one person or couple to another without proper legal process

Illegal or **black market adoptions** are often referred to as baby selling. They are brokered by individuals who collect a substantial fee for locating a child who is transferred from one person or couple to another without proper legal process. Historically, black market adoptions have been pursued by individuals who do not qualify as adoptive parents under agency standards, or who seek to adopt children in high demand (commonly infants). Such "arrangements" are high risk and likely to be deemed void if challenged at a later date. Some courts have held that surrogacy agreements constitute a form of baby selling. Before approving or enforcing a surrogacy agreement, most courts will scrutinize it to determine whether or not the gestational mother was paid for anything beyond reasonable medical costs such that the agreement constitutes the sale of a baby in violation of public policy and the law.

Paralegal **Application 14.1**

Do You Want to Learn More About International Adoption?

One of the best ways to learn more about the complexities of international adoption is to visit the website of the U.S. Department of State's Bureau of Consular Affairs on Intercountry Adoption *www.adoption.state.gov*. This site literally addresses this topic from A to Z. It provides a wealth of information, including, for example:

- an excellent description of the international adoption process (along with several forms)

- responses to frequently asked questions (FAQs) and information on who can adopt
- background information about various countries and variations in the adoption process in Hague and non-Hague Convention member countries
- state links for approved/accredited U.S.-based adoption service providers for Hague Convention adoption cases

(Continued)

- information about all members of the international adoption community, including adopters and adoptees, judges, social workers, and agencies
- a description of the Child Citizenship Act of 2000 and its requirements and instructions for obtaining a visa for a child adopted from another country
- a Glossary of related terms

PARALEGAL PRACTICE TIP

The Hague Convention on the Protection of Children and Co-operation in Respect of Inter-Country Adoption (Hague Adoption Convention) is an international agreement to establish safeguards designed to ensure that intercountry adoptions take place in the best interests of the child. The Convention went into effect in the United States in April 2008. The Hague Adoption Convention applies to adoptions between the United States and the other countries that have joined it. Based on government data, 11,059 children were adopted from other nations in 2010. To learn more, visit *www.hcch.net*, the site for the Hague Conference on Private International Law. You can find a link to this site at *www.pearsonhighered.com/wilson* in the companion website material for Chapter 14 under "Resources."

PARALEGAL PRACTICE TIP

To see some of the forms used in international adoptions, visit *www.adoption.state.gov*, the website of the U.S. Department of State's Bureau of Consular Affairs. There are two processes for intercountry adoptions, one for Hague Convention countries and one for non-Hague Convention countries. You can find a link to this site at *www.pearsonhighered.com/wilson* in the companion website material for Chapter 14 under "Forms."

Open and Closed Adoptions

Adoptions in the United States fall along a continuum from closed to open. In a **closed adoption,** the biological and adoptive parents essentially know nothing about each other, and adoptees have no access to their original birth certificates or any identifying or nonidentifying information about their biological parents. In an **open adoption,** the biological parents, the adoptive parents, and the adoptee have varying degrees of contact with each other.

CLOSED ADOPTION

Most adoptions are still initially closed adoptions, in which the biological and adoptive parents do not know each other's identities. The general rule is that once an adoption is finalized, the court orders the record sealed, and a new birth certificate is issued in an effort to protect the privacy of the birth parents and the security of the adoptive parents from interference with the new family bond. However, these interests have not stopped adoptees from challenging the constitutionality of confidentiality laws. (See Paralegal Application 14.2.)

Closed adoption
an adoption in which biological and adoptive parents essentially know nothing about each other, and adoptees have no access to their original birth certificates or identifying information about their biological parents

Open adoption
an adoption in which biological parents, adoptive parents, and the adoptee have varying degrees of contact with each other

Paralegal **Application 14.2**

Adoptee Challenges to Sealed Records

Adoptees occasionally challenge the confidentiality of adoption records through the courts. In one early landmark case, *Alma Society Inc. v. Mellon,* 601 F.2d 1225 (2d Cir. 1979), the appellants were an association of individual adult adoptees who claimed the New York statutes that required the sealing of adoption records violated their Fourteenth Amendment Equal Protection and Due Process rights. They also raised the novel argument that the statutes violated the Thirteenth Amendment prohibiting slavery because much like slavery they in effect abolish the parental relationship.

The appellants characterized adoptees as being much like slave children "sold off" and separated from their parents while too young to consent to, or even know, what was happening.

They claimed that upon reaching adulthood they should be entitled, without a showing of cause, to obtain their sealed adoption records, including the names of their natural parents. Some appellants argued that lack of access caused serious psychological trauma, pain, and suffering; potential medical problems and misdiagnoses due to a lack of medical history; the

(Continued)

danger of unwitting incest; and an impairment of religious freedom due to not being reared in the religion of their natural parents.

The District Court dismissed their Complaint, and the second circuit appellate court affirmed that decision. The courts emphasized that the statutes serve important interests such as erasing the stigma of illegitimacy from the adopted child's life by sealing his or her original birth certificate and issuing a new one under his or her new surname; encouraging natural parents to use the adoption process, when they are unwilling or unable to care for their offspring, by protecting their choice of privacy; and promoting the security of the newly formed family unit. The courts took this position even though they acknowledged that once an adopted child reaches adulthood, some of the considerations that apply at the time of adoption and throughout the child's tender years may no longer apply. Today, many biological mothers are willing to have their adult adopted children contact them, and many adoptive parents would not object to, or would even encourage, the adopted child to seek out the identity of or a relationship with a natural parent.

Sidebar

The policy of closed adoption is a source of controversy among adoption professionals. What are the primary arguments on each side of this issue? What is your position? The court suggests that the proper target for the appellants' claim in the *Alma Society* case is the adoption laws themselves rather than the sealed-records laws. Do you agree? Do you believe the appellants would prevail in that context? Explain your response.

PARALEGAL PRACTICE TIP

To learn about more about accessing adoption information, visit *www.childwelfare.gov.* You can find a link to this site at *www. pearsonhighered.com/wilson* in the companion website material related to Chapter 14 under "Resources."

PARALEGAL PRACTICE TIP

The opinion in *Alma Society Inc. v. Mellon* is available at *www. pearsonhighered.com/wilson* in the companion website material related to Chapter 14 under "Cases" and in the Case Resources Section of the MyLegalStudiesLab.

Generally, the child's desire to establish his or her roots and personal identity is not deemed sufficient for the records to be opened by court order, although over the years some exceptions to the rule of secrecy have developed in unusual or emergency circumstances.

- Some states have established an exception for medical reasons when the adoptee or a child of the adoptee requires information about inherited diseases and medical conditions or is in need of a bone marrow or organ transplant.

Adoption/reunion registry
a vehicle available in some states that allows adoptees after a certain age (usually eighteen) to try to contact their biological parents and siblings

- Several states (including Colorado, for example)[4] maintain **adoption** or **reunion registries** that allow adoptees after a certain age (usually eighteen) to try to contact their biological parents and siblings. Once contacted by the adoptee, the registry attempts to contact the birth parents, and if they consent, arrangements are made to put the child and the birth parents in touch with each other. If a birth parent refuses, no further contact is made.

PARALEGAL PRACTICE TIP

To see examples of Application for Adoption Registry forms for parents, adoptees, and relatives, visit *www.dcfs.state.nv.us.* (Nevada) You can find a link to this site at *www.pearsonhighered.com/wilson* in the companion website material for Chapter 14 under "Forms."

- Some states have statutes providing for the release to adoptees of nonidentifying information about their biological parents. Such information usually includes medical, ethnic, socioeconomic, and educational information and, in some cases, information about the circumstances under which the adopted person became available for adoption.[5]
- A small number of states, including Alabama, Alaska, Kansas, and Oregon[6] have legislated that an adoptee, upon reaching the age of majority (usually eighteen), may request a copy of his or her original birth certificate.

OPEN ADOPTION

An open adoption is a form of adoption in which the birth parents, the adoptive parents, and the adoptee maintain a degree of postadoption contact with each other. The contact may assume a variety of forms, including, for example, the sending of annual or seasonal photographs, written or electronic correspondence with or about the child, and visits. In states where open adoptions are permitted, the terms of the agreement are customarily expressed in a contract submitted for approval by the court.

PARALEGAL PRACTICE TIP

To see the statute governing open adoption agreements in Oregon, go to *www.pearsonhighered.com/ wilson*. Look in the companion website material related to Chapter 14 under "Statutes."

The Adoption Process

Adoption is a creation of statute and is subject to applicable state and federal laws. Each state has enacted its own adoption procedures and practices, which vary considerably from one jurisdiction to another. However, the basic steps in the adoption process in virtually all states include the following:

1. Determine the rights of the biological parents
2. Terminate the biological parents' rights
   By consent
   By involuntary termination
3. Identify potential adoptive parents and adoptees
   Who can adopt?
   Who can be adopted?
4. Conduct home study(ies) (depending on the jurisdiction and type of adoption)
5. Determine proper jurisdiction and venue
6. File a Petition for Adoption
7. Serve Notice on all interested parties
8. Conduct a Preliminary Hearing
9. Issue an Interlocutory Decree granting temporary custody to the adoptive parents
10. Arrange Preadoption Placement of the child with the adoptive parents
11. Issue a Final Decree
12. Consider challenges to the Adoption Decree, if any

These steps are carried out by several actors, whose precise roles and relationships depend on governing law and the facts of the case: the biological parents, the adoptive parents, attorneys, agency personnel, third-party facilitators, and the courts.

PARALEGAL PRACTICE TIP

The states vary with respect to whether dual representation of biological parents and adoptive parents is permitted. Very few states expressly permit it, and some states, including Kentucky, Maine, Minnesota, and Wisconsin, expressly prohibit dual representation by statute.

PARALEGAL PRACTICE TIP

Although the National Conference of Commissioners on Uniform State Laws approved a new Uniform Adoption Act (UAA) in 1994 in an effort to standardize adoption law, as of 2011 it has only been adopted in the state of Vermont. The earlier 1969 version was adopted in a handful of states. To learn more about the Act and see its text, visit *www.nccusl.org*. You can find a link to this site at *www.pearsonhighered.com/ wilson* in the companion website material for Chapter 12 under "Resources."

The Rights of Biological Parents in the Adoption Context

THE BIOLOGICAL MOTHER

As discussed in Chapter 7, a mother's parental rights are essentially already established at birth. The biological mother has the right to choose to place her child for adoption by voluntarily surrendering her parental rights to an agency and/or consenting to an adoption. If the state seeks to terminate her parental rights involuntarily, it can do so only based upon clear and convincing evidence of parental unfitness.

THE MARRIED FATHER

If the biological mother is married, under a marital presumption her husband commonly is deemed to be the father of any child born during their marriage or within 300 days of its termination. If no other man has been ruled the legal father of her child, an adoption cannot take place unless the married father's rights are terminated or he surrenders his parental rights and/or consents to the adoption.

THE FATHER WHOSE IDENTITY OR WHEREABOUTS ARE UNKNOWN

In the event the mother does not know the identity of the father, she (or the agency to which she has relinquished custody) usually must file an affidavit attesting to that fact before the adoption can proceed. If the identity of the father is known but he cannot be located, a diligent search must be made to locate him, and proof of the effort may be required by the court. The effort may involve a search of telephone, military, and post office records; driver and voter registration rolls; and publication of notice in newspapers published in areas where the father has been known to reside. A number of locater services are now available online. A failure to conduct a proper search may result in a later challenge to the adoption on the grounds that the father did not receive proper notice, to which he was constitutionally entitled.

THE NONMARITAL BIOLOGICAL FATHER

Under common law, the father of an illegitimate child had no standing to intervene in an action to adopt his biological child, and prior to 1972, there was little case law specifically addressing the rights of unwed fathers with respect to their children in the adoption context.

The Uniform Adoption Act

. . . distinguishes between fathers who willfully abandon their children and those whose attempts at fatherhood have been thwarted. The thwarted father has somehow been prevented from meeting his parental responsibilities, because the mother either never informed him of her pregnancy or the child's birth, lied to him about her plans for the child, disappeared with the child, named another man as the birth father, or was married to another man in a state that presumes the legitimacy of a

---

PARALEGAL PRACTICE TIP

An attorney's duty of due diligence may even include "a duty to Google" when searching for a lost father. It is remarkable how much information a simple search on a name may generate: addresses, death notices with names and locations of relatives, arrests, notable accomplishments, etc.

child born to a married woman. According to the UAA, the unmarried father in these circumstances has not willfully abandoned his child but has instead been externally prevented from carrying out his parental responsibilities. Thwarted fathers can assert parental rights during the pendency of adoption proceedings, but they must prove a compelling reason for not having performed their parental duties. The thwarted father must also defend against other parties who try to prove that termination of his rights is necessary to avoid "detriment or a risk of substantial harm to the child."[7]

Four key cases decided by the U.S. Supreme Court between 1972 and 1983 began to define the rights of unwed fathers. Beginning with the *Stanley* case in 1972,[8] the Court established that fathers of nonmarital children have constitutionally protected legal rights as parents under the Equal Protection Clause of the Fourteenth Amendment and a privacy interest in children they have sired and raised, such that the state cannot terminate their parental rights without affording them notice and an opportunity to be heard. However, the unmarried father's rights are neither automatic nor unlimited. Under the **biology-plus rule**, an unmarried father must take affirmative steps to demonstrate his parental commitment. Depending on the jurisdiction and the extent of demonstrated commitment, the rights of an unmarried father may include the following:

Biology-plus rule
the rule that an unwed father's rights are worthy of constitutional protection if the father grasps the opportunity to develop a relationship with and accept responsibility for his child

- He may be entitled to notice of an adoption proceeding as an interested party who may not be able to block the adoption but who can speak to whether it will be in the best interests of the child.
- He may be entitled to an opportunity to prove to the court that his consent should be required because he has taken sufficient steps to establish a relationship with his child, because his efforts to do so have been actively thwarted, or because his failure to do so should be excused for some other legitimate reason.
- Once his right to consent is established, he may have the capacity to block the adoption unless he is determined to be unfit and his parental rights are involuntarily terminated.

The four landmark Supreme Court decisions addressing the rights of nonmarital fathers in the adoption context are the following:

- *Stanley v. Illinois*, 405 U.S. 645 (1972)
- *Quilloin v. Walcott*, 434 U.S. 246 (1978)
- *Caban v. Mohammed*, 441 U.S. 380 (1979)
- *Lehr v. Robertson*, 463 U.S. 248 (1983)

PARALEGAL PRACTICE TIP

A description of each of the four landmark cases can be found at *www.pearsonhighered.com/wilson* in the companion website material related to Chapter 14 under "Resources."

The unifying theme emerging from these decisions is summarized in the following quote from the *Lehr* case:

> The significance of the biological connection [between father and child] is that it offers the natural father an opportunity that no other male possesses to develop a relationship with his offspring. If he grasps that opportunity and accepts some measure of responsibility for the child's future, he may enjoy the blessings of the parent-child relationship and make uniquely valuable contributions to the child's development. If he fails to do so, the Federal Constitution will not automatically compel a State to listen to his opinion of where the child's best interests lie.[9]

PARALEGAL PRACTICE TIP

There is no clear indicator of what a biological father must do to preserve his parental rights. It is a fact-intensive decision that varies case to case. For example, in some states, an unwed father may lose his parental rights by failing to establish a relationship with his newborn child by not supporting the mother emotionally and financially during the pregnancy, not being present at the birth, and not visiting the mother and child in the hospital.[10] An unwed father who has established a parent-child relationship may lose that relationship as a result of failing to comply with technical requirements such as those imposed by putative father registries.[11] An unwed father's parental rights may be lost as a result of the birth mother's deceit and/or concealment of a pregnancy until after an adoption is approved.

Paralegal Application 14.3

A "New" Cause of Action—Tortious Interference with Parental Relationships

The Facts

What remedy should an unwed father have when he diligently seeks to exercise his parental rights while the birth mother conceals her whereabouts and places the child for adoption against his wishes and with knowledge of a judgment determining him to be the child's natural father? What if she accomplishes this with active and knowing assistance from members of her family and her attorney? In 1998, a West Virginia father who was confronted with these circumstances sued the mother, her parents, her brother, and her attorney for fraud, civil conspiracy, tortious interference with parental relationships, outrage, and violation of constitutional rights. In a 118-page opinion, a West Virginia appellate court affirmed a $7.85-million judgment against all of the defendants (including the attorney) and, in its opinion, created a new cause of action imposing civil liability on anyone who conspires to conceal the whereabouts of a newborn from a parent seeking information about the child's location:

> . . . where a person has knowledge of information concerning a newborn child's birth or physical location, or indicating where and in whose care the child may be found, and the child's parent inquires of such person regarding his or her child's birth or physical location, and/or where and in whose care his/her child may be found, such person may be held liable for fraudulently concealing information if he/she affirmatively, intentionally, and willfully fails to provide such information to the child's parent pursuant to his/her request for such information, and such concealment unduly hinders or otherwise irreparably harms the parent's ability to establish a parent-child relationship with his or her child.[12]

Sidebar

The cause of action established in this case opens the door to considerable civil liability by imposing an affirmative duty on the public at large. Do you agree with the court that such a cause of action is appropriate? How far do you think that liability should extend? What challenges do such actions pose for a plaintiff?

STATE INITIATIVES ON BEHALF OF NONMARITAL FATHERS

There is a lack of uniformity among the states with respect to the level of support available to nonmarital fathers in the adoption context beyond the limited protection afforded by federal law. Many states have taken steps to protect their interests in assuming a role in the future of their children. The two primary methods used to do so are putative father registries and publication notice requirements.

Putative fathers serving in the armed forces may have additional protections under the Sailors and Soldiers Relief Act. This resource should be considered if a client is serving in the armed forces at the time an adoption of his or her child is pending.

Putative Father Registries

A **putative father** is a man who may be a child's father but his paternity has not yet been established by voluntary acknowledgment or in a court proceeding and he was not married to the child's mother before or when the child was born. When a putative father registers with a **putative father registry,** he is registering his intent to assert his rights and responsibilities as a parent. If he registers within a specified time frame, he will be given notice of a proposed adoption of his child and petition for termination of his parental rights. The notice advises the putative father that the action has been filed and includes the date, place, and time of any scheduled hearing.

Putative father registries of one form or another have been established by law in a majority of states. Although the states differ with respect to the information maintained in their registries, they typically include the following:

- Registration date
- Name, address, Social Security number, and date of birth of both the putative father and the birth mother
- Child's name and date of birth, if known, or anticipated month and year of birth

The features of putative father registries vary state to state with respect to:

- the time frame within which a putative father must register (ranging from prior to the child's birth to any time prior to the filing of an adoption petition)
- the consequences of a failure to register (usually an irrevocable implied consent to adoption and/or loss of the right to notice)
- the permissible exceptions to the registration requirement, if any (such as a failure to register due to the mother's concealment of the pregnancy)
- whether or not a putative father who registers can subsequently revoke or rescind a notice of intent to claim paternity

Putative father

a man who is reputed or believed to be the father of a child but who was not married to the mother when the child was born and whose paternity has not yet been established by legal process

Putative father registry

a vehicle available in several states that is designed to protect a putative father's parental rights by giving him notice of a pending adoption proceeding without his having to rely on the birth mother or prospective adoptive parents for such information

At *www.adoptioninstitute.org* you can find links to state putative father registries. To find a link to this site go to *www.pearsonhighered.com/wilson* in the companion website material for Chapter 14 under "Resources."

To see the Ohio Application for Search of Putative Father Registry "Registration Form for Fathers," visit *www.pearsonhighered.com/wilson* and look in the companion website material related to Chapter 14 under "Forms."

The information contained in the registry is essentially confidential and usually is available only to "interested parties," such as birth mothers, adoption agencies, state departments of social services and child support enforcement, adoptive parents, courts, attorneys for parties in a case, and others for good cause shown.

Registries are ostensibly designed to protect the parental rights of a putative father who has registered by giving him notice of a pending adoption proceeding without his having to rely on the birth mother or prospective adoptive parents for such information. By default or design, they serve a number of additional purposes:

- They help reassure the birth mother and prospective adoptive parents that an adoption will not be disrupted at a later date when the father, whose whereabouts or identity was previously unknown, appears and challenges the validity of the adoption.
- Consistent with Supreme Court decisions, they satisfy in part the requirement for an assumption of responsibility by a putative father who wants to establish a relationship with his child.
- They allow the birth mother to protect her privacy by not having to publish details of her personal life, and they relieve the pressure on her to perjure herself if she is unwilling or unable to identify the putative father and wants to receive public assistance.
- They generate revenue for the states through modest filing fees and potential establishment of paternal responsibility for child support and the expenses of the mother's prenatal and birth expenses.

Although touted as a protection for the rights of unknown fathers, the long-term impact and effectiveness of registries are yet to be measured. Critics argue that registries unreasonably restrict realization of the rights of putative fathers and serve instead to facilitate adoption and promote early bonding with adoptive parents. One commentator phrased her concerns in these terms:

> The draconian nature of most registry acts protects neither the interests of responsible fathers nor the long-term emotional interests of the child. In actuality, the function of most registries is usually to cut off the birth father's rights, often before he knows of the child's birth or whereabouts. In an astonishing number of instances, the unwed father has been actively deceived by the birth mother into believing that the baby died. In other cases, the birth mother leads the father to believe the baby is not his, or she never allows him to know that she is pregnant. Such statutes' interest in identifying the father is suspect and borders upon the pretextual, considering the absurdly short periods of time in which the father's rights are terminated for failure to file with the correct registry. The result is catastrophic for the child. . . .[13]

Additional criticisms and concerns include the following:

- In Alabama the Putative Father Registry has been designated by the legislature as the exclusive vehicle entitling a putative father to notice of and the opportunity to contest an adoption proceeding.[14] In addition, under the Alabama prebirth abandonment statute, a father can be deemed to have abandoned his child and by implication consented both to termination of his parental rights and to an adoption by failing, with reasonable knowledge of the pregnancy, to offer financial and/or emotional support to the mother for a period of six months prior to the birth, OR failing to file with the putative father registry within thirty days of the birth.[15]

- No registry presently requires the mother to inform a putative father of her pregnancy, although some state registries have a provision recognizing that some mothers may intentionally conceal their pregnancy to deceive the father. Such registries allow him to register when he discovers the existence of the baby. For example, the applicable Minnesota statute provides that a putative father will be considered to have timely filed if he proves by clear and convincing evidence that (1) it was not possible for him to register timely; (2) his failure to register was through no fault of his own; and (3) he registered within ten days after it became possible for him to do so.[16]

- Some states such as Arizona, Missouri,[17] and Utah do not accept a putative father's ignorance of a pregnancy or birth as an excuse for not registering. For example, a Utah statute provides that "[a]n unmarried biological father, by virtue of the fact he has engaged in a sexual relationship with a woman: (i) is considered to be on notice that a pregnancy and an adoption proceeding regarding the child may occur; and (ii) has a duty to protect his own rights and interests."[18]

- The burden is placed on the unmarried biological father to establish his claim of paternity by registering, and yet many putative fathers are unaware of the existence of putative father registries and may lose their parental rights by default, as most states provide that failure to register in a timely manner constitutes a waiver and surrender of any parental rights to notice. A small number of states make a special effort to publicize the existence of their putative father registries. Missouri does so through public service announcements and by requiring the Department of Health and Senior Services to provide, on request, pamphlets describing the registry to hospitals, libraries, medical clinics, schools, universities, and other providers of child-related services.[19]

Publication Notice Requirements

Publication requirements are not in place in all states, and in states that do have them, they vary widely. At one extreme is a Utah adoption statute that provides: ". . . an unmarried mother has a right of privacy with regard to her pregnancy and adoption plan, and therefore has no legal obligation to disclose the identity of an unmarried biological father prior to or during an adoption proceeding, and has no obligation to volunteer information to the court with respect to the father."[20]

At the other extreme is Florida's "Scarlet Letter law," enacted in 2001 and subsequently held unconstitutional on privacy grounds in 2003[21] and replaced with that state's Putative Father Registry. A Florida District Court essentially held that the Florida Constitution protects the privacy rights of individuals to avoid disclosure of personal matters and to make certain decisions independently. In effect, the law had required a genetic mother who could not identify or locate the father of the child she wanted to place for adoption to publish detailed information about dates and places where she had engaged in sexual relations and descriptions of partners who might be the child's father.[22] Some states, such as Kansas,[23] require the court in which the adoption petition is pending to provide publication notice to unknown putative fathers, while other states leave it to the court's discretion. Still other states, such as North Carolina,[24] place the burden of publication on the individual petitioning for adoption.

Paralegal **Application 14.4**

A Double Standard?

In some states, an unwed father who fails to provide emotional and financial prebirth support to the mother of their child may forfeit his parental rights to the child. A fit unwed father may have his paternal rights terminated for "abandoning" a child prebirth or for merely failing to sign the correct form, in the correct court, within the correct number of days after his child's birth.[25] Despite being warned of its harmful effects a pregnant mother continues to use cocaine and gives birth to an addicted newborn. The state of Connecticut seeks to terminate the mother's parental rights, but the court declines to do so despite her long drug history and the serious injury inflicted upon the child, concluding that the infant was not a child prior to birth and the mother's prebirth conduct could neither be considered abuse or neglect.[26]

Sidebar

What is your opinion with respect to the following questions? Explain your responses.

1. Should the mother's and father's parental rights be considered equal prior to their child's birth? Should they be subject to termination?

2. Should putative fathers have as long to establish their paternity rights as the states have to establish fathers' paternity for purposes of imposing financial obligations (i.e., at any time before the child attains eighteen years of age)?

3. Should all unwed genetic fathers be treated alike with respect to affording them an opportunity to develop a parent-child relationship with their offspring? How about a rapist? A statutory rapist? A male participant in a "one-night stand"? An abusive spouse who rapes his spouse? A man who has sexual relations with a woman after giving her a "date rape" drug without her knowledge? A man who solicits a prostitute or who has relations with a woman in exchange for drugs?

Termination of Parental Rights

Prior to the 1960s, public policy in the United States favored preservation of the biological family as a priority. When a child was removed from a home, voluntarily or involuntarily, the move was considered temporary whenever possible. The priority articulated by state legislatures and social services agencies was reunification of the biological family after effective completion of a service plan for the parents and children. For better or worse, today the focus is on permanency planning for the thousands of children in state care who have lost their parents to death, abandonment, incarceration, and/or abuse and neglect. **Permanency planning** is designed to move children as soon as possible into healthy, stable, and "permanent" homes.

Permanency planning
planning for the return home of a child following removal or for termination of parental rights within a legally specified period of time in an effort to promote stability for the child

PARALEGAL PRACTICE TIP

To view an example of a Petition for Permanency Planning Hearing used in Virginia, visit *www.courts. state.va.us.* You can find a link to this site at *www.pearsonhighered.com/wilson* in the companion website material for Chapter 14 under "Forms."

The Adoption and Safe Families Act of 1997 (ASFA)[27] requires state agencies to petition for termination of parental rights when a child has been in state care for fifteen of the prior twenty-two months. Although the Act appears to serve the best interests of children by not leaving them in limbo indefinitely, some commentators contend that this requirement does a disservice to poor families in particular. "Formerly, poor parents encountering housing, marital, economic, or health crises had foster care as a 'safety net' to provide temporary substitute care at public expense while they got back on their feet. Now, even voluntary placements by good parents in difficult times can rapidly lead to disintegration of a family and permanent loss of family ties."[28]

In order for an adoption to proceed, the groundwork usually is laid for extinguishing the biological parents' rights, through voluntary consent or involuntary termination, in one of four ways:

- The parents voluntarily surrender their parental rights, and the court transfers custody of the child to an agency, which then places the child in foster care or some other residential setting, depending on the circumstances. If and when the child is subsequently adopted, it is the state agency that consents to the adoption. In some states, the voluntary surrender effectively terminates the parents' rights. In other states, the surrender allows the agency to petition the court for a termination.
- The biological parents consent to the adoption directly, and their consents are filed with the petition for adoption.
- The biological parents' rights are terminated by the court for cause, and the state is granted custody of the child pending adoption.
- One of the biological parents, a third party, or a prospective adoptive parent asks the court to dispense with parental consent given the circumstances of the case. For instance, the mother of a child who has been in long-term foster care may be willing to consent to adoption, but the father who is serving an extended sentence in prison for battery on the child unreasonably refuses to consent.

PARALEGAL PRACTICE TIP

To see examples of a number of adoption forms used in Michigan, visit *www.courts.michigan.gov.* Note in particular: the various consent forms (by adoptee, agency, guardian and parent); Order Placing Child after Consent; Order Placing Child (Stepparent Adoption); Release of Child by Parent; Order Terminating Parental Rights after Release or Consent; Petition for Direct Placement Adoption; Order of Adoption; Petition for Rescission of Adoption and Order. You can find a link to this site at *www.pearsonhighered.com/wilson* in the companion website material for Chapter 14 under "Forms."

Ideally, the rights of both biological parents are extinguished by consent or court-ordered termination, in order to minimize the risk that the validity of the adoption may be challenged at a later date. However, this is not always possible, particularly in cases involving abandoned newborns, unknown fathers, or children left at **safe havens.** Virtually all states permit **at-risk adoptions** of children in such circumstances as an alternative to having children remain in permanent foster care placements. Parents who adopt at-risk children knowingly assume the risk that a biological parent may later appear and attempt to challenge the adoption.

Safe haven law
a law that allows a parent, or an agent of a parent, of an unwanted newborn to anonymously leave the baby at a safe haven center, such as a hospital emergency room, without fear of legal charges of abandonment or child endangerment, etc., provided there is no evidence of abuse

At-risk adoption
an adoption that is at risk of being challenged at a later date because the rights of one or both biological parents have not been terminated; an alternative to permanent foster care

Paralegal **Application 14.5**

Safe Haven Laws: State-Sponsored Abandonment of Newborns? Whom Do They Protect and Whom Do They Harm?

PARALEGAL PRACTICE TIP

To learn about the safe haven laws of various states, visit *www.childwelfare.gov.* You can find a link to this site at *www.pearsonhighered.com/wilson* in the companion website material for Chapter 14 under "Resources."

Beginning in 1999, when Texas passed its "Baby Moses" law, a majority of the states enacted safe haven laws allowing a parent, or an agent of a parent, of an unwanted newborn to anonymously leave the baby at a "safe haven" center without fear of legal charges of abandonment or child endangerment, etc., provided there is no evidence

(Continued)

of abuse. The applicable Florida statute provides: "Except where there is actual or suspected child abuse or neglect, any parent who leaves a newborn infant . . . has the absolute right to remain anonymous and to leave at any time and may not be pursued or followed unless the parent seeks to reclaim the newborn infant."[29]

Safe haven centers are usually located at medical facilities and police and fire stations. The center subsequently delivers the newborn to the appropriate child-protective agency. Although the parent is not required to provide or accept any information, some states require the safe haven provider to whom the newborn is relinquished to ask the parent for medical and family information and to give the parent information regarding adoption resources. No two states' safe haven laws are exactly the same, but all set maximum age limits for babies that can be left, with most ranging from three to thirty days of age (although Missouri R.S.Mo. §210.950 and North Dakota N.D. Cent. Code §27-20-02 cover children up to a year old). In some states, the parent may be able to reclaim the child within a certain period of time by following prescribed procedures. In the case of abandoned babies, the identity and whereabouts of both biological parents are unknown, and the burden of making a good-faith effort to identify and notify them of a petition for adoption eventually rests with the state's primary social services agency.

Sidebar

Safe haven laws protect newborns from infanticide and abandonment in dumpsters, high school lavatories, and other sites where they are at considerable risk. They provide an incentive to mothers to bring their babies to locations where they will receive appropriate care and medical attention and be placed in nurturing homes pending adoption. This serves mothers and babies well, but what about the fathers of these children? Do safe haven laws violate their rights to notice and an opportunity to be heard and consent before their children are effectively abandoned and placed for adoption?

CONSENT

Each state establishes by statute or administrative regulation the requirements governing consent to the kind(s) of adoption permitted in the jurisdiction: who must consent, the form of the consent, when the consent can be given, and under what circumstances it can be revoked. The rules are designed to respect and balance the constitutionally protected rights of birth parents and the rights of the adoptive parents who are seeking to establish a new family unit with confidence in its permanence.

PARALEGAL PRACTICE TIP

The family law team must carefully follow all of the prescribed steps in the adoption process, and the paralegal should be alert to any red flags requiring the attention of the supervising attorney. For example, does it appear that the parent's consent to the adoption is being given under duress? Is the biological mother falsely denying knowledge of the biological father's whereabouts in order to expedite the adoption? Has the biological mother actively thwarted the efforts of the nonmarital father to establish a relationship with his child?

PARALEGAL PRACTICE TIP

To learn about consent laws in each state, visit *www.childwelfare.gov*. You can find a link to this site at *www. pearsonhighered.com/wilson* in the companion website material for Chapter 14 under "Resources."

Who Must Consent?

Absent involuntary termination, the mother's consent (or surrender of parental rights) is required, and the father's consent may be required depending on the circumstances (whether he is married to the mother, has an established relationship with the child, etc.). Depending on the jurisdiction, the consent may be solely to a termination of parental rights or both to termination of parental rights and to the specific adoption, as in an independent adoption. In the case of a step-parent adoption, the consent of the custodial spouse/parent is solely to the adoption and not to a termination of his or her parental rights. If the adoptee has attained the age of majority, parental consent is not required. In most states, courts will consider the wishes of the child, and in some states, the adoptee's consent may be required if he or she has reached a certain age (usually twelve to fourteen).[30] If the parental rights of the biological parents have been terminated, parental consent to the adoption is not required, and the parent(s) cannot block an adoption of their child.

In What Form Is the Consent Given?

If the birth parents are willing to relinquish their parental rights, this is usually accomplished by their executing a formal document commonly called a **surrender** of parental rights or a consent to adoption and termination of parental rights. The consent must be in an impartially witnessed and notarized writing that clearly identifies the child and the parental rights being terminated. To be valid, it must be fully informed and free from duress, fraud, and undue influence. In some states, a voluntary surrender must be followed by a court order confirming the termination of parental rights.

Surrender
a formal document in which a legal (usually biological) parent gives up his or her parental rights to a specific child

Paralegal Application 14.6

Making Consent Count

The Child Welfare League of America and other advocates and practitioners recommend that, in order for a mother's consent to adoption to be meaningful and binding, certain precautions be taken even if not mandated by state law or administrative regulation. Such steps protect both the biological mother, by informing her decision, and the prospective adoptive parents, by promoting finality in adoptive placements. They also help to balance the power relationship between mothers with few resources who are experiencing maximum stress and adoptive parents, who are more likely to be economically secure, emotionally stable, and eager for the adoption to proceed. Suggested measures include:

- **Counseling:** More than half the states require that the mother participate in some degree of counseling before placing her child for adoption. "Counseling for parents, . . . can help parents to 'own' their decisions. . . . Counseling for mothers should include providing information about alternatives to adoption, options within adoption, legal steps and consequences involved in adoption, and possible effects of adoption on themselves and their children. Ideally, counseling will also help mothers resolve issues that arise with the fathers and family members."[31] The

counselor should be a neutral third person who has no interest in the mother's ultimate decision.
- **Legal advice:** Mothers should be given copies of all documents they will be asked to sign and have an opportunity to review them and raise questions with an attorney. They should be advised about "whether they may give binding consent before the birth, after the birth, or only after the passage of a certain number of days or hours after the birth. They should be informed about whether they have any right to revoke their consent and, if so, when and how to do so and whether revocation means automatic return of the child or a judicial best-interests determination. If any agreements are contemplated between the mother and the prospective adoptive parents, such as agreements concerning providing information about the child's development, they should be informed about whether and under what circumstances the agreements are enforceable."[32]
- **Sufficient time:** Mothers relinquishing their parental rights and consenting to adoption should not be rushed into the decision, a luxury most state laws do not afford them.

When Can the Consent Be Given?

Ideally, if the consent is voluntary, it should (and in some states must) be given prior to or simultaneously with filing of the adoption petition. If the adoption is of a newborn, some states permit consent to be given prior to the birth of the child, but the majority of states specify that it can be given only after a certain period following the birth (generally three days). The rationale for such restrictions is to minimize the situations in which a birth mother experiencing the emotional impact of delivering the child changes her mind and claims that an earlier consent was given under duress. Once the consent is given, some states provide a time limit within which it can be revoked.

PARALEGAL PRACTICE TIP

The Indian Child Welfare Act prevents a mother from consenting to an adoption until ten days after the child's birth and allows her to revoke her consent until the adoption is final.

Under What Circumstances Can Consent Be Revoked?

Most states provide that a consumer has seventy-two hours to rescind an ordinary business contract and yet, in many states, a mother's consent to adoption may be given and become irrevocable in fewer than four days after a child's birth. The general rule is that a consent to adoption that is given voluntarily, knowingly, and intelligently cannot be revoked absent proof that the consent was obtained by means of fraud, duress, or undue influence. Absent such circumstances, many states do not permit revocations.

When revocation is permitted, it usually must be written, witnessed, and notarized and given within a limited period of time. Generally, the revocation must be submitted to the court and may or may not be approved based on the court's discretion and standards, which vary from state to state. Simple changes of heart are usually insufficient, but a minor's claim that she received no counseling, was provided with no information about other options, and was coerced to consent by her parents may well prevail. (See Paralegal Application 14.7.) When the matter is considered by the court, the adoptive parents may contest the revocation and ask that the court dispense with the parental consent requirement in the best interests of the child.

Paralegal **Application 14.7**

You Be the Judge

The Facts

When T.F. was sixteen years old, she and her boyfriend, R.O., had A.L.O., a baby girl. T.F. correctly indicated her age to her doctor and on the certified paternity acknowledgment she and R.O. executed. They initially planned to raise A.L.O. but, after three weeks, decided they were not able to handle the responsibility. The father then asked if his sister and brother-in-law, Jennifer and Branch Martin, would consider adopting the child, and they agreed to do so.

During the relinquishment and adoption process, the mother misrepresented her age as over eighteen on all the documents, and everyone apparently believed her. However, when she went through counseling and signed the papers, she was actually only seventeen and still a minor. Under Montana law (MCA Section 42-2-405(2)), "In a direct parental placement adoption, a relinquishment and consent to adopt executed by a parent who is a minor is not valid unless the minor parent has been ad-

vised by an attorney who does not represent the prospective adoptive parent" and the legal fees "are an allowable expense that may be paid by prospective adoptive parents. . . ." The Martins were aware of the requirement but claimed they did not know T.F. was a minor, and T.F. stated she was unaware the Martins would have paid for an attorney for her.

Despite the Montana law prohibiting revocation of consent more than thirty days after termination of parental rights, T.F. filed a motion to set aside the adoption because she was a minor without legal representation at the time she signed the relinquishment papers. She testified that she had trouble understanding the paperwork and that it all looked the same to her. She also claimed that Jennifer Martin and Jennifer's mother called her daily, encouraging her to sign the papers and assuring her that she could see A.L.O. any time she wanted, but later, after signing, she learned she would not be able to do so.

(Continued)

The District Court set aside the termination of parental rights and voided the decree of adoption. The Martins appealed the order and sought a reversal and return of A.L.O. to their care, claiming equitable and judicial estoppel among other theories.

Sidebar

How do you think the Montana Supreme Court should decide this case? Does it make a difference that it involves an independent/private adoption? Why? What are the arguments in favor of T.F.? The Martins? What would be in the best interests of the child, or don't the child's interests matter in this context? Read the case (*In Re Adoption of A.L.O.*, 2006 MT 59, 331 Mont. 334, 132 P.3d 543 (2006) to see what the court did.

PARALEGAL PRACTICE TIP

The opinion in *In re Adoption of A.L.O.* is available at *www. pearsonhighered.com/wilson* in the companion website material related to Chapter 14 under "Cases" and in the Case Resources Section of the MyLegalStudiesLab.

INVOLUNTARY TERMINATION OF PARENTAL RIGHTS

Because parents have a constitutionally protected right in the parent-child relationship, their rights as parents generally cannot be terminated without notice and an opportunity to be heard in a termination proceeding. Although there is no parallel constitutional requirement that they be provided with counsel if they cannot afford an attorney, in most states parents have a right to counsel when the state seeks to terminate their parental rights.

PARALEGAL PRACTICE TIP

Adoptive parents, like biological parents, may have their parental rights terminated if they prove to be unfit to care for their adopted children.

PARALEGAL PRACTICE TIP

To review examples of a Petition for Termination of Parental Rights and an Answer to a Petition for Termination of Parental Rights, visit *www.courts.delaware.gov/forms*. You can find a link to this site at *www. pearsonhighered.com/wilson* in the companion website material related to Chapter 14 under "Forms."

PARALEGAL PRACTICE TIP

"The ethical duty to provide competent and zealous representation extends to all clients, including those faced with potential termination of their parental rights. Personal biases cannot compromise advocacy on behalf of the client. The vast majority of parents in termination proceedings are indigent, which often means that their counsel is appointed by the court or provided through a public defender or contract system. The representation of parents by overworked and underpaid attorneys results in claims by parents that their counsel was ineffective."[33]

The states establish by statute, administrative regulation, and case law the circumstances in which termination may occur, given clear and convincing evidence of parental unfitness and the best interest of a child. Paralegals are often surprised and troubled about the degree of "unfitness" that must be present in order for a parent's rights to be terminated. Given that parental rights are afforded a high degree of constitutional protection, before they can be terminated there must be clear and convincing evidence of severe inadequacies in parenting that place the child at risk. It is not necessarily enough that parents are overly strict or lax in discipline; that they fail to supervise their children and "let them run wild"; that the home is messy; that "negative" influences are present; or that the parents drink to excess, use "recreational" drugs, or have been convicted of crimes. Circumstances that may result in a termination include:

- Failure to support the child's basic needs, although nonsupport alone may not be enough
- Failure to see or contact the child for a specified period of time
- Failure to provide a safe environment for the child
- Incarceration of a parent for serious crimes against the child and/or the other parent of the child(ren)
- Failure to participate in a court-ordered rehabilitation or family-reunification plan
- Legal determination of incompetence of the parent and placement under guardianship

Even if these factors all are present, before rights can be terminated, the parent must be given a reasonable opportunity to address his or her parental deficiencies with or without the child being present in the home. In the final analysis however, the best interests of the child standard is the paramount consideration as the courts weigh the impact of parental inadequacies on the child's physical, emotional, and mental welfare and need for a stable home and continuity in care. To the extent feasible, many courts will consider "the child's opinion of his or her own best interests in the matter."[34]

PARALEGAL PRACTICE TIP

The Americans with Disabilities Act (ADA) provides: ". . . no qualified individual with a disability shall, by reason of such disability, be excluded from participation in or denied the benefits of the services, programs, or activities of a public entity, or be subjected to discrimination by any such entity."[35] Under the Act, a disability includes a physical or mental impairment that substantially limits one or more of a person's major life activities. The states are divided with respect to the question of whether or not the ADA applies to termination proceedings. Courts in states such as Iowa, Maine, and Washington have held that it does apply, whereas courts in Connecticut, Vermont, and Wisconsin have concluded that it does not. If it does apply, the state may be required to accommodate the special needs of parents with recognized disabilities that impact their parenting skills when those individuals are threatened with termination of their parental rights.

Paralegal **Application 14.8**

Would You Give Mom Another Chance?

The Facts

A mother of five children had an extensive history of substance abuse and dysfunctional relationships with a series of men, three of whom had abused both her and some of the children. Her problem with drugs over the years impaired her ability to parent and exposed the children to drugs, drug paraphernalia, and other drug users. She had come to the attention of the Department of Social Services on multiple occasions, based on complaints that she was neglecting the children, and the children were removed from the home. For two years, she failed to cooperate in the service plan designed to reunify the family.

The department eventually changed the goal of the plan for the family from reunification to adoption. Six weeks before the initially scheduled trial on termination of her parental rights, the mother entered a four- to six-month residential treatment program from which she successfully graduated. The mother presented evidence that she had participated successfully in a drug rehabilitation program. She was responding well to therapy and had submitted to required drug screens, all of which were negative. She was actively involved in outpatient services including substance abuse programming that encompassed five AA meetings a week, early-recovery and

(Continued)

relapse-prevention counseling, and domestic violence therapy. She was living with her mother, working two jobs, and visiting her five children once a month.

Sidebar

When deciding whether to terminate the rights of a parent, what factors do you think the court should consider? What if the parent's lack of fitness is "temporary" rather than chronic? What if the parent is taking steps and making significant progress toward addressing his or her inadequacies as a parent? How much leeway should be given to parents when an indeterminate period of time will be required for their recovery? Would you terminate the mother's parental rights in this particular case? To see what the Massachusetts Supreme Judicial Court decided to do and why, read the opinion in the case *Adoption of Elena*, 446 Mass. 24, 841 N.E.2d 252 (2006).

PARALEGAL PRACTICE TIP

The opinion in *Adoption of Elena* is available at *www.pearsonhighered.com/wilson* in the companion website material related to Chapter 14 under "Cases" and in the Case Resources Section of the MyLegalStudiesLab.

Identification of Potential Adoptive Parents and Adoptees

WHO CAN ADOPT?

Basic threshold requirements for potential adoptive parents vary but customarily relate to age, family/marital status, race, religion, health, and sexual orientation. Additional factors relating to parenting skills, emotional stability, financial resources, and nature of the home environment are also scrutinized, generally in the context of home studies conducted prior to placement and finalization of an adoption.

Age

Adoption statutes usually require that the petitioner be an adult under state law (typically at least eighteen to twenty-one years of age). Although there is customarily no maximum age set, given the basic purpose of adoption, adoptive parents usually must be older than the adoptee and of such an age that they are able to provide continuity of care to adoptees until they reach the age of majority.

Paralegal **Application 14.9**

Can a Person Ever Be Too Old to Become an Adoptive Parent?

The Facts

This case involves a seventy-seven-year-old paternal great-aunt's petition to adopt a four-year-old child who has lived with her since the age of two months. Evidence was presented that the child's mother:

- had evicted the child and her father from the family home when the child was an infant and put their belongings in the street in inclement weather
- had neglected the child and failed to protect her from sexual abuse by her half-brother
- had failed to cooperate with the child's treatment plan or the service plan designed to address the neglect

- used marijuana and cocaine and was convicted of distributing cocaine prior to the child's birth
- had a history of unstable relationships with men
- functioned poorly under stress
- failed to comply with a child support order

Although the child has supervised visits with her mother every two weeks, the great-aunt has provided a stable and loving home for the child for virtually all her life and has done so with little support from either of the child's parents. In the event of her death or disability, she has arranged for two backup caretakers, aged forty-one and sixty-seven, who are family members well known to the

(Continued)

child. She has also made financial arrangements to provide for the child. The mother opposes termination of her parental rights and granting of the petition.

Sidebar

Assuming that the father has consented to the adoption, what do you think the court should do, given these facts? Explain your response. Read the opinion and see if you agree with the appellate court's decision in this case, *In re A.C.G.*, 894 A.2d 436 (D.C. App. Ct. 2006).

PARALEGAL PRACTICE TIP

The full opinion in *In re A.C.G.* is available at *www.pearsonhighered.com/wilson* in the companion website material related to Chapter 14 under "Cases" and in the Case Resources Section of the MyLegalStudiesLab.

Family/Marital Status

Children may be adopted by family members, step-parents, married couples, single persons, and co-parents, depending on the jurisdiction.

PARALEGAL PRACTICE TIP

Foster parent
a person or persons who provide a temporary home for a child when his or her parents are temporarily unwilling or unable to do so, usually through a child welfare agency for a modest payment

For many years, several states did not allow foster parents to petition to adopt a child in their care. That bar has now been lifted in virtually all states. Although foster parents now have standing to petition for adoption, they cannot block an adoption. However, in some states, a **foster parent** has standing to petition for termination of the parental rights of one or both parents of a child in foster care, on the grounds that the parent has abandoned the child. The highly publicized *Kingsley* case (*Kingsley v. Kingsley*, 623 So. 2d 780 (Fla. Dist. Ct. App. 1993)) initially involved the effort of a minor child to, in effect, divorce his mother by petitioning to have her parental rights terminated. The court denied the child's petition based on a minor child's lack of standing to initiate legal proceedings in his or her own name. However, the child's foster parent subsequently was able to accomplish the desired result and eventually adopted the child.

Family Member

Several states establish by statute or administrative regulation a preference for adoption by family members such as aunts, uncles, and grandparents, ostensibly to minimize disruption and maintain some degree of family connectedness for children. However, states also may place restrictions on adoptions of family members. For example, the Massachusetts adoption statute provides, "A person of full age may petition the probate court . . . for leave to adopt as his child another person younger than himself, unless such other person is his or her wife or husband, or brother, sister, uncle or aunt, of the whole or half blood."[36]

Step-parent

Cut-off rule
the rule requiring that a biological parent's rights to his or her child be terminated prior to adoption of the child by a third party; not applicable when a step- or co-parent is adopting the child

A step-parent adoption occurs when the spouse of a divorced or widowed and remarried custodial biological parent or the spouse of a parent of a nonmarital child seeks to adopt the child. The child retains a legal relationship with one parent, but his or her other parent (if living and known) generally must voluntarily consent to the adoption or have his or her parental rights involuntarily terminated as in other adoptions. Unlike a typical adoption, in which both biological parents' rights are extinguished, the **cut-off rule** does not apply to the custodial biological parent who remains in the new family unit. Although the adoption still must be approved by the court, most states have in place simplified procedures designed to expedite step-parent adoptions. Depending on the circumstances and extent of the relationship between the child and the parent whose rights are being terminated, the court may grant some degree of postadoption contact similar to that provided in an open adoption agreement.

Married Couple

The most common form of adoption is one in which a married couple seeks to adopt a child who is biologically unrelated. The couple is usually required to file a **joint petition for adoption.** Several states expressly prefer married couples as adoptive parents and are reluctant to grant adoptions to unmarried couples (heterosexual or homosexual) seeking to adopt a child. Some biological parents condition placement of their child with an agency on eventual adoption by a married couple.

Single Parent

Today, both single persons and married couples are eligible to adopt in most all states. However, historically, some states have prohibited single persons (regardless of sexual orientation) from adopting and others have not considered them desirable candidates as adoptive parents. Old attitudes die hard, and some agencies still have biases, expressed or masked, in favor of placing children with married couples.

Co-parent

In **co-parent** adoptions (sometimes labeled second-parent adoptions), one partner in an unmarried couple has or adopts a child and the other partner seeks co-parent status. That status affords the second partner parental rights, including the right to make decisions regarding the child's health, education, and welfare, along with the responsibility of providing financial support. Should the parties' relationship terminate, both parties have custodial and visitation rights.

Some states are slow to accept and accord rights to nontraditional family units. For example, a Utah statute provides as of 2011, "A child may not be adopted by a person who is cohabiting in a relationship that is not a legally valid and binding marriage under the laws of this state."[37] However, courts in a number of states have granted adoptions to unmarried partners, either heterosexual or homosexual, when they find them to be in the best interest of the children involved.

Race

The pendulum has swung back and forth with respect to the role of race in adoption decisions. Prior to the 1950s, many states banned transracial adoptions by statute until such laws were struck down as unconstitutional. In the 1950s and 1960s, transracial adoptions became more common, given a decline in white infants available for adoption. However, by the 1970s, black advocacy groups took a strong stand against the adoption of black children by white families, even if it delayed placement, claiming that only black families could appropriately address the unique developmental needs of black children. Racial matching once again became the norm, motivated not by racial discrimination but rather by a concern for the best interests of minority children. The roller coaster finally stopped in 1994 when Congress passed the Multiethnic Placement Act (MEPA), which provides:

> A person or government that is involved in adoption or foster care placements may not (A) deny to any individual the opportunity to become an adoptive or a foster parent, on the basis of race, color, or national origin of the individual, or of the child involved; or (B) delay or deny the placement of a child for adoption or into foster care, on the basis of the race, color or national origin of the adoptive or foster parent, or the child, involved.[38]

As with custody decisions, race should not be used as the sole basis for adoption decisions, subject to limited exceptions. However, the court can consider race as a factor when determining if a particular placement will be in the best interests of the child. As a practical matter, courts and agencies often prefer to place a child with parents of the same race and ethnic background if possible. In the case of American Indian children, under federal law race MUST be considered, in an effort to address a congressional finding that a high percentage of Indian families are broken up by the removal of their children by nontribal public and private agencies and placement in non-Indian foster and adoptive homes and institutions.[39] The Indian Child Welfare Act provides: "In any adoptive placement of an Indian child under state law, a preference shall be given, in the absence of good cause to the contrary, to a placement with (1) a member of the child's extended family; (2) other members of the Indian child's tribe; or (3) other Indian families."[40] The Act is intended to protect the best interests of Indian children and to promote the stability and security of Indian tribes and families. To that end, it established heightened standards that must be applied in child custody actions involving Indian children (including adoptions and actions to terminate parental rights). The Act defines an "Indian child" as "an unmarried person who is under eighteen and . . . (b) is eligible for membership in an Indian tribe and is the biological child of a member of an Indian tribe."[41]

Religion

As a matter of practice, agencies customarily place children in homes practicing the same religion as their biological parents, especially when the child is older and has already begun practicing a particular religion. However, interfaith adoptions are not constitutionally prohibited.

Health

An individual with a disability should not be discriminated against as a potential adoptive parent, provided the disability does not unduly interfere with the capacity to parent such that an adoption would not be in the best interests of the child.

Sexual Preference

Increasing numbers of same-sex couples are seeking legal recognition not only of their relationships but also of their status as parents. Some have custody of children born to prior heterosexual marriages. Others have used reproductive technology to create the children they are parenting. Co-parents of the same sex seeking to adopt under these or other circumstances encounter distinctly different results depending on where they reside. When the decisions in such cases are not prescribed by statute or regulation, they are left to the court's discretion and are generally decided according to a best-interests-of-the-child standard. Lingering biases with respect to homosexuality may still influence these decisions in some cases.

PARALEGAL PRACTICE TIP

To learn more about lesbian, gay, bisexual, and transgender families, visit *www.childwelfare.gov*. Also check *www.adoptionchildwelfarelaw.org*. In addition to same-sex adoption, you can also search by other topics such as "Who can adopt," "Stepparent adoption," and "Form and Filing of Petition," among many other options. You can find a link to both of these sites at *www.pearsonhighered.com/wilson* in the companion website material for Chapter 14 under "Resources."

Paralegal **Application 14.10**

Where Do You Stand?

Some states, such as California, Connecticut, and Vermont, have enacted legislation allowing adoption by same-sex partners.[42] Vermont provides by statute that (1) any person may adopt or be adopted by another person for the purpose of creating the relationship of parent and child between them; (2) if a family unit consists of a parent and the parent's partner, and adoption is in the best interests of the child, the partner of a parent may adopt the child of the parent.[43] Appellate courts in several states, such as Illinois, New Jersey, New York, Ohio, and Tennessee, have interpreted their respective general adoption laws to allow same-sex partners or couples to adopt. In 2010, after an appellate court upheld a lower court's decision that Florida's three-decade-old ban on gay adoption was unconstitutional, that state began permitting adoption by gays. On the other hand, as of 2010 Arkansas and Utah still banned any unmarried gay or heterosexual couples from adopting, and Mississippi bans gay couples but not single gays from adopting.

Assume that you work for a legislator in a state that is considering restricting adoption to heterosexual married couples. She has solicited your opinion on the subject. How would you respond? What are the arguments in support of such legislation? Against it?

WHO MAY BE ADOPTED?

Although in the vast majority of cases the individual adopted (the adoptee) is a child, in most states both children and adults may be adopted, provided that all of the requirements for a valid adoption are satisfied. However, adoptions of one partner by the other in a same-sex couple are not permitted in some states.

PARALEGAL PRACTICE TIP

To view an example of a Petition for Adult Adoption, visit *www.vermontjudiciary.org/eforms.* You can find a link to this site at *www.pearsonhighered.com/wilson* in the companion website material for Chapter 14 under "Forms."

Home Studies

Home studies commonly occur at two points during the adoption process: before and after temporary placement with the adoptive family. Although not usually required in independent adoptions, in agency adoptions all states require that a home study be conducted to ensure the suitability of the adoptive home prior to placement. Virtually all states require postplacement studies, with limited exceptions such as in step-parent adoptions. An example of the nature and focus of home studies is provided in Exhibit 14.1, which contains an excerpt from provisions of the Iowa Administrative Code for the Human Services Department governing adoption services.

Home studies customarily involve multiple visits. The first home study is designed to screen the adoptive parents and usually involves extensive interviews with the parents themselves regarding their goals and expectations with respect to the adoption as well as their attitudes and beliefs about childrearing. It may also include interviews with the parents' neighbors, school personnel, employers, extended-family members, and other references in an effort to assess the adoptive parents' emotional and financial stability, character, work history, and relationships with others. The second home study is designed to assess the child's adjustment to the adoptive home before the adoption is finalized.

Home visits are usually conducted by state-licensed social workers who prepare reports and make recommendations to the court, much as GALs appointed by

Home studies
assessments of prospective adoptive parents and home environments, customarily conducted by social workers licensed by the state

the courts do in contested custody cases. Although sometimes criticized by prospective adoptive parents as unwarranted, overly intrusive, and biased toward the middle-class concept of the ideal family, most social workers would agree that home visits serve to protect the safety and well-being of adopted children. Agencies and courts will not knowingly place adoptees in homes in which the parents have a documented history of substance abuse, violence, or criminal activity.

Courts recognize that there is no such thing as a perfect parent, but prospective adoptive parents need to be able to effectively care for children in a manner that supports and promotes the children's best interests. The prospective adoptive parents do not need to be wealthy, but they should at least be financially responsible and have sufficient resources to adequately provide for each individual child's unique needs. In some cases, those needs may be substantial. For example, a child may have a serious medical condition requiring around-the-clock care and major modifications to the physical structure of the adoptive home.

EXHIBIT 14.1 Iowa Administrative Code/Human Services Department [441]/ Chapter 108 Licensing and Regulation of Child-Placing Agencies/441-108.9(238)(4) Services to Adoptive Applicants (c) Adoptive Home Study and (d) Record checks

c. Adoptive home study. The home study consists of a family assessment which shall include at least two face-to-face interviews with the applicant and at least one face-to-face interview with each member of the household. At least one interview shall take place in the applicant's home. The assessment shall include, but need not be limited to, the following:
 1. Motivation for adoption and whether the family has biological, adopted or foster children.
 2. Family and extended family's attitude toward accepting an adopted child, and plans for discussing adoption with the child.
 3. The attitude toward adoption of the significant other people involved with the family.
 4. Emotional stability; marital history, including verification of marriages and divorces; assessment of marital relationship; and compatibility of the adoptive parents.
 5. Ability to cope with problems, stress, frustrations, crises, separation and loss.
 6. Medical, mental, or emotional conditions which may affect the applicant's ability to parent a child.
 7. Ability to provide for the child's physical and emotional needs and respect the child's cultural and religious identity.
 8. Adjustment of biological and previously adopted children, if any, including their attitudes toward adoption, relationship with others, and school performance.
 9. Capacity to give and receive affection.
 10. Statements from at least three references provided by the family and other unsolicited references that the agency may wish to contact.
 11. Attitudes of the adoptive applicants toward the birth parents and the reasons the child is available for adoption.
 12. Income information, ability to provide for a child, and a statement as to the need for adoption subsidy for a special needs child, or children.
 13. Disciplinary practices that will be used.
 14. History of abuse by family members and treatment.
 15. Assessment of, commitment to, and capacity to maintain other significant relationships.
 16. Substance use or abuse by members of the family and treatment.
 17. Recommendations for type of child, number, age, sex, characteristics, and special needs of children best parented by this family.
d. Record checks. The licensed child-placing agency shall submit record checks for each applicant and for anyone who is 14 years of age or older living in the home of the applicant to determine whether they have any founded child abuse reports or criminal convictions or have been placed on the sex offender registry. . . .

Jurisdiction and Venue

In order for a court to grant an adoption, the court must have subject matter jurisdiction over adoption. Subject matter jurisdiction is established by statute and may reside in a court of general jurisdiction such as a Superior Court, or in courts of limited jurisdiction such as a Probate, Family, or Juvenile Court. Venue is commonly proper in the county where the child or the biological or the adoptive parent(s) reside.

Any adoption, other than one involving a step-parent, relative, or guardian, that involves adoption of a child who is born or lives in one state (the "sending state") by someone who resides in another state (the "receiving state") must comply with the requirements of the Interstate Compact on the Placement of Children (ICPC), adopted in all fifty states. Each state has a designated ICPC office charged with responsibility for coordinating interstate adoptions. When an adoption is proposed by a court in a sending state, the ICPC office in that state provides written notice of the proposed adoption to the ICPC office in the receiving state. The notice includes basic identifying information about the child, the child's parents or guardian, and the proposed placement, along with the reason for the placement. The receiving state then conducts a home study and, if approved, notifies the sending state that approval for the child's entry to the receiving state to be placed has been granted. A failure to comply with ICPC requirements can result in a voiding of the adoption.

PARALEGAL PRACTICE TIP

To locate Interstate Compact on the Placement of Children (ICPC) Forms and information in Utah, visit *www.hsdcfs.utah.gov.* You will be able to find both forms and other useful resources, particularly documents titled "The Seven Steps to ICPC" and "ICPC Basics Handbook." You can find a link to this site at *www.pearsonhighered.com/wilson* in the companion website material for Chapter 14 under "Forms."

Petition for Adoption

An adoption action is usually commenced when a Petition for Adoption is filed in the name of the child by the prospective adoptive parents or the agency (see the detailed Colorado Petition provided in Exhibit 14.2). In most jurisdictions, the Petition must be accompanied by the affidavits or consent forms from the biological parents surrendering their rights. The form and content of the petition varies state to state but usually includes the following at a minimum:

- The name(s) and address of the petitioners
- The nature of their relationship to each other (married, unmarried, partners)
- Data about the petitioners, such as their ages and occupations
- The name, sex, age (date of birth), and religion of the child
- The name by which the adoptive child will be known once adopted
- Documentation of any prior custodial actions involving the child
- Consents to the adoption attached or an indication of why there is no consent
- Type of adoption (agency, independent, etc.)
- Certification that there are no additional persons interested in the proceeding

EXHIBIT 14.2 Petition for Adoption

Courtesy of the State of Colorado

☐District Court ☐Denver Juvenile Court _____County, Colorado Court Address:	
IN THE MATTER OF THE PETITION OF: _____ (name of person(s) seeking to adopt)	
FOR THE ADOPTION OF A CHILD	▲ **COURT USE ONLY** ▲
Attorney or Party Without Attorney (Name and Address):	Case Number:
Phone Number: E-mail: FAX Number: Atty. Reg. #:	Division Courtroom

PETITION FOR ADOPTION

The Petitioner(s) being desirous of adopting a child so as to make said child for all intents and purposes the legal child of Petitioner(s) and to render him/her capable of inheriting their estate, state(s) the following facts:

Information about the Petitioner(s):

Petitioner #1: _____ (Full Name)

    Date of Birth: _____ Race: _____ Place of Birth: _____

    Current Mailing Address: _____

    City & Zip: _____

    Home Phone #: _____ Work Phone #: _____ Cell #: _____

    Length of Residence in Colorado: _____ Occupation: _____

    Place of residence at the time of birth of the child.

Street Address	City	State	Zip Code

Petitioner #2: _____ (Full Name)

    Date of Birth: _____ Race: _____ Place of Birth: _____

    Current Mailing Address: _____

    City & Zip: _____

    Home Phone #: _____ Work Phone #: _____ Cell #: _____

    Length of Residence in Colorado: _____ Occupation: _____

    Place of residence at the time of birth of the child.

Street Address	City	State	Zip Code

☐ If applicable, maiden name of adopting mother: _____ Date of Marriage: _____

☐ The Petitioner(s) has/have attached as "Attachment A" a current fingerprint-based criminal history records check as required by §19-5-207(2.5)(a)(I)-(IV), C.R.S.

☐ The Petitioner(s) has/have attached as "Attachment B" the TRAILS background check as required by §19-5-207, C.R.S.

(Continued)

EXHIBIT 14.2 *(Continued)*

If the Petitioner(s) has/have been convicted of a felony or misdemeanor in any of the following areas, please check the appropriate box and identify for the Court the date of the conviction and if it was a felony or misdemeanor.

- ❑ child abuse or neglect on _____ (date). ❑Felony❑Misdemeanor
- ❑ spousal abuse on _____ (date). ❑Felony❑Misdemeanor
- ❑ any crime against a child on _____ (date). ❑Felony❑Misdemeanor
- ❑ any crime, the underlying factual basis of which has been found by the Court to include an act of domestic violence on _____ (date). ❑Felony❑Misdemeanor
- ❑ violation of a Protection/Restraining Order on _____ (date). ❑Felony❑Misdemeanor
- ❑ any crime involving violence, rape, sexual assault, or homicide on _____ (date). ❑Felony❑Misdemeanor
- ❑ any felony involving physical assault or battery on _____ (date). ❑Felony❑Misdemeanor
- ❑ any felony drug-related conviction within the past five years, at a minimum on _____(date). ❑Felony❑Misdemeanor

Identify all children of the Petitioner(s) (both natural and adopted and both living and deceased).

Full Name of Child	Full Name of Child

Facts concerning the child to be adopted. (Do not fill in if placement is by an agency or Department of Social Services.)

Full Name: _____   Date of Birth: _____

Place of Birth: _____ Relationship of child to Petitioner(s), if any _____

Place of Residence: _____

The child ❑is ❑is not a member or eligible to be a member of an Indian tribe as defined by the Indian Welfare Act.   If applicable, name of tribe _____.

- ❑ Notice of this Petition has been provided to the parent or Indian custodian of the child and to the tribal agent of the tribe, as required by §19-1-126(1)(c), C.R.S.

- ❑ Reasonable efforts have been made to send notice to the identified persons as follows:

  _____
  _____

  Attach the postal receipts to this petition, indicating that notice was properly sent. If the postal receipts have not been returned at the time of filing, the postal receipts or copies shall be filed with the Court within ten days of the filing of this petition.

- ❑ If applicable, inquiries have been made by the County Department of Social Services or child placement agency to determine whether the child is an Indian child as follows:

  _____
  _____

The child has been in the care and custody of Petitioner(s) since _____ (date).

The legal custody of the child is with _____ (name).

(Continued)

EXHIBIT 14.2 (*Continued*)

Full description of the property of the child, if any: _____

_____

Name and address of the Guardian(s) of the child and estate of the child, if any, have been appointed:

_____

Name of agency, if any, to which custody of the child has been given by proper order of the Court:

_____

Information about the Birth Parents of the Child:

Full Name of Birth father: _____

_____

| Street Address | City | State | Zip Code |

Full Name of Birth Mother: _____

_____

| Street Address | City | State | Zip Code |

The written consent(s) of the birth parent(s) ☐is/are attached **or** ☐is/are not attached.

The child will not be the subject of a pending dependency and neglect action when the adoption is heard.

If parental rights are relinquished, are terminated, or are being terminated in this action pursuant to §§19-5-101-108, C.R.S., as amended, or parent is deceased, state details:

_____

_____

_____

_____

Wherefore, the Petitioner(s) pray(s) that a Decree of Adoption be entered herein declaring said child to be the child of Petitioner(s) and that the name of said child be changed to: _____ (full name) and that said child shall be entitled to all of the rights and privileges and be subject to all of the obligations now conferred and imposed by law.

VERIFICATION AND ACKNOWLEDGEMENT

I swear/affirm under oath that I have read the foregoing Petition and that the statements set forth herein are true and correct to the best of my knowledge and belief.

| Petitioner Signature | Date | Petitioner Signature | Date |

Petitioner's Attorney Signature, if any | Petitioner's Attorney Signature, if any

Subscribed and affirmed, or sworn to before me in the County of _____, State of _____, this _____ day of _____, 20 ____.

My Commission Expires: _____

_____
Notary Public/Deputy Clerk

Subscribed and affirmed, or sworn to before me in the County of _____, State of _____, this _____ day of _____, 20 ____.

My Commission Expires: _____

_____
Notary Public/Deputy Clerk

PARALEGAL PRACTICE TIP

If the child is a nonmarital child and the biological father has neither consented to the adoption nor had his parental rights terminated, he should be served with notice of the petition for adoption—by personal service or by publication if necessary. Other interested parties who may be given notice include foster parents, relatives who may have been caring for the child, and preadoptive parents if an agency is filing the petition.

Notice, Preliminary Hearing, Interlocutory Decree, Pre-Adoption Placement, and Final Decree

Once the Petition is filed and served on all interested parties, the court schedules a preliminary hearing in which the pending adoption may or may not be contested. If it is uncontested or not successfully contested, the court customarily then issues an interlocutory decree granting temporary custody of the child to the adoptive parents. The adoption is generally not finalized until the final hearing is held six months to a year later. During that period, a follow-up home study is usually conducted.

Whatever their type, all adoptions must be approved by the court. The court makes a determination as to whether or not all statutory requirements have been met and the adoption will be in the best interests of the child. Most adoption final hearings are joyful events and may be conducted in the judge's chambers, depending on the circumstances. Even if held in the courtroom, the proceedings are closed to the public and the related records are sealed. Once the adoption is finalized, a Final Decree of Adoption is issued by the court, and a new birth certificate designating the adoptive parents as the child's legal parents is issued for the public record.

Challenges to the Adoption

In general, adoptions are considered final, but challenges do arise. The three most common sources of challenges are unwed biological fathers who never received notice of their child's adoption (see Case 14.1), biological parents who seek to revoke their consents, and adoptive parents who seek to **abrogate** an adoption they believe was wrongfully procured by an agency or individual.

Adoption abrogation
an annulment, repeal, or undoing of an adoption

CASE 14.1 *In Re Doe*, 159 Ill. 2d 347, 638 N.E.2d 181 (1994)

THE FACTS

Similar to the "Baby Jessica" case[44] in 1993, this high-profile case, popularly known as the "Baby Richard" case, caused a national media frenzy. Baby Richard was the biological child of Daniella Janikova and Otakar Kirchner. When he was born, his parents were not married. At the time of the birth, the father was out of the country taking care of his dying grandmother in Czechoslovakia. Four days after the child was born, Daniella consented to have the child adopted by John and Jane Doe after being told by a relative of the father that Otakar was involved with another woman. She subsequently told Otakar that the baby had died at birth. He was suspicious of her story and promptly began checking birth and death records and even checked the garbage at the mother's home to look for evidence that a baby was living there. Approximately two months after the birth, he learned the truth. Daniella and Otakar subsequently reconciled and were married about six months after the child's birth and sought the return of the child. They challenged the legality of the adoption and alleged that the father's consent was required, because he had not abandoned the child and there was no evidence that he was an unfit parent. He further argued that his lack of contact with the baby immediately after birth was solely due to the mother's fraudulent conduct.

(Continued)

PARALEGAL PRACTICE TIP

The *In re Doe* opinion is available at *www.pearsonhighered.com/wilson* in the companion website material related to Chapter 14 under "Cases" and in the Case Resources Section of the MyLegalStudiesLab.

The trial court held that the father was unfit because he had failed to demonstrate a reasonable degree of interest, concern, or responsibility for his son during the first thirty days of his life as required by statute, and thus his consent was not required. The court determined it was in Richard's best interests to remain with his adoptive parents, with whom he had lived since he was four days old. The trial court's decision was upheld by the appeals court, basing its decision on the best interests of the child. The appeals court stated:

> Fortunately, the time has long past when children in our society were considered the property of their parents. Slowly, but finally, when it comes to children even the law has rid itself of the Dred Scott mentality that a human being can be considered a piece of property "belonging" to another human being. To hold that a child is the property of his parents is to deny the humanity of the child. Thus, in the present case we start with the premise that Richard is not a piece of property with property rights belonging to either his biological or adoptive parents. Richard "belongs" to no one but himself.
>
> . . .
>
> A child's best interest is not part of an equation. It is not to be balanced against any other interest.[45]

The Illinois Supreme Court disagreed, finding that the father had been wrongfully deprived of the opportunity to express his interest in the child. It focused in its analysis of the situation on the preemptive rights of a natural parent in his own children apart from the best interest of the child.

Multiple appeals by the adoptive parents eventually failed despite a national public outcry and efforts by both the governor and state legislature of Illinois to influence the outcome by enacting a bill that provided for a hearing to consider a child's best interests when an adoption is denied or revoked on appeal as it was in this case. At the age of four, the crying child was taken from his adoptive mother's arms and handed over to his biological father in the bright media glare.

SIDEBAR

This case basically involved the weighing of the best interests of the child against the biological father's right to consent to the adoption of his child. What relative weight do you think should be given in such situations to the best interests of the child? The interests of the adoptive parents? The conduct of the mother? The interests of the nonmarital father? Should it matter whether the nonmarital father learns about the adoption before or after it is finalized? Do you agree with the outcome in this case? Explain your response.

Adoptive parents are no different from biological parents in the sense that their adopted children do not always turn out as they might hope. However, neither biological nor adoptive parents get to trade in their children for models they like better! Much as the courts are resistant to allowing biological parents to revoke their consents to adoption, they are likewise reluctant to permit adoptive parents to abrogate (undo) an adoption. The majority view is that adoptions cannot be abrogated by an adoptive parent.

However, a few states, by statute or case law, permit adoptive parents to abrogate an adoption in exceptional circumstances. In isolated cases, adoptive parents do not get what they believe they bargained for because an adoption agency or biological parent failed to inform (or actively deceived) them with respect to a major issue relating to the adoptee. For example, an agency may have failed to disclose the existence of a serious or costly medical condition or a history of psychiatric and behavioral problems, including fire setting, animal abuse, or violent conduct. Adoption agencies cannot warranty the children they place, but they do have a duty to provide accurate information known to them, on the basis of which adoptive parents can make informed decisions. When they fail to do so, the adoptive parents may seek to revoke the adoption and bring an action against the agency for the tort of **wrongful adoption**.

The Paralegal's Role in Adoption Cases

The paralegal's role in adoption cases depends primarily on four factors:

1. the extent to which the firm where the paralegal is employed specializes in adoption
2. the type of adoption involved
3. the client's role in the litigation: Is he or she the petitioner? Is he or she seeking to block the adoption? Is the client an agency?
4. the nature and level of the paralegal's skills

   Primary tasks performed may include the following:

   - researching state and federal statutes, case law, and procedural rules and regulations governing adoption in the applicable jurisdiction(s)
   - creating websites and marketing strategies to recruit prospective adoptive parents and locate potential adoptees
   - interviewing prospective adoptive parents, parents considering relinquishing their rights, and parents facing involuntary termination of their rights, to gather information relevant to the client's case
   - researching issues such as the rights of nonmarital fathers to object to an adoption, the right of a child to consent to his or her adoption, involuntary termination of parental rights, and adoption by single persons or same-sex partners
   - conducting a thorough search for a biological father whose whereabouts are unknown
   - locating, drafting and filing necessary paperwork, including petitions, consents, surrenders, ICPC paperwork, etc.
   - drafting open adoption agreements
   - scheduling and calendaring events such as home studies, hearings, and client meetings
   - providing support to clients as they progress through the often emotionally draining adoption process
   - monitoring payments for medical expenses to a birth mother intending to give up her child for adoption

Wrongful adoption
a tort action that an adoptive parent can bring against an adoption agency for failure to provide accurate and sufficient information regarding an adoptive child prior to adoption

PARALEGAL PRACTICE TIP

For more information about wrongful adoption, visit *www.childwelfare.gov.* You can find a link to this site at *www.pearsonhighered.com/wilson* in the companion website material for Chapter 14 under "Resources."

CHAPTER SUMMARY

This chapter opens by defining the nature and purposes of adoption. Various types of adoptions are classified and described and the major steps required to effect an adoption are introduced. Special emphasis is given to the contrast between the rights of nonmarital fathers and the rights of nonmarital mothers in case law and practice, the nature and role of putative father registries, and the importance of effective consents. Several additional topics related to adoption are discussed and illustrated in cases, paralegal applications, and practice tips, including termination of parental rights, characteristics of prospective adoptive parents (including co-parents), safe haven laws, home studies, and challenges to adoptions. Multistate variations in adoption law and procedure are highlighted. The chapter closes with a description of the roles a paralegal might be called upon to play in the context of adoption cases.

CONCEPT REVIEW AND REINFORCEMENT

KEY **TERMS**

Adoptee
Adoption
Adoption abrogation
Adoption registry
Agency adoption
At-risk adoption
Biology-plus rule
Closed adoption
Co-parent
Cut-off rule

De facto adoption
Equitable adoption/adoption by
    estoppel
Foster parent
Home studies
Illegal/black market adoption
Independent adoption
International adoption
Joint petition for adoption
Open adoption

Permanency planning
Putative father
Putative father registry
Safe haven law
Standing
Surrender (of parental rights)
Termination of parental rights
Wrongful adoption

REVIEW **QUESTIONS**

1. Identify and distinguish among various types of adoption.
2. Distinguish between an open and a closed adoption and identify the merits of each approach.
3. Identify the basic steps in the adoption process.
4. Describe the nature and significance of the "biology-plus rule."
5. Describe the nature and purpose of putative father registries.
6. Identify the kinds of circumstances in which a parent's rights may be terminated.

7. Identify who must consent to an adoption and under what circumstances a consent can be revoked.
8. Describe the role each of the following plays in adoption determinations: race, age, marital status, and sexual orientation.
9. Describe the nature and purpose of a home study.
10. Identify three circumstances in which an adoption may be challenged.

DEVELOPING YOUR PARALEGAL SKILLS

FOCUS ON **THE JOB**

In this Focus, the student will draft three documents tailored to a specific fact pattern: a Petition for Adoption, a Surrender and Consent to Adoption, and a Proposed Open Adoption Agreement.

The Facts

Jessica and Scott met in 2007 at a local tavern, where Jessica was tending bar and dealing drugs on a small scale, essentially to support her own habit. They quickly became involved. Scott did not join Jessica in using drugs until after he was involved in an automobile accident and was initially prescribed Oxycontin for pain. A year after they met, Jessica became pregnant. Although she did not entirely stop using drugs while pregnant, she did cut back and eventually gave birth on June 23, 2009, to a healthy baby boy they named Michael ("Mike") after Jessica's father. Scott formally acknowledged paternity, and his name appears on the child's birth certificate. The couple (along with the baby) lived with Jessica's parents until Scott lost his job

and the parents found out about the couple's drug use. The parents blamed all of Jessica's problems on Scott and threw him out of the house but allowed her to continue living there.

Scott was unemployed and homeless for about two months before he entered detox for a week, a secure rehabilitation facility for a month, and then a halfway house for six months. He regularly visited Mike and sent whatever financial support he could to Jessica, although he feared it simply went toward her cocaine addiction. He eventually got a job in construction (earning approximately $48,000 a year) and met and married Hayley, a high school English teacher (earning $45,000 a year) who is a caring and supportive partner eager to make a good life with him and raise Mike. Jessica is relieved at the prospect of not being responsible for the boy and is willing to consent to a step-parent adoption by Hayley as long as they will allow her to visit with the child twice a year for an afternoon and send her pictures and letters on a monthly basis.

Jessica's last name is Olivio and Scott's is Martinelli. The baby was given the father's last name at birth. Jessica's date of birth is February 9, 1981 and her current address is 33 Main Street in your city and state. Scott is living with Hayley in her home at 903 Hale Street in your city and state. Scott was born on October 21, 1980, and Hayley was born on November 17, 1982. They are members of a Unitarian church. Jessica was formerly a practicing Catholic but has left the church. She is presently unemployed. She was receiving public assistance for the benefit of Mike, but now Scott pays monthly child support through the state's IV-D agency.

The Assignment

Assume that you are employed by Attorney Juliana Dimitry, whose office is located at 390 Main Street in your city and state, and that she represents Scott and Hayley in this matter. Research the appropriate forms used in your state and draft the following:

1. A Petition for Adoption
2. A Surrender and Consent to Adoption
3. A proposed open adoption agreement, assuming that such agreements are permitted in your jurisdiction.

FOCUS ON **ETHICS**

In this Focus, the student will discuss ethical issues raised in a client meeting, particularly with respect to privilege confidentiality and candor.

The Assignment

Assume that you are employed by Attorney Kelly Brantley, whose office is located at 220 High Street in your city and state. She has an established general practice and is well respected by her colleagues. The office has been retained to represent Jessica in the adoption action described in the above comprehensive fact pattern. In the initial interview you were assigned to conduct with Jessica, she asks if everything she tells you is "private," and you assure her that yes, all of her communications with the family law team working on her case are protected by the attorney-client privilege. She then tells you that Scott is not actually Mike's father, but

that she convinced him he was so that he would acknowledge paternity and she would have no problem applying for public assistance. It all worked out, she says, because Scott has gotten his life back together and has turned out to be a great father. She says everything is going well now and she doesn't want to upset the applecart by telling the truth. She just wants to give up her legal rights and get the adoption finalized as soon as possible. In a 1–2 page paper describe what you are going to do in response to this conversation. Personally, you would really like to see the adoption take place because it is clearly in the best interests of the child. Relate your response to the ethical canons for paralegals promulgated by the National Association of Legal Assistants which are contained in Appendix A. Although he is not your client, would any other options potentially be available to Scott if and when the truth comes out?

FOCUS ON **CASE LAW**

In this activity, the student has an opportunity to brief a case on a topic relating to adoption.

The Assignment

Locate and brief a case decided in your state within the past three years on one of the following topics:

1. Termination of parental rights
2. Revocation of parental consent to an adoption
3. Co-parent adoption
4. The state's putative father registry, if any
5. Access to adoption records

A format for briefing a case can be found at *www.pearsonhighered.com/wilson* in the material related to Chapter 1 under "Resources."

FOCUS ON **STATE LAW AND PROCEDURE**

This Focus requires students to research laws and procedures governing adoptions in their respective jurisdictions.

The Assignment

Locate, review, and prepare a summary of the laws and procedures governing adoption in your state of residence and then answer the following questions:

1. Under what circumstances, if any, may a parent have his or her parental rights terminated?
2. Who is required to consent to an adoption?
3. Is a parent permitted to revoke a consent to adoption and, if so, under what circumstances?
4. What kinds of adoptions are permitted?
5. Does your state have a safe haven law? If yes, describe its provisions.
6. Who may adopt and who may be adopted?
7. Does your state have a putative father registry? If yes, describe its provisions.
8. Are adult adoptees permitted to contact their biological parents? If yes, how do they go about doing so?

FOCUS ON **TECHNOLOGY**

In addition to the links throughout the chapter, this activity provides a series of useful websites for reference along with technology-related assignments for completion.

Websites of Interest

Links to all of the listed websites are provided at *www.pearsonhighered.com/wilson* in the companion website material for Chapter 14 under "Resources."

www.abcadoptions.com

This site contains information about the adoption process and includes adoption postings. It serves as a support for both birth parents seeking adoptive parents and adoptive parents seeking children. It provides information for both populations and appears to act as a "meeting ground."

www.adoptionchildwelfarelaw.org

This is the Adoption and Child Welfare Lawsite, a service of the National Center for Adoption Law and Policy at Capital University Law School. It allows the visitor to search cases, statutes, and articles about adoption on a state-by-state basis.

www.adoptioninstitute.org

This is the website for the Evan P. Donaldson Adoption Institute. It contains links to putative father registries, open records information, state registries, and confidentiality statutes. It states as its mission, "To provide leadership that improves adoption laws, policies, and practices—through sound research, education, and advocacy—in order to better the lives of everyone touched by adoption."

www.chask.org

"CHASK" is an acronym for Christian Homes and Special Kids. It is a Christian service organization that serves as a meeting place for adoptive parents and birth mothers seeking adoptive homes for their children with special needs.

www.childwelfare.gov

This is the website for the Child Welfare Information Gateway, an organization of the Department of Health and Human Services. This site contains links to a number of sites addressing topics such as open adoption, access to adoption records, single-parent adoption, and gay and lesbian adoptive parents. It provides links to federal and state laws, fact sheets, statistics, and publications.

www.law.cornell.edu

This site provides links to the adoption laws of all fifty states.

Assignments

1. Locate websites for three adoption reunion registries and describe their content. Begin with the Georgia Adoption Reunion Registry, located at *www.adoptions. dhr.state.ga.us/reunion.htm*.
2. Locate websites for putative father registries in three states. Begin with the Illinois Registry at *www.state. il.us/dcfs/putative.htm*.
3. Locate three websites that offer information and support to gays and lesbians seeking to adopt.

PORTFOLIO PRODUCTS

1. Surrender and Consent to Adoption
2. Petition for Adoption
3. Proposed Open Adoption Agreement
4. 1–2 page paper concerning ethical issues in a hypothetical case
5. Brief of an adoption case
6. List of selected laws and procedures governing adoption in the student's jurisdiction

Endnotes

Chapter 1

1. The NALA definition has been adopted in whole or in large part by other bodies. See, for example, the North Dakota Rules of Professional Conduct and South Dakota Supreme Court Rule 92–5.
2. For example, the revised Rules of Professional Conduct for New Hampshire Attorneys (effective January 1, 2008) expressly permit lawyers from different firms to share fees if the fees are divided "in reasonable proportion to the services performed or responsibilities or risks assumed by each" or "based on an agreement with the referring lawyer" (sometimes called a naked referral). The client must agree to the fee division in writing, and the total fee cannot be increased as a consequence of the fee division.
3. NY CLS Dom Rel Appx §1400.1 (2007).
4. *Missouri v. Jenkins,* 491 U.S. 274, 109 S. Ct. 2463, 105 L. Ed. 2d 229 (1989). See Footnote 10 in the opinion.
5. *Smith v. Lewis,* 530 P.2d 589 at 596 (Cal. 1975).
6. See *Hendrix v. Page,* 986 F.2d 195 (7th Cir. 1993). In this case, an appellant failed to cite the only case that was on point for the issue under appeal. The court stated that when an attorney knowingly conceals dispositive adverse authority, it constitutes professional misconduct.
7. William D. Farber, J.D., L.L.M., Legal Malpractice in Domestic Relations, American Jurisprudence 44 Am. Jur. Proof of Facts 2d 377 (as of Aug. 2004).
8. *Hodges v. Carter,* 329 N.C. 517, 519, 520, 80 S.E.2d 144, 145, 146 (1954).
9. See Debra Levy Martinelli, *Are You Riding a Fine Line? Learn to Identify and Avoid Issues Involving the Unauthorized Practice of Law,* 15 Utah Bar J. 18 (2002).
10. See *United States v. Hardy,* 681 F. Supp. 1326, 1328–29 (N.D. Ill. 1988), as quoted in *Monroe v. Horwitch* et al., 820 F. Supp. 682 (D. Conn. 1993), a case involving a paralegal who advertised her availability to prepare uncontested divorce papers for clients.
11. 5 U.S.C.A. §555 (1967) allows a person appearing before a federal administrative agency to be represented by an attorney or a nonattorney deemed a "qualified representative" if the agency permits.
12. National Federation of Paralegal Associations Model Code (Definitions).
13. *Bates v. State Bar of Arizona,* 433 U.S. 350, 97 S. Ct. 2691, 53 L. Ed. 2d 810 (1977), rehearing denied 434 U.S. 881, 98 S. Ct. 242, 54 L. Ed.2d 164 (1977).

Chapter 2

1. U.S. Census Bureau, 2005 American Community Survey.
2. *America's Family and Living Arrangements 2010 from the 2010 Current Population Survey.*
3. Pew Research Center calculations based on U.S. Census Data for 2008.
4. Pamela Smock, *Cohabitation in the United States,* Annual Review of Sociology (2000).
5. See Hillary Greene, *Note: Undead Laws: The Use of Historically Unenforced Criminal Statutes in Noncriminal Litigation,* 16 Yale L. & Pol'y Rev. 169 (1997), for an extensive discussion of the secondary enforcement of criminal laws that have essentially been abandoned by state criminal prosecutors.
6. In 2007, the North Dakota legislature repealed its statute criminalizing cohabitation. An earlier effort to do so in 2003 had failed (discussed in *North Dakota Senate Decides to Keep Cohabitation Illegal,* State Capitals Newsletters, Family Relations, Alexandria, VA, Apr. 7, 2003, at 9. The law had provided that a person is guilty of a misdemeanor "if he or she lives openly and notoriously with a person of the opposite sex as a married couple without being married to the other person." N.D. Cent. Code 12.1–20–10 (1997). The maximum penalty if convicted was thirty days' incarceration and a fine of $1,000. N.D. Cent. Code 12.1–32–01 (1997). In 1999, the North Dakota Supreme Court thwarted the efforts of an angry spouse to compel the state to prosecute his unfaithful spouse for criminal cohabitation. See *Olsen v. Koppy,* 593 N.W.2d 762 (N.D. 1999).
7. Mich. Comp. Laws Ann. 750.335 (Supp 2003).
8. The American Law Institute's Principles of the Law of Family Dissolution take the position that there is no difference between enforcement of premarital and postmarital agreements, but some states distinguish between them by case law or statute. A leading case is that of *Casto v. Casto,* 508 So. 2d 330 (Fla. 1987), and another interesting case on point is *In re Marriage of Friedman,* 100 Cal. App. 4th 65 (2002).
9. See, e.g., *Curry v. Curry,* 260 Ga. App. 302 (1990); *Yeich v. Yeich,* 11 Va. App. 509 (1990); *Flansburg v. Flansburg,* 581 N.E. 2d 430 (Ind. App. 1990); and *Gilley v. Gilley,* 778 S.W.2d 862 (Tenn. App. 1989).
10. See, e.g., *Hastings v. Dickinson,* 7 Mass. 153 (1810).
11. Arline Dubin, *Prenups for Lovers: A Romantic Guide to Prenuptial Agreements,* Random House, p. 15 (1999).
12. Donna Beck Weaver, CFLS, *The Collaborative Law Process for Premarital Agreements,* 4 Pepp. Disp. Resol. L.J. 337 (2004).
13. *Ibid.*
14. In some states, such as California, the general Statute of Frauds (§1624, subd. (a) of the Civil Code) provides that the requirement that a contract be in writing is subject to an implied exception for "part performance" of the contract's terms, but the Family Code provides that an interspousal transaction that changes the nature of community or separate property is not valid unless made in writing by an express declaration approved by the adversely affected spouse. See *In re Marriage of Benson,* 36 Cal. 4th 1096, 116 P.3d 1152, 32 Cal. Rptr. 3d 471 (2005). In Florida, the statute generally barring any action based on an agreement in consideration of marriage, unless in writing, has been interpreted as permitting oral premarital contracts if performed within one year or if there has been partial performance of the contract. See *O'Shea v. O'Shea,* 221 So. 2d 223 (Fla. 4th DCA 1969). In Massachusetts, the agreement must be in writing, but may consist of an exchange of letters.
15. See Judith T. Younger, *Lovers' Contracts in the Courts: Forsaking the Minimum Decencies,* 13 Wm. & Mary Journal of Women & L. 349 (2007).
16. *Ex Parte Walters,* 580 So. 2d 1352 (Ala. 1991).
17. *Fletcher v. Fletcher,* 628 N.E.2d 1343 (Ohio 1994).
18. See, e.g., *Spritz v. Lishner,* 355 Mass. 162, 243 N.E.2d 163 (1969), in which the court held that, absent fraud, the contract was binding regardless of whether its terms were understood.
19. Joanna L. Grama, *The New Newlyweds: Marriage Among the Elderly. Suggestions to the Elder Law Practitioner,* 7 Elder L. J. 379 (1999).
20. See, e.g., *Waton v. Waton,* 887 So. 2d 419 (FLA. APP. 2004).
21. See, e.g., *Zummo v. Zummo,* 574 A.2d 1130 (Pa. Super. Ct. 1990), in which the court refused to enforce a verbal provision of a prenuptial agreement stipulating the religious upbringing of children from the marriage on the grounds that enforcement would involve excessive entanglement and encroachment by the state on a fundamental right of religious freedom protected by the First Amendment. But see *Ramon v. Ramon,* 34 N.Y.S.2d 100 (N.Y. Fam. CT. 1942). For further information on questionable provisions, see Jonathan E. Fields, *Forbidden Provisions in Prenuptial Agreements: Legal and Practical Considerations for the Matrimonial Lawyer,* 21 J. AM. Acad. Matrimonial Law, 413 (2008).
22. An interesting decision on point is *Avitzur v. Avitzur,* 58 N.Y.2d 108, 459 N.Y.S.2d 572, 446 N.E.2d 136 (1983), cert. denied 464 U.S. 817, 104 S. Ct. 76, 78 L. Ed. 2d 88 (1983). In this case, the court enforced an

agreement in which the husband agreed that if a civil divorce was obtained, he would appear before a rabbinical court, the Beth Din, so that the wife would be able to marry again under Jewish law.

23. *Favrot v. Barnes,* 332 So. 2d 873 (La. Ct. App. 1976), rev'd on other grounds; *Favrot v. Barnes,* 339 So. 2d 843 (La. 1976).

24. For a comprehensive treatment of this topic, see Joline F. Sikaitis, *Comment: A New Form of Family Planning? The Enforceability of No-Child Provisions in Prenuptial Agreements,* 54 Cath. U.L. Rev. 335 (Fall 2004).

25. ERISA requires private pension plans to offer spousal benefits for couples married for at least one full year before retirement or death, absent a written waiver. Waivers of ERISA and REA benefits must meet specific requirements.

   a. An effective waiver of a spouse's interest can be made only after the spouse is in fact married to the participant.

   b. The waiver must be in writing, witnessed by a plan administrator or notary public.

   c. The waiver must designate a different beneficiary or form of benefits, which may not be changed without spousal consent.

   d. The waiver must acknowledge the effect of the election.

   A good case on point is *Hagwood v. Newton,* 282 F.3d 285 (4th Circ. Ct. App. 2002).

26. See, e.g., Massachusetts General Laws Chapter 209 Section 26, which requires that to be effective against third parties, a premarital agreement must be recorded at an appropriate Registry of Deeds within 90 days of execution.

27. Under California law, parties to a premarital agreement are not considered fiduciaries, and basic contract law will apply. In Maryland, parties to a premarital agreement are considered fiduciaries, and enforcement will be judged on a higher standard of fairness, full disclosure, and voluntary execution. See *Cannon v. Cannon,* 384 Md. 537, 865 A.2d 563 (2005). See also *DeLorean v. DeLorean,* 211 N.J. Super. 432, 511 A.2d 1257 (1986), for an analysis of the choice of law conflict between New Jersey and California (although the enforceability of the DeLorean agreement was held to have been determined in an arbitration proceeding).

28. See, e.g., *MacFarlane v. Rich,* 132 N.H. 608 (1989). New Hampshire RSA 460:2-a invests prenuptial agreements with a presumption of validity that can be rebutted only if one or more of three standards of fairness have not been met:

   a. The agreement was not obtained through fraud, duress, or mistake, or through misrepresentation or nondisclosure of a material fact.

   b. The agreement is not unconscionable.

   c. The facts and circumstances have not changed since the agreement was executed so as to make the agreement unenforceable.

Chapter 3

1. In 23 Pa, C.S. § 1103, the Pennsylvania legislature provided that "No common law marriage contracted after January 1, 2005 shall be valid." Any common law marriage entered prior to that date remains valid. A more complete break with common law marriage has been unsuccessfully sought in South Carolina.

2. *Inhabitants of Milford v. Inhabitants of Worcester,* 7 Mass. 48 (1810).

3. *Goodridge v. Department of Public Health,* 440 Mass. 309, 343, 798 N.E.2d 941, 969 (2003) (Marshall, C.J.).

4. *Id.*

5. *Loving v. Virginia.,* 388 U.S. 1, 87 S. Ct. 1817, 18 L. Ed. 2d 1010 (1967), citing *Skinner v. Oklahoma,* 316 U.S. 535, 542, 62 S. Ct. 1110, 86 L. Ed. 1655 (1942).

6. *Zablocki v. Redhail,* 434 U.S. 374, 98 S. Ct. 673, 54 L. Ed. 2d 618 (1978).

7. *Salisbury v. List,* 501 F. Supp. 105 (D. Nev. 1980).

8. *Turner v. Safley,* 482 U.S. 78, 107 S. Ct. 2254, 96 L. Ed. 64 (1987).

9. *Palmore v. Sidoti,* 466 U.S. 429, 104 S. Ct. 1879, 80 L. Ed. 2d 421 (1984), appeal after remand 472 So. 2d 843 (Fla. App. 1985).

10. *M.T. v. J.T.,* 140 N.J. Super. 7, 355 A.2d 204 (1976).

11. See, e.g., *Littleton v. Prang,* 9 S.W.3d 223 (Tex. App. 1999).

12. On this topic, see Tom Green, *Common-Law Marriage and the Illegality of Putative Polygamy,* 17 BYU J. Pub. L. 141 (2002). See also Maura Strassberg, *The Crime of Polygamy,* 12 Temp. Pol. & Civ. Rts. L. Rev. 353 (2003).

13. A report of the National Society of Genetic Counselors indicates that the increased risk of significant birth defects in children born to first-cousin unions is only 1.7% to 2.8% above the risk level for the general population. See Robin L. Bennett et al., *Genetic Counseling and Screening of Consanguineous Couples and Their Offspring: Recommendations of the National Society of Genetic Counselors,* 11 Journal of Genetic Counseling 97 (2002).

14. *Johnson v. Johnson,* 104 N.W.2d 8, 14 (N.D. 1960).

15. See, e.g., R.R.S. Neb. § 42–102, which provides, "No person who is afflicted with a venereal disease shall marry in this state."

16. Cynthia Grant Bowman, *ARTICLE: A Feminist Proposal to Bring Back Common Law Marriage,* 75 Or. L. Rev. 709, 779 (Fall 1996).

17. *Meister v. Moore,* 96 U.S. 76, 24 L. Ed. 826 (1877).

18. Immigration Marriage Fraud Amendments of 1986.

19. See, e.g., *Dommer v. Dommer,* 829 N.E.2d 125 (Ind. App. 2005).

20. *Baehr v. Lewin,* 74 Haw. 530, 852 P.2d 44 (1993).

21. Hawaii Revised Statutes § 572–1. The state of Hawaii subsequently enacted "reciprocal beneficiaries" legislation affording some of the rights of marriage to same-sex couples, blood relatives, and housemates and as of 1/1/2012 will permit civil unions.

22. *Goodridge v. Department of Public Health,* 440 Mass. 309, 343, 798 N.E.2d 941, 969 (2003).

23. Lynn Wardle, *The End of Marriage,* 44 Fam. Ct. Rev. 45, 54 (January 2006).

24. *Lawrence v. Texas,* 123 S. Ct. 2472, 2490, 156 L. Ed. 2d 508 (2003).

25. Robert Wintemute, *Same-Sex Marriage: When Will It Reach Utah?* 20 BYU J. Pub. L. 527 (2006).

26. Edward A. Zelinsky, *Deregulating Marriage: The Pro-Marriage Case for Abolishing Civil Marriage,* 27 Cardozo L. Rev. 1161, 1163 (January 2006).

27. 1 U.S.C.S. § 7.

28. U.S.C.S. § 1738C.

29. The Honorable J. Harvey Wilkinson III, *Essay: Gay Rights and American Constitutionalism,* 56 Duke L.J. 545 at 562, 563 (2006).

30. House Bill 2007 (HB 2007-A) §2 (3) can be found at *www.leg.state.or.us/07reg/measures/hb2000.dir/hb2007.en.html.*

31. See *In the Matter of Adult Anonymous II,* 88 A.D.2d 30, 452 N.Y.S.2d 198 (N.Y. App. Div. 1982). But see *Matter of Robert Paul P.,* 63 N.Y.2d 233, 471 N.E.2d 424, 481 N.Y.S.2d 652 (1984).

32. *Braschi v. Stahl Associates Co.,* 74 N.Y.2d 201, 543 N.E.2d at 55 (1989).

33. American Law Institute, *Principles of the Law of Family Dissolution: Analysis and Recommendations,* 6.03(1).

34. 22 M.R.S. § 2710 2.

35. The city of Berkeley, CA, was the first municipality to extend domestic partnership benefits to its employees in 1984. Many other cities across the country followed (such as Boston and Cambridge, MA; New York City; San Francisco, CA; and Seattle, WA) and extended employee benefits to domestic partners under a policy that recognized them as spousal equivalents and/or because of a nondiscrimination policy encompassing sexual orientation. Most recognized both opposite-sex and same-sex partnerships broadly defined.

36. *Baker v. State,* 170 Vt. 194, 744 A.2d 864 (1999).

37. Conn. Gen. Stat. §§ 46b-38aa. through 46b-38pp. and 46b-39.

Chapter 4

1. *Nerini v. Nerini,* 11 Conn. Sup. 361, 364–365 (1943).

2. Tenn. Code Ann. 1 §36–4–101(2) (2011).

3. For a Tennessee case addressing these issues, see *Janna Sheya Falk v. Geary Falk,* 2005 Tenn. App. LEXIS 34.

4. Internal Revenue Service Publication 504, *Tax Information for Divorced or Separated Individuals,* p. 3. (2011 edition).

5. *Davis v. Davis,* 119 Conn. 194, 175 A. 574 (Conn. 1934).
6. *Irving v. Irving,* 134 P.3d 718 (Nev. 2006).
7. *Brown v. Watson,* 2005 Tenn. App. LEXIS 387.
8. See *Nave v. Nave,* 173 S.W.3d 766 (Tenn. App. 2005), in which a conservator filed a petition to annul the marriage of her ward—her father—on the ground that he was mentally incapable of entering a marriage contract at the time of the ceremony. Before the court rendered its decision granting the annulment, the ward died. A Tennessee Court of Appeals held that the annulment action did not abate at the moment of death, and the conservator was not deprived of standing to continue to pursue the annulment action. The judgment was entered *nunc pro tunc,* making the judgment effective prior to the death.
9. For an interesting unpublished case on this topic, see *Estate of Julia Dominguez, Deceased,* 2002 NY Slip Op 50481U, 2002 N.Y. Misc. LEXIS 1596. In this case, the "husband" in a "sham" marriage entered to assist him with his immigration status sought to be designated as administrator of his wife's estate after she was killed in a plane accident. The deceased wife's daughter also sought to be named administratrix of her mother's estate and to have the alleged husband disqualified as a surviving spouse based on the fact the marriage was a sham.
10. See, e.g., N.C. Gen. Stat. § 51–3 (2006). The statute provides that no marriage followed by cohabitation and the birth of issue shall be declared void after the death of either of the parties for any cause except bigamy.
11. *In re the Marriage of Linda A. and Robert S. Owen,* 2002 Cal. App. Unpub. LEXIS 1500 at 6.
12. See, e.g., Hawaii Revised Statutes §572–6 application; license; limitations.
13. See, e.g., *Tagupa v. Tagupa,* 108 Haw. 459, 121 P.3d 924 (Haw. App. 2005).
14. *M.T. v. J.T.,* 140 N.J. Super. 77, 355 A.2d 204 (1976).
15. *Kantaras v. Kantaras,* 884 So. 2d 155 (Fla. App. 2004).
16. See, e.g., *Meagher v. Maleki,* 131 Cal. App. 4th 1, 31 Cal. Rptr. 3d 663 (2005).
17. See 4 Am. Jur. 2d. Annulment §11 (2002). However, the long-standing rule in most jurisdictions is that an annulment will not be granted on the basis of fraud if one partner conceals from the other partner a serious drinking problem for which he or she refuses to seek help even if it interferes with the parties' sexual relationship. See, e.g., *Schaub v. Schaub,* 71 Cal. App.2d 467, 162 P.2d 966 (1945).
18. *V.J.S. v. M.J.B.,* 249 N.J. Super. 318, 592 A.2d 328 (1991).
19. *Robertson v. Roth,* 163 Minn. 501, 204 N.W. 329 (Minn. 1925).
20. *Tam v. Chen,* 2004 Cal. App. Unpub. LEXIS 6283.
21. See *Fryar v. Roberts,* 346 Ark. 432, 57 S.W.3d 727 (Ark. 2001). In this case, the Arkansas Supreme Court addresses this issue in considerable detail.
22. *Mayo v. Mayo,* 172 N.C. App. 844, 617 S.E.2d 672 (N.C. App. 2005).
23. *Adler v. Adler,* 805 So. 2d 952 (Fla. App. 2001).
24. *In re Marriage of Kramer,* 253 Ill. App. 3d 923, 625 N.E.2d 808 (Ill. App. 1993).
25. See, e.g., *Guzman v. Guzman Alvares,* 205 S.W.3d 375 (Tenn. 2006).
26. *Mayo v. Mayo,* 172 N.C. App. 844, 617 S.E.2d 672 (2005), quoting *Weil v. Herring,* 207 N.C. 6, 175 S.E. 836 (N.C. 1934).
27. Gibson's Suits in Chancery, § 42 (4th ed.).
28. See, e.g., the Connecticut annulment statute, General Statutes 46b-60.
29. *In re State ex rel. Dep't. of Econ. Sec. v. Demetz,* 212 Ariz. 287, 130 P.3d 986 (Ariz. App. 2006).

Chapter 5

1. Honey Hastings, *Dispute Resolution Options in Divorce and Custody Cases,* New Hampshire Bar Journal, Volume 46, Number 2 Summer 2005, p. 54. Although this article focuses specifically on the use of alternative dispute resolution options in New Hampshire, it is an excellent, well-researched discussion of the basic nature of several ADR options.
2. See, e.g., *Kelm v. Kelm,* 623 N.E.2d 39 (Ohio 1993).
3. *Williams v. North Carolina,* 317 U.S. 287, 298–299, 63 S. Ct. 207, 87 L. Ed. 279 (1942).
4. *Kulko v. Kulko,* 436 U.S. 84, 98 S. Ct. 1690, 56 L. Ed. 132 (1978).

5. *Burnham v. Superior Court,* 495 U.S. 604, 628, 110 S. Ct. 2105, 2119, 109 L. Ed. 2d 631, 650 (1990).
6. *Russo v. Russo,* 714 A.2d 466 (Pa. Sup. Ct. 1998).
7. Utah Code Ann. § 30–3–1. (3)(j).
8. See, e.g., *Ricketts v. Ricketts,* 393 Md. 479, 903 A.2d 857 (Ct. App. 2006). In this case, a Maryland appellate court reversed a lower court's dismissal of a complaint for a limited divorce on the ground of constructive desertion based on an alleged denial of marital relations while the parties continued to live under the same roof in separate bedrooms.
9. *Shaffer v. Shaffer,* Not reported in S.E.2d, 2003 WL 21739039 (Va. App.).
10. § 750 ILCS 5/401 (1).
11. *Verplatse v. Verplatse,* 17 Ohio App. 3d 99, 477 N.E.2d 648 (1984). Also see, e.g., *Hoppes v. Hoppes,* 5 Ohio Misc. 159, 214 N.E.2d 860 (cP 1964).
12. See, e.g., *Routhier v. Routhier,* 128 N.H. 439, 514 A.2d 825 (1986).
13. M.G.L. c.208 §1.
14. O.C.G.A. § 19–5–3 (9) and (12).
15. 750 ILCS 5/401 (1).
16. Md. FAMILY LAW Code Ann. § 7–103 (a)(4).
17. O.C.G.A. § 19–5–3 (8).
18. ORC Ann. 3105.01 (H).
19. Va. Code Ann. § 20–91 A. (3).
20. See, e.g., 750 ILCS 5/401 (1).
21. See N.H. Rev. Stat. Ann. §458:7 VIII.
22. See, e.g., Conn. Gen. Stat. § 46b-40 (c)(10).
23. Md. FAMILY LAW Code Ann. § 7–103 (a)(8).
24. Utah Code Ann. § 30–3–1 (3)(d).
25. ORC Ann. 3105.01 (F).
26. *In re Hightower,* 830 N.E.2d 862 (Ill. App. Ct. 2005), quoting *Quagliano v. Quagliano,* 94 Ill. App. 2d 233, 237, 236 N.E.2d 748 (1968).
27. See *Vandevort v. Vandevort,* 134 P.3d 892 (Okla. Civ. App. 2005).
28. 50 U.S.C. § 521 (1982).
29. *Long v. Long,* 196 S.W.3d 460 (Tex. App. 2006).
30. See, e.g., Mark Chinn, *The Exit Interview,* Family Advocate, Fall 2006, American Bar Association.

Chapter 6

1. *Hickman v. Taylor,* 329 U.S. 495, 67 S. Ct. 385, 91 L. Ed. 451 (1947). (Jackson, J., concurring).
2. Supp.Dom.Rel.P. Rule 410 Mandatory Self-Disclosure of Financial Documents.
3. For a comprehensive treatment of Internet research, see the two-volume set, Carole A. Levitt and Mark E. Rosch, *Find Info Like a Pro,* ABA Law Practice Management Section, 2010.
4. Shelagh C. N. Michaud in New Hampshire Bar News 16 April 2010.
5. The content of this segment reflects, in part, observations made in a workshop handout prepared by Hon. Geoffrey A. Wilson, Franklin Probate and Family Court, titled "A Judge's Thoughts on Financial Statements (A Work in Progress)" and reprinted in several publications, including Donald G. Tye et al., *Trying Divorce Cases,* Volume I, MCLE, Inc. (2005).

Chapter 7

1. Several courts across the country have held that both parents have a support obligation to a child who is the product of statutory rape. See, e.g., *State of Kansas ex rel Hermesmann v. Seyer,* 252 Kan. 646, 847 P.2d 1273 (1993).
2. E. Gary Spitko, *Sexual Orientation: Public Perceptions: From Queer to Paternity: How Primary Gay Fathers Are Changing Fatherhood and Gay Identity,* 24 St. Louis U. Pub. L. Rev. 195 at 216 (2005).
3. See Cynthia R. Mabry, *Who Is the Baby's Daddy (And Why Is It Important for the Child to Know)?* 34 U. Balt. L. Rev. 211 (Winter 2004). Based on the Census data cited, 48% of children not living with their fathers

were African-American; 25% were Latino. Asian families reported the lowest number of children who lived with their single mothers, 13%.

4. The Court held that the biological father had no constitutionally protected relationship with his child. The plurality essentially reasoned that a natural father may have a protected right, but only if his rights do not conflict with the rights of the husband of the marriage into which the child was born.

5. See Katharine Baker, *Bargaining or Biology? The History and Future of Paternity Law and Parental Status*, 14 Cornell J. L. & Pub. Pol'y 1 at 6 (Fall 2004), for a comprehensive discussion of the rationale for and implementation of the duty of paternity support initially in the criminal context as "punishment for fornication and bastardy."

6. Nancy E. Dowd, *Essay: From Genes, Marriage and Money to Nurture: Redefining Fatherhood*, 10 Cardozo Women's L.J. 132 at 138 (Fall 2003).

7. *Levy v. Louisiana*, 391 U.S. 68 (1968).

8. *Lehr v. Robertson*, 463 U.S. 248, 103 S. Ct. 2985, 77 L. Ed. 2d 614 (1983).

9. *Nguyen v. Immigration and Naturalization Services*, 533 U.S. 53, 121 S. Ct. 2053, 150. L. Ed. 2d 115 (2001).

10. 8 U.S.C.S. §1409.

11. *Id*. at §1409(c).

12. *Id*. at §1409(a).

13. *Supra* n.9 at 62.

14. Uniform Parentage Act of 2000 (as amended 2002), Article 2 §201.

15. *Barnes v. Jeudevine*, 475 Mich. 696, at 715, 718 N.W.2d 311 (2006) (Markman, J., dissenting).

16. 41 U.S.C. 666(a)(5)(D).

17. 41 U.S.C. 666(a)(5)(D)(i).

18. Niccol D. Kording, *Little White Lies That Destroy Children's Lives— Recreating Paternity Fraud Laws to Protect Children's Interests*, 6 J.L. Fam. Stud. 237, 245 (2004).

19. Alaska Stat. § 25.27.166. Exception: Disestablishment is not permitted if paternity has been acknowledged or admitted or established through genetic testing.

20. O.C.G.A. § 19–7–54.

21. Md. Code Ann., Fam. Law § 5–1038(a)(2)(i)2. Exception: Cannot disestablish paternity if father has previously acknowledged paternity knowing he was not the father.

22. Ohio Revised Code Sections 3119.961 and 3119.962. Exception: Cannot disestablish paternity if father has previously acknowledged paternity knowing he was not the father. Two Ohio courts of appeal have declared the statutes unconstitutional because the legislature, in effect, was dictating to the courts what to do with paternity judgments rendered years before, in violation of the separation of powers doctrine.

23. See, e.g., *Doran v. Doran*, 2003 PA Super 129, 820 A.2d 1279 (2003), in which the court denied a request for an award in the amount of previously paid child support; but see *Denzik v. Denzik*, 197 S.W.3d 108 (Ky. 2006), in which the Kentucky Supreme Court reinstated a jury verdict in a husband's fraudulent misrepresentation action and allowed "restitution, albeit with considerations to limit the rate of payment in order to prevent detriment to the child(ren) supported."

24. *Langston v. Riffe*, 359 Md. 396 at 437, 754 A.2d 389 (Ct. App. 2000).

25. *Id*. at 416.

26. *Williams v. Williams*, 843 So. 2d 720 at 723 (Miss. 2003).

27. *Godin v. Godin*, 168 Vt. 514 at 523, 725 A.2d 904 (1998).

28. Mabry, *supra* n. 3 at 213, reflecting decisions of courts in New Jersey, Pennsylvania, Kansas, and Delaware.

29. *Betty L.W. v. William E.W.*, 212 W. Va. 1 at 12, 569 S.E.2d 77 (2002) (Maynard, J. dissenting).

30. *www.paternityfraud.com*.

31. Kording, *supra* n. 18, at 237.

32. Bruce Lord Wilder, *Current Status of Assisted Reproduction Technology: An Overview and Glance at the Future*, 39 FAM. L. Q. 573 (at 1) (No. 3 Fall 2005).

33. 750 ILCS 47.

34. N.H. Rev. Stat. §168-B: 19 and 14.

35. Mass. Gen. Laws Ch. 112 §12J.

36. 18 Pa. C. S. Ann. §3213(e).

37. Ark. Code Ann. § 23–85–137.

38. Md. Code Ann. §15–810(d) re limits and (b)(1) re mandates.

39. Mich. Comp. Laws Ann. §722.855.

40. Mich. Comp. Laws Ann. §722.857.

41. 750 ILCS 47/15.

42. N.H. Rev. Stat. Ann. §168-B:16(I)(b).

43. Utah Code Ann. §78B-15-801.

44. Va. Code Ann. 20–165 (A)(B).

45. Wash. Rev. Code §26.26.240.

46. Nev. Rev. Stat. Ann. §126.045 (3).

47. Ky. Rev. Stat. Ann. §199.590(4).

48. *Hodas v. Morin*, 442 Mass. 544, 814 N.E.2d 320 (Mass. 2004).

49. Cal. Fam. Code §7630 (f). For an excellent resource on prebirth parentage orders, see Steven H. Snyder and Mary Patricia Byrn, *The Use of Prebirth Parentage Orders in Surrogacy Proceedings*, 39 Fam. L. Q. 633–662 (No. 3 Fall 2005). The article includes as an appendix a state-by-state list of laws affecting surrogacy and prebirth order proceedings.

50. *Doe v. Doe*, 710 A.2d 1297 (Conn. 1998).

51. *Johnson v. Calvert*, 5 Cal. 4th 84, 93, 851 P.2d 776, 19 Cal. Rptr. 2d 494(1993), cert. denied 510 U.S. 874, 114 S. Ct. 206, 126 L. Ed. 2d 163(1993).

52. *Id*.

53. *Id*. at 93.

54. *In the Matter of Baby M.*, 109 N.J. 396, 537 A.2d 1227 (1988).

55. *Id*. at 441, 442.

56. See Charles P. Kindregan and Maureen McBrien, *Embryo Donation: Unresolved Legal Issues in the Transfer of Surplus Cryopreserved Embryos*, 49 Vill. L. Rev. 169 at 170 (2004).

57. See Naomi D. Johnson, *Excess Embryos: Is Embryo Adoption a New Solution or a Temporary Fix*, 68 Brook. L. Rev. 853 (2003).

58. See N.H. Rev. Stat. Ann. § 168-B:15 and La. Rev. Stat. Ann. § 9:129.

59. See generally La. Rev. Stat. Ann. §§9:129.

60. Fla. Stat. Ann. § 742.17.

61. 10 Okla. St. § 556.

62. *Davis v. Davis*, 842 S.W.2d 588 (Tenn. 1992).

63. *Id*. at 597.

64. *Id*. at 601.

65. *Id*. at 602.

66. *Kass v. Kass*, 91 N.Y.2d 554, 696 N.E.2d 174, 673 N.Y.S.2d 350 (N.Y. 1998).

67. *Id*. at 180.

68. See Charles P. Kindregan and Maureen McBrien, *Assisted Reproductive Technology: A Lawyer's Guide to Emerging Law and Science*, American Bar Association, 2005. Chapter 10 contains helpful pointers on the drafting of documents relating to assisted reproduction arrangements.

69. *Supra* n. 14 Article 7 Section 707.

70. Fla. Stat. §742.17.

71. La. R.S. 9:391.1A.

72. See, e.g., *Gillett-Netting v. Barnhart*, 371 F. 3d 593 (9th Cir, Ariz. 2004). See also 42 U.S.C. §402(d)(1) and 416(h)(2)(A).

73. See *In re Estate of Kolacy*, 753 A.2d 1257 (N.J. Super. Ct. Ch. Div. 2000), in which the court held that twins born eighteen months after their father's death were his legal heirs.

74. *Woodward v. Comm'r of Soc. Sec.*, 435 Mass. 536, 760 N.E.2d 257 (2002).

75. See *Kazmierazak v. Query*, 736 So. 2d 106 (Fla. Dist. Ct. App. 1999); *In re C.B.L.*, 723 N.E.2d 316 (Ill. App. Ct. 1999); *McGuffen v. Overton*, 542 N.W. 2d 288 (Mich. Ct. App. 1995); *Alison D. v. Virginia M.*, 572 N.E.2d 27 (N.Y. 1991); *In re Jones*, 2002 WL 940195 (Ohio Ct. App. 2002); and *In re Thompson*, 11 S.W.3d 913 (Tenn. Ct. App. 1999).

76. See, e.g., *Nancy S. v. Michele G.*, 279 Cal. Rptr. 212 (Ct. App. 1991).

77. *Jhordan C. v. Mary K.*, 179 Cal. App. 3d 386, 224 Cal. Rptr. 530 (Cal. App. 1986).

78. *Principles of the Law of Family Dissolution: Analysis and Recommendations*, American Law Institute, Philadelphia, PA, *www.ali.org*.

79. See Lars Noah, *Assisted Reproductive Technologies and the Pitfalls of Unregulated Biomedical Innovation,* 55 FLA. L. REV. 603 (2003).

80. *Gleitman v. Cosgrove,* 227 A.2d 689, 695 (N.J. 1967). In this case, the plaintiff claimed that a physician's failure to inform or advise a pregnant mother of the dangers of birth defects when she contracted rubella deprived her of the opportunity to terminate the pregnancy and allowed the child to be born with birth defects.

81. *Harbeson v. Parke-Davis, Inc.,* 656 P.2d 483 (Wash. 1983).

82. See, e.g., *Morgan v. Christman,* 1990 WL 137405 (D. Kan.), a case in which the use of the drug Clomid resulted in the premature birth of four children who suffered from various impairments and deformities.

83. *Stiver v. Parker,* 975 F.2d 261 (6th Cir. 1992).

84. CAL. PENAL CODE §367g.

85. See Cyrene Grothaus-Day, *Criminal Conception: Behind the White Coat,* 39 FAM. L. Q, 707 (2005).

86. *Perry-Rogers v. Fasano,* 276 A.D. 67, 715 N.Y.S.2d 19 (2000).

87. See *Perry-Rogers v. Obasaju,* 282 A.D.2d 231 (N.Y. App. Div. 2001), in which the court denied the defendant's motion to dismiss and held it was foreseeable that implantation of the plaintiff's embryo in another woman would cause emotional distress.

88. *Fasano v. Nash,* 282 A.D.2d 277 (N.Y. App. Div. 2001). See also Raizil Liebler, *Are You My Parent? Are You My Child? The Role of Genetics and Race in Defining Relationships After Reproductive Technological Mistakes,* 5 DEPAUL J. HEALTH CARE L. 15, pp. 42–52 (2002).

89. See, e.g., *Jeter v. Mayo Clinic of Arizona,* 121 P.3d 1256 (Ariz. App. Div. 1 2005).

Chapter 8

1. *Garska v. McCoy,* 167 W.Va. 59, 278 S.E.2d at 360 (1981).

2. American Law Institute Principles of Marital Dissolution §2.03 (1). The American Law Institute's Principles of Marital Dissolution refer to "allocation of parental responsibilities" rather than to "visitation" and "custody."

3. New Hampshire RSA 461-A:1, 2. Proposed by a Family Law Task Force after a two-year study, the Act went into effect in 2005. Similar to other jurisdictions moving in this direction, it supports "frequent and continuing contact between each child and both parents" and encourages parents "to develop their own parenting plans" and "to share in the rights and responsibilities of raising their children. . . ." RSA 461-A:2. "custody."

4. The Uniform Child Custody Jurisdiction Act, 9(1A) U.L.A. 261 (1968).

5. The Uniform Child Custody Jurisdiction and Enforcement Act, 9(1A) U.L.A. 649 (1997).

6. Federal Parental Kidnapping Act, P.L. 96–611 § 6–10.

7. Convention on the Civil Aspects of International Child Abduction, held at The Hague on October 25, 1980. The language of the Convention can be found in Appendix 2 to the Department of State Notice, 51 FR 10498 March 26, 1986. The federal legislation that makes the terms of the Convention available as a judicial remedy in the United States is the International Child Abduction Remedies Act (ICARA), Sec. 1 of P.L. 100–300, 42 U.S.C.A.11601 *et seq.* The Federal Regulations that define the State Department's role in implementing the Convention are found in 22 C.F.R. 94.4.

8. National Child Search Assistance Act, 42 USC §§ 5779 and 5780.

9. The International Parental Kidnapping Crime Act 18 USC §1204.

10. The Fugitive Felon Act, 18 USC §1073.

11. The International Child Abduction Remedies Act, 42 USC §11601 *et seq.*

12. Arizona Revised Statutes Annotated 25-403 Custody; Best interest of the child. . . .

13. *Ibid.*

14. MCLS § 722.23.

15. In Texas, custody cases may be heard by juries. See Texas Family Code Article 105.002.

16. *In re Milovich,* 105 Ill. App.3d 596, 434 N.E.2d 811 (1982).

17. See, e.g., *Burchard v. Garay,* 724 P.2d 486 (Cal. 1986.); *Maureen F.G. v. George W.G.,* 445 A.2d 934 (Del. 1982); *Agudo v. Agudo,* 411So. 2d 249 (Fla. Dist. Ct. App 1982); *Rolde v. Rolde,* 12 Mass. App. Ct. 398, 425 N.E.2d 388 (1981); *Maxfield v. Maxfield,* 452 N.W.2d 219 (Minn. 1990); *Riaz v. Riaz,* 789 S.W.2d 224 (Mo. App. Ct. 1990); *Burleigh v. Burleigh,* 650 P.2d 753 (Mont. 1982); *Crum v. Crum,* 505 N.Y.S.2d 656 (App. Div. 1986); *Moore v. Moore,* 574 A.2d 105 (Pa. Super. Ct. 1990); *Pusey v. Pusey,* 728 P.2d 117 (Utah 1986); *Harris v. Harris,* 546 A.2d 208 (Vt. 1988); and *Garska v. McCoy,* 167 W.Va. 59, 278 S.E.2d at (360 1981).

18. See *Pascale v. Pascale,* 140 N.J. 583, 660 A.2d 485 (N.J. 1995).

19. American Law Institute, Principles of the Law of Family Dissolution: Analysis and Recommendations, §208.

20. *Silva v. Silva,* 136 P.3d 371 (Idaho App. 2006).

21. *Kilsing v. Allison,* 343 S.C. 674, 541 S.E.2d 273 (S.C. App. 2001).

22. § 452.375 R.S. Mo.

23. *Source:* U.S. Census Bureau, Current Population Survey, April 1994–2002.

24. MCLS § 722.23.

25. *Garrett v. Garrett,* 527 N.W.2d 213, 221–222 (Neb. Ct. App. 1995).

26. *Hicks v. Hicks,* 2005 PA Super. 58, 868 A.2d 1245 (2005). There are those who might argue that the court violates the Constitution by, in effect, preferring one religion over the other. Occasionally, a dispute is about a particular religious practice between two parents who share the same faith. See *Sagar v. Sagar,* 57 Mass. App. Ct. 71, 781 N.E.2d 54 (2003).

27. *In re Stopher,* 328 Ill. App. 3d 1037, 263 Ill. Dec. 199, 767 N.E.2d 925 (2002). Other courts have reached a different result if, for example, the child had a serious medical problem that required complicated care and complex calculation and administration of medication.

28. *Matta v. Matta,* 44 Mass. App. Ct. 946, 693 N.E.2d 1063 (1998).

29. *Newton v. Riley,* 899 S.W.2d 509 (Ky. Ct. App. 1995).

30. *Taylor v. Taylor,* 345 Ark. 300, 47 S.W.3d 222 (2001).

31. See, e.g., *Boyle v. Boyle,* 12 Neb. App. 681, 684 N.W. 2d 49 (2004).

32. *McGriff v. McGriff,* 140 Idaho 642, 99P.3d 11 (2004).

33. *Supra* note 24.

34. *Anderson v. Anderson,* 278 Ga. 713, 606 S.E.2d 251 (2004).

35. Ill. Rev. Stat. § 750 ILCS 5/602.

36. *Resigno v. Annino,* 869 So. 2d 741 (Fla. 2004).

37. Wyo. Stat. Ann. §20–2–201(a)(iii).

38. *In re Julie Anne,* 121 Ohio Misc. 2d 20, 2002 Ohio 4489, 780 N.E.2d 635 (Ohio Com. Pleas 2002).

39. But in an Illinois case, the appeals court noted that "Neither the legislature or case law in Illinois has seen fit to set forth a rule of law that the killing of one parent by the other in the presence of the children, no matter what the circumstances, standing alone is sufficient to deprive that parent of his or her children on the basis of unfitness." *Tranel v. Lutgen,* 177 Ill. App. 3d 954, 127 Ill. Dec. 147, 532 N.E.2d 976 (2 Dist. 1988).

40. S.C. Code . § 63–15–30 (2008).

41. *Bodne v. Bodne,* 277 Ga. 445, 588 S.E.2d 95 (Ga. App. 2002).

42. Sometimes innovative strategies are used, such as having parents who cannot talk reasonably with each other in person communicate by writing basic messages in a notebook. *Shenk v. Shenk,* 159 Md. App. 548, 860 A.2d 408 (2004).

43. See, e.g., *Beck v. Beck,* 86 N.J. 480; 432 A.2d 63 (1981).

44. See, e.g., *Cohen v. Cohen,* 162 Md. App. 599, 875 A.2d 814 (2005).

45. *Cleri v. Cleri,* No. 01D-0009-D1 (Conn. Prob. Ct. July 2, 2002), as cited in Sarah L. Gottfried, *Virtual Visitation: The New Wave of Communication Between Children and Parents in Relocation Cases,* 9 Cardozo Women's L. J. 567, 582–583 Endnote 175 (2003).

46. *McCoy v. McCoy,* 336 N.J. Super. 172, 764 A. 2d 449 (N.J. Super. App. Div. 2001). See also *McCubbin v. Taylor,* 5 S.W.3d 202 (Mo. App. 1999); *Hartinger v. Hartinger,* 2000 WL 33418385 (Mich. App. 2000).

47. *Lazarevic v. Fogelquist,* 668 N.Y.S.2d 320 (1997).

48. Rev. Code Wash. (ARCW) § 2609.184.

49. The states that have adopted the UMDA as of January 2011 include Arizona, Colorado (in part), Illinois, Kentucky, Minnesota, Missouri, Montana, and Washington.

50. See, e.g., *Spahmer v. Gullette,* 113 P.3d 158 (Colo. 2005).

51. *Hawkes v. Spence,* 2005 VT 57, 178 Vt. 161, 878 A.2d 273 (2005).

52. William G. Austin, *Relocation Law and the Threshold of Harm: Integrating Legal and Behavioral Perspectives,* 34 Fam. L. Q. 63, 65 (Spring 2000), as quoted in *Fenwick v. Fenwick,* 114 S.W.3d 767 (Ky. 2003). See also *Tibor v. Tibor,* 598 N.W.2d 480, 485 (N.D. 1999), in which the court acknowledges that a "move which benefits the health and well-being of a custodial parent is certainly beneficial to the parent's child, and is consequently in the child's best interest."

53. California Family Code Article 3048; Minnesota Statute Article 518.175; Revised Statutes of Missouri Article 452.377; and CRS 14-10-129.

54. *Morgan v. Foretich,* 546 A.2d 407 (D.C. App. 1988). See also *Morgan v. Foretich,* 564 A.2d 1 (D.C. App. 1989), in which the contempt judgment was overturned.

55. Gupta-Kagan, *Children, Kin, and Court: Designing Third Party Custody Policy to Protect Children, Third Parties, and Parents,* 12 N.Y.U. J. Legis. & Pub. Pol'y 43 at 48 (2008).

56. HAW. REV. STAT. § 571–46(2) (Supp. 2006). Given the decision in the *Troxel* case, this statute is likely unconstitutionally broad but has not yet been declared so.

57. Mary Ann Mason and Nicole Zayac, *Rethinking Stepparent Rights: Has the ALI Found a Better Definition?* 36 Fam. L. Q. No. 2 (Summer 2002).

58. See, e.g., *Michael H. v. Gerald D.,* 491 U.S. 110, 109 S. Ct. 2333, 105 L. Ed. 2d 91 (1989). In this case, the child had known both "fathers" in a paternal capacity. The Supreme Court upheld a California court's decision recognizing the mother's husband as the child's legal father rather than the biological father who sought to establish paternity.

59. *Supra* note 57.

60. Some of the states imposing such obligations include Delaware, Hawaii, Iowa, Kentucky, Montana, North Carolina, and North Dakota.

61. In a Michigan case, for example, a court extended parental status to a step-parent, applying the concept of "equitable parenthood" under circumstances in which: (1) the husband and child mutually acknowledge a relationship as father and child, or the mother of the child has cooperated in the development of such a relationship over a time prior to the filing of the complaint for divorce, (2) the husband desires to have the rights afforded to a parent, and (3) the husband is willing to take on the responsibility of paying child support. *Atkinson v. Atkinson,* 160 Mich. App. 601, 408 N.W.2d 516 (1987). In the Minnesota case *Simmons v. Simmons,* 486 N.W.2d 788 (Minn. App. 1992), the court relied on the *in loco parentis* doctrine when it awarded visitation to a step-father over the mother's objection.

62. 50 USCS Appx. § 501 *et seq.*

63. *In re Marriage of Rayman,* 273 Kan. 996, 47 P.3d 413 (Kan. 2002).

64. U.S. Department of Commerce, Census Bureau, *Children's Living Arrangements and Characteristics, March 2002* (June 2003).

65. See *Troxel v. Granville,* 530 U.S. 57 at 74 (2000).

66. See, e.g., *Blixt v. Blixt,* 437 Mass. 649, 774 N.E.2d 1052 (Mass. 2002).

67. Sandra Martinez, *The Misinterpretation of Troxel v. Granville: Construing the New Standard for Third-Party Visitation,* 36 Fam. L. Q. No. 3, Fall 2002 at p. 495.

68. *J.A.L. v. E.P.H.,* 453 Pa. Super. 78, 88–89; 682 A.2d 1314, 1319–1320 (1996).

69. See, e.g., *V.C. v. M.L.B.,* 163 N.J. 200, 748 A.2d 539 (2000).

70. The U.S. Supreme Court has recognized the rights of a "mature" minor in some contexts, such as in the making of abortion decisions.

71. Barbara Bennett Woodhouse, *Talking About Children's Rights in Judicial Custody and Visitation Decision-Making,* 36 FAM. L. Q. Number 1, Spring 2002, p. 105 at 129.

72. *Lawrence v. Lawrence,* 2004 WI App. 170; 276 Wis. 2d 403, 687 N.W.2d 748 (2004).

73. *Kendall v. Kendall,* 426 Mass. 238, 687 N.E.2d 1228 (1997).

74. Jeff Atkinson, *Modern Child Custody Practice,* Vol. 1, § 4.1.

75. John DeWitt Gregory, *Family Privacy and the Custody and Visitation Rights of Adult Outsiders,* 36 FAM. L. Q. No. 1, Spring 2002 p. 163 at 168.

Chapter 9

1. *Kirkpatrick v. O'Neal,* 197 S.W.3d 674 (Tenn. 2006).

2. 42 U.S.C. §666(a)(5)(D)(ii).

3. *Rodney P. v. Stacy B.,* 169 S.W.3d 834 (Ky. 2005). The Guidelines will usually be used to determine the level of each parent's obligation. The basic premise is that a parent who has the ability to pay should not be relieved of the duty to do so solely because the child is removed from his or her custody. However, the total payment from the parents to the government agency should not exceed the actual costs to the agency of caring for the child. See also *In re Katherine C.,* 390 Md. 554, 890 A.2d 295 (Md. 2006).

4. See *In the Matter of the Marriage of Risley Doney, and Risley,* 41 Kan. App. 2d 294, 201 P.3d 770 (2009) and Section 25-320, A.R.S.

5. 11 U.S.C. §§ 523(a)(5) and 507(a).

6. Pub. L. No. 93–647, 88 Stat. 2361 (codified as amended at 42 U.S.C. §§651–662).

7. Child Support Enforcement Amendments of 1984, Pub. L. No. 98–378, 98 Stat. 1321 (1984) (42 U.S.C. §667).

8. 42 U.S.C. § 666(a)(5).

9. Pub. L. No. 100–485, 102 Stat. 2343 (1988) as codified in U.S.C. 42 § 667(b).

10. Uniform Interstate Family Support Act. 9(1) U.L.A., 201 (Supp. 1996).

11. Pub. L. No. 100–485, 102 Stat. 2343 (1988) as codified in U.S.C. 42 § 666.

12. Pub. L. No. 104–193, 110 Stat. 2105 (42 U.S.C. § 601 *et seq.*).

13. 28 U.S.C. § 1738B. This Act is similar in structure and intent to UIFSA, and the Acts are largely complementary and not contradictory. It was passed before UIFSA was adopted by all states in response to federal mandate.

14. 45 C.F.R. § 302.56.

15. Jo Michelle Beld and Len Biernat, *Federal Intent for State Child Support Guidelines: Income Shares, Cost Shares, and the Realities of Shared Parenting,* 37 Fam. Law Q. No. 2 (Summer 2003).

16. For a discussion of this approach, see *Maturo v. Maturo,* 296 Conn. 80, 995 A.2d 1 (2010).

17. An excellent case on this topic is *Caplan v. Caplan,* 182 N.J. 250, 864 A.2d 1108 (2005).

18. See, e.g., *In re the Marriage of Jack and Cindie Alter,* 171 Cal. App. 4th 718, 89 Cal. Rptr. 3d 849 (2009) and *In re Marriage of Rogers,* 213 Ill.2d 129, 820 N.E.2d 386 (2004).

19. See, e.g., *In re State (Taylor),* 153 N.H. 700, 904 A.2d 619 (2006).

20. Tori R. A. Kricken, *Child Support and Social Security Dependent Benefits: A Comprehensive Analysis and Proposal for Wyoming,* 2 Wyo. L. Rev. 39 (2002). This article provides an in-depth review of how various states deal with SSDI benefits. The author concluded that Wyoming should adopt the majority position of including the benefit in the obligor's income and subsequently allowing a setoff of his or her support obligations.

21. See, e.g., *Brown v. Brown,* 849 N.E.2d 610, (Ind. 2006); *Metz v. Metz,* 120 Nev. 786, 101 P.3d 779 (Nev. 2004); and *Groenstein v. Groenstein,* 2005 WY 6, 104 P. 3d 765, (Wyo. 2005), which are good examples of cases addressing this topic.

22. 42 U.S.C. §407(a).

23. See, e.g., *In the Matter of Takiyah Massey and David Evans,* 68 A.D.3d 79, 886 N.Y.S.2d 280 (2009).

24. 10 U.S.C.A. §1408 (c),(d), and (e)(1998 and Supp. 2004).

25. La.R.S. 9:315.

26. See, e.g., *In re Bazemore,* 153 N.H. 351, 899 A.2d 225 (2006).

27. 45 C.F.R. §302.56 (c).

28. Office of Child Support Enforcement, *Essentials for Attorneys in Child Support Enforcement,* Chapter 9 (3rd edition, 2002).

29. See *Wilkins v. Wilkins,* 269 Neb. 937, 697 N.W.2d 280 (2005). R.R.S. Neb. § 42-364.16 (2006) establishes that the Supreme Court of Nebraska shall provide child support guidelines by court rules. The language cited in the text is found in Neb. Ct. R., Child Support Guideline T (2006).

30. *Busse v. Busse,* 141 Idaho 566, 113 P.3d 224 (2005).

31. RSA 461-A:14 (2006).
32. C.R.S. 14–10–115 §(1.5)(c), (1.6), (1.7) (1997).
33. M.G.L. c. 208 §28.
34. *In re Marriage of Vannausdle,* 668 N.W.2d 885 (Iowa 2003). See also *Gac v. Gac,* 186 N.J. 535, 897 A.2d 1018 (2006). This is a good case illustrating a court's consideration of factors related to coverage of the costs of higher education.
35. WISC. Admin. Code Chapter DCF 150.
36. ARIZ. REV. STAT. §25.320 (2001).
37. COLO. REV. STAT. ANN. § 14–10–115 (West 1997 & Supp. 1998)
38. 19-A M.R.S. § 2006 (5)(D-1). See *Jabar v. Jabar,* 2006 Me.74, 899 A.2d 796 (2006). In 2003, the state of Maine enacted new child support guidelines that mandate an alternative method for calculating child support when the parties provide "substantially equal care for a child."
39. N.J. Court Rules, R., Appx. IX-A 2006 13.
40. Oklahoma Child Support Guidelines: 43 Okl. St. § 118E.
41. TEX. FAM. CODE §157.008. See, e.g., *In the Interest of A.M.,* 192 S.W.3d 570 (Tex. 2006).
42. N.D. Admin. Code, Section 75-02-04.1-08.2. (2003). Under North Dakota case law, the split custody offset will apply even when one parent assigns his or her right to receive child support to the state. See, e.g., *Simon v. Simon,* 2006 ND 29, 709 N.W.2d 4 (N.D. 2006).
43. An excellent case on this topic is *Gladis v. Gladisova,* 382 Md. 654, 856 A.2d 703 (2004).
44. *Smith v. Freeman,* 149 Md. App. 1, 814 A.2d 65 (Md. Spec. App. 2002).
45. In the case of *Scott-Lasley v. Lasley,* the Georgia Supreme Court held that when "an award of child support is made for several children and the trial court provides for reductions in child support as the children reach majority, the trial court may not reduce the child support on a pro rata per child basis, but must instead do so in accordance with the child support guidelines." *Scott-Lasley v. Lasley,* 278 Ga. 671, 604 S.E.2d 761 (2004).
46. 42 U.S.C.A. §666(a)10).
47. New York State Bar Association Committee on Professional Ethics, Op. 569 (Feb. 7, 1985).
48. See, e.g., *Prisco v. Stroup,* 2004 D.C. Super. LEXIS 23 (2004) and Pub. L, No. 105–187, 112 Stat. 618 (1998) (codified at 18 U.S.C. § 228)—an amendment to the Child Support Recovery Act of 1992; Pub. L. No. 102–521, 106 Stat. 3403.
49. MCL 600.5809(4).
50. MCL 767.24(5). For a related case see, e.g., *People v. Monaco,* 474 Mich. 48, 710 N.W.2d 46 (2005).
51. Pub. L, No. 105–187, 112 Stat. 618 (1998) (codified at 18 U.S.C. § 228)—an amendment to the Child Support Recovery Act of 1992; Pub. L. No. 102–521, 106 Stat. 3403.
52. 18 U.S.C.A. § 228.
53. 42 U.S.C. § 666(a)(4).
54. 42 U.S.C. §666(a)(7).
55. *Zablocki v. Redhail,* 434 U.S. 374, 98 S. Ct. 673, 54 L. Ed. 2d 618 (1978).
56. *State v. Oakley,* 2001 WI 103, 245 Wis. 2d 447, 629 N.W.2d 200 (Wis. 2001).
57. There are three exceptions to the general rule: (1) The decree or parties' agreement provides that the noncustodial parent is entitled to the deduction 26 U.S.C. §152(e)(2)(A); (2) the noncustodial parent furnishes at least $600 in support, and a pre-1985 instrument provides that the noncustodial parent is entitled to the deduction 26 U.S.C. §152(e)(3)(A); and (3) a multiple-support agreement provides that the child is to be claimed as a dependent by a taxpayer other than the custodial parent 26 U.S.C. §152(e)(5). The exemption gets reduced or even eliminated in the case of taxpayers with higher incomes (I.R.C. §151(d)(3)).
58. I.R.C. §24(b). The child tax credit phases out at a lower income level than does the dependency exemption.
59. See, e.g., *Columbus Bar Ass'n v. Albrecht,* 106 Ohio St. 3d 301, 2005 Ohio 4984, 834 N.E.2d 812 (2005).

Chapter 10

1. The Divorce Act of 1857 20 & 21 Vict. C. 85.
2. Richard Chused, *Married Women's Property Law, 1800–1850,* 71 Georgetown Law Journal 1359 (1983). This article provides an overview of these laws along with passage dates.
3. *Orr v. Orr,* 440 U.S. 268, 279-280, 283, 99 S. Ct. 1102, 59 L. Ed. 2d 306 (1979).
4. See, e.g., *In re Marriage of Thornley,* 361 Ill. App.3d 1067, 838 N.E. 2d 981 (2005).
5. See, e.g., *Austin v. Austin,* 445 Mass. 601, 839 N.E.2d 837 (2005).
6. *Chappelow v. Savastano,* 195 Misc. 2d 346, 758 N.Y.S.2d 782 (N.Y. Sup. 2003).
7. *Pendleton v. Pendleton,* 5 P.3d 839 (Cal. 2000).
8. Definitions based on *Black's Law Dictionary,* Abridged Eighth Edition, Bryan A. Garner, Editor in Chief, Thomson West (2005).
9. Uniform Marriage and Divorce Act (UMDA) 1970, as amended in 1971 and 1973 (U.L.A.) §308.
10. See Patricia Barbaruto, *Standard of Living: What's It REALLY Mean?* New Jersey Lawyer, Trends in Family Law, Volume 14, Number 36, p. A3. This is an interesting article on proving standard of living in New Jersey in particular.
11. See, e.g., *Trs. of the AFTRA Health Fund v. Biondi,* 303 F.3d 765 (7th Cir. 2002).
12. *Miller v. Miller,* 356 Mass. 846, 314 N.E.2d 443 (1974).
13. The spousal support rules are located in the Internal Revenue Service Code, 26 U.S.C. §71 (1988).
14. *In re Sarah,* 163 F.3d 397, 401 (6th Cir. 1998).
15. As of 2011, about one-fifth of the states have adopted the act in whole or part.
16. Va. Code Ann. § 20–107.1 (2006).
17. See Utah Code Ann. section 30–3–5 subsection 8 (b) (Supp. 1995); see also *Riley v. Riley,* 2006 UT App 214, 138 P.3d 84 (Utah App. 2006). In the *Riley* case, a Utah appellate court opined that the "Husband's engagement in extramarital affairs and his prolonged deceitful conduct that led to the divorce—present precisely the type of situation where the legislature intended the trial court to consider fault. Indeed, Husband's fault goes a long way in explaining the propriety of a $900 per month alimony award, even though such an award would be too high if only economic factors were considered."
18. See, e.g., Edward M. Ginsburg, *The Place of Alimony in the Scheme of Things,* Massachusetts Family Law Journal, Volume 14, Number 5, January 1997. This article proposes guidelines that the author believes would be applicable in the great majority of cases. Now retired, Judge Ginsburg began applying "guidelines" in his alimony cases in western Massachusetts in the late 1970s in hopes of fostering predictability and limiting litigation regarding what constitutes reasonable need and ability to pay. His position was that need is a function of available income and that making an equitable division of available income can prevent the difficulties inherent in an open-ended, case-by-case approach.
19. On spousal support guidelines, see Victoria M. Ho and Jennifer J. Cohen, *An Update on Florida Alimony Case Law: Alimony Guidelines a Part of Our Future,* 77 Fla. Bar J. 85 (2003); Marie Gordon, *Spousal Support Guidelines and the American Experience: Moving Beyond Discretion,* 19 Can. J. Fam. L. 247 (2002); and June Carbone, *The Futility of Coherence: The ALI's Principles of the Law of Family Dissolution, Compensatory and Spousal Support Payments,* 43 J. L. & Fam. Stud. 43 (2002).
20. *Bak v. Bak,* 24 Mass. App. Ct. 608 n.14, 511 N.E.2d 625 n.14 (1987).
21. § 750 ILCS 5/504.

Chapter 11

1. See *Solomon v. Solomon,* 383 Md. 176, 857 A.2d 1109 (2004), for an example of a case in which the court held that a non-equity club membership

lacked the fundamental characteristics of property and was, therefore, not part of the marital estate.

2. See, e.g., *In re Marriage of Keedy,* 249 Mont. 47, 813 P.2d 442 (1991). In this case, the Montana Supreme Court upheld a lower court's decision that a baseball card collection consisting of more than 100,000 cards was marital property worth $208,000, less the $5,000 portion the husband brought into the marriage.

3. See *Stageberg v. Stageberg,* 695 N.W.2d 609 (Minn. App. 2005). In this case involving contingent attorney's fees, a Minnesota appellate court upheld a lower court's conclusion that "the portion of a contingent fee for work in progress on the valuation date that is attributable to work done before the valuation date shall be treated as marital property for dissolution purposes."

4. See, e.g., *In re Marriage of Anderson,* 811 P.2d 419 (Colo. App. 1990), finding that the portion of the husband's contract as a professional basketball player paid, but not expended, during the marriage was marital property subject to division.

5. See, e.g., *Campbell v. Campbell,* 213 A.D.2d 1027, 624 N.Y.S.2d 493 (N.Y. App. Div. 1995). This case involves a determination that a spouse's share of lottery winnings on a ticket purchased with ten co-workers was marital property.

6. See the New York case involving two roommates in which the court reached a decision based less on an ownership of property and more on a sentimental, pet-centered best interests custody analysis. *Raymond v. Lachman,* 264 A.D.2d 340, 695 N.Y.S.2d 308 (N.Y. App. Div. 1999).

7. See *In re Marriage of Rogers,* 352 Ill. App.3d 896, 817 N.E.2d 562 (2004). In this case, an Illinois appellate court held that social security benefits may be considered in calculation of maintenance awards, although they are not subject to division upon dissolution of a marriage. The court noted: "Section 407(a) of the Social Security Act prohibits a beneficiary from transferring or assigning his or her benefits to another and imposes a broad bar against the use of any legal process to reach social security benefits. . . . however . . . Congress has carved out a narrow exception to this rule to allow the collection of past-due child support or alimony (maintenance). . . . A trial court dividing assets in a marital dissolution proceeding should simply not give any consideration to federal social security benefits; those benefits have already been divided by the Congress."

8. See *Brebaugh v. Deane,* 211 Ariz. 95, 118 P.3d 43 (Ariz. App. 2005), a case of first impression in Arizona addressing the issue of whether stock options that had not vested before the petition for dissolution was served can be divided as community property. The court examined approaches taken in other states before holding that unvested stock options received prior to service of the dissolution petition constitute community property based on the employer's intent, to the extent that they compensate the employee for past or present service and not as an incentive for future performance.

9. See *In re Marriage of Schriner,* 695 N.W.2d 493 (Iowa 2005), in which the Supreme Court of Iowa considered as a matter of first impression whether worker's compensation benefits awarded to one spouse during the marriage are divisible property at the time of divorce. After reviewing approaches taken in other jurisdictions, the Iowa Supreme Court held "that workers' compensation benefits received up to the time of the dissolution are property subject to an equitable division to the extent they have been retained and not spent. Benefits received after the divorce constitute separate property of the injured spouse." See also *Drake v. Drake,* 555 Pa. 481, 725 A.2d 717 (1999).

10. See *Landis & Landis,* 200 Ore. App. 107, 113 P.3d 456 (2003). In this case, an Oregon appeals court affirmed a lower court's decision to reopen a case based on the wife's discovery that, in listing his assets, the husband did not mention or account for a $16,687 lump sum payment he had received as a Veteran's Disability Benefit.

11. *Buckl v. Buckl,* 373 Pa. Super. 521, 542 A.2d 65 (1988), quoting *White v. Rairdon,* 52 D. & C. 558, 559 (Delaware County 1944).

12. See, e.g., *Baker v. Baker,* 2004 PA Super 413, 861 A.2d 298 (2004).

13. See Elizabeth Paek, *Fido Seeks Full Membership in the Family: Dismantling the Property Classification of Companion Animals by Statute,* 25 Hawaii L. Rev. 481 (2003). See also end note 6 above.

14. *Archer v. Archer,* 303 Md. 347, 357, 493 A.2d .74, at 1079 (1985).

15. *Supra* n.1.

16. S.C. Code Ann. § 20 -7- 473 (2006).

17. See *Quinn v. Quinn,* 13 Neb. App. 155, 689 N.W.2d 605 (2004).

18. See, e.g., *Conrad v. Conrad,* 216 W. Va. 696, 612 S.E.2d 772 (2005). See also *Villasenor v. Villasenor,* 134 Ariz. 476, 657 P.2d 889 (Ariz. App. 1982), holding that the husband's disability compensation had both a disability component deemed separate property and a retirement component considered community property; *Gay v. Gay,* 573 So.2d 180 (Fla. App. 1991), holding that disability benefits are separate property because they replace future income; and *Allard v. Allard,* 708 A.2d 554 (R.I. 1998), holding that the disability pension at issue was separate property to the extent it compensated for lost earning capacity but marital property to the extent it constituted retirement pay earned by the disabled spouse during the marriage.

19. *Huber v. Huber,* 200 W. Va. 446, 490 S.E.2d 48 (W. Va. 1997).

20. See *Abrell v. Abrell,* 236 Ill. 2d 249, 923 N.E.2d 791 (2010). In this opinion, the Illinois Supreme Court provides an excellent review of various approaches taken by courts across the country to classification of accrued vacation and sick leave benefits.

21. See, e.g., *Bacon v. Bacon,* 26 Mass. App. Ct. 117, 524 N.E.2d 401 (1988), a case in which the assets derived from one spouse's family and the appreciation on it was due to inflation and sound investment advice received from that spouse's family. In such cases, courts will usually consider whether the parents intended a gift or a loan, as evidenced by appropriate documentation such as a letter and promissory note.

22. See, e.g., *Wiese v. Wiese,* 46 Va. App. 399, 617 S.E.2d 427 (2005). This is a case of first impression in Virginia that addresses the question of whether refinancing precludes the possibility of tracing separate property or constitutes a transmutation of separate property into marital property. See also *Schmitz v. Schmitz,* 88 P.3d 1116 (Alas. 2004). This case addresses the complexities of appreciation, tracing, transmutation, and commingling issues in a determination of separate and marital property. See also Thomas J. Oldham, *Tracing, Commingling, and Transmutation,* 23 Fam. L. Q. 219 (1989), for a discussion of tracing.

23. See, e.g., *Painter v. Painter,* 65 N.J. 196, 320 A.2d 484 (1974).

24. Wisconsin adopted the Uniform Marital Property Act in 1986 (Wis. Stat. §766.31), which incorporates many community property principles. The IRS subsequently ruled that Wisconsin marital property is the equivalent of community property for income tax purposes. (Rev. Rul. 87–13, 1987–1 C.B. 20). The Wisconsin Act is different in several respects from other "community property" states, and property division upon divorce can be complex. In case law, the Wisconsin Supreme Court has held that the legislature did not intend, as a general rule, that the Marital Property Act change the state's statutory equitable distribution principles and that classification of property under the Marital Property Act is not necessarily determinative of property division on divorce. *Mausing v. Mausing,* 146 Wis. 2d 92, 429 N.W.2d 768 (1988). The Marital Property Act is concerned primarily with the spouses' ownership of property during the marriage and at their death, not on dissolution. *Kuhlman v. Kuhlman,* 146 Wis. 2d 588, 432 N.W.2d 295 (1988).

25. Alaska Statute § 34.77.030 (2011). Although not generally considered a community property state, the Alaska legislature enacted the Alaska Community Property Act, effective in 1998. The Act essentially adopts the Uniform Marital Property Act as Wisconsin had done in 1986. The Act is unique in that it allows, but does not require, a married couple who are both Alaska residents to elect to classify property as community property in a community property agreement or a community property trust. In addition, under the Act, nonresident spouses may transfer property to an Alaska Community Property Trust (a form of Marital Property Agreement), and the property will be characterized as community property under Alaska law, provided at least one trustee is a "qualified" individual (essentially, a resident of Alaska).

26. Ibid.
27. Wis. Stat. § 766.55.
28. Internal Revenue Code §1041(b)(6). The one exception to this rule is that if separate property is converted to community property within a year of the decedent's death, it will pass back to the donor spouse and not receive a step-up in basis. Sec. 1014(e).
29. See, e.g., RCW 26.16.030 (2011).
30. *In re Estate of Erikson,* 368 N.W.2d 525 (N.D. 1985).
31. Restatement (Second) of Conflicts of Laws, Introduction and §§ 258, 259.
32. *In re Marriage of Welchel,* 476 N.W.2d 104 (Iowa App. 1991).
33. See, e.g., *Horner v. Horner,* 2004 ND 165, 686 N.W.2d 131 (2004).
34. See, e.g., *Thompson v. Thompson,* 105 P.3d 346 (Okla. App. 2004).
35. *Bratcher v. Bratcher,* 26 S.W.3d 797 (Ky. App. 2000).
36. See Dylan A. Wilde, *Obtaining an Equitable Distribution of Retirement Plans in a Divorce Action,* 49 S.D. L. Rev. 141 (2003). See also Susan J. Prather, *Characterization, Valuation, and Distribution of Pensions at Divorce,* 15 J. Am. Acad. Matrimonial Law, 443 (1998).
37. See, e.g., *Moore v. Moore,* 376 N.J. Super. 246, 870 A.2d 303 (2005). See also *Andrukiewicz v. Andrukiewicz,* 860 A.2d 235 (R.I. 2004), in which the Supreme Court of Rhode Island bound a husband who chose not to retire at "normal retirement age" to the terms of a written property settlement agreement between the parties incorporated in a Qualified Domestic Relations Order. The Agreement provided as follows: "The Husband agrees and acknowledges that the Wife will receive the first $583.00 of the monthly benefit that he will be entitled to receive at the time of his normal retirement date under the Husband's Pension Trust Benefit Plan that he has through the Town of Coventry. . . ."
38. See *Fabich v. Fabich,* 144 N.H. 577, 744 A.2d 615 (1999). In this case of first impression in New Hampshire, the state Supreme Court adopted a functional approach to determining whether or not a retirement disability pension is divisible marital property after discussing the various approaches applied in other jurisdictions.
39. QDROs are not favored by plan administrators because they create additional "paperwork," or by parties who want their pensions to remain intact. Prior to 1984, companies were not permitted to distribute pension benefits to payees other than the employee participant.
40. See, e.g., *Kazel v. Kazel,* 3 N.Y.3d 331, 819 N.E.2d 1036, 786 N.Y.S.2d 420 (N.Y. 2004). In this case, a New York court of appeals held that "A judgment of divorce and qualified domestic relations order (QDRO) awarding an interest in the husband's pension plan do not automatically include pre-retirement death benefits available under the plan. If the intent is to distribute such benefits, that should be separately, and explicitly stated."
41. *Hardy v. Hardy,* 311 S.C. 433, 429 S.E.2d 811 (S.C. App. 1992).
42. Internal Revenue Code §1041. See generally, Craig D. Bell, *Need-to-Know Divorce Tax Law for Legal Assistance Officers,* 177 Mil. L. Rev. (2003).
43. The *Solomon* case referenced in endnotes 1 and 15 above includes a good discussion by the court regarding the issue of whether tax liabilities may be considered as "another factor" under the Maryland statute for purposes of distributing a marital property award.
44. See *Keff v. Keff,* 757 So. 2d 450 (Ala. Civ. App. 2000). In this case the court might have adopted the husband's position that his stock options should have been valued as of the date of the divorce, but the appellate court affirmed the lower court's decision, stating, "He cites no authority in support of this contention. An appellant's failure to cite supporting authority for his or her arguments leaves the court with no alternative but to affirm." In an Oregon case, *Timm & Timm,* 200 Ore. App. 621, 117 P.3d 301 (2005), the court remanded a case involving premarital contribution to marital assets, because the parties had relied on authority that was no longer controlling.
45. See, e.g., *Rodrigue v. Rodrigue,* 55 F. Supp.2d 534 (E.D. La. 1999). This case involved a conflict between federal copyright law and the state of Louisiana's community property law concerning certain artworks produced by the husband, in which the wife claimed a copyright interest.

See also *Coon v. Coon,* 364 S.C. 563, 614 S.E.2d 616 (2005), in which the South Carolina Supreme Court examined the relationship between federal and state law governing disposable military retirement pay. The court held that under federal law, states may treat disposable retired pay payable to a service member either as property solely of the member or as property of the member and his spouse, provided the award does not exceed 50% of the disposable retirement pay. The court held that South Carolina had elected to treat it as marital property.

Chapter 12

1. *Dominick v. Dominick,* 18 Mass. App. Ct. 85, 463 N.E.2d 564 (1984).
2. They may also ask that a constructive trust be imposed over the proceeds of the policy received by the new wife.

Chapter 13

1. Richard Gelles, *Intimate Violence in Families,* Third Edition, Thousand Oaks, CA, 1997, Sage, as quoted in Henry H. Brownstein, *The Social Reality of Violence and Violent Crime,* Allyn & Bacon, 2000, p. 77.
2. *Id.*
3. See Anne E. Appel and George W. Holden, *The Co-Occurrence of Spouse and Physical Child Abuse: A Review and Appraisal,* 12(4) Journal of Family Psychology. 578-599 (1998). See also S. M. Ross, *Risk of Physical Abuse to Children of Spouse Abusing Parents,* 20(7) Child Abuse & Neglect 589–598 (1996) (asserting that intimate partner violence increases the risk of child abuse from 5% after one abusive act to 100% after fifty acts of intimate partner violence).
4. Kathleen Finley Duthu, *Feature: Why Do [We] Need to Know [About] Domestic Violence? How Attorneys Can Recognize and Address the Problem,* 53 LA Bar Jnl. 20 (June, July 2005).
5. Patricia Tjaden and Nancy Thoennes, National Institute of Justice and the Centers of Disease Control and Prevention, "Extent, Nature and Consequences of Intimate Partner Violence: Findings from the National Violence Against Women Survey" (2000).
6. Bureau of Justice Statistics Crime Data Brief, Intimate Partner Violence, 1993–2001, February 2003.
7. Costs of Intimate Partner Violence Against Women in the United States. 2003. Centers for Disease Control and Prevention, National Centers for Injury Prevention and Control. Atlanta, GA.
8. Patricia Tjaden, *Symposium on Integrating Responses to Domestic Violence: Extent and Nature of Intimate Partner Violence as Measured by the National Violence Against Women Survey,* 47 Loy. L. Rev. 41, 54 (2001).
9. Constance M. Weimann et al., *Pregnant Adolescents: Experiences and Behaviors Associated with Physical Assault by an Intimate Partner,* 4 Maternal & Child Health J. 93 (2000).
10. Pamela B. Teaster et al., *2004 Survey of State Adult Protective Services: Abuse of Vulnerable Adults 18 Years of Age and Older,* National Adult Protective Services Association.
11. *Id.*
12. The American Bar Association's Commission on Domestic Violence provides a comprehensive survey of recent statistics "as a service to legal practitioners and advocates who may find it useful to include current statistical data in their arguments to the court." The survey references a number of resources for data on domestic violence by race and ethnicity.
13. Shannon Catalano, Bureau of Justice Statistics, *Intimate Partner Violence in the United States,* December 2007.
14. *Supra* at n. 5.
15. *Supra* at n. 13.
16. Hilary Mayell, *Thousands of Women Killed for Family Honor,* National Geographic News, February 2, 2002.
17. Violence Against Women Reauthorization Act of 2005, Pub. L. No. 109–162, 119 Stat. 2960 (2006). See Leila Abolfazli, *Violence Against Women Act,* 7 Geo. J. Gender and L. 863 (2006), for a description of the provisions of the successive VAWA acts.

18. See Erin L. Han, *Mandatory Arrest and No-Drop Policies: Victim Empowerment in Domestic Violence Cases,* 23 B.C. Third World L.J. 159, 176 (2003).

19. Laurie S. Kohn, *Why Doesn't She Leave? The Collision of First Amendment Rights and Effective Court Remedies for Victims of Domestic Violence,* 29 Hastings Const. L.Q. 1 at 5 ("Literature examining same-sex battering routinely refers to the fear of HIV 'outing' as being a primary cause of the secrecy that characterizes same-sex domestic violence.") ("Fearing homophobic responses, gay men and women often hide their sexual orientation from employers and family members. This fear gives batterers a manipulative tool to force victims to endure additional abuse. As long as a victim knows that a batterer intends to publicize this information and finds his threats credible, he may well stay in an abusive relationship rather than face the potential repercussions, which could include loss of child custody, employment, and family and personal relationships.")

20. Patricia Tjaden and Nancy Thoennes, *Stalking in America: Findings from the National Violence Against Women Survey,* U.S. Department of Justice, National Institute of Justice, Washington, D.C., as reported on the website of the National Center for Victims of Crime Stalking Resource Center in a fact sheet titled "Stalking in America—National Violence Against Women Survey (NVAW)."

21. See, e.g., *Heacock v. Heacock,* 402 Mass. 21, 520 N. E. 2d 151 (1988), and *Heacock v. Heacock,* 30 Mass. App. Ct. 304, 568 N. E. 2d 621 (1991). (The Superior court dismissed a wife's tort action for unreasonable delay in serving process. In an effort to gain a tactical advantage in the parties' divorce action, the wife filed a tort action relating to an event that allegedly occurred during the marriage but did not attempt to serve it prior to the divorce, in order to avoid alerting her husband to the pending claim. The Appellate Court affirmed. The Supreme Court transferred the case from the Appellate Court and reversed on other grounds.)

22. See the Federal Gun Control Act of 1968 as amended codified at 18 U.S.C. §922 (g)(8).

23. Kohn *supra* n. 19 at page 10–11. This article provides an excellent discussion of the constitutionality of such speech restrictions in protective orders. ("Although at least one court has granted such a restriction, none has resulted in an appellate decision. Because privacy invading speech in a domestic violence context does not fall into one of the predetermined categories of unprotected speech, the court would therefore engage in balancing, weighing the value of the speech against the countervailing interests to be protected by the injunction.")

24. *Supra* at n. 5.

25. See Wis. Stat. 968.075(3)(a)1.b.

26. Ruth Jones, *Guardianship for Coercively Controlled Battered Women: Breaking the Control of the Abuser,* 88 Geo. L.J. 605, 612 (April 2000).

27. *Id.* at 609.

28. *Supra* n. 19 at 59.

29. Much of this exhibit is based on a series of presentations by Douglas Gaudette, Director of the Family Safety Project at Holy Family Hospital in Methuen, Massachusetts.

30. *Child Maltreatment 2009,* Administration for Children and Families, report available online at *www.acf.hhs.gov/programs/cb.*

31. The Child Abuse Prevention and Treatment Act of 1974 (CAPTA) codified at 42 U.S.C. 5101 through 5107 as most recently amended by the Keeping Children and Families Safe Act of 2003.

32. 42 U.S.C.A. §5106g (2).

33. *Definitions of Child Abuse and Neglect: Summary of State Laws,* Child Information Gateway accessed May 2012 at *www.childwelfare.gov.*

34. Definitions of various types of neglect are provided in the National Child Abuse and Neglect Data Collection System.

35. 42 U.S.C. § 5106i .

36. *Supra* n. 33.

37. *Supra* n. 33.

38. *State v. Wilder,* 2000 ME 32, 748 A.2d 444, 449 n.6 (Me. 2000) (quoting William Blackstone, *Blackstone's Commentaries on the Laws of England*

440 (Oxford reprint 1966), and William Blackstone, *Blackstone's Commentaries on the Law of England 120* (1768)).

39. *Wisconsin v. Yoder,* 406 U.S. 205, 213–215, 92 S.Ct. 1526, 32 L. Ed. 2d 15 (1972); *Pierce v. Society of Sisters,* 268 U.S. 510, 534–535, 45 S. Ct. 571, 69 L. Ed. 1070 (1925).

40. *State v. Adaranijo,* 153 Ohio App. 3d 266, 2003 Ohio 3822, 792 N.E.2d 1138, 1140 (2003).

41. *State v. Singleton,* 41 Wn. App. 721, 705 P.2d 825, 827 (Wash. App. 1985).

42. *State v. Thorpe,* 429 A.2d 785, 788, (R.I. 1981).

43. *State v. Kimberly B.,* 2005 WI App 115, 283 Wis. 2d 731, 699 N.W.2d 641 at 650 (Wis. App. 2005).

44. American Humane Association, *Shaken Baby Syndrome,* accessed May 2011 at *www.americanhumane.org.*

45. *Id.*

46. *Supra* n. 33.

47. American Humane Association, *Emotional Abuse,* accessed May 2012 at *www.americanhumane.org.*

48. 42 U.S.C.A. § 5106g(4).

49. *Parental Drug Abuse as Child Abuse: Summary of State Laws,* Child Welfare Information Gateway available online at *www.childwelfare.gov.*

50. Wis. Stat. §§ 48.02 and 48.133.

51. *In re Baby Boy Blackshear,* 90 Ohio St. 3d 197, 2000 Ohio 173, 736 N.E.3d 462 (2000).

52. N.J. Stat. Ann. §9:6–8.10.

53. *Id.* at Article 9:6–8.13.

54. *Id.* at Article 9:6–8.14. See Lauren E. Parsonage, *Note: Caught Between a Rock and a Hard Place: Harmonizing Victim Confidentiality Rights With Children's Best Interests,* 70 Mo. L. Rev. 863 (Summer 2005).

55. Pub. L. No. 96–272, 94 Stat. 500 (codified at 42 U.S.C. §§620-628 and 670–679).

56. See Kathleen Bean, *Reasonable Efforts: What State Courts Think,* 36 U. Tol. L. Rev. 321 (Winter 2005), for a comprehensive discussion of the federal reunification requirements and the states' interpretations and applications of those requirements.

57. *DeShaney v. Winnebago Department of Social Services,* 489 U.S. 189, 109 S. Ct. 998, 103 L. Ed.2d 249 (1989).

58. For an argument favoring imposition of liability on state actors for failure to protect victims of domestic violence and child abuse, see G. Kristian Miccio, *Notes From the Underground: Battered Women, the State, and Conceptions of Accountability,* 23 Harv. Women's L.J. 133 (Spring 2000).

59. Alicia Hehr, *A Child Shall Lead Them: Developing and Using Child Protection Mediation to Better Serve the Interests of the Child,* 22 Ohio St. J. on Disp. Resol. 443 at 455–456 (2007).

60. *Id.* at 457–458.

61. 25 U.S.C. § 1901 *et seq.*

62. See, e.g., California Rules of Court, rule 1439(f); RCW 13.34.070 (Washington); and Title 10 O.S. 20 §40, the Oklahoma Indian Child Welfare Act, which essentially codifies the holding in *Mississippi Band of Choctaw Indians v. Holyfield,* 490 U.S. 30, 109 S. Ct. 1597, 104 L. Ed. 2d 29 (1989).

63. National Council of Juvenile and Family Court Judges, Family Violence: Model Code on Domestic and Family Violence, Chapter 4, Section 401 (1994). The Council has published a useful resource for judges entitled *Navigating Custody & Visitation Evaluations in Cases With Domestic Violence: A Judge's Guide.*

64. Nancy Ver Steegh, *Differentiating Types of Violence: Implications for Child Custody,* 65 La. L. Rev. 1379 at 1477 (Summer 2005), referencing Howard Davidson, *The Impact of Domestic Violence on Children, a Report to the President of the American Bar Association 13* (1994).

65. Laurel Kent, *Comment: Addressing the Impact of Domestic Violence on Children: Alternatives to Laws Criminalizing the Commission of Domestic Violence in the Presence of a Child,* 2001 Wis. L. Rev 1337 at 1342, referencing K. J. Wilson, *When Violence Begins at Home: A Comprehensive Guide to Understanding and Ending Domestic Abuse,* p. 31 (1997),

and Honore Hughes, *Impact of Spouse Abuse on Children of Battered Women: Implications for Practice,* Violence Update, Aug. 1992, at 1.

66. *Id.* at 1342.

67. Prentice L. White, *You May Never See Your Child Again: Adjusting the Batterer's Visitation Rights to Protect Children From Future Abuse,* 13 Am. U.J. Gender Soc. Pol'y & L. 327, 334 (2005).

68. See American Judges Foundation, *Domestic Violence and the Court House: Understanding the Problem . . . Knowing the Victim,* available at *aja.ncsc.dni.us/domviol* (indicating that such abusive fathers are successful approximately 70% of the time).

69. A majority of the effects identified in this application are commonly accepted and well documented in Laurel A. Kent, *supra* n. 65. The content draws on additional sources, including Dawn Bradley Berry, *The Domestic Violence Sourcebook* 8 (1998); Laura Crites and Donna Coker, *What Therapists See That Judges May Miss: A Unique Guide to Custody Decisions When Spouse Abuse Is Charged,* 27 Judges' J. (Spring 1988); John W. Fantuzzo and Wanda Mohr, *Prevalence and Effects of Child Exposure to Domestic Violence,* 9 Future of Children 21 (1999); K. J. Wilson, *When Violence Begins at Home: A Comprehensive Guide to Understanding and Ending Domestic Abuse* (1997).

70. "Research indicates that children who witness or experience abuse are one thousand times more likely to abuse a spouse or partner than children from non-violent homes." Kent, *supra* n. 73 at 1345, referencing Dawn Bradley Berry, *The Domestic Violence Sourcebook* at 121 (1998).

71. "Studies assessing children living in domestic violence shelters for posttraumatic stress disorder have found incidence rates ranging from 13% to more than 50%." Hon. Donna J. Hitchens and Patricia Van Horn, Ph.D., J.D., *Courts Responding to Domestic Violence: The Court's Role in Supporting and Protecting Children Exposed to Domestic Violence,* 6 J. Center for Fam. Child. & Cts. 31 at 33 (2005).

72. This practice is not universally accepted. For example, in *Nicholson et al. v. Scopetta,* 3 N.Y.3d 357, 820 N.E. 2d 840 (N.Y. 2004), New York's high court held that it is inappropriate to remove children from a parent based solely on the ground that they have been exposed to a parent's domestic violence. The victim's "failure to protect" the child must be understood in context before a determination of neglect can be reached. See Justine A. Dunlap, *Sometimes I Feel Like a Motherless Child: The Error of Pursuing Battered Mothers for Failure to Protect,* 50 Loy. L. Rev. 565 (Fall 2004).

73. Ver Steegh *supra* note 64 at 1412. See Association of Family and Conciliation Courts (AFCC) Task Force on Parenting Coordination, *Parenting Coordination: Implementation Issues,* 41 Fam. Ct. Rev. 533 (2003).

74. *Id.* at 1413–1414 referencing Christine A. Coates et al., *Parenting Coordination for High Conflict Families,* 42 Fam. Ct. Rev. 246, 247 (2004).

75. Jennifer M. Collins, *Crime and Parenthood: The Uneasy Case for Prosecuting Negligent Parents,* 100 Nw. U.L. Rev. 807, 810–811 (Winter 2006).

76. *Id.* at 809.

77. *Dempsey v. Frazier,* 119 Miss. 1, 80 So. 341, 342 (1918).

78. Miss. Code. Ann. §§97–37–14 and 15.

79. Sara Buel and Margeret Drew, *Do Ask and Do Tell: Rethinking the Lawyer's Duty to Ward in Domestic Violence Cases,* 75 U. Cin. L. Rev. 447 (Winter 2006). This article provides a detailed survey of disclosure rules in various states.

80. See Adrienne Jennings Lockie, *Salt in the Wounds: Why Attorneys Should Not Be Mandated Reporters of Child Abuse,* 36 N.M.L. Rev. 125 (Winter 2006).

81. Mo. Rev. Stat. § 210.140 (2000).

82. Tx. R. Prof. Conduct 1.05(e).

83. Opinion 280, 97 N.J.L.T. 362 (1974).

84. Wis. Stat. 48.981(2)(c).

85. Buel and Drew *supra* at n. 79 at pages 450–451.

Chapter 14

1. Barbara Bennett Woodhouse, *Waiting for Loving: The Child's Fundamental Right to Adoption,* 34 Cap. U. L. Rev. 297, 328 (Winter, 2005).

2. U.S. Census Bureau, *Adopted Children and Stepchildren: 2000* (2003) (*www.census.gov/prod/2003pubs/censr-6.pdf*).

3. Elizabeth J. Samuels, *Time to Decide? The Laws Governing Mothers' Consents to the Adoption of Their Newborn Infants,* 72 Tenn. L. Rev. 509, 518 (Winter 2005), referencing Sue Zeidler, "Internet Transforms U.S. Adoption Process," Reuters, May 21, 2004.

4. See, e.g., Colo. Rev. Stat. §25–2–113.5.

5. See, e.g., Massachusetts General Laws Chapter 210 Section 5D.

6. Ala. Code § 22–9A-12(c); Alaska Stat. § 18.50.500(a); Kan. Stat. Ann. 65–§2423(a); and Or. Rev. Stat. § 432.240(1) (at age 21).

7. Erin Green, *Unwed Fathers' Rights in Adoption: The Virginia Code vs. The Uniform Adoption Act,* 11 Wm. & Mary J. of Women & L. 267, 273 (Winter 2005).

8. *Stanley v. Illinois,* 405 U.S. 645, 92 S. Ct. 1208, 31 L. Ed 2d 551 (1972).

9. *Lehr v. Robertson,* 463 U.S. 248 at 262, 103 S. Ct. 2985, 77 L. Ed. 2d 614 (1983).

10. For an interesting New Mexico case addressing whether or not a father's conduct prior to his child's birth can be used to terminate parental rights under a presumptive abandonment statute, see *Helen G. v. Mark J. H. (In re Adoption Petition of Romero),* 2006 NMCA 136, 145 P.3d 98 (2006).

11. See, e.g., *In re Adoption of Reeves,* 831 S.W.2d 607 (Ark. 1992). In this Arkansas case, an unwed father was not notified of a petition for adoption of his two children. The mother and step-father, who adopted one of the children, swore that the father was "unknown." The Arkansas Supreme Court upheld the adoption despite the mother's and step-father's deceit and the fact that the father had alleged he was the child's natural father, had established a substantial *de facto* relationship with the child, and had received no notice of the paternity proceeding. The adoption was upheld because the father was not registered in the state's putative father registry.

12. *Kessel v. Leavitt,* 511 S.E.2d 720, 756 (W. Va. 1998).

13. Shirley Darby Howell, *Adoption: When Psychology and Law Collide,* 28 Hamline L. Rev. 29, 54 (Winter 2005). For a more extensive discussion of this topic, see Robbin Potz Gonzalez, *The Rights of Putative Fathers to Their Infant Children in Contested Adoptions: Strengthening State Laws That Currently Deny Adequate Protection,* 13 Mich. J. Gender 7 L. 39 (2006).

14. Code of Ala. § 26–10C-1(i).

15. Code of Ala. § 26–10A-9(a).

16. Minn. Stat. § 259.52(8). See also 750 Ill. Comp. Stat. § 50/12.1 (2011).

17. Ariz. Rev. Stat. §8–106.01(F); see also R.S.Mo. §192.016.

18. Utah Code Ann. § 78B–6-110 (2011).

19. See Mo. Ann. Stat. § 192.016(9)(2,3).

20. Utah Code Ann. 78B–6-102 (2011).

21. *G.P. v. State,* 842 So. 2d 1059 (Fla. Dist. Ct. App. 2003), invalidating Fla. Stat. Ann. §§ 63.087, 63.088, commonly known as the Scarlet Letter Provisions.

22. Kimberly Barton, *Who's Your Daddy? State Adoption Statutes and the Unknown Biological Father,* 32 Cap. U.L. Rev. 113 (Fall 2003). See also Jeffrey A. Parness, *Adoption Notices to Genetic Fathers: No to Scarlet Letters, Yes to Good Faith Cooperation,* 36 Cumb. L. Rev. 63 (2005/2006).

23. Kan. Stat. Ann. § 59–2136(c) requires the court to order publication notice of the adoption hearing if no person is identified as the father or a possible father.

24. N.C. Gen. Stat. §§ 48–2–401(c)(3) and 48–2–402(b).

25. *Supra* n. 13 Howell at 46.

26. *Supra* n. 13 Howell at 47, describing *In re Valerie D.,* 223 Conn. 492, 613 A.2d 748 (1992).

27. 105 P.L. 89, 111 Stat. 2115 (codified as amended in scattered sections of 2 U.S.C. and 42 U.S.C.).

28. *Supra* n. 1 at 303.

29. Fla. Stat. Ann. §383.50 (5). For a multistate review of the nature and complexity of safe haven laws, see Dayna R. Cooper, *Fathers Are Parents Too: Challenging Safe Haven Laws With Procedural Due Process,* 31 Hofstra L. Rev. 877 (2003), and Jeffrey A. Parness, *Deserting Mothers, Abandoned Babies, Lost Fathers: Dangers in Safe Havens,* 24 Quinnipiac L. Rev. 335 (2006).

30. See, e.g., Massachusetts General Laws Chapter 210 Section 2.

31. Samuels *supra* n. 3 at 526, 527.

32. Samuels *supra* n. 3 at 528. For an example of a state statute regarding requirements for effective consents, see the following Vermont Statutes: 15A V.S.A. § 2–405 and 15A V.S.A. § 2–406. For an excellent resource, see Ann McLane Kuster and Marilyn T. Mahoney, *A Practitioner's Guide to Creating a Secure Adoption,* New Hampshire Bar Journal March 1996.

33. Susan Calkins, *Ineffective Assistance of Counsel in Parental-Rights Termination Cases: The Challenge for Appellate Courts,* 6 J. App. Prac. 179 (Fall 2004). A problem sometimes arises when the adoption of a child is approved while termination of a parent's rights is under appeal. For a discussion of cases involving such situations, see Kate M. Heideman, *Avoiding the Need to "Unscramble the Egg": A Proposal for the Automatic Stay of Subsequent Adoption Proceedings When Parents Appeal a Judgment Terminating Their Parental Rights,* 24 St. Louis U. Pub. L. Rev. 445 (2005).

34. D.C. Code 16–2353(b)(4).

35. 42 U.S.C.A. §12132.

36. M.G.L. Chapter 210 Section 1.

37. Utah Code Ann. §78B–6–117 (2011).

38. 42 U.S.C.A. § 1996b.

39. 25 U.S.C.A. § 1901.

40. 25 U.S.C.A. §1915(a) codifies this provision of the Indian Welfare Act. The Bureau of Indian Affairs has published Guidelines for state courts' implementation of the Act in 44 Fed. Reg. 67, 584. Guideline F.3 provides that good cause may be based on a request of the biological parents, established extraordinary physical or emotional needs of the child, or the unavailability of suitable families for placement after a diligent search. For a case applying this guideline, see *In re Adoption of B.G.J.,* 281 Kan. 552, 133 P.3d 1 (2006), decided by the Supreme Court of Kansas.

41. 25 U.S.C. §1903(4). For examples of cases addressing the requirements and application of the Indian Child Welfare Act, see *In re Dependency of T.L.G. et al.,* 126 Wn. App. 181, 108 P.3d 156 (2005), and *In the Matter of Baby Boy L.,* 2004 OK 93, 103 P.3d 1099 (2004).

42. See Cal. Fam. Code 9000(b); Conn. Gen. Stat. Ann. 45a-724(a)(3); and Vt. Stat. Ann. Tit. 15A, 1–102(b).

43. VSA 1–102.

44. *DeBoer v. DeBoer,* 509 U.S. 1301, 114 S. Ct. 1, 125 L. Ed. 2d 755 (1993).

45. *In re Doe,* 254 Ill. App. 3d 405, 627 N.E.2d 648 at 651–652 (Ill.App. 1 Dist. 1993).

appendix A

NATIONAL ASSOCIATION OF LEGAL ASSISTANTS (NALA) CODE OF ETHICS AND PROFESSIONAL RESPONSIBILITY

First adopted by the NALA membership in May of 1975, the Code of Ethics and Professional Responsibility is the foundation of ethical practices of paralegals in the legal community.

A paralegal must adhere strictly to the accepted standards of legal ethics and to the general principles of proper conduct. The performance of the duties of the paralegal shall be governed by specific canons as defined herein so that justice will be served and goals of the profession attained.

The canons of ethics set forth hereafter are adopted by the National Association of Legal Assistants, Inc., as a general guide intended to aid paralegals and attorneys. The enumeration of these rules does not mean there are not others of equal importance although not specifically mentioned. Court rules, agency rules and statutes must be taken into consideration when interpreting the canons.

Definition: Legal assistants, also known as paralegals, are a distinguishable group of persons who assist attorneys in the delivery of legal services. Through formal education, training and experience, legal assistants have knowledge and expertise regarding the legal system and substantive and procedural law which qualify them to do work of a legal nature under the supervision of an attorney.

In **2001**, NALA members also adopted the ABA definition of a legal assistant/paralegal, as follows:

A legal assistant or paralegal is a person qualified by education, training or work experience who is employed or retained by a lawyer, law office, corporation, governmental agency or other entity who performs specifically delegated substantive legal work for which a lawyer is responsible. (Adopted by the ABA in 1997)

Canon 1

A paralegal must not perform any of the duties that attorneys only may perform nor take any actions that attorneys may not take.

Canon 2

A paralegal may perform any task which is properly delegated and supervised by an attorney, as long as the attorney is ultimately responsible to the client, maintains a direct relationship with the client, and assumes professional responsibility for the work product.

Canon 3

A paralegal must not: (a) engage in, encourage, or contribute to any act which could constitute the unauthorized practice of law; and (b) establish attorney-client relationships, set fees, give legal opinions or advice or represent a client before a court or agency unless so authorized by that court or agency; and (c) engage in conduct or take any action which would assist or involve the attorney in a violation of professional ethics or give the appearance of professional impropriety.

Canon 4

A paralegal must use discretion and professional judgment commensurate with knowledge and experience but must not render independent legal judgment in place of an attorney. The services of an attorney are essential in the public interest whenever such legal judgment is required.

Canon 5

A paralegal must disclose his or her status as a paralegal at the outset of any professional relationship with a client, attorney, a court or administrative agency or personnel thereof, or a member of the general public. A paralegal must act prudently in determining the extent to which a client may be assisted without the presence of an attorney.

Canon 6

A paralegal must strive to maintain integrity and a high degree of competency through education and training with respect to professional responsibility, local rules and practice, and through continuing education in substantive areas of law to better assist the legal profession in fulfilling its duty to provide legal service.

Canon 7

A paralegal must protect the confidences of a client and must not violate any rule or statute now in effect or hereafter enacted controlling the doctrine of privileged communications between a client and an attorney.

Canon 8

A paralegal must disclose to his or her employer or prospective employer any pre-existing client or personal relationship that may conflict with the interests of the employer or prospective employer and/or their clients.

Canon 9

A paralegal must do all other things incidental, necessary, or expedient for the attainment of the ethics and responsibilities as defined by statute or rule of court.

Canon 10

A paralegal's conduct is guided by bar associations' codes of professional responsibility and rules of professional conduct.

appendix B

WEBSITES OF
GENERAL INTEREST

Note: The World Wide Web offers a wealth of freely accessible and rapidly changing information that may be immensely useful, but it should be verified when appropriate. The following URLs were all operational as of January 2012.

GOVERNMENT SITES

www.acf.hhs.gov

This is the site for the Administration for Children and Families (ACF). It provides links to a number of topics related to family law including adoption and foster care, child abuse and neglect, child support, etc.

www.acf.hhs.gov/programs/cse

This is the website for the federal Office of Child Support Enforcement (OCSE). There is a wealth of material available on this website including the publication, "Essentials for Attorneys in Child Support Enforcement." It also includes a list of, and links to, child support (IV-D) agencies in each state.

www.bioethics.gov

Sponsored by the President's Council on Bioethics, this site offers a rich variety of sources, including transcripts, reports, background materials, and books. The reports may either be downloaded or ordered in print form.

www.cdc.gov/nchs

This is the site for the Centers for Disease Control and Prevention National Center for Health Statistics. It provides an alphabetical directory to offices of vital records in the individual states and territories. A variety of useful statistical reports are available at this site on topics such as abuse and intimate partner violence.

www.census.gov

A number of statistical reports relevant to family law topics are available on this government site.

www.childwelfare.gov

This is the website for the Child Information Gateway, previously known as the National Adoption Information Clearinghouse, an activity of the Department of Health and Human Services. This site contains links to federal and state laws, fact sheets, statistics, and publications on a variety of child-related topics, including adoption, types of abuse, grounds for termination of parental rights, infant safe haven laws, and parental drug abuse. The text of the most recent Child Maltreatment Report is available at this site.

www.dol.gov/ebsa

This is the Department of Labor's site for the Employee Benefits Security Administration. Available at this site is an informative forty-eight page publication on QDROs produced by the United States Department of Labor. Extensive information is also available at the DOL site on occupational statistics and labor market trends.

www.irs.gov

This is the home page of the Internal Revenue Service, which provides access to general tax information, forms, and specific treasury regulations.

www.ncea.aoa.gov

The National Center on Elder Abuse (NCEA) is the major source of available statistics on elder abuse, neglect, and exploitation in the United States, including abuse in family settings. The website provides links to resources for locating state statutes, codes, and case law.

www.ojp.usdoj.gov/bjs

This is the foremost site for "official" crime statistics.

TOPICAL SITES

Adoption

www.adoptioncouncil.org

This is the website for the National Council for Adoption, a not-for-profit organization that engages in research, education, and advocacy for adoption. The 2007 Fact Book available at this site provides facts, statistics, and an analysis of state adoption laws.

www.adoptionattorneys.org

This is the site for the American Academy of Adoption Attorneys.

www.adoptioninstitute.org

This is the website for the Evan P. Donaldson Adoption Institute. It provides links to state putative father registries, open records information, state registries, and confidentiality statutes. It provides reports on the effectiveness of safe havens and the rights of all parties interested in the adoption process.

Assisted Reproductive Technology

www.asrm.org

This is the site for the American Society for Reproductive Medicine. It provides links to articles and websites on virtually every form of ART.

Child Advocacy

www.casanet.org

This is the website for the National Court Appointed Special Advocates for Children (CASA) Association. The site provides links to state CASA programs.

www.childrensdefense.org

This is the site for the Children's Defense Fund, an advocacy organization for children. Among other things, the site provides data links and fact sheets on grandparents raising children.

www.crckids.org

This is the site for the Children's Rights Council. Available at this site are links to state codes, contact numbers for legislators, information on pending legislation, etc.

www.cwla.org

This is the site for the Child Welfare League of America.

Child Support

www.supportguidelines.com/main.html

This is a comprehensive resource on child support guidelines in the United States. It provides a number of useful resources and links to state material. It addresses additional topics relating to divorce and custody in particular.

Courts

www.ncjfcj.org

This is the site for the National Council of Juvenile and Family Court Judges.

Custody

www.ancpr.com

This is the site for the Alliance for Non-Custodial Parents' Rights, an organization that provides assistance to noncustodial parents on issues related to child support, custody, and visitation. It provides information about legal resources, UIFSA, recent cases, and obtaining school records. It also offers a "Winning Strategies Handbook" for sale.

www.coloradodivorcemediation.com

This is a court-sponsored site providing information about the psychological effects of divorce on children who are not physically close to their noncustodial parent. It offers age-specific suggestions on fostering the parent-child relationship through long-distance parenting.

www.deltabravo.net/custody/pplan3.htm

The stated goal of this site is to ensure that children of divorce have access to both parents regardless of marital status. It offers links to a variety of resources, including one featuring an online parenting-plan generator.

www.stepfamily.org

This is the site for the StepFamily Foundation.

Domestic Violence/Child Abuse

www.bwjp.org

This is the site for the Battered Women's Justice Project Civil and Criminal Justice Office. This project serves as a national clearinghouse for information about domestic violence and the policing, prosecuting, sentencing, and monitoring of domestic violence offenders. The site provides links to state domestic violence coalitions.

www.childfindofamerica.org

This site provides facts and statistics and offers free investigation and location services, kidnap prevention programs, and referral, media, and support services in parental abduction cases.

www.ncadv.org

This is the site for the National Coalition Against Domestic Violence.

www.ncmec.org

This is the website for the National Center for Missing and Exploited Children. This site provides resources in English and Spanish for parents, grandparents, childcare providers, law enforcement personnel, and attorneys.

www.ncvc.org

This is the site for the National Center for Victims of Crime. Available at this site is a stalking resource center that provides links to federal and state stalking laws and a digest of relevant cases. A dating-violence resource center is also available at this site.

www.ndvh.org

This is the site for the National Domestic Violence Hotline (800-799-SAFE; 800-787-3224). The line provides 24/7 access for calls from all states with translation services available in 140 languages.

www.lrcvaw.org

This is the site for the Legal Resource Center on Violence Against Women (funded by VAWA). The primary focus of the Center is on improving legal representation for domestic violence survivors particularly in interstate custody cases. It features links to national and state resources on topics including crisis lines, abuse later in life, and immigration issues. It also provides state-by-state links to child custody jurisdictional statutes, long-arm statutes, and relocation statutes.

Ethics

www.legalethics.com

This site abstracts and provides links to recently published articles on a number of topics related to legal ethics. It also provides links to other ethics-related sites.

Gender-Based Issues

www.feministmajority.org

This is the website for the Feminist Majority Foundation.

www.lambdalegal.org

This is the site for Lambda Legal's National Headquarters. The site provides extensive information regarding states, municipalities, and other entities offering domestic partnerships and civil union benefits. It also provides information on hot topics related to divorce, marriage, relationships, and family law.

www.mensdefense.org

This is the site for the Men's Defense Organization, which provides Web assistance to men, particularly fathers.

www.now.org

This is the site for the National Organization for Women.

www.orgformen.org

This is the website for the National Organization for Men.

www.thetaskforce.org

This is the site for the National Gay and Lesbian Task Force.

Legislation

www.ncsl.org

This site for the National Conference of State Legislatures provides summaries of enacted and proposed legislation in the various states.

www.nccusl.org

This is the site for the National Commission on Uniform State Laws. It provides copies of various iterations of uniform state laws and indicates which state(s) have adopted each act in whole or in part.

Nonmarital Families

www.unmarried.org

This is the site for Alternatives to Marriage, a national nonprofit organization advocating for equality and fairness for unmarried persons. It contains information and statistics on cohabitation, living single, domestic partner benefits, common law marriage, etc., as well as information on current news events, statistics, and advocacy efforts, particularly with respect to opposition to state constitutional amendments.

www.palimony.com

This is the site for Unmarried Couples and the Law.

Paralegal Organizations/Associations

www.nala.org

This is the website for the National Association of Legal Assistants (NALA). In addition to providing links to NALA-affiliated paralegal/legal assistant associations in thirty-five states, this site also contains the NALA Model Standards and Guidelines for Utilization of Legal Assistants. The Addendum to the Guidelines includes case references on a variety of ethical issues, including Unauthorized Practice of Law (UPL).

www.paralegals.org

This is the website for the National Federation of Paralegal Associations (NFPA).

www.nationalparalegal.org

This is the website for the National Paralegal Association (NPA).

Parental Rights

www.parentsrights.net

This is the site for the Coalition for the Restoration of Parents' Rights. It provides links to data sources and state statutes and cases on third-party visitation (including grandparent visitation).

www.acfc.org

This is the site for the American Coalition for Fathers and Children.

Professional Organizations

www.aaml.org

This is the site for the American Academy of Matrimonial Lawyers. It provides links to family law organizations, courts and cases, the IRS, relevant federal statutes, and sites addressing topics such as ADR, divorce, adoption, custody, parental kidnapping, etc.

www.americanbar.org

This is the site for the American Bar Association (ABA). The ABA has several sections and centers that offer helpful information, such as the ABA Juvenile Justice Center, Commission on Domestic Violence, and the Family Law Section. Of particular assistance are the Tables produced by the ABA each year on various aspects of family law in the fifty states, including, for example, alimony/spousal support, custody, child support, grounds for divorce, property division, and third-party visitation.

www.socialworkers.org

This is the website for the National Association of Social Workers.

Research

www.alllaw.com

This site provides articles on many aspects of family law. It includes a generic child support guidelines calculator feature.

www.divorcelinks.com

A divorce and child custody law site with direct links to state and federal divorce laws by topic. As of January 2012, the site placed a heavy emphasis on parenting plans.

www.divorcenet.com

This site contains information on a number of family law topics. Search by topic and/ or by state. This site offers links to state divorce laws and provides statutory references and brief narratives on topics such as grounds for divorce, approaches to division of property, alimony, and child custody, visitation, and support.

www.divorceonline.com

This site provides a wide range of articles and information on various aspects of divorce along with links to state divorce laws.

www.findlaw.com

In Findlaw's "Family Law Center," the user can search specific topic areas and narrow down and focus research. The Center provides generic articles as well as state-by-state links to laws relating to virtually every family law area including, among others, marriage, divorce, child custody, adoption, abuse, surrogacy, paternity, support, and parental liability. Some of the links it provides to divorce forms by state contain sample separation agreements and parenting plans. Findlaw's Legal Technology Center has an Electronic Discovery Rule Wizard, an online interactive tool to help legal professionals understand the amended Federal Rules of Civil Procedure and improve their use of e-discovery methods and procedures.

www.law.cornell.edu

This is the site for Cornell Law School. It provides a variety of links to federal and state codes. For example, see *www.law.cornell.edu/wex/table_marriage* on state marriage laws. The master topic list includes adoption, divorce, emancipation of children, and marriage.

www.library.law.emory.edu

This Law Library resource provides links to state codes and selected cases. It also provides an Internet legal research guide.

www.lectlaw.com

Among other resources, this site provides articles on a range of topics related to marriage and divorce, custody and support, etc.

www.megalaw.com/top/family.php

The Megalaw Family Law Center provides links to a range of family law resources, including landmark and recent court cases, federal and state statutes, uniform acts, organizations, and forms. State-specific resources are provided for California, Colorado, Florida, Illinois, Michigan, New Jersey, New York, Ohio, and Texas.

appendix C

STATE WEBSITES FOR FORMS AND STATUTES

State	Statutes	Forms
AL	www.legislature.state.al.us	eforms.alacourt.gov
AK	www.alaska.gov	www.courts.alaska.gov/forms.htm
AR	portal.arkansas.gov	courts.arkansas.gov/aoc/forms.cfm
AZ	www.azleg.gov/ArizonaRevisedStatutes.asp	azcourts.gov/selfservicecenter
CA	www.leginfo.ca.gov/calaw.html	www.courts.ca.gov/forms.htm
CO	michie.com/colorado	www.courts.state.co.us
CT	www.cga.ct.gov	www.jud.ct.gov
DC	www.dccouncil.washington.dc.us/legislation	www.dccourts.gov/dccourts/superior/family/forms.jsp
DE	michie.com/delaware	www.courts.delaware.gov/forms
FL	www.leg.state.fl.us/Statutes	www.flcourts.org
GA	www.legis.ga.gov (Georgia Code)	www.georgiacourts.org
HI	www.capitol.hawaii.gov	www.courts.state.hi.us
ID	www3.idaho.gov	www.courtselfhelp.idaho.gov
IL	www.ilga.gov	www.cookcountyclerkofcourt.org
IN	www.in.gov/legislative/index.htm	www.in.gov
IO	www.legis.iowa.gov	www.iowacourts.gov
KS	www.kslegislature.org	www.kscourts.org
KY	www.lrc.ky.gov	courts.ky.gov/forms
LA	www.legis.louisiana.gov	www.familycourt.org
MA	www.malegislature.gov	www.lawlib.state.ma.us
MC	www.legislature.mi.gov	www.courts.michigan.gov
MD	michie.com/maryland	www.courts.state.md.us
ME	www.maine.gov/legis	www.maine.gov (Court Forms)
MI	www.revisor.mn.gov	www.mncourts.gov
MO	www.moga.mo.gov	www.courts.mo.gov
MS	michie.com/mississippi	(available to MS Bar members or via commercial sites)
MT	courts.mt.gov	courts.mt.gov
NC	www.ncga.state.nc.us	www.nccourts.org
ND	www.legis.nd.gov	www.ndcourts.gov (only for pro se)
NE	nebraskalegislature.gov	www.supremecourt.ne.gov/forms

(continued)

State	Statutes	Forms
NH	www.nh.gov	www.courts.state.nh.us/fdpp/forms
NJ	www.njleg.state.nj.us	www.judiciary.state.nj.us/forms.htm
NM	www.nmlegis.gov	supremecourtlawlibrary.org
NV	www.leg.state.nv.us	lawlibrary.nevadajudiciary.us
NY	assembly.state.ny.us/leg	www.nycourts.gov/forms
OH	codes.ohio.gov	(attorneys and commercial sites)
OK	www.oklegislature.gov	(available from attorneys)
OR	www.leg.state.or.us	courts.oregon.gov/OJD
PA	www.legis.state.pa.us	(attorneys and commercial sites)
RI	www.rilin.state.ri.us	www.courts.ri.gov/PublicResources/forms (very sparse)
SC	www.scstatehouse.gov	www.judicial.state.sc.us/forms
SD	legis.state.sd.us/statutes	www.sdjudicial.com/forms
TN	michie.com/tennessee	www.tncourts.gov
TX	www.statutes.legis.state.tx.us	http://www.co.travis.tx.us/courts/
UT	www.le.state.ut.us	www.utcourts.gov
VA	Leg1.state.va.us	www.courts.state.va.us
VT	michie.com/vermont	www.vermontjudiciary.org/eforms
WA	apps.leg.wa.gov/rcw	www.courts.wa.gov/forms
WI	www.legis.wisconsin.gov	www.wicourts.gov
WV	www.legis.state.wv.us	www.courtswv.gov (Court Forms under Legal Community)
WY	michie.com/wyoming	www.courts.state.wy.us

GLOSSARY

Note: This Glossary defines terms as they are applied in the family law context.

A

Abandonment   (1) a fault ground for divorce in some states sometimes termed desertion; (2) a type of child neglect that occurs when the whereabouts of a child's parents are unknown, the parent has left the child in unsafe circumstances, and/or has failed for an extended period of time to maintain contact with or provide support for the child.

Absolute divorce   a total divorce of husband and wife, dissolving the marital bond and releasing the parties wholly from their matrimonial obligations; frees the parties to remarry. See also **Divorce *a vinculo matrimonii*.**

Abuse   the causing of harm to another, often in the family setting; may include physical, emotional, sexual, and other forms of abuse

Abuse of discretion   the failure of a court to exercise sound, reasonable, impartial, and legal decision making

Acceptance of service   acceptance and acknowledgment of receipt of a summons and complaint or other legal document

Acknowledgment of paternity   a voluntary acknowledgment of paternity by the father of a child in a sworn (notarized) affidavit of parentage; sometimes a joint acknowledgment with the child's mother

Active appreciation   increase in the value of an asset that results from effort rather than market forces or the passage of time

Actual service of process   actual delivery of notice to the person for whom it is intended

Actuary   a statistician who determines the present value of a future event; one who calculates insurance and pension values on the basis of empirically based tables

Adjudication of paternity   a judicial decision declaring a man to be the legal father of a child

Adjusted gross income   income after nonvoluntary deductions are taken out, such as federal and state tax obligations, social security withholding, union dues, wage assignments related to prior support orders, etc.

Adoptee   in an adoption, the individual who is adopted

Adoption   the judicial process by which a new parent-child relationship is created and an adoptive parent assumes the legal rights and duties of a biological parent

Adoption abrogation   an annulment, repeal, or undoing of an adoption

Adoption registry   a vehicle available in some states that allows adoptees after a certain age (usually eighteen) to try to contact their biological parents and siblings

Adoptive parent   a person who, by means of legal process, becomes a parent of a child to whom he or she is biologically unrelated

Adultery   voluntary sexual intercourse between a married person and a person other than his or her spouse; a fault ground for divorce recognized in some states

Affidavit   a written statement of facts based on firsthand knowledge, information, or belief and signed by the affiant under pain and penalty of perjury

Affidavit of competency   an affidavit from a physician that an individual is competent to perform a particular act

Affinity   the relationship a spouse has to the blood relatives of the other spouse; relationship by marriage

Age of consent   the age at which a person becomes eligible to consent to his or her marriage without parental permission

Age of majority   the age, usually eighteen, at which a person attains adulthood and associated legal rights

Agency adoption   an adoption facilitated by an agency licensed by the state

Alimony   See **Spousal support**.

Alimony in gross   sometimes called lump-sum alimony; alimony ordered payable in the form of a definite sum, usually in a single or limited number of installments; usually not subject to modification

Alimony *pendente lite*   [Latin: while the action is pending] support awarded to a dependent spouse in order to maintain the status quo as to financial circumstances while a marital action is pending

Alimony recapture rule   the IRS rule that the government can recover a tax benefit (such as the prior claiming of a deduction for payment of alimony) by taxing the income that no longer qualifies for the benefit

All property states   states in which divorce courts may reach and distribute all property without distinguishing between separate and marital property if necessary to achieve an equitable division of property upon divorce

Alternate payee   a recipient of a pension payment other than the plan participant

Alternative dispute resolution (ADR)   a procedure for settling a dispute by means other than litigation, such as mediation or arbitration

Annulment   the legal procedure for declaring that a marriage is null and void because of an impediment existing at its inception

Answer   a pleading filed by a defendant setting forth the defendant's allegations, defenses, and counterclaims in response to a plaintiff's complaint

Antenuptial agreement   See **Premarital agreement**.

Antiheartbalm statutes   state laws that abolish the cause of action for breach of promise

Appearance   (1) coming into court as a party in a lawsuit; (2) a document filed with the court by an attorney indicating that he or she will be representing one of the parties in a matter before the court

Appellant   the party bringing an appeal of a lower court's judgment

Appellee   the party against whom an appeal is brought

Appreciation   an increase in value; active appreciation results from effort applied, and passive appreciation refers to an increase that would have occurred anyway, without any expenditure of effort

Approximation rule   the rule that the custodial responsibilities of the parents at dissolution should be allocated in a manner that approximates the proportion of time each parent spent caring for a child when the family was intact

Arbitration   an alternative dispute resolution process in which one or more neutral third persons, who are trained arbitrators, hear arguments, review evidence, and render a decision with respect to the issues selected for arbitration by the parties involved in a dispute

Arrearage   a payment that is due but has not been made

Artificial insemination   the process of inseminating a woman by means other than sexual intercourse

Assisted reproductive technology (ART)   treatment or procedures designed to make parenthood possible for persons with fertility problems or individuals who are otherwise unable or personally unwilling to reproduce

At-risk adoption   an adoption that is at risk of being challenged at a later date because the parental rights of one or both biological parents have not been terminated; an alternative to permanent or long-term foster care

Attorney-client privilege   the client's right to refuse to disclose and to prevent the attorney from disclosing confidential communications between the client and his or her attorney unless the communication concerns future commission of a serious crime; the privilege is established by statute. See also **Rule of attorney-client confidentiality**.

B

Bankruptcy   a legal proceeding in which a party seeks to be relieved of responsibility for paying his or her debts

Basis   the value assigned by the IRS to a taxpayer's investment in property

Battered woman's syndrome   the psychological condition of a woman who has been abused for a sustained period of time; sometimes used as a defense to justify the act or mitigate the penalty when the woman attacks her abuser

Beneficiary   the person named in a document (such as a will, trust, or insurance policy) to receive property, money, or some other benefit

Best interest of the child   a legal standard for resolving custody disputes that focuses on the needs of the child over the rights or wishes of the parents; the position that determination of legal parentage should be based on who is best able to fulfill the social and legal responsibilities of parenthood

Bifurcated divorce   a divorce in which the dissolution of marriage is resolved in one proceeding, and all other issues such as property division and child custody are resolved in one or more later proceedings in the same or another state

Bigamy   the act of entering a subsequent marriage while a prior marriage of one or both of the parties is still in effect; a ground for annulment and/or divorce in all states

Binding arbitration   arbitration in which the parties agree to abide by the arbitrator's decision as final and unappealable

Biological parent   a blood-related parent who contributes half of a child's genetic material by means of a reproductive cell (egg or sperm); sometimes called a genetic or natural parent

Biology-plus rule   the rule that an unwed father's parental rights are worthy of constitutional protection if the father grasps the opportunity to develop a relationship with and accept responsibility for his child

Black market adoption   an adoption brokered by an individual who collects a substantial fee for locating a child who is transferred from one person or couple to another without proper legal process

Blog (web log)   a website feature in which an individual maintains a chronicle—frequently on a single topic

Boilerplate   standard language commonly used in a particular kind of document; usually does not require negotiation

Bottom line   the limit beyond which a party will not go in a negotiation

Breach of promise   under common law, the breaking of an engagement without justification, entitling the innocent party to damages

Burden of proof   the requirement that a party or defendant prove a disputed assertion or charge

C

Canon law   church law; a body of law developed within a particular religious tradition

Capacity   the legal power to perform a particular act and to understand the nature and effect of that act

Capital gains tax   a tax on income derived from the sale of a capital asset as defined by the Internal Revenue Code

Care and protection proceeding   a court proceeding in which the state seeks custody of a child and termination of parental rights, if warranted

CASA program   a national program that trains court-appointed volunteer advocates to work one-on-one with abused and endangered children; CASA (Court Appointed Special Advocate) volunteers provide objective recommendations to the court concerning the environment that will best ensure a particular child's safety and well-being

Case law   the body of law contained in court opinions

Case of first impression   a case involving an issue being addressed for the first time in a given jurisdiction

Case registry   a federally mandated statewide database containing basic information on all child support

orders issued by courts within the state; there exists a federal case registry as well

Cause of action   the fact or combination of facts that gives a person the right to seek judicial redress or relief against another; a legal theory on which a lawsuit can reasonably be based, given a particular set of facts

Ceremonial marriage   a marriage that complies with statutory requirements, such as obtaining a license and having the marriage performed by an authorized person

Child support   a parent's legal obligation to contribute to the economic maintenance of his or her child; the payments made by a parent to meet his or her legal obligation to contribute to the economic maintenance of a child until the age of majority or emancipation or some other time or circumstance set by a court

Child support guidelines   guidelines developed by states in response to federal mandate that are presumed to generate an appropriate amount of child support, given a particular set of assumptions and circumstances

Chose in action   a pending right to recover something in a lawsuit, such as an action for wrongful termination

Civil contempt   a sanction for failure to obey a court order issued for another's benefit; a civil contempt proceeding is remedial in nature and its purpose is to promote compliance with the order. See also **Criminal contempt**.

Civil law   one of the two primary legal systems in the Western world, originating in the Roman Empire and influential in several parts of the world and a small number of states

Civil union   a formal legal status that provides a same-sex couple with the rights, benefits, protections, and responsibilities that a married heterosexual couple has under state but not federal law

Clear and convincing evidence   a standard of proof requiring that the evidence show it is highly probable or reasonably certain that an alleged fact is true or false as claimed; a greater burden than preponderance of the evidence, but less than proof beyond a reasonable doubt, the standard for criminal trials

Cloning   the genetic replication of a living organism

Closed adoption   an adoption in which biological and adoptive parents essentially know nothing about each other, and adoptees have no access to their original birth certificates or identifying information about their parents

Cloud computing Internet-based computing in which both the software and the data storage reside on an Internet site or network of sites

Cohabitation two unmarried people living together, commonly in an intimate relationship

Cohabitation agreement an agreement between two unmarried individuals who live or intend to live together, defining their intentions, rights, and obligations with respect to one another while living together and upon termination of their relationship

Collaborative law an approach to reaching agreements and resolving differences that stresses cooperation, joint problem solving, and the avoidance of litigation

Collusion an agreement by the parties to a divorce action to jointly deceive the court as to the true nature and purpose of the action; e.g., to seek a divorce in order to obtain an economic benefit without an intention of living apart

Comity, doctrine of the practice of giving effect to the laws and judicial decisions of another jurisdiction (e.g., nation or state) out of mutual respect even if not legally obligated to do so

Commingling mixing together a spouse's separate property with marital property, or mixing together the separate property of both spouses

Common law judge-made law; the legal system that originated in England based on evolving case law and statutes

Common law marriage a form of marriage created by the conduct of the parties rather than in a formal ceremony; usually requires capacity and intent to marry, cohabitation, and a holding out to the public as husband and wife; recognized in a limited number of states

Common law property property acquired during the marriage and generally viewed as owned by the spouse who acquired or earned it; with limited exceptions, property acquired during the marriage is divided equitably upon divorce in common law property states

Community property assets owned in common by a husband and wife as a result of having been acquired during the marriage by means other than an inheritance or gift to one of the spouses, each spouse generally holding a one-half interest in the property no matter in whose name it is held

Community property states states in which a husband and wife hold property acquired during the marriage

(exclusive of gifts and inheritances) in common, with each spouse entitled to a one-half interest in the property upon divorce

Comparative rectitude, doctrine of in the divorce context, the granting of a divorce to the party who is least at fault when both parties have committed marital wrongdoing

Compensatory damages damages designed to compensate an injured person for a loss suffered

Complaint the main pleading in a civil case that sets forth the nature of the action and the request for relief; called a petition in some states

Complaint for contempt a complaint to obtain compliance with a court order or to punish a person for noncompliance.

Complaint for modification a complaint seeking an alteration in an existing order based on a change of circumstances.

Conclusions of law statements as to how governing law applies to a case

Concurrent jurisdiction the circumstance in which two or more courts have simultaneous jurisdiction over the same subject matter

Condonation a defense to a divorce complaint claiming the forgiveness of an alleged matrimonial offense

Conflict of interest a situation or circumstance that interferes with the attorney's or paralegal's duties of zealous advocacy and loyalty to the client

Conflict of law a conflict arising out of a difference between the laws of two jurisdictions, such as two states or two nations

Connivance a traditional defense in which the defendant alleges the plaintiff consented to, or participated in, the act complained of in the complaint

Consanguinity a blood relationship between individuals

Consent the approval, permission, or assent to some act or purpose, given voluntarily by a competent person, as in consent to an adoption

Consideration a bargained-for exchange or mutual promises underlying the formation of a contract

Consortium companionship, affection, and, in the case of spouses, sexual relations, that one is entitled to receive from another based on existence of a legally recognized relationship (e.g., husband-wife, parent-child)

Constructive desertion a situation in which a spouse's objectionable conduct is so abusive or otherwise intolerable that it renders continuation of the marital relationship impossible and forces the "innocent spouse" either to move out or into a separate area within the marital residence in order to maintain his or her health, safety, or self-respect

Constructive trust a trust imposed by the court on an asset of a party who improperly or wrongfully acquired the property

Consummation making a marriage complete by engaging in sexual intercourse

Contingent fee the payment of a certain percentage of the amount recovered by the client in a settlement or court judgment (plus fees and costs) based on results obtained; common in personal injury cases but generally not permitted in divorce cases except in limited circumstances such as collection of past-due child support

Continuing jurisdiction when a court has acquired proper jurisdiction (as in a child custody case), the retention of that jurisdiction over the matter to the exclusion of other courts for purposes of modification, etc.

Contract an agreement that establishes legally enforceable rights and obligations between two or more parties

Co-parent a person who is engaged in a nonmarital relationship with the legal parent of a child and who regards himself or herself as a parent rather than as a legal stranger to the child; a person who shares childrearing responsibilities with a partner with or without benefit of a legally recognized relationship

Co-respondent a person alleged to have had sexual intercourse with a defendant charged with adultery

Counterclaim a defendant's claim against the plaintiff

Court of equity a court that has authority to decide controversies in accordance with rules and principles of equity (principles of fairness)

Coverture (**archaic, "couverture"**) the legal doctrine that upon marriage, a husband and wife become one person (the husband), and that the wife loses many of the legal rights she possessed prior to marriage

Covenant marriage a type of marriage that emphasizes the permanence of marriage and limits the availability of divorce to fault grounds

Criminal contempt a punishment for failure to comply with a court order; a criminal contempt proceeding is punitive in nature and designed to punish an attack on the integrity of the court

Criminal conversation a tort action for adultery brought against a third party who has sexual intercourse with another's spouse; abolished as a cause of action in most jurisdictions

Cruel and abusive treatment a fault ground for divorce available in some states; conduct that is so physically or mentally damaging that it endangers the spouse's health, safety, or reason

Cryopreservation freezing and storage of genetic material for later use in procreation or research

Curtesy at common law, the right of a husband to lifetime use of land owned by his deceased wife during the marriage if children were born of the marriage

Custodial parent the parent with whom the child primarily resides; the parent who has the right to have the child live with him or her

Cut-off rule the rule requiring that a biological parent's rights to his or her child be terminated prior to adoption of the child by a third party; not applicable to a custodial biological parent who remains in the new family unit

Cyberstalking repeated use of the Internet, text messaging, e-mail, or other forms of electronic communication with intent to harass, intimidate, torment, or embarrass another person

D

Decree *nisi* [Latin: unless] a provisional judgment of divorce that ripens into a final decree after a certain period of time (usually ninety days) absent a challenge or request of the parties to vacate the judgment

Declaratory judgment a binding adjudication that establishes the rights, status, or other legal relations between the parties

***De facto* adoption** [Latin: in point of fact] an adoption that does not meet formal statutory requirements but is considered an adoption based on the conduct of the parties and the surrounding circumstances; sometimes called an equitable adoption or adoption by estoppel

***De facto* parent** [Latin: in point of fact] an individual who performs a caretaking role without compensation for an extended period knowing he or she is not a child's legal parent; often with the consent of the legal parent(s)

Default judgment a judgment entered against a defendant who fails to respond to a complaint or otherwise defend the action

Defense   a defendant's stated reason why a plaintiff has no valid claim or why the court should not grant the relief requested

Defense of Marriage Act (DOMA)   a federal law restricting the definition of marriage to the union of one man and one woman for purposes of federal law and allowing the states to deny full faith and credit to same-sex marriages valid in a sister state

Defined-benefit plan   a retirement plan in which the amount of the benefit is usually determined according to a formula based on the participant's earnings, length of service, or a target monthly benefit

Defined-contribution plan   a retirement plan funded by the employee's contributions and the employer's contributions (usually in a preset amount) in which the eventual benefit is based on the amount of contributions and investment earnings in the years during which the employee is covered by the plan

Dependency exemption   a deduction a taxpayer may take for a person principally dependent on him or her for support; in the custody context, usually taken by the parent with primary physical custody of a child, although the parties may agree otherwise

Dependency proceeding   See **Care and protection proceeding**.

Deponent   the individual who is asked to respond under oath to questions asked in a deposition

Deposition   a method of pretrial discovery in which one party questions the other party or a third person (the deponent) under oath; responses to oral or written questions are reduced to writing for possible later use in a court proceeding

Desertion   See **Abandonment**.

Directory of new hires   federally mandated databases maintained by both the state and federal governments and containing basic information from employers regarding all newly hired employees and applicants for unemployment

Discharge a debt   to relieve an obligor of the legal obligation to pay a debt; the method by which a legal duty to pay a debt is extinguished

Discovery   the process of gathering information relevant to a matter at issue; includes both formal and informal methods

Disestablishment of paternity   a court order vacating an earlier paternity judgment or acknowledgment based on evidence the man is not the child's father, in effect disestablishing a previously existing father-child relationship

Dissipation   the use of an asset for an illegal or inequitable purpose, such as when a spouse uses or expends marital property for personal benefit while a divorce is pending

Divisible divorce   See **Bifurcated divorce**.

Divorce   a judicial determination that a marriage is legally terminated

Divorce *a mensa et thoro*   [Latin: from board and hearth] a divorce from bed and board only; a legal separation

Divorce *a vinculo matrimonii*   [Latin: from the chains of marriage] literally, a divorce from the chains or bonds of matrimony; an absolute divorce that frees the parties to remarry

DNA (deoxyribonucleic acid) test   a test used to determine inherited characteristics and establish parentage

Docket number   the number assigned to a case by the court for organizational and reference purposes; the number appears on all papers filed in the case; sometimes called a calendar number

Domestic partnership   a status granted to an unmarried couple who live together and receive a variety of economic and noneconomic benefits customarily granted to spouses

Domestic violence   See **Family violence**.

Domicile   a person's legal residence; the place a person considers his or her permanent home and to which he or she intends to return when away

Donee   the one to whom a gift is made

Donor   the one who gives a gift; in ART, a person who donates genetic material

Dower   a widow's right to lifetime use of one-third of the land owned by her deceased husband during the marriage

Dual divorce   a divorce granted to both parties

Dual property states   states that distinguish between marital and separate property for distribution purposes and permit only marital property to be divided and distributed upon divorce

Due process   the constitutional requirement that legal proceedings be conducted according to established rules and principles, including notice and the right to a fair hearing

Durable power of attorney   a document that grants someone authority to act in the grantor's stead for convenience and/or in the event of incapacity; the authority survives incapacity but terminates on the death of the grantor

Duress   a threat of harm made to compel a person to do something contrary to his or her free will or judgment

E

Ecclesiastical law   (syn. **Canon law**) the law governing the doctrine and discipline of a particular church

Educational neglect   a parent's failure to use his or her best efforts to ensure that a child of mandatory school age attends a legally recognized school or program of home schooling

Electronic discovery   discovery of information in electronic form; refers to any information created, stored, or utilized with computerized technology of any sort

Emancipation   the point at which a child is considered an adult; usually occurs at the age of majority (eighteen in most states) or upon the occurrence of certain acts or events, such as marriage or entering the armed services; usually frees the parent from a child support obligation

Emergency jurisdiction   jurisdiction based on a child's physical presence in a state and need for emergency protection

Emotional neglect   a pattern of rejecting, isolating, and ignoring a child's needs for nurturance, stimulation, and social contact

Employee Retirement Income Security Act (ERISA)   a federal statute designed to protect qualified employee pensions in the event an employer goes out of business or declares bankruptcy; ERISA governs retirement plans that do not discriminate in favor of highly compensated employees.

Equal protection   constitutional protection provided by the Fourteenth Amendment that prevents states from imposing arbitrary and discriminatory legislative classifications that treat citizens unfairly or unequally based on race, religion, disability, sex, age, or national origin

Equitable adoption   an adoption in which prospective adoptive parents accept a child into their home and raise the child as their own without ever formally finalizing the adoption; treated by some courts as an adoption to promote fairness and serve the ends of justice; sometimes called an adoption by estoppel

Equitable division/distribution   the legal concept that upon divorce property accumulated during a marriage should be divided between the parties equitably, but not necessarily equally, based upon principles of fairness

Equitable estoppel   preventing a party from asserting a claim or a defense because it would be unfair to an opposing party to do otherwise

Equitable parenthood   parenthood established on the basis of equitable principles of fairness rather than on biological connection; the equitable parent doctrine extends parental status to an individual who is willing and able to assume parental rights and responsibilities and who has done so in the past

Equity   in its broadest sense, equity is fairness; as a legal system, it is a body of law that addresses concerns that fall outside the jurisdiction of common law; in real estate law, it refers to the fair market value of a property less any encumbrances (mortgage, loans, tax liens, etc.)

Equitable remedy   a remedy used by a court to achieve a just and fair result in situations not covered by existing laws

Error of law   a mistake made by a court in applying the law to the facts of a case

Estoppel   the doctrine that a person should be prevented by his or her prior conduct from claiming or denying the right of another person who has reasonably relied on that conduct

Escalation clause   a provision in an agreement that provides for an automatic increase in an amount owed, such as in an alimony payment

Ethical wall   a screening mechanism designed to protect a client from a conflict of interest by preventing one or more lawyers (or paralegals) within a firm from participating in a legal matter involving that client

Ethics   the standards or rules of conduct to which members of a profession are expected to conform

Evidence-based prosecution   in abuse cases, prosecution of a defendant that relies on physical evidence and testimony of persons other than the victim, such as police officers; formerly called "victimless" prosecutions

Exhibit notebook   a notebook, prepared for the convenience of the court and counsel, containing all exhibits to be introduced at trial by either or both parties

Ex parte   without advance notice to or hearing argument from the opposing party based on the urgency of the matter or the harm that might otherwise result

Ex parte **motion**   [Latin: from the part] a motion made without advance notice to the opposing party; a motion considered and initially ruled on by the court without hearing from both parties

Expectation damages   compensation awarded for the loss of what a person reasonably anticipated from a contract or transaction that was not completed

Expert   a person who, through education or experience, has developed special skill or knowledge in a particular subject

Express contract   a contract that is created by an actual articulated agreement of the parties as to certain terms of their relationship expressed orally or in writing

Extraordinary expense   an unusual, unanticipated childrearing expense that is substantial in amount and/or duration

F

Fair market value   the price a willing buyer would pay a willing seller in an arm's-length transaction when neither party is under any compulsion to buy or sell

Family law   the body of the law that deals with marriage, divorce, custody, adoption, support, paternity, and other domestic relations issues, including matters related to nonmarital family units

Family violence   a pattern of coercive behavior designed to exert power and control over a person in a familial relationship; sometimes called domestic or intimate partner violence

Fault grounds   grounds for divorce based on the fault of one of the parties

Federal Parent Locator Service (FPLS)   a service operated by the Office of Child Support Enforcement (OCSE) for the purpose of locating parents delinquent in meeting their child support obligations when multiple states are involved

Fee agreement   a contract between an attorney and a client regarding payment for the attorney's professional services

Fiduciary   a person who owes another a duty of good faith, trust, loyalty, and candor

Fiduciary duty   a duty of good faith, trust, loyalty, and candor owed by one person to another based upon the existence of a special relationship

Filius nullius   [Latin: the son of no one] the child of no one

Final judgment/judgment absolute   the court's final decision determining the rights of the parties and issues in dispute

Financial statement   a party's statement of his or her assets and liabilities signed under pain and penalty of perjury; sometimes called a financial affidavit or case information statement (CIS)

Flat fee   a fixed dollar amount charged to handle a specific legal matter, such as the negotiating and drafting of a cohabitation agreement

Foreign divorce   a divorce obtained in another state or country

Forensic   gathered as potential evidence in a lawsuit

Forensic accountant   an accountant who applies accounting principles and analysis to gather and present evidence in a lawsuit

Formal discovery   discovery methods that are subject to procedural and court rules

Forum   a location where disputes are heard and decided; a website feature in which a thread (specific topic within a subject area) or multiple simultaneous threads can be discussed

Forum non conveniens   [Latin: an unsuitable court] a situation in which the forum where an action is filed is not convenient for one or both of the parties, usually the defendant; the court, in its discretion, may find that justice would be better served if the matter is heard in another court

Forum shopping   seeking a court that will grant the most favorable ruling in a case

Foster parent   a person or persons who provide a temporary home for a child when his or her parents are temporarily unwilling or unable to do so, usually through a child welfare agency for a modest payment

"Four corners"   the face of a written instrument

IV-D agency   the state agency charged with responsibility for enforcing child support obligations

Fraud   a false statement of a material fact with intent that another rely on the statement to his or her detriment

Front loading   the making of substantial payments to a former spouse shortly after a divorce in an effort to disguise a property division as deductible alimony

Full faith and credit   the recognition, acceptance, and enforcement of the laws, orders, and judgments of another jurisdiction

G

Genetic parent   a biological parent who is genetically related to the child

Genetic test   the position taken in parentage determinations that the individuals who contribute a child's genetic material should be considered his or her legal parents

Gestational mother   a woman who carries and gives birth to a child; the woman may or may not be biologically related to the child

Gestational test   the position taken in maternity determinations that the woman who carries and delivers a child should be deemed the child's legal mother

Get   a "bill of divorce" in the Jewish religion

Green card   a document (registration card) evidencing a resident alien's status as a permanent resident of the United States; a "green card marriage" is a sham marriage in which a United States citizen marries a foreign citizen for the sole purpose of allowing the foreign citizen to become a permanent United States resident

Gross income   total income from all sources before any deductions are made

Ground for divorce   the reason for filing the action, the basis on which relief is sought in a divorce action; may be a fault or no-fault ground

Guardian   an individual appointed by the court to have legal authority for another's person and/or property during a period of minority or incapacitation

Guardian *ad litem*   [Latin: for the suit] a person, usually a lawyer, appointed by the court to conduct an investigation or to represent a party who is a minor or otherwise unable to represent himself or herself in a legal proceeding; the guardian's role may be limited to a particular matter, such as custody

H

Health care proxy   a document granting another person the authority to make health care decisions for the grantor in the event of his or her incapacity

Hold harmless (indemnity) provision   a provision specifying that a particular spouse will be solely responsible for payment of certain debts and that the other spouse shall be free and clear of any obligation

regarding those debts and will be indemnified by the debtor spouse if forced to pay the debt

Home state   jurisdiction in custody matters, based on where a child has lived for a specified period of time; under UIFSA, the UCCJEA, and the PKPA, the state where the child has lived for six consecutive months prior to the filing or since birth if the child is less than six months old

Home study   a means of assessing prospective adoptive parents and home environments; customarily conducted by social workers licensed by the state

I

Ignorantia legis non excusat   [Latin: ignorance of the law is not an excuse]

Illegal adoption   See **Black market adoption.**

Illegitimate child   a child born to unmarried parents; a term abandoned in most states

Impediment   a legal obstacle to formation of a valid marriage or contract

Implied-in-fact contract   a judicially created contract the existence of which is inferred from the conduct of the parties

Implied partnership/Joint venture   a judicially created partnership, the existence of which is inferred from the conduct of the parties

Impotence   lack of capacity to procreate due to inability to have sexual intercourse or due to incompetent sperm or ova

Impounded   kept in the custody of the court and not available to the public, and, in some instances, to other parties

Imputed income   income that is attributed to a party based upon his or her earning capacity rather than on actual earnings

In camera   in the judge's chambers

Inception of title theory   a theory/rule that fixes ownership of property at the time it is acquired and holds that contributions are of no effect

Incest   sexual intercourse between two people who are too closely related as defined by civil and criminal statutes; a term used in some states to describe prohibited degrees of consanguinity and affinity in the marriage context

Income withholding   an automatic deduction of an obligation such as child support from an obligor's paycheck

Incompatibility a no-fault ground for divorce that exists when there is such discord in the marriage that the parties are unable to live together in a normal marital relationship

Incorporation (by reference) adoption by reference; inclusion of the content of a document such as a separation agreement by referencing the agreement in a divorce judgment and indicating that the agreement should be treated as part of the divorce decree

Independent adoption an adoption usually facilitated by a third party such as a physician or attorney, rather than by a licensed state agency; sometimes called a private, designated, or identified adoption

Independent legal significance a property of a contract or other document that is legally binding in its own right

Informal discovery information gathering not governed by specific procedural rules, such as searches of public records and researching "Blue Book" values

In loco parentis [Latin: in the place of the parent] taking on some or all of the responsibilities of a parent

Innocent spouse a spouse who may be relieved of liability for taxes incurred if the other spouse prepared the tax forms, controlled the information that went into them, and is responsible for errors, omissions, and/or fraud that resulted in significant penalties; also generally refers to a spouse who did not engage in marital misconduct

In rem jurisdiction [Latin: against a thing] the authority a court has over a property or thing (rather than over persons) located within its jurisdictional borders

Intangible property property that has no physical presence or form, such as legal claims, patents, and trademarks

Intent test the position taken in parentage determinations that the individual(s) who set the procreative process in motion with the intent of raising any resulting children should be deemed the legal parents of those children

Interlocutory order or decree an interim decree; a decree that is not final

International adoption an adoption in which a child residing in one country is adopted by a resident of another country

Interrogatories a method of discovery in which one party submits a series of written questions to an opposing party to be responded to in writing within a certain period of time under pain and penalty of perjury

Interspousal immunity a doctrine preventing spouses from suing each other in civil actions

Intestacy laws the laws governing distribution of property when a decedent dies without a valid will.

Intestate the condition of not having a will

In vitro fertilization [Latin] a technology that involves retrieval of eggs from a female to be fertilized in a laboratory by sperm from a male

Irreconcilable differences a no-fault ground for divorce, the essence of which is that the marriage has irreparably broken down due to serious differences between the parties

Irremediable breakdown See **Irreconcilable differences**.

J

Joint award an award made to both parties as in a joint custody award

Joint custody an arrangement in which both parents share in the responsibility for and authority over the child at all times, although one parent may exercise primary physical custody

Joint petition for adoption a petition to adopt a child that is brought by both parties to a marriage or by co-parents

Joint tenant with right of survivorship a form of ownership of property by two or more persons in which each tenant owns an identical interest in the property, and each joint tenant has a right of survivorship in the others' shares

Joint venture an express or implied agreement to conduct a common enterprise in which the parties have a mutual right of control

Judicial estoppel an equitable doctrine designed to prevent a party from gaining an unfair advantage over another party by making inconsistent statements on the same issue in different lawsuits

Judicial notice a court's acceptance of a well-known fact without requiring proof

Jurisdiction (1) a geographical area in which a certain law or procedure is governing; (2) the authority of a court to issue enforceable orders concerning a particular type of legal matter, person, or thing

L

Laches unreasonable delay in pursuing a right or claim that prejudices the other party's rights

Last resort jurisdiction   jurisdiction based on the fact no other state is willing or able to exercise jurisdiction and, in the case of child custody and support, it is in the best interest of the child for the court to do so

Laws of descent and distribution   the laws governing inheritance of property by heirs when a decedent dies without leaving a valid will

Lay witness   a witness who is not an expert on a matter at issue in a legal proceeding and who testifies as to facts and opinions based on firsthand knowledge

Legal custody   custody relating to decision-making authority with respect to major issues affecting a child; may be sole or joint

Legal parent   a person who is recognized as a child's parent under state and/or federal law

Legal separation   a judicial decree that allows spouses to live separate and apart without dissolving their legal relationship as husband and wife; sometimes called a limited divorce

Letter of engagement   a letter from an attorney to a client confirming that the attorney agrees to represent the client in a particular legal matter

Letter of nonengagement/declination   a letter from an attorney to an individual confirming that the attorney will NOT be representing that individual with respect to a particular legal matter

Letters rogatory   documents issued by a court in one state to a court in another state requesting that the "foreign" court serve process on an individual within the foreign jurisdiction

Liabilities   legal obligations, responsibilities, and debts

Lien   an encumbrance on a property that operates as a cloud against clear title to the property

Limited scope agreement   an agreement between an attorney and a client that specifically limits the nature and extent of the professional representation to be provided

Liquidated damages   an amount agreed to in a contract as the measure of damages to be paid by the breaching party to the nonbreaching party

Living separate and apart   a no-fault ground for divorce based on the fact that, due to a breakdown of the marriage, the parties have lived apart from each other for a requisite period of time

Long-arm statute   a statute setting forth the circumstances in which a state may exercise personal jurisdiction over a nonresident defendant; identifies the minimum contacts a defendant must have with the territory where the statute is in effect

Lord Mansfield's rule   the evidentiary rule that prohibited either spouse from testifying as to a husband's access to his wife at the time of conception if the testimony would tend to render the child illegitimate

Lump-sum alimony   See **Alimony in gross**.

M

Malpractice   intentional or negligent professional misconduct of an attorney that may occur in the form of a failure to properly supervise a paralegal

Mandatory reporter   an individual, who by virtue of his or her employment as a police officer, nurse, etc., is required by statute to report suspected child abuse and neglect

Mandatory self-disclosure   material specified by statute or court rule that each party in a particular legal action must provide to the other party within a certain period after filing and service of a summons and complaint

Marital communications privilege   the privilege that allows a spouse to refuse to testify, and to prevent others from testifying, about confidential communications between the spouses during their marriage; does not apply in certain contexts, such as cases involving child custody and/or abuse

Marital debt   debt incurred during the marriage for the benefit of the marital enterprise, regardless of which party incurred the obligation

Marital estate   See **Marital property**.

Marital presumption   the presumption that when a woman gives birth to a child while married or within 300 days of termination of the marriage, her husband is the child's legal father

Marital property   property acquired by either or both parties during the marriage, other than by gift or inheritance, that is subject to division at the time of marital dissolution

Marriage   a legal status that two people attain by entering a government-approved and -regulated contract with each other; a civil contract between a man and a woman or between two partners of the same sex in a state that permits same-sex marriage

Marriage restriction laws   state laws that prevent certain persons from marrying each other, such as persons closely related by blood

Married Women's Property Acts   state statutes that extended to women various rights that had been denied to them under common law, such as the right to own and control property

Material change in circumstances   a change in the physical, emotional, or financial condition of one or both of the parties (or their child) sufficient to warrant a change in a court order; a change that, if known at the time of the divorce decree, would have resulted in a different outcome

Maternal preference   the concept that custody should be awarded to a mother over a father provided she is fit

Mediation   an approach to resolving differences in which a neutral third person helps the parties identify and clarify their differences, consider their options, and structure a mutually acceptable agreement

Medical neglect   the failure of a parent or caretaker to provide appropriate health care for a child

Meeting of the minds   a shared understanding with respect to the terms and conditions of a contract

Memorandum of *lis pendens*   [Latin: a pending lawsuit] a notice that ownership and disposition of certain real property is subject to a pending legal action and any interest acquired during the pendency of that action is subject to its outcome; usually filed in a registry of deeds where the property is located

Meretricious sex   unlawful or illicit sexual relations, such as prostitution or sex outside of marriage

Merger   the process by which a separation agreement is incorporated in a divorce judgment and does not survive but rather loses its identity as a separate and independent contract

Metadata   information that is stored or transmitted electronically together with a file or message that describes the file or message

Military affidavit   an affidavit submitted by a party stating, under pain and penalties of perjury, that an absent party is currently not serving in the armed services

Minor child   a child who has not reached full legal age

Modification   a change in a court's order or judgment based on a change in circumstances; customarily sought by motion of one of the parties

Motion   a written or oral request that a court issue a particular ruling or order

Motion to dismiss   a request that the court dismiss a case because of some procedural or other defect, such as lack of jurisdiction or failure to state a claim on which relief can be based

Motion to vacate the judgment   a motion requesting the court to nullify or cancel a judgment

Motion *in limine*   [Latin: at the outset] a motion asking the court to exclude or limit the use of certain evidence at trial

N

Natural parent   biological (genetic) parent of a child

Necessaries, doctrine of   under common law, a husband's duty to pay debts incurred by his wife or children for "necessaries" indispensable to living, such as food, shelter, and clothing

Neglect   failure by a caregiver to provide needed, age-appropriate care although financially able to do so, or offered financial or other means to do so

Negligence   a failure to exercise reasonable care that results in harm to a person to whom one owes a duty of care

Negligent supervision   a cause of action based on parents' duty to society to exercise reasonable care in the supervision of their minor children in order to prevent them from intentionally causing injury to others

Net income   total income from all sources minus voluntary and nonvoluntary deductions

Neutral case evaluation   a process in which a neutral third party, usually an experienced trial attorney or judge, listens to the parties' positions and offers an opinion about settlement potential and the likely outcome if the matter proceeds to trial

Nexus   a connection or link; in the custody context, a requirement that there be a connection between parental conduct and a detrimental effect on a child before the conduct will be considered by the court

No-contact order   a court order prohibiting an individual from having contact of any kind with a person he or she has threatened and/or abused in some manner

No-fault divorce   divorce based on an irremediable breakdown of the marital relationship rather than on the fault of one or both of the parties

No-fault ground   a ground for divorce based on the irremediable breakdown of the marital relationship rather than on the fault of one or both of the parties

Nonage   the condition of being below the minimum age established by law to perform a particular act

Nonbinding arbitration   arbitration in which the parties are free to accept or reject the arbitrator's decision

Noncustodial parent   a parent who does not have sole or primary physical custody of a child but who is still a legal parent with enforceable rights and responsibilities

Notice of deposition   the notification sent to an opponent (or his or her attorney, if represented) of an intention to depose him or her at a certain date, place, and time

O

Obligee   a person to whom a duty is owed

Obligor   a person who owes a duty; in the child custody context, the parent who owes the duty of support

Open adoption   an adoption in which biological parents, adoptive parents, and the adoptee have varying degrees of contact with each other

Operation of law   a process by which a result occurs automatically because the law mandates it regardless of whether or not a party agrees or intends that result; a party does not need to take any further action to bring about the result

Order to show cause   an order directing a party to appear in court and explain why he or she took, or failed to take, some action and why relief should not be granted

P

Palimony   a court-ordered allowance paid by one cohabitant to the other after their relationship terminates; recognized in case law in some states, but generally not by statute; a term that originated in the media

Parens patriae doctrine   [Latin: parent of the country] the doctrine holding that the government, as parent of the country, has standing to act on behalf of a citizen, particularly one who is a minor or under a disability

Parent locator service (PLS)   a federal or state government program that helps locate parents, particularly those who are delinquent in child support payments

Parental alienation syndrome   a condition in which a child involved in a custody dispute comes to idealize one parent and demonize the other parent as a result of the former parent's pressure and manipulation

Parental responsibility law   a statute that imposes vicarious liability on parents for the torts committed by their children

Parent by estoppel   essentially provides that a person may be designated the legal parent of a child if he or she has held himself or herself out as the child's parent and has supported the child emotionally and financially; a theory used to establish parenting rights that asserts a legal parent should not be permitted to deny a co-parent's parental status based on a prior agreement with the legal parent, on which the co-parent relied, to raise a child together; parenthood based on the fact an individual has functioned as a parent with the approval of a child's legal parents

Parenting coordinator   an individual, usually appointed by the court, who assists with creation and implementation of a parenting agreement and/or enforcement of a decree in a high-conflict case involving minor children

Parenting plan   a written agreement in which parents lay out plans for taking care of their children postseparation and/or postdivorce

Parol evidence rule   the rule that when a writing is intended to embody the entire agreement between the parties, its terms cannot later be varied or contradicted by evidence of earlier or contemporaneous agreements

Passive appreciation   increase in the value of an asset that results without effort and as a result of market forces and/or the passage of time

Paternal preference   the common law doctrine that fathers had an absolute right to the care and custody of their children

Paternity fraud   fraud in which a mother has intentionally misled a man into believing he is the father of a child to whom he is genetically unrelated

Pendente lite   [Latin: while the action is pending]

Pension   a job-related retirement benefit acquired by an employee and funded through contributions by the employer, the employee, or a combination of both

Permanency planning   planning for the return home of a child following removal or for termination of parental rights within a legally specified period of time in an effort to promote stability for the child

Permanent alimony   alimony usually payable in weekly or monthly installments either indefinitely or until a time or circumstance specified in a court order

Permissive reporter   an individual who may, but is not required to, report suspected child abuse

Per se **rule** [Latin: by itself] without reference to additional facts; an agreement against the law or a strong public policy may be deemed *per se* invalid, invalid in and of itself, standing alone, without reference to any additional facts or circumstances

Personal jurisdiction the authority of a court to issue and enforce orders binding a particular individual; sometimes called *in personam* jurisdiction

Personal property any movable or intangible thing that is subject to ownership and not classified as real property

Physical custody custody relating to where and with whom the child resides; can be either sole or joint

Physical neglect inadequate supervision and/or a failure to provide adequate food, shelter, and clothing, such that the child's health, safety, growth, and development are endangered

Pleading a document in which a party to a legal proceeding sets forth or responds to a claim, allegation, defense, or denial

Polyandry the practice of a woman having more than one husband at the same time

Polygamy the practice of a spouse having more than one spouse at a time; a term that includes both polyandry and polygyny

Polygyny the practice of having more than one wife at a time

Posthumous reproduction reproduction that occurs after the death of one or both of the gamete contributors

Postmarital agreement (postmarital contract, postnuptial agreement) an agreement made by two people already married to each other who want both to continue their marriage and also to define their respective rights upon separation, divorce, or death of one of them

Precedent a higher court's decision regarding a question of law that provides a basis for determining later cases that involve similar facts or issues in a given jurisdiction

Premarital agreement an agreement made by two persons about to be married defining for themselves their respective rights, duties, and responsibilities in the event their marriage terminates by death, annulment, separation, or divorce

Preponderance of the evidence a standard of proof requiring that the evidence show that it is more likely than not that an alleged fact is true or false as claimed

Presumption an assumption of fact that can reasonably be drawn based on other established facts

Presumptive child support guidelines See **Child support guidelines**.

Prima facie **showing** [Latin: first face] a legally rebuttable showing

Primary authority authority created by a governmental body such as a legislature or court—includes statutes, constitutions, and case law

Primary caretaker the individual who has performed most of the significant parenting tasks for the child since birth or in the years preceding the divorce

Privilege a legal right or exemption granted to a person or a class of persons to not testify in a legal proceeding; generally based on the existence of a special relationship

Pro rata **theory** [Latin] See **Source of funds theory**.

Pro se [Latin: for self] the condition under which a person represents himself or herself in a legal proceeding without the assistance of an attorney

Procedural fairness fairness in the negotiation and execution of an agreement

Procedural law the technical rules for bringing and defending actions before a court or administrative agency, e.g., the steps to be followed in seeking child support

Property division the distribution upon divorce of property accumulated during the marriage; if not agreed upon by the parties, the division will be based on community property or equitable distribution principles depending on the jurisdiction

Proposed findings of fact facts that a party asks a court to accept as true

Protective order (1) a court order restricting or prohibiting a party from unduly burdening an opposing party or third-party witness during the discovery process; (2) in the context of family violence cases, a court order directing a person to refrain from harming, intimidating, or harassing another person

Provocation a traditional defense to divorce, claiming that the plaintiff provoked the conduct alleged in the complaint and therefore should be denied relief

Proxy marriage a marriage ceremony in which a designated agent stands in for and acts on behalf of one of the absent parties (prohibited in most states)

Psychological parent the individual who has the strongest "parental" bond with the child, who has provided the most significant care in quality and quantity, and whom the child often regards as the "parent"

Public assistance programs government programs providing financial and other forms of assistance to poor and low-income families

Public charge   a person dependent on public assistance programs for necessaries

Public policy   an idea or principle that is considered right and fair and in the best interest of the general public

Putative father   a man who is reputed or believed to be the father of a child but who was not married to the mother when the child was born and whose paternity has not yet been established by legal process

Putative father registry   a vehicle available in several states that is designed to protect a putative father's parental rights by giving him notice of a pending adoption proceeding without his having to rely on the birth mother or prospective adoptive parents for information

Putative spouse   a person who believes in good faith that his or her invalid marriage is legally valid

Q

Qualified Domestic Relations Order (QDRO)   a court order directing the administrator of a pension plan to pay a specified portion of a current or former employee's pension to an alternate payee to satisfy a support or other marital obligation

Qualified Medical Child Support Order (QMCSO)   a court order requiring provision of medical support or health benefits for the child of a parent covered by a group insurance plan

Quantum meruit   [Latin: as much as he deserved] a basis for establishing damages based on the reasonable value of services one person has provided to another

Quasi-community property   [Latin, *quasi*: as if] property acquired during a marriage in a non-community-property state that would be marital property if acquired in a community property state

Quasi-contract/Implied-in-law contract   [Latin, *quasi*: as if] a contract imposed by a court to prevent unjust enrichment of one party at the expense of the other

Quasi-marital property   [Latin, *quasi*: as if] property treated as if it was acquired by the parties during the marriage even though the marriage was never valid

Quid pro quo   [Latin: this for that] an action or thing exchanged for another action or thing of relatively equal value

R

Ratification   acceptance or confirmation of a previous act, thereby making it valid from the moment it was done

Real property   land and anything growing on, attached to, or erected on it, excluding anything that may be severed without injury to the land

Reasonable efforts   the level of effort a child protective agency must make to prevent removal of a child from his or her home, or, if removed, to reunify the family within a specified period of time

Rebuttable presumption   an inference drawn from certain facts that can be overcome by the introduction of additional or contradictory evidence

Recapture rule   the IRS rule that provides for the government's recovery of a tax benefit (such as a claimed deduction or credit) by taxing income or property that no longer qualifies for the benefit

Reciprocal beneficiaries   a nonmarital family status, available in a limited number of states, in which two adults residing together may register for certain benefits available to married persons

Recrimination   a defense to divorce raised when the defendant alleges the plaintiff has also committed a marital wrong and therefore should not be granted a divorce

Rehabilitative alimony   alimony designed to assist a divorced person in acquiring the education or training required to find employment outside the home or to reenter the labor force; sometimes called limited or transitional alimony

Reimbursement alimony   See **Restitution alimony**.

Reliance damages   damages awarded to a plaintiff for losses incurred from having acted in reliance on a contract that was breached by the other party

Relocation   moving from one place to another

Request for admissions   a discovery method in which a party makes written requests to an opposing party calling for an admission or denial of specific facts at issue or verification or denial of the genuineness of documents relevant to a case

Request for physical or mental examination   a method of discovery in which one party requests that the court order the other party (or, in some instances, a third party) to submit to a physical or mental examination

Request for production of documents or things   a method of pretrial discovery in which a party makes a written request that the other party, or a third person, produce specified documents or other tangible things for inspection and/or copying

Res judicata   [Latin: a thing adjudicated] an issue that has been definitively settled by judicial decision;

requires three essential elements: (1) an earlier decision on the issue, (2) a final judgment on the merits, and (3) the involvement of the original parties

Rescission the cancellation or unmaking of a contract for a legally sufficient reason

Respondeat superior, doctrine of [Latin: let the superior make answer] the doctrine under which an attorney may be held vicariously liable for the acts of his or her employees performed within the scope of employment

Restitution alimony alimony designed to repay a spouse who made financial contributions during the marriage that directly enhanced the future earning capacity of the other spouse; sometimes called reimbursement alimony

Restraining order a court order, commonly issued in domestic violence cases, restricting an individual from threatening and/or harassing another individual or individuals; an order prohibiting a party from taking a certain action or actions, such as selling a piece of property or removing the parties' children from the jurisdiction where the action is pending

Resulting trust a trust created by the court when one party contributes funds or services towards the acquisition of property and title to that property is held in the name of another party

Retainer used in general to describe a form of contract between an attorney and a client, particularly with respect to fees; most commonly, the client advances a lump-sum payment to an attorney for deposit in a client trust fund account, the attorney withdraws funds from the retainer as the client incurs fees and costs, and any unused portion of a retainer is returned to the client at the conclusion of the representation

Right of survivorship the right of surviving joint tenants to succeed to the whole estate upon the death of one or more of the other joint tenants

Rule of attorney-client confidentiality the duty of an attorney not to reveal any information relating to representation of a client; an ethical rule established in codes of professional conduct

S

Safe haven law a law that allows a parent, or an agent of a parent, of an unwanted newborn to anonymously leave the baby at a designated safe haven center, such as a hospital emergency room, without fear of legal charges of abandonment or child endangerment, etc., provided there is no evidence of abuse

Safety plan a plan prepared by a victim of family violence (sometimes with assistance) outlining actions to be taken in the event the victim needs to protect herself or himself and/or escape from the presence of the abuser

Sanctions penalties imposed by a court when, for example, a party fails to comply with court rules or orders

Second look doctrine an approach adopted by some courts to determining enforceability of premarital agreements which involves examining the terms of a premarital agreement for fairness at the time of performance as well as at the time of execution

Secondary authority publications that discuss but do not establish law including, for example, treatises, annotations, and law review articles

Separate maintenance court-ordered spousal support while the parties are living separate and apart but not divorced

Separate property property that a spouse owned before marriage or acquired during marriage by inheritance or gift from a third party; may include property acquired during marriage in exchange for separate property

Separate support See **Separate maintenance**.

Separation agreement an agreement made between spouses in anticipation of a divorce or legal separation concerning the terms of the divorce or separation and any continuing obligations of the parties to each other

Service of process the delivery of a summons and complaint to a defendant in a manner consistent with local procedural rules; usually accomplished by personal "in hand" service by an authorized individual such as a sheriff or by publication in a newspaper and mailing to the defendant's last known address

Service plan a plan developed by a child protection agency outlining services to be provided to parents to help them care for their children and identifying obligations the parents must perform in order for their children to remain in or be returned to the home

Shaken baby syndrome a condition that results from repeated, vigorous shaking of a baby that causes brain damage and sometimes death that can result from a single incident or a more prolonged pattern of abuse

Sham marriage a marriage in which one or both of the parties has no intention of fulfilling the responsibilities of marriage

Significant connection jurisdiction jurisdiction based on the existence in a state of substantial evidence concerning a child

Social network a collection of people connected electronically by reason of something they have in common

Social networking site an Internet-based service that promotes the formation of social networks by providing a means for people to describe (profile) themselves and to search for others whose public profiles match theirs in some respect

Sole award an award made to one party only; may apply to legal or physical custody

Sole legal custody an arrangement by which one parent has full control and sole decision-making responsibility—to the exclusion of the other parent—on matters such as health, education, religion and living arrangements; sole custody can also apply to physical custody awards

Source of funds theory a theory/rule that bases ownership of property on contribution; an asset may be characterized as both separate and marital in proportion to the respective contributions of the parties before and during the marriage

Specific performance a court-ordered remedy for breach of contract requiring that the terms of a contract be fulfilled as fully as practicable when money damages are inappropriate or inadequate

Split custody a custody arrangement in which each parent has sole legal and/or physical custody of one or more of the parties' children

Spousal support an allowance for support and maintenance that one spouse may be ordered by a court to pay to the other spouse while they are living apart or divorced; also called alimony, maintenance, and separate support. depending on the circumstances and the jurisdiction

Stalking a knowing and willful course of conduct intended to cause another substantial emotional distress or fear for his or her safety; includes behaviors such as following, telephoning, or watching a person's place of residence or employment

Standing an individual's right to bring a matter before the court and seek relief based on a claim that he or she has a stake in the outcome of the case

Stare decisis [Latin: let the decision stand] the doctrine that requires a lower court to follow the precedent of a higher court in its jurisdiction (e.g., application of earlier case law to current cases)

State Case Registry See **Case registry**.

State Directory of New Hires See **Directory of New Hires**.

State Parent Locator Service (SPLS) See **Parent Locator Service**.

Statute of Frauds the requirement that certain types of contracts be in writing, such as a contract that by its terms cannot be completed within a year or a contract for the sale of land; in most states includes a contract made in contemplation of marriage

Statute of limitations a statute that bars a certain type of claim after a specified period of time

Stay away order a court order requiring a person to keep away from another individual wherever he or she may be (home, work, school, etc.)

Step-parent a parent by virtue of marriage to a child's legal parent

Stipulation an agreement between the parties concerning some matter; may be filed with the court to be considered and entered as an order

Subject matter jurisdiction the authority of a court to hear and decide a particular type of claim or controversy

Subpoena a document ordering a witness to appear and provide testimony in a legal proceeding such as a deposition, court hearing, or trial

Subpoena *duces tecum* [Latin: bring with you] a subpoena ordering a witness to appear in a legal proceeding such as a deposition, court hearing, or trial, and to bring with him or her specified documents, records, or things

Substantive fairness fairness in the specific terms of an agreement

Substantive law laws that relate to rights and obligations/duties (e.g., the right to child support) rather than to technical procedures

Summons a formal notice from a court informing a defendant of an action filed against him or her and ordering the defendant to respond and answer the allegations of the plaintiff within a certain period or risk entry of a default judgment

Surrender in the context of parenthood, a formal document/process in which a legal (usually biological) parent gives up his or her parental rights to a specific child

Surrogate mother a woman who agrees to carry and deliver a baby with an understanding that she will surrender the child to the intended parents at birth or shortly thereafter; she may or may not be biologically related to the child

Surviving agreement   an agreement of the parties incorporated in a court's divorce decree that also retains its existence as an independent contract enforceable under basic principles of contract law

T

Talak   an Arabic word that means to release or divorce

Tangible property   property that has a physical form capable of being touched and seen

Temporary alimony   See **Alimony** *pendente lite*.

Temporary orders   orders designed to protect the parties and maintain the status quo while a matter is pending before the court

Tender years doctrine   the doctrine holding that custody of very young children should be awarded to a mother rather than a father unless she is found to be unfit

Term alimony   alimony payable in weekly or monthly installments that continue for a set period of time or until a condition specified in a court order or agreement

Termination of parental rights   the judicial severing of the legal relationship between a parent and child; may be voluntary or involuntary based on clear and convincing evidence of parental unfitness

Third-party beneficiary   a person who, though not a party to a contract, benefits from performance of the contract

Tort   a civil wrong (other than breach of contract) for which a court provides a remedy, usually in the form of money damages; the wrong must involve harm resulting from breach of a duty owed to another

Tracing   the process of tracking ownership of a property from the time of inception to the present, usually in an effort to establish its character as separate or marital property

Transitional Assistance to Needy Families (TANF)   the welfare system that replaced the former Aid to Families with Dependent Children Program (AFDC)

Transmutation   a change in the classification of an asset from separate to marital or marital to separate

Trial notebook   a term used loosely to describe the organizational system used by an attorney to assemble all of the material needed for a trial

Trust   a legal construct in which legal title to property is held by one or more persons (trustee(s)) for the benefit of another (the beneficiary)

Trustee process   a legal process by which a third party holds the property of a party in trust at the direction of a court

U

Unallocated support   support payments made to a former spouse that do not distinguish between alimony/spousal support and child support

Unauthorized practice of law (UPL)   the practice of law without a license

Unbundling of legal services   an alternative to full representation in which an attorney performs discrete tasks rather than comprehensive representation in a legal matter, usually at a substantial overall savings to the client

Unconscionable   so substantially unfair in terms or result as to shock the conscience

Unclean hands   the principle that a party should not be granted relief if he or she has acted unfairly, wrongfully, or illegally

Undue influence   the improper use of power or trust in a way that deprives a person of his or her free will and substitutes another's purposes in its place

Unearned income   income derived from investment rather than labor

Uniform Interstate Family Support Act (UIFSA)   adopted in all fifty states, a model act designed to facilitate establishment and enforcement of interstate child support orders

Uniform Law   an unofficial law proposed as legislation by the National Conference of Commissioners on Uniform State Laws for adoption by the states as written in the interest of promoting greater consistency among state laws such as the Uniform Marriage and Divorce Act (UMDA)

V

Valuation   the process of assessing the financial worth of property, real or personal

Venue   refers to the geographical location within which a particular action should be filed

Vest   gives a person an immediate, fixed right of ownership and present or future enjoyment; a vested interest is fixed or accrued and is usually unable to be taken away by subsequent events or circumstances

Virtual visitation   communication between parents and children through the use of technology

Visitation   a noncustodial parent's period of access to a child

Void   invalid and of no legal effect

Void *ab initio*   [Latin: from the beginning] of no legal effect from the outset; a contract may be void *ab initio* if it seriously offends law or public policy

Voidable marriage   a marriage capable of being nullified because of a circumstance existing at the time it was established

W

Wage assignment/withholding   an order directing a support obligor's employer to take support payments directly out of that person's paycheck for the benefit of the obligee

Waiver   the giving up of a right or privilege

Work product   written or oral material prepared for or by an attorney in preparation for litigation either planned or in progress; not subject to discovery absent a court's finding of special need

Writ *ne exeat*   [Latin: that he not depart] a court order restraining a person from leaving the jurisdiction until the petitioner's claim has been satisfied

Wrongful adoption   a tort action that an adoptive parent can bring against an adoption agency for failure to provide accurate and sufficient information regarding an adoptive child prior to adoption

Wrongful birth   an action brought by parents claiming that the defendant's negligent conduct resulted in the birth of a child with serious defects or disabilities, thereby causing the parents serious emotional distress and expense

Wrongful life   an action brought by a plaintiff who claims he or she was brought into the world with a disability that was foreseeable and could have been prevented by a competent physician exercising due care

INDEX

PHOTO CREDITS